FLP 汉英对照经典读本·古典精华

西 游 记 （节选）

JOURNEY TO THE WEST
(Condensed Version)

吴承恩　著
詹纳尔　译

By WU CHENG'EN
Translated by W.J.F. Jenner

外文出版社
FOREIGN LANGUAGES PRESS

图书在版编目(CIP)数据

西游记:节选本:汉英对照/(明)吴承恩著.-北京
:外文出版社,1999
(FLP汉英对照经典读本·古典精华;1)
ISBN 7-119-02291-1

Ⅰ.西… Ⅱ.吴… Ⅲ.古典小说:章回小说:长篇小说-
中国-明代-对照读物-汉、英 Ⅳ.H319.4:I

中国版本图书馆 CIP 数据核字(98)第 34899 号

外文出版社网址:
http://www.flp.com.cn
外文出版社电子信箱:
info@flp.com.cn
sales@flp.com.cn

FLP汉英对照经典读本·古典精华①
西游记(节选)

作　　者　吴承恩

责任编辑　余冰清
封面设计　蔡　荣
出版发行　外文出版社
社　　址　北京市百万庄大街24号　　　　邮政编码　100037
电　　话　(010)68320579(总编室)
　　　　　(010)68329514/68327211(推广发行部)
印　　刷　北京建筑工业印刷厂
经　　销　新华书店/外文书店
开　　本　64开　　　　　　　　　字　　数　434千字
印　　数　5001—8000册　　　　　印　　张　10
版　　次　1999年第1版　2001年第1版第2次印刷
装　　别　盒装
书　　号　ISBN 7-119-02291-1/I·562(外)
定　　价　60.00元(盒)

出版前言

本社专事外文图书的编辑出版，几十年来用英文翻译出版了大量的中国文化典籍、文学作品及重要文献，内容涉及文学、政治、经济、法律等诸多方面。这些英译图书均取自相关领域著名的、权威的作品，英译则出自国内外译界名家。每本图书的编选、翻译过程均极其审慎严肃，精雕细琢，中文作品及相应的英译版本均堪称经典。在全面而准确地译介中国文化及政治、经济情况等方面，这些图书起着相当重要的作用。

我们意识到，这些英译精品，不单有对外译介的意义，而且对国内英文学习者、爱好者及英语工作者，也是极有价值的读本。为此，我们对这些英译精品做了认真的遴选，编排成汉英对照的形式，陆续推出，以飨读者。

我们相信，这套配以典雅插图的系列读本，一方面将有助于读者对中国文化典籍、文学作品做自由、轻松而有趣的阅读体认，另一方面也将有助于读者对语言的深入的、生动的理解、把握和学习——因其中文作品和英文译本的双重经典性质，本系列读本不仅对国内的英语学习者爱好者有用，对国外的汉语学习者来说也不失为极好的汉教参考读物。

我们在陆续推出本系列的同时，将不断使之更加完善。在此，我们十分感谢读者诸君和专家们的支持与帮助，并甚盼你们不吝指教。

外文出版社
1999 年

Publisher's Note

The Foreign Languages Press is dedicated to the editing, translating and publishing of books in foreign languages. For several decades it has published, in English, a great number of China's ancient books and records, literary works and important documents relating to literature, politics, economy and laws. These books in the original are famous and authoritative in their respective fields, and their English translations are masterworks produced by notable translators both at home and abroad. Each book is carefully compiled and translated with minute precision. Consequently, the English versions as well as their Chinese originals may be rated as classics. They play important roles in introducing Chinese culture, politics and economy to the outside world in an all-round and accurate way.

We realize that these English translations are not only significant for introducing China to the outside world but also useful reading materials for domestic English learners and translators. For this reason, we have carefully selected some of these books, and will publish them successively in Chinese-English bilingual form.

We believe that this series of outstanding works, containing fine illustrations, will help the readers acquire a broad understanding of China's cultural classics and literary works in an attractive and entertaining manner, while assisting in the study of the two languages.

In the process of publishing this series of books we will constantly strive to improve its quality. Meanwhile, we would like to take this opportunity to extend our heartfelt thanks to the experts and readers for their help and support, and hope that they will offer their comments and suggestions.

Foreign Languages Press

目　　录

Contents

1. 乱蟠桃大圣偷丹
反天宫诸神捉怪

（石卵爆裂产生的猴王孙悟空，拜师学艺，练就了七十二般变化，一个筋头可翻十万八千里，可谓神通广大。他从龙宫借来了兵器，又在幽冥地府的生死簿上勾掉自己的名字。龙王、地藏王上奏玉帝，请求派天兵剿除。但天兵天将也奈何他不得，玉皇大帝只好顺从他的意思，封他做了个有官无禄、无权无事的"齐天大圣"。）

【1】　话表齐天大圣到底是个妖猴，更不知官衔品从，也不较俸禄高低，但只注名便了。那齐天府下二司仙吏，早晚伏侍，只知日食三餐，夜眠一榻，无事牵萦，自由自在。闲时节会友游宫，交朋结义。见三清，称个"老"字，逢四帝，道个"陛下"。与那九曜星、五方将、二十八宿、四大天王、十二元辰、五方五老、普天星相、河汉群神，俱以弟兄相待，彼此称呼。今日东游，明日西荡，云去云来，行踪不定。

【2】　一日，玉帝早朝，班部中闪出许旌阳真人，俯囟启奏道："今有齐天大圣，无事闲游，结交天上众星宿，不论高低，俱称朋友。恐后闲中生事。不若与他一件事管，庶免别生事端。"玉帝闻言，即时宣诏。那猴王欣欣然而至，道："陛下，诏老孙有何升赏？"玉帝道："朕见你身闲无事，与你件执事。你且权管那蟠桃园，早晚好生在意。"大圣欢喜谢恩，朝上唱喏而退。

【3】　他等不得穷忙，即入蟠桃园内查勘。本园中有个土地拦住，问道："大圣何往？"大圣道："吾奉玉帝点差，代管蟠桃园，今来查勘也。"那土地连忙施礼，即呼那一班锄树力士、运水力士、修桃力士、打扫力士都来见大圣磕头，引他进去。但见那

1

孫行者

夭夭灼灼，颗颗株株。夭夭灼灼花盈树，颗颗株株果压枝。果压枝头垂锦弹，花盈树上簇胭脂。时开时结千年熟，无夏无冬万载迟。先熟的，酡颜醉脸；还生的，带蒂青皮。凝烟肌带绿，映日显丹姿。树下奇葩并异卉，四时不谢色齐齐。左右楼台并馆舍，盈空常见罩云霓。不是玄都凡俗种，瑶池王母自栽培。

大圣看玩多时，问土地道："此树有多少株树？"土地道："有三千六百株：前面一千二百株，花微果小，三千年一熟，人吃了成仙了道，体健身轻。中间一千二百株，层花甘实，六千年一熟，人吃了霞举飞升，长生不老。后面一千二百株，紫纹缃核，九千年一熟，人吃了与天地齐寿，日月同庚。"大圣闻言，欢喜无任。当日查明了株树，点看了亭阁，回府。自此后，三五日一次赏玩，也不交友，也不他游。

【4】　一日，见老树梢头，桃熟大半，他心里要吃个尝新。奈何本园土地、力士并齐天府仙吏紧随不便。忽设一计道："汝等且出门外伺候，让我在这亭上少憩片时。"那众仙果退。只见那猴王脱了冠服，爬上大树，拣那熟透的大桃，摘了许多，就在树枝上自在受用。吃了一饱，却才跳下树来，簪冠着服，唤众仙从回府。迟三二日，又去设法偷桃，尽他享用。

【5】　一朝，王母娘娘设宴，大开宝阁，瑶池中做"蟠桃胜会"，即着那红衣仙女、青衣仙女、素衣仙女、皂衣仙女、紫衣仙女、绿衣仙女，各顶花篮，去蟠桃园摘桃建会。七衣仙女直至园门首，只见蟠桃园土地、力士同齐天府二司仙吏，都在那里把门。仙女近前道："我等奉王母懿旨，到此摘桃设宴。"土地道："仙娥且住。今岁不比往年了，玉帝点差齐天大圣在此督理，须是报大圣得知，方敢开园。"仙女道："大圣何在？"土地道："大圣在园内，因困倦，自家在亭子上睡哩。"仙女道："既如此，寻他去来，不可迟误。"土地即与同行。寻至తీ宫不见，但有衣冠在亭，不知何往。四下里都没寻处。原来大圣耍了一会，吃了几个桃子，变做二寸长的个人儿，在那大树梢头浓叶之下睡着了。七衣仙女道："我等奉旨前来，寻不见大圣，怎敢空回？"旁有仙使道："仙娥既奉旨来，不必迟疑。我大圣闲游惯了，想是出园会友去

了。汝等且去摘桃。我们替你回话便是。"那仙女依言，入树林之下摘桃。先在前树摘了二篮，又在中树摘了三篮；到后树上摘取，只见那树上花果稀疏，止有几个毛蒂青皮的。原来熟的都是猴王吃了。七仙女张望东西，只见向南枝上止有一个半红半白的桃子。青衣女用手扯下枝来，红衣女摘了，却将枝子望上一放。原来那大圣变化了，正睡在此枝，被他惊醒。大圣即现本相，耳朵里擘出金箍，幌一幌，碗来粗细，咄的一声道："你是那方怪物，敢大胆偷摘我桃!"慌得那七仙女一齐跪下道："大圣息怒。我等不是妖怪，乃王母娘娘差来的七衣仙女，摘取仙桃，大开宝阁，做'蟠桃胜会'。适至此间，先见了本园土地等神，寻大圣不见。我等恐迟了王母懿旨，是以等不得大圣，故先在此摘桃，万望恕罪。"大圣闻言，回嗔作喜道："仙娥请起。王母开阁设宴，请的是谁?"仙女道："上会自有旧规。请的是西天佛老、菩萨、圣僧、罗汉，南方南极观音，东方崇恩圣帝、十洲三岛仙翁，北方北极玄灵，中央黄极黄角大仙，这个是五方五老。还有五斗星君，上八洞三清、四帝、太乙天仙等众，中八洞玉皇、九垒、海岛神仙；下八洞幽冥教主、注世地仙。各宫各殿大小尊神，俱一齐赴蟠桃嘉会。"大圣笑道："可请我么?"仙女道："不曾听得说。"大圣道："我乃齐天大圣，就请我老孙做个席尊，有何不可?"仙女道："此是上会旧规，今会不知如何。"大圣道："此言也是，难怪汝等。你且立下，待老孙先去打听个消息，看可请老孙不请。"

【6】 好大圣，捻着诀，念声咒语，对众仙女道："住!住!住!"这原来是个定身法，把那七衣仙女，一个个瞪瞪睁睁，白着眼，都站在桃树之下。大圣纵朵祥云，跳出园内，竟奔瑶池路上而去。正行时，只见那壁厢：

　　一天瑞霭光摇曳，五色祥云飞不绝。
　　白鹤声鸣振九皋，紫芝色秀分千叶。
　　中间现出一尊仙，相貌昂然丰采别。
　　神舞虹霓幌汉霄，腰悬宝篆无生灭。
　　名称赤脚大罗仙，特赴蟠桃添寿节。

那赤脚大仙觌面撞见大圣，大圣低头定计，赚哄真仙，他要暗去，却问："老道何往?"大仙道："蒙王母见诏，去赴蟠桃嘉会。"

乱蟠桃大聖偷丹 開聖宮諸神赴妖

大圣道:"道道不知。玉帝因老孙筋斗云疾,着老孙五路邀请列位,先至通明殿下演礼,后方去赴宴。"大仙是个光明正大之人,就以他的诳语做真。道:"常年就在瑶池演礼谢恩,如何先去通明殿演礼,方去瑶池赴会?"无奈,只得拨转祥云,径往通明殿去了。

【7】 大圣驾着云,念声咒语,摇身一变,就变做赤脚大仙模样,前奔瑶池。不多时,直至宝阁,按住云头,轻轻移步,走入里面。只见那里:

> 琼香缭绕,瑞霭缤纷。瑶台铺彩结,宝阁散氤氲。凤翥鸾翔形缥缈,金花玉萼影浮沉。上排着九凤丹霞庆,八宝紫霓墩。五彩描金桌,千花碧玉盆。桌上有龙肝和凤髓,熊掌与猩唇。珍馐百味般般美,异果嘉肴色色新。

那里铺设得齐齐整整,却还未有仙来。这大圣点看不尽,忽闻得一阵酒香扑鼻;忽转头,见右壁厢长廊之下,有几个造酒的仙官,盘糟的力士,领几个运水的道人,烧火的童子,在那里洗缸刷瓮,已造成了玉液琼浆,香醪佳酿。大圣止不住口角流涎,就要去吃,奈何那些人都在这里。他就弄了个神通,把毫毛拔下几根,丢入口中嚼碎,喷将出去,念声咒语,叫"变!"即变做几个瞌睡虫,奔在众人脸上。你看那伙人,手软头低,闭眉合眼,丢了执事,都去盹睡。大圣却拿了些百味八珍,佳肴异品,走入长廊里面,就着缸,挨着瓮,放开量,痛饮一番。吃勾了多时,酕醄醉了。自揣自摸道:"不好!不好!再过会,请的客来,却不怪我?一时拿住,怎生是好?不如早回府中睡去也。"

【8】 好大圣,摇摇摆摆,仗着酒,任情乱撞,一会把路差了;不是齐天府,却是兜率天宫。一见了,顿然醒悟道:"兜率宫是三十三天之上,乃离恨天太上老君之处,如何错到此间?——也罢!也罢!一向要来望此老,不曾得来,今趁此残步,就望他一望也好。"即整衣撞进去。那里不见老君,四无人迹。原来那老君与燃灯古佛在三层高阁朱陵丹台上讲道,众仙童、仙将、仙官、仙吏,都侍立左右听讲。这大圣直至丹房里面,寻访不遇,但见丹灶之旁,炉中有火。炉左右安放着五个葫芦,葫芦里都是炼就的金丹。大圣喜道:"此物乃仙家之至宝。老孙自了道以来,识破了内外相同之理,也要炼些金丹济人,不期到家无暇;今日有缘,却

又撞着此物，趁老子不在，等我吃他几丸尝新。"他就把那葫芦都倾出来，就都吃了，如吃炒豆相似。

【9】　一时间丹满酒醒，又自己揣度道："不好！不好！这场祸，比天还大；若惊动玉帝，性命难存。走！走！走！不如下界为王去也！"他就跑出兜率宫，不行旧路，从西天门，使个隐身法逃去。即按云头，回至花果山界。但见那旌旗闪灼，戈戟光辉，原来是四健将与七十二洞妖王，在那里演习武艺。大圣高声叫道："小的们！我来也！"众怪丢了器械，跪倒道："大圣好宽心，丢下我等许久，不来相顾！"大圣道："没多时！没多时！"且说且行，径入洞天深处。四健将打扫安歇，叩头礼拜毕。俱道："大圣在天这百十年，实受何职？"大圣笑道："我记得才半年光景，怎么就说百十年话？"健将道："在天一日，即在下方一年也。"大圣道："且喜这番玉帝相爱，果封做'齐天大圣'，起一座齐天府，又设安静、宁神二司，司设仙吏侍立。向后见我无事，着我代管蟠桃园。近因王母娘娘设'蟠桃大会'，8未曾请我，是我不待他请，先赴瑶池，把他那仙品、仙酒，都是我偷吃了。走出瑶池，踉踉跄跄误人老君宫阙，又把他五个葫芦金丹也偷吃了。但恐玉帝见罪，方才走出天门来。"

【10】　众怪闻言大喜。即安排酒果接风，将椰酒满斟一石碗奉上。大圣喝了一口，即咨牙俫嘴道："不好吃！不好吃！"崩、芭二将道："大圣在天宫，吃了仙酒、仙肴，是以椰酒不甚美口。常言道：'美不美，乡中水。'"你们都曾尝着。待我再去偷他几瓶回来，你们各饮半杯，一个个也长生不老。"众猴欢喜不胜。大圣即出洞门，又翻一筋斗，使个隐身法，径至蟠桃会上。进孺池宫阙，只见那几个造酒、盘糟、运水、烧火的，还鼾睡未醒。他将大的从左右胁下挟了两个，两手提了两个，即拨转云头回来，会众猴在于洞中，就做个"仙酒会"，各饮了几杯，快乐不题。

【11】　却说那七衣仙女自受了大圣的定身法术，一周天方能解脱。各提花篮，回奏王母，说道："齐天大圣使术法困住我等，故此来迟。"王母问道："汝等摘了多少蟠桃？"仙女道："只有两篮小

桃，三篮中桃。至后面，大桃半个也无，想都是大圣偷吃了。及正寻间，不期大圣走将出来，行凶拷打，又问设宴请谁。我等把上会事说了一遍，他就定住我等，不知去向。直到如今，才得醒解回来。"

王母闻言，即去见玉帝，备陈前事。说不了，又见那造酒的一班人，同仙官等来奏："不知甚么人，搅乱了'蟠桃大会'，偷吃了玉液琼浆，其八珍百味，亦俱偷吃了。"又有四个大天师来奏上："太上道祖来了。"玉帝即同王母出迎。老君朝礼毕，道："老道宫中，炼了些'九转金丹'，伺候陛下做'丹元大会'，不期被贼偷去，特启陛下知之。"玉帝见奏，悚惧。少时，又有齐天府仙吏叩头道："孙大圣不守执事，自昨日出游，至今未转，更不知去向。"玉帝又添疑虑。只见那赤脚大仙又颏囟上奏道："臣蒙王母诏昨日赴会，偶遇齐天大圣，对臣言万岁有旨，着他邀臣等先赴通明殿演礼，方去赴会。臣依他言语，即返至通明殿外，不见万岁龙车凤辇，又急来此俟候。"玉帝越发大惊道："这厮假传旨意，赚哄贤卿，快着纠察巡官缉访这厮踪迹！"

【12】 灵官领旨，即出殿遍访，尽得其详细。回奏道："搅乱天宫者，乃齐天大圣也。"又将前事告诉一番。玉帝大恼。即差四大天王，协同李天王并哪吒太子，点二十八宿、九曜星官、十二元辰、五方揭谛、四值功曹、东西星斗、南北二神、五岳四渎、普天星相，共十万天兵，布一十八架天罗地网下界，去花果山围困，定捉获那厮处治。众神即时兴师，离了天宫。这一去，但见那：

黄风滚滚遮天障，紫雾腾腾罩地昏。只为妖猴欺上帝，致令众圣降凡尘。四大天王，五方揭谛：四大天王权总制，五方揭谛调多兵。李托塔中军掌号，恶哪吒前部先锋。罗睺星为头检点，计都星随后峥嵘。太阴星精神抖擞，太阳星照耀分明。五行星偏能豪杰，九曜星最喜相争。元辰星子午卯酉，一个个都是大力天丁。五瘟五岳东西摆，六丁六甲左右行。四渎龙神分上下，二十八宿密层层。角亢氐房为总领，奎娄胃昂惯翻腾。斗牛女虚危室壁，心尾箕星个个能，井鬼柳星张翼轸，轮枪舞剑显威灵。停云降雾临凡世，花果山前扎下营。

诗曰：

　　天产猴王变化多，偷丹偷酒乐山窝。

　　只因搅乱蟠桃会，十万天兵布网罗。

　　当时李天王传了令，着众天兵扎了营，把那花果山围得水泄不通。上下布了十八架天罗地网，先差九曜恶星出战。九曜即提兵径至洞外，只见那洞外大小群猴跳跃顽耍。星官厉声高叫道："那小猴！你那大圣在那里？我等乃上界差调的天神，到此降你这造反的大圣。教他快快来归降；若違半个'不'字，教汝等一概遭诛！"那妖慌忙传入道："大圣，祸事了！祸事了！外面有九个凶神，口称上界差来的天神，收降大圣。"

【13】那大圣正与七十二洞妖王，并四健将分饮仙酒，一闻此报，公然不理道："'今朝有酒今朝醉，莫管门前是与非。'"说不了，一起小妖又跳来道："那九个凶神，恶言泼语，在门前骂战哩！"大圣笑道："莫采他。'诗酒且图今日乐，功名休问几时成。'"说犹未了，又一起小妖来道："爷爷！那九个凶神已把门打破，杀进来也！"大圣怒道："这泼毛神，老大无礼！本待不与他计较，如何上门来欺我？"即命独角鬼王，领帅七十二洞妖王出阵，"老孙领四健将随后。"那鬼王疾帅妖兵，出门迎敌，却被九曜恶星一齐掩杀，抵住在铁板桥头，莫能得出。

【14】正嚷间，大圣到了。叫一声"开路！"掣开铁棒，幌一幌，碗来粗细，丈二长短，丢开架子，打将出来。九曜星那个敢抵，一时打退。那九曜星立停阵势道："你这不知死活的弼马温！你犯了十恶之罪，先偷桃，后偷酒，搅乱了蟠桃大会，又窃了老君仙丹，又将御酒偷来此处享乐，你罪上加罪，岂不知之？"大圣笑道："这几桩事，实有！实有！但如今你怎么？"九曜星道："吾奉玉帝金旨，帅众到此收降你，快早皈依！免教这些生灵纳命。不然，就踏平了此山，掀翻了此洞也！"大圣大怒道："量你这些毛神，有何法力，敢出浪言。不要走，请吃老孙一棒！"这九曜星一齐踊跃。那美猴王不惧分毫，轮起金箍棒，左遮右挡，把那九曜星战得筋疲力软，一个个倒拖器械，败阵而走，急入中军帐下，对托塔天王道："那猴王果十分骁勇！我等奈他不过，败阵来了。"李天王即调四大天王与二十八宿，一路出师来斗。大圣也公然不惧，调出独

角鬼王，七十二洞妖王与四个健将，就于洞门外列成阵势。你看这场混战好惊人也：

> 寒风飒飒，怪雾阴阴。那壁厢旌旗飞彩，这壁厢戈戟生辉。滚滚盔明，层层甲亮。滚滚盔明映太阳，如撞天的银磬；层层甲亮砌岩崖，似压地的冰山。大捍刀，飞云掣电，楮白枪，度雾穿云。方天戟，虎眼鞭，麻林摆列；青铜剑，四明铲，密树排阵。弯弓硬弩雕翎箭，短棍蛇矛挟了魂。大圣一条如意棒，翻来复去战天神。杀得那空中飞鸟过，山内虎狼奔；扬砂走石乾坤黑，播土飞尘宇宙昏。只听兵兵扑扑惊天地，煞煞威威振鬼神。

这一场自辰时布阵，混杀到日落西山。那独角鬼王与七十二洞妖怪，尽被众天神捉拿去了，止走了四健将与那群猴，深藏在水帘洞底。这大圣一条棒，抵住了四大天神与李托塔、哪吒太子，俱在半空中，——杀彀多时，大圣见天色晚，即拔毫毛一把，丢在口中，嚼碎了，喷将出去，叫声"变！"就变成了千百个大圣，都使的是金箍棒，打退了哪吒太子，战败了五个天王。

【15】 大圣得胜，收了毫毛，急转身回洞，早又见铁板桥头，四个健将，领众叩接那大圣，哽哽咽咽大哭三声，又唏唏哈哈大笑三声。大圣道："汝等见了我，又哭又笑，何也？"四健将道："今早帅众将与天王交战，把七十二洞妖王与独角鬼王，尽被天神捉了，我等逃生，故此该哭。这见大圣得胜回来，未曾伤损，故此该笑。"大圣道："胜负乃兵家之常。古人云：'杀人一万，自损三千。'况捉了去的头目乃是虎豹、狼虫、獾獐、狐狢之类，我同类者未伤一个，何须烦恼？他虽被我使个分身法杀退，他还要安营在我山脚下。我等且紧紧防守，饱食一顿，安心睡觉，养养精神。天明看我使个大神通，拿这些天将，与众报仇。"四将与众猴将椰酒吃了几碗，安心睡觉不题。

【16】 那四大天王收兵罢战，众各报功：有拿住虎豹的，有拿住狮象的，有拿住狼虫狐狢的，更不曾捉往一个猴精。当时又安辕营，下大寨，赏犒了得功之兵，吩咐了天罗地网之兵，各各提铃喝号，围困了花果山，专待明早大战。各人得令，一处处谨守。此正是：妖猴作乱惊天地，布网张罗昼夜看。毕竟天晓后如何处治，且听下回分解。

Chapter 1
After Chaos Among the Peaches the Great Sage Steals the Pills;
In the Revolt Against Heaven the Gods Capture the Demons

(The Monkey King Sun Wukong was born bursting out of an egg of stone. He pledged himself to a Master who taught him his mystic arts. His training complete, his magical powers were great. He was adept at the seventy-two transformations and able to travel 108,000 li with a single somersault. He took a gold-banded cudgel from the Dragon King's Palace and descended to yamen of the Netherworld to scratch his name from the Book of Life and Death. The Dragon King and the Lord of the Netherworld petitioned the Jade Emperor begging him to dispatch the Heavenly Armies to suppress the obstreperous Sun Wukong. But how could the Heavenly Generals and Heavenly Armies prevail? The Jade Emperor could only yield to Sun Wukong's wish, conferring upon him the title "Great Sage Equal to Heaven," an official post, but one without remuneration, without authority and without duties.)

【1】 The story goes on to relate that the Great Sage Equalling Heaven, a mere monkey devil after all, was quite satisfied that his name was on the register of office without caring about the grading of his job and his own rank, or the size of his salary. The immortal clerks in the two offices in his residence were in constant attendance on him, he had three meals a day and a bed to sleep on at night, and he lived a free and easy life without worries. In his spare time he would visit the other palaces, get together with his old friends, and make new ones. When he saw the Three Pure Ones, he would address them as "venerable," and when he met the Four Emperors he called them "Your Majesty." He was on fraternal terms with the Nine Bright Shiners, the Generals of the Five Regions, the Twenty-Eight Constellations, the Four Great

Heavenly Kings, the Gods of the Twelve Branches, the Five Ancients of the Five Regions, the star ministers of the whole sky, and the countless gods of the Milky Way. Today he would wander east, and tomorrow he would go west, coming and going by cloud, and never staying anywhere for long.

[2] When the Jade Emperor was holding his morning court one day the Immortal Xu of Jingyang came forward from the body of officials, kowtowed, and suggested, "The Great Sage Equalling Heaven is spending his time in idle travel, and is making the acquaintance of all the stars in the sky, calling them all his friends irrespective of their rank. It would be as well to give him some responsibility, and prevent his idleness leading to trouble later on." The Jade Emperor's response to this suggestion was to send for the Monkey King at once. He came in a cheerful mood and asked, "What promotion and reward have you summoned me here to receive, Your Majesty?" "Seeing that you are idle and have nothing to do," replied the Jade Emperor, "we are giving you a job. You are to administer the Peach Orchard, and you will give it your attention day and night." The Great Sage was overjoyed, and after expressing his thanks and chanting "na-a-aw" he withdrew.

[3] In his eagerness to be at work he went straight to the Peach Orchard to have a look round. When he got there he was stopped by a local tutelary god who asked him, "Where are you going, Great Sage?" "I've been put in charge of the Peach Orchard by the Jade Emperor, and I've come to inspect it." The local god hastened to greet him formally, and he called the men who weeded, brought water, looked after the trees, and swept the grounds to come and kowtow to the Great Sage. When Sun Wukong was taken inside this is what he saw:

> *Charming,*
> *Every tree.*
> *Charming and luxuriant the full blossom;*
> *Every tree weighed down with fruit.*
> *The fruit-laden branches bend like carding-bows;*

12

The blossoming trees are covered with powder and rouge.
Always blossoming, always in fruit, they are ripe for a
thousand years;
They know no summer or winter, but linger for ever.
The early ripeners
Look red-faced and tipsy;
The ones still growing
Are green in stalk and skin.
When the dew forms, their flesh has a touch of blue,
While the sun picks out their vermilion beauty.
Below the trees exotic flowers grow,
Bright and unfading throughout the year.
On either side stand towers and pavilions,
And a rainbow always arches the sky.
These are not the common breeds of the Dark Earth
Capital,
But are tended by the Queen Mother of the Jade Pool.

After taking a good look at this the Great Sage asked the local god, "How many of these trees are there?" "Three thousand six hundred all together," the local god replied. "The ones growing at the front have tiny blossoms and small fruits, and they ripen every three thousand years. Anyone who eats them becomes an Immortal and understands the Way, and his body becomes both light and strong. The twelve hundred in the middle have multiple blossoms and sweet fruits, and ripen every six thousand years; whoever eats them can fly and enjoy eternal youth. The back twelve hundred are streaked with purple and have pale yellow stones. They ripen once every nine thousand years, and anyone who eats them becomes as eternal as Heaven and Earth, as long-lived as the Sun and Moon." The Great Sage was beside himself with joy on learning this, and that day he checked the number of the trees and looked over the buildings in the orchard before going back to his residence. From then on he went to admire them every three or four days. He dropped his friends, and made no more pleasure jaunts.

13

[4] One day he noticed that the peaches near the end of the branches of one old tree were all but ripe, and he felt like trying one; but as the local god, the workmen, and the immortal clerks from his residence were close on his heels it was impossible. Suddenly he had an idea, and he said, "Go and wait for me outside the gates while I take a nap in this summerhouse." All the Immortals thereupon withdrew, and the Monkey King took off his official hat and clothes, climbed one of the bigger trees, and chose some large, ripe peaches. When he had picked a good number he sat at his ease in the branches and ate his fill of them, then jumped down from the tree, pinned on his hat, put on his clothes, and shouted for all his attendants to go back to his residence with him. Two or three days later he thought of another trick to steal some more peaches, and he ate his fill of them.

[5] One day the Queen Mother arranged a banquet, opening many precious pavilions for a feast of peaches by the Jade Pool. She sent the Red Fairy, the Blue Fairy, the White Fairy, the Black Fairy, the Purple Fairy, the Yellow Fairy, and the Green Fairy to the Peach Orchard with their baskets to pick peaches for the feast. The seven fairies went straight to the orchard gates, the workmen of the orchard and the immortal superintendents of the two offices of the Equalling Heaven Residence were guarding the gate. The fairies went up to them and said, "We have come on the orders of the Queen Mother to pick peaches for a feast." "Wait a moment please, Immortal Beauties," said the local god. "Things are different this year. The Jade Emperor has appointed the Great Sage Equalling Heaven to be the guardian of this orchard, and we must ask him before we can open the orchard to you." "Where is the Great Sage?" the fairies asked, and the local god replied, "Inside the orchard. As he was feeling tired he is having a nap by himself in a summerhouse." "In that case, please find him without delay," requested the fairies, and the local god took them into the orchard. But all they could find of him in the summerhouse were his hat and clothes. They had no idea where he could have gone, and looked everywhere without success. The

14

Great Sage had in fact made himself only two inches long after eating some of the peaches for fun, and he was sleeping under a large leaf at the top of one of the big trees.

"We have come by decree, and we can't go back empty-handed, although the Great Sage is nowhere to be found," said the fairies. One of the immortal superintendents who was standing nearby replied, "As you Immortal Beauties have come by order of the Queen Mother, we must not delay you. Our Great Sage is always wandering off, so I expect that he has gone away to visit some of his friends. You had better pick the peaches; it will be all right if we inform him." The fairies did as he suggested and went into the orchard to pick peaches. First they filled two baskets from the trees in front, and then they picked three basketfuls from the trees in the middle; but when they came to the trees at the back, they saw that peaches and blossoms were few and far between. Only a few unripe fruits with furry stalks and green skins were left. All the ripe ones had been eaten up by the Monkey King. The seven fairies looked everywhere, but all they could see was a single red and white peach on a southern branch. The Blue Fairy pulled the branch down, the Red Fairy picked the peach, and then they let the branch go again. This woke up the Great Sage, who had changed himself into this peach to take a nap on this branch. He resumed his own form, took his gold-banded cudgel from his ear, shook it till it was as thick as a ricebowl, and shouted at them, "Where are you from, you thieving fiends?" The seven fairies fell on their knees in confusion. "Please don't be angry with us, Great Sage. We're not fiends but seven fairies sent by Her Majesty the Queen Mother of the West to pick peaches of immortality and open the precious halls here for a Feast of Peaches. When we arrived here we saw the local god and other deities of the place, but we could not find you, Great Sage. We could not delay carrying out the Queen Mother's orders, so we went ahead and picked the peaches without waiting for you, Great Sage. We very much hope that you will forgive us." These words turned the Great Sage's bad mood into a good one, and he said, "Please rise, Fairy Beauties.

15

Who is the Queen Mother inviting to this feast?" "There are old rules about who attends: The Buddha of the Western Heaven, Bodhisattvas, holy monks, Arhats, the Guanyin of the South Pole, the Merciful and Sage Emperor of the East, the Venerable Immortals of the Ten Continents and the Three Islands, the Mystic Divinity of the North Pole, and the Great Yellow-horned Immortal of the Yellow Pole at the Centre. These make up the Five Venerable Ones of the Five Regions. There will also be the Star Lords of the Five Constellation; the Three Pure Ones, the Four Emperors and the Heavenly Immortal of the Great Monad from the Eight High Caves; the Jade Emperor, the immortals of the Nine Mounds, and the gods of the Seas and Mountains and the Ruler of the Nether World from the Eight Lower Caves; and the terrestrial deities. All the major and minor gods of all the halls and palaces will come to the Feast of Peaches." "Will I be invited?" asked the Great Sage with an ingratiating smile. "Not as far as we've heard," the fairies replied. "I'm the Great Sage Equalling Heaven, so why shouldn't I be asked?" said the Great Sage. "That was what happened before: we don't know about this time," the fairies replied. "You're right," he said. "Just wait here while I go and find out whether I'm invited."

[6] Splendid Great Sage. Making a magic with his hands as he spoke the words of the spell, he said to the fairies, "Stay where you are! Stay where you are!" As this was an immobilizing spell, the seven fairies were left standing in a daze under the peach tree with their eyes wide open as the Great Sage leapt out of the orchard on a somersault cloud and headed for the Jade Pool. As he travelled he saw that

> *The sky shimmered with auspicious light*
> *As clouds of many colours streamed across it.*
> *The white stork's cry made the heavens shake;*
> *A thousand leaves grew on the purple asphodel.*
> *Amid it all an Immortal appeared,*
> *Carrying himself with heaven-sent elegance,*
> *As he danced on the rainbow, cloaked by the Milky Way,*

With a talisman at his waist to ward off birth and death.
His name was Bare-foot Immortal,
And he was going to the feast of longevity-giving peaches.

As the Bare-foot Immortal saw him, the Great Sage lowered his head and thought of a plan by which to trick the Immortal and get to the banquet himself. "Where are you going, reverend sir?" he asked; and the Immortal replied, "I'm going to the Peach Banquet by the invitation of the Queen Mother." "There is something you do not know, venerable sir," said the Great Sage. "As my somersault cloud is so fast, the Jade Emperor has sent me everywhere to tell all you gentlemen to go to the Hall of Universal Brightness for a ceremony before going on to the banquet." As the Immortal was an open and upright man, he took this lie for the truth, but wondered, "The thanksgiving ceremony is usually held by the Jade Pool, so why are we having the ceremony in the Hall of Universal Brightness before going to the Jade Pool for the banquet?" Nevertheless, he turned his propitious cloud around and went to the Hall of Universal Brightness.

【7】 As the Great Sage rode his cloud he said a spell, shook himself, took the form of the Bare-foot Immortal, and hurried to the Jade Pool. He reached the pavilion there a moment later, stopped his cloud, and went quietly inside. He saw

Fabulous perfumes coiling,
A confusion of auspicious clouds;
The jade tower set with colour,
The precious pavilions scattering mists;
The phoenix soars till almost lost to view,
And jewelled flowers seem to rise and fall.
Above a nine-phoenix screen
A rainbow stool of the eight precious things,
A coloured golden table,
Green jade bowls with a thousand flowers.
On the table were dragon livers and marrow of phoenix bone,

> *Bears' paws and apes' lips—*
> *A hundred different dishes, and all of them good;*
> *Rare fruits and fine delicacies, every one unique.*

Everything was neatly set out, but no Immortals had yet arrived. The Great Sage had not finished looking when he smelt wine; and as he whirled round he saw under a portico to the right several immortal officials in charge of brewing liquor with some workmen who stirred the lees, a number of novices who carried water and some boys who looked after the fires. They were washing the vats and scrubbing the pots, having made jade liquor and a fragrant fermentation of the lees. The Great Sage could not stop himself from drooling, and he longed to drink some, but unfortunately all those people were there. So he performed a spell by pulling several hairs from his body, chewing them up, spitting them up, saying the magic words, and shouting "Change"; whereupon the hairs turned into sleep insects, which flew into the faces of all the liquor-makers. Watch them as their hands go limp, their heads droop, their eyes close, and they drop their symbols of office and all fall asleep. Whereupon the Great Sage grabbed the rare delicacies and exotic foods, then went under the portico and drank from the vats and pots until he was completely drunk. Only then did he think, "This won't do at all. When the guests come for the banquet they'll be furious with me, and I'll be for it if I'm caught. I'd better get back to the residence as soon as I can and sleep it off."

[8] Our dear Great Sage staggered and swayed, charging about all over the place under the influence of the liquor, and going the wrong way. He arrived not at the Equalling Heaven Residence but at the Tushita Heavenly Palace. As soon as he saw this he sobered up and said to himself, "The Tushita Palace is the highest of the thirty-three heavens, where Lord Lao Zi of the Great Monad reigns. However did I get here? Never managed to come here before. I might as well go and have a look at him now that I'm passing this way." He straightened his clothes and rushed in, but did not see Lord Lao Zi. There was no sign of anyone. This

was because Lao Zi and the ancient Buddha Dipamkara were expounding the Way from a red dais in a triple-storeyed pavilion, and all the immortal boys, generals, officials and petty functionaries were standing to right and left listening to the lecture. The Great Sage went straight to the room in which the elixir was kept, and although he could not find Lao Zi there he saw that there was a small fire in the stove beside the range over which pills were made. On either side of the stove were five gourds, full of golden pills of refined elixir. "This is the Immortals' greatest treasure," he exclaimed in delight. "I've wanted to refine some of these golden pills to save people with ever since I understood the Way and mastered the principle of the correspondence of the Esoteric and Exoteric, but I've never had time to come here. Today I'm in luck—I've found them. As Lao Zi isn't here I'll try a few." He emptied the gourds of their contents and ate up all the pills as if he were eating fried beans.

[9] Before long he was full of pills and quite sober. "This is terrible," he thought, "this is a colossal disaster. If the Jade Emperor is shocked by this, I'm done for. I must get out of here. I'd be much better off as a king in the lower world." He rushed out of the Tushita Palace, avoiding his usual route. Using a spell to make himself invisible, he left by the West Gate of Heaven, and went straight down to the Mountain of Flowers and Fruit by cloud. When he got there he saw flags, banners, spears and halberds gleaming in the sun: the four Stalwart Generals and the seventy-two kings of the monsters were holding military exercises. "Children, I'm back," shouted the Great Sage in a loud voice, and all the fiends dropped their weapons and fell to their knees. "You don't care, do you, Great Sage?" they said. "It's been so long since you left us, and you never came back to see us." "I haven't been long, I haven't been long," protested the Great Sage, and as they talked they walked into the innermost part of the cave. When the four Stalwart Generals had tidied the place up and made him sit down, they kowtowed to him and asked, "What office did you hold, Great Sage, during your century and more in Heaven?" the Great Sage laughed and said,

"As far as I can remember it was only six months, so why do you say it was over a century?" "A day in Heaven is the same as a year on earth," the Stalwart Generals replied. "I was lucky this time," said the Great Sage. "The Jade Emperor took a liking to me and ennobled me as the Great Sage Equalling Heaven. He had an Equalling Heaven Residence built for me, complete with a Tranquillity Office and a Calm Divinity Office with Immortal functionaries, attendants and guards. Later on, when he saw that I had nothing to do, he put me in charge of the Peach Orchard. Recently the Queen Mother Goddess gave a Peach Banquet, but she didn't invite me. Instead of waiting for an invitation, I went to the Jade Pool and stole all the immortal food and drink. I staggered away from the Jade Pool and blundered into Lord Lao Zi's palace, and there I ate up his five gourds of pills of immortality. Then I got out through the heavenly gates and came here because I was scared that the Jade Emperor was going to punish me."

[10]   All the fiends were delighted with what they heard, and they laid on liquor and fruit with which to welcome him back. They filled a stone bowl with coconut toddy and handed it to him, but when he tasted it the Great Sage grimaced and said, "It's awful, it's awful." Two of his Stalwart generals, Beng and Ba, explained, "You don't find coconut toddy very tasty because you have drunk immortal liquor and eaten immortal food in the heavenly palace, Great Sage. But as the saying goes, 'Sweet or not, it's water from home'." To this the Great Sage replied, "And all of you, whether related to me or not, are from my home. When I was enjoying myself beside the Jade Pool today I saw jars and jars of jade liquor under a portico there. As none of you have ever tasted it I'll go and pinch you a few jars; then you can each have a little drink, and live for ever." All the monkeys were beside themselves with glee. The Great Sage then went out of the cave, turned a somersault, made himself invisible, and went straight to the Peach Banquet. As he went through the gates of the Jade Pool he saw that the men who made the wine, stirred the lees, carried the water, and looked after the fire were still

snoring away. He tucked two big jars of wine under his arms, took two more in his hands, then turned his cloud round and went back to have a feast of immortal wine with the monkey masses in the cave. They all drank several cups and were very happy, but we will not go into this.

[11]   The story returns to the seven fairies, who were only able to free themselves a whole day after Sun Wukong had immobilized them with his magic. They picked up their baskets and went back to report to the Queen Mother that they were late because the Great Sage Equalling Heaven had held them there by magic. "How many peaches did you pick?" the Queen Mother asked. "Two baskets of little ones and three baskets of medium ones. But when we got to the back we could not find a single big one; we think that they were all eaten by the Great Sage. While we were looking for some the Great Sage suddenly appeared, and he beat and tortured us to make us tell him who had been invited to the banquet. After we had told him he immobilized us there, and we don't know where he went. We only came round and freed ourselves a moment ago."

On hearing this the Queen Mother went to see the Jade Emperor and gave him a full account of what had happened. Before she had finished, the liquor-makers arrived with their immortal officials to report that an unknown person had thrown the Grand Peach Banquet into confusion and stolen the jade liquor as well as the precious delicacies of a hundred flavours. Then came Four Heavenly Teachers to announce that the Supreme Patriarch of the Way, Lao Zi, had arrived. The Jade Emperor went out with the Queen Mother to meet him, and after doing obeisance Lao Zi said, "I had refined some Golden Pills of the Nine Transformations in my palace for a Feast of Elixir Pills with Your Majesty, but a thief has stolen them. This is what I have come to report to Your Majesty." This news made the Jade Emperor tremble with fear. Not long afterwards the immortal administrators from the Equalling Heaven Residence came to kowtow and report: "The Great Sage Sun Wukong abandoned his post and went wandering off yesterday. He has not come back yet

21

and we do not know where he has gone." The Jade Emperor, now more suspicious than ever, then saw the Bare-foot Immortal bow his head to the ground. "Your subject was going to the banquet on a summons from the Queen Mother," he reported, "when I happened to meet the Great Sage Equalling Heaven. He told me, O Lord of Ten Thousand Years, that you had issued a decree ordering him to tell all the rest of us to go to the Hall of Universal Brightness for a ceremony before going to the banquet. Your subject went back to the Hall of Universal Brightness as he had told me to, but as I did not see the Imperial Dragon and Phoenix Chariot outside I hurried here to await orders." "This wretch has the impudence to invent fraudulent decrees and deceive eminent ministers," exclaimed the Jade Emperor with anger and astonishment. "The Miraculous Investigator is to find out at once what he has been up to."

【12】　The Miraculous Investigator left the palace in obedience to the edict, and by making thorough enquiries he found out all the details of what had happened. "The wrecker of the Heavenly Palace was Sun Wukong," he reported, and he went on to give a full account. The Jade Emperor was furiously angry, and he ordered the Four Great Heavenly Kings along with Heavenly King Li and Prince Nezha to mobilize the Twenty-eight Constellations, the Nine Bright Shiners, the Twelve Gods of the Twelve Branches, the Revealers of the Truth of the Five Regions, the Four Duty Gods, the Constellations of the East and West, the Gods of the North and South, the Deities of the Five Mountains and the Four Rivers, the star ministers of all Heaven, and a total of a hundred thousand heavenly soldiers. They were to descend to the lower world with eighteen heaven-and-earth nets, surround the Mountain of Flowers and Fruit, and capture that wretch for punishment. The gods called out their troops at once, and left the heavenly palace.

> *A gusty sandstorm blotted out the heavens,*
> *Purple fog threw the earth into darkness.*
> *Just because the monkey fiend offended the Supreme*

Emperor

Heavenly hosts were sent down to the mortal dust.

The Four Great Heavenly Kings,

The Revealers of the Truth of the Five Regions.

The Four Great Heavenly Kings held the supreme command,

And the Revealers controlled the soldiers' movements.

Li the Pagoda Carrier commanded the central corps,

Nezha the deadly led the van.

The star Rahu ordered the leading ranks,

And the star Ketu towered behind.

The Sun revealed his divinity,

And radiance shone from the Moon.

The stars of the Five Elements were mighty in valour,

And the Nine Bright Shiners were fond of battle.

The stars of the Branches Zi, Wu, Mao and You,

Were all great heavenly warriors.

The Five Plagues and the Five Mountains were drawn up on the east and west,

While the Six Ding and Six Jia marched to right and left.

The Dragon Gods of the Four Rivers stood above and below,

And the Twenty-eight Constellations were drawn up in serried ranks:

Horn, Gullet, Base, and Chamber were the officers commanding,

Strider, Harvester, Stomach, and Mane wheeled and soared;

Dipper, Ox, Woman, Barrens, Roof, House, and Wall, Heart, Tail, and

Winnower—all able stars—

Well, Ghost, Willow, Spread, Wing and Axletree

Wielded their swords and spears, showed forth their power,

Halted their clouds and descended in mists to the mortal world,

Pitching camp before the Mountain of Flowers and Fruit.

There is a poem that runs:

Many the transformations of the heaven-born Monkey King
Happy in his lair after stealing the pills and wine.
Just because he wrecked the banquet of peaches,
A hundred thousand heavenly troops now spread their nets.

Heavenly King Li gave the order for the heavenly soldiers to pitch camp and throw a watertight cordon round the Mountain of Flowers and Fruit. Above and below they spread eighteen heaven-and-earth nets, and the Nine Bright Shiners were sent out to start the battle. They took their soldiers to the outside of the cave, where they saw the monkeys, big and small, leaping and fooling around. The star officers shouted in harsh voices, "Little goblins, where's that Great Sage of yours? We are gods sent from the upper world to subdue your mutinous Great Sage. Tell him to surrender at once—and if there's so much as a hint of a 'no' from him, we will exterminate every last one of you." The little monkeys went rushing in to report, "Great Sage, a disaster, a disaster. There are nine evil gods outside who say they've been sent from the upper world to subdue you."

[13] The Great Sage, who was just then sharing the immortal liquor with the seventy-two kings of the monsters and his four Stalwart Generals, paid no attention to the report, saying:

"Today we have wine so today we celebrate;
To hell with what's happening outside the gate."

But before the words were out of his mouth another group of little devils came in. "Those nine evil gods are using foul and provocative language to challenge us to fight," they announced. "Never mind them," said the Great Sage with a laugh.

"With verse and wine we're happy today;
Who cares when fame will come our way?"

But before these words were out of his mouth yet another group of devils came rushing in. "Sir, those nine evil gods have smashed the gates and are charging in." "The stinking gods!" exploded the Great Sage, "What bloody cheek! I never wanted a fight with them, so why should they come here to push us around?" He thereupon ordered the One-horned Monster King to lead to seventy-two monster kings into battle while he followed them with the four Stalwart Generals. The monster king hastily assembled the devil soldiers and sallied forth to meet the enemy. They were all stopped by a charge by the Nine Bright Shiners, who held the head of the iron bridge so that no one could enter or leave.

[14] During the tumult the Great Sage came on the scene, and shouting "Make way" he raised his iron cudgel, shook it till it was as thick as a bowl and twelve feet long, and struck and parried as he came charging out. The Nine Bright Shiners, who were no match for him, fell back. "You reckless Protector of the Horses," they shouted when they were back in the safety of their own positions. "You have committed the most terrible crimes. You stole the peaches and the wine, wrecked the Peach Banquet, and pilfered the immortality pills of Lord Lao Zi. On top of all this you brought some of the immortal liquor you stole back here. Don't you realize that you have piled crime upon crime?" The Great Sage laughed. "It's true, it's true," he said, "but what are you going to do about it?" "In obedience to a golden edict of the Jade Emperor," the Nine Bright Shiners replied, "we have led our troops here to subdue you. Submit at once, or else all these creatures of yours will have to pay with their lives. If you refuse, we shall trample this mountain flat and turn your cave upside-down." "You hairy gods," roared the Great Sage in a fury, "what magic powers have you got to let you talk so big? Clear off, or I'll give you a taste of my cudgel." The Nine Bright Shiners did a war-dance together, which did not frighten the Handsome Monkey King in the least. He whirled his gold-banded cudgel, parrying to right and left, and fought the Nine Bright Shiners till their muscles were weak and their strength was gone; then each of them broke ranks and fled, dragging their weapons

25

behind them. They rushed to the command post of the central corps and reported to the Pagoda-Bearing Heavenly King Li that the Monkey King was so ferocious that they had fled from the battlefield, unable to defeat him. Heavenly King Li then sent the Four Heavenly Kings and the Twenty-eight Constellations into battle. The Great Sage, not at all frightened at this, ordered the One-horned Demon King, the seventy-two kings of the monsters, and the four Stalwart Generals to draw up their line of battle outside the gates of the cave. The ensuing melee was really terrifying.

> Howling winds,
> Dark, sinister clouds.
> On one side flags and standards colourfully flying,
> On the other side the gleam of spears and halberds.
> Round helmets shine,
> Layered armour gleams.
> The shining round helmets reflect the sun,
> Like silver boulders reaching to the sky;
> Gleaming layers of armour are built into a wall
> Like a mountain of ice weighing down the earth.
> Long-handled swords
> Flash through the clouds like lightning;
> Paper-white spears
> Pierce mists and fogs;
> Heaven-shaped halberds,
> Tiger-eye chains,
> Bristling like a field of hemp;
> Bronze swords,
> And four-brightness spears
> Drawn up like a dense forest.
> Bows and crossbows, eagle-feathered arrows,
> Short clubs and snaky spears to terrify the soul.
> Wielding his single as-you-will cudgel,
> The Great Sage fights against the heavenly gods.
> Such is the slaughter that no bird flies over it;

And tigers and wolves flee in terror.
The swirling stones and clouds of sand make everything dark,
The dirt and the dust blot out the heavens.
The clash of arms startles the universe
As the battle strikes awe into gods and demons.

The battle started in the morning and went on till the sun set behind the mountains in the west. By then the One-horned Demon King and the seventy-two kings of the monsters had all been captured by the heavenly hosts. Only the four Stalwart Generals and the monkeys had got away, and they were now hiding in the innermost recesses of the Water Curtain Cave. The Great Sage's solitary cudgel had fought off the Four Heavenly Kings, Li the Pagoda-bearer and Prince Nezha, who were all in the sky. After the battle had gone on for a long time the Great Sage saw that night was drawing on, so he plucked out one of his hairs, munched it up, spat out the pieces and shouted, "Change!" They changed into thousands of Great Sages, all with gold-banded cudgels, who forced Prince Nezha and the five Heavenly Kings to withdraw.

[15] After winning this victory the Great Sage put back his hair and hurried back to the cave, where the four Stalwart Generals at once led the monkeys out to kowtow at the head of the iron bridge to welcome him back. They sobbed three times and then laughed three times. "Why are you laughing and crying at the sight of me?" the Great Sage asked. "When we led all the commanders into battle against the heavenly kings this morning," replied the Stalwart Generals, "the seventy-two kings of the monsters and the One-horned Demon King were all captured by the gods, and we had to flee for our lives. That is why we cried. We laughed because you, Great Sage, have come back victorious and unharmed." To this the Great Sage replied, "Victory and defeat are all the soldier's lot. As the ancients said, 'To kill ten thousand of the enemy you must lose three thousand of your own.' Anyhow, the officers of ours who were captured were all

27

tigers, leopards, wolves, badgers, river-deer, foxes, and racoon-dogs. Not one of our own kind was even wounded, so there's no need for us to be bothered about it. But although I forced the enemy to withdraw by dividing up my body through magic, they're still encamped at the foot of our mountain, so we'll have to remain on our guard. Meanwhile we must eat a good meal and get a good night's sleep to build up our energy. Tomorrow morning I'll use powerful magic to capture those heavenly generals and avenge our people. " After the four Stalwart Generals and the other monkey commanders had drunk several cups of coconut toddy, they went to bed with their worries calmed.

[16] When the four Heavenly Kings had withdrawn their troops and ended the battle, those who had distinguished themselves reported what they had done. Some had captured tigers and leopards, some lions and elephants, and others wolves and racoon-dogs, but not one single monkey goblin had been taken. Then they built a mighty stockade around their camp. Commanders who had distinguished themselves were rewarded, and the soldiers who made up the heaven-and-earth nets were ordered to surround the Mountain of Flowers and Fruit, holding bells and shouting, ready for a great battle the next day. Every man heard the orders, and they were strictly obeyed. Indeed,

> A wicked monkey made chaos, shocking heaven and earth,
> So they spread their nets and watched by night and day.

Listen to the next instalment to hear how he was dealt with the following morning.

2. 观音赴会问原因
小圣施威降大圣

【1】　且不言天神围绕、大圣安歇。话表南海普陀落伽山大慈大悲救苦救难寻感观音菩萨，自王母娘娘请赴蟠桃大会，与大徒弟惠岸行者，同登宝阁瑶池，见那里荒荒凉凉，席面残乱；虽有几位天仙，俱不就座，都在那里乱纷纷讲论。菩萨与众仙相见毕，众仙备言前事。菩萨道："既无盛会，又不传杯，汝等可跟贫僧去见玉帝。"众仙怡然随往。至通明殿前，早有四大天师、赤脚大仙等众，俱在此迎着菩萨，即道玉帝烦恼，调遣天兵，擒怪未回等因。菩萨道："我要见玉帝，烦为转奏。"天师邱弘济、即入灵霄宝殿，启知宣入。时有太上老君在上，王母娘娘在后。

【2】　菩萨引众同入里面，与玉帝礼毕，又与老君、王母相见，各坐下。便问："蟠桃盛会如何？"玉帝道："每年请会，喜喜欢欢，今年被妖猴作乱，甚是虚邀也。"菩萨道："妖猴是何出处？"玉帝道："妖猴乃是东胜神洲傲来国花果山石卵化生的。当时生出，即目运金光，射冲斗府。始不介意，继而成精，降龙伏虎，自削死籍。当有龙王、阎王启奏。朕欲擒拿，是长庚星启奏道：'三界之中，凡有九窍者，可以成仙。'朕即施教育贤，宣他上界，封为御马监弼马温官。那厮嫌恶官小，反了天宫。即差李天王与哪吒太子收降，又降诏抚安，宣至上界，就封他做个'齐天大圣'，只是有官无禄。他因没事干管理，东游西荡。朕又恐别生事端，着他代管蟠桃园。他又不遵法律，将olive老树大桃，尽行偷吃。及至设会，他乃无禄人员，不曾请他；他就设计赚哄赤脚大仙，却自变他相貌入会，将仙肴仙酒尽偷吃了，又偷老君仙丹，又偷御酒若干，去与本山众猴享乐。朕心为此烦恼，故调十万天兵，天罗地网收伏。这一日不见回报，不知胜负如何。"

【3】　菩萨闻言，即命惠岸行者道："你可快下天宫，到花果山，打

29

探军情如何。如遇相敌，就相助一功，务必的实回话。"惠岸行者整整衣裙，执一条铁棍，驾云离阙，径至山前。见那天罗地网，密密层层，各营门提铃喝号，将那山围绕的水泄不通。惠岸立住，叫："把营门的天丁，烦你传报：我乃李天王二太子木叉，南海观音大徒弟惠岸，特来打探军情。"那营里五岳神兵，即传入辕门之内。早有虚日鼠、昴日鸡、星日马、房日兔，将言传到中军帐下。李天王发下令旗，教开天罗地网，放他进来。此时东方才亮。惠岸随旗进入，见四大天王与李天王下拜。拜讫，李天王道："孩儿，你自哪厢来者？"惠岸道："愚男随菩萨赴蟠桃会，菩萨见胜会荒凉，瑶池寂寞，引众仙并愚男去见玉帝。玉帝备言父王等下界收伏妖猴，一日不见回报，胜负未知，菩萨因命愚男到此打听虚实。"李天王道："昨日到此安营下寨，着九曜星挑战，被这厮大弄神通，九曜星俱败走而回。后我等亲自提兵，那厮也排开阵势。我等十万天兵，与他混战至晚，他使个分身法战退。及收兵着勘时，止捉得些狼虫虎豹之类，不曾捉得他半个妖猴。今日还未出战。"

　　说不了，只见辕门外有人来报道："那大圣引一群猴精，在外面叫战。"四大天王与李天王并太子正议出兵。木叉道："父王，愚男蒙菩萨吩咐，下来打探消息，就说若遇战时，可助一功。今不才愿往，看他怎么个大圣！"天王道："孩儿，你随菩萨修行这几年，想必也有些神通，切须在意。"

【4】　好太子，双手抡着铁棍，束一束绣衣，跳出辕门，高叫："那个是齐天大圣？"大圣挺如意棒，应声道："老孙便是。你是甚人，辄敢问我？"木叉道："吾乃李天王第二太子木叉，今在观音菩萨宝座前为徒弟护教，法名惠岸是也。"大圣道："你不在南海修行，却来此见我做甚？"木叉道："我蒙师父差来打探军情，见你这般猖獗，特来擒你！"大圣道："你敢说那等大话！且休走！吃老孙这一棒！"木叉全然不惧，使铁棍劈手相迎。他两个立那半山中，辕门外，这场好斗：

　　棍虽对棍铁各异，兵纵交兵人不同。一个是太乙散仙呼大圣，一个是观音徒弟正元龙。浑铁棍乃千锤打，六丁六甲运神功；如意棒是天河定，镇海神珍法力洪。两个相逢真对手，往来解数实无穷。这个阴手棍，万千凶，绕腰贯索疾如风；那个的夹枪棒，不放空，左遮右挡怎相容？那阵上旄旗闪闪，这阵上鼍鼓冬冬。万员天将团团绕，一洞妖猴簇簇丛。怪雾愁云漫地府，猴烟煞气射天宫。昨朝混战还犹可，今日争持更又凶。堪羡猴王真本事，木叉复败又逃生。

【5】　这大圣与惠岸战经五六十合，惠岸臂膊酸麻，不能迎敌，虚幌一幌，败阵而走。大圣也收了猴兵，安扎在洞门之外。只见天王营门外，大小天兵，接住了太子，让开大路，径入辕门，对四天王、李托塔、哪吒，气哈哈的，喘息未定："好大圣！好大圣！着实神通广大！孩儿战不过，又败阵而来也！"李天王见了心惊，即命写表求助，便差大力鬼王与木叉太子上天启奏。

　　二人当时不敢停留，闯出天罗地网，驾起瑞霭祥云。须臾，径至通明殿下，见了四大天师，引至灵霄宝殿，呈上表章。惠岸又见菩萨施礼。菩萨道："你打探的如何？"惠岸道："始领命到花果山，叫开天罗地网门，见了父亲，道明父亲命之意。父王道：'昨日与那猴王战了一场，止捉得他虎豹狮象之类，更未捉他一个猴精。'正讲间，他又索战，是弟子使铁棒与他战经五六十合，不能取胜，败走回营。父亲因此差大力鬼王同弟子上界求助。"菩萨低头思忖。

【6】　却说玉帝拆开表章，见有求助之言，笑道：叵耐这个猴精，能有多大手段，就敢敌过我天兵？"李天王又来求助，却将那路神兵助之？"言未毕，观音合掌启奏："陛下宽心，贫僧举一神，可擒此猴。"玉帝道："所举者何神？"菩萨道："乃陛下令甥显圣二郎真君，见居灌州灌江口，享受下方香火。他昔日曾力诛六怪，又有梅山兄弟与帐前一千二百草头神，神通广大。奈他只是听调不听宣，陛下可降一道调兵旨意，着他助力，便可擒也。"玉帝闻言，即传调兵的旨意，就差大力鬼王赍调。

【7】　那鬼王领了旨，即驾起云，径至灌江口。不消半个时辰，直至真君之庙。早有把门的鬼判，传报至里道："外有天使，捧旨而至。"二郎即与众弟兄，出门迎接旨意，焚香开读。旨意上云："花果山妖猴齐天大圣作乱。因在宫偷桃、偷酒、偷丹，搅乱蟠桃大会，见着十万天兵，一十八架天罗地网，围山收伏，未曾得

胜，今特调贤甥同义兄弟即赴花果山助力剿除。成功之后，高升重赏。"真君大喜道："天使请回，吾当就去拔刀相助也。"鬼王回奏不题。

【8】　这真君即唤梅山六兄弟——乃康、张、姚、李四太尉，郭申、直健二将军，聚集殿前道："适才玉帝调遣我等往花果山收降妖猴，同去去来。"众兄弟忻然愿往。即点本部神兵，驾鹰牵犬，搭弩张弓，纵狂风，霎时过了东洋大海，径至花果山。见那天罗地网，密密层层，不能前进，因叫道："把天罗地网的神将听着：吾乃二郎显圣真君，蒙玉帝调来，擒拿妖猴者，快开营门放行。"一时，各神一层层传入。四大天王与李天王俱出辕门迎接。相见毕，问及胜败之事，天王将上项事备陈一遍。真君笑道："小圣来此，必须与他斗个变化。列公将天罗地网，不要幔了顶上，只四围紧密，让我赌斗。若我输与他，不必列公相助，我自有兄弟扶持；若赢了他，也不必列公绑缚，我自有兄弟动手。只请托塔天王与我使个照妖镜，住立空中。恐他一时败阵，逃窜他方，切须与我照耀明白，勿走了他。"天王各居四维，众天兵各挨排列阵去讫。

【9】　这真君领着四太尉、二将军，连本身七兄弟，出营挑战，分付众将，紧守营盘，收了鹰犬。众草头神得令，真君只到那水帘洞外，见那一群猴，齐齐整整，排作个蟠龙阵势；中军里，立一竿旗，上书"齐天大圣"四字。真君道："那泼妖，怎么称得起齐天之职？"梅山六弟道："且休赞叹，叫战去来。"那营口小猴见了真君，急走去报知。那猴王即擎金箍棒，整黄金甲，登步云履，按一按紫金冠，腾出营门，急睁睛观看，那真君的相貌，果是清奇，打扮得又秀气。真个是：

> 仪容清俊貌堂堂，两耳垂肩目有光。
> 头戴三山飞凤帽，身穿一领淡鹅黄。
> 缕金靴衬盘龙袜，玉带团花八宝妆。
> 腰挎弹弓新月样，手执三尖两刃枪。
> 斧劈桃山曾救母，弹打棱罗双凤凰。
> 力诛八怪声名远，义结梅山六圣行。
> 心高不认天家眷，性傲归神住灌江。

　　赤城昭惠英灵圣，显化无边号二郎。

　　大圣见了，笑嘻嘻的，将金箍棒擎起，高叫道："你是何方小将，辄敢大胆到此挑战？"真君喝道："你这厮有眼无珠，认不得我么！吾乃玉帝外甥，敕封昭惠灵显王二郎是也。今蒙上命，到此擒你这反天宫的弼马温猢狲，你还不知死活！"大圣道："我记得当年玉帝妹子思凡下界，配合杨君，生一男子，曾使斧劈桃山的，是你么？我行要骂你几声，曾奈无甚冤仇；待要打你一棒，可惜了你的性命。你这郎君小辈，可急急回去，唤你四大天王出来。"真君闻言，心中大怒道："泼猴！休得无礼！吃吾一刃！"大圣侧身躲过，疾举金箍棒，劈手相还。他两个这场好杀：

　　昭惠二郎神，齐天孙大圣，这个心高欺敌美猴王，那个面生压伏真梁栋。两个乍相逢，各人皆赌兴。从来未识浅和深，今日方知轻与重。铁棒赛飞龙，神锋如舞凤。左挡右攻，前迎后映。这阵上梅山六弟助威风，那阵上马流四将传军令。摇旗擂鼓各齐心，呐喊筛锣都助兴。两个钢刀有见机，一来一往无丝缝。金箍棒是海中珍，变化飞腾能取胜。若还身慢命该休，但要差池命蹭蹬。

　　【10】　真君与大圣斗经三百余合，不知胜负。那真君抖擞神威，摇身一变，变得身高万丈，两只手，举着三尖两刃神锋，好便似华山顶上之峰，青脸獠牙，朱红头发，恶狠狠，望大圣着头就砍。这大圣也使神通，变得与二郎身躯一样，嘴脸一般，举一条如意金箍棒，却就如昆仑顶上的擎天之柱，抵住二郎神：唬得那马、流元帅，战兢兢，摇不得旌旗；am芭二将，虚怯怯，使不得刀剑。这阵上，康、张、姚、李、郭申、直健，传号令，撒放草头神，向他那水帘洞外，纵着鹰犬，搭弩张弓，一齐掩杀。可怜冲散妖猴四健将，捉拿灵怪二三千！那些猴，抛戈弃甲，撇剑丢枪；跑的跑，喊的喊；上山的上山，归洞的归洞：好似夜猫惊宿鸟，飞洒满天星。众兄弟得胜不题。

　　【11】　却说真君与大圣变做法天象地的规模，正斗时，大圣忽见本营中妖猴惊散，自觉心慌，收了法象，掣棒抽身就走。真君见他败走，大步赶上道："那里走？趁早归降，饶你性命！"大圣不恋战，只情跑起。将近洞口，正撞着康、张、姚、李四太尉，郭申、直

健二将军，一齐帅众挡住道："泼猴！那里走！"大圣慌了手脚，就把金箍棒捏做绣花针，藏在耳内，摇身一变，变做个麻雀儿，飞在树梢头钉住。那六兄弟，慌慌张张，前后寻觅不见，一齐吆喝道："走了这猴精也！走了这猴精也！"

【12】 正嚷处，真君到了，问："兄弟们，赶到那厢不见了？"众神道："才在这里围住，就不见了。"二郎圆睁睁凤目观看，见大圣变了麻雀儿，钉在树上，撒了法象，卸下弹弓，摇身一变，变做个饿鹰儿，抖开翅，飞将去扑打。大圣见了，搜的一翅飞起去，变做一只大鹚老，冲天而去。二郎见了，急抖翎毛，摇身一变，变做一只大海鹤，钻在云霄来嗛。大圣又将身按下，入涧中，变做一个鱼儿，淬入水内。二郎赶至涧边，不见踪迹。心中暗想道："这猢狲必然下水去也，定变做鱼虾之类。等我再变变拿他。"果一变变作个鱼鹰儿，飘荡在下溜头波面上，等待片时。那大圣变鱼儿，顺水正游，忽见一只飞禽，似青鹞，毛片不青；似鹭鸶，顶上无缨；似老鹳，腿又不红……"想是二郎变化了等我哩！……"急转头，打个花就走。二郎看见道："打花的鱼儿，似鲤鱼，尾巴不红；似鳜鱼，花鳞不见；似黑鱼，头上无星；似鲂鱼，鳃上无针。他怎么见了我就回去了？必然是那猴变的。"赶上来，刷的啄一嘴。那大圣就撺出水中，一变，变做一条水蛇，游近岸，钻入草中。二郎因嗛他不着，他见水响中，见一条蛇撺出去，认得是大圣，急转身，又变了一只朱绣顶的灰鹤，伸着一个长嘴，与一把尖头铁钳子相似，径来吃这水蛇。水蛇跳一跳，又变做一只花鸨，木木樗樗的，立在蓼汀之上。二郎见他变得低贱——花鸨乃鸟中至贱至淫之物，不拘鸾、凤、鹰、鸦都与交群——故此不去拢傍，即现原身，走将去，取过弹弓拽满，一弹子把他打个躘踵。

【13】 那大圣趁着机会，滚下山崖，伏在那里又变，变一座土地庙儿：大张着口，似个庙门，牙齿变做门扇，舌头变做菩萨，眼睛变做窗棂。只有尾巴不好收拾，竖在后面，变做一根旗竿。真君赶到崖下，不见打倒的鸨鸟，只有一间小庙；急睁凤眼，见旗竿立在后面，笑道："是这猢狲了！他今又在那里哄我。我也曾见庙宇，更不曾见一个旗竿竖在后面的。断是这畜生弄喧！他若哄我进去，他便一口咬住。我怎肯进去？等我拳先捣窗棂，后踢门

扇!"大圣听得,心惊道:"好狠!好狠!门扇是我牙齿,窗棂是我眼眼;若打了牙,捣了眼,却怎么是好?"扑的一个虎跳,又冒在空中不见。

真君前前后后乱赶,只见四太尉、二将军,一齐拥至道:"兄长,拿住大圣了么?"真君笑道:"那猴儿才自变座庙宇哄我。我正要捣他窗棂,踢他门扇,他就纵一纵,又渺无踪迹。可怪!可怪!"众皆愕然,四望更无形影。真君道:"兄弟们在此看守巡逻,等我上去寻他。"急纵身驾云,起在半空。见那李天王高擎照妖镜,与哪吒住立云端,真君道:"天王,曾见那猴王么?"天王道:"不曾上来。我这里照着他哩。"真君把那赌变化,弄神通,拿群猴一事说毕,却道:"他变庙宇,正打处,就走了。"李天王闻言,又把照妖镜四方一照,呵呵的笑道:"真君,快去!快去!那猴使了个隐身法,走出营围,往你那灌江口去也。"二郎听说,即取神锋,回灌江口来赶。

【14】　却说那大圣已至灌江口,摇身一变,变做二郎爷爷的模样,按下云头,径入庙里。鬼判不能相认,一个个磕头迎接。他坐中间,点查香火:见李虎拜还的三牲,张龙许下的保福,赵甲求子的文书,钱丙告病的良愿。正看处,有人报:"又一个爷爷来了。"众鬼判急急观看,无不惊心。真君却道:"有个甚么齐天大圣,才来这里否?"众鬼判道:"不曾见甚么大圣,只有一个爷爷在里面查点哩。"真君撞进门,大圣见了,现出本相道:"郎君不消嚷,庙宇已姓孙了!"这真君即举三尖两刃神锋,劈脸就砍。那猴王使个身法,让过神锋,掣出那绣花针儿,幌一幌,碗来粗细,赶到前,对面相还。两个嚷嚷闹闹,打出庙门,半雾半云,且行且战,复打到花果山,慌得那四大天王等众,提防愈紧。这康、张太尉等迎着真君,合心努力,把那美猴王围绕不题。

【15】　话表大力鬼王既调了真君与六兄弟提兵擒魔去后,却上界回奏。玉帝与观音菩萨、王母并众仙卿,正在灵霄殿讲话,道:"既是二郎已去赴战,这一日还不见回报。"观音合掌道:"贫僧请陛下同道祖出南天门外,亲去看看虚实如何?"玉帝道:"言之有理。"即摆驾,同道祖、观音、王母与众仙卿至南天门。早有些天丁、力士接着,开门遥观,只见众天丁布罗网,围住四面;李天王

与哪吒，擎照妖镜，立在空中；真君把大圣围绕中间，纷纷赌斗哩。菩萨开口对老君说："贫僧所举二郎神何如？——果有神通，已把那大圣围困，只是未得擒拿。我如今助他一功，决拿住他也。"老君道："菩萨将甚兵器？怎么助他？"菩萨道："我将那净瓶杨柳抛下去，打那猴头；即不能打死，也打个一跌，教二郎小圣好去拿他。"老君道："你这瓶乃磁器，准打着他便罢，若打不着他的头，或撞着他的铁棒，却不打碎了？你且莫动手，等我老君助他一功。"菩萨道："你有甚么兵器？"老君道："有，有，有。"将起衣袖，左膊上，取下一个圈子，道："这件兵器，乃锟钢抟炼的，被我将还丹点就，养就一身灵气，善能变化，水火不侵，又能套诸物；一名'金钢琢'，又名'金刚套'。当年过函关，化胡为佛，甚是亏他。早晚最可防身。等我丢下去打他一下。"

　　话毕，自天门上往下一掼，滴流流，径落花果山营盘里，可可的着猴王头上一下。猴王顾苦战七圣，却不知天上坠下这兵器，打中了天灵，立不稳脚，跌了一跤，爬将起来就跑；被二郎爷爷的细犬赶上，照腿肚子上一口，又扯了一跌。他睡倒在地，骂道："这个亡人，你不去妨家长，却来咬老孙！"急翻身爬不起来，被七圣一拥按住，即将绳索捆绑，使勾刀穿了琵琶骨，再不能变化。

　　【16】那老君收了金钢琢，请玉帝同观音、王母、众仙等，俱回灵霄殿。这下面四大天王与李天王诸神，俱收兵拔营，近前向小圣贺喜。都道："此小圣之功也！"小圣道："此乃天尊洪福，众神威权，我何功之有？"康、张、姚、李道："兄长不必多叙，且押这厮去上界见玉帝，请旨发落去也。"真君道："贤弟，汝等未受天箓，不得面见玉帝。教甲神兵押着，我同天王等上界回旨。你们帅众在此搜山，搜净之后，仍回灌口。待我请了赏，讨了功，回来同乐。"四太尉、二将军，依言领诺。这真君与众即驾云头，唱凯歌，得胜朝天。不多时，到通明殿外。天师启奏道："四大天王等众已捉了妖猴齐天大圣了，今来进献。"玉帝传旨，即命大力鬼王与天丁等众，押至斩妖台，将这厮碎剁其尸。咦！正是：欺诳今遭刑宪苦，英雄气概等时休。毕竟不知那猴王性命何如，且听下回分解。

Chapter 2
Guanyin Comes to the Feast and Asks the Reason Why; The Little Sage Uses His Might to Subdue the Great Sage

[1] We shall leave for the moment the Heavenly Generals making their encirclement and the soundly sleeping Great Sage. The story goes on to tell how the Compassionate and Merciful Miraculous Saviour from Suffering, the Bodhisattva Guanyin of Mount Potaraka in the Southern Sea, having been invited by the Queen Mother to the Peach Banquet, went to the precious pavilions at the Jade Pool with her great disciple Huian the Novice. She found the place deserted and the banquet ruined. The few Immortals present were not sitting at their places but holding confused discussions. When greetings were over the Immortals gave the Bodhisattva an account of what had happened. "If there is to be no banquet and no drinking," said the Bodhisattva, "you had better all come with me to the Jade Emperor." The Immortals were delighted to follow her, and when they arrived before the Hall of Universal Brightness the Four Heavenly Teachers, the Bare-foot Immortal and many others were all there to greet the Bodhisattva. They told her that the Jade Emperor had sent heavenly armies to capture the demon, but they had not yet returned. "I wish to see the Jade Emperor," said the Bodhisattva, "so may I trouble you to inform him on my behalf?" The heavenly teacher Qiu Hongji then went to the Hall of Miraculous Mist, and the Bodhisattva was invited in. She found that Lord Lao Zi was there in the place of honour, and that the Queen Mother was behind him.

[2] The Bodhisattva went in at the head of the others, and when she had done obeisance to the Jade Emperor she greeted Lao

37

Zi and the Queen Mother. After they had all sat down she asked what had happened at the Peach Banquet. "The banquet is held every year, and it is normally a very happy occasion," the Jade Emperor replied, "but this year that monkey fiend wrecked it, so that your invitation was worth nothing." "Where does this monkey fiend come from?" asked the Bodhisattva. "He was born from a stone egg on the Mountain of Flowers and Fruit in the land of Aolai in the Eastern Continent of Superior Body," the Jade Emperor replied. "When he was born golden beams flashed from his eyes that reached to the star palace. At first we paid no attention to him, but later on he became a spirit, subduing dragons and tigers, and erasing his own name from the registers of death. The Dragon Kings and King Yama of the underworld informed us of this in memorials, and we wanted to capture him, but the Star of Longevity memorialized that in the Three Worlds all beings with nine orifices can become Immortals. We therefore extended education to the worthy by summoning him to the upper world and appointing him Protector of the Horses in the Imperial Stable. But this was not good enough for the scoundrel, who rebelled against Heaven. We sent Heavenly King Li and Prince Nezha to accept his surrender, extended him an amnesty, and summoned him back to the upper world. We made him a 'Great Sage Equalling Heaven', though this carried no salary. As he had nothing to do he would go wandering all over the place, and for fear that this might lead to trouble we had him look after the Peach Orchard. Once again he flouted the law by stealing and eating every single one of the big peaches from the old trees. When the banquet was to be held he was not invited as his position was purely an honorary one; so he played a trick on the Bare-foot Immortal, went to the banquet looking like him, ate all the immortal delicacies, and drank all the immortal liquor. On top of this he stole Lord Lao Zi's pills of immortality and some imperial liquor, which he took to his mountain for the monkeys to enjoy. This made us very angry so we sent a hundred thousand heavenly troops to spread heaven-and-earth nets and subdue him. But we have received no reports today, so we do not know whether we have been victorious."

【3】 When the Bodhisattva heard this she said to Huian the Novice, "Hurry down from Heaven to the Mountain of Flowers and Fruit and find out about the military situation. If you meet with any opposition you may do your bit to help, but the important thing is to bring an accurate report back." Huian the Novice straightened his robes, took his iron staff, left the palace by cloud, and went straight to the mountain. He saw that with the layer upon layer of heaven-and-earth nets, and the men holding bells and shouting passwords at the gates of the camp, the cordon round the mountain was watertight. Huian stopped and called, "Heavenly soldiers at the gates of the camp, I would trouble you to report that I, Moksa, the second son of Heavenly King Li, also known as Huian, the senior disciple of Guanyin of the Southern Sea, have come to ask about the military situation." Then the divine soldiers of the Five Mountains inside the camp went in through the gates of the headquarters, where the Rat, the Cock, the Horse and the Hare stars reported the news to the commander of the central corps. Heavenly King Li sent a flag of command with the order that the heaven-and-earth nets were to be opened to let Huian in. The east was just beginning to grow light as Huian followed the flag in and bowed to Heavenly King Li and the four other heavenly kings. "Where have you come from, my son?" asked Heavenly King Li. "Your stupid son accompanied the Bodhisattva to the Peach Banquet, and when she found the banquet deserted and nobody at the Jade Pool, she took me and the other immortals to see the Jade Emperor. The Jade Emperor told her that you, father, and the other kings had gone down to the lower world to capture this monkey fiend. As the Jade Emperor has received no news all day on the outcome of the battle, the Bodhisattva sent me here to find out what has happened." "We arrived here and encamped yesterday," Heavenly King Li replied, "then sent the Nine Bright Shiners to challenge the enemy to battle, but that wretch used such tremendous magic powers that the Nine Bright Shiners all came back defeated. Then we led our own soldiers into action, and the

39

wretch also drew up his line of battle. Our hundred thousand heavenly soldiers fought an indecisive engagements with him till dusk when he used a spell to divide up his body and force us back. When we withdrew our forces and held an investigation, we found that we had only captured wolves, tigers, leopards, and so on, and had not even taken half a monkey fiend. We have not yet given battle today."

Before he had finished speaking someone appeared outside the gates of the headquarters to report that the Great Sage was outside at the head of a crowd of monkey spirits, clamouring for battle. The four other Heavenly Kings, Heavenly King Li, and Prince Nezha were all for committing their forces, but Moksa said, "Father, when your stupid son was instructed by the Bodhisattva to come here and find out the news, I was also told that if there was a battle I could do my bit to help. May I please go and see what sort of a 'Great Sage' he is, untalented though I am?" "My boy," said Heavenly King Li, "you have been cultivating your conduct with the Bodhisattva for some years now so I suppose that you must have acquired some magic powers, but do be very careful."

【4】 The splendid Prince Moksa hitched up his embroidered robes and charged out through the gates of the headquarters waving his iron staff with both hands. "Which of you is the Great Sage Equalling Heaven?" he shouted. "I am," answered the Great Sage, brandishing his as-you-will cudgel. "But who do you think you are, asking a question like that?" "I am Prince Moksa, the second son of Heavenly King Li, and I am now a disciple and a guard before the throne of the Bodhisattva Guanyin. My Buddhist name is Huian." "Why have you come here to see me instead of staying in the Southern Sea and cultivating your conduct?" asked the Great Sage, and Moksa replied, "My teacher sent me here to find out about the military situation, but now that I've seen your savagery I've come to capture you." "You talk big, don't you," said the Great Sage. "Well then, don't go away, try a taste of my cudgel." Moksa, not in the least frightened, struck at him with his iron staff. It was a fine fight

they fought, half-way up the mountainside outside the gates of
the headquarters.

> *The staves were matched, but made of different iron;*
> *The weapons clashed, but their masters were not the same.*
> *One was a wayward Immortal known as the Great Sage,*
> *The other a true dragon disciple of Guanyin.*
> *The cast-iron staff, beaten with a thousand hammers,*
> *Had been forged by the art of the Ding and the Jia.*
> *The as-you-will cudgel once anchored the Milky Way:*
> *As the Treasure Stilling the Sea its magic power was great.*
> *When the two met they were well matched indeed,*
> *And they parried and lunged at each other without end.*
> *The sinister cudgel,*
> *Infinitely murderous,*
> *Could whirl round your waist as quick as the wind,*
> *The spear-catching staff,*
> *Never yielding an opening,*
> *Was irresistible, parrying to right and left.*
> *On the one side the flags and banners fly,*
> *On the other the camel drums roll.*
> *Ten thousand heavenly generals in multiple encirclement;*
> *A cave of monkey devils densely packed together.*
> *Monstrous fogs and evil clouds cover the earth,*
> *While the smoke of deadly battle rises to the sky.*
> *Yesterday's fighting was bad enough;*
> *Today's struggle is even worse.*
> *The admirable skills of the Monkey King*
> *Put Moksa to flight, utterly defeated.*

【5】 After they had fought some fifty or sixty rounds, Huian's
arm and shoulders were numbed and aching, and he could resist
the Great Sage no longer. Waving his staff in a feint, he turned
away and ran. The Great Sage then withdrew his monkey soldiers
and encamped outside the gates of the cave. The big and little
heavenly soldiers at the gates of the other camp received Huian

41

and let him go straight to the headquarters, where he gasped and panted for breath as he said to the Four Heavenly Kings, Li the Pagoda-bearer, and his brother Prince Nezha, "What a Great Sage! What a Great Sage! His magic powers are too much for me. He beat me." Startled by this news, Heavenly King Li had a request for reinforcements written and sent the Strongarm Devil King and Prince Moksa up to Heaven to submit.

Not daring to waste a moment, the two messengers rushed out through the heaven-and-earth nets and mounted their propitious clouds. A moment later they arrived outside the Hall of Universal Brightness, where they greeted the Four Heavenly Teachers, who led them to the Hall of Miraculous Mist and handed up their memorial. Prince Moksa, or Huian, did homage to the Bodhisattva, who asked him what he had found out. "As you instructed me, I went to the Mountain of Flowers and Fruit," reported Huian, "asked them to open the gates of the heaven-and-earth nets, saw my father, and told him of the orders you had given him. His Majesty my father said that they fought against the Monkey King yesterday but did not capture a single monkey spirit—only tigers, leopards, lions, elephants and so on. While he was telling me this the Monkey King demanded battle again, so your disciple fought some fifty or sixty rounds against him with my iron staff, but I was no match for him. He beat me, and drove me back to the camp. This is why my father has sent me and the Strongarm Devil King up to Heaven to ask for reinforcements." The Bodhisattva lowered her head in deep thought.

[6] The Jade Emperor opened the memorial and saw that it contained a request for help. "This intolerable monkey spirit has enough tricks to fight off a hundred thousand heavenly soldiers," he observed with a smile. "Heavenly King Li has asked for reinforcements. Which heavenly soldiers should I send him?" Before the words were out of his mouth, Guanyin put her hands together and said, "Do not worry, Your Majesty. I can recommend a god to capture this monkey." "Which god?" the Jade Emperor asked, and the Bodhisattva replied, "Your

Majesty's nephew, the Illustrious Sage and True Lord Erlang, who is now living at Guanjiangkou in Guanzhou, enjoying the incense that the lower beings burn to him. In the past he exterminated the Six Bogies. He has the Brothers of Plum Hill and the twelve hundred straw-headed gods, and his magical powers are enormous. He will agree to be sent though he would not obey a summons to come here, so Your Majesty might like to issue a decree ordering him to take his troops to the rescue." The Jade Emperor then issued such a decree and sent the Strongarm Devil King to deliver it.

【7】 The devil king took the decree, mounted his cloud, and went straight to Guanjiangkou. He reached the temple of the True Lord within an hour. When the demon judges guarding the gates went in to report that there was an envoy from Heaven standing outside with an imperial decree, Erlang went with the brothers to receive the decree outside the gates, and incense was burned as he read.

> The Great Sage Equalling Heaven, the monkey fiend of the Mountain of Flowers and Fruit, has rebelled. Because he stole peaches, wine and pills while in Heaven and wrecked the Peach Banquet, we have despatched a hundred thousand heavenly soldiers and eighteen heaven-and-earth nets to surround the mountain and force him to submit, but we have not yet succeeded. We do now therefore especially appoint our worthy nephew and his sworn brothers to go to the Mountain of Flowers and Fruit and give their help in eliminating him. When you succeed, large rewards and high office shall be yours.

Erlang was delighted. He told the envoy from Heaven to go back and report that he would be putting his sword to the Emperor's service. We need not describe how the devil king reported back to Heaven.

【8】 The True Lord Erlang called the six sworn brothers of Plum Hill—Marshals Kang, Zhang, Yao, and Li, and Generals

43

Guo Shen and Shi Jian—together before the hall. "The Jade Emperor has just ordered us to the Mountain of Flowers and Fruit to subdue a monkey fiend," he said. "You are all coming with me." The brothers were all eager to go, and mustering their divine troops they unleashed a gale wind. In an instant they had crossed the Eastern Ocean, riding eagles and leading dogs, pulling their bows and drawing their crossbows, and had reached the Mountain of Flowers and Fruit. Finding that the many layers of heaven-and-earth nets were impenetrable, Erlang shouted, "Listen, all you generals in charge of the heaven-and-earth nets. I am the True Lord and the Illustrious Sage Erlang, and I have been sent here by the Jade Emperor to capture the monkey fiend. Open the gates of the camp and let me in at once." Each line of gods forming the nets let them through, and the four other Heavenly Kings and Heavenly King Li all came to welcome him outside the headquarters. When the introductions were over he asked how the fighting had gone, and the Heavenly Kings gave him a full account of what had happened. "Now that I, the Little Sage, have come here I shall have to match a few transformations with him," said Erlang with a smile. "I hope that all you gentlemen will maintain a close cordon with your heaven-and-earth nets, but don't screen off the top of the mountain; then I'll be able to fight him. If he beats me I shan't need the help of you gentlemen, as I have my brothers to support me; and if I beat him I won't have to trouble you to tie him up as my brothers can do it. I would just like to ask Heavenly King Li to stand in the sky and operate his fiend-detecting mirror. I'm worried that if he's beaten he may go and hide somewhere, so you will have to give me a clear view of him and not let him get away." The Heavenly Kings stayed in the four quarters, and all the heavenly soldiers were drawn up in their battle positions.

[9]   The True Lord Erlang went out at the head of the four marshals and the two generals—making seven sworn brothers with himself included—to challenge the enemy to battle; and he ordered his other officers to defend the camp firmly and keep the eagles and dogs under control. All the straw-headed gods

acknowledged the order. Erlang then went to the outside of the Water Curtain Cave, where he saw the monkey hordes neatly drawn up in a coiled-dragon battle line; in the middle of the central corps stood a pole with a banner on it reading "Great Sage Equalling Heaven." "What business has that loathsome fiend to call himself the equal of Heaven?" Erlang asked; and the six sworn brothers of Plum Hill replied, "Stop admiring him and challenge him to battle." When the junior monkeys at the gate of the camp saw the True Lord Erlang they rushed back to report, whereupon the Monkey King took his gold-banded cudgel, adjusted his golden armour, put on his cloud-walking shoes, felt his golden helmet, and leapt out through the gates of the camp. He saw at first sight how cool and remarkable Erlang looked, and how elegantly he was dressed. Indeed,

> His bearing was refined, his visage noble,
> His ears hung down to his shoulders, and his eyes shone.
> The hat on his head had three peaks and phoenixes flying,
> And his robe was of a pale goose-yellow.
> His boots were lined with cloth of gold; dragons coiled round his socks;
> His jade belt was decorated with the eight jewels,
> At his waist was a bow, curved like the moon,
> In his hand a double-edged trident.
> His axe had split open Peach Mountain when he rescued his mother,
> His bow had killed the twin phoenixes of Zongluo.
> Widespread was his fame for killing the Eight Bogies,
> And he had become one of Plum Hill's seven sages.
> His heart was too lofty to acknowledge his relatives in heaven;
> In his pride he went back to be a god at Guanjiang.
> He was the Merciful and Miraculous Sage of the red city,
> Erlang, whose transformations were numberless.

When the Great Sage saw him he laughed with delight,

raised his gold-banded cudgel, and shouted, " Where are you from, little general, that you have the audacity to challenge me?" "You must be blind, you wretch, if you can't recognize me. I am the nephew of the Jade Emperor, and my title is Merciful and Miraculous King Erlang. I am here on imperial orders to arrest you, Protector of the Horses, you rebel against Heaven, you reckless baboon." " Now I remember who you are, " replied the Great Sage. "Some years ago the Jade Emperor's younger sister wanted to be mortal and came down to the lower world, where she married a Mr. Yang and gave birth to a son, who split the Peach Mountain open with his axe. Is that who you are? I should really fling you a few curses, but I've got no quarrel with you; and it would be a pity to kill you by hitting you with my cudgel. So why don't you hurry back, young sir, and tell those four Heavenly Kings of yours to come out?" When the True Lord Erlang heard this he burst out angrily, "Damned monkey! Where are your manners? Try this blade of mine!" The Great Sage dodged the blow and instantly raised his gold-banded club to hit back. There was a fine battle between the two of them:

> The Merciful God Erlang,
> The Great Sage Equalling Heaven:
> One is the Handsome Monkey King, the proud deceiver of
> his enemies;
> The other a true pillar, the unknown subduer.
> When the two met
> They were both in a fighting mood.
> He who had no respect before
> Today learnt a sense of proportion.
> The iron staff raced with the flying dragons,
> The divine cudgel seemed like a dancing phoenix.
> Parrying to the left, thrusting to the right,
> Advancing to meet a blow, flashing behind.
> The brothers of Plum Hill add to one side's might,
> While the other has the four Stalwart Generals to transmit
> orders.

As the flags wave and the drums roll each side is as one;
Battle-cries and gongs raise everyone's morale.
The two steel blades each watch for their chance,
But neither leaves an opening as they come and go,
The gold-banded cudgel, the treasure from the sea,
Can fly and transform itself to win the victory.
A moment's delay and life is lost;
A single mistake will be the last.

[10]   After Erlang and the Great Sage had fought over three hundred rounds the outcome of the fight was still undecided. Erlang braced himself, and with a shake became ten thousand fathoms tall; in his hands his two-bladed trident looked like the peaks of Mount Hua. His face was black, his fangs were long, and his hair was bright red: he looked ferociously evil. He hacked at the Great Sage's head. The Great Sage, also resorting to magic, gave himself a body as big as Erlang's and a face as frightening; and he raised his as-you-will gold-banded cudgel, which was now like the pillar of Heaven on the summit of the Kunlun Mountain, to ward off Erlang's blow. This reduced the two ape field marshals Ma and Liu to such trembling terror that they could no longer wave their banners, while the gibbon generals Seng and Ba were too scared to use their swords. On the other side Kang, Zhang, Yao, Li, Guo Shen and Zhi Jian threw the straw-headed gods into an assault on the Water Curtain Cave, with the dogs and eagles unleashed and their bows and crossbows drawn. This attack put the four monkey generals to flight, and two or three thousand devils were captured. The monkeys threw away their spears, tore off their armour, abandoned their swords and halberds, and fled screaming. Some went up the mountain and some returned to the cave, like roosting birds frightened by an owl, or stars scattered across the sky. That is all we have to say about the sworn brothers' victory.

[11]   The story goes on to tell how the True Lord Erlang and the Great Sage, having turned themselves into figures on the scale of Heaven and Earth, were locked in battle when the Great Sage

was suddenly appalled to notice that the monkey fiends in his camp had scattered in terror. Putting off his magic appearance he broke away and fled, his cudgel in his hand. Seeing him go, the True Lord Erlang hurried after him with long strides. "Where are you going?" he asked. "If you surrender at once, your life will be spared." The Great Sage, who had no heart left for the fight, was running as fast as he could. As he approached the mouth of the cave he came up against Marshals Kang, Zhang, Yao and Li, as well as Generals Guo Shen and Zhi Jian, blocking his way at the head of their armies. "Where are you going, damned monkey?" they asked, and the Great Sage hastily squeezed his gold-banded cudgel till it was the size of an embroidery needle and hid it in his ear. Then he shook himself, turned into a sparrow, flew up into a tree, and perched on one of its branches. The six sworn brothers looked for him very hard but could find him nowhere, so they all shouted in unison, "The monkey fiend has escaped, the monkey fiend has escaped."

[12] As they were shouting the True Lord Erlang arrived and asked them, "Brothers, where had you chased him to when he disappeared?" "We had him surrounded here just now, but he vanished." Erlang opened his phoenix eyes till they were quite round and looked about him. He saw that the Great Sage had changed himself into a sparrow and was perching on a branch; so he put off his magical appearance, threw down his divine trident, and took the pellet bow from his waist. Then he shook himself, changed into a kite, spread his wings, and swooped in to attack. As soon as the Great Sage saw this he took off and turned himself into a big cormorant, soaring up into the sky. Erlang saw him, and with a quick shake of his feathers and a twist of his body he transformed himself into a crane and pierced the clouds as he tried to catch him. The Great Sage landed on a mountain stream and, changing into a fish, plunged into the water. Erlang, who had pursued him to the bank of the stream, could see no trace of him. "That macaque must have gone into the water and changed himself into some kind of fish or shrimp," he thought. "I'll transform myself again, then I'll get him." He turned into a fish-

hawk and soared above the lower reaches of the stream and the first waves of the sea. He waited there for a time. Meanwhile the Great Sage, who was in the form of a fish, swam with the stream until he noticed a bird flying above him. It was quite like a blue kite, except that its feathers were not blue; it was quite like an egret, but it had no crest on its head; and it was quite like a stork, but its legs were not red. "That must be what Erlang turned himself into while waiting for me," he thought, turned round quickly, and went away. "The fish who turned round," thought Erlang when he saw this, "is like a carp but its tail isn't red; it's like a mandarin fish, but I can't see the pattern on its scales; it's like a snake-fish, but without a star on its head; and like a bream, but it has no needles on its gills. Why did it turn round the moment it saw me? It must be that monkey transformed." He swooped down and snapped at the Great Sage with his beak. The Great Sage leapt out of the water, turned into a water-snake, swam to the bank, and slid into the grass. Failing to catch the fish in his beak, Erlang saw a snake jump out of the water and realized it was the Great Sage. He changed himself at once into a red-crested grey crane, and stretched out his long beak that was like a pair of pointed pincers to eat up the water-snake. The snake gave a jump and became a bustard standing stiffly on a smartweed-covered bank. When Erlang saw that he had turned himself into so low a creature—for the bustard is the lowest and lewdest of birds, not caring whether it mates with phoenix, eagle or crow—he kept his distance, reverted to his own body, went away to fetch and load his pellet bow, and knocked him flying with a single shot.

[13]   The Great Sage seized the chance as he rolled down the precipice to crouch there and turn himself into a temple to a local god. He opened his mouth wide to look like the entrance to the temple and turned his teeth into the doors; he made his tongue into a statue of a god and his eyes into windows and lattice. He could not tuck his tail away, so he stuck it up behind him as a flagpole. When Erlang came to the foot of the precipice he could not see the bustard he had shot over, and anxiously opening his

phoenix eyes he looked carefully around and saw a temple with its flagpole at the back. "It must be that monkey over there," he observed with a smile. "He's trying to fool me again. I've seen temples before, but never one with the flagpole at the back. I'm sure it is that beast up to his tricks again. If he'd managed to lure me in, he'd have been able to get me with a single bite. Of course I won't go in. I'll smash his windows in with my fist, then I'll kick his door down." "Vicious, really vicious," thought the Great Sage with horror when he heard him say this. "Those doors are my teeth, and the windows are my eyes; and if he smashes my teeth and bashes in my eyes, what sort of a state will that leave me in?" With a tiger leap he disappeared into the sky.

The True Lord Erlang rushed around wildly, but he could only see his six sworn brothers, who crowded round him and asked, "Elder brother, did you catch the Great Sage?" "That monkey turned himself into a temple to fool me," he replied with a laugh. "Just when I was going to smash his windows and kick in his door he gave a jump and vanished without a trace. Strange, very strange." They were all astonished, and although they looked all around they could see no sign of him. "Brothers, you patrol this area while I go to look for him above," said Erlang, and with a quick jump he was riding a cloud in mid-air. When he saw Heavenly King Li holding high the fiend-detecting mirror and standing with Nezha at the edge of a cloud, the True Lord asked, "Your Heavenly Majesty, have you seen that Monkey King?" "He hasn't come up here—I've been keeping a lookout for him with this mirror," the Heavenly King replied. The True Lord Erlang then told him how he had used transformations and magic to capture the monkey hordes. "He changed into a temple," Erlang went on, "but got away just when I was going to hit him." On hearing this, Heavenly King Li turned the fiend-detecting mirror in all four directions, then said with a laugh, "Hurry away, True Lord, hurry away. The monkey made himself invisible to get through the encirclement, and he's gone to your place, Guanjiangkou." Erlang took his divine trident and returned to Guanjiangkou in pursuit.

【14】 The Great Sage had already arrived there, changed himself into the likeness of the god Erlang with a shake of his body, put away his cloud, and gone into the temple. The demon judges did not realize who he really was, so they all kowtowed to welcome him. He took his seat in the middle of the temple, and inspected the offerings: the beef, mutton and pork presented by one Li Hu, the ex-voto promised by a Zhang Long, the letter from a Zhao Jia asking for a son, and one Qian Bing's prayer for recovery from illness. As he was looking round it was announced that another Lord Erlang had arrived. All the demon judges hurried to look, and they were all astonished. The True Lord Erlang asked, "Has a so-called Great Sage Equalling Heaven been here?" "We haven't seen any Great Sages," they replied, "only another god who's looking around inside." The True Lord rushed in through the gates, and as soon as the Great Sage saw him he reverted to his own appearance and said, "There's no point in shouting, sir. This temple's mine now." The True Lord raised his double-bladed trident and swung at the Monkey King's head, but the Monkey King dodged the blow by magic, took his embroidery needle, shook it till it was as thick as a bowl, and rushed forward to meet the attack. Shouting and yelling, they fought their way out through the gates, and went on fighting through the mists and clouds all the way back to the Mountain of Flowers and Fruit. The Four Heavenly Kings and all their soldiers were so alarmed that they kept an even tighter guard. Marshals Kang and Zhang and the others came to meet the True Lord, and combined their efforts to surround the Handsome Monkey King. But of this no more for now.

【15】 After the Strongarm Demon King had sent the True Lord Erlang and his six sworn brothers with their troops to capture the fiend, he had gone back to Heaven to report. He found the Jade Emperor, the Bodhisattva Guanyin, the Queen Mother and all his immortal ministers in conference. "Although Erlang has joined the fight, we have had no reports on it all day," the Jade Emperor said. Guanyin put her hands together and replied, "May I suggest that Your Majesty go out through the Southern Gate of

Heaven with Lord Lao Zi to see for yourself what is happening."
"A good idea," said the Emperor, and he went by chariot with
Lao Zi, the Queen Mother, and all the immortal ministers to the
Southern Gate of Heaven. Here they were met by a number of
heavenly soldiers and strongmen. When the gates were opened
and they looked into the distance they saw that the heavenly hosts
were spread all around in a net; Heavenly King Li and Nezha
were standing in mid-air with the fiend-detecting mirror, and
Erlang was struggling with the Great Sage within the encircling
ring. The Bodhisattva addressed Lao Zi and asked, "What do you
think of the god Erlang I recommended? He really does have
divine powers. He's just got that Great Sage cornered, and all he
has to do now is to catch him. If I give him a little help now he
will certainly be able to do it." "What weapon would you use,
Bodhisattva? How could you help him?" Lao Zi asked. "I'll drop
that pure vase of willow twigs on the monkey's head. Even if it
doesn't kill him it will knock him off balance and enable the Little
Sage to catch him." "That vase of yours is made of porcelain,"
Lao Zi replied, "and if you hit the target that will be fine. But if
it were to miss his head and smash into his iron club, it would be
shattered. Just hold your hand while I give him a little help."
"What sort of weapon do you have?" the Bodhisattva asked, and
Lord Lao Zi replied, "I've got one all right." He pulled up his
sleeve and took a bracelet off his right arm. "This weapon," he
said, "is made of tempered steel to which I have added the magic
elixir. It preserves my miraculous essence, can transform itself, is
proof against fire and water, and can snare anything. One of its
names is Diamond Jade and the other is Diamond Noose. When I
went out through the Han Pass some years ago to turn into a
foreigner and become a Buddha, I had a great deal to thank it for.
It's the best protection at any time. Just watch which I throw it
down and hit him."

As soon as he had finished speaking he threw it down from
outside the heavenly gate, and it fell into the camp on the
Mountain of Flowers and Fruit, hitting the Monkey King neatly
on the head. The Monkey King was too preoccupied with fighting

the seven sages to notice this weapon falling on him from heaven, and when it struck him on the forehead he lost his balance and stumbled, then picked himself up and started to run. The slim dog of the god Erlang caught him up and bit him in the calf, bringing him down again. As he lay on the ground he cursed at the dog. "You don't bother your own master, damn you; why pick on me to bite?" He rolled over and tried unsuccessfully to get up, but the seven sages all held him down, roped him up, and put a sickle-shaped blade round his collar-bone to prevent him from making any more transformations.

[16] Lord Lao Zi then recovered his Diamond Jade and invited the Jade Emperor, Guanyin, the Queen Mother, and all the immortal ministers to return to the Hall of Miraculous Mist. Down below, Heavenly King Li and the four other Heavenly Kings assembled their troops and pulled up the stockade. They went over to congratulate the Little Sage and said, "It was all thanks to you, Little Sage." "No, it was thanks to the great blessings of His Celestial Majesty and the might of all the gods—it was nothing I did," replied the Little Sage. "No time to talk now, elder brother," said the four marshals Kang, Zhang, Yao, and Li. "Let's take this wretch up to Heaven to see the Jade Emperor and ask what is to be done with him." "Worthy brothers," Erlang replied, "you never received any heavenly commission, so it would not be right for you to see the Jade Emperor. The heavenly soldiers can escort him while I go up there with the Heavenly Kings to report back. You should comb this mountain with your troops, and when you've finished go back to Guanjiangkou. When I've asked for our rewards I'll come back and we can celebrate together." The four marshals and the two generals accepted their orders, and the rest mounted their clouds and went to Heaven triumphantly singing victory songs. Before long they were outside the Hall of Universal Brightness. The heavenly teachers reported to the throne that the Four Great Heavenly Kings and the rest of them had captured the monkey devil, the Great Sage Equalling Heaven, and were now waiting to be summoned. The Jade Emperor then issued an edict ordering

53

the Strongarm Demon King and the heavenly soldiers to march him to the Demon-beheading Tower, where the wretch was to have his body chopped to mincemeat. Goodness!

The bully and cheat now meets with a bitter punishment,
The heroic spirit must now come to an end.

If you don't know what happened to the Monkey King's life, then listen to the explanation in the next instalment.

3. 八卦炉中逃大圣
五行山下定心猿

【1】　富贵功名，前缘分定，为人切莫欺心。正大光明，忠良善果弥深。些些狂妄天加谴，眼前不遇待时临。问东君因甚，如今祸害相侵。只为心高图阔极，不分上下乱规箴。

【2】　话表齐天大圣被天兵押去斩妖台下，绑在降妖柱上，刀砍斧剁，枪刺剑刳，莫想伤及其身。南斗星奋令火部众神，放火煨烧，亦不能烧着。又教雷部众神，以雷屑钉打，越发不能伤损一毫。那大力鬼王与众启奏道："万岁，这大圣不知是何处学得这护身之法，臣等用刀砍斧剁，雷打火烧，一毫不能伤损，即如之何？"玉帝闻言道："这厮这等，这等……如何处治？"太上老君即奏道："那猴吃了蟠桃，饮了御酒，又盗了仙丹，——我那五壶丹，有生有熟，被他都吃在肚里，运用三昧火，煅成一块，所以浑做金钢之躯，急不能伤。不若与老道领去，放在八卦炉中，以文武火煅炼。炼出我的丹来，他身自为灰烬矣。"玉帝闻言，却教六丁、六甲，将他解下，付与老君。老君领旨去讫。一壁厢宣二郎显圣，赏赐金花百朵，御酒百瓶，还丹百粒，异宝明珠，锦绣等件，教与义兄弟分享。真君谢恩，回灌江口不题。

【3】　那老君到兜率宫，将大圣解去绳索，放了穿琵琶骨之器，推入八卦炉中，命看炉的道人，架火的童子，将火扇起煅炼。原来那炉是乾、坎、艮、震、巽、离、坤、兑八卦。他即将身钻在"巽宫"位下。巽乃风也，有风则无火。只是风搅得烟来，把一双眼灼红了，弄做个老害病眼，故唤作"火眼金睛"。

【4】　真个光阴迅速，不觉七七四十九日，老君的火候俱全。忽一日，开炉取丹。那大圣双手侮着眼，正自揉搓流涕，只听得炉头声响。猛睁睛看见光明，他就忍不住，将身一纵，跳出丹炉，唿喇一声，蹬倒八卦炉，往外就走。慌得那架火、看炉，与丁甲一班

55

人来扯，被他一个个都放倒，好似癫痫的白额虎，风狂的独角龙。老君赶上抓一把，被他一捽，捽了个倒栽葱，脱身走了。即去耳中掣出如意棒，迎风幌一幌，碗来粗细，依然拿在手中，不分好歹，却又大乱天宫，打得那九曜星闭门闭户，四天王无影无踪。好猴精！有诗为证。诗曰：

> 混元体正合先天，万劫千番只自然。
> 渺渺无为浑太乙，如如不动号初玄。
> 炉中久炼非铅汞，物外长生是本仙。
> 变化无穷还变化，三皈五戒总休言。

又诗：

> 一点灵光彻太虚，那条拄杖亦如之：
> 或长或短随人用，横竖横排任卷舒。

又诗：

> 猿猴道体配人心，心即猿猴意思深。
> 大圣齐天非假论，官封"弼马"是知音。
> 马猿合作心和意，紧缚牢拴莫外寻。
> 万相归真从一理，如来同契住双林。

【5】 这一番，那猴王不分上下，使铁棒东打西敌，更无一神可挡。只打到通明殿里，灵霄殿外。幸有佑圣真君的佐使王灵官执殿。他看大圣纵横，掣金鞭近前挡住道："泼猴何往！有吾在此，切莫猖狂！"这大圣不由分说，举棒就打。那灵官鞭起相迎。两个在灵霄殿前厮浑一处。好杀：

赤胆忠良名誉大，欺天诳上声名坏。一低一好幸相持，豪杰英雄同赛赛。铁棒凶，金鞭快，正直无私怎忍耐？这个是太乙雷声应化尊，那个是齐天大圣猿猴怪。金鞭铁棒两家能，都是神宫仙器械。今日在灵霄宝殿开威风，各展雄才真可爱。一个欺心要夺斗牛宫，一个竭力匡扶玄圣界。苦争不让显神通，鞭棒往来无胜败。

他两个斗在一处，胜败未分，早有佑圣真君，又差将佐发文到雷府，调三十六员雷将齐来，把大圣围在核心，各骋凶恶鏖战。那大圣全无一毫惧色，使一条如意棒，左遮右挡，后架前迎。一时，见那众雷将的刀枪剑戟、鞭简挝锤、钺斧金瓜、旄镰月铲，来的甚紧，他即摇身一变，变做三头六臂，把如意棒幌一幌，变做三条；六只手使开三条棒，好便似纺车儿一般，滴流流，在那垓心里飞舞。众雷神莫能相近。真个是：

> 圆陀陀，光灼灼，亘古常存人怎学？人火不能焚，人水何曾溺？光明一颗摩尼珠，剑戟刀枪伤不着。也能善，也能恶，眼前善恶凭他做。善时成佛与成仙，恶处披毛并带角。无穷变化闹天宫，雷将神兵不可捉。

当时众神把大圣攒在一处，却不能近身，乱嚷乱斗，早惊动玉帝。遂传旨着游奕灵官同翊圣真君上西方请佛老降伏。

【6】　那二圣得了旨，径到灵山胜境，雷音宝刹之前，对四金刚、八菩萨礼毕，叫烦转达。众神随至宝莲台下启知，如来召请。二圣礼佛三匝，侍立台下。如来问："玉帝何事，烦二圣下临？"二圣即启道："向时花果山产一猴，在那里弄神通，聚众猴搅乱世界。玉帝降招安旨，封为'弼马温'，他嫌官小反去。当遣李天王、哪吒太子擒拿未获，复招安他，封做'齐天大圣'，先有官无禄。着他代管蟠桃园，他即偷桃；又走至瑶池，偷肴，偷酒，搅乱大会；仗酒又暗入兜率宫，偷老君仙丹，反出天宫。玉帝复遣十万天兵，亦不能收伏。后观音举二郎真君同他义兄弟追杀，他变化多端，亏老君抛金钢琢打重，二郎方得拿住。解赴御前，即命斩之。刀砍斧剁，火烧雷打，俱不能伤，老君奏准领去，以火煅炼。四十九日开鼎，他却又跳出八卦炉，打退天丁，径入通明殿里，灵霄殿外；被佑圣真君的佐使王灵官挡住苦战，又调三十六员雷将，把他困在垓心，终不能相拿。事在紧急，玉帝特请如来救驾。"如来闻诏，即对众菩萨道："汝等在此稳坐法堂，休得乱了禅位，待我炼魔救驾去来。"

【7】　如来即唤阿傩、迦叶二尊者相随，离了雷音，径至灵霄门外。忽听得喊声振耳，乃三十六员雷将围困着大圣哩。佛祖传法旨："教雷将停息干戈，放开营所，叫那大圣出来，等我问他有何法力。"众将果退。大圣也收了法象，现出原身近前，怒气昂昂，厉声高叫道："你是那方善士，敢来止住刀兵问我？"如来笑道："我是西方极乐世界释迦牟尼尊者，南无阿弥陀佛。今闻你猖狂村野，屡反天宫，不知是何方生长，何年得道，为何这等暴

横?"大圣道:"我本:

天地生成灵混仙,花果山中一老猿。
水帘洞里为家业,拜友寻师悟太玄。
炼就长生多少法,学来变化广无边。
因在凡间嫌地窄,立心端要住瑶天。
灵霄宝殿非他久,历代人王有分传。
强者为尊该让我,英雄只此敢争先。

佛祖听言,呵呵冷笑道:"你那厮乃是个猴子成精,焉敢欺心,要夺玉皇上帝龙位?他自幼修持,苦历过一千七百五十劫。每劫该十二万九千六百年。你算,他该多少年数,方能享受此无极大道?你那个初世为人的畜生,如何出此大言!不当人子!不当人子!折了你的寿算!趁早皈依,切莫胡说!但恐遭了毒手,性命顷刻而休,可惜了你的本来面目!"大圣道:"他虽年劫修长,也不应久占在此。常言道:'皇帝轮流做,明年到我家。'只教他搬出去,将天宫让与我,便罢了;若还不让,定要搅攘,永不清平!"佛祖道:"你除了长生变化之法,再有何能,敢占天宫胜境?"大圣道:"我的手段多哩!我有七十二般变化,万劫不老长生。会驾筋斗云,一纵十万八千里。如何坐不得天位?"佛祖道:"我与你打个赌赛:你若有本事,一筋斗打出我这右手掌中,算你赢,再不用动刀兵苦争战,就请玉帝到西方居住,把天宫让你,若不能打出手掌,你还下界为妖,再修几劫,却来争吵。"

【8】那大圣闻言,暗笑道:"这如来十分好呆!我老孙一筋斗去十万八千里。他那手掌,方圆不满一尺,如何跳不出去?"急发声道:"既如此说,你可做得主张?"佛祖道:"做得!做得!"伸开手,却似个荷叶大小。那大圣收了如意棒,抖擞神威,将身一纵,站在佛祖手心里,却道声:"我出去也!"你看他一路云光,无影无形去了。佛祖慧眼观看,见那猴王风车子一般相似不住,只管前进。大圣行时,忽见有五根肉红柱子,撑着一股青气。他道:"此间乃尽头路了。这番回去,如来作证,灵霄宫定是我坐也。"又思量说:"且住!等我留下些记号,方好与如来说话。"拔下一根毫毛,吹口仙气,叫"变!"变做一管浓墨双毫笔,在那中间柱子上写一行大字云:"齐天大圣,到此一游。"写毕,收了毫毛。又不庄

尊，却在第一根柱子根下撒了一泡猴尿。翻转筋斗云，径回本处，站在如来掌内道："我已去，今来了。你教玉帝让天宫与我。"

如来骂道："我把你这个尿精猴子！你正好不曾离了我掌哩！"大圣道："你是不知，我去到天尽头，见五根肉红柱，撑着一股青气，我留个记在那里，你敢和我同去看么？"如来道："不消去，你只低头看看。"那大圣睁圆火眼金睛，低头看时，原来佛祖右手中指写着"齐天大圣，到此一游"。大指丫里，还有些猴尿臊气，大圣吃了一惊道："有这等事！有这等事！我将此字写在撑天柱上，如何却在他手指上，莫非有个未卜先知的法术。我决不信！不信！等我再去来！"

好大圣，急纵身又要跳出，被佛祖翻掌一扑，把这猴王推出西天门外，将五指化作金、木、水、火、土五座联山，唤名"五行山"，轻轻的把他压住。众雷神与阿傩、迦叶，一个个合掌称扬道："善哉！善哉！

　　当年卵化学为人，立志修行果道真。

　　万劫无移居胜境，一朝有变散精神。

　　欺天罔上思高位，凌圣偷丹乱大伦。

　　恶贯满盈今有报，不知何日得翻身。"

【9】　如来佛祖殄灭了妖猴，即唤阿傩、迦叶同转西方极乐世界。时有天蓬、天佑急出灵霄宝殿道："请如来少待，我主大驾来也。"佛祖闻言，回首瞻仰。须臾，果见八景鸾舆，九光宝盖；声奏玄歌妙乐，咏唱无量神章；散宝花，喷真香，直至佛前谢доб："多蒙大法收殄妖邪，望如来少停一日，请诸仙做一会筵奉谢。"如来不敢违悖，即合掌谢道："老僧承大天尊宣命来此，有何法力？还是天尊与众神洪福。敢劳致谢？"天帝传旨，即着雷部众神，分头请三清、四御、五老、六司、七元、八极、九曜、十都、千真万圣，来此赴会，同谢佛恩。又命四大天师、九天仙女，大开玉京金阙、太玄宝宫、洞阳玉馆，请如来高座七宝灵台，调设各班坐位，安排龙肝凤髓，玉液蟠桃。

【10】　不一时，那太清元始天尊、上清灵宝天尊、太清道德天尊、五炁真君、五斗星君、三官四圣、九曜真君、左辅、右弼、天王、哪吒，玄虚一应灵通对对旌旗，双双幡盖，都捧着明珠异宝，寿果

奇花，向佛前拜献曰："感如来无量法力，收伏妖猴。蒙大天尊设宴呼唤，我等皆来陈谢。请如来将此会立一名，如何？"如来领众神之托曰："今欲立名，可做个'安天大会'。"各仙老异口同声，俱道："好个'安天大会'！"言讫，各坐座位，走斝传觞，簪花鼓瑟，果好会也。有诗为证。诗曰：

> 宴设蟠桃猴搅乱，安天大会胜蟠桃。
> 龙旗鸾辂祥光蔼，宝节幢幡瑞气飘。
> 仙乐玄歌音韵美，凤箫玉管响声高。
> 琼香缭绕群仙集，宇宙清平贺圣朝。

【11】 众皆畅然喜会，只见王母娘娘引一班仙子、仙娥、美姬、毛女，飘飘荡荡舞向佛前，施礼曰："前被妖猴搅乱蟠桃嘉会，请众仙众佛，俱未成功。今蒙如来大法链锁顽猴，喜庆'安天大会'，无物可谢，今是我净手亲摘大株蟠桃数颗奉献。"真个是：

> 半红半绿喷甘香，艳丽仙根万载长。
> 堪笑武陵源上种，争如天府更奇强！
> 紫纹娇嫩宴中少，缃核清甜世莫双。
> 延寿延年能易体，有缘食者自非常。

佛祖合掌向王母谢讫。王母又着仙姬、仙子唱的唱，舞的舞。满会群仙，又皆赏赞。正是：

> 缥缈天香满座，缤纷仙蕊仙花。玉京金阙大荣华，异品奇珍无价。对对与天齐寿，双双万劫增加。桑田沧海任更差，他自无惊无讶。

王母正着仙姬仙子歌舞，觥筹交错，不多时，忽又闻得：

> 一阵异香来鼻嗅，惊动满堂星与宿。
> 天仙佛祖把杯停，各各抬头迎目候。
> 霄汉中间现老人，手捧灵芝飞蔼绣。
> 葫芦藏蓄万年丹，宝箓名书千纪寿。
> 洞里乾坤任自由，壶中日月随成就。
> 遨游四海乐清闲，散淡十洲容辐辏。
> 曾赴蟠桃醉几遭，醒时明月还依旧。
> 长头大耳短身躯，南极之方称老寿。

寿星又到。见玉帝礼毕，又见如来，申谢曰："始闻那妖猴被老君引至兜率宫煅炼，以为必致平安，不期他又反出。幸如来善伏此怪，设宴奉谢，故此闻风而来。更无他物可献，特具紫芝瑶草，碧藕金丹奉上。"诗曰：

　　碧藕金丹奉释迦，如来万寿若恒沙。
　　清平永乐三乘锦，康泰生长九品花。
　　无相门中真法主，色空天上是仙家。
　　乾坤大地皆称祖，丈六金身福寿赊。

如来欣然领谢。喜星得座，依然走举传觞。只见赤脚大仙又至。向玉帝前颜凶礼毕，又对佛祖谢道："深感法力，降伏妖猴。无物可以表敬，特具交梨二颗，火枣数枚奉献。"诗曰：

　　大仙赤脚枣梨香，敬献弥陀寿算长。
　　七宝莲台山样稳，千金花座锦般妆。
　　寿同天地言非谬，福比洪波话岂狂。
　　福寿如期真个是，清闲极乐那西方。

如来又称谢了。叫阿傩、迦叶，将各所献之物，一一收起，方向玉帝前谢宴。众各酩酊。只见个巡视灵官来报道："那大圣伸出头来了。"佛祖道："不妨，不妨。"袖中只取出一张帖子，上有六个字："唵、嘛、呢、叭、𡄰、吽"递与阿傩，叫贴在那山顶上。这尊者即领帖子，拿出天门，到那五行山顶上，紧紧的贴在一块四方石上。那座山即生根合缝，可运用呼吸之气，手儿爬出，可以摇挣摇挣。阿傩回报道："已将帖子贴了。"

【12】　如来即辞了玉帝众神，与二尊者出天门之外，又发一个慈悲心，念动真言咒语，将五行山，召一尊土地神祇，会同五方揭谛，居住此山监押。但他饥时，与他铁丸子吃；渴时，与他溶化的铜汁饮。待他灾愆满日，自有人救他。正是：

　　妖猴大胆反天宫，却被如来伏手降。
　　渴饮溶铜捱岁月，饥餐铁弹度时光。
　　天灾苦困遭磨折，人事凄凉喜命长。
　　若得英雄重展挣，他年奉佛上西方。

又诗曰：

　　伏逞豪强大势兴，降龙伏虎弄乖能。
　　偷桃偷酒游天府，受箓承恩在玉京。

　　恶贯满盈身受困，善根不绝气还升。
　　果然脱得如来手，且待唐朝出圣僧。
　　毕竟不知向后何年何月，方满灾殃，且听下回分解。

Chapter 3
The Great Sage Escapes from the Eight Trigrams Furnace; The Mind Ape Is Fixed Beneath Five Elements Mountain

[1] *Wealth and honour, glory and fame,*
Are predetermined by fate:
No one should act against conscience to covet any of them.
Far-going and deep
Are the good results of true enlightenment and loyalty.
Heaven punishes all wild and wicked deeds
If not at once then later on.
Ask the Lord of the East the reason why
Disasters now strike him.
It is because his ambition was high, his plans far-reaching,
He did not respect authority, and he smashed convention.

[2] The story goes on to tell how the Great Sage Equalling Heaven was escorted by the hosts of heavenly soldiers to the Demon-beheading Tower and tied to the Demon-subduing Pillar. They hacked at him with sabres, sliced at him with axes, lunged at him with spears and cut at him with swords, but they were unable to inflict a single wound on him. The Southern Dipper angrily ordered all the gods of the Department of Fire to set him alight and burn him up, but he would not ignite. He told the gods of the Department of Thunder to nail splinters of thunder into him, but however hard they tried they could not harm a hair of his body. The Strongarm Demon King and the rest of them then reported this to the throne. "Your Majesty," they said, "this Great Sage has learnt somewhere or other how to protect himself by magic. Although your subjects have hacked at him with sabres, sliced at him with axes, struck at him with thunder and

tried to burn him with fire, we have not been able to harm a hair of his body. What are we to do?" "How can we deal with a wretch like this?" the Jade Emperor asked, and the Lord Lao Zi replied to this in a memorial: "That monkey has eaten the peaches of immortality, drunk the imperial liquor, and stolen the pills of elixir. He swallowed those five gourds of pills of mine, fresh ones and mature ones alike. Now we have used the fire of samadhi on him, which has tempered his body and made it a diamond one that cannot be harmed. The best course would be to let me take him and put him in my Eight Trigrams Furnace, where I can refine out my elixir with the civil and martial fire and reduce him to ashes at the same time. The Jade Emperor then ordered the Six Dings and the Six Jias to untie him and hand him over to the Lord Lao Zi, who took him away in obedience to the imperial decree. At the same time the Jade Emperor summoned the Illustrious Sage Erlang to his presence and rewarded him with a hundred golden flowers, a hundred jars of imperial liquor, a hundred pills of elixir, rare jewels, lustrous pearls, brocade, embroidery, and other gifts to share with his sworn brothers. The True Lord Erlang thanked him for his bounty and returned to Guanjiangkou.

[3]　When he reached the Tushita Palace, Lord Lao Zi had the Great Sage untied, took the hook from his collar-bone, pushed him into the Eight Trigrams Furnace, and ordered the priests in charge of it and the fire-boys to fan the fire up to refine him. Now this furnace was made up of the Eight Trigrams—Qian, Kan, Gen, Zhen, Sun, Li, Kun, and Dui—so he squeezed himself into the "Palace of Sun, as Sun was the wind, and where there was wind there could be no fire. All that happened was that the wind stirred up the smoke, which made both his eyes red and left him somewhat blind with the illness called "fire eyes with golden pupils."

[4]　Time soon passed, and without him realizing it the seven times seven, or forty-nine, days had passed, and Lord Lao Zi's fire had reached the required temperature and burned for long enough. One day the furnace was opened for the elixir to be taken out. The Great Sage, who was shielding his eyes with both hands and wiping away his tears, heard a noise at the top of the

furnace. He looked hard and saw daylight; and, unable to stand being in there a moment longer, leapt out of the furnace, kicked it over with a crash, and was off. In the ensuing chaos the fireboys, the keepers of the furnace, the Dings and the Jias all tried to grab him, but he knocked them all down. He was like a white-browed tiger gone berserk, a single-horned dragon raving mad. Lord Lao Zi rushed up to seize him, but was thrown head over heels as the Great Sage freed himself. He took the as-you-will cudgel from his ear, and shook it in the wind till it was thick as a bowl, and once more created total chaos in the Palace of Heaven, not caring in the least what he did. He laid about him to such effect that the Nine Bright Shiners shut their windows and doors, and not a sign was to be seen of the Four Heavenly Kings. Marvellous monkey spirit! As the poem has it,

> His primordial body matches an earlier heaven,
> Completely natural throughout ten thousand ages;
> Vast and passive, blended with the Great Monad;
> Always immobile, known as the Prime Mystery.
> After so much refining in the furnace he is not lead or mercury;
> Having lived long outside the ordinary he is a natural Immortal.
> His changes are inexhaustible, and still he has more,
> So say nothing about the Three Refuges or Five Abstentions.

Another poem says:

> A single point of magic light can fill the whole of space;
> Likewise that staff of his:
> Longer or shorter, depending on his needs,
> Upright or horizontal, it can shrink or grow.

Yet another poem runs:

> To the ape's immortal body is matched a human mind:

That the mind is an ape is deeply meaningful.
It was quite true that the Great Sage equalled Heaven:
The appointment as Protector of the Horse showed no
discernment.
Horse and ape together make mind and thought;
Bind them tightly together, and do not seek elsewhere.
When all phenomena are reduced to truth they follow a
single pattern;
Like the Tathagatha reaching nirvana under the two trees.

[5]   This time the Monkey King made no distinctions between
high and humble as he laid about him to east and west with his
iron club. Not a single god opposed him. He fought his way into
the Hall of Universal Brightness outside the Hall of Miraculous
Mist, where the Kingly Spirit Officer, the lieutenant of the
Helpful Sage and True Lord, fortunately was on duty. When he
saw the Great Sage charging around he took up his golden mace
and went forward to resist him. "Where are you going, damned
monkey?" he asked. "If you go wild you'll have me to deal
with." The Great Sage was not in a position to argue with him,
so he raised his cudgel to strike him. The Spirit Officer lifted his
mace and advanced to meet him. It was a fine fight:

Great was the fame of the brave and loyal officer,
Evil the name of the rebel who bullied Heaven.
The low one and the good one were well matched;
Valiant heroes fighting each other.
Vicious the iron cudgel,
Quick the golden mace.
Both were straight, merciless, and terrible.
One of them is a deity formed from the Great Monad's
thunder;
The other is the monkey spirit, the Great Sage Equalling
Heaven.
With golden mace or iron cudgel each is a master;
Both are weapons from the palaces of the gods.

Today they show their might in the Hall of Miraculous Mist,
A wonderful display of courage and skill.
One in his folly wanting to capture the Palace of the Dipper and the Bull,
The other exerting all his strength to support the world of the gods.
The fight is too hard to allow the use of magic,
As mace and cudgel struggle without result.

As they fought together without either of them emerging as victor, the True Lord sent an officer with a message to the Thunder Palace ordering the thirty-six thunder generals to surround the Great Sage. Although they all fought with the utmost ferocity, the Great Sage was not in the least frightened, and parried and blocked to left and right with his as-you-will cudgel, resisting his opponents in front and behind. Before long he found that the pressure was too great from the sabres, spears, swords, halberds, clubs, maces, claws-and-ropes, hammers, pole-axes, battle-axes, grabs, pennoned hooks, and moon-shaped bills of the thunder generals; so he shook himself and grew three heads and six arms. Then he shook his as-you-will cudgel and changed it into three cudgels, and wielding the three cudgels in his six hands he flew round and round inside the encirclement like a spinning wheel. None of the thunder generals could get anywhere near him. Indeed,

Perfectly round,
Gleaming bright,
How can men learn to live for ever?
He can enter fire without being burned,
And go in the water but not be drowned.
He is as bright as a Mani pearl,
Swords and spears cannot harm him.
He is capable of good,
And capable of evil:

67

> *When faced with the choice between good and evil he might do either.*
> *If he is good he becomes a Buddha or an Immortal,*
> *If bad, he grows fur and horns.*
> *With his boundless transformations he wrecked the Heavenly Palace,*
> *Nor can thunder generals and divine troops take him.*

Although the gods had the Great Sage cornered, they were unable to get near him. The noise of the shouting and the fighting had already alarmed the Jade Emperor, who ordered the Miracle Official Youyi to go to the West with the Helpful Sage and True Lord and ask the Buddha to subdue him.

[6] When these two sages received the order they went to the wonderful land of the Miraculous Mountain, where they offered their greetings to the Four Vajrapanis and Eight Bodhisattvas before the Thunder Monastery and asked them to pass on their message. The gods went to the foot of the lotus seat to inform the Tathagata, who invited the two sages to his presence. When the sages had performed the threefold obeisance to the Buddha they stood in attendance below the throne. "Why has the Jade Emperor troubled you two sages to come here?" asked the Buddha. "A monkey," they reported, "who was born on the Mountain of Flowers and Fruit, has used his magic powers to unite all the monkeys and throw the world into confusion. The Jade Emperor sent down an edict of amnesty and appointed him Protector of the Horses, but this was not good enough for him, so he left Heaven again. When Heavenly King Li and Prince Nezha were unsuccessful in their attempt to capture him the Jade Emperor sent down another amnesty with his appointment as a 'Great Sage Equalling Heaven.' At first this appointment was purely nominal, but later he was told to look after the Peach Orchard. But he stole the peaches and then went to the Jade Pool where he stole the delicacies and the liquor and wrecked the banquet. In his drunkenness he staggered into the Tushita Palace, stole Lord Lao Zi's pills of immortality, and left Heaven

again. The Jade Emperor sent a hundred thousand heavenly troops, but they were still unable to subdue him. Then Guanyin recommended the True Lord Erlang and his sworn brothers to go after the monkey, and he used many a transformation until he was finally able to capture the monkey after the Lord Lao Zi hit him with his Diamond Jade. The monkey was then taken to the imperial presence, and the order for his execution was given. But although he was hacked at with sabres, chopped at with axes, burned with fire, and struck with thunder, none of this did him any damage; so Lord Lao Zi requested permission to take him away and refine him with fire. But when the cauldron was opened after forty-nine days he jumped out of the Eight Trigrams Furnace, routed the heavenly troops, and went straight to the Hall of Universal Brightness in front of the Hall of Miraculous Mist. Here he has been stopped and engaged in fierce combat by the Kingly Spirit Officer, the lieutenant of the Helpful Sage and True Lord Erlang, thunder generals have been sent there to encircle him; but no one has been able to get close to him. In this crisis the Jade Emperor makes a special appeal to you, the Tathagata, to save his throne." On hearing this the Tathagata said to the assembled Bodhisattvas, "You stay here quietly in this dharma hall and behave yourselves in your seats of meditation while I go to deal with the demon and save the throne."

[7]   Telling the Venerable Ananda and the Venerable Kasyapa to accompany him, the Tathagata left the Thunder Monastery and went straight to the gate of the Hall of Miraculous Mist, where his ears were shaken by the sound of shouting as the thirty-six thunder generals surrounded the Great Sage. The Buddha issued a decree that ran: "Tell the thunder generals to stop fighting, open up their camp, and call on that Great Sage to come out, so that I may ask him what divine powers he has." The generals then withdrew, whereupon the Great Sage put away his magic appearance and came forward in his own body. He was in a raging temper as he asked, "Where are you from? You are a good man. You've got a nerve, stopping the fighting and questioning me!" "I am the Venerable Sakyamuni from the Western Land of

69

Perfect Bliss," replied the Buddha with a smile. "I have heard of your wild and boorish behaviour, and of your repeated rebellions against Heaven, and I would like to know where you were born, when you found the Way, and why you have been so ferocious." "I am," the Great Sage said,

> "A miracle-working Immortal born of Heaven and Earth,
> An old ape from the Mountain of Flowers and Fruit.
> My home is in the Water Curtain Cave,
> I sought friends and teachers, and became aware of the
> Great Mystery.
> I have practised many a method for obtaining eternal life,
> Infinite are the transformations I have learned.
> That is why I found the mortal world too cramped,
> And decided to live in the Jade Heaven.
> None can reign for ever in the Hall of Miraculous Mist;
> Kings throughout history have had to pass on their power.
> The strong should be honoured—he should give way to me:
> This is the only reason I wage my heroic fight."

The Buddha laughed mockingly. "You wretch! You are only a monkey spirit and you have the effrontery to want to grab the throne of the Jade Emperor. He has trained himself since childhood, and suffered hardship for one thousand, seven hundred and fifty kalpas. Each kalpa is 129,600 years, so you can work out for yourself how long it has taken him to be able to enjoy this great and infinite Way. But you are a beast who has only just become a man for the first time. How dare you talk so big? You're not human, not even human! I'll shorten your life-span. Accept my teaching at once and stop talking such nonsense! Otherwise you'll be in for trouble and your life will very shortly be over; and that will be so much the worse for your original form too." "Although he has trained himself for a long time, ever since he was a child, he still has no right to occupy this place for ever," the Great Sage said. "As the saying goes, 'Emperors are made by turn; next year it may be me.' If he can be persuaded to move out

70

and make Heaven over to me, that'll be fine. But is he doesn't abdicate in my favour I'll most certainly make things hot for him, and he'll never know peace and quiet again." "What have you got, besides immortality and the ability to transform yourself, that gives you the never to try to seize the Heavenly Palace?" the Buddha asked. "I can do many tricks indeed," the Great Sage replied. "I can perform seventy-two transformations, and I can preserve my youth for two thousand kalpas. I can ride a somersault cloud that takes me thirty-six thousand miles at a single jump. So why shouldn't I sit on the throne of Heaven?" "I'll have a wager with you then," said the Buddha. "If you're clever enough to get out of my right hand with a single somersault, you will be the winner, and there will be no more need for weapons or fighting: I shall invite the Jade Emperor to come and live in the west and abdicate the Heavenly Palace to you. But if you can't get out of the palm of my hand you will have to go down to the world below as a devil and train yourself for several more kalpas before coming to argue about it again."

[8] When he heard this offer the Great Sage smiled to himself and thought, "This Buddha is a complete idiot. I can cover thirty-six thousand miles with a somersault, so how could I fail to jump out of the palm of his hand, which is less than a foot across?" With this in his mind he asked eagerly, "Do you guarantee that yourself?" "Yes, yes," the Buddha replied, and he stretched out his right hand, which seemed to be about the size of a lotus leaf. Putting away his as-you-will cudgel, the Great Sage summoned up all his divine powers, jumped into the palm of the Buddha's hand, and said, "I'm off." Watch him as he goes like a streak of light and disappears completely. The Buddha, who was watching him with his wise eyes, saw the Monkey King whirling forward like a windmill and not stopping until he saw five flesh-pink pillars topped by dark vapours. "This is the end of the road," he said, "so now I'll go back. The Buddha will be witness, and the Hall of Miraculous Mist will be mine." Then he thought again, "Wait a moment. I'll leave my mark here to prove my case when I talk to the Buddha." He pulled out a hair,

71

breathed on it with his magic breath, and shouted "Change." It turned into a writing brush dipped in ink, and with it he wrote THE GREAT SAGE EQUALLING HEAVEN WAS HERE in big letters on the middle pillar. When that was done he put the hair back on, and, not standing on his dignity, made a pool of monkey piss at the foot of the pillar. Then he turned his somersault round and went back to where he had started from. "I went, and now I'm back. Tell the Jade Emperor to hand the Heavenly Palace over to me," he said, standing in the Buddha's palm.

"I've got you, you piss-spirit of a monkey," roared the Buddha at him. "You never left the palm of my hand." "You're wrong there," the Great Sage replied. "I went to the farthest point of Heaven, where I saw five flesh-pink pillars topped by dark vapours. I left my mark there: do you dare come and see it with me?" "There's no need to go. Just look down." The Great Sage looked down with his fire eyes with golden pupils to see the words "The Great Sage Equalling Heaven Was Here" written on the middle finger of the Buddha's right hand. The stink of monkey-piss rose from the fold at the bottom of the finger. "What a thing to happen," exclaimed the Great Sage in astonishment. "I wrote this on one of the pillars supporting the sky, so how can it be on his finger now? He must have used divination to know what I was going to do. I don't believe it. I refuse to believe it! I'll go there and come back again."

The dear Great Sage hurriedly braced himself to jump, but the Buddha turned his hand over and pushed the Monkey King out through the Western Gate of Heaven. He turned his fine fingers into a mountain chain belonging to the elements Metal, Wood, Water, Fire, and Earth, renamed them the Five Elements Mountain, and gently held him down. All the thunder gods and the disciples Ananda and Kasyapa put their hands together to praise the Buddha: "Wonderful, wonderful,

An egg learnt to be a man,
Cultivated his conduct, and achieved the Way.

72

Heaven had been undisturbed for ten thousand kalpas,
Until one day the spirits and gods were scattered.
The rebel against Heaven, wanting high position,
Insulted Immortals, stole the pills, and destroyed morality.
Today his terrible sins are being punished,
Who knows when he will be able to rise again?"

[9]　When he had eliminated the monkey fiend the Buddha told Ananda and Kasyapa to return with him to the western paradise. At that moment Tian Peng and Tian You hurried out of the Hall of Miraculous Mist to say, "We beg the Tathagata to wait a moment as the Jade Emperor's chariot is coming." The Buddha turned round and looked up, and an instant later he saw an eight-splendour imperial chariot and a nine-shining jewelled canopy appear to the sound of strange and exquisite music, and the chanting of countless sacred verses. Precious flowers were scattered and incense was burned. The Jade Emperor went straight up to the Buddha and said, "We are deeply indebted to the great Buddha's powers for wiping out the demon, and we hope that the Tathagata will spend a day here so that we may invite all the Immortals to a feast of thanksgiving." The Buddha did not dare refuse, so putting his hands together he replied, "This old monk only came here in obedience to Your Celestial Majesty's command. What magic powers can I pretend to? This was all due to the wonderful good fortune of Your Celestial Majesty and the other gods. How could I possibly allow you to thank me?" The Jade Emperor then ordered all the gods of the Department of Thunder to split up and invite the Three Pure Ones, the Four Emperors, the Five Ancients, the Six Superintendents, the Seven Main Stars, the Eight Points of the Compass, the Nine Bright Shiners, the Ten Chiefs, the Thousand Immortals, and the Ten Thousand Sages to a banquet to thank the Buddha for his mercy. Then he ordered the Four Great Heavenly Teachers and the Nine Heavenly Maidens to open the golden gates of the jade capital, and Palace of the Great

73

Mystery, and the Tong Yang Jade Palace, invite the Tathagata to take his seat on the Throne of the Seven Precious Things, arrange the places for all the different groups of guests, and set out the dragon liver, phoenix bone-marrow, jade liquor, and magic peaches.

[10] Before long the Original Celestial Jade Pure One, the High Celestial Precious Pure One, the Heavenly Celestial Pure One of the Way, the True Lords of the Five Humours, the Star Lords of the Five Constellations, the Three Officers, the Four Sages, the Left Assistant, the Right Support, the Heavenly Kings, Nezha, and the whole of space responded to the invitations that had been sent out magically. Their standards and canopies came two by two as they brought shining pearls, rare jewels, fruit of longevity, and exotic flowers, and presented them to the Buddha with bows. "We thank the Tathagata for subduing the monkey fiend with his infinite powers. His Celestial Majesty has asked us all to come to his banquet to express our thanks. We beg the Tathagata to give this banquet a title." The Buddha accepted this commission and said, "Since you want a name for it, we could call it the 'Banquet to Celebrate Peace in Heaven'." "Splendid, 'Banquet to Celebrate Peace in Heaven', splendid," exclaimed all the Immortals with one voice, and then they all sat down in their places, put flowers in their hair, and played the lyre. It was indeed a splendid banquet, and here are some verses to prove it:

> The Banquet to Celebrate Peace in Heaven far surpasses
> The Banquet of Peaches that the monkey wrecked.
> Radiance shines from dragon flags and imperial chariots;
> Auspicious vapours float above streamers and symbols of office.
> Melodious the fair music and mysterious songs;
> Loud sound the tones of phoenix flute and pipe of jade
> The rarest of perfumes waft around the Immortals, assembled calm in the sky.
> To congratulate the court on Pacifying the Universe.

[11] When the Immortals were all enjoying the feast the Queen

Mother and a group of fairies, immortal beauties, and houris, floated through the air as they danced towards the Buddha, and after paying her respects the Queen Mother said, "My Peach Banquet was ruined by that monkey fiend, and this Banquet to Celebrate Peace in Heaven is being given because the Tathagata has used his great powers to chain down the evil monkey. Having nothing else with which to express my gratitude, I have picked a number of peaches of immortality with my own pure hands as an offering." They were

Half red, half green, sweet-smelling beauties
Growing every ten thousand years from immortal roots.
The peaches of Wulingyuan seem laughable:
How can they compare with those of Heaven?
Purple-veined and tender, rare even in the sky,
Yellow-stoned, and matchless on earth for their sweetness.
They are able to adapt the body and make it live for ever;
Those lucky enough to eat them are no ordinary beings.

The Buddha put his hands together to thank the Queen Mother, who instructed the fairies and houris to sing and dance again, and their performance met with the praises of the whole assembly. Indeed,

Misty heavenly incense filled the room;
A chaos of heavenly petals and flowers.
Great is the splendour of the jade city and golden gates,
Priceless the strange treasures and rare jewels.
Two by two, coeval with Heaven,
Pair by pair, outliving ten thousand kalpas:
Even if land and sea changed places
They would not be astonished or alarmed.

Soon after the Queen Mother had ordered the fairies and houris to sing and dance, and when wine cups and chopsticks were weaving to and fro, suddenly

A strange scent reached their noses,
Startling the stars and constellations in the hall.
Immortals and the Buddha put down their cups,
Each of them raising their heads to look.
An old man appeared in the middle of the Milky Way
Holding a sacred mushroom.
His gourd contains ten-thousand-year elixir.
On the sacred rolls his name is written Eternal Life.
In his cave Heaven and Earth are free.
In his bottle Sun and Moon were created.
As he wanders around the Four Seas in pure idleness
Taking his ease in the Ten Continents, enjoying the bustle.
When he went to Peach Banquets he often got drunk
But when he came round, the moon was as bright as ever.
A long head, big ears and a short body,
Known as Longevity from the Southern Pole.

The Star of Longevity had arrived. When he had made his greetings to the Jade Emperor and the Buddha he made a speech of thanks. "When I heard that the monkey fiend had been taken by the Lord Lao Zi to his Tushita Palace to be refined I thought that this was bound to restore peace," he said, "and I never expected he would rebel again. Happily the demon was quelled by the Tathagata, and so when I heard that this feast was being given to thank him I came at once. As I have nothing else to offer I have brought with me purple magic mushrooms, jasper herbs, greenish jade lotus-root, and golden pills of immortality: these I humbly present." The poem says

Offering the jade lotus-root and golden pills to Sakyamuni,
To give him as many years as the grains of sand of the Ganges.
Peace and eternal joy decorate the Three Vehicles;
Prosperity and eternal life make the nine grades of immortals glorious.

Within the gate of No-Phenomena the true Law rules;
Above the Heaven of Nothingness is his immortal home.
Heaven and Earth both call him their ancestor,
His golden body provides blessings and long life.

The Buddha happily accepted his thanks, and after the Star of Longevity had taken his place the wine-cups started to circulate once more. Then the Bare-foot Immortal appeared, kowtowed to the Jade Emperor, and thanked the Buddha. "I am deeply grateful to you for subduing the monkey fiend with your divine powers. As I have nothing else with which to express my respect, I offer you two magic pears and a number of fire-dates."

Sweet are the Bare-foot Immortal's pears and dates,
And long will be the life of the Buddha to whom they are offered.
The lotus seat of the seven treasures is as firm as a mountain,
His thousand-golden-flower throne is as gorgeous as brocade.
Coeval with Heaven and Earth—this is no lie;
It is true that his blessings are greater than a flood.
His Western Paradise of leisure and bliss
Truly provides all the long life and blessings one could hope.

The Buddha thanked him too, and telling Ananda and Kasyapa to collect together all the offerings he went over to the Jade Emperor to thank him for the banquet. When all the guests were thoroughly drunk the Miraculous Patrolling Officer reported that the Great Sage had poked his head out. "It doesn't matter," the Buddha said, producing from his sleeve a strip of paper on which were written the golden words: Om mani padme hum. He gave this piece of paper to Ananda and told him to stick it on the summit of the mountains. The Venerable Ananda took it through the gates of Heaven and pasted it firmly to a square boulder on the

77

top of the Five Elements Mountain. When this was done the mountain sank roots and joined up all its seams. The Monkey King was still able to breathe and he could still stick his hands out and move them. Ananda went back to Heaven and reported that he had pasted the paper in place.

[12]　The Buddha then took his leave of the Jade Emperor and all the other deities. When he and his two disciples had gone out through the gates of Heaven his merciful heart moved him to chant a spell ordering a local tutelary god and the Revealers of the Truth of the Five Regions to live on the mountain and keep guard over him. When he was hungry they were to feed him iron pellets, and when he was thirsty they were to give him molten copper to drink. When the time of his punishment was over, someone would come and rescue him. Indeed,

> The monkey fiend was bold enough to rebel against Heaven,
> But was subdued by the Tathagata's hand.
> He endures the months and years, drinking molten copper
for his thirst,
> And blunts his hunger on iron pellets, serving his time.
> Suffering the blows of Heaven, he undergoes torment,
> Yet even in the bleakest time a happy fate awaits.
> If some hero is ready to struggle for him,
> One year he will go to the West in the service of the
Buddha.

Another poem goes:

> His great power grew as he humbled the mighty,
> He used his wicked talents to subdue tigers and dragons.
> He stole the peaches and wine as he wandered round
Heaven,
> Was graciously given office in the Jade Capital.
> When his wickedness went too far his body suffered,
> But his roots of goodness were not severed, and his breath
still rose.

He will escape from the hand of the Buddha,
And wait till the Tang produces a saintly monk.

If you don't know in what month of what year his sufferings ended, listen to the explanation in the next instalment.

4. 我佛造经传极乐
观音奉旨上长安

【1】 试问禅关，参求无数，往往到头虚老。磨砖做镜，积雪为粮，迷了几多年少？毛吞大海，芥纳须弥，金色头陀微笑。悟时超十地三乘，凝滞了四生六道。谁听得绝想崖前，无阴树下，杜宇一声春晓？曹溪路险，鹫岭云深，此处故人音杳。千丈冰崖，五叶莲开，古殿帘垂香袅。那时节，识破源流，便见龙王三宝。

这一篇词，名《苏武慢》。话表我佛如来，辞别了玉帝，回至雷音宝刹，但见那三千诸佛、五百阿罗、八大金刚、无边菩萨，一个个都执着幢幡宝盖，异宝仙花，摆列在灵山仙境，婆罗双林之下接迎。如来驾住祥云，对众道："我以

甚深般若，遍观三界。根本性原，毕竟寂灭。同虚空相，一无所有。珍伏乖猴，是事莫识，名生死始，法相如是。"

说罢，放舍利之光，满空有白虹四十二道，南北通连。大众见了，皈身礼拜。少顷间，聚庆云彩雾，登上品莲台，端然坐下。那三千诸佛、五百罗汉、八金刚、四菩萨，合掌近前礼毕，问曰："闹天宫搅乱蟠桃者，何也？"如来道："那厮乃花果山产的一妖猴，罪恶滔天，不可名状；概天神将，俱莫能降状；虽二郎捉获，老君用火煅炼，亦莫能伤损。我去时，正在雷将中间，扬威耀武，卖弄精神，被我止住戈，问他来历，他言有神通，会变化，又驾筋斗云，一去十万八千里。我与他打了个赌赛，他出不得我手，却将他一把抓住，指化五行山，封压他在那里。玉帝大开金阙瑶宫，请我坐了首席，"立'安天大会'谢我，却方辞驾而回。"大众听言喜悦，极口称扬。谢罢，各分班而退，各执乃事，共乐天真。果然是：

瑞霭漫天竺，虹光拥世尊。西方称第一，无代法王门。常见玄猿献果，麋鹿衔花；青鸾舞，彩凤鸣；灵龟捧寿，仙鹤噙芝。安享净土祇园，受用龙宫法界。日日花开，时时果熟。习静归真，

80

参禅果正。不灭不生,不增不减。烟霞缥缈随来往,寒暑无侵不记年。

诗曰:

> 去来自在任优游,也无恐怖也无愁。
> 极乐场中俱坦荡,大千之处没春秋。

【2】佛祖居于灵山大雷音宝刹之间,一日,唤聚诸佛、阿罗、揭谛、菩萨、金刚、比丘僧、尼等众于:"自伏乖猿安天之后,我处不知年月,料凡间有半千年矣。今值秋望日,我有一宝盆,盆中具设百祥奇花,千般异果等物,与汝等享此'盂兰盆会',如何?"概众一个个合掌,礼佛三匝领会。如来却将宝盆中花果品物,着阿傩捧定,着迦叶布散。大众感激,各献诗伸谢。

福诗曰:

> 福星光耀世尊前,福纳弥深远更绵。
> 福德无疆同地久,福缘有庆与天连。
> 福田广种年年盛,福海洪深岁岁坚。
> 福满乾坤多福荫,福增无量永周全。

禄诗曰:

> 禄重如山彩凤鸣,禄随时泰祝长庚。
> 禄添万斛身康健,禄享千种世太平。
> 禄俸齐天还永固,禄名似海更澄清。
> 禄恩远继多瞻仰,禄爵无边万国荣。

寿诗曰:

> 寿星献彩对如来,寿域光华自此开。
> 寿果满盘生瑞霭,寿花新采插莲台。
> 寿诗清雅多奇妙,寿曲调音按美才。
> 寿命延长同日月,寿如山海更悠哉。

众菩萨献毕。因请如来明示根本,指解源流。那如来微开善口,敷演大法,宣扬正果,讲的是三乘妙典,五蕴楞严。但见那天龙围绕,花雨缤纷。正是:禅心朗照千江月,真性清涵万里天。

【3】如来讲罢,对众言曰:"我观四大部洲,众生善恶,各方不一:东胜神洲者,敬天礼地,心爽气平;北巨芦洲者,虽好杀生,只因糊口,性拙情疏,无多作践;我西牛贺洲者,不贪不杀,养气潜

灵,虽无上真,人人固寿;但那南赡部洲者,贪淫乐祸,多杀多争,正所谓口舌凶场,是非恶海。我今有三藏真经,可以劝人为善。"诸菩萨闻言,合掌皈依。向佛前问曰:"如来有那三藏真经?"如来曰:"我有《法》一藏,谈天;《论》一藏,说地;《经》一藏,度鬼。三藏共计三十五部,该一万五千一百四十四卷,乃是修真之经,正善之门。我待要送上东土,叵耐那方众生愚蠢,毁谤真言,不识我法门之旨意,怠慢了瑜迦之正宗。怎么得一个有法力的,去东土寻一个善信,教他苦历千山,询经万水,到我处求取真经,永传东土,劝化众生,却乃是个山大的福缘,海深的善庆。谁肯去走一遭来?"当有观音菩萨,行近莲台,礼佛三匝道:"弟子不才,愿上东土寻一个取经人来也。"诸众抬头观看,那菩萨——

> 理圆四德,智满金身。缨络垂珠翠,香环结宝明。乌云巧迭盘龙髻,绣带轻飘彩凤翎。碧玉纽,素罗袍,祥光笼罩;锦绒裙,金落索,瑞气遮迎。眉如小月,眼似双星。玉面天生喜,朱唇一点红。净瓶甘露年年盛,斜插垂杨岁岁青。解八难,度群生,大慈悯:故镇太山,居南海,救苦寻声,万称万应,千圣千灵。兰心欣紫竹,惠性爱香藤。他是落伽山上慈悲主,潮音洞里活观音。

如来见了,心中大喜道:"别个是也去不得,须是观音尊者,神通广大,方可去得。"菩萨道:"弟子此去东土,有甚言语吩咐?"如来道:"这一去,要踏看路道,不许在霄汉中行,须是要半云半雾:目过山水,谨记程途远近之数,叮咛那取经人。但恐善信难行,我与你五件宝贝。"即命阿傩、迦叶,取出"锦襕袈裟"一领,"九环锡杖"一根,对菩萨言曰:"这袈裟、锡杖,可与那取经人亲用。若肯坚心来此,穿我的袈裟,免堕轮回;持我的锡杖,不遭毒害。"这菩萨皈依拜领。如来又取出三个箍儿,递与菩萨道:"此宝唤做'紧箍儿';虽是一样三个,但只是用各不同。我有'金紧禁'的咒语三篇。假若路上撞见神通广大的妖魔,你须是劝他学好,跟那取经人做个徒弟。他若不伏使唤,可将此箍儿与他藏在头上,自然见肉生根。各依所用的咒语念一念,眼胀头痛,脑门皆裂,管教他入我门来。"

【4】那菩萨闻言,踊跃作礼而退。即唤惠岸行者随行。那惠岸

使一条浑铁棍，重有千斤，只在菩萨左右，做一个降魔的大力士。菩萨遂将锦襕袈裟，做一个包裹，令他背了。菩萨将金箍藏了，执了锡杖，径下灵山。这一去，有分教：佛子还来归本愿，金蝉长老裹栴檀。

那菩萨到山脚下，有玉真观金顶大仙在观门首接住，请菩萨献茶。菩萨不敢久停，曰："今领如来法旨，上东土寻取经人去。"大仙道："取经人几时方到？"菩萨道："未定，约摸二三年间，或可至此。"遂辞了大仙，半云半雾，约记程途。有诗为证。诗曰：

万里相寻自不言，却云谁得意难全？
求人忽若浑如此，是我平生岂偶然？
伟道有方成妄语，说明无信也虚传。
愿倾肝胆寻相识，料想前头必有缘。

【5】　师徒二人正走间，忽然见弱水三千，乃是流沙河界。菩萨道："徒弟呀，此处却是难行。取经人浊骨凡胎，如何得渡？"惠岸道："师父，你看河有多远？"那菩萨停立云步看时，只见：

东连沙碛，西抵诸番；南达乌戈，北通鞑靼。经过有八百里遥，上下有千万里远。水流一似地翻身，浪滚却如山耸背。洋洋浩浩，漠漠茫茫，十里遥闻万丈洪。仙槎难到此，莲叶莫能浮。衰草斜阳流曲浦，黄云影日暗长堤。那里得客商来往？何曾有渔叟依栖？平沙无雁落，远岸有猿啼。只是红蓼花蘩知景色，白苹香细任依依。

菩萨正然点看，只见那河中，泼剌一声响亮，水波里跳出一个妖魔来，十分丑恶。他生得：

青不青，黑不黑，晦气色脸；长不长，短不短，赤脚筋躯。眼光闪烁，好似灶底双灯；口角丫叉，就如屠家火钵。獠牙撑剑刃，红发乱蓬松。一声叱咤如雷吼，两脚奔波似滚风。

【6】　那怪物手执一根宝杖，走上岸就捉菩萨，却被惠岸掣浑铁棒挡住，喝声"休走！"那怪物就持宝杖来迎。两个在流沙河边，这一场恶杀，真个惊人：

木叉浑铁棒，护法显神通；怪物降妖杖，努力逞英雄。双条银蟒河边舞，一对神僧岸上冲。那一个威镇流沙施本事，这一个力保观音建大功。那一个翻波跃浪，这一个吐雾喷

沙僧

风。翻波跃浪乾坤暗，吐雾喷风日月昏。那个降妖杖，好便似出山的白虎；这个浑铁棒，却就如卧道的黄龙。那个使将来，寻蛇拨草；这个丢过去，扑鹞分松。只杀得昏漠漠，星辰灿烂；雾腾腾，天地朦胧。那个久住弱水惟他狠，这个初出灵山第一功。

他两个来来往往，战上数十合，不分胜负。那怪物架住了铁棒道："你是那里和尚，敢来与我抵敌？"木叉道："我是托塔天王二太子木叉惠岸行者。今保我师父往东土寻取经人去。你是何怪，敢大胆阻路？"那怪方才醒悟道："我记得你跟南海观音在紫竹林中修行，你为何来此？"木叉道："那岸上不是我师父？"

【7】　怪物闻言，连声喏喏：收了宝杖，让木叉揪了去，见观音纳头下拜。告道："菩萨，恕我之罪，待我诉告。我不是妖邪，我是灵霄殿下侍銮舆的卷帘大将。只因在蟠桃会上，失手打碎了玻璃盏，玉帝把我打了八百，贬下界来，变得这般模样。又教七日一次，将飞剑来穿我胸胁百余下下方而行，故此这般苦恼。没奈何，饥寒难忍，三二日间，出波涛寻一个行人食用。不期今日无知，冲撞了大慈菩萨。"菩萨道："你在天有罪，既贬下来，今又这等伤生，正所谓罪上加罪。我今领了佛旨，上东土寻取经人。你何不入我门来，皈依善果，跟那取经人做个徒弟，上西天拜佛求经？我教飞剑不来穿你。那时节功成免罪，复你本职，心下如何？"那怪道："我愿皈正果。"又向前道："菩萨，我在此间吃人无数，向来有几次取经人，都被我吃了。凡吃的人头，抛落流沙，竟沉水底。这个水，鹅毛也不能浮。惟有九个取经人的骷髅，浮在水面，再不能沉。我以为异物，将索儿穿在一处，闲时拿来玩耍。这去，但恐取经人不得到此，却不是反误了我的前程也？"菩萨曰："岂有不到之理？你可将骷髅儿挂在头项下，等候取经人，自有用处。"怪物道："既然如此，愿领教诲。"菩萨方与他摩顶受戒，指沙为姓，就姓了沙；起个法名，叫做个沙悟净。当时入了沙门，送菩萨过了河，他洗心涤虑，再不伤生，专等取经人。

【8】　菩萨与他别了，同木叉径奔东土。行了多时，又见一座高山，山上有恶气遮漫，不能步上。正欲驾云过山，不觉狂风起处，又闪上一个妖魔。他生得又甚凶险。但见他：

> 卷脏莲蓬吊搭嘴，耳如蒲扇显金睛。
> 猴牙利刻如钢锉，长嘴张开似火盆。
> 金盔紧系腮边带，勒甲丝绦蟒退鳞。
> 手执钉钯龙探爪，腰挎弯弓月半轮。
> 纠纠威风欺太岁，昂昂志气压天神。

他撞上来，不分好歹，望菩萨举钉钯就筑。被木叉行者挡住，大喝一声道："那泼怪，休得无礼！看棒！"妖魔道："这和尚不知死活！看钯！"两个在山底下，一冲一撞，赌斗输赢。真个好杀：

> 妖魔凶猛，惠岸威能。铁棒分心捣，钉钯劈面迎。播土扬
> 尘天地暗，飞砂走石鬼神惊。九齿钯，光耀耀，双环响喨；
> 一条棒，黑悠悠，两手飞腾。这个是天王太子，那个是元帅
> 精灵。一个在普陀为护法，一个在山洞做妖精。这场相遇
> 争高下，不知那个亏输那个赢。

【9】 他两个正杀到好处，消息在半空中，抛下莲花，隔开钯杖。怪物见了心惊，便问："你是那里和尚，敢弄甚么眼前花儿哄我？"木叉道："我把你个肉眼凡胎的泼物！我是南海菩萨的徒弟。这是我师父抛来的莲花，你也不认得哩！"那怪道："南海菩萨，可是扫三灾救八难的观世音么？"木叉道："不是他是谁？"怪物撇了钉钯，纳头下礼道："老兄，菩萨在那里？累烦你引见一见。"木叉仰面指道："那不是？"怪物朝上磕头，厉声高叫道："菩萨，恕罪！恕罪！"观音按下云头，前来问道："你是那里成精的野豕，何方作怪的老彘，敢在此间挡我？"那怪道："我不是野豕，亦不是老彘，我本是天河里天蓬元帅。只因带酒戏弄嫦娥，玉帝把我打了二千锤，贬下尘凡。一灵真性，竟来夺舍投胎，不期错了道路，投在个母猪胎里，变得这般模样。是我咬杀母猪，可群群彘，在此处占了山场，吃人度日。不期撞着菩萨，万望拔救，拔救。"菩萨道："此山叫做甚么山？"怪物道："叫做福陵山。山中有一洞，叫做云栈洞。洞里原有个卵二姐。他见我有些武艺，招我做了家长，又唤做'倒踏门'。不上一年，他死了，将一洞的家当，尽归我受用。在此日久年深，没有个赡身的勾当，只是依本等吃人度日。万望菩萨恕罪。"菩萨道："古人云：'若要有前程，莫俺没前程。'你既上界违法，今又不改凶心，伤生造孽，却不是二罪俱

猪八戒

罚?"那怪道:"前程!前程!若依你,教我嗑风!常言道:'依着官法打杀,依着佛法饿杀。'去也!去也!还不如捉个行人,肥腻腻的吃他家娘!管甚么二罪,三罪,千罪,万罪!"菩萨道:"'人有善愿,天必从之。'汝若肯归依正果,自有养身之处。世有五谷,尽能济饥,为何吃人度日?"怪物闻言,似梦方觉。向菩萨施礼道:"我欲从正,奈何'获罪于天,无所祷也'!"菩萨道:"我领了佛旨,上东土寻取经人。你可跟他做个徒弟,往西天走一遭来,将功折罪,管教你脱离灾瘴。"那怪满口道:"愿随!愿随!"菩萨才与他摩顶受戒,指身为姓,就姓了猪;替他起个法名,就叫做猪悟能。遂此领命归真,持斋把素,断绝了五荤三厌,专候那取经人。

【10】 菩萨却与木叉,辞了悟能,半兴云雾前来。正走处,只见空中有一条玉龙叫唤。菩萨近前问曰:"你是何龙,在此受罪?"那龙道:"我是西海龙王敖闰之子。因纵火烧了殿上明珠,我父王表奏龙王,告了忤逆。玉帝把我吊在空中,打了三百,不日遭诛。望菩萨搭救,搭救。"

观音闻言,即与木叉撞上南天门里,早有邱、张二天师接着,问道:"何往?"菩萨道:"贫僧要见玉帝一面。"二天师即忙上奏。玉帝遂下殿迎接。菩萨上前礼毕道;"贫僧领佛旨上东土寻取经人,路遇孽龙悬吊,特来启奏,饶他性命,赐与贫僧,教他与取经人做个脚力。"玉帝闻言,即传旨赦宥,差天将解放,送与菩萨。菩萨谢恩而出。这小龙叩头谢活命之恩,听从菩萨使唤。菩萨把他送在深涧之中,只等取经人来,变做白马,上西方立功。小龙领命潜身不题。

【11】 菩萨带引木叉行者过了此山,又奔东土。行不多时,忽见金光万道,瑞气千条。木叉道:"师父,那放光之处,乃是五行山了,见有如来的'压帖'在那里。"菩萨道:"此却是那搅乱蟠桃会大闹天宫的齐天大圣,今乃压在此也。"木叉道:"正是,正是。"师徒俱上山来,观看帖子,乃是"唵、嘛、呢、叭、咪、吽"六字真言。菩萨看罢,叹惜不已,做诗一首,诗曰:

"堪叹妖猴不奉公,当年狂妄逞英雄。
欺心搅乱蟠桃会,大胆私行兜率宫。
十万军中无敌手,九重天上有威风。

自遭我佛如来困，何日舒伸再显功！"

【12】　师徒们正说处，早惊动了那大圣。大圣在山根下，高叫道："是那个在山上吟诗，揭我的短哩？"菩萨闻言，径下山来寻看。只见那石崖之下，有土地、山神、监押大圣的天将，都来拜接了菩萨，引至那大圣面前。看时，他原来压于石匣之中，口能言，身不能动。菩萨道："姓孙的，你认得我么？"大圣睁开火眼金睛，点着头儿高叫道："我怎么不认得你。你好的是那南海普陀落伽山救苦救难大慈大悲南无观世音菩萨。承看顾！承看顾！我在此度日如年，更无一个相知的来看我一看。你从那里来也？"菩萨道："我奉佛旨，上东土寻取经人去，从此经过，特留残步看你。"大圣道，"如来哄了我，把我压在此山，五百余年了，不能展挣。万望菩萨方便一二，救我老孙一救！"菩萨道："你这厮罪业弥深，救你出来，恐你又生祸害，反为不美。"大圣道："我已知悔了。但愿大慈悲指条门路，情愿修行。"这才是：

　　人心生一念，天地尽皆知。善恶若无报，乾坤必有私。

那菩萨闻得此言，满心欢喜，对大圣道："圣经云：'出其言善，则千里之外应之；出其言不善，则千里之上违之。'你既有此心，待我到了东土大唐国寻一个取经的人来，教他救你。你可跟他做个徒弟，秉教伽持，入我门门，再修正果，如何？"大圣声声道："愿去！愿去！"菩萨道："既有善果，我与你起个法名。"大圣道："我已有名了，叫做孙悟空。"菩萨又喜道："我前面也有二人归降，正是'悟'字排行。你今也是'悟'字，却与他相合，甚好，甚好。这等也不消叮嘱，我去也。"那大圣见性明心归佛教，这菩萨留情在意访神僧。

【13】　他与木叉离得此处，一直东来，不一日就到了长安大唐国。敛雾收云，师徒们变做两个疥癞游僧，入长安城里，早不觉天晚。行至大市街旁，见一座土地神祠，二人径入，唬得那土地心慌，鬼兵胆战。知是菩萨，叩头接入。那土地又急跑报与城隍、社令，及满长安各庙神祇，都知是菩萨，参见告道："菩萨，恕众神接迟之罪。"菩萨道："汝等切不可走漏一毫消息。我奉佛旨，特来此处寻访取经人。借你庙宇，权住几日，待访着真僧即回。"

Chapter 4
Our Buddha Creates the Scriptures and Passes on Perfect Bliss; Guanyin Obeys a Decree and Goes to Chang'an

[1] *If you try to ask about the dhyana*
   Or investigate the innumerable
   You will waste your life and achieve nothing.
   Polishing bricks to make mirrors,
   Or piling up snow to turn it into grain—
   However many years have you wasted like that?
   A hair can contain an ocean,
   A mustard-seed can hold a mountain,
   And the golden Kasyapa only smiles.
   When you are awakened you will surpass the Ten Stages and the Three Vehicles,
      And stop the four kinds of birth and the six types of reincarnation.
      Who has ever heard, before the cliff of thoughts extinguished,
      Under the tree that has no shadow,
      The sound of the cuckoo in a spring dawn?
      The path by the Cao Stream is dangerous,
      The Vulture Peak is high in the clouds:
      Here the voice of the ancients was a mystery.
      On a cliff ten thousand feet high
      Five-leaved lotuses bloom
      As scent coils round the shutters of the old palace.
      At that time
      Your knowledge smashes all the currents of thought;
      The Dragon King and the Three Treasures can be seen.

This lyric poem is set to the tune *Sun Wu Man*. Our story

goes on to how our Buddha, the Tathagata, left the Jade Emperor and went back to the Thunder Monastery, where he saw the three thousand Buddhas, five hundred Arhats, eight great Vajrapanis and countless Bodhisattvas standing under the pairs of sala trees at the foot of the Vulture Peak, all holding banners, canopies, jewels and magical flowers. The Tathagata brought his propitious cloud to a halt and addressed them thus:

> *"With my deep insight*
> *I surveyed the Three Worlds.*
> *The origin of nature*
> *Is ultimately emptiness,*
> *Like the great void,*
> *Containing nothing at all.*
> *The subjection of this evil monkey*
> *Was a mystery beyond understanding.*
> *It is called the beginning of life and death:*
> *Such is the appearance of things."*

When he had spoken a sacred light filled the sky with forty-two rainbows that linked north and south together. All who saw them bowed, and a moment later the Buddha gathered together some felicitious cloud and climbed to the supreme Lotus Throne, where he seated himself in majesty. Then the three thousand Buddhas, the five hundred Arhats, the eight Vajrapanis and the four Bodhisattvas came forward to bow to him with their hands together and ask, "Who was it who wrecked the Heavenly Palace and ruined the Peach Banquet?" they asked. "The wretch was a monkey fiend born on the Mountain of Flowers and Fruit," the Buddha replied, "whose towering crimes would beggar description. None of the heavenly generals were able subdue him, and when Lord Lao Zi refined him with fire after Erlang had captured him, he was unharmed. When I went there he was in the middle of the thunder generals, giving a great display of his martial prowess and his spirit. I stopped the fighting and asked him what it was all about. He said that he had divine powers, was able to do transformations, and could ride a somersault cloud for thirty-six thousand miles at a single jump. I made a wager with him that he could not jump out of my hand, then grabbed him, turned my fingers into the Five Elements Mountain, and sealed him under it. The Jade Emperor opened wide the golden gates of the Jade Palace, and invited me to be the guest of honour at a Banquet to Celebrate Peace in Heaven he gave to thank me. After that I took my leave of him and came back here." They were all delighted by the news and they congratulated him effusively, after which they withdrew group by group, each to go about his duties as all rejoiced in the divine truth. Indeed,

Propitious vapours filled Paradise,
Rainbows surround the Venerable One.
The Western Paradise, known as the best,
Is ruled by the dharma King of non-phenomenon.
Black apes are always offering fruit,
Deer hold flowers in their mouths;
Blue phoenixes dance,
Coloured birds call;
Sacred turtles offer long life,
Immortal cranes present magic mushrooms.
Here they peacefully enjoy the Pure Land of the Jetavana
Park,
The infinite realms of the Dragon Palace.
Every day flowers bloom,
Fruit is always ripe.
Through practising silence they return to the truth,
Achieving reality by contemplation.
There is no birth nor death;
They neither wax nor wane.
Mists follow them as they come and go;
Untouched by heat or cold, they do not notice the years.

【2】 One day, as the Buddha dwelt in the Thunder Monastery on the Vulture Peak, he called together all the other Buddhas,

Arhats, guardian deities, Bodhisattvas, Vajrapanis, monks and nuns and said, "As we are beyond time, I don't know how long it has been since the crafty ape was subdued and Heaven pacified, but by earthly reckoning it must be about five hundred years. As today is a fine early autumn day and I have a precious bowl filled with a hundred kinds of rare flowers and a thousand varieties of exotic fruit, what would you say to our having an Ullambana Feast?" They all put their hands together and performed the reverence of going round him three times in acceptance. The Buddha then ordered Ananda to hold the bowl of flowers and fruit while Kasyapa laid them out. The hosts were moved to gratitude, which they expressed in verse.

The poem on happiness went:

> *The Star of Happiness shines bright before the Venerable One;*
> *Gifts of happiness spread wide and deep, ever richer.*
> *Fortune is boundless and lasts as long as the Earth;*
> *A happy fate has the luck to be linked with Heaven.*
> *Fields of happiness are widely sown and flourish every year;*
> *The sea of happiness is mighty and deep, never changing.*
> *Happiness fills Heaven and Earth, leaving legacies of happiness*
> *Happiness grows beyond measure, eternally complete.*

The poem on official rank went:

> *With rank as high as a mountain, coloured phoenixes call;*
> *With rank ever increasing, we praise the evening star.*
> *Salary raised to ten thousand bushels, and a healthy body;*
> *Salary raise to a thousand tons, and the world at peace.*
> *Rank and salary equalling Heaven, and eternal too;*
> *Rank and fame as great as the sea, and even clearer.*
> *Rank and favour continuing for ever, greatly to be admired;*

93

Rank and nobility without bounds, like ten thousand kingdoms.

The poem on longevity went:

The Star of Longevity shines towards the Buddha;
The glories of the land of longevity start from here.
Fruits of longevity fill the bowls, glowing with good omen;
Longevity's flowers are newly plucked and placed on the lotus throne.
Poems of longevity, pure and elegant, full of rare conceits,
Songs of longevity sung with exquisite talent.
Life as long as sun and moon,
Life that will outlast both mountains and seas.

When the Bodhisattvas had presented all the poems they asked the Buddha to expound the fundamentals to them. Then the Tathagata opened his excellent mouth and expounded the great Law and retribution. He spoke about the wonderful scriptures of the Three Vehicles and the theory of the Five Aggregates as contained in the Surangama-sutra; the deities and nagas gathered round, and flowers came raining down in profusion. Indeed,

The meditating heart shines like the moon in a thousand rivers;
The true nature embraces ten thousand miles of sky.

[3] When the Buddha had finished his sermon he said to the host, "I have observed that the morality of the living creatures of the four continents varies. In the Eastern Continent of Superior Body they worship Heaven and Earth, their minds are lively and they are even-tempered. In the Northern Kuru Continent they are given to killing living things, but they only do it to feed

themselves; they are stupid and lazy by nature, but they do not trample much on others. Our Western Continent of Cattle—gift has people who neither covet nor kill. They nourish the vital essence and submerge the spirit; and although they produce no saints of the highest order, they all live to a ripe old age. But in the Southern Jambu Continent they are greedy and lecherous and delight in the sufferings of others; they go in for a great deal of killing and quarrelling. That continent can with truth be called a vicious field of tongues and mouths, an evil sea of disputation. I now have *Three Stores of True Scriptures* with which they can be persuaded to be good." On hearing this, all the Bodhisattvas put their hands together in submission, then went forward to ask, "What *Three Stores of True Scriptures* does the Tathagata have?" "I have one store of the *Vinaya*, the law, which is about Heaven; one of *Sastras*, expositions which are concerned with Earth; and one of *Sutras*, or scriptures, which save ghosts. The Three Stores consist of fifteen thousand one hundred and forty-four scrolls in thirty-five classes. They are the scriptures for cultivating the truth, and the gate to real goodness. I want to send them to the eastern lands because it is intolerable that the beings of that quarter should all be such stupid wretches who slander and defame the true word, do not understand the gist of my Law, and have lapsed from the orthodox Yogacara Sect. How am I to find one with the magic powers to go to the east, choose a worthy believer and bid him make the arduous crossing of a thousand mountains and ten thousand rivers in search of the scriptures until he finally comes to this abode of mine to receive them? When he does come they will be sent to the East for ever to convert all living beings, which will be a blessing as big as a mountain, a cause for congratulation as deep as the sea. Is anyone willing to go and find him?" The Bodhisattva Guanyin went up to the lotus throne, and after going round the Buddha three times by way of salutation she said, "Your untalented disciple wishes to go to the East to find a man to come and fetch the scriptures." All present raised their heads to look at the Bodhisattva:

Her understanding filling out the four virtues,

Wisdom filling her golden body.
From her necklace hang pearls and jade,
Her bracelet is made of jewels.
Her hair is black clouds skilfully piled like coiling dragons;
Her embroidered girdle lightly sways, a phoenix wing.
Seagreen jade buttons,
A gown of white silk gauze,
Bathed with sacred light;
Brocade skirts,
A girdle of gold,
Shielded by propitious vapours.
Eyebrows like crescent moons,
Eyes like a pair of stars.
A jade face full of heavenly happiness,
Scarlet lips making a touch of red.
Her pure bottle of sweet dew is ever full,
The willow twigs in it are always green.
She delivers from the eight disasters,
Saves all living beings,
Great is her compassion.
She stays on Mount Tai,
Lives in the Southern Sea,
Rescues the suffering when she hears their cries,
Never failing to answer every call,
Infinitely divine and miraculous.
Her orchid heart admires the purple bamboo;
Her orchid nature loves the fragrant creeper.
She is the merciful ruler of Potaraka Island,
The living Guanyin of the Tide Cave.

The Buddha was very pleased to see her. "No one but the venerable Guanyin, whose divine powers are so great, will do for this mission," he said. "What instructions have you for your disciple as she goes to the East?" Guanyin asked. "You must watch the route all the way," said the Buddha. "You may not go via the Milky Way, but if necessary you may have a little cloud or mist. As you cross mountains and rivers you must note the distances carefully to enable you to give full instructions to the man who will come to fetch the scriptures. But that true believer will, I'm afraid, have a difficult journey, so I shall give you five treasures for him." The Buddha ordered Ananda and Kasyapa to bring out a brocade cassock and a nine-ringed monk's staff. "Give this cassock and staff to him who will come to fetch the scriptures: they are for him to use. If he is determined to come here, he can avoid the Wheel of Reincarnation by wearing this cassock, and he will be free from evil if he carries this staff." The Bodhisattva bowed and took them. The Buddha then produced three bands. "These precious things are called 'tight bands'," he told the Bodhisattva as he handed them to her. "Although all three of them look the same, they have different uses. I also have three Band-Tightening Spells. If you meet any devils with great magic powers on your journey you should persuade them to reform and become the disciples of the pilgrim who will come to fetch the scriptures. If they do not do as they are told these bands should be put on their heads, where they will of themselves take root in the flesh. If the appropriate spell for each one is recited the victim's eyes will bulge, his head will ache, and his forehead will split open. He will thus be certainly induced to adopt our religion."

[4]   When he finished speaking the Bodhisattva bowed eagerly and withdrew. She told Huian the Novice to accompany her, and he took his iron staff weighing a thousand pounds with him so that he could as a demon-quelling strongman for the Bodhisattva. The Bodhisattva wrapped the cassock up in a bundle and gave it to him to carry. She then put the golden bands away safely and went down the Vulture Peak with the staff in her hand. This journey was to have consequences:

> The Buddha's disciple comes back to his original vow;
> The Venerable Golden Cicada is dressed in sandalwood.

When the Bodhisattva reached the foot of the mountain the

Gold-headed Immortal of the Jade Truth Temple stopped her at the temple gate and invited her to take some tea. But she dared not stop for long, and so she said, "I have been given a sacred command by the Tathagata to go to the East and find a man who will come to fetch the scriptures." "When will he arrive?" the Immortal asked. "It is not definite," the Bodhisattva replied, "but he will probably reach here in two or three years' time." She took her leave of the Immortal and as she travelled amid cloud and mist she estimated the distances. There are some verses to prove it:

> *She cared nothing of the journey of ten thousand miles to find him,*
> *But worried about finding the right man.*
> *Looking for the man seemed to be very chancy,*
> *But how can it be a mere coincidence?*
> *One who teaches the Way for the wrong motives will distort it;*
> *He who explains it without faith will preach in vain.*
> *Whoever will try and know it with his whole being,*
> *Is bound to have a future ahead of him.*

【5】 As the teacher and her disciple were on their journey they suddenly noticed a thousand miles of weak water, which was the River of Flowing Sands. "Disciple," said the Bodhisattva, "this will be hard to cross for the man who will come to fetch the scriptures, as he will be of impure bone and mortal flesh. How will he do it?" "Teacher, how wide does the river look to you?" asked Huian. The Bodhisattva stopped her cloud to investigate. She saw:

> *Joining up with the deserts to the east,*
> *Reaching the foreign kingdoms in the west,*
> *Wuge in the south*
> *The Tatars in the north.*
> *It was about three hundred miles across,*
> *And three million miles long.*
> *As the waters flowed it was like the earth turning over,*

The waves were like rearing mountains.
Broad and boundless,
Vast and mighty:
From three miles' distance the mighty flood is heard.
Immortals' rafts do not reach here,
Lotus leaves cannot float on it.
The sun slants through withered plants and bathes the
crooked shore;
Brown clouds block its light and darken the long bank.
How could merchants pass this way?
Has a fisherman ever moored here?
No geese alight on the sandbanks,
But apes cry on the distant shore.
Its colour comes from bountiful red smartweed,
While delicate white duckweed drifts together.

As the Bodhisattva was surveying the scene she heard a splash and saw a hideous ogre leap out of the waves. He was

Not really blue,
Not really black,
With an evil face;
Neither tall,
Nor short,
Bare legs and a muscular body.
His eyes flashed
Like a pair of tortoise-shell lanterns;
The corners of his mouth were as sinister
As a butcher's cauldron.
Protruding fangs like swords,
Red hair, matted and unkempt,
He roared like a clap of thunder,
And ran across the waves with the speed of wind.

【6】 This ogre climbed up the bank with a pole in his hands to catch the Bodhisattva, but was stopped by Huian's staff. "Don't run away," Huian shouted as the ogre advanced towards him. The battle that ensued between them was quite terrifying:

> Moksa with his iron club,
> Using his divine powers to protect the Bodhisattva;
> The ogre with his demon-quelling pole
> Displaying his valour for all he was worth.
> A pair of silver dragons dancing by the river;
> Two holy monks in battle on the bank.
> The one used his skill to control the River of Flowing Sands
> The other had distinguished himself in protecting Guanyin.
> The one could make the waves leap and roll,
> The other could breathe out fogs and gales.
> When the waves leapt and rolled, Heaven and Earth were darkened;
> In the fogs and gales, sun and moon were dimmed.
> The demon-quelling pole
> Was like a white tiger coming down from the mountain;
> The iron club
> Was like a crouching yellow dragon.
> When one goes into action
> It beats the undergrowth to start the snakes;
> When the other lashes out,
> It parts the pines to flush the sparrowhawks.
> They fight till the sky goes dark
> And the stars twinkle.
> Then the mist rises,
> And earth and sky are dim.
> The one has long been unrivalled in the Weak Waters;
> The other has always been the hero of Vulture Peak.

When the pair of them had fought several dozen rounds inconclusively the ogre blocked his opponent's iron staff and asked, "Where are you from, monk, that you dare to take me on?" "I am Prince Moksa, the second son of the Pagoda-bearing

Heavenly King Li," the other replied. "I am also Huian the Novice. I am now protecting my teacher on her journey to the East to find the man who will fetch the scriptures. Which monster are you? How dare you stand in our way?" The ogre then realized who he was. "I remember," he said, "you used to cultivate your conduct with Guanyin of the Southern Sea in the Purple Bamboo Grove. Why have you come here?" "Can't you see my teacher standing there on the bank?"

【7】 When the ogre heard this he chanted "na-a-aw" several times to show his respect, withdrew his pole and let Moksa seize it. Then he bowed to Guanyin and said, " Forgive me, Bodhisattva, and listen to what I have to tell you. I am not a demon, but the Curtain Raising General who used to stand in attendance by the imperial chariot in the Hall of Miraculous Mist. Just because I accidentally smashed a crystal dish at a Peach Banquet the Jade Emperor had me given eight hundred strokes of the rod, exiled me to the lower world, and made me look like this. And on top of it all every seven days he sends a flying sword here to stab my chest over a hundred times before it goes back again. It's agony. I get so unbearably cold and hungry that I have to emerge from the waves every two or three days to devour a traveller. I never thought that in my ignorance I would insult the merciful Bodhisattva today." "You were exiled here for a crime against Heaven, but now you are deepening your guilt by harming living beings. I am now going to the East on the Buddha's orders to find the man who will fetch the scriptures. Why don't you become one of us and ensure yourself good retribution in future by accompanying the pilgrim as a disciple and ascending to the Western Heaven to pay homage to the Buddha and seek the scriptures? I will see to it that the flying sword stops coming to pierce you, and when you are successful you will be forgiven your crimes and your old job will be given back to you. What do you think of that?" "I am willing to return to the truth," the ogre replied, then went closer as he continued, "Bodhisattva, I have lost count of the number of people I have eaten here, and I have even devoured some pilgrims who were trying to fetch scriptures.

101

I throw the heads of all my victims into the river, and they all sink to the bottom as not even goose-down will float on this water. But the skeletons of those nine pilgrims floated and would not sink. I was so impressed by this that I threaded them together with rope and play with them in my spare time. But I am afraid that the man who is to fetch the scriptures may not get this far, which would wreck my future." "Of course he'll get here," the Bodhisattva replied. "You should hang those skeletons from your head and wait for him. They will come in useful." "In that case," the ogre said, "I shall await your instructions." The Bodhisattva then laid her hands on his head and administered the monastic rules to him, chose for him the surname Sha ("Sand") and gave him the Buddhist name of Wujing ("Awakened to Purity"). Then he entered monkish life and took the Bodhisattva across the river. He washed his heart, cleansed his thoughts, and stopped killing living creatures. All he did now was to wait for the pilgrim who would come to fetch the scriptures.

[8] After leaving him the Bodhisattva and Huian hurried on towards the east. When they had been travelling for a long time they saw a high mountain veiled with an evil mist, and they were unable to climb it on foot. Just when they were intending to cross the mountain by cloud, a gale wind blew up and a monster suddenly appeared. He too was very menacing to behold:

> *His entrails hung from his mouth, rolled up and knotted;*
> *His ears were like rush fans, his eyes shone gold.*
> *His teeth were sharp as steel files,*
> *And when he opened his mouth it was like a brazier.*
> *His golden helmet was tied firmly round his cheeks;*
> *His armour, bound with a silken sash, was a python's sloughed-off skin.*
> *In his hands he held a nailed rake like a dragon's claw,*
> *At his waist hung a curved bow the shape of a half-moon.*
> *His martial might overawed the Year Planet;*
> *His overweening spirit threatened the heavenly gods.*

He rushed upon them, and without a second thought smote at the Bodhisattva with his rake. Moksa the Novice parried his blow, and shouted at the top of his voice, "Remember your manners, damned monster, and watch out for my staff." "Monk," the other replied, "you don't know how to keep yourself in one piece. Mind my rake!" At the foot of the mountain the pair of them rushed upon each other as they struggled for supremacy. It was a fine battle:

> The fierce and murderous ogre;
> Huian, imposing and able.
> The iron staff could pulverize the heart;
> The rake struck at the face.
> The dust thrown up darkened Heaven and Earth;
> The flying sand and stones startled gods and ghouls.
> The nine-toothed rake
> Gleamed and flashed
> As its pair of rings resounded;
> The lone staff
> Was ominously black
> As it whirled in its owner's hands
> One was the heir of a Heavenly King,
> One defended the Law on Potaraka Island.
> The other was an evil fiend in a mountain cave.
> In their battle for mastery,
> None knew who the winner would be.

[9] Just when the fight was getting really good, Guanyin threw down a lotus flower from mid-air to separate the two weapons. The monster, shocked at the sight of it, asked, "Where are you from, monk? How dare you try to fool me with a 'flower in front of the eyes'?" "I'll get you, you stinking, flesh-eyed mortal," replied Moksa. "I am a disciple of the Bodhisattva of the Southern Sea, and this lotus was thrown down by her. Don't you know that?" "By the Bodhisattva of the Southern Sea do you mean Guanyin Who Eliminates the Three Calamities and Saves from the

103

Eight Disasters?" the monster asked. "Who else could I mean?" retorted Moksa. The monster threw down his rake, bowed to him, and asked, "Where is the Bodhisattva, elder brother? May I trouble you to introduce me?" Moksa looked up and pointed. "There she is," he said. The monster kowtowed to her and shouted in a shrill voice, "Forgive me, Bodhisattva, forgive me." Guanyin brought her cloud down to earth, went over to him and asked, "Are you a wild boar become a devil or a pig turned monster? How dare you block my way?" "I'm neither a wild boar nor a pig," the monster replied. "I used to be Marshal Tian Peng in the Milky Way. Because I took some wine to seduce the moon maiden, the Jade Emperor sentenced me to two thousand hammer blows and exile in the mortal world. My spirit had to find a womb to occupy, but I lost my way and entered the womb of a sow. That's why I look like this. I ate up my sow mother, drove all the other pigs away, and seized this mountain, where I keep myself by eating people. I never meant to offend you, Bodhisattva. Save, save, I beg you." "What is this mountain called?" the Bodhisattva asked. "It's called the Mount of Blessing, and the cave in it is called the Cloud Pathway Cave. Second Sister Luan, who used to live there, saw that I knew how to fight and asked me to be the head of her household as her husband, but she died within a year and all her property became mine. As the days lengthened into years I found that I had no way of supporting myself, so I had to eat people to keep myself going as I had done before. Forgive me my sins, I beg of you, Bodhisattva." "There is an old saying," the Bodhisattva replied, "that goes, 'If you want to have a future, don't do anything with no future in it.' You broke the law in the upper world, and since then your vicious nature has not been reformed. You have further sinned by taking life, so this surely means that you will be doubly punished." "Future!" said the monster angrily. "According to you I should have lived on air! As the saying goes, 'By the government's law you're beaten to death, and by the Buddha's law you starve to death.' Clear off! Clear off! If you don't I'll capture this pilgrim and eat this plump and tender old woman. I 'don't give a hoot if it's double sinning, triple sinning, or sinning a thousand or ten thousand times over." " 'If a man wishes to be good, Heaven will certainly allow him to be'," said the Bodhisattva. "If you are prepared to submit to the truth, there are of course, ways to feed yourself. There are the five kinds of food-grains, and they are sufficient to assuage hunger, so why eat people to keep alive?"

When the monster heard these words it was as if he awoke from a dream, and he said to the Bodhisattva, "I would love to reform, but isn't it true that 'a sinner against Heaven has nowhere to pray to'?" "I'm going to the East on the orders of the Buddha to find the man who will fetch the scriptures," she replied. "You can be a disciple of his and make this journey to the Western Heaven; thus you will gain merit and atone for your crimes, and I will see to it that you are freed from disaster." "I'll go with him, I'll go with him," the monster said over and over again. The Budhisattva then laid her hands on his head and he accepted the monastic rules. She gave him the surname Zhu ("Pig") because of his appearance, and gave him the Buddhist name Zhu Wuneng ("Pig Awakened to Power"). She ordered him to adhere to the truth and eat only vegetarian food, cutting out the five pungent vegetables as well as the three forbidden things; wild goose, dog and fish. He was now to wait single-mindedly for the pilgrim who would come to fetch the scriptures.

[10]   The Bodhisattva and Moksa then took their leave of the Pig Awakened to Power and continued on their way by low-altitude cloud. As they were travelling along they heard a jade dragon call to them in mid-air. "Which dragon are you?" the Bodhisattva asked as she went up to him. "And why are you undergoing punishment here?" "I am the son of Ao Run, the Dragon King of the Western Sea. Because I burnt up the bright pearls in the palace, my father reported me to the court of Heaven as a rebel. The Jade Emperor had me hung up in mid-air and given three hundred strokes, and I am to be executed any day now. I beg you to save me, Bodhisattva."

When she heard his plea the Bodhisattva went in through the

Southern Gates of Heaven with Moksa. Here they were met by the Heavenly Teachers Qiu and Zhang, who asked them, "Where are you going?" "I would like an audience with the Jade Emperor." The two Heavenly Teachers hurried in to announce her, and the Jade Emperor came out of his palace to receive her. The Bodhisattva went forward to greet him and said, "On my way to the East on the orders of the Buddha to find the man to fetch the scriptures, I met a wicked dragon suspended in mid-air. I have come here especially to ask you to spare his life and give him to me so that I can teach him to serve the pilgrim with his legs." On hearing this the Jade Emperor issued a decree pardoning him, and he sent a heavenly general to release him and give him to the Bodhisattva. The Bodhisattva thanked him for his generosity and left. The young dragon kowtowed to show how grateful he was for having his life spared, and he obediently did what the Bodhisattva told him to. She took him to a deep ravine, where he was to wait until the pilgrim came. When that happened he was to turn into a white horse and achieve merit by going to the Western Heaven. On receiving his orders the young dragon hid himself.

【11】 The Bodhisattva led Moksa the Novice across this mountain, and they hurried on towards the east. Before they had gone much further they suddenly saw ten thousand beams of golden light and a thousand wisps of propitious vapour. "Teacher," said Moksa, "the place where all the light is coming from is the Five Elements Mountain, where the Tathagata's restriction order is posted." "This must be cause that Great Sage Equalling Heaven who wrecked the Peach Banquet and threw the Heavenly Palace into chaos is imprisoned there." "That's right," Moksa replied, and teacher and pupil climbed the mountain together to look at the paper. On it were written the true words Om mani padme hum, and when the Bodhisattva saw them she sighed deeply and composed a poem that went:

"Pity the evil monkey who did not obey the lord
In his arrogance he showed off his valour in the old days,

In his folly he wrecked the Peach Banquet,
And he had the effrontery to sin in the Tushita Palace.
In the army of a hundred thousand there was none to match him;
His might was felt above the ninefold heavens.
But now he has been caught by our Tathagata, the Buddha:
Will he ever be able to unleash his talents and win more glory?"

【12】 The conversation between teacher and disciple had disturbed the Great Sage, who shouted from under the roots of the mountain, "Who's that up there?" When she heard this the Bodhisattva hurried down the mountain to visit him. At the foot of the Mountainside the local gods, the mountain gods and the heavenly generals who were guarding the Great Sage all bowed to the Bodhisattva in greeting and took her to the Great Sage. She saw that he was pressed down inside a stone box, so that he could speak but could not move his body. "Monkey," the Bodhisattva said, "do you know who I am?" The Great Sage opened wide his fiery eyes with their golden pupils, nodded his head and shouted at the top of his voice, "Of course I recognize you. You, thank goodness, are the All-Compassionate, All-Merciful Deliverer from Suffering, the Bodhisattva Guanyin from Potaraka Island in the Southern Sea. You're a very welcome visitor. Every day here seems like a year, and nobody I know has ever come to see me. Where have you come from?" "I have received a mandate from the Buddha to go to the East and find the man who will fetch the scriptures," she replied, "and as I was passing this way I decided to come over and see you." "The Buddha fooled me and crushed me under this mountain—I haven't been able to stretch myself for five hundred years. I desperately hope that you will be obliging enough to rescue me, Bodhisattva." "You wretch," she replied, "you have such an appalling criminal record that I'm afraid you'd only make more trouble if I got you out." "I have already repented," he said, "and hope that you will show me the road I

107

should follow. I want to cultivate my conduct." Indeed,

> *When an idea is born in a man's mind*
> *It is known throughout Heaven and Earth.*
> *If good and evil are not rewarded and punished*
> *The world is bound to go to the bad.*

The Bodhisattva was delighted to hear what he had to say. "The sacred scriptures say," she replied, " ' If one's words are good, they will meet with a response from even a thousand miles away; if they are bad, they will be opposed from the same distance.' If this is your state of mind, then wait while I go to the East to find the man who will fetch the scriptures; I'll tell him to rescue you. You can be his disciple, observe and uphold the faith, enter our Buddha's religion, and cultivate good retribution for yourself in the future. What do you say to that?" "I'll go, I'll go," the Great Sage repeated over and over again. "As you have reformed," she said, "I'll give you a Buddhist name." "I've already got a name. It's Sun Wukong." The Bodhisattva, very pleased, said, "I made two converts earlier, and their names both contained Wu ('Awakened'). There's no need to give you any further instructions, so I'll be off." The Great Sage, now aware of his own Buddha-nature, was converted to the Buddha's religion; and the Bodhisattva devotedly continued her search for a saintly monk.

[13] After leaving that place she and Huian carried straight on to the east, and before long they reached Chang'an, the capital of the Great Tang. Putting away their mists and clouds, teacher and pupil turned themselves into a pair of scabby itinerant monks and went inside the city of Chang'an. It was already dark, and beside the great market street they saw a shrine to a local tutelary god and went in. The local god was thrown into confusion at the sight of them, and the devil soldiers quaked with terror; they knew that she was a Bodhisattva, and kowtowed to her in greeting. The local god then scurried off to tell the City God, the Lord of the Altar, and the gods of all the other shrines in Chang'an.

When they knew that the Bodhisattva had come they all went to report to her and said, "Bodhisattva, please forgive us for our crime in being late to welcome you." "You mustn't let a whisper of this get out," she said. "I have come here on a decree from the Buddha to find someone to fetch the scriptures. I shall be borrowing your temple for a few days while I find this true monk, and then I shall go back."

5. 观音院僧谋宝贝
黑风山怪窃袈裟

(唐三藏在孙悟空的保护下，前往西天取经。靠观音菩萨的帮助，他们在鹰愁洞收了白龙马，继续西行。一天，日色西沉，遥见前方像有座寺院，他们欲去投宿。)

【1】 却说他师徒两个，策马前去，直至山门首观看，果然是一座寺院。但见那：

层层殿阁，迭迭廊房。三山门外，巍巍万道彩云遮；五福堂前，艳艳千条红雾绕。两路松篁，一林桧柏。两路松篁，无年无纪自清幽；一林桧柏，有色有颜随öld丽。又见那钟鼓楼高，浮屠塔峻。安禅僧定性，啼树鸟音闲。寂寞无尘真寂寞，清虚有道果清虚。

诗曰：

上刹祇园隐翠窝，招提胜景赛娑婆。
果然净土人间少，天下名山僧占多。

长老下了马，行者歇了担，正欲进门，只见那门里走出一众僧来。你看他怎生模样：

头戴左笄帽，身穿无垢衣。
铜环双坠耳，绢带束腰围。
草履行来稳，木鱼手内提。
口中常作念，般若总皈依。

三藏见了，侍立门旁，道个问讯，那和尚连忙答礼。笑道："失瞻。"问："是那里来的？请入方丈献茶。"三藏道："我弟子乃东土钦差，上雷音寺拜佛求经。至此处天色将晚，欲借上刹一宵。"那和尚道："请进里坐，请进里坐。"三藏方唤行者牵马进来。那和尚

110

唐僧

忽见行者相貌，有些害怕，便问："那牵马的是个甚么东西？"三藏道："悄言！悄言！他的性急，若听见你说是甚么东西，他就恼了。——他是我的徒弟。"那和尚打了个寒噤，咬着指头道："这般一个丑头怪脑的，好招他做徒弟！"三藏道："你看不出来哩，丑自丑，甚是有用。"

【2】 那和尚只得同三藏与行者进了山门。山门里，又见那正殿上书四个大字，是："观音禅院"。三藏又大喜道："弟子屡感菩萨圣恩，未及叩谢；今遇禅院，就如见菩萨一般，甚好拜谢。"那和尚闻言，即命道人开了殿门，请三藏朝拜。那行者拴了马，丢了行李，同三藏上殿。三藏展背舒身，铺胸纳地，望金像叩头。那和尚便去打鼓，行者就去撞钟。三藏俯伏台前，倾心祝祷。祝拜已毕，那和尚住了鼓，行者还只管撞钟不歇，或紧或慢，撞了许久。那道人道："拜已毕了，还撞钟怎么？"行者方丢了钟杵，笑道："你那晓得！我这是'做一日和尚撞一日钟'的。"此时却惊动了那寺里大小僧人、上下房长老，听得钟声乱响，一齐拥出道："那个野人在这里乱敲钟鼓？"行者跳将出来，咄的一声道："是你孙外公撞了耍子的！"那些和尚一见，唬得跌跌滚滚，都爬在地下道："雷公爷爷！"行者道："雷公是我的重孙儿哩！起来，起来，不要怕，我们是东土大唐来的老爷。"众僧方才礼拜，见了三藏，都放心不怕。内有本寺院主请道："老爷们到后方丈中奉茶。"遂即解缰牵马，抬了行李，转过正殿，径入后房，序что坐次。

【3】 那童献了茶，又安排斋供。天光尚早，只见那后面有两个小童，搀着一个老僧出来。看他怎生打扮：

头上戴一顶毗卢方帽，猫睛石的宝顶光辉；身上穿一领锦绒褊衫，翡翠毛的金边晃亮。一对僧鞋攒八宝，一根拄杖嵌云星。满面皱痕，好似骊山老母；一双昏眼，却如东海龙君。口不关风因齿落，腰驼背屈为筋挛。

众僧道："师祖来了。"三藏躬身施礼迎接道："老院主，弟子拜揖。"那老僧还了礼，又各叙坐。老僧道："适间小的们说，东土唐朝来的老爷，我才出来奉见。"三藏道："轻造宝山，不知好歹，恕罪！恕罪！"老僧道："不敢！不敢！"因问："老弟，东土到此，有多少路程？"三藏道："出长安边界，有五千余里；过两界山，收了一众小徒，一路来，行过西番哈咇国，经两个月，又有五六千里，才到了贵处。”老僧道：“也有万里之遥了。我弟子虚度一生，山门也不曾出去，诚所谓‘坐井观天’，樗朽之辈。”三藏又问：“老院主高寿几何？”老僧道：“痴长二百七十岁了。”行者听见道：“这还是我万代孙儿哩！”三藏瞅了他一眼道：“谨言！莫要不识高低，冲撞人。”那和尚便问：“老爷，你有多少年纪了？”行者道：不敢说。”那老僧也只当一句疯话，便不介意，也不再问，只叫献茶。有一个小幸童，拿出一个羊脂玉的盘儿，有三个法蓝镶金的茶钟；又一童，提一把白铜壶儿，斟了三杯香茶。真个是色欺榴蕊艳，味胜桂花香。三藏见了，夸爱不尽道：“好物件！好物件！真是美食美器！”那老僧道：“污眼！污眼！老爷乃天朝上国，广览奇珍，似这般器具，何足过奖？老爷自上邦来，可有甚么宝贝，借与弟子一观？”三藏道；“可怜！我那东土，无甚宝贝；就有时，路程遥远，也不能带得。”

【4】　行者在旁道；“师父，我前日在包袱里，曾见那领袈裟，不是件宝贝？拿与他看看何如？”众僧听说袈裟，一个个冷笑。行者道：“你笑怎的？”院主道；“老爷才说袈裟是件宝贝，言实可笑。若说袈裟，似我等辈者，不止二三十件；若论我师祖，在此处做了二百五六十年和尚，足有七八百件！”叫：“拿出来看看。”那老和尚，也是他一时卖弄，便叫道人开库房，头陀抬柜子，就抬出十二柜，放在天井中，开了锁，两边设下衣架，四围牵了绳子，将袈裟一件件抖开挂起，请三藏观看。果然是满堂绮绣，四壁绫罗！

行者一一观之，都是些穿花纳锦，刺绣销金之物。笑道：“好，好，好！收起！收起！把我们的也取出来看看。”三藏把行者扯住，悄悄的道：“徒弟，莫要与人斗富。你我是单身在外，只恐有错。”行者道：“看看袈裟，有何差错？”三藏道：“你不曾理会得。古人有云：“珍奇玩好之物，不可使见贪婪奸伪之人。”倘若一经入目，必动其心；既动其心，必生其计。汝是个畏祸的，索之而必应其求，可也；不然，则殒身灭命，皆起于此，事不小矣。”行者道：“放心！放心！都在老孙身上！”你看他不由分说，急急的走了去，把个包袱解开，早有霞光迸迸；尚有两层油纸裹定，去了纸，取出袈裟，抖开时，红光满室，彩气盈庭。众僧见了，无一个不心欢口赞。真个好袈裟！上头有：

> 千般巧妙明珠坠，万样稀奇佛宝攒。
> 上下龙须铺彩绮，兜罗四面锦沿边。
> 体挂魍魉从此灭，身披魑魅入黄泉。
> 托化天仙亲手制，不是真僧不敢穿。

【5】那老和尚见了这般宝贝，果然动了好心，走上前，对三藏跪下，眼中垂泪道："我弟子真是没缘！"三藏搀起道："老院师有何话说？"他道："老爷这件宝贝，方才展开，天色晚了，奈何眼目昏花，不能看得明白，岂不是无缘！"三藏教："掌上灯来，让你再看。"那老僧道："爷爷的宝贝，已是光亮；再点了灯，一发晃眼，莫想看得仔细。"行者道："你要怎的看才好？"老僧道："老爷若是宽恩放心，教弟子拿到后房，细细的看一夜，明早送老爷西去，不知尊意如何？"三藏听说，吃了一惊，埋怨行者道："都是你！都是你！"行者笑道："怕他怎的？等我包起来，教他拿去看。但有疏虞，尽是老孙管整。"那三藏阻拦不住，他把袈裟递与老僧道："凭你看去；只是明早照旧还我，不得损污色须。"老僧喜喜欢欢，着幸童将袈裟拿进去，却吩咐众僧，将前面禅堂扫净，取两张藤床，安setting铺盖，请二位老爷安歇；一壁厢又教安排明早斋送行，遂而各散。师徒们关了禅堂，睡下不题。

【6】却说那和尚把袈裟骗到手，拿在后房灯下，对袈裟号陶痛哭，慌得那本寺僧，不敢先睡。小幸童也不知为何，却去报与众僧道："公公哭到二更时候，还不歇声。"有两个徒孙，是他心爱之人，上前问道："师公，你哭怎么？"老僧道："我哭无缘，看不得唐僧宝贝！"小和尚道："公公年纪高大，发过了。他的袈裟，放在你面前，你只消解开看便罢了，何须痛哭？"老僧道："看的不长久。我今年二百七十岁，空挣了几百件袈裟。怎么得他这一件？怎么得做个唐僧？"小和尚道："师公差了。唐僧乃是离乡背井的一个行脚僧。你这等年高，享用也够了，倒要像他做行脚僧，何也？"老僧道："我虽是坐家自在，乐乎晚景，却不得他这袈裟穿穿。若教我穿得一日儿，就死也闭眼，——只是我来阳世间为僧一场！"众僧道："好没正经！你要穿他的，有何难处？我们明日留他住一日，你就穿他一日；留他住十日，你就穿他十日，便罢了。

何苦这般痛哭？"老僧道："纵然留他住了半截，也只穿得半截，到底也不得气长。他要去时，只得与他去，怎生留得长远？"

【7】　正说话处，有一个小和尚，名唤广智，出头道："公公，要得长远，也容易。"老僧闻言，就欢喜起来道："我儿，你有甚么高见？"广智道："那唐僧两个是走路的人，辛苦之甚，如今已睡着了。我们想几个有力量的，拿了枪刀，打开禅堂，将他一刀一个，尽皆杀了，把尸首埋在后园，只我一家知道，却又谋了他的白马、行囊，却把那袈裟留下，以为传家之宝，岂非子孙长久之计耶？"老和尚见说，满心欢喜，却才揩了眼泪道："好！好！好！此计绝妙！"即便收拾枪刀。

内中又有一个小和尚，名唤广谋，就是那广智的师弟，上前来道："此计不妙。若要杀他，须要看看动静。那个白脸的似易，那个毛脸的似难；万一不得他死，却不反招一祸？我有一个不动刀枪之法，不知你尊意何如？"老僧道："我儿，你有何法？"广谋道："依小孙之见，如今唤聚东山大小房头，每人要干柴一束，舍了那三间禅堂，放起火来，教他欲走无门，连马一火焚之。就是山前山后人家看见，只说是他自不小心，走了火，将我禅堂都烧了。那两个和尚，却不都烧死？又好掩人耳目。袈裟岂不是我们传家之宝？"那些和尚闻言，无不欢喜。都道："强！强！强！此计更妙！更妙！"遂教各房头搬柴来。唉！这一计，正是弄得个高寿老僧该尽命，观音禅院化为尘！原来他那寺里，有七八十个房头，大小有二百余众。当夜一拥搬柴，把个禅堂，前前后后，四面围绕不通，安排放火不题。

【8】　却说三藏师徒，安歇已定。那行者却是个灵猴，虽然睡着，只是存神炼气，朦胧着醒眼。忽听得外面不住的人走，揸揸的柴响风生。他心疑惑道："此时夜静，如何有人行得脚步之声？莫敢是贼盗，谋害我们的？……"他就一骨鲁跳起。欲要开门出看，又恐惊醒师父。你看他弄个精神，摇身一变，变做一个蜜蜂儿。真个是：

口甜尾毒，腰细身轻。穿花度柳飞如箭，粘絮寻香似落星。小小微躯能负重，器器薄翅会乘风。却自椽棱下，钻出看分明。

只见那众僧们，搬柴运草，已围住禅堂放火哩。行者暗笑道："果依我师父之言！他要害我们性命，谋我的袈裟，故起这等歹心。我待要拿棍打他啊，可怜又不禁打，一顿棍都打死了，师父又怪我凶。——罢，罢，罢！与他个'顺手牵羊，将计就计'，教他化不成罢！"好行者，一筋斗跳上南天门里，唬得个庞、刘、苟、毕四身，马、赵、温、关控背，俱道："不好了！不好了！那闹天宫的主子又来了！"行者摇着手道："列位免礼，休惊。我来寻广目天王的。"

【9】　说不了，却遇天王早到，迎着行者道："久阔，久阔。前闻得观音菩萨来见玉帝，借了四值功曹、六丁六甲并揭谛等，保护唐僧往西天取经去，说你与他做了徒弟，今日怎么得闲到此？"行者道："且休叙阔。唐僧路遇歹人，放火烧他，事在万分紧急，特来寻你借'辟火罩儿'，救他一救。快些拿来使使，即刻返上。"天王道："你差了！既是歹人放火，只该借水救他，如何要辟火罩？"行者道："你那里晓得就里。借水救之，却烧不起来，倒相应了他；只是借此罩，护住了唐僧无伤，其余管他，尽他烧去。快些！快些！此时恐已无及。莫误了我下边干事！"那天王笑道："这猴子还是这等起不善之心，只顾了自家，就不管别人。"行者道："快着！快着！莫要调嘴，害了大事！"那天王不敢不借，遂将罩儿递与行者。

行者拿了，按着云头，径到禅堂房脊上，罩住了唐僧与白马、行李。他却去那后面老和尚住的方丈上头坐上，着意保护那袈裟。看那些人放起火来，他转捻诀念咒，望巽地上吸一口气吹去，一阵风起，把那火转刮得烘烘乱着。好火！好火！但见：

黑烟漠漠，红焰腾腾。黑烟漠漠，长空不见一天星；红焰腾腾，大地有光千里赤。起初时，灼灼金蛇；次后来，威威血马。南方三炁逞英雄，回禄大神施法力。燥干柴烧烈火性，说甚么燧人钻木；熟油门前飘彩焰，赛过了老祖开炉。正是那无情火发，怎禁这有意行凶；不再预灾，反行助虐。风随火势，焰飞有引上千高；火趁风威，灰进上九霄云。乒乒乓乓，好便似残年爆竹；泼泼喇喇，却就如军中炮声。烧得那当场佛像莫能逃，东院伽蓝无处躲。胜如赤壁夜鏖兵，赛过阿房宫内火！

【10】　这正是星星之火，能烧万顷之田。须臾间，风狂火盛，把一座观音院，处处通红。你看那众和尚，搬箱抬笼，抢桌端锅，满院里叫苦连天。孙行者护住了后边方丈，辟火罩罩住了前面禅堂，其余前后火光大发，真个是照天红焰辉煌，透壁金光照耀！

【11】　不期火起之时，惊动了一山兽怪。这观音院正南二十里远近，有座黑风山，山中有一个黑风洞，洞中有一个妖精，正在睡醒翻身。只见那窗门透亮，只道是天明。起来看时，却是正北下的火光晃亮，妖精大惊道："呀！这必是观音院里失了火！这些和尚好不小心！我看时，与他救一救来。"好妖精，纵起云头，即至烟火之下，果然冲天之火，前面殿宇皆空，两廊烟火方灼。他大拽步，撞将进去，正呼唤叫取水来，只见那后房无火，房脊上有一个放风。他却情知如此，急入里面看，见那方丈中间有些霞光彩气，台案上有一个青毡包袱。他解开一看，见是一领锦袈裟，乃佛门之异宝。正是财动人心，他也不救火，他也不叫水，拿着那袈裟，趁哄打劫，拽回云步，径转东山而去。

那场火只烧到五更天明，方才灭息。你看那众僧们，赤赤精精，啼啼哭哭，都去那灰内寻铜铁，拨腐炭，扑金银。有的在墙筐里，苦搭窝棚；有的赤壁根头，支锅造饭。叫冤叫屈，乱嚷乱闹不题。

【12】　却说行者取了辟火罩，一筋斗送上南天门，交与广目天王道："谢借！谢借！"天王收了道："大圣至诚了。我正愁你不还我的宝贝，无处寻讨，且喜就送来也。"行者道："老孙可是那当面骗物之人？这叫做'好借好还，再借不难。'"天王道："许久不面，请到宫少坐一时，何如？"行者道："老孙比在前不同，'烂板凳，高谈阔论'了；如今保唐僧，不得身闲。容叙！容叙！"急辞别坠云，又见那太阳星上。径来到禅堂前，摇身一变，变做个蜜蜂儿，飞将进去，现了本像方叮，那师父还沉睡着哩。

行者叫道："师父，天亮了，起来罢。"三藏才醒觉，翻身道："正是。"穿了衣服，开门出来，忽抬头，只见些僻壁红墙，不见楼台殿宇。大惊道："呀！怎么这般殿宇俱无？都是红墙，何也？"行者道："你还做梦哩！今夜走了火的。"三藏道："我怎不知？"行者道:"是老孙护了禅堂,见师父浓睡,不曾惊动。"三藏道:"你有本事护了禅堂,如何就不救别房之火?"行者笑道:"好教师父得知。果然依你昨日之言,他爱上我们的袈裟,算计要烧杀我们。若不是老孙知觉,到如今皆成灰骨矣!"三藏闻得,害怕道:"是他们放的火么?"行者道:"不是他是谁?"三藏道:"莫不是怠慢了你,你干的这个勾当?"行者道:"老孙是这等惫懒之人,干这等不良之事?实实是他家放的。老孙见他心毒,果是不曾与他救火,只是与他略略助些风的。"三藏道:"天那!天那!火起时,只该助水,怎转助风?"行者道:"你可知古人云:'人没伤虎心,虎没伤人意。'他不弄火,我怎肯弄风?"三藏道:"袈裟何在?敢莫是烧坏了也?"行者道:"没事!没事!烧不坏!那放袈裟的方丈无火。"三藏恨道:"我不管你!但是有些儿伤损,我只把那话儿念动念动,你就是死了!"行者慌了道:"师父,莫念!莫念!管寻还你袈裟便是了。等我去拿来走路。"三藏才牵着马,行者挑了担,出了禅堂,径往后方丈去。

【13】 却说那些和尚,正悲切间,忽的看见他师徒牵马挑担而来,唬得一个个魂飞魄散道:"冤魂索命来了!"行者喝道:"甚么冤魂索命?快还我袈裟来!"众僧一齐跪倒,叩头道:"爷爷呀!冤有冤家,债有债主。要索命不干我们事,都是广谋与老和尚定计害你的,莫问我们讨命。"行者咄的一声道:"我把你这些该死的畜生!那个问你讨甚么命?只拿袈裟来还我走路!"其间有两个胆量大的和尚道:"老爷,你们在禅堂里已烧死了,如今又来讨袈裟,端的还是人,是鬼?"行者笑道:"这伙蠢畜!那里有甚么火来?你去前面看看禅堂,再来说话!"众僧们爬起来往前观看,那禅堂外面的门窗隔扇,更不曾燎灼了半分。众人悚惧,才认得三藏是种神僧,行者是尊护法。一齐上前叩头道:"我等有眼无珠,不识真人下界!你的袈裟在后面方丈中老师祖处哩。"三藏行过了三五层败壁破墙,嗟叹不已。只见方丈果然无火,众僧抢入里面,叫道:"公公!唐僧乃是神人,未曾烧死,如今反害了自己家当!趁早拿出袈裟,还他去也。"

【14】 原来这和尚寻不见袈裟,又烧了本寺的房屋,正在万分烦恼焦燥之处,一闻此言,怎敢答应,因寻思无计,进退无方,拽开

步,躬着腰,往那墙上着实撞了一头,可怜只撞得脑破血流魂魄散,咽喉气断染红沙!有诗为证。诗曰:

> 堪叹老衲性愚蠢,枉做人间一寿翁。
> 欲得袈裟传世久,岂知佛宝不凡同!
> 但将容易为长久,定是萧条取败功。
> 广智广谋成甚用,损人利己一场空!

慌得个小僧哭道:"师公已撞杀了,又不见袈裟,怎生是好?"行者道:"想是汝等盗藏起也!都出来!开具花名手本,等老孙逐一查点!"那上下房的院主,将本寺和尚、头陀、幸童、道人尽行开具手本二张,大小人等,共计二百三十名。行者请师父高坐,他却一一从头唱名搜检,都要解放衣襟,分明点过,更无袈裟。又将那各房头搬抢出去的箱笼物件,从头细细寻遍,那里得有踪迹。三藏心中烦恼,懊恨行者不尽,却坐在上面念那咒。行者扑的跌倒在地,抱着头,十分难禁,只教"莫念!莫念!管寻还了袈裟!"那众僧见了,一个个战兢兢的,上面跪下劝解,三藏才合口不念。行者一骨鲁跳起来,耳朵里掣出铁棒,要打那些和尚,被三藏喝住道:"这猴头!你头痛还不怕,还要无礼?休动手!且莫伤人!再与我审问一问!"众僧们磕头礼拜,哀告三藏道:"老爷饶命!我等委实的不曾看见。这都是那老死鬼的不是。他昨晚看着你的袈裟,只哭到更深时候,看也不曾敢看,思量要图长久,做个传家之宝,设计定策,要烧杀老爷;自火起之候,狂风大作,各人只顾救火,搬抢物件,我却不知袈裟去向。"

【15】 行者大怒,走进方丈屋里,把那触死鬼尸首抬出,选剥了细看,浑身更无那件宝贝;就把个方丈掘地三尺,也无踪影。行者忖量半晌,问道:"你这里可有甚么妖怪成精么?院主道:"老爷不问,莫想得知。我这里正东南有座黑风山。黑风洞内有一个黑大王。我这老死鬼常与他讲道。他便是个妖精。别无甚物。"行者道:"那山离此有多远近?"院主道:"只有二十里,那望见山头的就是。"行者笑道:"师父放心,不须讲了。一定是那黑怪偷去无疑。"三藏道:"他那厢离此有二十里,如何就断得是他?"行者道:"你不曾见夜间那火,光腾万里,亮透三天,且休说二十里,就是二百里也照见了!坐定是他见火光焜耀,趁着机会,暗暗的

来到这里，看见我们袈裟是件宝贝，必然趁哄掳去也。等老孙去寻他一寻。"三藏道："你去了时，我却何倚？"行者道："这个放心，暗中自有神灵保护，明中等我叫那些和尚伏侍。"即唤众和尚过来，道："汝等着几个去埋那老鬼，着几个伏侍我师父，看守我白马！"众僧领诺。行者又道："汝等莫顺口儿答应，等我去了，你就不来奉承。看师父的，要怡颜悦色；养白马的，要水草调匀；假有一毫儿差了，照依这个样棍，与你们看看！"他掣出棍子，照那火烧的砖墙扑的一下，把那墙打得粉碎，又震倒了有七八层墙。众僧见了，个个骨软身麻，跪着磕头滴泪道："爷爷宽心前去，我等竭力度心，供奉老爷，决不敢一毫怠慢！"好行者，急纵筋斗，径上黑风山，寻找这袈裟。正是那：

> 金禅求正出京畿，仗锡投西涉翠微。
> 虎豹独虫行处有，工商士客见时稀。
> 路逢异国愚僧妒，全仗齐天大圣威。
> 火发风生禅院废，黑熊夜盗锦襕衣。

毕竟此去不知袈裟有无，吉凶如何，且听下回分解。

Chapter 5
The Monks of the Guanyin Monastery
Plot to Take the Treasure;
The Monster of the Black Wind Mountain
Steals the Cassock

(*The monk Sanzang traveled to the west under Sun Wukong's protection. With the Boddhisattva Guanyin's help, the monk Sanzang received the White Dragon Horse from out of the waters of the Eagle's Dread Ravine and continued on westward. One day, as the sun sank in the west, what seemed to be a temple appeared far off in the distance. There they thought to pass the night.*)

【1】　The master whipped on his horse and hurried straight to the temple gate with his disciple to have a look. They saw that it was indeed a monastery:

> Hall upon hall,
> Cloister after cloister.
> Beyond the triple gates
> Countless coloured clouds are massed;
> Before the Hall of Five Blessings
> Coil a thousand wisps of red mist.
> Two rows of pine and bamboo,
> A forest of locust and cypress trees.
> The two rows of pine and bamboo
> Are ageless in their elegant purity;
> The forest of locust and cypress trees
> Has colour and beauty.
> See how high the drum and bell towers are,
> How tall the pagoda.
> In peaceful mediation the monks make firm their natures,
> As birds sing in the trees outside.

> *Peace beyond mortal dust is the only true peace;*
> *Emptiness with the Way is the real emptiness.*

As the poem goes,

> *A supreme Jetavana hidden in a green valley,*
> *A monastery set in scenery unbeaten in the world.*
> *Such pure lands are rare on earth;*
> *On most of the famous mountains dwell monks.*

Sanzang dismounted, Monkey laid down his burden, and they were just on the point of going in when a crowd of monks came out. This is how they were dressed:

> *On their heads they wore hats pinned on the left,*
> *On their bodies were clothes of purity.*
> *Copper rings hung from their ears,*
> *And silken belts were tied around their waists.*
> *Slowly they walked on sandals of straw,*
> *As they held wooden clappers in their hands.*
> *With their mouths they were always chanting*
> *Their devotion to the Wisdom.*

When Sanzang saw them he stood respectfully beside the gate and greeted them. A monk hastily returned his greeting and apologized for not noticing him before. "Where are you from?" he asked, "please come to the abbot's rooms and have some tea." "I have been sent from the East on an imperial mission to worship the Buddha in the Thunder Monastery and ask for the scriptures," Sanzang replied, "and as it is almost night we would like to ask for a night's lodging now that we are here." "Come inside and sit down, come inside and sit down," the monk said. When Sanzang told Monkey to lead the horse over, the monk was frightened at the sudden sight of him and asked, "What's that thing leading the horse?" "Keep your voice down," Sanzang urged, "keep your voice down. He has a quick temper, and if he hears you referring to him as 'that thing', he'll be furious. He's my disciple." The monk shuddered and bit his finger as he remarked, "Fancy taking a monstrously ugly creature like that for a disciple." "He may not look it," Sanzang replied, "but ugly as he is, he has his uses."

【2】 The monk had no choice but to go through the monastery gate with Sanzang and Monkey, and inside they saw the words CHAN MONASTERY OF GUANYIN written in large letters on the main hall. Sanzang was delighted. "I have often been the grateful beneficiary of the Bodhisattva's divine mercy," he exclaimed, "but I have not yet been able to kowtow to her in thanks. To worship her in this monastery will be just as good as seeing her in person." On hearing this, the monk, ordering a lay brother to open the doors, invited Sanzang to go in and worship. Monkey tethered the horse, put the luggage down, and went up into the hall with Sanzang, who prostrated himself and put his head on the floor before the golden statue. When the monk went to beat the drum, Monkey started striking the bell. Sanzang lay before the image, praying with all his heart, and when he had finished the monk stopped beating the drum. Monkey, however, was so engrossed in striking the bell, sometimes fast and sometimes slow, that he went on for a very long time. "He's finished his devotions," a lay brother said, "so what are you still beating the bell for?" Monkey threw down the bell hammer and said with a grin, "You're ignorant, aren't you? 'Whoever is a monk for a day strikes the bell for a day': that's me." By then all the monks in the monastery, senior and junior, as well as the abbot and his assistant, had been so startled by the wild noises from the bell that they all came crowding out to ask what savage was making such a din with the bell and drum. Monkey jumped out and cursed them: "Your grandfather Sun Wukong was having some fun." All the monks collapsed with shock at the sight of him and said as they knelt on the ground, "Lord Thunder God, Lord Thunder God." "The Thunder God is my great grandson," Monkey replied. "Get up, get up, you've nothing to fear. I'm a lord from the land of the Great Tang empire in the East." The

123

monks all bowed to him, and could not feel easy until Sanzang appeared. "Please come and drink tea in my rooms," said the abbot of the monastery. The horse was unloaded and led off, while they went round the main hall to a room at the back where they sat down according to their seniority.

【3】 The abbot gave them tea and arranged for food to be brought, and after the meal it was still early. As Sanzang was expressing his thanks, two servant boys appeared behind them supporting an aged monk. This is what he looked like:

> A Vairocana mitre on his head
> Topped with a gleaming cat's-eye jewel.
> On his body a gown of brocade,
> Edged with gold-mounted kingfisher feathers.
> A pair of monkish shoes studded with the Eight Treasures,
> A walking stick inlaid with clouds and stars.
> A face covered with wrinkles,
> Like the Old Goddess of Mount Li;
> A pair of purblind eyes,
> Like the Dragon King of the Eastern Sea.
> His mouth can't keep out the wind as his teeth have gone;
> His back is bent because his muscles are stiff.

"The Patriarch has come," the monks all said. Sanzang bowed low to him in greeting and said, "Your disciple pays his respects, venerable abbot." The aged monk returned his greeting and they both sat down. "The youngsters have just told me that gentlemen have come from the Tang Empire in the East," he said, "so I have come out to see you." "Please forgive us for blundering into your monastery so rudely," Sanzang replied. "Don't put it like that," the aged monk said, going on to ask, "How long a journey is it from the eastern lands to here?" "It was over sixteen hundred miles from Chang'an to the Double Boundary Mountain, where I took on this disciple," Sanzang replied. "We travelled on together through the land of Hami, and as that took two months we must have covered getting on for another two thousand miles before reaching here." "Over three thousand miles," said the aged monk. "I have spent a life of piety and have never been outside the monastery gates, so you could really say that I have been 'looking at heaven from the bottom of a well', and call mine a wasted life." "How great is your age, venerable abbot?" Sanzang asked. "In my stupid way I have lived to be two hundred and seventy," the old monk replied. "Then you're my ten-thousandth-great grandson," put in Monkey. "Talk properly," said Sanzang, glaring at him, "Don't be so disrespectful and rude." "How old are you, sir?" the aged monk asked. "I don't venture to mention it," Monkey replied. The aged monk then thought that he must have been raving, so he put the matter out of his mind, said no more about it, and ordered tea to be brought for them. A young page brought in three cloisonne teacups on a jade tray the colour of mutton fat, and another carried in a white alloy teapot from which he poured out three cups of fragrant tea. It had a better colour than pomegranate blossom, and its aroma was finer than cassia. When Sanzang saw all this he was full of praise. "What splendid things," he said, "what splendid things. Wonderful tea in wonderful vessels." "They're not worth looking at," the old monk replied. "After all, sir, you come from a superior and heavenly court, and have seen many rare things in your wide travels; so how can you give such exaggerated praise to things like that? What treasures did you bring with you from your superior country that I could have a look at?" "I'm afraid our eastern land has no great treasures, and even if it did, I would have been unable to bring them on so long a journey."

[4] "Master," put in Monkey, who was sitting beside him, "isn't that cassock I saw in our bundle the other day a treasure? Why don't I take it out for him to see?" When the monks heard him mention the cassock, they smiled sinister smiles. "What are you smiling at?" Monkey asked. "We thought it was very funny when you said that a cassock was a treasure," the abbot of the monastery replied. "A priest of my rank has two or three dozen, and our Patriarch, who has been a monk here for two hundred

125

and fifty or sixty years, has seven or eight hundred." He ordered them to be brought out and displayed. The old monk, who was also in on the game, told the lay brothers to open the store-rooms, while friars carried twelve chests out into the courtyard, and unlocked them. Then they set up clothes frames, put rope all around, shook the cassocks open one by one, and hung them up for Sanzang to see. Indeed, the whole building was full of brocade, and the four walls covered with silk.

Monkey examined them one by one and saw that some were made of brocade and some were embroidered with gold. "Enough, enough, enough," he said. "Put them away, put them away. I'll bring ours out for you to take a look at." Sanzang drew Monkey aside and whispered to him, "Disciple, never try to compete with other people's wealth. You and I are alone in this foreign land, and I'm afraid that there may be trouble." "What trouble can come from letting him look at the cassock?" Monkey asked. "You don't understand," Sanzang replied. "The ancients used to say, 'Don't let greedy and treacherous men see rare or amusing things.' If he lays his eyes on it, his mind will be disturbed, and if his mind is disturbed, he's bound to start scheming. If you were cautious, you would only have let him see it if he'd insisted; but as it is, this is no trifling matter, and may well be the end of us." "Don't worry, don't worry," said Brother Monkey, "I'll look after everything." Watch as without another word of argument he rushed off and opened the bundle, which was already giving off a radiant glow. It still had two layers of oiled paper round it, and when he removed it to take out the cassock and shake it open the hall was bathed in red light and clouds of coloured vapours filled the courtyard. When the monks saw it their hearts were filled with delight and their mouths with praise. It really was a fine cassock.

> Hung with pearls of unrivalled quality,
> Studded with Buddhist treasures infinitely rare.
> Above and below a dragon beard sparkles,
> On grass-cloth edged with brocade.

126

> *If it is worn, all demons are extinguished;*
> *When donned it sends all monsters down to hell.*
> *It was made by the hands of heavenly Immortals,*
> *And none but a true monk should dare put it on.*

[5]   When the aged monk saw how rare a treasure it was, his
heart was indeed disturbed. He went up to Sanzang and knelt
before him. "My fate is indeed a wretched one," he lamented,
tears pouring down his cheeks. Sanzang helped him to his feet
again and asked, "Why do you say that, venerable Patriarch?"
"You have unfolded this treasure of yours, sir," the aged monk
replied, "when it is already evening, so that my eyes are too dim
to see it clearly. That is why I say my fate is wretched." "Send
for a candle and take another look," Sanzang suggested. "My
lord, your precious cassock is already shining brightly, so I don't
think I would see more distinctly even if a candle were lit,"
replied the aged monk. "How would you like to look at it then?"
asked Sanzang. "If, sir, you were in your mercy to set aside your
fears and let me take it to my room to examine it closely during
the night, I will return it to you in the morning to take to the
West. What do you say to that?" This request startled Sanzang,
who grumbled at Brother Monkey, "It's all your fault, all your
fault." "He's nothing to be frightened of." Monkey replied with
a grin. "I'll pack it up and tell him to take it away to look at. If
anything goes wrong, I'll be responsible." As there was nothing
he could do to stop him, Sanzang handed the cassock to the old
monk with the words, "I'll let you take it, but you must give it
back to me tomorrow morning in the condition it's in now. I
won't have you getting it at all dirty." The old monk gleefully
told a page to take the cassock to his room, and instructed the
other monks to sweep out the front meditation hall, move two
rattan beds in, spread out the bedding on them, and invite the
two gentlemen to spend the night there; he also arranged for
them to be given breakfast and seen off the next morning. Then
everyone went off to bed. Sanzang and his disciple shut the doors
of the meditation hall and went to sleep.

127

[6]   Now that the old monk had tricked them into giving him
the cassock, he held it under the lamp in the back room as he
wept and wailed over it. This so alarmed the monks that none of
them dared go to sleep before he did. The young page, not
knowing what to do, went to tell the other monks, "Grandad's
still crying although it's getting on for eleven." Two junior
monks, who why among the old man's favorites, went over to
ask him why he was crying. "I'm crying because my accursed fate
won't allow me to see the Tang Priest's treasure," he said; to
which they replied, "Granddad, in your old age you have
succeeded. His cassock is laid before you, and all you have to do is
open your eyes and look. There's no need for tears." "But I can't
look at it for long," the aged monk answered. "I'm two hundred
and seventy this year, and I've collected all those hundreds of
cassocks for nothing. However am I to get hold of that one of his?
However am I to become like the Tang Priest?" "Master, you've
got it all wrong," the junior monks said. "The Tang Priest is a
pilgrim far from home. You should be satisfied with your great
seniority and wealth; why ever would you want to be a pilgrim
like him?" "Although I live at home and enjoy my declining
years, I've got no cassock like his to wear," the aged monk
replied. "If I could wear it for a day, I would close my eyes in
peace. I'd be as happy as if I were a monk in my next life."
"What nonsense," the junior monks said. "if you want to wear
his cassock, there'll be no problem about that. We'll keep him for
another day tomorrow, and you can wear it for another day. Or
we can keep him for ten days and you can wear it for ten days. So
why get so upset about it?" "Even if we kept him for a year,"
the old monk replied, "I'd only be able to wear it for a year, which
wouldn't bring me any glory. I'll still have to give it to him when
he went: I can't keep him here for ever."
[7]   As they were talking a young monk called Broad Wisdom
spoke out. "Granddad," he said, "if you want it for a long time,
that's easy to arrange too." "What brilliant idea have you got,
child?" the aged monk asked, cheering up. "That Tang Priest
and his disciple were so exhausted after their journey that they are

both asleep by now," Broad Wisdom replied, "if we arm some strong monks with swords and spears to break into the meditation hall and kill them, they can be buried in the back garden, and nobody but us will be any the wiser. This way we get their white horse and their luggage as well as the cassock, which will become an heirloom of the monastery. We would be doing this for posterity." The old monk was very pleased with this suggestion, and he wiped the tears from his eyes as he said, "Very good, very good, a marvellous plan."

Another young monk called Broad Plans, a fellow-student of Broad Wisdom's, came forward and said, "This plan's no good. If we are to kill them, we'll have to keep a sharp eye on them. That old pale-faced one looks easy enough, but the hairy-faced one could be tricky; and if by any chance we fail to kill him, we'll be in deep trouble. I have a way that doesn't involve using weapons, but I don't know what you'll think of it." "What do you suggest, my child?" the aged monk asked. "In my humble opinion," he replied, "we should assemble the head monks of all the cells, senior and junior, and get everyone to put a bundle of firewood outside the meditation hall. When it's set alight, those two will have no escape, and will be burnt to death together with their horse. Even if the people who live around this mountain see the blaze, they'll think that those two burnt down the meditation hall by carelessly starting a fire. This way they'll both be burnt to death and nobody will know how it happened. Then the cassock will become our monastery's treasure for ever." All the monks present were pleased with this suggestion, exclaiming, "Great, great, great; an even better plan." The head of every cell was told to bring firewood, a scheme that was to bring death to the venerable and aged monk, and reduce the Guanyin Monastery to ashes. Now there were seventy or eighty cells in the monastery, and over two hundred junior and senior monks. They shifted firewood all night, piled it up all round the meditation hall so that there was no way out, and prepared to set it alight.

[8] Although Sanzang and he had gone to bed, the magical Monkey's spirit remained alert and his eyes half open even when

he was asleep. His suspicions were aroused by the sound of people moving around outside and the rustling of firewood in the breeze. "Why can I hear footsteps in the still of the night?" he wondered. "Perhaps bandits are planning to murder us." He bounded out of bed, and was on the point of opening the door to take a look when he remembered that this might disturb his master, so instead he used his miraculous powers to turn himself into a bee with a shake of his body.

> Sweet his mouth and venomous his tail,
> Slender his waist and light his body.
> He flew like an arrow, threading through willows and flowers,
> Seeking their nectar like a shooting star.
> A tiny body that could bear great weights,
> Carried on the breeze by his frail and buzzing wings.
> Thus did he emerge from under the rafters,
> Going out to take a look.

He saw that the monks had piled firewood and straw all around the meditation hall and were setting it alight. Smiling to himself he thought, "So my master was right. This is their idea. They want to kill us and keep our cassock. I wish I could lay into them with my cudgel. If only I wasn't forbidden to use it, I could kill the lot of them; but the master would only be angry with me for murdering them. Too bad. I'll just have to take my chances as they come, and finish them off." The splendid Monkey leapt in through the Southern Gate of Heaven with a single somersault, startling the heavenly warriors Pang, Liu, Gou and Bi into bowing, and Ma, Zhao, Wen and Guan into bending low as they all said, "Oh no, oh no! The fellow who turned Heaven upside down is here again." "There's no need to stand on courtesy or be alarmed, gentlemen," said Monkey with a wave of his hand, "I've come to find the Broad-Visioned Heavenly King."

[9] Before the words were out of his mouth the Heavenly King was there and greeting Monkey with, "Haven't seen you for

ages. I heard the other day that the Bodhisattva Guanyin came to see the Jade Emperor to borrow the four Duty Gods, the Six Dings and Jias and the Revealers of the Truth to look after the Tang Priest on his pilgrimage to the Western Heaven to fetch the scriptures. They were also saying that you were his disciple, so how is it that you have the spare time to come here?" "Let's cut the cackle," said Monkey. "The Tang Priest has run into some villains who have started a fire to burn him to death. It's very urgent, which is why I've come to ask you for the loan of your Anti-fire Cover to save him with. Fetch it at once; I'll bring it straight back." "You've got it all wrong," the Heavenly King replied. "If villains are trying to burn him, you should rescue him with water. What do you need my Anti-fire Cover for?" "You don't understand," Monkey continued. "If I try to save him with water, he may still be hurt even if he isn't burnt up. I can only keep him free from injury if you lend me that cover; and with that it doesn't matter how much burning they do. Buck up, buck up! It may be too late already. Don't mess up what I've got to do down there." "You monkey," said the Heavenly King with a laugh, "you're as wicked as ever, thinking only of yourself and never of others." "Hurry up, hurry up," Monkey pleaded. "You'll ruin everything if you go on nattering." The Heavenly King, no longer able to refuse, handed the cover to Monkey.

Taking the cover, Monkey pressed down on his cloud and went straight to the roof of the meditation hall, where he spread the cover over the Tang Priest, the dragon horse, and the luggage. Then he went to sit on top of the aged monk's room to protect the cassock. As he watched them starting the fire he kept on reciting a spell and blew some magic breath towards the southwest, at which a wind arose and fanned the flames up into a wild and roaring blaze. What a fire!

> Spreading black smoke,
> Leaping red flames;
> The spreading black smoke blotted out all the stars in the
sky,

131

    The leaping red flames made the earth glow red for
hundreds of miles.

    When it started
    It was a gleaming golden snake;
    Later on
    It was a spirited horse.
    The Three Spirits of the South showed their might,
    The Fire God Huilu wielded his magic power.
    The bone-dry kindling burned ferociously,
    As when the Emperor Suiren drilled wood to start a fire.
    Flames leapt up from the boiling oil before the doors,
    Brighter than when Lord Lao Zi opens his furnace.
    As the cruel fire spreads,
    What can stop this wilful murder?
    Instead of dealing with the disaster
    They abetted it.
    As the wind fanned the fire,
    The flames flew many miles high;
    As the fire grew in the might of the wind,
    Sparks burst through the Nine Heavens.
    Cracking and banging,
    Like firecrackers at the end of the year;
    Popping and bursting,
    Like cannon-fire in battle.
    None of the Buddha statues could escape the blaze,
    And the guardian gods in the eastern court had nowhere to
hide.
    It was fiercer that the fire-attack at Red Cliff,
    Or the burning of the Epang Palace.

[10]   A single spark can start a prairie fire. In a few moments
the raging wind had blown the fire up into an inferno, and the
whole Guanyin Monastery was red. Look at the monks as they
move away boxes and baskets, grabbing tables and carrying
cooking-pots on their heads. The whole monastery was full of the
sound of shouting and weeping. Brother Monkey protected the

abbot's rooms at the back, and the Anti-fire Cover covered the meditation hall in front; everywhere else the fire raged its red flames reflected in the sky and its dazzling brightness shining through the wall.

[11]   When the fire broke out, all the animals and devils of the mountain were disturbed. Seven miles due south of the Guanyin Monastery was the Black Wind Mountain, on which there was a Black Wind Cave. In this cave a monster awoke and sat up. Seeing light streaming in through his window, he thought it must be dawn, but when he got up to take a better look he saw a fire blazing to the north. "Blimey," the monster exclaimed with astonishment, "those careless monks must have set the Guanyin Monastery on fire. I'd better go and help them." The good monster leapt off on a cloud and went down below the smoke and flames that reached up to the sky. The front halls were all empty, and the fire was burning bright in the cloisters on either side. He rushed forward with long strides and was just calling for water when he noticed that the rooms at the back were not burning as there was someone on the roof keeping the wind away. The moment he realized this and rushed in to look, he saw a magic glow and propitious vapours coming from a black felt bundle on the table. On opening it he found it contained a brocade cassock that was a rare treasure of the Buddhist religion. His mind disturbed by the sight of this valuable object, he forgot about putting out the fire or calling for water and grabbed the cassock, which he made off with in the general confusion. Then he went straight back to his cave by cloud.

The fire blazed on till dawn before burning itself out. The undraped monks howled and wailed as they searched through the ashes for bronze and iron, and picked over the cinders to find gold and silver. Some of them fixed up thatched shelters in what remained of the frames of the buildings, and others were rigging up pots to cook food at the bases of the exposed walls. We will not describe the weeping, the shouting and the confused hubbub.

[12]   Brother Monkey grabbed the Anti-fire Cover, took it back to the Southern Gate of Heaven with a single somersault, and

133

returned it to the Broad-visioned Heavenly King with thanks. "Great Sage," said the Heavenly King as he accepted it. "You are as good as your word. I was so worried that if you didn't give me back my treasure, I'd never be able to find you and get it off you. Thank goodness you've returned it." "Am I the sort of bloke who'd cheat someone to his face?" asked Monkey. "After all, 'If you return a thing properly when you borrow it, it'll be easier to borrow it next time'." "As we haven't met for so long, why don't you come into the palace for a while?" said the Heavenly King. "I'm no longer the man to 'sit on the bench till it rots, talking about the universe'." Monkey replied. "I'm too busy now that I have to look after the Tang Monk. Please excuse me." Leaving with all speed, he went down on his cloud, and saw that the sun was rising as he went straight to the meditation hall, where he shook himself, turned into a bee, and flew in. On reverting to his true form he saw that his master was still sound asleep.

"Master, get up, it's dawn," he called. Sanzang woke up, rolled over, and said, "Yes, so it is." When he had dressed he opened the doors, went outside, and saw the walls reddened and in ruins, and the halls and towers gone. "Goodness," he exclaimed in great astonishment, "why have the buildings all disappeared? Why is there nothing but reddened walls?" "You're still asleep," Monkey replied. "There was a fire last night." "Why didn't I know about it?" Sanzang asked. "I was protecting the meditation hall, and as I could see you were asleep, master, I didn't disturb you," Monkey replied. "If you were able to protect the meditation hall, why didn't you put out the fire in the other buildings?" Sanzang asked. Monkey laughed. "I'll tell you, master. What you predicted actually happened. They fancied that cassock of ours and planned to burn us to death. If I hadn't noticed, we'd be bones and ashes by now." "Did they start the fire?" asked Sanzang who was horrified to learn this. "Who else?" replied Monkey. "Are you sure that you didn't cook this up because they were rude to you?" Sanzang asked. "I'm not such a rascal as to do a thing like that," said Monkey. "Honestly and truly, they started it. Of course, when I saw how vicious they were I didn't help put the blaze out. I helped them with a slight breeze instead." "Heavens! Heavens! When a fire starts you should bring water, not wind." "You must know the old saying—'If people didn't harm tigers, tigers wouldn't hurt people.' If they hadn't started a fire, I wouldn't have caused a wind." "Where's the cassock? Don't say that it's been burnt too." "It's all right; it hasn't been burnt. The abbots' cell where it was kept didn't catch fire." "I don't care what you say. If it's come to any harm, I'll recite that spell till it kills you." "Don't do that," pleaded Monkey desperately, "I promise to bring that cassock back to you. Wait while I fetch it for you, and then we'll be on our way." With Sanzang leading the horse, and Monkey carrying the luggage, they went out of the meditation hall and straight to the abbot's lodgings at the back.

【13】 When the grief-stricken monks of the monastery suddenly saw master and disciple emerge with horse and luggage from the meditation hall they were terrified out of their wits, and screamed, "Their avenging ghosts have come to demand our lives." "What do you mean, avenging ghosts coming to demand your lives?" Monkey shouted. "Give us back our cassock at once." The monks all fell to their knees and kowtowed, saying, "Masters, wrongs are always avenged, and debts always have to be paid. If you want lives, it's nothing to do with us. It was the old monk and Broad Plans who cooked up the plot to kill you. Please don't punish us." Monkey snorted with anger and roared, "I'll get you, you damned animals. Who asked for anyone's life? Just bring out that cassock and we'll be on our way." Two brave men from among the monks said, "Masters, you were burnt to death in the meditation hall, and now you come back to ask for the cassock. Are you men or ghosts?" "You cattle," sneered Monkey, "there wasn't any fire. Go and look at the meditation hall and then we'll see what you have to say." The monks rose to their feet, and when they went forward to look, they saw that there was not even the slightest trace of scorching on the door and the window-frames. The monks, now struck with fear, realized

135

that Sanzang was a divine priest, and Monkey a guardian god. They all kowtowed to the pair of them and said, "Our eyes are blind. We failed to recognize saints sent down from Heaven. Your cassock is in the abbot's rooms at the back." Sanzang went past a number of ruined walls and buildings, sighing endlessly, and saw that the abbot's rooms at the back had indeed not been burnt. The monks all rushed in shouting, "Grandad, the Tang Priest is a saint, and instead of being burnt to death he's wrecked our home. Bring the cassock out at once and give it back to him."

[14] Now the old monk had been unable to find the cassock, which coming on top of the destruction of the monastery had him distraught with worry. When the monks asked him for it, he was unable reply. Seeing no way out of his quandary, he bent his head down and dashed it against the wall. He smashed his skull open and expired as his blood poured all over the floor. There are some verses about it:

> Alas that the aged monk in his folly
> Lived so long a life for nothing.
> He wanted the cassock as an heirloom for the monastery,
> Forgetting that what is Buddha's is not as mortal things.
> As he took the changeable for the eternal,
> His sorry end was quite inevitable.
> What use were Broad Wisdom and Broad Plans?
> To harm others for gain always fails.

The other monks began to howl in desperation, "Our Patriarch has dashed his brains out, and we can't find the cassock, so whatever shall we do?" "I think you've hidden it somewhere," Monkey said. "Come out, all of you, and bring me all the registers. I'm going to check that you're all here." The senior and junior abbots brought the two registers in which all the monks, novices, pages, and servants were registered. There were a total of two hundred and thirty names in them. Asking his master to sit in the place of honour, Monkey called out and marked off each of the names, making the monks open up their clothes for his inspection. When he had checked each one carefully there was no sign of the cassock. Then he searched carefully through all the boxes and baskets that had been saved from the flames, but again he could find no trace of it. Sanzang, now absolutely furious with Brother Monkey, started to recite the spell as he sat up high. Monkey fell to the ground in great agony, clutching his head and pleading, "Stop, stop, I swear to return the cassock to you." The monks, trembling at the sight, begged him to stop, and only then did he shut his mouth and desist. Monkey leapt to his feet, took his iron cudgel from behind his ear, and was going to hit the monks when Sanzang shouted, "You ape, aren't you afraid of another headache? Are you going to misbehave again? Don't move your hand or hurt anyone. I want you to question them again instead." The monks all kowtowed to him and entreated him most pitifully to spare their lives. "We've honestly not seen it. It's all that dead old bastard's fault. After he saw your cassock yesterday evening he cried till late into the night, not even wanting to look at it as he worked out a plan by which it could belong to the monastery for ever. He wanted to burn you to death, masters, but when the fire started, a gale wind blew up, and we were all busy trying to put the blaze out and move away what stuff we could. We don't know where the cassock went."

[15]   Monkey went into the abbot's quarters at the back in a great rage and carried out the corpse of the old monk who had killed himself. When he stripped the body he found no treasures on it, so he dug up the floor of his room to a depth of three feet, again without finding a sign of the cassock. Monkey thought for a moment and then asked, "Are there any monsters turned spirits around here?" "If you hadn't asked, sir, I'd never have imagined you wanted to know," the abbot replied. "There is a mountain due south of here called the Black Wind Mountain, and in the Black Wind Cave on it there lives a Great Black King. That old dead bastard of ours was always discussing the Way with him. There aren't any other evil spirits apart from." "How far is the mountain from here?" Monkey asked. "Only about seven miles,"

the abbot replied. "It's the mountain you can see over there."
Monkey smiled and said to Sanzang, "Don't worry, master,
there's no need to ask any more questions. No doubt about it: it
must have been stolen by that black monster." "But his place is
seven miles from here, so how can you be sure it was him?"
Sanzang asked. "You didn't see the fire last night," Brother
Monkey retorted. "The flames were leaping up hundreds of miles
high, and the glow penetrated the triple heavens. You could have
seen it seventy miles away, let alone seven. I'm convinced that he
saw the glare and took the chance to slip over here quietly. When
he saw that our cassock was a treasure, he must have stolen it in
the confusion. Just wait while I go and find him." "If you go,
who's going to protect me?" asked Sanzang. "Don't worry, gods
are watching over you in secret, and in the visible sphere I'll make
these monks serve you." With that he called the community
together and said, "I want some of you to go and bury that old
ghost, and some of you to serve my master and look after our
white horse." The monks all assented obediently, and Monkey
continued, "I won't have you agreeing glibly now but not waiting
on them when I've gone. Those of you who look after my master
must do so with pleasant expressions on your faces, and those
who feed the horse must make sure he gets the right amount of
hay and water. If there's the slightest mistake, I'll hit you like
this." He pulled out his cudgel, and smashed a fire-baked brick
wall to smithereens; the shock from this shook down seven or
eight more walls. At the sight of this the monks' bones turned to
jelly, and they knelt down and kowtowed to him with tears
pouring down their cheeks. "Don't worry, master, you can go—
we'll look after him. We promise not to show any disrespect."
The splendid Monkey then went straight to the Black Wind
Mountain with a leap of his somersault cloud to look for the
cassock.

> *The Golden Cicada left the capital in search of the truth,*
> *Leaning on his staff as he went to the distant west.*
> *Along his route were tigers, leopards and wolves;*

Few were the artisans, merchants, or scholars he met.
In a foreign land he encountered a stupid and covetous monk,
And depended entirely on the mighty Great Sage Equalling Heaven.
When fire and wind destroyed the monastery,
A black bear came one night to steal the silken cassock.

If you don't know whether the cassock was found on this journey or how things turned out, listen to the explanation in the next instalment.

6. 孙行者大闹黑风山 观世音收伏熊罴怪

【1】 话说孙行者一筋斗跳将起去，唬得那观音院大小和尚并头陀、幸童、道人等一个个朝天礼拜道："爷爷呀！原来是腾云驾雾的神圣下界！怪道火不能伤！恨我那个不识人的老剥皮，使心用心，今日反害了自己！"三藏道："列位请起，不须恨了。这去寻着袈裟，万事皆休；但恐找寻不着，我那徒弟性子有些不好，汝等性命不知如何，恐一人不能脱也。"众僧闻得此言，一个个提心吊胆，告天许愿，只要寻得袈裟，各全性命不题。

【2】 却说孙大圣到空中，把腰儿扭了一扭，早来到黑风山上。住了云头，仔细看，果然是座好山。况正值春光时节，但见：

> 万壑争流，千崖竞秀。鸟啼人不见，花落树犹香。雨过天连青壁润，风来松卷翠屏张。山草发，野花开，悬崖峭嶂；薜萝生，佳木丽，峻岭平岗。不遇幽人，那寻樵子？洞边双鹤饮，石上野猿狂。蠢蠢堆螺排黛色，巍巍拥翠弄岚光。

那行者正观山景，忽听得芳草坡前，有人言语。他却轻步潜踪，闪在那石崖之下，偷睛观看。原来是三个妖魔，席地而坐：上面的是一条黑汉，左首下是一个道人，右首下是一个白衣秀士。都在那里高谈阔论。讲的是立鼎安炉，抟砂炼汞；白雪黄芽；傍门外道。正说中间，那黑汉笑道："后日是我母难之日，二公可光顾光顾？"白衣秀士道："年年与大王上寿，今年岂有不来之理？"黑汉道："我夜来得了一件宝贝，名唤锦襴佛衣，诚然是件玩好之物。我明日就以他为寿，大开筵宴，邀请各山道官，庆贺佛衣，称为'佛衣会'如何？"道人笑道："妙！妙！妙！我明日先来拜寿，后日再来赴宴。"行者闻得佛衣之言，定以为是他宝贝。他就忍不住怒气，跳出石崖，双手举起金箍棒，高叫道："我把你这伙贼怪！你偷了我的袈裟，要做甚么'佛衣会'！趁早儿将来还我！"

140

喝一声"休走!"抡起棒，照头一下，慌得那黑汉化风而逃，道人驾云而走；只把一个白衣秀士，一棒打死。拖将过来看处，却是一条白花蛇怪。索性提起，摔作五七断，径入深山，找寻那个黑汉。转过尖峰，抹过峻岭，又见那壁陡崖前，耸出一座洞府，但见那：

　　烟霞渺渺，松柏森森。烟霞渺渺采盈门，松柏森森青绕户。桥踏枯槎木，峰巅绕薜萝。鸟衔红蕊来云壑，鹿践芳丛上石台。那门前时催花发，风送花香。临堤绿柳转黄鹂，傍岸夭桃翻粉蝶。虽然旷野不堪夸，却赛蓬莱山下景。

【3】　行者到于门首，又见那两扇石门，关得甚紧。门上有一横石板，明书六个大字，乃"黑风山黑风洞"。即便抡棒，叫声"开门!"那里面有把门的小妖，开了门出来，问道:"你是何人，敢来击吾仙洞?"行者骂道:"你个作死的孽畜!甚么个去处，敢称仙洞?'仙'字是你称的?快进去报与你那黑汉，教他快送老爷的袈裟出来，饶你一窝性命!"小妖急急跑到里面，报道:"大王!'佛衣会'做不成了!门外有一个毛脸雷公嘴的和尚，来讨袈裟哩!"那黑汉被你在芳草坡前赶将来，却才关了门，坐还未稳。又听得那话，心中暗想道:"这厮不知是那里来的，这般无礼，他敢嚷上我的门来!"教:"取披挂。"随即束了，绰一杆黑缨枪，走出门来。这行者闪在门外，执着铁棒，睁睛观看，只见那怪果生得凶险:

　　碗子铁盔火漆光，乌金铠甲亮辉煌。皂罗袍罩风兜袖，黑绿丝绦攒穗长。手执黑缨枪一杆，足踏乌皮靴一双。眼幌金睛如掣电，正是山中黑风王。

行者暗笑道:"这厮真个如烧窑的一般，筑煤的无二!想必是在此处刷炭为生，怎么这等一身乌黑?"那怪厉声高叫道:"你是个甚么和尚，敢在我这里大胆?"行者执铁棒，撞至面前，大吒一声道:"不要闲讲!快还你老外公的袈裟来!"那怪道:"你是那寺里和尚?你的袈裟在那里失落了，敢来我这里索取?"行者道:"我的袈裟，在直北观音院后方丈里放着，只因那院里失了火，你这厮，趁哄抢掠，盗了来，要做'佛衣会'庆寿，怎敢抵赖?快快还我，饶你性命!若牙迸半个'不'字，我推倒了黑风山，踏平了黑风洞，把你这一洞妖邪，都碾为齑粉!"

141

【4】那怪闻言，呵呵冷笑道："你这个泼物！原来昨夜那火就是你放的！你在那方丈屋上，行凶招风，是我把一件袈裟拿来了，你待怎么！你是那里来的？姓甚名谁？有多大手段，敢那等海口浪言！"行者道："是你也认不得你老外公哩！你老外公乃大唐上国驾前御弟三藏法师之徒弟，姓孙，名悟空行者，若问老孙的手段，说出来，教你魂飞魄散，死在眼前！"那怪道："我不曾会你，有甚么手段，说来我听。"行者笑道："我儿子，你站稳着，仔细听之！我：

> 自小神通手段高，随风变化逞英豪。
> 养性修真熬日月，跳出轮回把命逃。
> 一点诚心曾访道，灵台山上采药苗。
> 那山有个老仙长，寿年十万八千高。
> 老孙拜他为师父，指我长生路一条。
> 他说身内有丹药，外边采取枉徒劳。
> 得传大品天仙诀，若无根本实难熬。
> 回光内照宁心坐，身中日月坎离交。
> 万事不思全寡欲，六根清净体坚牢。
> 返老还童容易得，超凡入圣路非遥。
> 三年无漏成仙体，不同俗辈受煎熬。
> 十洲三岛还游戏，海角天涯转一遭。
> 活该三百多余岁，不得飞升上九霄。
> 下海降龙真宝贝，才有金箍棒一条。
> 花果山前为帅首，水帘洞里聚群妖。
> 玉皇大帝传宣诏，封我齐天极品高。
> 几番大闹灵霄殿，数次曾偷王母桃。
> 天兵十万来降我，层层密密布枪刀。
> 战退天王归上界，哪吒负痛领兵逃。
> 显圣真君能变化，老孙硬赌跌平交。
> 道祖观同玉帝，南天门上看降妖。
> 却被老君助一阵，二郎擒我到天曹。
> 将身绑在降妖柱，即命神兵把首枭。
> 刀砍锤敲不得坏，又教雷打火来烧。

老孙其实有手段，全然不怕半分毫。

送在老君炉里炼，六丁神火慢煎熬。

日满开炉我跳出，手持铁棒绕天跑。

纵横到处无遮挡，三十三天闹一遭。

我佛如来施法力，五行山压老孙腰。

整整压该五百载，幸逢三藏出唐朝。

吾今饭正西方去，转上雷音见玉毫。

你去乾坤四海问一问，我是历代驰名第一妖！"

【5】　那怪闻言笑道："你原来是那闹天宫的弼马温么？"行者最恼的是人叫他弼马温；听见这一声，心中大怒。骂道："你这贼怪！偷了袈裟不还，倒伤老爷！不要走！看棍！"那黑汉侧身躲过，绰长枪，壁手来迎。两家这场好杀：

如意棒，黑缨枪，二人洞口逞刚强。分心劈脸刺，着臂照头伤。这个横丢闷棍手，那个直拖急三枪。白虎爬山来探爪，黄龙卧道转身忙。喷彩雾，吐毫光，两个妖仙不可量——一个是修正齐天圣，一个是成精黑大王。这场山里相处处，只为袈裟不良。

那怪与行者斗了十数回合，不分胜负。渐渐红日当午，那黑汉举枪架住铁棒道："孙行者，我两个且收兵，等我进了膳来，再与你赌斗。"行者道："你这个孽畜，叫做汉子？好汉子，半日儿就要吃饭？似老孙在山根下，整压了五百余年，也未曾尝些汤水，那里便饿哩？莫推故！休走！还我袈裟来，方让你去吃饭！"那怪虚幌一枪，撤身入洞，关了石门，收回小怪，且安排筵宴，书写请帖，邀请各山魔王庆会不题。

【6】　却说行者攻门不开，也只得回观音院。那本寺僧人已葬埋了那老和尚，都在方丈里伏侍唐僧。早斋已毕，又摆上午斋。正那里添汤换水，只见行者从空降下，众僧礼拜道，接入方丈，见了三藏。三藏道："悟空，你来了？袈裟如何？"行者道："已有了根由。早是不曾冤了这些和尚。原来是那黑风山妖怪偷了。老孙去暗暗的寻他，只见他与一个白衣秀士，一个老道人，坐在那芳草坡前讲话。也是个不打自招的怪物，他忽然说道："后日是他母难之日，邀请诸亲来做生日；夜来得了一件锦襕佛衣，要以此为寿，作一大宴，唤做'庆赏佛衣会'。是老孙抢到面前，打了

143

一棍，那黑汉化风而走，道人也不见了，只把个白衣秀士打死，乃是一条白花蛇成精。我又急急赶到他洞口，叫他出来与他赌斗。他已承认了，是他拿回。战毕这半日，不分胜负。那怪回洞，却要吃饭，关了石门，惧战不出。老孙却来回看师父，先报此信。已是有了袈裟的下落，不怕他不还我。"

【7】 众僧闻言，合掌的合掌，磕头的磕头，都念声"南无阿弥陀佛！今日寻着下落，我等方有了性命矣！"行者道："你且休喜欢畅快，我还未曾到手，师父还未曾出门哩。只等有了袈裟，打发得我师父好好的出门，才是你们的安乐处；若稍有些须不虞，老孙可是好惹的主子！可曾有好茶饭与我师父吃？可曾有好草料喂马？"众僧俱满口答应道："有！有！有！更不曾一毫待慢了老爷。"三藏道："自你去了这半日，我已吃过了三次茶汤，两餐斋供了。他俱不曾敢慢我。但只是你还尽心竭力去寻取袈裟回来。"行者道："莫忙！既有下落，管情拿住这厮，还你原物。放心，放心！"

正说处，那上房院主，又整治素供，请孙老爷吃斋。行者却吃了些须，复驾祥云，又去找寻。正行间，只见一个小怪，左胁下夹着一个花梨木匣儿，从大路而来。行者度他匣内必有甚么柬札，举起棒，劈头一下，可怜不禁打，就打得像个肉饼一般；却拖在路旁，揭开匣儿观看，果然是一封请帖。帖上写着：

"侍生熊罴顿首拜，启上大阐金池老上人丹房：屡承佳惠，感激渊深。夜观回禄之难，有失救护，谅仙机必无他害。生偶得佛衣一件，欲作雅会，谨具花酌，奉饭清赏。至期，千乞仙驾过临一叙。是荷。先二日具。"

【8】 行者见了，呵呵大笑道："那个老剥皮，死得他一毫儿也不亏！他原来与妖精结党！怪道他也活了二百七十岁。想是那妖精，传他些甚么服气的小法儿，故有此寿。老孙还记得他的模样，等我变做那和尚，往他洞里走走，看我那袈裟放在何处。假若得手，即便拿回，却也省力。"

好大圣，念动咒语，迎着风一变，果然就像那老和尚一般，藏了铁棒，拽开步，径来洞口，叫声"开门"。那小妖开了门，见是这般模样，急转身报道："大王，金池长老来了。"那怪大惊道："刚才差了小的去下简帖请他，这时候还未到那里哩，如何他就来得这等迅速？想是小的不曾撞着他，断是孙行者呼他来讨袈裟的。管事的，可把袈裟藏了，莫教他看见。"

【9】　行者进了前门，但见那天井中，松篁交翠，桃李争妍，丛丛花发，簇簇兰香，却也是个洞天之处。又见那二门上有一联对子，写着："静隐深山无俗虑，幽居仙洞乐天真。"

行者暗道："这厮也是个脱俗离尘，知命的怪物。"入门里，往前又进，到于三层门里，都是些画栋雕梁，明窗彩户。只见那黑汉子，穿的是黑绿纻丝祆袄，罩一领鸦青花绫披风，戴一顶乌角软巾，穿一双麂皮皂靴；见行者进来，整顿衣巾，降阶迎接道："金池老友，连日欠亲。请坐，请坐。"行者以礼相见。见毕而坐，坐定而茶。茶罢，妖精欠身道："适有小简奉启，后日一叙，何老友今日就下顾也？"行者道："正来进拜，不期路遇华翰，见有'佛衣雅会'，故此急急奔来，愿求见见。"那怪笑道："老友差矣。这袈裟本是唐僧的，他在你处住札，你岂不曾看见，反来就我看看？"行者道："贫僧借来，因夜晚还不曾展看，不期被大王取去，又被火烧了荒山，失落了家私。那唐僧的徒弟，又有些骁勇，乱忙中，四下里都寻觅不见。原来是大王的洪福收来，故特来一见。"

【10】　正讲处，只见有个巡山的小妖，来报道："大王！祸事了！下请书的小校，被孙行者打死在大路旁边，他绰着经儿，变化做金池长老，来骗佛衣也！"那怪闻得，暗道："我说那长老怎么今日就来，又来得迅速，果然是他！"急纵身，拿过枪来，就刺行者。行者耳朵里急掣出棍子，现了本相，架住枪尖，就在他那中厅里跳出，自天井中，斗到前门，唬得那洞里群魔都丧胆，家间老幼尽无魂。这场在山头好赌斗，比前番更是不同。好杀：

那猴王胆大充和尚，这黑汉心灵隐佛衣。语去言来机会巧，随机应变不差池。袈裟欲见无由见，宝贝玄微真妙微。小怪寻山言祸事，老妖发怒显神威。翻身打出黑风洞，枪棒争持辩是非。棒架长枪声响亮，枪迎铁棒放光辉。悟空变化人间少，妖怪神通世上稀。这一个要把佛衣来庆寿，那一个不得袈裟肯善归？这番苦战难分手，就是活佛临凡也解不得围。

他两个从洞口打上山头，自山头杀在云外，吐雾喷风，飞砂走石，只斗到红日沉西，不分胜败。那怪道："姓孙的，你且住了手。今日天晚，不好相持。你去，你去！待明早来，与你定个死活。"行者叫道："儿子莫走！要战便像个战的，不可以天晚相推。"看他没头没脸的，只情使棍子打来，这黑汉又化阵清风，转回本洞，紧闭石门不出。

【11】　行者却无计策奈何，只得也回观音院里。按落云头，道声"师父"。那三藏眼儿巴巴的，正望他哩。忽见到了面前，甚喜，又见他手里没袈裟，又惧；问道："怎么这番还不曾有袈裟来？"行者袖中取出个简帖儿来，递与三藏道："师父，那怪物与这死的老剥皮，原是朋友。他着一个小妖送此帖来，还请他去赴'佛衣会'。是老孙就把那小妖打死，变做那和尚，进他洞去，骗了一钟茶吃。欲问他讨袈裟看看，他不肯拿出。正坐间，忽被一个甚么巡风的，走了风信，他就与我打将起来。我斗到这早晚，不分上下。他见天晚，回归洞去，紧闭石门。老孙无奈，也暂回来。"三藏道："你手段比他何如？"行者道："我也硬不多儿，只战个手平。"三藏才看了简帖，又递与那院主："你师父敢莫也是妖精么？"那院主慌忙跪下道："老爷，我师父是人；只因那黑大王修成人道，常来寺里与我师父讲话，他传了我师父些养神服气之术，故以朋友相称。"行者道："这伙和尚没甚妖气，他一个个头圆顶天，足方履地，但比老孙肥胖长大些儿，非妖精也。你看那帖儿上写着'侍生熊罴'，此物必定是个大黑熊成精。"三藏道："我闻得古人云：'熊与猩猩相类。'都是兽类，他却怎么又成精？"行者笑道："老孙是兽类，见做了齐天大圣，与他何异？大抵世间之物，凡有九窍者，皆可以修行成仙。"三藏又道："你才说他本事与你手平，你却怎生得胜，取我袈裟回来？"行者道："莫管，莫管，我有处治。"

【12】　正商议间，众僧摆上晚斋，请他师徒们吃了。三藏教掌灯，仍是前面禅堂安歇。众僧都挨墙倚壁，苦搭窝棚，各各睡下，只把个上方让与那上下院主安身。此时夜静，但见：

　　银河现影，玉宇无尘。满天星灿烂，一水浪收痕。万籁声宁，千山鸟绝。溪边渔火息，塔上佛灯昏。昨夜闻黎钟鼓响，今宵一遍哭声闻。

是夜在禅堂歇宿。那三藏想着袈裟，那里得稳睡？忽翻身见窗外透白，急起叫道："悟空，天明了，快寻袈裟去。"行者一骨鲁跳将起来。早见众僧侍立，供奉汤水，行者道："你等用心伏侍我师父，老孙去也。"三藏下床，扯住道："你往那里去？"行者道："我想这桩事都是观音菩萨没理，他有这个禅院在此，受了人家香火，又容那妖精邻住。我去南海寻他，与他讲三讲，教他亲来问妖精讨袈裟还我。"三藏道："你这去，几时回来？"行者道："时少只在饭罢，时多只在晌午，就成功了。那些和尚，可好伏侍，老孙去也。"

【13】说声去，早已无踪。须臾间，到了南海，停云观看，但见那：

汪洋海远，水势连天。祥光笼宇宙，瑞气照山川。千层雪浪吼青霄，万迭烟波滔白昼。水飞四野，浪滚周遭。水飞四野振轰雷，浪滚周遭鸣霹雳。休言水势，且看中间。五色朦胧宝迭山，红黄紫绿缘和蓝。才见观音真胜境，试看南海落伽山。好去处！山峰高耸，顶透虚空。中间有千祥奇花，百般瑞草。风摇宝树，日映金莲。观音殿瓦盖琉璃，潮音洞门铺玳瑁。绿杨影里语鹦哥，紫竹林中啼孔雀。罗纹石上，护法威严；玛瑙滩前，木叉雄壮。

这行者观不尽那异景非常，径直趋到紫竹林之下。早有诸天迎接道："菩萨前者对众言大圣归善，甚是宣扬。今保唐僧，如何得暇到此？"行者道："因保唐僧，路逢一事，特见菩萨，烦为通报。"诸天遂来洞口报知。菩萨唤入。行者遵法而行，宝莲台下拜了。菩萨问曰："你来何干？"行者道："我师父路遇你的禅院，你受了人间香火，容一个黑熊精在那里邻住，着他偷了我师父袈裟，屡次取讨不与，今特来问你要的。"菩萨道："这猴子说话，这等无状！既是熊精偷了你的袈裟，你怎幺问我取讨？都是你这个孽猴大胆，将你宝贝卖弄，拿与小人看见，你却又行凶？唤风发火，烧了我的留云下院，反来我处放刁！"行者见菩萨说出这话，知他晓得过去未来之事，慌忙礼拜道："菩萨，乞恕弟子之罪，果是这般这等。但恨那怪物不肯与我袈裟，师父又要念那话儿咒语，老孙忍不得头疼，故此来拜烦菩萨。望菩萨慈悲之心，助我去拿那妖精，取衣西进也。"菩萨道："那怪物有许多神通，却也不亚于你。也罢，我看唐僧面上，和你去走一遭。"行者闻言，谢恩再拜。即请菩萨出门，遂同驾祥云，早到黑风山。坠落云头，依路找洞。

【14】 正行处，只见那山坡前，走出一个道人，手拿着一个玻璃盘儿，盘内安着两粒仙丹，往前正走；被行者撞个满怀，掣出铁棒，就照头一下，打得脑里浆流出，腔中血进溅。菩萨大惊道："你这个猴子，还是这等放泼！他又不曾偷你袈裟，又不与你相识，又无甚冤仇，你怎么就将他打死？"行者道："菩萨，你认他不得。他是那黑熊精的朋友。他昨日和一个白衣秀士，都在芳草坡前坐讲。后日是黑精的生日，请他们来庆'佛衣会'。今日他先来拜寿，明日来庆'佛衣会'，所以我认得。定是今日替那妖去上寿。"菩萨说："既是这等说来，也罢。"行者去把那道人提起来看，却是一只苍狼。旁边那个盘底下有字样，刻道："凌虚子制"。

行者见了，笑道："造化！造化！老孙也是便益，菩萨也是省力。这怪叫做不打自招，那怪教他今日了劣。"菩萨说道："悟空，这教怎么说？"行者道："菩萨，我悟空有一句话儿，叫做将计就计，不知菩萨可肯依我？"菩萨道："你说。"行者说道："菩萨，你看这盘儿中是两粒仙丹，便是我们与那妖魔的赆见；这盘儿后面刻的四个字，说'凌虚子制'，便是我们与那妖魔的勾头。菩萨若要依得我时，我好替你做个计较，也就不须动得干戈，也不须劳得征战，妖魔可一时而得也。"菩萨道："你不依时，我悟空往东，佛衣只当相送，唐三藏只当落空。"菩萨笑道："这猴熟嘴！"行者道："不敢，倒是一个计较。"菩萨道："你这计较怎说？"行者道："这盘上刻那'凌虚子制'，想这道人就叫做凌虚子。菩萨，你要依我时，可就变做这个道人，我把这丹吃了一粒，变上一粒，略大些儿。菩萨你就捧了这个盘儿，两粒仙丹，去与那妖上寿，把这丸大些的让与那妖。待那妖一口吞之，老孙便于中取事，他若不肯献出佛衣，老孙与他肚肠，就也织将一件出来。"

【15】 菩萨没法，只得也点点头儿。行者笑道："如何？"尔时菩萨乃以广大慈悲，无边法力，亿万化身，以心会意，以意会身，恍

惚之间,变做凌虚仙子:

鹤氅仙风飒,飘飘欲步虚。
苍颜松柏老,秀色古今无。
去去还无住,如如自有殊。
总来归一法,只是隔邪躯。

行者看道:“妙啊!妙啊!还是妖精菩萨,还是菩萨妖精?”菩萨笑道:“悟空,菩萨、妖精,总是一念;若论本来,皆属无有。”行者心下顿悟,转身却就变做一粒仙丹:

走盘无不定,圆明未有方。
三三勾漏合,六六少翁商。
瓦铄黄金焰,牟尼白昼光。
外边铅与汞,未许易论量。

行者变了那颗丹,终是略大些儿。菩萨认定,拿了那个玻璃盘儿,径到妖洞门口,看时,果然是:

崖深岫险,云生岭上;柏苍松翠,风飒林间。崖深岫险,晃是妖邪出没人烟少;柏苍松翠,也可仙真修隐道情多。山有涧,涧有泉,潺潺流水鸣琴,便堪洗耳;崖有鹿,林有鹤,幽幽仙籁动闲岑,亦可赏心。这是妖仙有分降菩提,弘誓无边垂恻隐。

菩萨看了,心中暗喜道:“这孽畜占了这座山洞,却是也有些道分。”因此心中已此有个慈悲。

【16】 走到洞口,只见守洞小妖,都有些认得道:“凌虚仙长来了。”一边传报,一边接引。那妖早已迎出二门道:“凌虚,有劳仙驾珍顾,蓬荜有辉。”菩萨道:“小道敬献一粒仙丹,敢称千寿。”他二人拜毕,方才坐定,又叙起他昨日之事。菩萨不答,连忙拿丹盘道:“大王,且见小道鄙意。”觑定一粒大的,推与那妖道:“愿大王千寿!”那妖亦推一粒,递与菩萨道:“愿与凌虚子同之。”让毕,那妖才待要咽,那药顺口儿一直滚下。现了本相,理起四平,那妖滚倒在地。菩萨现相,问妖取了佛衣。行者早已从鼻孔中出去。菩萨又怕那妖无礼,却把一个箍儿,丢在那妖头上。那妖起来,提枪要刺,行者、菩萨早已起在空中,菩萨将真言念起。那怪依旧头疼,丢了枪,满地乱滚。半空里笑倒个美猴王,平地下滚

坏个黑熊怪。

菩萨道："孽畜！你如今可皈依么？"那怪满口道："心愿皈依，只望饶命！"行者道："恐耽搁了工夫，"意欲就打。菩萨急止住道："休伤他命。我有用他处哩。"行者道："这样怪物，不打死他，反留他在何处用哩？"菩萨道："我那落伽山后，无人看管，我要带他去做个守山大神。"行者笑道："诚然是个救苦慈尊，一灵不损。若是老孙有这样咒语，就念上他娘千遍！这回儿就有许多黑熊，都教他了帐！"却说那怪苏醒多时，公道难禁疼痛，只得跪在地下哀告道："但饶性命，愿皈正果！"菩萨方坠落祥光，又与他摩顶受戒，教他执了长枪，跟随左右。那黑熊才一片野心今日定，无穷顽性此时收。菩萨吩咐道："悟空，你回去罢。好生伏侍唐僧，休懈惰生事。"行者道："深感菩萨远来，弟子还当回送回送。"菩萨道："免送。"行者才捧着袈裟，叩头而别。菩萨亦带了熊罴，径回大海。

Chapter 6
Brother Monkey Makes Trouble on the Black Wind Mountain; Guanyin Subdues the Bear Spirit

【1】 As Monkey leapt up with a somersault, the senior and junior monks, the novices, the page-boys, and the servants of the monastery all bowed low to the sky and said, "Master, you must be a cloud-riding Immortal come down from Heaven. No wonder that fire can't burn you. Damn that stupid old skinflint of ours: he destroyed himself with his own scheming." "Please rise, gentlemen," replied Sanzang, "there's no need to hate him. If my disciple finds the cassock our troubles will all come to an end; but if he doesn't find it, he has rather a nasty temper, and I'm afraid that none of you will escape with your lives." When they heard this warning, the monks' hearts were in their mouths, and they implored Heaven to let him find the cassock and spare their lives.

【2】 Once in mid-air, the Great Sage Sun Wukong reached at the Black Wind Mountain with one twist of his waist. Stopping his cloud while he took a careful look around, he saw that it was indeed a fine mountain. It was a spring day:

> The myriad valleys' streams compete,
> A thousand precipices vie in beauty.
> Where the birds call, no man is;
> When the blossoms fall, the trees are still fragrant.
> After the rain, the sky and the lowering cliff are moist;
> As the pines bend in the wind, they spread an emerald
screen.
> The mountain herbs grow,
> The wild flowers blossom,

151

Hanging over beetling crags;
The wild fig thrives
And fine trees flourish
On craggy range and flat-topped hill.
You meet no hermits,
And can find no wood-cutters.
Beside the stream a pair of cranes drink,
And wild apes gambol on the rocks.
Peaks like mussel-shells, gleaming black,
Lofty and green as they shine through the mist.

As Monkey was looking at the mountain scenery he heard voices from in front of the grassy slope. He slipped off to conceal himself under the rock-face and take a discreet look. He saw three fiends sitting on the ground. At the head was a dark fellow, to his left was a Taoist, and to his right a white-robed scholar, and they were all talking about lofty and broad matters: about refining cinnabar and mercury with tripods and cauldrons; and about the white snow, mercury, the yellow sprout, lead, and other esoteric teachings. In the middle of this the dark fellow said, "As it's my birthday tomorrow, I hope you two gentlemen will do me the honour of coming along." "We celebrate your birthday every year, Your Majesty," the white-robed scholar replied, "so of course we shall come this year." "I came by a treasure last night," the dark fellow went on, "a brocade cassock for a Buddha, and it's a wonderful thing. I'm going to give a big banquet for it the day after tomorrow and I'm inviting all you mountain officials to come and congratulate me, which is why I'm calling it a 'Buddha's Robe Banquet'." "Wonderful, wonderful," the Taoist exclaimed with a smile. "Tomorrow I'll come to congratulate you on your birthday, and the day after I'll come again for the banquet." As soon as Monkey heard him mention the Buddha's robe he was sure it was their treasure, and unable to hold back his anger he leapt out from the cliff brandishing his gold-banded cudgel with both hands and shouting, "I'll get you, you gang of devils. You stole our cassock, and now you think you're going to have a 'Buddha's Robe Banquet'. Give it back to me at once." "Don't move," he barked, swinging the cudgel and bringing it down towards the monster's head. The dark fellow turned into a wind to flee in terror, and the Taoist rode off on a cloud; so Monkey was only able to slay the white-robed scholar with a blow from the club. When he dragged the body over to look at it, he saw that it was a white-patterned snake spirit. In his anger he picked the corpse up and tore it to pieces, then went into the recesses of the mountain in search of the dark fellow. Rounding a sharp pinnacle and traversing a dizzy precipice, he saw a cave palace in the cliff:

> Thick, misty clouds,
> Dense with cypress and pine.
> The thick and misty clouds fill the gates with colour;
> The dense stands of cypress and pine surround the door
> with green.
> For a bridge there is a dried-out log,
> And wild fig coils around the mountain peaks.
> Birds carry red petals to the cloud-filled valley;
> Deer tread on scented bushes as they climb the stone tower.
> Before the season brings out flowers;
> As the wind wafts their fragrance.
> Around the willows on the dike the golden orioles wheel;
> Butterflies flit among the peach-trees on the bank.
> This ordinary scene can yet compete
> With lesser views in Fairyland.

[3] When he reached the gates Monkey saw that they were very strongly fastened, and above them was a stone tablet inscribed with the words Black Wind Cave of the Black Wind Mountain in large letters. He brandished his cudgel and shouted, "Open up!" at which the junior devil who was on the gates opened them and asked, "Who are you, and how dare you come and attack our Immortals' cave?" "You damned cur," Monkey railed at him. "How dare you call a place like this an 'Immortals'

153

cave'? What right have you to use the word 'Immortals'? Go in and tell that dark fellow of yours that if he gives back my cassock at once, I'll spare your lives." The junior devil rushed in and reported, "The 'Buddha's Robe Banquet' is off, Your Majesty. There's a hairy-faced thunder god outside the gates who's demanding the cassock." The dark fellow, who had barely had time to shut the gates and had not even sat down properly since Brother Monkey chased him away from the grassy slope, thought on hearing this news, "This wretch has come from I don't know where, and now he has the effrontery to come yelling at my gates." He called for his armour, tightened his belt, and strode out of the gates with a black-tasselled spear in his hands. Monkey appeared outside the gates holding his iron cudgel and glaring wide-eyed at that ferocious-looking monster.

> His bowl-shaped iron helmet shone like fire;
> His black bronze armour gleamed.
> A black silk gown with billowing sleeves;
> A dark green silken sash with fringes.
> In his hands a spear with black tassels,
> On his feet a pair of dark leather boots.
> Lightning flashed from his golden pupils;
> He was indeed the Black Wind King of the mountains.

"This wretch looks as though he's been a brick-burner or a coal-digger," Monkey thought as he smiled to himself. "He's so black he must be the local soot-painter." "What gives you the nerve to act so big round here, monk, and what the hell are you?" shouted the monster at the top of his voice. Monkey rushed him with his cudgel and roared, "Cut the cackle, and give me back the cassock at once, kid." "What monastery d'you come from? Where did you lose the cassock? Why come and ask for it here?" "My cassock was in the rear abbot's lodgings at the Guanyin Monastery due north of here. When the monastery caught fire you made the most of the confusion to do a bit of looting and brought it back here, you wretch, and now you're planning to hold a 'Buddha's Robe Banquet'. Don't try to brazen it out. Give it back at once, and I'll spare your life, but if even a hint of a 'no' gets past your teeth I'll push the Black Wind Mountain over, trample your cave flat, and flatten every one of you fiends into noodles."

[4]   The monster laughed evilly and replied, "You've got a nerve. You were the one who started the fire last night. You were sitting on the roof of the abbot's lodgings and calling up a wind to make it worse. What's it to you if I did take a cassock? Where are you from? Who are you? You must have a lot of tricks up your sleeve if you have the nerve to talk so big." "You can't recognize your own grandfather," Brother Monkey replied. "I, your grandfather, am the disciple of His Highness the Patriarch Sanzang, the younger brother of the Emperor of the Great Tang. My name is Brother Sun Wukong. If you want to know about my tricks, just give me the word. I'll slaughter you here and now, and send your souls flying." "I've never heard of these tricks of yours, so you'd better tell me about them." "Stand still and listen to me, my child," Monkey replied, and went on to say:

'Great have been my magic powers since childhood;
Changing with the wind, I show my might.
Nourishing my nature and cultivating the truth,
I have lived out the days and months,
Saving my life by jumping beyond the cycle of rebirth.
Once I searched sincerely for the Way
Climbing the Spirit Terrace Mountain to pick medicinal
herbs.
On that mountain lives an ancient Immortal
One hundred and eight thousand years old.
I took him as my master,
Hoping that he would show me a road to immortality.
He said that the elixir is in one's own body—
It is a waste of effort to seek it outside.
I learnt a great spell of immortality.
I could scarcely have survived without it.

155

Turning my gaze inwards, I sat and calmed my mind,
While the sun and moon in my body intermingled.
Ignoring the affairs of the world, I made my desires few.
When sense, body, and mind were purified, my body was
firm.
Reversing the years and returning to youth is then easily
done;
The road to immortality and sagehood was not long.
In three years I acquired a magic body,
That did not suffer like a common one.
I wandered around the Ten Continents and Three Islands,
The corners of the sea and the edge of the sky.
I was due to live over three hundred years
But could not yet fly up to the Nine Heavens.
I got a real treasure for subduing sea dragons:
An iron cudgel banded with gold.
On the Mountain of Flowers and Fruit I was supreme
commander;
In the Water Curtain Cave I assembled the fiendish hosts.
The Great Jade Emperor sent me a decree
Conferring high rank and the title 'Equalling Heaven.'
More than once I wrecked the Hall of Miraculous Mist,
And stole the Queen Mother's peaches several times.
A hundred thousand heavenly soldiers in serried ranks
Came with spears and swords to put me down.
I sent the heavenly kings back up there in defeat,
Made Nezha flee in pain at the head of his men.
The True Lord Erlang, skilled at transformations,
Lao Zi, Guanyin and the Jade Emperor
Watched me being subdued from the Southern Gate of
Heaven.
As he was given some help by Lord Lao Zi,
Erlang captured me and took to Heaven.
I was tied to the Demon-subduing Pillar,
And divine soldiers were ordered to cut off my head.
Though hacked with swords and pounded with hammers I

remained unharmed.

>*So then I was struck with thunder and burned with fire.*
>*As I really do have magic powers,*
>*I was not in the slightest bit afraid.*
>*They took me to Lao Zi's furnace to be refined.*
>*The Six Dings roasted me slowly with divine fire.*
>*When the time was up and the furnace opened, out I jumped,*
>*And rushed round Heaven, my cudgel in my hand.*
>*No one could stop me making trouble everywhere,*
>*And I cause chaos in the thirty-three Heavens.*
>*Then our Tathagata Buddha used his Dharma power*
>*And dropped the Five Elements Mountain on my back.*
>*There I was crushed for full five hundred years,*
>*Until Sanzang came from the land of Tang.*
>*Now I have reformed and am going to the West*
>*To climb the Thunder Peak and see the Buddha.*
>*Enquire throughout the Four Seas, Heaven and Earth:*
>*You'll find that I'm the greatest monster ever.*

【5】 On hearing this the fiend laughed and said, "So you're the Protector of the Horses who wrecked Heaven, are you?" Monkey, who got angrier at being addressed by this title than at anything else, was furious. "You vicious monster. You steal the cassock and refuse to give it back, and on top of that you insult your lord and master. Just hold it, and see how you like my club." The dark fellow dodged the blow and then riposted with his spear. The pair of them fought a fine battle.

>*An as-you-will cudgel,*
>*A black-tasselled spear,*
>*And two men showing their toughness at the mouth of a cave.*
>*One stabs at heart and face,*
>*The other tries for arm and head.*
>*This one strikes cunning sideswipes with a club,*

> *That one brandishes his spear in three swift movements.*
> *The white tiger climbs the mountain to sink in his claws;*
> *The yellow dragon lying on the road turns round fast.*
> *Snorting out coloured mists,*
> *Disgorging rays of light,*
> *The two immortal fiends are hard to choose between:*
> *One is the Sage Equalling Heaven who has cultivated the truth;*
> *The other is the Great Black King become a spirit.*
> *On this battlefield in the mountains*
> *The pair of them fight for the cassock.*

The fiend fought some ten inconclusive rounds with Monkey, and as the sun was now rising steadily towards the zenith, the dark fellow raised his halberd to block the iron cudgel and said, "Brother Monkey, let's lay down our arms. I'll come back and fight you again after I've eaten." "You accursed beast," Monkey replied, "how can you call yourself a real man? If you were, you wouldn't be needing to eat after only half a day. I never even tasted water once in those five hundred years I spent under the mountain, but I wasn't hungry. Stop making excuses, and don't go. I'll let you have your meal if you give me back my cassock." The fiend waved his halberd in a feint, withdrew into the cave, and shut the doors fast behind him. Summoning his junior goblins, he ordered that a banquet be spread and wrote invitations asking all the devil kings of the mountain to come to the celebratory feast.

[6] Monkey charged the gates but was unable to force them open, so he had to go back to the Guanyin Monastery, where the monks had buried the old patriarch and were now all in attendance on the Tang Priest in the abbot's quarters. Breakfast was over, and lunch was being brought in. Just as they were bringing soup and more hot water, Monkey descended from the sky. The monks all bowed low and took him into the abbot's room to see Sanzang. "Ah, you're back, Wukong," he said. "What about the cassock?" "I've found the answer. We misjudged these

monks. It was in fact stolen by a fiend from the Black Wind Mountain. I went to have a quiet look for him and found him sitting in front of a grassy slope talking to a white-gowned scholar and an old Taoist. He's a self-confessed monster, and he said with his own mouth that he was inviting all the evil spirits to come and celebrate his birthday tomorrow, and that as he had come by a brocade Buddha's robe last night he wanted to celebrate that too, so he was going to give a great feast that he called an 'Assembly for the Celebration and Admiration of the Buddha's Robe'. I rushed him and took a swipe at him with my club, but the dark fellow turned into a puff of wind and fled. The Taoist disappeared too, and I was only able to kill the white-clad scholar, who was a white snake turned spirit. I went to the mouth of his cave as fast as I could and told him to come out and fight me. He admitted that he had carried it off. We fought for half a day without either of us winning, and then the monster went back to his cave for lunch and shut the stone gates behind him. He was too scared to come out again, so I came back to give you this news, master. Now we know where the cassock is, there's no need to worry that he won't give it back."

[7] On hearing this, the monks put their hands together or kowtowed as they invoked Amitabha Buddha and exclaimed, "He's found where it is—we're saved." "Don't be so happy about it," Monkey warned, "I haven't got it yet, and my master hasn't left your monastery yet. You'll have to wait till I've recovered the cassock and my master has been seen off properly from here before you can consider yourselves safe. And if there is the slightest mistake, remember that I'm a very quick-tempered boss. Have you given my master the best food and tea? Have you given my horse the best fodder?" "Yes, yes, yes," the monks hastened to assure him. "We haven't been remiss in any way while looking after his Reverence." "While you were away all morning I've drunk tea three times and eaten twice, and they have not been at all offhand with me," Sanzang explained. "You'd better go back and do everything possible to recover that cassock." "Don't be in such a hurry," Monkey replied. "I know

159

where it is, and I guarantee that I'll capture this wretch and return the cassock to you. There's no need to worry."

As he was talking the senior abbot came in, set out the vegetarian meal, and invited Lord Monkey to eat. After swallowing a few mouthfuls, Monkey mounted his magic cloud once more and went off on his hunt. On his way he saw a junior goblin going along the main path with a rosewood box under his left arm. Guessing that there must be some kind of letter in the box Monkey raised his cudgel and brought it down on his head. The blow did not just kill the goblin: it left him looking like a hamburger. Throwing his remains aside, Brother Monkey wrenched open the box and saw that it contained an invitation:

> Your pupil Bear presents his humble greetings to Your Excellency, the Supreme and Venerable One of the Golden Pool:
>
> I am deeply grateful for the magnificent kindness that I have so frequently received from you. When I saw the fire last night I failed to put it out, but I am sure that your divine intelligence will have suffered no harm from it. As your pupil has been lucky enough to obtain a Buddha's robe, I am giving a banquet, to which I hope you will come to appreciate the robe. I would be profoundly grateful if you would honour me with your presence at the appointed time. Written two days beforehand.

[8] On reading this, Monkey roared with laughter and said, "That crooked old monk. He thoroughly deserved to be killed. He'd been ganging up with evil spirits, had he? It's odd that he should have lived to be two hundred and seventy. I suppose that evil spirit must have taught him a few tricks about controlling his vital essence, which was why he lived so long. I can remember what he looked like, so I think I'll make myself look like him and go into that cave. This way I can see where he's put that cassock, and if I'm lucky I'll be able to get back and save a lot of trouble."

The splendid Great Sage recited a spell, faced the wind, and made himself look just like the old monk. He hid his cudgel, walked straight to the entrance of the cave, and shouted, "Open up." The junior goblin opened up, and as soon as he saw him he rushed back to report, "Your Majesty, the Elder of the Golden Pool is here." The monster was astounded. "I've only just sent a youngster with an invitation for him, and the message can't have reached him yet. How could he possibly have got here so fast? The youngster can't even have met him. Obviously Brother Monkey has sent him here to ask for the cassock. Steward, hide that cassock somewhere where he won't see it."

【9】 As he came to the front gates Monkey saw that the courtyard was green with bamboo and cypress, while peach and plum trees vied in beauty amid blossoming shrubs and fragrant orchids. It was a cave paradise. He also saw a couplet inscribed on the gates that read:

> In peaceful retirement deep in the hills, one is free of vulgar worries;
> Dwelling quietly in a magic cave, happy in divine simplicity.

"This wretch has escaped from the dirt and dust of the world," thought Monkey, "and is a fiend who understands life." Going through the gates he went further inside and passed through a triple gate. Here were carved and painted beams, light windows and coloured doors. He saw that the dark fellow was wearing a dark green silken tunic over which was slung a black patterned silk cloak; on his head was a soft black hat, and on his feet a pair of dusky deerskin boots. When he saw Monkey approaching he straightened his clothes and came down the steps to greet him with the words, "I've been looking forward to seeing you for days, Golden Pool. Please take a seat." Monkey returned his courtesies, and when they had finished greeting each other they sat down and drank tea. Then the evil spirit bowed and said, "I sent you a note just now asking you to come over the day after tomorrow. Why is it that you've come to see me today, old

161

friend?" "I was on my way here to visit you when I happened to see your message that you were giving a 'Buddha's Robe Banquet', so I hurried over to ask you to let me have a look." "You've misunderstood, old friend," replied the evil monster with a smile. "It's the Tang Priest's cassock, and as he's been staying at your place you must have seen it there. Why come here to see it?" "When I borrowed it," Monkey said, "it was too late at night for me to be able to look at it. Since then, to my great surprise, it has been taken by Your Majesty. On top of that, the monastery has been burnt down and I have lost everything I own. That disciple of the Tang Priest's is quite a bold fellow, but he could not find it anywhere. I have come here to look at it as Your Majesty has had the great good fortune to recover it."

【10】 As they were talking, a junior goblin came in from patrolling the mountain to announce, "Your Majesty, a terrible thing's happened. Brother Monkey has killed the lieutenant who was taking the invitation by the main path, and taken the chance of making himself look like the Elder of the Golden Pool to come here and trick the Buddha's robe out of you." "I wondered why the elder came today," the monster thought, "and why he came so soon, and now I see that it's really him." He leapt to his feet, grabbed his halberd, and thrust at Monkey. Monkey pulled the cudgel from his ear in a flash, reverted to his true form, parried the halberd's blade, jumped out from the main room into the courtyard, and fought his way back out through the front gates. This terrified all the fiends in the cave, scaring the wits out of young and old alike. The fine combat on the mountain that ensued was even better than the previous one.

The courageous Monkey King was now a monk,
The cunning dark fellow had hidden the Buddha's robe.
At matching words they were both masters;
In making the most of chances there was nothing between them.
The cassock could not be seen, whatever one wished;
A hidden treasure is a true wonder.

When the junior demon on mountain patrol announced a disaster,

> *The old fiend in his fury showed his might.*

Monkey transformed himself and fought his way out of the cave,

> *As halberd and cudgel strove to decide the issue.*

The club blocked the lengthy halberd with resounding clangs;

> *The halberd gleamed as it parried the iron club.*

Sun Wukong's transformations were rare on earth;

Few could rival the foul fiend's magic.

One wanted to take the robe to bring himself long life;

One had to have the cassock to return with honour.

This bitter struggle was not to be broken up;

Even a Living Buddha could not have resolved it.

From the mouth of the cave the pair of them fought to the top of the mountain, and from the top of the mountain they battled their way beyond the clouds. They breathed out wind and mist, set sand and stones flying, and struggled till the red sun set in the west, but the contest was still undecided. Then the monster said, "Stop for the moment, Monkey. It's too late to go on fighting tonight. Go away, go away. Come back tomorrow, and we'll see which of us is to live and which to die." "Don't go, my child," Monkey shouted back. "If you want to fight, fight properly. Don't use the time of day as an excuse to get out of it." With that he struck wildly at the dark fellow, who changed himself into a puff of wind, went back to his cave, and fastened the stone gates tightly shut.

[11] Monkey could think of no alternative to going back to the Guanyin Monastery. Bringing his cloud down, he called to his master, who had been waiting for him anxiously until he appeared suddenly before his eyes. Sanzang was very glad, until seeing that there was no cassock in Monkey's hands his happiness turned to fear. "Why haven't you got the cassock this time either?" he asked. Brother Monkey produced the invitation from his sleeve,

163

and as he handed it to Sanzang he said, "Master, that fiend was friends with that dead crook. He sent a junior goblin with this invitation asking him to go to a 'Buddha's Robe Banquet'. I killed the goblin, made myself look like the old monk, went into the cave, and tricked a cup of tea out of them. I asked him to let me see the cassock, but he wouldn't bring it out. Then as we were sitting there a mountain patrolman of some sort gave the game away, so he started to fight me. We fought till just now, and neither of us was on top, when he saw that it was late, shot back to his cave and shut the stone doors behind him. This meant that I had to come back for the moment." "How do your tricks compare with his?" Sanzang asked. "I'm not much better than him," Monkey replied, "and I can only keep my end up." Sanzang read the invitation and handed it to the prelate. "Can it be that your Patriarch was an evil spirit?" he said. The prelate fell to knees as fast as he could and said, "My lord, he was human. But because the Great Black King was cultivating the ways of humanity he often came to our temple to discuss the scriptures with our Patriarch, and taught him some of the arts of nourishing the divine and controlling the vital essence. That was why they were on friendly terms." "None of these monks have anything satanic about them," Monkey said. "They all have their heads in the air and their feet on the ground, and are taller and fatter than I am. They're not evil spirits. Do you see where it says 'Your pupil Bear' on the invitation? He must be a black bear who has become a spirit." To this Sanzang said, "There's an old saying that 'Bears and baboons are alike'. If they are all animals, how can they become spirits?" Monkey laughed and replied, "I'm just the same as him. All the creatures on heaven and earth that have nine openings to their bodies can cultivate their conduct and become Immortals." "Just now you said his abilities were the same as yours, so how are you going to beat him and get the cassock back?" Sanzang went on to ask. "Don't worry, don't worry," Monkey replied, "I can manage."

[12] As they were talking, the monks brought their evening meal and invited them to eat. Then Sanzang asked for a lamp and

went to bed in the front meditation hall as before. The monks all slept under thatched shelters rigged up against the walls, leaving the abbot's quarters at the back for the senior and junior prelate. It was a peaceful night.

The Milky Way was clear,
The jade firmament free of dust.
The sky was full of coruscating stars,
A single wave wiped out the traces.
Stilled were all sounds,
And the birds were silent on a thousand hills.
The fisherman's light beside the bank was out,
The Buddha-lamp in the pagoda dimmed.
Last night the abbot's bell and drum had sounded;
This evening the air was filled with weeping.

This night he spent asleep in the monastery. Sanzang, however, could not sleep for thinking about the cassock. He turned over, and seeing that the sky was growing light outside the window, got straight out of bed and said, "Monkey, it's light, go and get the cassock." Brother Monkey bounded out of bed, and in an instant a host of monks was in attendance, offering hot water. "Look after my master properly," he said. "I'm off." Sanzang got out of bed and seized hold of him. "Where are you going?" he asked. "I've been thinking," said Monkey, "that this whole business is the Bodhisattva Guanyin's fault. Although this is her monastery and she receives the worship of all these monks, she allows that evil spirit to live in the neighbourhood. I'm going to the Southern Sea to find her and ask her to come here herself to make that evil spirit give us back the cassock." "When will you come back?" Sanzang asked. "After you've finished breakfast at the earliest, and by midday at latest, I'll have done the job. Those monks had better look after you well. I'm off now."

【13】 No sooner were the words out of his mouth than he had disappeared without a trace and reached the Southern Sea. Stopping his cloud to take a look, he saw:

165

A vast expanse of ocean,
Waters stretching till they joined the sky.
Propitious light filled the firmament,
Auspicious vapours shone over mountains and rivers.
A thousand snow-capped breakers roared at the azure
vault,
A myriad misty waves reared at the sky.
Water flew in all directions,
Torrents poured everywhere.
As the water flew in all directions it echoed like thunder;
As the torrents poured everywhere they crashed and roared.
Let us leave the sea,
And consider what lay in it:
A precious mountain in many a misty colour—
Red, yellow, purple, black, green, and blue.
Then did he see the beautiful land of Guanyin,
Potaraka Island in the Southern Sea.
What a wonderful place to go—
Towering peaks
Cutting through the sky,
With a thousand kinds of exotic flowers below them,
And every type of magical herb.
The wind shook priceless trees,
The sun shone on golden lotus.
Guanyin's palace was roofed with glazed tiles,
The gates of the Tide Cave were set with tortoise shell.
In the shade of green willows parrots talked,
While peacocks called amid purple bamboo.
On the marbled stone
The protecting gods are majestically severe;
Before the agate strand
Stands the mighty Moksa.

Not pausing to take in the whole of this exotic scene,
Monkey brought his cloud straight down to land under the
bamboo grove. A number of devas were already there to meet

him, and they said, "The Bodhisattva told us some time ago that you had been converted, Great Sage, and praised you very warmly. But if you are now protecting the Tang Priest, how have you found the time to come here?" "Because something has happened while I've been escorting him on his journey. Please go and tell the Bodhisattva that I'd like an audience with her." When the devas went into the cave to report this, Guanyin summoned him inside. Monkey did as he was told and bowed to her beneath the lotus throne. "What have you come for?" the Bodhisattva asked. "My master's journey has brought him to a monastery of yours," Monkey replied, "and I find that although you accept incense from its monks, you allow a black bear spirit to live in the neighbourhood, and have let him steal my master's cassock. I've tried to take it off him a number of times but got nowhere, so now I've come to ask you to demand it from him." "What nonsense, you ape," the Bodhisattva retorted. "Even if a bear spirit has stolen your cassock, what business have you to ask me to go and demand it for you? It all happened because you wanted to show it off, you big-headed and evil baboon, in front of petty-minded people. On top of that, in your wickedness you called up the wind to spread the fire that burnt down my monastery. And now you have the nerve to try your tricks here." These words from the Bodhisattva made Monkey realize that she knew all about the past and the future, so he hastily bowed down in reverence and pleaded, "Bodhisattva, forgive your disciple his sins, everything you say is true. All the same, my master will recite that spell again because that monster won't give back the cassock, and I couldn't bear the agonizing headache. That's why I came to bother you, Bodhisattva. I beg you in your mercy to help me catch that evil spirit, get the cassock back, and carry on towards the west." "That monster's magical powers are certainly no weaker than yours," the Bodhisattva said. "Very well then, out of consideration for the Tang Priest I'll go there with you." Monkey thanked her and bowed again, asked her to come out, and rode on the same magic cloud as her. In next to no time they reached the Black Wind Mountain, where they landed the cloud and headed for the cave on foot.

[14]   As they were on their way, a Taoist priest appeared on the mountain slope. He was carrying a glass salver on which were two pills of the elixir of immortality. Monkey was immediately suspicious of him, so he struck straight at his head with the iron cudgel, sending blood splattering out from brain and chest. "Are you still as wild as this, you ape?" the shocked Bodhisattva asked. "He didn't steal your cassock, you didn't even know him, and he was no enemy of yours. Why kill him?" "You may not know him, Bodhisattva," Monkey replied, "but he was a friend of the Black Bear Spirit. Yesterday they and a white-clad scholar were sitting talking in front of the grassy mountainside. Today is the Black Spirit's birthday, and tomorrow he was coming to the 'Buddha's Robe Banquet'. That's why I recognized him. I'm sure that he was coming to greet that monster on his birthday." "If that's the way it is, very well then," said the Bodhisattva. Monkey then went to lift up the Taoist to take a look at him, and he saw that he had been a grey wolf. There was an inscription under the glass salver that lay beside him. It read, "Made by Master Emptiness-reached".

Brother Monkey laughed and said, "What luck, what luck. This helps me and will save you trouble too, Bodhisattva. This monster has confessed of his own free will, and the other monster there can be finished off today." "What do you mean?" the Bodhisattva asked. "I have a saying," he replied, "that goes 'beat him at his own game'. Are you willing to let me do things my way?" "Tell me about it," the Bodhisattva said. "The two pills of immortality you see on that salver will be the present we take to visit him with," said Monkey, "and the words inscribed underneath—'Made by Master Emptiness-reached'—are the bait we'll set for him. If you do as I say, I have a plan for you that does not call for force or fighting. The fiend will collapse before our eyes, and the cassock will appear. If you won't let me have my way, then you go west, I'll go east, we can say goodbye to the Buddha's robe, and Sanzang will be up the creek." "You've got a cheek, you ape," replied the Bodhisattva with a smile.

"No, no, I really have got a plan," Monkey protested. "Tell me about it then," said Guanyin. "You know it says on the salver, 'Made by Master Emptiness-reached'. Well, Master Emptiness-reached must be his name. Bodhisattva, if you're prepared to let me have my way, then change yourself into that Taoist. I shall eat one of those pills and then change myself into a pill, though I'll be a bit on the big side. You are to take the tray with the two pills on it and go to wish the fiend many happy returns. Give him the bigger of the pills, and when he's swallowed me, I'll take over inside him. If he doesn't hand the cassock over then, I'll weave a substitute out of his guts."

[15]   The Bodhisattva could only nod her agreement. "What about it then?" said the laughing Monkey, and at this the Bodhisattva in her great mercy used her unbounded divine power and her infinite capacity for transformation to control her will with her heart and her body with her will—in an instant she turned into Master Emptiness-reached.

> *The wind of immortality blew around his gown,*
> *As he hovered, about to rise to emptiness.*
> *His dark features were as ancient as a cypress,*
> *His elegant expression unmatched in time.*
> *Going and yet staying nowhere,*
> *Similar but unique.*
> *In the last resort all comes down to a single law,*
> *From which he is only separated by an evil body.*

"Great, great," exclaimed Brother Monkey at the sight. "Are you a Bodhisattva disguised an evil spirit, or a Bodhisattva who really is an evil spirit?" "Monkey," she replied with a laugh, "evil spirit and Bodhisattva are all the same in the last analysis— they both belong to non-being." Suddenly enlightened by this, Monkey curled up and turned himself into a pill of immortality:

> *Rolling across the plate but not unstable,*
> *Round and bright without any corners.*

169

> *The double three was compounded by Ge Hong,*
> *The double six was worked out by Shao Weng.*
> *Pebbles of golden flame,*
> *Pearls that shone in the daylight.*
> *On the outside were lead and mercury,*
> *But I cannot reveal the formula.*

The pill he changed himself into was indeed a little larger than the other one. The Bodhisattva noted this and went with the glass salver to the entrance of the fiend's cave. Here she saw

> *Towering crags and lofty precipices,*
> *Where clouds grow on the peaks;*
> *Blue cypresses and green pines*
> *Where the wind soughs in the forest.*
> *On towering crags and lofty precipices*
> *The devils come and go, and few men live.*
> *The blue cypresses and green pines*
> *Inspire Immortals to cultivate the hidden Way.*
> *The mountains have gullies,*
> *The gullies have springs,*
> *Whose gurgling waters sing like a guitar,*
> *Refreshing the ear.*
> *Deer on its banks,*
> *Cranes in the woods,*
> *Where the reticent Immortal's pipe is casually played*
> *To delight the heart.*
> *Here an evil spirit can attain enlightenment,*
> *And the boundless vow of the Buddha extends its mercy.*

When the Bodhisattva saw this she thought, "If the beast has chosen this cave, there must be some hope for him." And from then on she felt compassion for him.

[16]   When she reached the entrance of the cave, the junior goblins at the gates greeted her with the words, "Welcome, Immortal Elder Emptiness-reached." As some of them ran in to

170

announce her, the monster came out of the gates to meet her and say, "Master Emptiness-reached, how good of you to put yourself to this trouble. This is an honour for me." "Allow me to present you with this magic pill that, I venture to say, will confer immortality on you," the Bodhisattva replied. When the two of them had finished exchanging greetings they sat down, and the monster started to talk about the events of the previous day. The Bodhisattva quickly changed the subject by passing the salver to him and saying, "Please accept this token of my regard for you." She observed which was the bigger one and handed it to him with the words, "I wish Your Majesty eternal life." The monster handed the other pill to her and said, "I hope, Master Emptiness-reached, that you will share it with me." When they had finished declining politely, the fiend picked up the pill and was on the point of swallowing it when it went rolling into his mouth. Then Monkey resumed his true form and struck up some acrobatic postures, at which the fiend fell to the ground. The Bodhisattva too resumed her true form and asked the monster for the Buddha's cassock. As Monkey had now emerged through the monster's nostrils, she was worried that the evil spirit might misbehave again, so she threw a band over his head. He rose to his feet, ready to run them through with his spear but Monkey and the Bodhisattva were already up in mid-air, where she began to recite the spell. As the monster's head began to ache, he dropped the spear and writhed in agony on the ground. The Handsome Monkey King collapsed with laughter in the sky, while the Black Bear Spirit rolled in torment on the earth.

"Beast, will you return to the truth now?" asked the Bodhisattva. "I swear to, I swear to, if only you spare my life," the monster repeated over and over again. Monkey wanted to finish him off with no more ado, but the Bodhisattva stopped him at once: "Don't kill him—I've got a use for him." "What's the point in keeping that beast alive instead of killing him?" Monkey asked. "I've got nobody to look after the back of my Potaraka Island," she replied, "so I shall take him back with me to be an island-guarding deity." "You certainly are the all-merciful deliverer who doesn't allow a single soul to perish," said Monkey with a laugh. "If I knew a spell like that one of yours, I'd say it a thousand times over and finish off all the black bears I could find." Although the bear spirit had come round and the spell had stopped, he was still in great pain as he knelt on the ground and begged pitifully, "Spare my life and I promise I'll return to the truth." The Bodhisattva descended in a ray of light, placed her hands on his head, and administered the monastic discipline to him; then she told him to take up his spear and accompany her. The black bear's evil intentions ceased from that day on, and his unbounded perversity came to an end. "Sun Wukong," ordered the Bodhisattva, "go back now. Serve the Tang Priest well, don't be lazy and don't start trouble." "I'm very grateful to you for coming so far, Bodhisattva, and I must see you home," Monkey said. "That will not be necessary," she replied. Monkey took the cassock, kowtowed to her, and departed. The Bodhisattva took Bear back to the sea.

7. 万寿山大仙留故友
五庄观行者窃人参

（悟空保着唐僧西行，降妖捉怪，收了八戒和沙僧。
观音菩萨等四人，要试他师徒四人的禅心，化为美女，
要招他们为婿。唯八戒凡心不灭，结果被吊在树上。）

【1】　却说三藏、悟空、沙和尚穿林入里，只见那呆子绷在树上，声声叫喊，痛苦难禁。行者上前笑道："好女婿呀！这早晚还不起来谢亲，又不到师父处报喜，还在这里卖解儿耍子哩！——咄！你娘呢？你老婆呢？好个绷巴吊拷的女婿呀！"那呆子见他来抢白着羞，咬着牙，忍着疼，不敢叫喊。沙僧见了，老大不忍，放下行李，上前解了绳索救出。呆子对他们只是磕头礼拜，其实羞耻难当。有《西江月》为证：

> 色乃伤身之剑，贪之必定遭殃。佳人二八好容妆，更比夜叉凶壮。只有一个原本，再无微利添囊。好将资本谨收藏，坚守休教放荡。

那八戒撮土焚香，望空礼拜。行者道："你可认得那些菩萨么？"八戒道："我已此晕倒昏迷，眼花缭乱，那认得是谁？"行者把那简帖儿递与八戒。八戒见了是颂子，更加惭愧。沙僧笑道："二哥有这般好处哩，感得四位菩萨来与你做亲！"八戒道："兄弟再莫提起。不当人子了！从今后，再也不敢妄为。——就是累折骨头，也只是磨肩压担，随师父西域去也。"三藏道："既如此说才好。"

【2】　行者遂领师父上了大路。在路餐风宿水，行罢多时，忽有高山挡路。三藏勒马停鞭道："徒弟，前面一山，必须仔细，恐有妖魔作耗，侵害吾党。"行者道："马前但有我等三人，怕甚妖魔？"因此，长老安心前进。只见那座山，真是好山。

173

高山峻极，大势峥嵘。根接昆仑脉，顶摩霄汉中。白鹤每来栖桧柏，玄猿时复挂藤萝。日映晴林，迭迭千条红雾绕；风生阴壑，飘飘万道彩云飞。幽鸟乱啼青竹里，锦鸡齐斗野花间。只见那千年峰、五福峰、芙蓉峰，巍巍凛凛放毫光；万岁石、虎牙石、三尖石，突突磷磷生瑞气。崖前草秀，岭上梅香。荆棘密森森，兰芝清淡淡。深林鹰凤聚千禽，古洞麒麟辖万兽。涧水有情，曲曲弯弯多绕顾；峰峦不断，重重迭迭自周回。又见那绿的槐，斑的竹，青的松，依依千载斗秋华；白的李，红的桃，翠的柳，灼灼三春争艳丽。龙吟虎啸，鹤舞猿啼。麋鹿从花出，青鸾对日鸣。乃是仙山真福地，蓬莱阆苑只如然。又见些花开花谢山头景，云去云来岭上峰。

三藏在马上欢喜道："徒弟，我一向西来，经历许多山水，都是那崎峨险峻之处，更不似此山好景，果然的趣味非常。若是相近雷音不远路，我们好整肃端严见世尊。"行者笑道："早哩！早哩！正好不得到哩！"沙僧道："师兄，我们到雷音有多少远？"行者道："十万八千里。十停中还不曾走了一停哩！"八戒道："哥啊，要走几年才得到？"行者道："这些路，若论二位贤弟，便十来日也可到；若论我走，一日也好走五十遭，还见日色，若论师父走，莫想！莫想！"唐僧道："悟空，你说得几时方可到？"行者道："你自小时走到老，老了再小，老小千番也还难；只要你见性志诚，念念回首处，即是灵山。"沙僧道："师兄，此言虽不是雷音，观此景致，必有个好人居止。"行者道："此言却当。这里决无邪崇，一定是个圣僧、仙辈之乡。我们游玩慢行。"不题。

【3】　却说这座山名唤万寿山；山中有一座观，名唤五庄观；观里有一尊仙，道号镇元子，混名与世同君。那观里出一般异宝，乃是混沌初分，鸿蒙始判，天地未开之际，产成这颗灵根。盖天下四大部洲，惟西牛贺洲五庄观出此，唤名"草还丹"，又名"人参果"。三千年一开花，三千年一结果，再三千年才得熟，短头一万年方方得吃。似这万年，只结得三十个果子。果子的模样，就如三朝未满的小孩相似，四肢俱全，五官咸备。人若有缘，得那果子闻了一闻，就活三百六十岁；吃一个，就活四万七千年。

【4】　当日镇元大仙得元始天尊的简帖，邀他上上清天上弥罗宫中听讲"混元道果"。大仙门下出的散仙，也不计其数，见如今还有四十八个徒弟，都是得道的全真。当日带领四十六个上界去听讲，留下两个绝小的看家：一个唤做清风，一个唤做明月。清风只有一千三百二十岁，明月才交一千二百岁。镇元子吩咐二童道："不可违了大天尊的简帖，要往弥罗宫听讲，你两个在家仔细。不日有一个故人从此经过，却莫怠慢了他。可将我人参打两个与他吃，权表旧日之情。"二童道："师父的故人是谁？望说与弟子，好接待。"大仙道："他是东土大唐驾下的圣僧，道号三藏，今往西天拜佛求经的和尚。"二童笑道："孔子云：'道不同，不相为谋。'我等是太乙玄门，怎么与那和尚做甚相识！"大仙道："你那里得知。那和尚乃金蝉子转生，西方圣老如来佛第二个徒弟。五百年前，我与他在'兰盆会'上相识。他曾亲手传茶，佛子敬我，故此是个人也。"

　　二仙童闻言，谨遵师命。那大仙临行，又叮咛嘱咐道："我那果子有数，只许与他两个，不得多费。"清风道："开园时，大众共吃了两个，还有二十八个在树，不敢多费。"大仙道："唐三藏虽是故人，须要防备他手下人罗唣，不可惊动他知。"二童领命讫，那大仙承众徒弟飞升，径朝天界。

【5】　却说唐僧四众，在山游玩，忽抬头，见那松篁一簇，楼阁数层。唐僧道："悟空，你看那里是甚么去处？"行者看了道："那所在，不是观宇，定是寺院。我们走动些，到那厢方知端的。"不一时，来于门首观看，见那：

　　松坡冷淡，竹径清幽。往来白鹤送浮云，上下猿猴时献果。那门前池宽树影长，石裂苔花破。宫殿森罗紫极高，楼台缥缈丹霞堕。真个是福地灵区，蓬莱云ална。清虚人事少，寂静道心生。青鸟每传王母信，紫鸾常寄老君经。看不尽那巍巍道德之风，果然漠漠神仙之宅。

　　三藏离鞍下马，又见那山门左边有一通碑，碑上有十个大字，乃是"万寿山福地，五庄观洞天"。长老道："徒弟，真个是一座观宇。"沙僧道："师父，观此景鲜明，观里必有好人居住。我们进去看看，若行满东回，此间也是一景。"行者道："说得好。"遂都一

175

齐进去。又见那二门上有一对春联。

长生不老神仙府，与天同寿道人家。

行者笑道："这道士说大话唬人。我老孙五百年前大闹天宫时，在那太上老君门首，也不曾见有此话说。"八戒道："且莫管他，进去！进去！或者这道士有些德行，未可知也。"

及至二层门里，只见那里面急急忙忙，走出两个小童儿来。看他怎生打扮：

骨清神爽容颜丽，顶结丫髻短发鬅。

道服自然襟绕雾，羽衣偏是袖飘风。

环绦紧束龙头结，芒履轻缠蚕口绒。

丰采异常非俗辈，正是那清风明月二仙童。

那童子控背躬身，出来迎接道："老师父，失迎，请坐。长老欢喜，遂与二童子上了正殿观看。原来是向南的五间大殿，都是上明下暗的雕花格子。那仙童推开格子，请唐僧入殿，只见壁中间挂着五彩装成的"天地"二字，设一张朱红雕漆的香几，几上有一副黄金炉瓶，炉边有方便整香。

【6】 唐僧上前，以左手拈香注炉，三匝礼拜。拜毕，回头道："仙童，你五庄观真是西方仙界，何不供养三清、四帝、罗天诸宰，只将'天地'二字侍奉香火？"童子笑道："不瞒老师说。这两个字，上头的，礼上还当；下边的，还受不得我们的香火。是家师父诣佞出来的。"三藏道："何为诣佞？"童子道："三清是家师的朋友，四帝是家师的故人；九曜是家师的晚辈，元辰是家师的下宾。"

那行者闻言，笑得打跌。八戒道："哥啊，你笑怎的？"行者道："只讲老孙会捣鬼，原来这童子会捆风！"三藏："令师何在？"童子道："家师元始天尊降简请到上清天弥罗宫听讲'混天道果'去了，不在家。"

行者闻言，忍不住喝了一声道："这个臊道童！人也不认得，你在那个面前捣鬼，扯甚么空心架子？那弥罗宫有谁是太乙天仙？"斗起祸来。三藏见他发怒，恐怕那童子回言，认真的还骂，便陪个礼道："悟空，且休争竞。我们既进来就出去，且莫没了方情。常言道：'鹭鸶不吃鹭鸶肉。'他师既是不在，搅扰他做甚？你去山门前放马，沙僧看守行李，教八戒解包袱。取些米粮，借他锅灶，做顿饭吃，待临行，送他几文柴钱，便罢了。各依执事，让我在此歇息歇息，饭毕就行。"他三人果各依执事而去。

【7】　那明月、清风，暗自夸称不尽道："好和尚！真个是西方爱圣临凡，真元不昧。师父命我们接待唐僧，将人参果与他吃，以表故旧之情；又教防着他手下人罗唕。果然那三个嘴脸凶顽，性情粗糙。幸得就把他们剪开，若在边前，却不与他人参果见面了。"清风道："兄弟，还不知那和尚可是师父的故人。问他一问看，莫要错了。"二童子又上前道："启问老师可是大唐往西天取经的唐三藏？"长老回礼道："贫僧就是。仙童为何知我贱名？"童子道："我师临行，曾吩咐教弟子远接。不期车驾来促，有失迎逆。老师请坐，待弟子办茶来奉。"三藏道："不敢。"那明月急转本房，取一杯香茶，献与长老。茶毕，清风道："兄弟，不可违了师命，我和你去取果子来。"

【8】　二童别了三藏，同到房中，一个拿了金击子，一个拿了丹盘，又多将丝帕垫着盘底，径到人参园内。那清风爬上树去，使金击子敲果；明月在树下，以丹盘等接。须臾，敲下两个果来，接在盘中，径至前殿献道："唐师父，我五庄观土僻山荒，无物可奉，土仪素果二枚，权为解渴。"那长老见了，战战兢兢，远离三尺道："善哉！善哉！今岁倒也年丰时稔，怎么这观里作荒吃人？这个是三朝未满的孩童，如何与我解渴？"清风暗道："这和尚在那口舌场中，是非海里，弄得糊肉胎儿，不识我仙家异宝。"明月上前道："老师，此物叫做'人参果'，吃一个儿不妨。"三藏道："胡说！胡说！他那父母怀胎，不知受了多少苦楚，方生下来。未及三日，怎么就把他拿来当果子？"清风道："实是树上结的。"长老道："乱谈！乱谈！树上又会结出人来？拿过去，不当人子！"

那两个童儿，见千推万阻不吃，只得拿着盘子，转回本房。那果子却也跷蹊，久放不得；若放多时，即僵了，不中吃。二人到于房中，一家一个，坐在床边上，只情吃起。

【9】　噫！原来有这般事哩！他那道房，与那厨房紧紧的间壁。这边悄悄的言语，那边即便听见。八戒正在厨房里做饭，先前听见说，取金击子，拿丹盘，他已在心；又听见他说，唐僧不认得是

人参果，即拿在房里自吃，口里忍不住流涎道："怎得一个儿尝新！"自家身子又狼犺，不能彀得动，只等行者来，与他计较。他在那锅门前，更无心烧火，不时的伸头探脑，出来观看。不多时，见行者牵将马，拴在槐树上，径往后走。那呆子用手乱招道："这里来！这里来！"行者转身，到于厨房门首，道："呆子，你嚷甚的？想是饭不彀吃。且让老和尚吃饱，我们前边大人家，再化吃去罢。"八戒道："你进来，不是饭少。这观里有一个宝贝，你可晓得？"行者道："甚么宝贝？"八戒笑道："说与你，你不曾见；拿与你，你不认得。"行者道："这呆子笑话我老孙。老孙五百年前，因访仙道时，也曾云游在海角天涯。那般儿不曾见？"八戒道："哥啊，人参果你曾见么？"行者惊道："这个真不曾见。但只常闻人说，人参果乃是草还丹，人吃了极能延寿。如今那里有得？"八戒道："他这里有。那童子拿两个与师父吃，那老和尚不认得，道是三朝未满的孩儿，不曾敢吃。那童子老大惫懒，师父不吃，便该让我们，他就瞒着我哩，才自在这隔壁里，一家一个，唧唧哝哝的吃了出去，就急得我口水淬。——怎么得一个儿尝新？我想你有些溜撒，去他那园子里偷几个来尝尝，如何？"行者道："这个容易。老孙去，手到擒来。"急抽身，往前就走。八戒一把扯住道："哥啊，我听得他在这房里说，要拿甚么金击子去打哩。须是干得停当，不可走露风声。"行者道："我晓得，我晓得。"

【10】　那大圣使一个隐身法，闪进道房看时，原来那两个道童，吃了果子，上殿与唐僧说话，不在房里。行者四下里观看，看有甚么金击子，但只见窗棂上挂着一条赤金，有二尺长短，有指头粗细；底下是一个蒜疙疸的头子，上边有眼，系着一根绿绒绳儿。他道："想必就是此物叫做金击子。"他却取下来，出了道房，径入后边去，推开两扇门，抬头观看，——呀！却是一座花园！但见：

> 朱栏宝槛，曲砌峰山。奇花与丽日争妍，翠竹共青天斗碧。流杯亭外，一弯绿柳似拖烟；赏月台前，数簇乔松如泼靛。红拂拂，锦巢榴；绿依依，绣墩草。青茸茸，碧砂兰；攸荡荡，翠丝桐。丹桂映金井梧桐，锦槐傍朱栏玉砌。有的红或白丹竹桃，有的香或黄九秋菊。荼蘼架，映着牡丹亭；木槿台，相连芍药圃。看不尽傲霜君子竹，欺雪大夫松。更

在那鹤庄鹿宅，方沼圆池；泉流碎玉，地镍堆金；朔风触绽
梅花白，春来点破海棠红。——诚所谓人间第一仙景，西方
魁首ực丛。

那行者观看不尽，又见一层门，推开看处，却是一座菜园：

布种四时蔬菜，菠芹莙荙姜苔。
笋篃瓜瓟茭白，葱蒜芫荽韭薤。
窝蕖蕈蒿苦蕒，葫芦茄子须栽。
蔓菁萝卜羊头埋，红苋青菘紫荠。

行者笑道："他也是个自种自吃的道士。"走过菜园，又见一层门。
推开看处，呀！只见那正中间有根大树，真个是青枝馥郁，绿叶阴
森，那叶儿却似芭蕉模样，直上去有千尺余高，根下有七八丈围
圆。那行者倚在树下，往上一看，只见向南的枝上，露出一个人
参果，真个像孩儿一般。原来尾间上是个扢蒂，看它子在枝头，
手脚乱动，点头幌脑，真个像是风儿吹动似乎有声。行者欢喜不尽，暗自
称道："好东西呀！果然罕见！"他倚着树，飕的一声，攀上去。

[11]　那猴子原来第一会爬树偷果子。他把金击子敲了一下，
那果子扑的落将下来。他也随跳下来跟寻，寂然不见；四下里草
中找寻，更无踪影。行者道："跷蹊！跷蹊！想是有脚的会走；想
走也跳不出墙去。我知道了，想是花园中土地不许老孙偷他果
子，他收了去也。"他就捻着诀，念一口"唵"字咒，拘得那花园土
地面前来，对行者施礼道："大圣，呼唤小神，有何吩咐？"行者道：
"你不知老孙是盖天下有名的贼头。我当年偷蟠桃、盗御酒、窃
灵丹，也不曾有人敢与我分用；怎么今日偷他一个果子，你就抽
了我的头分去了！这果子是树上结的，空中过鸟也该有份，老孙
就吃他一个，有何大害？怎么刚打下来，你就捞了去？"土地道：
"大圣，错怪了小神也。这宝贝乃是地仙之物，小神是个鬼仙，怎
么敢拿去？就是闻也无福闻闻。"行者道："你既不曾拿去，如何打
下来就不见了？"土地道："大圣只知这宝贝延寿，更不知他的出
处哩。"

行者道："有甚出处？"土地道："这宝贝，三千年一开花，三千
年一结果，再三千年方得成熟。短头一万年，只结得三十个。有
缘的，闻一闻，就活三百六十岁；吃一个，就活四万七千年。却是

179

只与五行相畏。"行者道:"怎么与五行相畏?"土地道:"这果子遇金而落,遇木而枯,遇水而化,遇火而焦,遇土而入。敲时必用金器,方得下来。打下来,却将盘儿用丝帕衬垫方可;若受些木器,就枯了,吃也不得延寿。吃他须用磁器,清水化开食用,遇火即焦而无用。遇土而人者,大圣方才打落地上,他即钻下土去了。这个土有四万七千年,就是钢钻钻它也钻不动些须,比生铁也还硬三四分。人若吃了,所以长生。大圣不信,可把这地下打打儿看。"行者即揙金箍棒,筑了一下,响一声,迸起棒来,土上更无痕迹。行者道:"果然!果然!我这棍,打石头如粉碎,撞生铁也有痕。怎么这一下打不伤些儿?这等说,我却错怪了你,你回去罢。"那土地即回本庙去讫。

【12】 大圣却有算计:爬上树,一只手使击子,一只手将锦布直裰的襟儿扯起来做个兜子等住,他却串枝分叶,敲了三个果,兜在襟中。跳下树,一直来,径到厨房里去。那八戒笑道:"哥哥,可有么?"行者道:"这个不是?老孙的手到擒来。这个果子,也莫背了沙僧,可叫他一声。"八戒即招手叫道:"悟净,你来。"那沙僧撇下行李,跑进厨房道:"哥哥,叫我怎的?"行者放开衣兜道:"兄弟,你看这个是甚的东西?"沙僧见了道:"是人参果。"行者道:"好啊!你倒认得。你曾在哪里吃过的?"沙僧道:"小弟虽不曾吃,但旧时做卷帘大将,扶侍鸾舆赴蟠桃宴,尝见海外诸仙将此果与王母上寿。见便曾见,却未曾吃。哥哥,可与我些儿尝尝?"行者道:"不消讲,兄弟们一家一个。"

【13】 他三人将三个果各受用。那八戒食肠大,口又大,一则是听见童子吃时,便觉馋虫拱动,却才见了果子,拿过来,张开口,毂辘的囫囵吞咽下肚,却白着眼胡赖,向行者、沙僧道:"你两个吃的是甚么?"沙僧道:"人参果。"八戒道:"甚么味道?"行者道:"悟净,不要睬他!你倒先吃了,又来问谁?"八戒道:"哥哥,吃的忙了些,不像你们细嚼细咽,尝出些滋味。我也不知有核无核,就吞下去了。哥啊,为人为彻;已经调动我这馋虫,再去弄个儿来,老猪细细的吃吃。"行者道:"兄弟,你好不知止足!这个东西,比不得那米食面食,撞着尽饱。像这一万年只结得三十个,我们吃他一个,也是大有缘法,不等小可。罢罢罢!彀了耳!"他

欠起身来，把一个金击子，瞒窗眼儿，丢进他道房里，竟不睬他。

【14】　那呆子只管絮絮叨叨的唧哝，不期那两个道童复进房来取茶去献，只听得八戒还嚷甚么"人参果吃得不快活，再得一个儿吃吃才好。"清风听见，心疑道："明月，你听那长嘴和尚讲'人参果还要个吃吃'。师父别时叮咛，教防他手下人罗唣，莫敢是他偷了我们宝贝么？"明月回头道："哥哥，不好了！不好了！金击子如何落在地下！我们去园里看看来！"他两个急急忙忙的走去，只见花园开了。清风道："这门儿是我关的，如何开了？"又急转过花园，只见菜园门也开了。忙人人参园里，倚在树下，望上查数；颠倒来往，只得二十二个。明月道："你可会算帐？"清风道："我会，你说将来。"明月道："果子原是三十个。师父开园，分吃了两个，还有二十八个；适才打两个与唐僧吃，还有二十六个；如今止剩得二十二个，却不少了四个？不消讲，不消讲，定是那伙恶人偷了，我们只骂唐僧去来。

【15】　两个出了园门，径来殿上，指着唐僧，秃前秃后，秽语污言，不绝口的乱骂；贼头鼠脑，臭短臊长，没好气的胡嚷。唐僧听不过道："仙童啊，你闹的是甚么，消停些儿；有话慢说不妨，不要胡说散道的。"清风说："你的耳聋？我是蛮话，你不省得？你偷了人参果，怎么不容我说？"唐僧道："人参果怎么模样？"明月道："才拿来与你吃，你说像孩童的不是？"唐僧道："阿弥陀佛！那东西一见，我就心惊胆战，还敢偷它吃哩！就是害了馋痨，也不敢干这贼事。不要错怪了人。"清风道："你虽不曾吃，只手下人要偷吃的哩。"三藏道："这等也说得是，你且莫嚷，等我问他们看。果若是偷了，教他赔补。"明月道："赔呀！就有钱那里去买！"三藏道："纵有钱没处买呵，常言道：'仁义值千金。'教他陪你个礼，便罢了。——也还不知是他不是他哩。"明月道："怎的不是他？他那里分不均，还在那里嚷哩。"三藏叫声"徒弟，且都来！"沙僧听见道："不好了，决撒了！老师父叫我们，小童童胡厮骂，不是旧话儿走了风，却是甚的！"行者道："活羞杀人！只为一个吃饮食之类！若说出来，就是我们偷嘴了，只是莫认。"八戒道："正是，正是，昧了罢！"他三人只得出了厨房，走上殿去。咦！毕竟不知怎么与他抵赖，且听下回分解。

Chapter 7

On the Mountain of Infinite Longevity
a Great Immortal Entertains an Old Friend;
In the Wuzhuang Temple Monkey
Steals Manfruit

(Sun Wukong protected the Tang Monk as he traveled west, subduing evil spirits and capturing monsters. The Tang Monk accepted Pig and the Sand Monk as disciples. The Boddhisattva Guanyin and three other gods, wanting to test the meditative minds of the master and his three disciples, changed themselves into four beauties in search of husbands. Only Pig was unable to extinguish his mundane thought, and as a result found himself bound to a tree.)

[1] Sanzang, Monkey and Friar Sand went into the wood and saw the idiot tied up under a tree, yelling and howling in unbearable pain. Monkey went over to him and said with a laugh, "What a son-in-law! So late, and you still haven't got up to thank your mother-in-law or come to tell the good news to the master. Why are you still playing around here? Where's your mother-in-law? Where's your wife? You make a fine, strapped-up, well-beaten son-in-law!" The blockhead, burning with humiliation at being thus mocked, gritted his teeth to stop himself howling in his agony. Friar Sand was overcome with pity when he saw him, and putting down the luggage he went over and untied him. The idiot kowtowed to him in gratitude. He was suffering terrible remorse. There is a poem to the tune *The Moon in the West River* to prove it:

> *Sex is a sword that wounds the body:*
> *Whoever lusts for it will suffer.*
> *A pretty girl of sixteen*
> *Is far more dangerous than a yaksha demon.*

There is only one Origin,
And there are no extra profits to stuff in the sack.
Better store all your capital away,
Guard it well, and don't squander it.

Pig used a pinch of earth to represent burning incense and bowed in worship to Heaven. "Did you recognize the Bodhisattva?" Monkey asked. "I was lying here in a faint and my eyes were seeing stars, so I couldn't tell who it was." Monkey handed him the piece of paper, and when he saw the divine message, Pig was more ashamed than ever. "You're very lucky," said Friar Sand with a laugh, "you've got four Bodhisattvas as your relations now." "Please don't talk about it," said Pig. "I really don't deserve to be human. I'll never misbehave again in future, and even if the effort breaks my bones, I'll rub my shoulder and carry our master's luggage to the West." "That's more like it," said Sanzang.

【2】 Monkey then led his master along the main road. After they had been going for a long time, walking and resting, they saw a high mountain blocking their way. "Disciples," said Sanzang as he reined in the horse and stopped giving it the whip, "we must be very careful on that mountain. There may be fiends and demons on it who will attack us." "With us three followers," said Monkey, "you needn't fear demons." Sanzang, his worries ended, pressed forward. The mountain was certainly a fine one:

The mountain was very high
And craggy was its majesty.
Its roots joined the Kunlun range,
Its summit touched the Milky Way.
White crane came to perch in its locust and cypress trees,
Dark apes hung upside-down from its creepers.
When the sun shone bright on its forests,
It was enveloped in red haze;
When winds sprang from dark valleys,

Coloured clouds scudded across the sky.
Hidden birds called in the green bamboo,
Pheasants fought among the wild flowers.
Thousand-year peaks,
Five-blessing peaks,
Lotus peaks,
Majestically reflecting a delicate light;
Ten thousand year rocks,
Tiger-tooth rocks,
Three Heavens rocks,
Wreathed in subtle and auspicious vapours.
Luxuriant grass in front of the cliff,
The scent of plum blossom on the ridge.
Dense grew the jungle of thorns,
Pure and pale were the orchids.
Deep in the woods the birds gathered round the phoenix;
In an ancient cave a unicorn was chief of the animals.
A delightful stream in a gully
Twisted and turned as it wandered around;
Endless peaks
Coiled about in layer upon layer.
Then there were the green locust trees,
Mottled bamboo,
And bluish pines,
That had been competing in splendour for a thousand years.
White plum blossom,
Red peach,
And emerald willows
Were brilliant as they vied in beauty during spring.
Dragons called and tigers roared,
Cranes danced and apes howled.
Deer emerged from the flowers,
Pheasants sang to the sun.
This was a land of blessing, an Immortals' mountain,
Just like Penglai or Langyuan.

Flowers opened and withered on the mountain top,
Clouds came and went above the peaks along the ridge.

"Disciples," said Sanzang with delight as he sat on his horse, "I've crossed many mountains on my journey west, and they were all steep and rocky, but none of them could be compared to the extraordinarily beautiful scenery here. If this isn't far from the Thunder Monastery, we had better put ourselves in a solemn and reverent mood to meet the Buddha." "It's early days yet," said Monkey with a laugh. "That's not an easy place to get to." "How far are we from Thunder Monastery, elder brother?" asked Friar Sand. "Thirty-six thousand miles," Monkey replied, "and we haven't covered a tenth of it." "How many years will it take us to get there?" Pig asked. "You two younger brothers of mine could manage it in ten days or so, and I could go there fifty times over in a single day and still be back before sunset. But for our master it doesn't bear thinking about." "Tell me, Monkey! how long will it take?" asked Sanzang. "If you went from childhood to old age," said Monkey, "and from old age back to childhood again, and you did it a thousand times over, you'd still find it hard to get there. But if you see your true nature, are determined to be sincere, and always remember to turn your head back to enlightenment, then you will have reached Vulture Peak." "Even if this isn't the Thunder Monastery," said Friar Sand, "good people must live amid such fine scenery as this." "Quite right," said Monkey, "there couldn't be any evil creatures here. This must be the home of holy monks or Immortals. Let's look around here and take our time over it."

[3] This mountain was called the Mountain of Infinite Longevity, and there was a Taoist temple on it called the Wuzhuang Temple. In this temple lived an Immortal whose Taoist name was Zhen Yuan Zi. He was also known as Conjoint Lord of the Age. The temple had a rare treasure, a miraculous tree that had been formed when primeval chaos was first being divided, before the separation of Heaven and Earth. In the four great continents of the world, only the Western Continent of

Cattle-gift's Wuzhuang Temple had this treasure that was known as "Grass-returning Cinnabar" or "manfruit." It took three thousand years to blossom, three thousand years to form the fruit, and another three thousand years for the fruit to ripen, so that very nearly ten thousand years had to pass before the fruit could be eaten. Only thirty fruit were formed each ten thousand years, and they were shaped just like a newborn baby, complete with limbs and sense organs. Anyone whose destiny permitted him to smell one would live for three hundred and sixty years, and if you ate one you would live for forty-seven thousand years.

【4】 That day the Great Immortal Zhen Yuan had received an invitation from the Original Celestial Jade Pure One inviting him to the Miluo Palace in the Heaven of Supreme Purity to hear a lecture on the Product of Undifferentiated Unity. The Immortals who had studied under this great Immortal were too numerous to count, and he now had forty-eight disciples who had all attained to the full truth of the Way. That day, the Great Immortal took forty-six of them with him to hear the lecture in the upper world, leaving the two youngest, Pure Wind and Bright Moon, to look after the temple. Pure Wind was 1,320 years old, and Bright Moon had just turned 1,200. The Great Immortal gave his instructions to the two boys: "As I must obey the summons of the Original Celestial Jade Pure One and go to the Miluo Palace to hear a lecture, you two will have to look after the temple carefully. An old friend of mine will be coming this way before long, and you must entertain him very well indeed. You can pick two manfruits for him as a token of our old friendship." "Who is this old friend of yours, master?" the boys asked. "Please tell us who he is so that we can entertain him properly." "He is a priest sent by the Tang Emperor in the East," the Great Immortal replied, "and he is known as Sanzang. He is the monk going to worship the Buddha and ask for the scriptures in the Western Heaven." "Confucius said, 'Don't have anything to do with people of a different Way'," replied the boys with smiles. "Ours is the esoteric sect of the Great Monad, so why ever are you friends with that Buddhist monk?" "You are not aware," the

Great Immortal replied, "that he is a reincarnation of the Golden Cicada, the second disciple of the Tathagata Buddha, that ancient sage of the West. I made his acquaintance at an Ullambana assembly where he gave me tea with his own hands. As this disciple of the Buddha paid me such an honour, I regard him as an old friend."

When the two Immortal boys heard this, they accepted their master's orders. Just as he was on the point of setting out, the Great Immortal gave them some more instructions: "There are a limited number of those manfruits. You must only give two, and not one more." "When the garden was opened we all shared two," said the boys, "and there are twenty-eight now left on the tree. We won't use more than two." "Although the Tang Priest is an old friend of mine," said the Great Immortal, "you must be on your guard against his gangster underlings, and you mustn't let them know about the manfruit." The Great Immortal then flew up to Heaven with the rest of his disciples.

【5】 The Tang Priest and his three followers, meanwhile, were enjoying themselves strolling on the mountain when they noticed some tall buildings rising above a bamboo grove. "What do you think that is?" Sanzang asked Monkey, who replied, "It's either a Taoist temple or a Buddhist one. Let's go over and find out." It did not take them long to reach the gate, and they saw

> A cool pine-covered slope,
> A tranquil path through the bamboo.
> White cranes brought floating clouds,
> Monkeys and apes offered fruit.
> Before the gate was a wide pool, and the shadows of the trees were long;
> In the cracks of the rocks grew moss.
> Many a purple hall was massed together;
> A red aura enveloped the lofty towers.
> It certainly was a blessed place,
> A cloud cave on Penglai.
> In its pure emptiness little happened;

Its stillness gave birth to thoughts of the Way.
Green birds often brought letters from the Queen Mother;
Purple pheasants carried the classics of Lord Lao Zi.
There was a majestic air of the Way and its Power—
It was indeed a divine Immortal's home.

Sanzang dismounted and saw that there was a stone tablet outside the gate on which was inscribed in large letters:

BLESSED LAND OF THE MOUNTAIN OF INFINITE LONGEVITY
CAVE HEAVEN OF THE WUZHUANG TEMPLE

"You were right," said Sanzang, "it is a Taoist temple." "Good people must live in this temple," said Friar Sand, "set as it is in such fresh, light scenery. Let's go in and have a look round. When we go back to the East at the end of our journey; this will be one of the finest sights we'll have seen." "Well spoken," said Monkey, and they all went in. On the next gate was pasted the couplet:

"Residence of Divine Immortals Who Never Grow Old;
Home of Taoists as Ancient as Heaven."

"This Taoist tries to intimidate people by talking big," said Monkey with a laugh. "When I wrecked the Heavenly Palace five hundred years ago I never saw anything like that over the gate of the Supreme Lord Lao Zi." "Never mind him," said Pig. "Let's go in. This Taoist may well be quite a decent bloke."

As they went through the second gate they saw two boys come scurrying out. This is what they looked like:

Pure bones, lively spirits, pretty faces,
And hair tied in childish tufts.
Their Taoist robes naturally wreathed in mist,
The sleeves of their feather clothes were floating in the

188

wind.

> *Their jade belts were tied with dragon-head knots,*
> *Their grass sandals lightly fastened with silk.*
> *In their elegance they were unlike common mortals—*
> *The Taoist boys Pure Wind and Bright Moon.*

The two boys bowed and came out to greet them. "We are sorry we did not welcome you properly, venerable master," they said. "Please sit down." Sanzang was delighted, and he accompanied the two boys up to the main hall of the temple, which faced south. There was a patterned lattice window that let through the light on top of the door that the boys pushed open. They asked the Tang Priest to come in, and he saw two huge words executed in many colours hanging on the wall—Heaven and Earth. There was an incense table of red carved lacquer on which stood a pair of golden censers and a supply of incense.

【6】 Sanzang went over to the table and put a pinch of incense in the censers with his left hand while performing triple reverences. Then he turned round to the boys and said, "This temple is a home of Immortals in the Western Continent, so why don't you worship the Three Pure Ones, the Four Emperors, and all the ministers of Heaven? Why do you burn incense to the two words 'Heaven' and 'Earth'?" "To be frank with you, venerable teacher," the boys replied with smiles, "it's quite right to worship the top word, 'Heaven', but the bottom one, 'Earth', gets no incense from us. Our teacher only put them up to ingratiate himself." "How does he ingratiate himself?" Sanzang asked. "The Three Pure Ones and the Four Emperors are our teacher's friends," the boys replied, "the Nine Bright Shiners are his juniors, and the Constellations are his underlings."

When Monkey heard this he collapsed with laughter, and Pig asked him, "What are you laughing at?" "They say that I get up to no good, but these Taoist boys really tell whoppers." "Where is your teacher?" Sanzang asked them. "He had an invitation from the Original Celestial Jade Pure One and has gone to the Palace in the Heaven of Supreme Purity to hear a lecture on

189

the Product of Undifferentiated Unity, so he's not at home."

At this Monkey could not help roaring, "Stinking Taoist boys, you don't know who you're talking to. You play your dirty tricks in front of our faces and pretend to be oh-so-innocent. What Heavenly Immortal of the Great Monad lives in the Miluo Palace? Who invited your cow's hoof of a master to a lecture?" Sanzang was worried that now he had lost his temper the boys would answer back and spark off a disastrous fight, so he said, "Don't quarrel with them, Wukong. We'll be going in a minute, so we obviously need have nothing to do with them. Besides, as the saying goes, 'egrets don't eat egret flesh'. Their master isn't here anyway, so there would be no point in wrecking the place. Go and graze the horse outside the gate. Friar Sand, you look after the luggage, and tell Pig to take some rice from our bundles and use their kitchen to make our meal. When we go we shall give them a few coppers for the firewood. All do as I've told you and leave me here to rest. When we have eaten we shall be on our way again." The three of them went off to do their jobs.

[7] Bright Moon and Pure Wind were meanwhile quietly praising Sanzang to each other: "What a splendid monk. He is indeed the beloved sage of the West in mortal form, and his true nature is not at all befuddled. The master told us to entertain him and give him some manfruit as a token of their old friendship, and he also warned us to be on our guard against those gangsters of his. They have murderous-looking faces and coarse natures. Thank goodness he sent them away, because if they were still with him, we wouldn't be able to give him the manfruit." "We don't yet know whether this monk is our master's old friend or not," said Pure Wind. "We'd better ask him to make sure." The two of them then went over to Sanzang and said, "May we ask you, venerable master, whether you are the Sanzang of the Great Tang who is going to the Western Heaven to fetch the scriptures?" "Yes, I am," said Sanzang, returning their bows. "How did you know who I was?" "Our master told us before he went," they replied, "to go out to meet you long before you got here, but as you came faster then we expected we failed to do so.

Please sit down, teacher, while we fetch you some tea." "I am honoured," said Sanzang. Bright Moon hurried out and came back with a cup of fragrant tea for him. When Sanzang had drunk the tea, Pure Wind said to Bright Moon, "We must do as our teacher told us and fetch the fruit."

[8] The two boys left Sanzang and went to their room, where one of them picked up a golden rod and the other a red dish, on which he put many a silk handkerchief as cushioning. They went into the manfruit orchard, where Pure Wind climbed the tree and tapped the fruit with the golden rod while Bright Moon waited below to catch them in the dish. They only took a few moments to knock down and catch a couple, which they took to the front hall to offer to Sanzang with the words, "This temple of ours is on a remote and desolate mountain, master Sanzang, and there is no local delicacy we can offer you except these two pieces of fruit. We hope they will quench your thirst." At the sight of the manfruit the monk recoiled some three feet, shaking with horror. "Goodness me!" he exclaimed. "How could you be so reduced to starvation in this year of plenty as to eat human flesh? And how could I possibly quench my thirst with a newborn baby?" "This monk has developed eyes of flesh and a mortal body in the battlefield of mouths and tongues and the sea of disputation," thought Pure Wind, "and he can't recognize the treasures of this home of Immortals." "Venerable master," said Bright Moon, "this is what is called 'manfruit', and there is no reason why you should not eat one." "Nonsense, nonsense," said Sanzang. "They were conceived by their fathers and mothers and had to go through no end of suffering before they were born. How can you treat them as fruit when they haven't been alive for three days yet?" "They really and truly grew on a tree," said Pure Wind. "Stuff and rubbish," Sanzang replied. "Babies don't grow on trees. Take them away, you inhuman beasts."

As he refused absolutely to eat them, the two boys had to take the dish away and go back to their room. This fruit was rather difficult to handle, and did not keep for long without becoming hard and inedible, so the boys sat on their beds and ate

191

one each.

[9] Oh dear! What a thing to happen! There was only a wall separating their room from the kitchen, where their whispering could be clearly heard. Pig was in there cooking the rice when he heard them talk as they fetched the golden rod and the red dish. Later he heard them saying that the Tang Priest had not recognized the manfruit, which was why they took them back to their room to eat. "I'd love to try one, but I don't know how," thought Pig, unable to prevent his mouth from watering. Too stupid to do anything about it himself, he had to wait until he could talk it over with Brother Monkey. He had now lost all interest in stoking the stove as he stood in front of it, constantly poking his head outside the kitchen to look for Monkey. Before long Monkey appeared leading the horse, which he tethered to a locust tree. As he came round to the back, the blockhead waved frantically to him and said, "Come here, come here." Monkey turned round, came to the kitchen door, and said, "What are you yelling for, idiot? Not enough food for you? Let the old monk eat his fill, then we two can go to the next big house that lies ahead and beg for some more." "Come in," said Pig, "it's not that. Do you know that there's a treasure in this temple?" "What treasure?" Monkey asked. "I can't describe it because you've never seen it," said Pig, "and if I gave it to you, you wouldn't know what it was." "Don't try to make a fool of me, idiot," said Monkey. "When I studied the Way of Immortality five hundred years ago I travelled on my cloud to the corners of the ocean and the edge of the sky. I've seen everything." "Have you seen manfruit then?" Pig asked. "No, I haven't," said Monkey with astonishment. "But I've heard that manfruit is Grass-returning Cinnabar, and that anyone who eats it lives to a great old age. Where can we get some?" "Here," said Pig. "Those boys gave two to our master, but that old monk didn't know what they were and thought they were newborn babies. He wouldn't eat them. Those boys are disgraceful—instead of giving them to us as they should have done they sneaked off into their room and had one each, gobble, gobble, gobble—I was drooling. I wish I knew how I could try one. Surely you've got some dodge for getting into the orchard and pinching a few for us to taste. You have, haven't you?" "Easy," said Monkey. "I'll go in and pick some." As he rushed out Pig grabbed him and said, "I heard them saying in their room that they needed a golden rod to knock them down with. You must do this very carefully—nobody must know about it." "I know, I know," replied Monkey.

[10] The Great Sage made himself invisible and slipped into the boys' room, only to find that after eating the fruit they had gone to the front hall, where they were talking to Sanzang. Monkey looked all around the room for the golden rod until he saw a two-foot length of gold hanging from the window lattice. It was about as thick as a finger. At the bottom was a lump like a bulb of garlic, and at the top was a hole through which was fastened a green silk tassel. "So this must be what they call the golden rod," he thought as he took it down. He left the room and pushed open a pair of gates at the back. Goodness! He saw a garden

> With red, jewelled balconies
> And a twisting artificial hill.
> Rare flowers try to outshine the sun,
> The bamboo attempts to be bluer than the sky.
> Outside the Floating Cup Pavilion
> A curve of willows hangs like mist;
> Before the Platform to Admire the Moon
> Clumps of lofty pines make splashes of indigo.
> Bright, bright red,
> The pomegranate thicket;
> Deep, deep green,
> The cushions of grass.
> Richly blue
> Were the jade-coloured orchids;
> Rushing and powerful
> The water in the stream.
> Crimson cassia blazed beside golden wells and wutong
> trees.

Brocade-rich locust trees flanked red balconies and steps.
There was peach blossom in pink and white,
Yellow and fragrant chrysanthemums that have seen nine autumns.
Trellises of raspberries
Flourish by the peony pavilion;
Banks of hibiscus
Lead to beds of tree-peonies.
There is no end of noble bamboos that have held out against frost.
Or lordly pines that defy the snows.
Then there are nests of cranes and houses for deer,
Square ponds and round pools,
Spring water like fragments of jade,
Golden heaps of flowers.
The north wind bursts the white plum blossom open.
When spring comes, it touches the crab-apple with red.
It can be rightly called the most splendid view on Earth,
The finest garden in the west.

Before Monkey had time to take all of this in he saw another gate. When he pushed it open he saw

Vegetables for each of the four seasons—
Spinach, celery, beetroot, ginger, and kelp,
Bamboo shoots, sweet potato, melons, oblong gourd and wild rice stem,
Onions, garlic, coriander, scallion and shallots,
Lettuce, artemisia, and bitter alisma,
Gourds and aubergines that must be planted,
Rutabaga, turnips, docks,
Red amaranth, green cabbage, and purple mustard-plant.

"So they're Taoists who grow their own food," thought Monkey, smiling to himself. When he had crossed the vegetable garden he saw yet another gate, and when he opened it there was a huge tree in front of him with fragrant branches and shade-giving green leaves shaped rather like those of plantains. The tree was about a thousand feet high, and its trunk was some seventy or eighty feet round. Monkey leant against it and looked up, and on a branch that was pointing south he saw a manfruit, which really did look just like a newborn child. The stem came from its bottom, and as it hung from the branch its hands and feet waved wildly around and it shook its head. Monkey was thoroughly delighted, and he thought in admiration, "What a splendid thing—a real rarity, a real rarity." And with that thought he went shooting up the tree.

[11]   Now there is nothing that monkeys are better at than climbing trees to steal fruit, and one blow from the golden rod sent the manfruit tumbling down. He jumped down to fetch it, but it was nowhere to be seen. He searched the grass all around, but could find not a trace of it. "That's odd," he thought, "very odd indeed. It must be able to use its feet—but even then it won't be able to get past the wall. No, I've got it. The local deity of this garden has hidden it away to stop me stealing it." He made some finger magic and uttered the sacred sound "Om," which forced the garden deity to come forward, bow and say, "You summoned me, Great Sage. What are your orders?" "Surely you know," Monkey said, "that I am the most famous criminal on earth. When I stole the sacred peaches, the imperial wine, and the elixir of immortality some years ago, nobody dared to try and take a cut. How comes it that when I take some fruit today you pinch my very first one? This fruit grows on a tree, and the birds of the air must have their share of it, so what harm will be done if I eat one? Why did you snatch it the moment it fell down?" "Great Sage," the deity replied, "don't be angry with me. These treasures belong to the Immortals of the Earth, and I am a ghost Immortal, so I would never dare take one. I've never even had the good fortune to smell one." "If you didn't take it, why did it disappear the moment I knocked it down from the tree?" Monkey asked. "You may know that these treasures give eternal life, Great Sage," the deity replied, "but you don't know about their

origin."

"Where do they come from, then?" Monkey asked. "These treasures," the deity replied, "take three thousand years to blossom, another three thousand to form, and three thousand more to ripen. In almost ten thousand years only thirty grow. Anyone lucky enough to smell one will live for three hundred and sixty years, and if you eat one you will live to be forty-seven thousand. These fruit fear only the Five Elements." "What do you mean, 'fear only the Five Elements'?" Monkey asked. "If they meet metal," the deity said, "they fall; if they meet wood they rot; if they meet water they dissolve; if they meet fire they are burnt; and if they meet earth they go into it. If you tap them you have to use a golden rod, otherwise they won't drop; and when you knock them down you must catch them in a bowl padded with silk handkerchiefs. If they come in contact with wooden utensils they rot, and even if you eat one it won't make you live any longer. When you eat them you must do so off porcelain, and they should be cooked in clear water. If they come in contact with fire they become charred and useless, and they go into any earth they touch. When you knocked one to the ground just now it went straight in, and as the earth here will now live for forty-seven thousand years you wouldn't be able to make any impression on it even with a steel drill: it's much harder than wrought iron. But if a man eats one he wins long life. Try hitting the ground if you don't believe me." Monkey raised his gold-ringed cudgel and brought it down on the ground. There was a loud noise as the cudgel sprank back. The ground was unmarked. "So you're right," said Monkey, "you're right. This cudgel of mine can smash rocks to powder and even leave its mark on wrought iron, but this time it did no damage at all. This means that I was wrong to blame you. You may go back now." At this the local deity went back to his shrine.

【12】 The Great Sage now had a plan. He climbed the tree and then held the rod in one hand while he undid the lapel of his cloth tunic and made it into a kind of pouch. He pushed the leaves and branches aside and knocked down three manfruits, which he caught in his tunic. He jumped out of the tree and went straight to the kitchen, where a smiling Pig asked him if he had got any. "This is the stuff, isn't it?" said Monkey. "I was able to get some. We mustn't leave Friar Sand in the dark, so give him a shout." "Come here, Friar Sand," Pig called, waving his hand. Friar Sand put the luggage down, hurried into the kitchen, and asked, "Why did you call me?" "Do you know what these are?" Monkey asked, opening his tunic. "Manfruits," said Friar Sand as soon as he saw them. "Good," said Monkey, "you know what they are. Where have you eaten them?" "I've never eaten them," Friar Sand replied, "but when I was the Curtain-lifting General in the old days I used to escort the imperial carriage to the Peach Banquets, and I saw some that Immortals from over the seas brought as birthday presents for the Queen Mother. I've certainly seen them, but I've never tasted one. Please give me a bit to try." "No need to ask," said Monkey. "We're having one each."

[13]   So each of them had one manfruit to eat. Pig had both an enormous appetite and an enormous mouth, and had, moreover, been suffering pangs of hunger ever since hearing the Taoist boys eating. So the moment he saw the fruit he grabbed one, opened his mouth, and gulped it down whole; then he put on an innocent expression and shamelessly asked the other two what they were eating. "Manfruit," Friar Sand replied. "What does it taste like?" Pig asked. "Ignore him, Friar Sand," said Monkey. "He's already eaten his, and he's no business to ask you." "Brother," said Pig, "I ate mine too fast. I didn't nibble it delicately and taste the flavour like you two. I don't even know if it had a stone or not as I gulped it straight down. You should finish what you've started: you've whetted my appetite, so you ought to get me another to eat slowly." "You're never satisfied," Monkey replied. "These things aren't like rice or flour—you can't go stuffing yourself full of them. Only thirty grow in every ten thousand years, so we can think ourselves very lucky indeed to have a whole one each. Come off it, Pig, you've had enough." He got up, slipped into the Taoist boys' room with the golden rod, and put it back without letting himself be seen through the

197

window. He paid no more attention to Pig, who went on grumbling.

【14】 Before long the Taoist boys were back in their room, and they heard Pig moaning, "I didn't enjoy my manfruit; I wish I could have another." Pure Wind's suspicion were aroused, and he said to Bright Moon, "Did you hear that long-snouted monk saying he wished he could have another manfruit? Our master told us when he went that we were to be careful of those gangsters and not let them steal our treasures." "This is terrible, terrible," said Bright Moon. "What's the golden rod doing on the floor? We'd better go into the garden and take a look around." The two of them hurried out and found the garden gates open. "We shut this gate," said Pure Wind, "so why is it open?" They rushed round the flower garden, found the vegetable garden gate open too, and tore into the manfruit garden. They leant on the tree and looked up into it to count the fruit, but however often they added the number up, it always came to twenty-two. "Can you do arithmetic?" Bright Moon asked, and Pure Wind replied, "Yes. Tell me the figures." "There were originally thirty manfruits," said Bright Moon. "When our master opened the garden two were divided up and eaten, which left twenty-eight. Just now we knocked two down to give the Tang Priest, which left twenty-six. But there are only twenty-two now, which means that we're four short. It goes without saying that those bad men must have stolen them. Let's go and tell that Tang Priest what we think of him."

【15】 The two of them went from the garden to the front hall, where they pointed at Sanzang and poured the most filthy and stinking abuse on him, calling him "baldy" this and "baldy" that. It was more than Sanzang could stand, so he said, "What are you making all this fuss about, Immortal boys? Please stop. I wouldn't mind you being a bit offhand with me, but you can't talk in this outrageous way." "Are you deaf?" Pure Wind asked. "We're not talking a foreign language, and you can understand us perfectly well. You've stolen our manfruit, and you've no right to forbid us to mention it." "What does manfruit look like?"

Sanzang asked. "It's what we offered you just now and you said looked like babies." "Amitabha Buddha!" Sanzang exclaimed. "I shook with terror at the very sight of them—I couldn't possibly steal one. Even if I were being racked by the most terrible greed, I could never commit the crime of eating one of those. What do you mean by making so unjust an accusation?" "Although you didn't eat any," said Pure Wind, "those underlings of yours stole and ate some." "Even if they did, you shouldn't shout like that. Wait till I've questioned them. If they stole some, I'll see that they make it up to you." "Make it up?" said Bright Moon. "They are things that money can't buy." "Well then," said Sanzang, "if money won't buy them, 'decent behaviour is worth a thousand pieces of gold,' as the saying goes. I'll make them apologize to you, and that will be that. Besides, we still don't know whether they did it." "Of course they did," retorted Bright Moon. "They're still quarrelling in there because they were divided unfairly." "Come here, disciples," called Sanzang.

"We've had it," said Friar Sand when he heard Sanzang calling. "The game's up. Our master is calling us and the young Taoists are swearing and cursing. The cat must be out of the bag." "How disgraceful," said Monkey, "all that fuss about some food. But if we confess it, they'll say it was stealing food; the best thing is not to admit it at all." "Quite right, quite right, we'll cover it up," said Pig, and three of them went from the kitchen to the hall. If you don't know how they denied it, listen to the explanation in the next instalment.

8. 镇元仙赶捉取经僧
孙行者大闹五庄观

【1】　却说他兄弟三众，到了殿上，对师父道："饭将熟了，叫我们怎的？"三藏道："徒弟，不是问饭。他这观里，有甚么人参果，似孩子一般的东西，你们是那一个偷他的吃了？"八戒道："我老实。不晓得。不曾见。"清风道："笑的就是他！笑的就是他！"行者喝道："我老孙生的是这个笑容儿，莫成为你不见了甚么果子，就不容我笑？"三藏道："徒弟息怒。我们是出家人，休打诳语，莫吆昧心食。果然吃了他的，赔他个礼罢。何苦这般抵赖？"

【2】　行者见师父说得有理，他就实说道："师父，不干我事。是八戒隔壁听见那两个道童吃甚么人参果，他想一个儿尝新，着老孙打了三个，我兄弟各人吃了一个，如今吃也吃了，待要怎么？明月道："偷了我四个，这和尚还说不是贼哩！"八戒道："阿弥陀佛！既是偷了四个，怎么只拿出三个来分，预先就打起一个偏手？"那呆子倒转胡嚷。

【3】　二仙童问得是实，越加毁骂。就恨得个大圣钢牙咬响，火眼睁圆，把条金箍棒捏得了又揾，忍了又忍道："这童子这样可恶，只说当面打人，也罢，受他些气儿，等我送他个绝后计，教他大家都吃不成！"好行者，把脑后的毫毛拨下一根，吹口仙气，叫"变！"变做个假行者，跟定唐僧，陪着悟能、悟净，忍受着道童嚷骂；他的真身，出一个神，纵云头，跳将起来，径到人参园里，掣金箍棒往树上乒乓一下，又使个推山移岭的神力，把树一推推倒。可怜叶落桠开根出土，道人断绝草还丹！那大圣推倒树，却在枝儿上寻果子，那里得有半个。原来这宝贝遇金而落，他的棒刃头却是金裹之物，况铁又是五金之类，所以敲着就振下来了，既下来，又遇土而入，因此上边再没一个果子。他道："好！好！好！大家散火！"他收了铁棒，径往前走，把毫毛一抖，收上身来。那些人

200

肉眼凡胎,看不明白。

【4】 却说那仙童骂彀多时,清风道:“明月,这些和尚也受得气哩,我们就像骂鸡一般,骂了这半会,通没个招声。想必他不曾偷吃。倘或树高叶密,数得不明,不要诳骂了他。我和你再去查查。”明月道:“也说得是。”他两个果又到园中,只见那树倒桠开,果无叶落。唬得清风脚软跌跟头,明月腰酥打骸垢。那两个魂飞魄散。有诗为证。诗曰:

三藏西临万寿山,悟空断送草还丹。
桠开叶落仙根露,明月清风心胆寒。

他两个倒在尘埃,语言颠倒,只叫“怎的好!怎的好!害了我五庄观里的丹头,断绝我仙家的苗裔!师父来家,我两个怎的回话?”明月道:“师兄莫嚷。我们且整了衣冠,莫要惊张了这几个和尚。这个没有别人,定是那个毛脸雷公嘴的那厮,他来出神弄法,坏了我们的宝贝。若是与他分说,那厮毕竟抵赖,定要与他相争,争起来,就要交手相打,你想我们两个,怎么敌得过他四个?且不如去哄他一哄,只说果子不少,我们错数了,转与他陪个不是。他们的饭已熟了,等他吃饭时,再贴他些儿小菜。他一家拿着一个碗,你却站在门左,我却站在门右,扑的把门关倒,把锁锁住,将这几层门都锁了,不要放他。待师父来家,凭他怎的处置。他又是师父的故人,饶了他,也是师父的人情;不饶他,我们也拿住个贼在,庶几可以免我等之罪。”清风闻言道:“有理!有理!”

【5】 他两个强打精神,勉生欢喜,从后园中径来殿上,对唐僧控背躬身道:“师父,适间言语粗俗,多有冲撞,莫怪,莫怪。”三藏问道:“怎么说?”清风道:“果子不少,只因树高叶密,不曾看得明白;才然又去查查,还是原数。”那八戒就趁脚儿跷道:“你这个童儿,年幼不知事体,就来乱骂,白口咀咒,枉赖了我们也!不当人子!”行者心上明白,口里不言,心中暗想道:“是谎!是谎!果子已了了帐,怎的说这般话?…… 想必有起死回生之法。……”三藏道:“既如此,盛将饭来,我们吃了去罢。”

那八戒便去盛饭,沙僧安放桌椅。二童忙取小菜,却是些酱瓜、酱茄、糟萝卜、醋豆角、腌窝蕖、绰芥菜,共排了七八碟儿,与师徒们吃饭;又提一壶好茶,两个茶钟,伺侯左右。那师徒四众,却才拿起碗来，这童儿一边一个，扑的把门关上，插上一把两鑞铜锁。八戒笑道："这童子差了。你这里风俗不好，却怎的关了门里吃饭？"明月道："正是，正是，好歹吃了饭儿开门。"清风骂道："我把你这个害馋痨、偷嘴的秃贼！你偷吃了我的仙果，已该一个擅食田园瓜果之罪，却又把我的仙树推倒，坏了我五庄观里仙根，你还要说嘴哩！——若能彀到得西方参佛面，只除是转背摇车再托生！"三藏闻言，丢下饭碗，把个石头放在心上。那童子将那前山门、二山门，通都上了锁。却又去正殿门首，恶语恶言，贼前贼后，只骂到天色将晚，才去吃饭。饭毕，归房去了。

【6】 唐僧埋怨行者道："你这个猴头，番番撞祸！你偷吃了他的果子，就受他些气儿，让他骂几句便也罢了；怎么又推倒他的树！若论这般情由，告起状来，就是你老子做官，也说不通。"行者道："师父莫闹。那童儿都睡去了，只等他睡着了，我们连夜起身。"沙僧道："哥哥，几层门都上了锁，闭得甚紧，如何走么！"行者笑道："莫管！莫管！老孙自有法儿。"八戒道："愁你没有法儿哩！你一变，变甚么虫蛭儿，瞒格子眼里就飞将出去，只苦了我们不会变的，便在此顶缸受罪哩！"唐僧道："他若干出这个勾当，不同你我出去啊，我念念起旧话经儿，他却怎生消受！"八戒闻言，又愁又笑道："师父，你说的那里话？我只听得佛教中有卷《楞严经》、《法华经》、《孔雀经》、《观音经》、《金刚经》，不曾听见个甚那'旧话儿经'啊。"行者道："兄弟，你不知道。我顶上戴的这个箍儿，是观音菩萨赐与我师父的；师父哄我戴了，就如生根的一般，莫想拿得下来；——叫做《紧箍儿咒》，又叫做《紧箍儿经》。他念'旧话儿经'，即此是也。但若念动，我就头疼，故有这个法儿难我。师父，你莫念，我决不负你，管情大家一齐出去。"

【7】 说话肯，都已天昏，不觉东方月上。行者道："此时万籁无声，冰轮明显，正好走了去罢。"八戒道："哥啊，不要捣鬼。门俱锁闭，往那里走？"行者道："你看手段！"好行者，把金箍棒捻在手中，使一个"解锁法"，往门上一指，只听得突磮的一声响，几层门双鑞锁俱落，唿喇的开了门扇。八戒笑道："好本事！就是叫小炉儿匠使掭子，便也不像这等爽利！"行者道："这个门儿，有甚稀罕！就是南天门，指一指也开了。"却请师父出了门，上了马，八戒挑

着担，沙僧拢着马，径投西路而去。行者道："你们且慢行。"等老孙去照顾那两个童儿睡一个月。"三藏道："徒弟，不可伤他性命；不然，又一个得财伤人的罪了。"行者道："我晓得。"行者复进去，来到那童儿睡的房门外。他腰里有带的瞌睡虫儿，原来在东天门与增长天王猜枚耍子赢的。他摸出两个来，瞒窗眼儿弹将进去，径奔到那童子脸上，鼾鼾沉睡，再莫想得醒。他才拽开云步，赶上唐僧，顺大路一直西奔。

　　这一夜马不停蹄，只行到天晓。三藏道："这个猴头弄杀我也！你因为嘴，带累我一夜无眠！"行者道："不要只管埋怨。天色明了，你且在这路旁边树林中将就歇歇，养养精神再走。"那长老只得下马，倚松根权做禅床坐下。沙僧歇了担子打盹。八戒枕着石睡觉。孙大圣偏有心肠，你看他跳树扳枝顽耍。四众歇息不题。

【8】　　却说那大仙自元始宫散会，领众小仙出离兜率，径下瑶天，坠祥云，早来到万寿山五庄观门首。看时，见观门大开，地上干净。大仙道："清风、明月，却也中用。常时节，日高三丈，腰也不伸；今日我们不在，他倒肯起早，开门扫地。"众小仙惧悦。行至殿上，香火全无，人踪俱寂，那里有明月、清风！大仙道："他两个想是因我们不在，拐了东西走了。"大仙道："岂有此理！修仙的人，敢有这般坏心的事！想是昨晚忘却关门，就去睡了，今早还未醒哩。"众仙到他房门首着看处，真个关着房门，鼾鼾沉睡；这外边打门乱叫，那里叫得醒来。众仙撬开门板，着手扑下床来，也只是不醒。大仙笑道："好仙童啊！成仙的人，神满再不瞌睡，却怎么这般困倦？莫不是有人作弄了他也？快取水来。"一童急取水半瓯递与大仙。大仙念动咒语，喷一口水，喷在脸上，一随即解了睡魔。

【9】　　二人方醒，忽睁睛，抹抹脸，抬头观看，认得是仙师与世同君和师兄等众，慌得那清风顿首，明月叩头道："师父呵！你的故人，原是'东来的和尚，———一伙强盗'十分凶狠！"

　　大仙笑道："莫惊恐，慢慢的说来。"清风道："师父啊，当日别后不久，果有个东土唐僧，一行有四个和尚，连马五口。弟子不敢违了师命，问及来因，将人参果取了两个奉上。那长老俗眼愚

203

心，不识我们仙家的宝贝。他说是三朝未满的孩童，再三不吃，是弟子各吃了一个。不期他那手下有三个徒弟，有一个姓孙的，名悟空行者，先偷四个果子吃了。是弟子们向伊理说，实实的言语了几句，他却不容，暗自里弄了个出神的手段，——苦啊！……"二童子说到此处，止不住腮边泪落。众仙道："那和尚打来？"明月道："不曾打，只是把我们人参树打倒了。"大仙闻言，更不恼怒。道："莫哭！莫哭！你不知那姓孙的，也是个太乙金仙，也曾大闹天宫，神通广大。既然打倒了宝树，你可认得那些和尚？"清风道："都认得。"大仙道："既认得，都跟我来。众徒弟们，都收拾下刑具，等我回来打他。"

【10】 众仙领命。大仙与明月、清风纵起祥光，来赶三藏，倾刻间就有千里之遥。大仙在云端里平西观看，不见唐僧；及转头向东看时，倒多赶了九百余里。原来那长老一日马不停蹄，只行了一百二十里路，大仙的云头一纵，赶过了九百余里。仙童道："师父，那路旁树下坐的是唐僧。"大仙道："我已见了。你两个回去安排下绳索，等我自家拿他。清风……先回不题。

那大仙按落云头，摇身一变，变做个行脚全真。你道他怎生模样：

> 穿一领百衲袍，系一条吕公绦。手摇麈尾，渔鼓轻敲。三耳草鞋登脚下，九阳巾子把头包。飘飘风满袖，口唱月儿高。

径直来到树下，对唐僧高叫道："长老，贫道起手了。"那长老忙答礼道："失瞻！失瞻！"大仙问："长老是那方来的？为何在途中打坐？"三藏道："贫僧乃东土大唐差往西天取经者。路过此间，权为一歇。"大仙佯讶道："长老东来，可曾在荒山经过？"长老道："不知仙官是何宝山？"大仙道："万寿山五庄观，便是贫道栖止处。"

【11】 行者闻言，他心中有物的人，忙答道："不曾！不曾！我们是打上路来的。"那大仙指定笑道："我把你这个泼猴！你瞒谁哩？你倒在我观里，把我人参树打倒了，你连夜走在此间，还不招认，遮饰甚么！不要走！趁早去还我树来！"那行者闻言，心中恼怒，掣铁棒不容分说，望大仙劈头就打。大仙侧身躲过，踏祥光，径

204

到空中。行者也腾云，急赶上去。大仙在半空现了本相，你看他怎生扮扮：

> 头戴紫金冠，无忧鹤氅穿。履鞋登足下，丝带束腰间。体如童子貌，面似美人颜。三须飘领下，鸦翎叠鬓边。相迎行者无兵器，止将玉麈手中拈。

那行者没高没低的，棍子乱方三回合，使一个"袖里乾坤"的手段，在云端里把袍袖迎风轻轻的一展，刷地前来，把四僧连马一袖子笼住。八戒道："不好了！我们都装在袼褳里了！"行者道："呆子，不是袼褳，我们被他笼在衣袖中哩。"八戒道："这个不打紧；等我一顿钉钯，筑他个窟窿，脱将下去，只说他不小心，笼不牢，吊的了罢！"那呆子使钯乱筑，那里筑得动：手捏着虽然是个软的，筑起来就比铁还硬。

【12】那大仙转祥云，径落五庄观坐下，叫徒弟拿绳来。众小仙一一伺候。你看他从袖子里，却像捉揭偶一般，把唐僧拿出，缚在正殿檐柱上；又拿出他三个，每一根柱上，绑了一个；将马也拿出拴在庭下，与他些草料；行李抛在廊下，又道："徒弟，这和尚是出家人，不可用刀枪，不可加铁钺，且与我取出皮鞭来，打他一顿，与我人参果出气！"众仙即忙取出一条鞭，——不是甚么牛皮、羊皮、麂皮、犊皮的，原来是龙皮做的七星鞭，着水浸在那里。令一个有力量的小仙，把鞭执定道："师父，先打那个？"大仙道："唐三藏做大不尊，先打他。"

【13】行者闻言，心中暗道："我那老和尚不禁打；假若一顿鞭打坏了啊，却不是我造的业么？"他忍不住，开言道："先生差了。偷果子是我，吃果子是我，推倒树也是我，怎么不先打我，打他做甚？"大仙笑道："这泼猴倒言语膂劣。这等便先打他。"小仙问："打多少？"大仙道："照依果数，打三十鞭。"那小仙抢鞭就打。行者恐仙家法大，睁圆眼睛觑定，看他打那里。原来打腿。行者就把腰扭一扭，叫声"变！"变做两条熟铁腿，看他怎么打。那小仙一下一下的，打了三十，天早响午了。大仙又吩咐道："还该打三藏训教不严，纵放顽徒撒泼。"那仙又抢鞭来打。行者道："先生又差了。偷果时，我师父不知，他在殿上与二童讲话，是我兄弟们做的勾当。纵是有教训不严之罪，我为弟子的，也当替打。再打我

罢。"大仙笑道："这泼猴，虽是狡猾奸顽，却倒也有些孝意。既这等，还打他罢。"小仙又打了三十。行者低头看看，两只腿似明镜一般，通打亮了，更不知些疼痒。此时天色将晚。大仙道："且把鞭子浸在水里，待明朝再拷打他。"小仙且收鞭去浸，各各归房。晚斋已毕，尽皆安寝不题。

【14】　那长老泪眼双垂，怨他三个徒弟道："你等闯出祸来，却带累我在此受罪，这是怎的起？"行者道："且休报怨，打便先打我。你又不曾吃打，倒转嗟呀怎的？"唐僧道："虽然不曾打，却也绑得身上疼哩。"沙僧道："师父，还有陪绑的在这里哩。"行者道："都莫要嚷，再停会儿走路。"八戒道："哥哥又弄虚头了。这里麻绳喷水，紧紧的绑着，还比关在殿上，被你使解锁法撺开门去走哩！"行者道："不是夸口说，那怕他三股的麻绳喷上了水，——就是碗粗的棕缆，只好当秋风！"正说些，早已三籁无声，正是天街人静。好行者，把身子小一小，脱下索来道："师父去哩！"沙僧慌了道："哥哥，也救我们一救！"行者道："悄言！悄言！"他却解了三藏，放下八戒、沙僧，整束了偏衫，扣背了马匹，廊下拿了行李，一齐出了观门。又教八戒："你去把那崖边柳树伐四颗来。"八戒道："要他怎的？"行者道："有用处，快快取来！"

那呆子有些夯力，走了去，一嘴一颗，就拱了四颗，一抱抱来。行者将枝梢折了，教见弟二人复进去，将原锅照旧绑在柱上。那大圣念动咒语，咬破舌尖，将血喷在树上，叫"变！"一根变做长老，一根变做自身，那两根变做沙僧、八戒；都变得容貌一般，相貌皆同，问他也说话，叫名也答应。他两个却才放开步，赶上师父。这一夜依旧马不停蹄，躲离了五庄观。

只走到天明，那长老在马上摇桩打盹。行者见了，叫道："师父不济！出家人怎的这般辛苦？我老孙千夜不眠，也不晓得困倦。且下马来，莫教走路的人，看见笑我。权在山坡下藏风聚气，歇歇再走。"

【15】　不说他师徒在路暂住。且说那大仙，天明起来，吃了早斋，出在殿上。教拿鞭来："今日却该打唐三藏了。"那小仙抢着鞭，望唐僧道："打你哩！"那柳树也应道："打么。"乒乓打了三十。轮过鞭来，对八戒道："打你哩！"那柳树也应道："打么。"及打沙

僧,也应道:"打么"。及打到行者,那行者在路,偶然打个寒噤道:"不好了!"三藏问道:"怎么说?"行者道:"我将四颗柳树变做我师徒四众,我只说他昨日打了我两顿,今日想不打了,却又打我的化身,所以我真身打噤。收了法罢"。那行者慌忙念咒收法。

【16】你看那些道童害怕,丢了皮鞭,报道:"师父呀,为头打的是大唐和尚,这一会打的都是柳树之根!"大仙闻言,呵呵冷笑,夸不尽道:"孙行者,真是一个好猴王!曾闻他大闹天宫,布地网天罗,拿他不住,果有此理。——你走了便也罢,却怎么绑些柳树在此,冒名顶替?决莫饶他!赶去来!那大仙说声赶,纵起云头,往西一望,只见那和尚挑包策马,正然走路。大仙低下云头,"叫声"孙行者!往那里走!还我人参树来!"八戒听见道:"罢了!对头又来了!"行者道:"师父,且把善字儿包起,让我们使些凶恶,一发结果了他,脱身去罢。"唐僧闻言,战战兢兢,未曾答应,沙僧掣宝杖,八戒举钉钯,大圣使铁棒,一齐上前,把大仙围住在空中,乱打乱筑。这场恶斗,有诗为证。诗曰:

> 悟空不识镇元帅,与世同君妙更玄。
> 三件神兵施猛烈,一根麈尾自飘然。
> 左遮右挡随来往,后架前迎任转旋。
> 夜去朝来难脱体,淹留何日到西天!

【17】那师弟三众,各举神兵,一齐攻打,那大仙只把蝇帚儿演架。那里有半个时辰,他将袍袖一展,依然将四僧一马并行李,一袖笼去,返云头,又到观里。众仙接着,仙师坐于殿上。却又在袖儿里一个个搬出,将唐僧绑在阶下矮槐树上;八戒、沙僧各绑在两边树上;将行者捆倒,行者道:"想是调问哩。"不一时,捆绑停当,教把长头布取十四匹。行者笑道:"八戒!这先生好意思,拿出布来与我们做中袖哩!——减省些儿,做个口中罢了。"那小仙将家机布搬将出来。大仙道:"把唐三藏、猪八戒、沙和尚都使布裹了!"众仙一齐上前,果将三人都使布裹了!行者笑道:"好!好!夹活儿就大绑了!"须臾,缠裹已毕。又教拿出漆来。众仙即忙取了些自收自晒的生熟漆,把他三个布裹漆漆了,浑身俱裹漆,上留着头脸在外。八戒道:"先生,上头倒不打紧,只是下面还留孔儿,

我们好出恭。"那大仙又把锅大锅抬出来。行者笑道："八戒，造化！抬出锅来，想是煮饭我们吃哩。"八戒道："也罢了；让我们吃些饭儿，做个饱死的鬼也好看。"众仙果抬出一口锅支在阶下。大仙叫架起干柴，发起烈火，教："把清油拗上一锅，烧得滚了，将孙行者下油锅扎他一扎，与我人参树报仇！"

行者闻言，暗喜道："正可老孙之意。这一向不曾洗澡，有些儿皮肤燥痒，好刬荡荡，足感盛情。"顷刻间，那油锅将滚。大圣却又留心：恐他仙法难参，油锅里难做手脚，急回头四顾，只见那台下东边是一座日规台，西边是一个石狮子。行者将身一纵，滚到西边，咬破舌尖，把石狮子喷了一口，叫声"变！"变做他本身模样，也这般捆作一团；他却出了元神，起在云端里，低头看着道士。

只见那小仙报道："师父，油锅滚透了。"大仙教"把孙行者抬下去！"四个仙童抬不动；八个来，也抬不动；又加四个，也抬不动。众仙道："这猴子恋土难移，一心自小，倒也结实。"却着二十个小仙，扛将起来，往锅里一掼，烹的响了一声，溅起些滚油点子，把那小道士们脸上烫了几个燎浆大泡！只听得烧火的小童喊道："锅漏了！锅漏了！"说不了，油漏得罄尽，锅底打破。原来是一个石狮子放在里面。

【18】　大仙大怒道："这个泼猴，着然无礼！教他当面做了手脚！你走了便罢，怎么又捣了我的灶？这泼猴枉自也拿他不住；就拿住他，也似抟弄汞，提影捕风。——罢！罢！罢！饶他去罢。且将唐三藏解下，另换新锅，把他扎一扎，与人参树报仇罢。"那小仙真个动手，拆解布漆。

行者在半空里听得明白。他想着："师父不济：他若到了油锅里，一滚就死，二滚就焦，到三五滚，他就弄做个熻烂的和尚了！我还去救他一救。"好大圣，按落云头，上前叉手道："莫要拆坏了布漆，我来下油锅了。"那大仙惊骂道："你这猢猴！怎么弄手段捣了我的灶？"行者笑道："你遇着我就该倒灶，干我甚事？我才自也要领你些油汤油水之爱，但只是大小便急了，若在锅里开风，恐怕污了你的熟油，不好调菜吃；如今大小便通干净了，却好下锅。不要扎我师父，还来扎我。"那大仙闻言，呵呵冷笑，走出殿来，一把扯住。毕竟不知有何话说，端的怎么脱身，且听下回分解。

Chapter 8
The Immortal Zhen Yuan Captures
the Pilgrim Priest;
Monkey Makes Havoc in
the Wuzhuang Temple

【1】 "The meal is cooked," the three disciples said as they entered the hall, "what did you call us for?" "I'm not asking about the meal, disciples," said Sanzang. "This temple has things called manfruit or something that look like babies. Which of you stole and ate some?" "I don't know anything about it, honest I don't—I never saw any," said Pig. "That grinning one did it," said Pure Wind, "that grinning one." "I've had a smile on my face all my life," shouted Monkey. "Are you going to stop me smiling just because you can't find some fruit or other?" "Don't lose your temper, disciple," said Sanzang. "As men of religion we should control our tongues and not eat food that befuddles our minds. If you ate their fruit you should apologize to them, instead of trying to brazen it out like this."

【2】 Seeing that his master was talking sense, Brother Monkey began to tell the truth. "I didn't start it, master," he said. "Pig heard the Taoist boys eating something called manfruit next door to him and wanted to try one himself. He made me go and get three so that we three disciples could have one each. But now they've been eaten, there's no point in waiting around here." "How can these priests deny that they are criminals when they've stolen four of our manfruits?" said Bright Moon. "Amitabha Buddha," exclaimed Pig, "if he pinched four of them why did he only share out three? He must have done the dirty on us." He continued to shout wildly in this vein.

【3】 Now that they knew that the fruit really had been stolen, the two boys started to abuse them even more foully. The Great Sage ground his teeth of steel in his fury, glaring with his fiery

209

eyes and tightening his grip on his iron cudgel. "Damn those Taoist boys," he thought when he could restrain himself no longer. "If they'd hit us we could have taken it, but now they're insulting us to our faces like this, I'll finish their tree off, then none of them can have any more fruit." Splendid Monkey. He pulled a hair out from the back of his head, breathed a magic breath on it, said "Change," and turned it into an imitation Monkey who stayed with the Tang Priest, Pig and Friar Sand to endure the cursing and swearing of the Taoist boys, while the real Monkey used his divine powers to leap out of the hall by cloud. He went straight to the garden and struck the manfruit tree with his gold-banded cudgel. Then he used his supernatural strength that could move mountains to push the tree over with a single shove. The leaves fell, the branches splayed out, and the roots came out of the ground. The Taoists would have no more of their "Grass-returning Cinnabar." After pushing the tree over Monkey searched through the branches for manfruit, but he could not find a single one. These treasures dropped at the touch of metal, and as Monkey's cudgel was ringed with gold, while being made of iron, another of the five metals, one tap from it brought them all tumbling down, and when they hit the ground they went straight in, leaving none on the tree. "Great, great, great," he said, "that'll make them all cool down." He put the iron cudgel away, went back to the front of the temple, shook the magic hair, and put it back on his head. The others did not see what was happening as they had eyes of mortal flesh.

【4】 A long time later, when the two Taoist boys felt that they had railed at them for long enough, Pure Wind said to Bright Moon, "These monks will take anything we say. We've sworn at them as if we were swearing at chickens, but they haven't admitted anything. I don't think they can have stolen any, after all. The tree is so tall and the foliage is so dense that we may well have miscounted, and if we have, we shouldn't be cursing them so wildly. Let's go and check the number again." Bright Moon agreed, and the pair of them went back to the garden. When they saw that the tree was down with its branches bent out, the leaves fallen, and the fruit gone, they were horror-struck. Pure Wind's knees turned soft and he collapsed, while Bright Moon trembled and shook. Both of them passed out, and there is a verse to describe them:

When Sanzang came to the Mountain of Infinite Longevity,
Monkey finished the Grass-returning Cinnabar.
The branches were splayed out, the leaves fallen, and the tree down.
Bright Moon and Pure Wind's hearts both turned to ice.

The two of them lay in the dirt mumbling deliriously and saying, "What are we to do, what are we to do? The elixir of our Wuzhuang Temple has been destroyed and our community of Immortals is finished. Whatever are we going to say to the master when he comes back?" "Stop moaning, brother," said Bright Moon. "We must tidy ourselves up and not let those monks know anything's wrong. That hair-faced sod who looks like a thunder god must have done it. He must have used magic to destroy our treasure. But it's useless to argue with him as he'll deny everything, and if we start a quarrel with him and fighting breaks out, we two haven't a chance against the four of them. We'll have to fool them and say that no fruit is missing. We'll pretend we counted wrong before, and apologize to them. Their rice is cooked, and we can give them a few side dishes to eat with it. The moment they've each got a bowl of food you and I will stand on either side of the door, slam it shut, and lock it. After that we can lock all the gates, then they won't be able to get away. When our master comes back he can decide what to do with them. That old monk is a friend of his, so our master may want to forgive him as a favour. And if he doesn't feel forgiving, we've got the criminals under arrest and may possibly not get into trouble ourselves." "Absolutely right," said Pure Wind.
[5] The two of them pulled themselves together, forced themselves to look happy, and went back to the front hall.

211

"Master," they said, bowing low to Sanzang, "we were extremely rude to you just now. Please forgive us." "What do you mean?" asked Sanzang. "The fruit is all there," they replied. "We couldn't see it all before as the tree is so tall and the foliage so thick but when we checked just now the number was right." "You're too young to know what you're doing," said Pig, taking the chance to put the boot in. "Why did you swear and curse at us, and try to frame us up? You bastards." Monkey, who understood what the boys were up to, said nothing and thought, "Lies, lies. The fruit is all finished. Why ever are they saying this? Can it be that they know how to bring the tree back to life?" "Very well then," Sanzang was saying meanwhile, "bring our rice in and we'll be off after eating it."

Pig went off to fill their bowls and Friar Sand arranged a table and chairs. The two boys hurried out and fetched some side dishes—salted squash, salted eggplant, turnips in wine-lees, pickled bean, salted lettuce, and mustard plant, some seven or eight plates in all. These they gave to the pilgrims to eat with their rice, and then they waited on them with a pot of good tea and two cups. As soon as the four pilgrims had their ricebowls in their hands, the boys, who were on either side of the door-way, slammed the doors to and locked them with a double-sprung bronze lock. "You shouldn't do that, boys," said Pig with a smile. "Even if the people round here are a bit rough there's no need to shut the doors while we eat." "Yes, yes," said Bright Moon, "we'll open them after lunch." Pure Wind, however, was abusive. "I'll get you, you greedy, bald-headed food-thief," he said. "You ate our immortal fruit and deserve to be punished for the crime of stealing food from fields and gardens. On top of that you've pushed our tree over and ruined our temple's source of immortality. How dare you argue with us? Your only chance of reaching the Western Heaven and seeing the Buddha is to be reborn and be rocked in the cradle again." When Sanzang heard this he dropped his ricebowl, feeling as if a boulder was weighing down his heart. The two boys went and locked the main and the inner gates of the temple, then came back to the main hall to abuse them with filthy language and call them criminals and bandits till evening, when they went off to eat. The two of them returned to their rooms after supper.

[6]   "You're always causing trouble, you ape," grumbled Sanzang at Monkey. "You stole their fruit, so you should have let them lose their temper and swear at you, then that would have been the end of it. Why on earth did you push their tree over? If they took this to court you wouldn't be able to get off even if your own father were on the bench." "Don't make such a row, master," said Monkey. "Those boys have gone to bed, and when they're asleep we can do a midnight flit." "But all the gates have been locked," said Friar Sand, "and they've been shut very firmly, so how can we possibly get away?" "Don't let it bother you," said Monkey, "I have a way." "We weren't worried that you wouldn't have a way," said Pig. "You can turn yourself into an insect and fly out through the holes in the window lattice. But you'll be leaving poor old us, who can't turn ourselves into something else, to stay here and carry the can for you." "If he does a trick like that and doesn't take us with him I'll recite that old sutra—he won't get away scot-free then." Pig was both pleased and worried to hear this. "What do you mean, master?" he said. "I know that the Buddha's teachings include a *Lankavatara Sutra*, a *Lotus Sutra*, a *Peacock Sutra*, an *Avalokitesvara Sutra*, and a *Diamond Sutra*, but I never heard of any *Old Sutra*." "What you don't know, brother," said Monkey, "is that the Bodhisattva Guanyin gave this band I have round my head to our master. He tricked me into wearing it, and now it's virtually rooted there and I can't take it off. The spell or sutra for tightening this band is what he meant by the 'old sutra'. If he says it, my head aches. It's a way he has of making me suffer. Please don't recite it, master. I won't abandon you. I guarantee that we'll all get out."

[7]   It was now dark, and the moon had risen in the east. "It's quiet now," said Monkey, "and the moon is bright. This is the time to go." "Stop fooling about, brother," said Pig. "The gates are all locked, so where can we possibly go?" "Watch this trick,"

213

said Monkey, and gripping his cudgel in his hand he pointed at the doors and applied unlocking magic to them. There was a clanking sound, and the locks fell from all the doors and gates, which he pushed them open. "Not half clever," said Pig. "A locksmith with his skeleton keys couldn't have done it anything like as fast." "Nothing difficult about opening these doors," said Monkey. "I can open the Southern Gates of Heaven just by pointing at them." Then he asked his master to go out and mount the horse. Pig shouldered the luggage, Friar Sand led the horse, and they headed west. "You carry on," Monkey said, "while I go back to make sure that those two boys will stay asleep for a month." "Mind you don't kill them, disciple," said Sanzang, "or you'll be on a charge of murder in the pursuit of theft as well." "I'm aware of that," replied Monkey and went back into the temple. Standing outside the door of the room where the boys were sleeping, he took a couple of sleep insects from his belt. These were what he had used when he fooled the Heavenly King Virudhaka at the Eastern Gate of Heaven, and now he threw them in through a gap in the window lattice. They landed straight on the boys' faces, and made them fall into a deeper sleep from which they would not wake up for a long time. Then he streaked back by cloud and caught up with Sanzang. They headed west along the main road.

That night the horse never stopped, and they kept on till dawn. "You'll be the death of me, you ape," said Sanzang. "Because of your greed I've had to stay awake all night." "Stop grumbling," said Monkey. "Now that it's light you can rest in the forest beside the road and build your strength up before we move on." Sanzang obediently dismounted and sat down on the roots of a pine tree, using it as a makeshift meditation platform. Friar Sand put down the luggage and took a nap, while Pig pillowed his head on a rock and went to sleep. Monkey, the Great Sage, had his own ideas and amused himself leaping from tree to tree.

[8] After the lecture in the palace of the Original Celestial Jade Pure One the Great Immortal Zhen Yuan led his junior Immortals

down from the Tushita Heaven through the jade sky on auspicious clouds, and in a moment they were back at the gates of the Wuzhuang Temple. The gates, he saw, were wide open, and the ground was clean. "So Pure Wind and Bright Moon aren't so useless after all," he said. "Usually they're still in bed when the sun is high in the sky. But now, with us away, they got up early, opened the gates, and swept the grounds." All the junior Immortals were delighted. Yet when they went into the hall of worship there was no incense burning and nobody to be seen. Where were Bright Moon and Pure Wind, they wondered. "They probably thought that with us not here they could steal some stuff and clear out." "What an outrageous idea," said the Great Immortal. "As if men cultivating immortality could do anything so evil! I think they must have forgotten to shut the gates before they went to sleep last night and not have woken up yet." When the Immortals went to look in their room they found the doors closed and heard the boys snoring. They hammered on the doors and shouted for all they were worth, but the boys did not wake up. They forced the doors open and pulled the boys from their beds: the boys still did not wake up. "Fine Immortal boys you are," said the Great Immortal with a smile. "When you become an Immortal your divine spirit should be so full that you do not want to sleep. Why are they so tired? They must have been bewitched. Fetch some water at once." A boy hastily handed him half a bowl of water. He intoned a spell, took a mouthful of the water, and spruted it on their faces. This broke the enchantment.

[9] The two of them woke up, opened their eyes, rubbed their faces, looked around them, and saw the Great Immortal as well as all their Immortal brothers. Pure Wind bowed and Bright Moon kowtowed in their confusion, saying, "Master, that old friend of yours, the priest from the East ... a gang of bandits ... murderous, murderous...."

"Don't be afraid," said the Great Immortal with a smile. "Calm down and tell us all about it." "Master," said Pure Wind, "the Tang Priest from the East did come. It was quite soon after you had left. There were four monks and a horse—five of them altogether. We did as you had ordered us and picked two manfruits to offer him, but the venerable gentleman was too vulgar and stupid to know what our treasures were. He said that they were newborn babies and refused to eat any, so we ate one each. Little did we imagine that one of his three disciples called Brother Sun Wukong, or Monkey, would steal four manfruits for them to eat. We spoke to him very reasonably, but he denied it and secretly used his magic. It's terrible. . . ." At this point the two boys could no longer hold back the tears that now streamed down their cheeks. " Did the monk strike you?" asked the Immortals. " No," said Bright Moon, " he only felled our manfruit tree."

The Great Immortal did not lose his temper when he heard their story, "Don't cry," he said, "don't cry. What you don't realize is that Monkey is an Immortal of the Supreme Monad, and that he played tremendous havoc in the Heavenly Palace. He has vast magic powers. But he has knocked our tree over. Could you recognize those monks?" "I could recognize all of them," replied Pure Wind. "In that case come with me," said the Great Immortal. "The rest of you are to prepare the instruments of torture and be ready to flog them when we come back."

【10】 The other Immortals did as they were told while the Great Immortal, Bright Moon and Pure Wind pursued Sanzang on a beam of auspicious light. It took them but an instant to cover three hundred miles. The Great Immortal stood on the edge of the clouds and gazed to the west, but he did not see Sanzang; then he turned round to look east and saw that he had left Sanzang over two hundred and fifty miles behind. Even riding all night that venerable gentleman had covered only forty miles, which was why the Great Immortal's cloud had overshot him by a great distance. "Master," said one of the Immortal boys, "there's the Tang Priest, sitting under a tree by the side of the road." "Yes, I'd seen him myself," the Great Immortal replied. "You two go back and get some ropes ready, and I'll catch him myself." Pure Wind and Bright Moon went back.

The Great Immortal landed his cloud, shook himself, and turned into an itinerant Taoist. Do you know what he looked like?

He wore a patchwork gown,
Tied with Lu Dongbin sash,
Waving a fly-whisk in his hand
He tapped a musical drum.
The grass sandals on his feet had three ears,
His head was wrapped in a sun turban.
As the wind filled his sleeves
He sang The Moon is High.

"Greetings, venerable sir," he called, raising his hands. "Oh, I'm sorry I didn't notice you before," replied Sanzang hastily. "Where are you from?" the Great Immortal asked. "And why are you in meditation during your journey?" "I have been sent by the Great Tang in the East to fetch the scriptures from the Western Heaven," Sanzang said, "and I'm taking a rest along the way." "You must have crossed my desolate mountain if you have come from the East." "May I ask, Immortal sir, which mountain is yours?" "My humble abode is the Wuzhuang Temple on the Mountain of Infinite Longevity."

[11] "We didn't come that way," said Monkey, who realized what was happening. "We've only just started out." The Great Immortal pointed at him and laughed. "I'll show you, you damned ape. Who do you think you're fooling? I know that you knocked our manfruit tree down and came here during the night. You had better confess: you won't get away with concealing anything. Stay where you are, and give me back that tree at once." Monkey flared up at this, and with no further discussion he struck at the Great Immortal's head with his cudgel. The Great Immortal twisted away from the blow and went straight up into the sky on a beam of light, closely pursued by Monkey on a cloud. In mid-air the Great Immortal reverted to his true appearance, and this is what he looked like:

217

A golden crown on his head,
A No-worries cloak of crane's down on his body.
A pair of turned-up sandals on his feet,
And round his waist a belt of silk.
His body was like a child's,
His face was that of a beautiful woman.
A wispy beard floated down from his chin,
And the hair on his temples was crow-black.
He met Monkey unarmed
With only a jade-handled whisk in his hands.

Monkey struck wildly at him with his club, only to be parried to left and right by the Great Immortal's whisk. After two or three rounds the Great Immortal did a "Wrapping Heaven and Earth in His Sleeve" trick, waving his sleeve gently in the breeze as he stood amid the clouds, then sweeping it across the ground and gathering up the four pilgrims and their horse in it. "Hell," said Pig, "We're all caught in a bag." "It isn't a bag, you idiot," said Monkey, "he's caught us all in his sleeve." "It doesn't matter, anyhow," said Pig. "I can make a hole in it with a single blow of my rake that we can all get through. Then we'll be able to drop out when he relaxes his grip on us." But however desperately he struck at the fabric he could make no impression on it: although it was soft when held in the hand it was harder than iron when hit.

【12】 The Great Immortal turned his cloud round, went straight back to the Wuzhuang Temple, landed, sat down, and told his disciples to fetch rope. Then, with all the junior Immortals in attendance, he took the Tang Priest out of his sleeve as if he were a puppet and had him tied to one of the pillars of the main hall. After that he took the other three out and tied each of them to a pillar. The horse was taken out, tethered, and fed in the courtyard, and their luggage he threw under the covered walk. "Disciples," he said, "these priests are men of religion, so we cannot use swords, spears or axes on them. You'd better fetch a leather whip and give them a flogging for me—that will make me feel better about the manfruit." The disciples immediately produced a whip—not an oxhide, sheepskin, deerskin or calfskin whip, but a seven-starred dragon-skin one—and were told to soak it in water. A brawny young Immortal was told to take a firm grip on it. "Master," he said, "which of them shall I flog first?" "Sanzang is guilty of gross disrespect," the Great Immortal replied, "flog him first."

[13]   "That old priest of ours couldn't stand a flogging," thought Monkey when he heard this, "and if he died under the lash the fault would be mine." Finding the thought of this unbearable, he spoke up and said, "You're wrong, sir. I stole the fruit, I ate the fruit, and I pushed the tree over. Why flog him first when you ought to be flogging me?" "That damn monkey has a point," said the Great Immortal with a smile, "so you'd better flog him first." "How many strokes?" the junior Immortal asked. "Give him thirty," the Great Immortal replied, "to match the number of fruits." The junior Immortal whirled the lash and started to bring it down. Monkey, frightened that the Immortal would have great magical powers, opened his eyes wide and looked carefully to see where he was going to be hit, and it turned out to be on his legs. He twisted at the waist, shouted "Change!", turned them into a pair of wrought-iron legs, and watched the blows fall. The junior Immortal gave him thirty lashes, one after the other, until it was almost noon. "Sanzang must be flogged too," the Great Immortal commanded, "for training his wicked disciple so slackly and letting him run wild." The junior Immortal whirled the lash again and was going to strike Sanzang when Monkey said, "Sir, you're making another mistake. When I stole the fruit, my master knew nothing about it—he was talking to those two boys of yours in the main hall of the temple. This plot was hatched by us three disciples. Anyhow, even if he were guilty of slackness in training me, I'm his disciple and should take the flogging for him. Flog me again." "That damn monkey may be cunning and vicious, but he does have some sense of his obligations to his master. Very well then, flog him again." The junior Immortal gave him another thirty

219

strokes. Monkey looked down and watched his legs being flogged till they shone like mirrors but still he felt no pain. It was now drawing towards evening, and the Great Immortal said, "Put the lash to soak. We can continue the flogging tomorrow." The junior Immortal took the lash away to be soaked while everyone retired to their quarters, and after supper they all went to bed.

[14]   "It was because you three got me into this trouble that I was brought here to be punished," moaned the venerable Sanzang to his three disciples as tears streamed down from his eyes. "Is that how you ought to treat me?" "Don't grumble," Monkey replied. "I was the one to be flogged first, and you haven't felt the lash, so what have you got to groan about?" "I may not have been flogged," Sanzang replied, "but it's agony being tied up like this." "We're tied up too to keep you company," said Friar Sand. "Will you all stop shouting?" said Monkey "then we can be on our way again when we've taken a rest." "You're showing off again, elder brother," said Pig. "They've tied us up with hempen ropes and spurted water on them, so we're tightly bound. This isn't like the time we were shut up in the hall of the temple and you unlocked the doors to let us out." "I'm not boasting," said Monkey. "I don't give a damn about their three hempen ropes sprayed with water. Even if they were coir cables as thick as a ricebowl they would only be an autumn breeze." Apart from him speaking, all was now silence. Splendid Monkey made himself smaller, slipped out of his bonds, and said, "Let's go, master." "Save us too, elder brother," pleaded a worried Friar Sand. "Shut up, shut up," Monkey replied, then freed Sanzang, Pig and Friar Sand, straightened his tunic, tightened his belt, saddled the horse, collected their luggage from under the eaves, and went out through the temple gates with the others. "Go and cut down four of the willow-trees by that cliff," he told Pig, who asked, "Whatever do you want them for?" "I've got a use for them," Monkey replied. "Bring them here immediately."

The idiot Pig, who certainly had brute strength, went and felled each of them with a single bite, and came back holding them all in his arms. Monkey stripped off their tops and branches and told his two fellow-disciples to take the trunks back in and tie them up with the ropes as they themselves had been tied up. Then Monkey recited a spell, bit the tip of his tongue open, and spat blood over the trees. At his shout of "Change!" one of the trees turned into Sanzang, one turned into Monkey, and the other two became Friar Sand and Pig. They were all perfect likenesses; when questioned they would reply, and when called by their names they responded. The three disciples then hurried back to their master, and once more they travelled all night without stopping as they fled from the Wuzhuang Temple.

By the time it was dawn the venerable Sanzang was swaying to and fro as he dozed in the saddle. "Master," called Monkey when he noticed, "you're hopeless. You're a man of religion—how can you be finding it so exhausting? I can do without sleep for a thousand nights not feeling a bit tired. You'd better dismount and spare yourself the humiliation of being laughed at by a passer-by. Take a rest in one of the places under this hill where the wind is stored and the vapours gather before we go any further."

[15]　We shall leave them resting beside the path to tell how the Great Immortal got up at dawn, ate his meatless breakfast, and went to the hall. "Today Tang Sanzang is to be whipped," he announced as he sent for the lash. The junior whirled it around and said to the Tang Priest, "I'm going to flog you." "Flog away," the willow tree replied. When he had given it thirty resounding lashes he whirled the whip around once more and said to Pig, "Now I'm going to flog you." "Flog away," the willow tree replied. When he came to flog Friar Sand, he too told him to go ahead. But when he came to flog Monkey, the real Monkey on the road shuddered and said, "Oh, no!" "What do you mean?" Sanzàng asked. "When I turned the four willow trees into the four of us I thought that as he had me flogged twice yesterday he wouldn't flog me again today, but now he's lashing the magic body, my real body is feeling the pain. I'm putting an end to this magic." With that he hastily recited an incantation to break the spell.

221

[16]　　Look at the terror of the Taoist boys as they throw down their leather whips and report, "Master, at first we were flogging the Priest from the Great Tang, but all we are flogging now are willow trunks. The Great Immortal laughed bitterly on hearing this and was full of admiration. "Brother monkey really is a splendid Monkey King. I had heard that when he turned the Heavenly Palace upside-down, he could not even be caught with a Heaven and Earth Net, and now I see it must be true. I wouldn't mind your escaping, but why did you leave four willows tied up here to impersonate you? He shall be shown no mercy. After him!" As the words "After him" left his mouth, the Great Immortal sprang up on a cloud and looked west to see the monks carrying their bundles and spurring their horse as they went on their way. Bringing his cloud down he shouted, "Where are you going, Monkey? Give me back my manfruit tree." "We're done for," exclaimed Pig, "our enemy's come back." "Put all your piety away for now, master," said Monkey, "while we finish him off once and for all with a bit of evil; then we'll be able to escape." The Tang Priest shivered and shook on hearing this, and before he could answer, the three disciples rushed forward, Friar Sand wielding his staff, Pig with his rake held high, and the Great Sage Monkey brandishing his iron cudgel. They surrounded the Great Immortal in mid-air and struck wildly at him. There are some verses about this terrible fight:

> *Monkey did not know that the Immortal Zhen Yuan,*
> *The Conjoint Lord of the Age, had even deeper powers.*
> *While the three magic weapons fiercely whirled,*
> *His deer-tail fly-whisk gently waved.*
> *Parrying to left and right, he moved to and fro,*
> *Blocking blows from front and back he let them rush around.*
> *When night gave way to dawn they still were locked in combat.*
> *If they tarried here they would never reach the Western Heaven.*

【17】   The three of them went for him with their magic weapons, but the Great Immortal kept them at bay with his fly-whisk. After about an hour he opened wide his sleeve and caught up master, disciples, horse, and baggage in it once more. Then he turned his cloud around and went back to his temple, where all the Immortals greeted him. After taking his seat in the hall he took them out of his sleeve one by one. He had the Tang Priest tied to a stunted locust tree at the foot of the steps, with Pig and Friar Sand tied to trees next to him. Monkey was tied up upside-down, which made him think that he was going to be tortured and interrogated. When Monkey was tightly bound, the Great Immortal sent for ten long turban-cloths. "What a kind gentleman, Pig," said Monkey, "he's sent for some cloth to make sleeves for us—with a bit less he could have make us cassocks." The junior Immortals fetched home-woven cloth, and on being told by the Great Immortal to wrap up Pig and Friar Sand with it, they came forward to do so. "Excellent," said Monkey, "excellent—you're being encoffined alive." Within a few moments the three of them were wrapped up, and lacquer was then sent for. The Immortals quickly fetched some lacquer that they had tapped and dried themselves, with which they painted the three bandaged bodies all over except for the heads. "Never mind about our heads, sir," said Pig, "but please leave us a hole at the bottom to shit through." The Great Immortal then sent for a huge cauldron, at which Monkey said with a laugh, "You're in luck, Pig. I think they must have brought the cauldron out to cook us some rice in." "Fine," said Pig, "I hope they give us some rice first—we'll make much better-looking ghosts if we die with our bellies full." The Immortals carried out the large cauldron and put it under the steps, and the Great Immortal called for dry wood to be stacked up round it and set ablaze. "Ladle it full of pure oil," he commanded, "and when it is hot enough to bubble, deep-fry Monkey in it to pay me back for my manfruit."

Monkey was secretly delighted to hear this. "This is just what I want," he thought. "I haven't had a bath for ages, and

223

my skin's getting rather itchy. I'd thoroughly appreciate a hot bath." Very soon the oil was bubbling and Monkey was having reservations: he was afraid that the Immortal's magic might be hard for him to fathom, and that at first he might be unable to use his limbs in the cauldron. Hastily looking around him, he saw that there was a sundial to the east of the dais and a stone lion to the west. Monkey rolled towards it with a spring, bit off the end of his tongue, spurted blood all over the stone lion, and shouted "Change," at which it turned into his own image, tied up in a bundle like himself. Then he extracted his spirit and went up into the clouds, from where he looked down at the Taoists.

It was just at this moment that the junior Immortals reported, "The oil's boiling hard." "Carry Monkey down to it," the Great Immortal ordered, but when four of them tried to pick him up they could not. Eight then tried and failed, and four more made no difference. "This earth-infatuated ape is immovable," they said. "He may be small, but he's very solid." Twelve junior Immortals were then told to pick him up with the aid of carrying-poles, and when they threw him in there was a loud crash as drops of oil splashed about, raising blisters all over the junior Immortals' faces. "There's a hole in the cauldron—it's started leaking," the scalded Immortals cried, but before the words were out of their mouths the oil had all run out through the broken bottom of the cauldron. They realized that they had thrown a stone lion into it.

[18]   "Damn that ape for his insolence," said the Great Immortal in a terrible rage. "How dare he play his tricks in my presence! I don't mind so much about your getting away, but how dare you wreck my cauldron? It's useless trying to catch him, and even if you could it would be like grinding mercury out of sand, or trying to hold a shadow or the wind. Forget about him, let him go. Untie Tang Sanzang instead and fetch another pot. We can fry him to avenge the destruction of the tree." The junior Immortals set to and began to tear off Sanzang's lacquered bandages.

Monkey could hear all this clearly from mid-air. "The master will be done for," he thought. "If he goes into that cauldron it'll kill him. Then he'll be cooked, and after four or five fryings he'll be eaten as a really tender piece of monk. I must go back down and save him." The splendid Great Sage brought his cloud down to land, clasped his hands in front of him, and said, "Don't spoil the lacquered bands, and don't fry my master. Put me in the cauldron of oil instead." "I'll get you, you baboon," raged the Great Immortal in astonishment. "Why did you use one of your tricks to smash my cooking-pot?" "You must expect to be smashed up if you meet me—and what business is it of mine anyhow? I was going to accept your kind offer of some hot oil, but I was desperate for a shit and a piss, and if I'd done them in your cauldron, I'd have spoilt your oil and your food wouldn't have tasted right. Now I've done my stuff I'm ready for the cauldron. Please fry me instead of my master." The Great Immortal laughed coldly, came out of the hall, and seized him. If you don't know how the story goes or how he escaped, listen to the explanation in the next instalment.

9. 孙悟空三岛求方
观世音甘泉活树

【1】　诗曰：

　　　　处世须存心上刃，修身切记寸边而。
　　　　常言刃字为生意，但要三思戒怒欺。
　　　　上士无争传亘古，圣人怀德继当时。
　　　　刚强更有刚强辈，究竟终成空与非。

却说那镇元大仙用手搀着行者道："我也知道你的本事，我也闻得你的英名，只是你今番越理欺心，纵有腾那，脱不得我手。我就和你讲到西天，见了你那佛祖，也少不得还我人参果树。你莫弄神通。"行者笑道："你这先生，好小家子样！若要树活，有甚疑难！早说这话，可不省了一场争竞？"大仙道："不争竞，我肯善自饶你！"行者道："你解了我师父，我还你一棵活树如何？"大仙道："你若有此神通，医得树活，我与你八拜为交，结为兄弟。"行者道："不打紧。放了他们，老孙管教还你活树。"

【2】　大仙谅他走不脱，即命解放了三藏、八戒、沙僧。沙僧道："师父啊，不知师兄捣鬼是甚么鬼哩。"八戒道："甚么鬼！这叫做'当面人情鬼'！树死了，又可医得活？他弄个光皮散儿好看，着求医治树，单单了脱身走路，还顾得和我哩！"三藏道："他决不敢撇了我们。我们问他那里求医去？"遂叫道："悟空，你怎么哄了仙长，解放我等？"行者道："老孙是真言实语，怎么哄他？"三藏道："你往何处去求方？"行者道："古人云：'方从海上来。'我今要上东洋大海，遍游三岛十洲，访问仙翁圣老，求一个起死回生之法，管教医得со树活。"三藏道："此去几时可回？"行者道："只消三日。"三藏道："既如此，就依你说，与你三日之限。三日里来便罢；若三日之外不来，我就念那话儿经了。"行者道："遵命，遵命。"

226

【3】　你看他急整虎皮裙，出门来对大仙道："先生放心，我就去就来。你却要好生伏侍我师父，逐日家三茶六饭，不可欠缺。若少了些儿，老孙回来和你算帐，先捣塌你的锅底。衣服褴了，与他浆洗浆洗。脸儿黄了些儿，我不要，若瘦了些儿，不出门了。"那大仙道："你去，你去，定不教他忍饿。"

好猴王，急纵筋斗云，别了五庄观，径上东洋大海。在半空中，快如掣电，疾如流星，早到蓬莱仙境。按云头，仔细观看。真个好去处！有诗为证。诗曰：

> 大地仙乡列圣曹，蓬莱分合镇波涛。
> 瑶台影излу天心冷，巨阙光浮海面高。
> 五色烟霞含玉籁，九霄星月射金鳌。
> 西池王母常来此，奉祝三仙几次桃。

那行者看不尽仙景，径入蓬莱。正然走处，见白云洞外，松阴之下，有三个老儿围棋：观局者是福星、禄星。行者上前叫道："老弟们，作揖了。"那三星见了，拂退棋枰，回礼道："大圣何来？"行者道："特来寻你们耍子。"寿星道："我闻大圣弃道从释，脱性命保护唐僧往西天取经，遂日奔波山路，那些儿得闲，却来耍子？"行者道："实不瞒列位说，老孙因往西方，行在半路，有些儿阻滞，特来小事欲干，不知肯否？"福星道："是甚地方？是何阻滞？乞为明示，吾好裁处。"行者道："因路过万寿山五庄观有阻。"三老惊讶道："五庄观是镇元大仙的仙宫。你莫不是把他人参果偷吃了？"行者笑道："偷它了能值甚么？"三老道："你这猴子，不知好歹。那果子闻一闻，活三百六十岁；吃一个，活四万七千年；叫做'万寿草还丹'。我们的道，不及他多矣！他得之甚易，就可与天齐寿；我们还要养精、炼气、存神，调和龙虎，捉坎填离，不知费多少工夫。你怎么说他的能值甚黍？天下只有此种灵根！"行者道："灵根！灵根！我已弄了他个断根哩！"三老惊道："怎的断根？"行者道："我们前日在他观里，那大仙不在家，只有两个小童，接待了我，将两个人参果奉与我师。我师不认得，只说是三朝未满的孩童，再三不吃。那童子就拿去吃了，不曾让得我们。是老孙就去偷了他三个，我三兄弟吃了。那童子不知高低，贼前贼后的骂不住。是老孙恼了，把他树打了一棍，推倒在地，树上果子全无，桠开叶落，根出枝伤，已枯死了。不想那童子关住我们，又被孙扭开锁走了。次日清晨，那先生回家赶来，问答间，语言不和，遂与他赌斗；被他闪一闪，把袍袖展开，一袖子都笼去了。绳缠索绑，拷问鞭敲，就打了一日。是夜又进了，他又赶上，依旧笼去。他身无寸铁，只是把个麈尾遮架。我兄弟这等三般兵器，莫想打得着他。这一番仍旧摆布，将布裹漆了我师父与两师弟，却将我下油锅。我又做了个脱身本事走了，把他锅都打破。他见拿我不住，尽有几分醋气。是我又与他好讲，教他放了我师父、师弟，我与他医树管活，两家才得安宁。我想着'方从海上来'，故此特游仙境，访三位老弟。有甚医树的方儿，传我一个，急救唐僧苦苦。"

【4】 三星闻言，心中也闷道："你这猴儿，全不识人，那镇元子乃地仙之祖；我等乃神仙之宗；你虽是太乙散数，未人真流，你怎么脱得他手？若是大圣打杀了走兽飞禽，蠛虫鳞长，只用我黍米之丹，可以救活；那人参果乃仙木之根，如何医治？没方，没方。"那行者见说无方，却就眉峰双锁，额蹙千痕。福星道："大圣，此处无方，他处或有，怎么就生烦恼？"行者道："无方别访，果然容易；就是游遍海角天涯，转透三十六天，亦是小可；只是我那唐长老法严量窄，止与了我三日期限。三日以外不到，他就要念那《紧箍儿咒》哩。"三星笑道："好！好！好！若不是这个法儿拘束你，你又钻天了。"寿星道："大圣放心，不须烦恼。那大仙虽然上辈，却也与我等有识。一则久别，不曾拜望；二来是大圣的人情；如今我三人同去望他一望，就与你道此情，教那唐和尚莫念《紧箍儿咒》，休说三日五日，只等你求得方来，我们才别。"行者道："感激！感激！就请三位老弟行行，我去也。"大圣辞别三星不题。

【5】 却说这三星驾起祥光，即往五庄观而来。那观中合众人等，忽听得长天鹤唳，原来是三老光临。但见那：

盈空蔼蔼祥光簇，霄汉纷纷香馥郁。
彩雾千条护羽衣，轻云一朵擎仙足。
青鸾飞，丹凤翙，袖引香风满地扑。
拄杖悬龙喜笑生，皓髯垂玉胸前拂。

> 童颜欢悦更无忧，壮体雄威多有福。
> 执星筹，添海屋，腰挂葫芦并宝箓。
> 万纪千旬福寿长，十洲三岛随缘宿。
> 常来世上送千祥，每向人间增百福。
> 概乾坤，荣福禄，今喜得。
> 三老乘祥谒大仙，福堂和气皆无极。

那仙童看见，即忙报道："师父，海上三星来了。"镇元子正与唐僧师弟闲叙，闻报，即降阶奉迎。那八戒见了寿星，近前扯住，笑道："你这肉头老儿，许久不见，还是这般脱洒，帽儿也不带个来。"遂把自家一个僧帽，扑的套在他头上，扑着手呵呵大笑道："好！好！好！真是'加冠进禄'也！"那寿星将帽子掼了，骂道："你这个夯货，老大不知高低！"八戒道："我不是夯货，你等真是奴才！"福星道："你倒是个夯货，反到骂人是奴才！"八戒又笑道："既不是人家奴才，好道叫做'添寿'、'添福'、'添禄'？"

【6】　那三藏喝退了八戒，急整衣拜了三星。那三星以晚辈之礼见了大仙，方才叙坐。坐定，禄星道："我们一向久阔尊颜，有失恭敬。今因孙大圣搅扰仙山，特来相见。"大仙道："孙行者到蓬莱去的？"寿星道："是，因为伤了大仙的丹树，他来我处求方医治。我辈无方，他又到别处求访；但恐违了三僧三日之限，要念《紧箍儿咒》。我辈一来奉拜，二来讨个宽限。"三藏闻言，连声应道："不敢念，不敢念。"

正说处，八戒又跑进来，扯住福星，要讨果子吃。他去袖里乱摸，腰里乱吞，不住的揭他衣服搜检。三藏笑道："那八戒是甚么规矩！"八戒道："不是没规矩，此叫做'番番是福'。"三藏又令出去。那呆子蹯出门，瞅着福星，眼不转睛的发狠。福星道："夯货！我那里恼了你来，你这等恨我？"八戒道："不是恨你，这叫'回头望福'。"那呆子出得了门来，只见一个小童，拿了四把茶匙，方去寻锺取果看茶；被他一把夺过，跑上殿，拿着小锺儿，用手乱敲乱打，两头玩耍。大仙道："这个和尚，越发不尊重了！"八戒笑道："不是不尊重，这叫做'四时吉庆'。"

【7】　且不说八戒打诨乱缠。却表行者纵祥云离了蓬莱，又早到方丈仙山。这山真好去处。有诗为证。诗曰：

> 方丈巍峨别是天，太元宫府会神仙。
> 紫台光照三清路，花木香浮五色烟。
> 金凤自多桀蕊阙，玉膏谁逐灌芝田？
> 碧桃紫李新成熟，又换仙人信万年。

那行者按落云头，无心玩景。正走处，只闻得香风馥馥，玄鹤声鸣，那壁厢有个神仙。但见：

> 盈空万道霞光现，彩雾飘飘光不断。
> 丹凤衔花也更鲜，青鸾飞舞弄娇艳。
> 福如东海寿如山，貌似小童身体健。
> 壶隐洞天不老丹，腰悬与日长生箓。
> 人间数次降祯祥，世上几番消厄愿。
> 武帝曾宣加寿龄，瑶池每赴蟠桃宴。
> 教化众僧脱俗缘，指开大道明如电。
> 也曾跨海祝千秋，常去灵山参佛面。
> 圣号东华大帝君，烟霞第一神仙眷。

孙行者觑面相迎，叫声"帝君，起了了。"那帝君慌忙回礼道："大圣，失迎。请荒居奉茶。"遂与行者搀手而入。果然是贝阙仙宫，看不尽瑶池琼阁。方坐待茶，只见翠屏后转出一个童儿。他怎生打扮：

> 身穿道服飘霞烁，腰束丝绦光错落。
> 头戴纶巾布斗星，足登芳履游仙岳。
> 炼元真，脱本壳，功行成时遂意乐。
> 识破原流精气神，主人认得无虚错。
> 逃名今喜寿无疆，甲子周天管不着。
> 转回廊，登宝阁，天上蟠桃三度摸。
> 缥缈香云出翠屏，小仙乃是东方朔。

行者见了，笑道："这个小贼在这里哩！帝君处没有桃子你偷吃！"东方朔朝上进礼，笑道："老贼，你来这里怎的？我师父没有仙丹你偷吃。"

【8】帝君叫道："曼倩休乱言，看茶来也。"曼倩原是东方朔的道名。他急入里取茶二杯，饮讫。行者道："老孙此来，有一事奉干，未知允否？"帝君道："何事？自当领教。"行者道："近因保唐

僧西行，路过万寿山五庄观，因他那小童无状，是我一时发怒，把他人参果树推倒，因此阻滞，唐僧不得脱身，特来尊求赐一方医治，万望慨允。"帝君道："你这猴子，不管一二，到处里闯祸。那五庄观镇元子，圣号与世同君，乃地仙之祖。你怎么就冲撞出他？他那人参果树，乃草还丹。你偷吃了，尚说有罪；却又连树推倒，他肯干休？"行者道："正是呢。我们走脱了，被他赶上，把我们就当汗巾儿一般，一袖子都笼了去，没奈何，许他求方医治，故此拜求。"帝君道："我有一粒'九转太乙还丹'，但能治世间生灵，却不能医树。树乃水土之灵，天滋地润。若是凡间的果木，医治还可；这万寿山乃先天福地，五庄观乃贺洲洞天，人参果又是天开地辟之灵根，如何可治！无方！无方！"

【9】　行者道："既然无方，老孙告别。"帝君仍欲留奉玉液一杯，行者道："急救事紧，不敢久滞。"遂驾云复至瀛洲海岛。也好去处。有诗为证。诗曰：

> 珠树玲珑照紫烟，瀛洲宫阙接诸天。
> 青山绿水琪花艳，玉液锟铻铁石坚。
> 五色碧鸡啼海日，千年丹凤吸朱烟。
> 世人罔究壶中景，象外春光亿万年。

那大圣至瀛洲，只见那丹崖珠树之下，有几个皓发皤髯之辈，童颜鹤鬓之仙，在那里着棋饮酒，谈笑讴歌。真个是：

> 祥云光满，瑞霭香浮。彩鸾鸣洞口，玄鹤舞山头。碧藕水桃为按酒，交梨火枣寿千秋。一个个丹诏无闻，仙符有籍；逍遥随浪荡，散淡任清幽。周天甲子难拘管，大地乾坤只自由。献果玄猿，对对参随多美爱；衔花白鹿，双双拱伏甚绸缪。

那些老儿，正然洒乐。这行者厉声高叫道："带我耍耍儿，便怎的！"众仙见了，忙忙趋步相迎。有诗为证。诗曰：

> 人参果树灵根非，大圣访仙求妙诀。
> 缭绕丹霞出宝林，瀛洲九老来相接。

行者认得是九老，笑道："老兄弟们自在哩！"九老道："大圣当年若存正，不闹天宫，比我们还自在哩。如今好了，闻你归真向西拜佛，如何得暇至此？"行者将那医树求方之事，具陈了一遍。九

231

老也大惊道:"你也忒惹祸!惹祸!我等实是无方。"行者道:"既是无方,我且奉别。"

【10】 九老又留他饮琼浆,食碧藕。行者定不肯坐,止立饮了他一杯浆,吃了一块藕,急急离了瀛洲,径转东洋大海。早望见落伽山不远,遂落下云头,直到普陀岩上。见观音菩萨在紫竹林中与诸天大神、木叉、龙女,讲经说法。有诗为证。诗曰:

> 海主城高瑞气浓,更观奇异事无穷。
> 须知隐约千般外,尽出希微一品中。
> 四圣授时成正果,六凡听后脱樊笼。
> 少林别有真滋味,花果馨香满树红。

那菩萨早已看见行者来到,即命守山大神去迎。那大神出林来,叫声"孙悟空,那里去?"行者抬头见道:"你这个熊黑!我是你叫的悟空?当初不是老孙饶了你,你已此做个黑风山的尸鬼矣。如今现了菩萨,受了善果,居此仙山,常听法教,你叫不得我一声'老爷'?"那黑熊真个得了正果,在菩萨处镇守普陀,称为大神,是也亏了行者。他只得陪笑道:"大圣,古人云:'君子不念旧恶。'只管题他怎的!菩萨着我来迎你哩。"这行者就端肃尊诚,与大神到了紫竹林里,参拜菩萨。

菩萨道:"悟空,唐僧行到何处也?"行者道:"行到西牛贺洲万寿山了。"菩萨道:"那万寿山有座五庄观,镇元大仙,你曾会他么?"行者顿首道:"因是在五庄观,弟子不识镇元大仙,毁伤了他的人参果树,冲撞了他,他就困滞了我师父,不得前进。"那菩萨情知,怪道:"你这泼猴,不知好歹!他那人参果树,乃天开地辟的灵根;镇元子乃地仙之祖,我也让他三分;你怎么就打伤他树!"行者再拜道:"弟子实是不知。那一日,他不在家,只有两个仙童,候待我等。是猪悟能晓得他有果子,要一个尝新,弟子委偷了他三个,兄弟们分吃了。那童子知觉,骂我等无已,是弟子发怒,遂将他树推倒。他次日回来赶上,将我等一地笼云,绳绑鞭抽,拷打了一日。我等当夜走脱,又把他赶上,依然笼了。三番两次,其实难逃,又允了与他医树。却才自海上求方,遍游三岛,众神仙都没有本事。弟子因此志心朝礼,特拜告菩萨。伏望慈悯,俯赐一方,以救唐僧早早西去。"菩萨道:"你怎么不早来见我，却往岛上去寻找？"

行者闻得此言，心中暗道："造化了！造化了！菩萨一定有方也！"他又上前恳求。菩萨道："我这净瓶底的'甘露水'，善治得仙树灵苗。"行者道："可曾经验过么？"菩萨道："经验过的。"行者道："有何经验？"菩萨道："当年太上老君曾与我赌胜：他把我的杨柳枝拔了去，放在炼丹炉里，炙得焦干，送来还我。是我拿了插在瓶中，一昼夜，复得青枝绿叶，与旧相同。"行者笑道："真造化了！真造化了！烘焦了的尚能医活，况此推倒的，有何难哉！"菩萨吩咐大众："看守林中，我去去来。"遂手托净瓶，白鹦哥前边巧啭，孙大圣随后相从。有诗为证。诗曰：

玉毫金像世难论，正是慈悲救苦尊。
过去劫逢无垢佛，至今成得有为身。
几生欲海澄清浪，一片心田绝点尘。
甘露久经真妙法，管教宝树永长春。

【11】　却说那观里大仙与三老正然清话，忽见孙大圣按落云头，叫道："菩萨来了。快接！快接！"慌得那三星与镇元子共三藏师徒，一齐迎出宝殿。菩萨才住了祥云，先与镇元子陪了话；后与三星作礼。礼毕上坐。那阶前，行者引唐僧、八戒、沙僧都拜了。那观中诸仙，也来拜见。行者道："大仙不必迟疑，趁早儿陈设香案，请菩萨替你治那五显、果树去。"大仙躬身谢菩萨道："小可的勾当，怎么敢劳菩萨下降？"菩萨道："唐僧乃我之弟子，孙悟空冲撞了先生，理当赔修宝树。"三老道："既如此，不须谦讲了。请菩萨都到园中去看看。"

【12】　那大仙即命设具香案，打扫后园，请菩萨先行。三老随后。三藏师徒与本观众仙，都到园内观看时，那棵树倒在地下，土开根现，叶落枝枯。菩萨叫："悟空，伸手来。"那行者将左手伸开。菩萨将杨柳枝，蘸出瓶中甘露，把行者手心里画了一道起死回生的符字，教他放在树根底下，看水出为度。那行者捏着拳头，往那树根底下端着，须臾，有清泉一汪。菩萨道："那水不许犯五行之器，须用玉瓢舀出，扶起树来，从头浇下，自然根皮相合，叶长芽生，枝青果出。"行者道："小道士们，快取玉瓢来。"镇元子道："贫道荒山，没有玉瓢，只有玉茶盏、玉酒杯，可用得么？"

菩萨道："但是玉器,可舀得水的便罢,取将来看。"大仙即命小童子取出有二三十个茶盏,四五十个酒盏,却将那根下清泉舀出。行者、八戒、沙僧,扛起树来,扶得周正,拥上土,将玉器内甘泉,一瓯瓯捧与菩萨。菩萨将杨柳枝细细洒上,口中又念着经咒。不多时,洒净那舀出之水,只见那树果然依旧青绿叶阴森,上有二十三个人参果。清风、明月二童子道:"前日不见了果子时,颠倒只数得二十二个;今日回生,怎么又多了一个?"行者道:"'日久见人心。'前日老孙只偷了三个,那一个落下地来,土地说这宝遇土而入,八戒只嚷我打了偏手,故走了风信,只缠到如今,才见明白。"

【13】 菩萨道:"我方才不用五行之器者,知道此物与五行相畏故耳。"那大仙十分欢喜,急令取金击子来,把果子敲下十个,请菩萨与三老复回宝殿,一则谢劳,二来做个"人参果会"。众小仙遂调开桌椅,铺设丹盘,请菩萨坐了上面正席,三老左席,唐僧右席,镇元子前席相陪,各食了一个。有诗为证。诗曰:

> 万寿山中古洞天,人参一熟九千年。
> 灵根现出芽枝损,甘露滋生果叶全。
> 三老喜逢皆旧契,四僧幸遇是前缘。
> 自今会服人参果,尽是长生不老仙。

此时菩萨与三老各吃了一个,唐僧始知是仙家宝贝,也吃了一个。悟空三人,亦各吃一个。镇元子陪了一个。本观仙众分吃了一个。行者才谢了菩萨回上普陀岩,送三星径转蓬莱岛。镇元子却又安排蔬酒,与行者结为兄弟。这才是不打不成相识,两家合了一家。

Chapter 9
Sun Wukong Looks for the Formula in the Three Islands;
Guanyin Revives the Tree with a Spring of Sweet Water

[1] As the poem goes,

When living in the world you must be forbearing;
Patience is essential when training oneself.
Although it's often said that violence is good business,
Think before you act, and never bully or be angry.
True gentlemen who never strive are famed for ever;
The virtue-loving sages are renowned to this day.
Strong men always meet stronger than themselves,
And end up as failures who are in the wrong.

The Great Immortal Zhen Yuan held Monkey in his hand and said, "I've heard about your powers and your fame, but this time you have gone too far. Even if you manage to remove yourself, you won't escape my clutches. You and I shall argue it out as far as the Western Heaven, and even if you see that Buddha of yours, you'll still have to give me back my manfruit tree first. Don't try any of your magic now." "What a small-minded bloke you are, sir," Monkey replied with a laugh. "If you want your tree brought back to life, there's no problem. If you'd told me earlier we could have been spared all this quarrelling." "If you hadn't made trouble I'd have forgiven you," said the Great Immortal. "Would you agree to release my master if I gave you back the tree alive?" Monkey asked. "If your magic is strong enough to revive the tree," the Great Immortal replied, "I shall bow to you eight times and take you as my brother." "That's easy then," said Monkey. "Release them and I guarantee to give you back your tree alive."

235

【2】 Trust him not to escape, the Great Immortal ordered that Sanzang, Pig and Friar Sand be set free. "Master," said Friar Sand, "I wonder what sort of trick Monkey is up to." "I'll tell you what sort of trick," retorted Pig. "A pleading for favour trick. The tree's dead and can't possibly be revived. Finding a cure for the tree is an excuse for going off by himself without giving a damn for you or me." "He wouldn't dare abandon us," said Sanzang. "Let's ask him where he's going to find a doctor for it. Monkey," he continued, "why did you fool the Immortal elder into untying us?" "Every word I said was true," Monkey replied. "I wasn't having him on." "Where will you go to find a cure?" "There's an old saying that 'cures come from over the sea'. I'll go to the Eastern Sea and travel round the Three Islands and Ten Continents visiting the venerable Immortals and sages to find a formula for bringing the dead back to life. I promise that I'll cure that tree." "When will you come back?" "I'll only need three days." "In that case I'll give you three days. If you are back within that time, that will be all right, but if you are late I shall recite that spell." "I'll do as you say," said Monkey.

【3】 He immediately straightened up his tiger-skin kilt, went out through the door, and said to the Great Immortal, "Don't worry, sir, I'll soon be back. Mind you look after my master well. Give him tea three times a day and six meals, and don't leave any out. If you do, I'll settle that score when I come back, and I'll start by holing the bottoms of all your pans. If his clothes get dirty, wash them for him. I won't stand for it if he looks sallow, and if he loses weight you'll never see the back of me." "Go away, go away," the Great Immortal replied. "I certainly won't let him go hungry."

The splendid Monkey King left the Wuzhuang Temple with a bound of his somersault cloud and headed for the Eastern Sea. He went through the air as fast as a flash of lightning or a shooting star, and he was soon in the blessed land of Penglai. As he landed his cloud he looked around him and saw that it was indeed a wonderful place. A poem about it goes:

A great and sacred land where the Immortal sages
Still the waves as they come and go.
The shade of the jasper throne cools the heart of the sky;
The radiance of the great gate-pillars shimmers high above
the sea.
Hidden in the coloured mists are flutes of jade;
The moon and the stars shine on the golden leviathan.
The Queen Mother of the Western Pool often comes here
To give her peaches to the Three Immortals.

Gazing at the enchanted land that spread out before him,
Brother Monkey entered Penglai. As he was walking along, he
noticed three old men sitting round a chess table under the shade
of a pine tree outside a cloud-wreathed cave. The one watching
the game was the Star of Longevity, and the players were the
Star of Blessings and the Star of Office. "Greetings, respected
younger brothers," Monkey called to them, and when they saw
him they swept the pieces away, returned his salutation, and
said, "Why have you come here, Great Sage?" "To see you," he
replied. "I've heard" said the Star of Longevity, "that you have
given up the Way for the sake of the Buddha, and have thrown
aside your life to protect the Tang Priest on his journey to fetch
the scriptures from the Western Heaven. How can you spare the
time from your endless crossings of waters and mountains just to
see us?" "To tell you the truth," said Monkey, "I was on my
way to the West until a spot of bother held us up. I wonder if you
could do me a small favour." "Where did this happen?" asked the
Star of Blessings, "what has been holding you up? Please tell us
and we'll deal with it." "We've been held up because we went via
the Wuzhuang Temple on the Mountain of Infinite Longevity,"
said Monkey. "But the Wuzhuang Temple is the palace of the
Great Immortal Zhen Yuan," exclaimed the three Immortals with
alarm, "don't say that you've stolen some of his manfruit!"
"What if I had stolen and eaten some?" asked Monkey with a
grin. "You ignorant ape," the three Immortals replied. "A mere
whiff of that fruit makes a man live to be three hundred and

237

sixty, and anyone who eats one will live forty-seven thousand years. They are called ' Grass-returning Cinnabar of Ten Thousand Longevities', and our Way hasn't a patch on them. Manfruit makes you as immortal as Heaven with the greatest of ease, while it takes us goodness knows how long to nourish our essence, refine the spirit, preserve our soul, harmonize water and fire, capture the kan to fill out the li. How can you possibly ask whether it would matter? There is no other miraculous tree like it on earth. " " Miraculous tree, " scoffed Monkey, " miraculous tree! I've put an end to that miraculous tree. " " What? Put an end to it? " the three Immortals asked, struck with horror. "When I was in his temple the other day, " Monkey said, "the Great Immortal wasn't at home. There were only a couple of boys who received my master and gave him two manfruits. My master didn't know what they were and said that they were newborn babies; he refused to eat them. The boys took them away and ate them themselves instead of offering them to the rest of us, so I went and pinched three, one for each of us disciples. Those disrespectful boys swore and cursed at us no end, which made me so angry that I knocked their tree over with a single blow. All the fruit disappeared, the leaves fell, the roots came out, and the branches were smashed up. The tree was dead. To our surprise the two boys locked us in, but I opened the lock and we escaped. When the Great Immortal came home the next day, he came after us and found us. Our conversation didn't go too smoothly and we started to fight him, but he dodged us, spread his sleeve out, and caught us all up in it. After being tied up, then flogged and interrogated for a day, we escaped again, but he caught up with us and captured us again. Although he had not an inch of steel on him, he fought us off with his whisk, and even with our three weapons we couldn't touch him. He caught us the same way as before. He had my master and two brothers wrapped up in bandages and lacquered, and was going to throw me into a cauldron of oil, but I used a trick to take my body away and escape, smashing that pan of his. Now that he has realized he can't catch me and keep me he's getting a bit scared of me, and I had a good talk with him. I told him that if he released my master and my brothers I'd guarantee to cure the tree and bring it back to life, which would satisfy both parties. As it occurred to me that 'cures come from over the sea' I came here specially to visit you three brothers of mine. If you have any cures that will bring a tree back to life, please tell me one so that I can get the Tang Priest out of trouble as quickly as possible."

[4] "You ape," the Three Stars said gloomily when they heard this. "You don't know who you're up against. That Master Zhen Yuan is the Patriarch of the Immortals of the earth, and we are the chiefs of the divine Immortals. Although you have become a heavenly Immortal, you are still only one of the irregulars of the Great Monad, not one of the elite. You'll never be able to escape his clutches. If you'd killed some animal, bird, insect or reptile, Great Sage, we could have given you some pills made from sticky millet to bring it back to life, but the manfruit tree is a magic one and can't possibly be revived. There's no cure, none at all." When he heard that there was no cure, Monkey's brows locked in a frown, and his forehead was creased in a thousand wrinkles. "Great Sage" said the Star of Blessing, "even though we have no cure here, there may be some somewhere else. Why be so worried?" "If there were anywhere else for me to go," Monkey replied, "it would be easy. It wouldn't even matter if I had to go to the furthest corner of the ocean, or to the cliff at the end of the sky, or if I had to penetrate the Thirty-sixth Heaven. But the trouble is that the Tang Patriarch is very strict and has given me a time-limit of three days. If I'm not back in three days he'll recite the Band-tightening Spell." "Splendid, splendid," laughed the Three Stars. "If you weren't restricted by that spell you'd go up to Heaven again." "Calm down, Great Sage," said the Star of Longevity, "there's no need to worry. Although that Great Immortal is senior to us he is a friend of ours, and as we haven't visited him for a long time and would like to do you a favour we'll go and see him. We'll explain things for you and tell that Tang monk not to recite the Band-tightening Spell. We won't go away until you come back, however long you take, even if it's a lot

239

longer than three to five days." "Thank you very much," said Monkey. "May I ask you to set out now as I'm off?" With that he took his leave.

【5】　The Three Stars went off on beams of auspicious light to the Wuzhuang Temple, where all present heard cranes calling in the sky as the three of them arrived.

> *The void was bathed in blessed glow,*
> *The Milky Way heavy with fragrance.*
> *A thousand wisps of coloured mist enveloped the feather-clad ones:*
> *A single cloud supported the immortal feet.*
> *Green and red phoenixes circled and soared,*
> *As the aroma in their sleeves wafted over the earth.*
> *These dragons leant on their staffs and smiled,*
> *And jade-white beards waved before their chests.*
> *Their youthful faces were untroubled by sorrow,*
> *Their majestic bodies were rich with blessing.*
> *They carried star-chips to count their age,*
> *And at their waists hung gourds and talismans.*
> *Their life is infinitely long,*
> *And they live on the Ten Continents and Three Islands.*
> *They often come to bring blessings to mortals,*
> *Spreading good things a hundredfold among humans.*
> *The glory and blessings of the universe*
> *Come now as happiness unlimited.*
> *As these three elders visit the Great Immortal on auspicious light,*
> *There is no end to good fortune and peace.*

"Master," the immortal youths rushed to report when they saw them, "the Three Stars from the sea are here." The Great Immortal Zhen Yuan, who was talking with the Tang Priest, came down the steps to welcome them when he heard this. When Pig saw the Star of Longevity he went up and tugged at his clothes. "I haven't seen you for ages, you meat-headed old fellow," he said with a grin. "You're getting very free and easy, turning up without a hat." With these words he thrust his own clerical hat on the star's head, clapped his hands, and roared with laughter. "Great, great. You've been 'capped and promoted' all right." Flinging the hat down, the Star of Longevity cursed him for a disrespectful moron. "I'm no moron," said Pig, "but you're all slaves." "You're most certainly a moron," the Star of Blessing replied, "so how dare you call us slaves?" "If you aren't slaves then," Pig retorted, "why do people always ask you to 'bring us long life', 'bring us blessings', and 'bring us a good job'?"

[6]   Sanzang shouted at Pig to go away, then quickly tidied himself up and bowed to the Three Stars. The Three Stars greeted the Great Immortal as befitted members of a younger generation, after which they all sat down. "We have not seen your illustrious countenance for a long time," the Star of Office said, "which shows our great lack of respect. The reason we come to see you now is because the Great Sage Monkey has made trouble in your immortal temple." "Has Monkey been to Penglai?" the Great Immortal asked. "Yes," replied the Star of Longevity. "He came to our place to ask for a formula to restore the elixir tree that he killed. As we have no cure for it, he has had to go elsewhere in search of it. We are afraid that if he exceeds the three-day time-limit the holy priest has imposed, the Band-tightening Spell may be said. We have come in the first place to pay our respects and in the second to ask for an extension of the limit." "I won't recite it, I promise," answered Sanzang as soon as he heard this.

As they were talking Pig came rushing in again to grab hold of the Star of Blessing and demand some fruit from him. He started to feel in the star's sleeves and rummage round his waist, pulling his clothes apart as he searched everywhere. "What sort of behaviour is that?" asked Sanzang with a smile. "I'm not misbehaving," said Pig. "This is what's meant by the saying, 'blessings wherever you look'." Sanzang shouted at him to go away again. The idiot withdrew slowly, glaring at the Star of Blessing with unwavering hatred in his eyes. "I wasn't angry with you, you moron," said the Star, "so why do you hate me so?" "I don't hate you," said Pig. "This is what they call 'turning the head and seeing blessing'." As the idiot was going out he saw a young boy came in with four tea ladles, looking for bowls in the abbot's cell in which to put fruit and serve tea. Pig seized one of the ladles, ran to the main hall of the temple, snatched up a hand-bell, and started striking it wildly. He was enjoying himself enormously when the Great Immortal said, "This monk gets more and more disrespectful." "I'm not being disrespectful," Pig replied. "I'm 'ringing in happiness for the four seasons'."

[7]   While Pig was having his jokes and making trouble, Monkey had bounded away from Penglai by auspicious cloud and come to the magic mountain Fangzhang. This was a really wonderful place. As the poem goes,

The towering Fangzhang is another heaven,

Where gods and Immortals meet in the Palace of the Great Unity.

The purple throne illuminates the road to the Three Pure Ones,

The scent of flowers and trees drifts among the clouds.

Many a golden phoenix comes to rejoice around its flowery portals;

What makes the fields of magical mushrooms glisten like jade?

Pale peaches and purple plums are newly ripened,

Ready to give even longer life to the Immortals.

But as monkey brought his cloud down he was in no mood to enjoy the view. As he was walking along he smelt a fragrance in the wind, heard the cry of the black stork, and saw an Immortal:

The sky was filled with radiant light,

As multicoloured clouds shone and glowed.

Red phoenixes looked brighter than the flowers in their

beaks;

> *Sweetly sang green ones as they danced in flight.*
> *His blessings were as great as the Eastern Sea, his age that*
of a mountain;
> *Yet his face was a child's and his body was strong.*
> *In a bottle he kept his pills of eternal youth,*
> *And a charm for everlasting life hung from his waist.*
> *He had often sent blessings down to mankind,*
> *Several times saving mortals from difficulties.*
> *He once gave longer life to Emperor Wu,*
> *And always went to the Peach Banquets at the Jade Pool.*
> *He taught all monks to cast off worldly fates;*
> *His explanations of the great Way were clear as lightning.*
> *He had crossed the seas to pay his respects,*
> *And had seen the Buddha on the Vulture Peak.*
> *His title was Lord Emperor of Eastern Glory,*
> *The highest-ranked Immortal of the mists and clouds.*

When Brother Monkey saw him he hailed him with the words, "I salute you, Lord Emperor." The Lord Emperor hastened to return his greeting and say, "I should have welcomed you properly, Great Sage. May I ask you home for some tea?" He led Monkey by the hand to his palace of cowrie-shells, where there was no end of jasper pools and jade towers. They were sitting waiting for their tea when a boy appeared from behind an emerald screen. This is how he looked:

> *A Taoist robe that sparkled with colour hung from his*
body,
> *And light gleamed from the silken sash round his waist.*
> *On his head he wore a turban with the sign of the stars of*
the Dipper,
> *And the grass sandals on his feet had climbed all the*
magical mountains.
> *He was refining his True Being, shuffling off his shell,*
> *And when he had finished he would reach unbounded bliss.*

His understanding had broken through to the origins,

And his master knew that he was free from mistakes.

Avoiding fame and enjoying the present he had won long life

And did not care about the passing of time.

He had been along the crooked portico, climbed to the precious hall,

And three times received the peaches of Heaven.

Clouds of incense appeared to rise from behind the emerald screen;

This young Immortal was Dongfang Shuo himself.

"So you're here, you young thief," said Monkey with a smile when he saw him. "There are no peaches for you to steal here in the Lord Emperor's palace." Dongfang Shuo greeted him respectfully and replied, "What have you come for, you old thief? My master doesn't keep any pills of immortality here for you to pinch."

[8] "Stop talking nonsense, Manqian," the Lord Emperor shouted, "and bring some tea." Manqian was Dongfang Shuo's Taoist name. He hurried inside and brought out two cups of tea. When the two of them had drunk it, Monkey said, "I came here to ask you to do something for me. I wonder if you'd be prepared to." "What is it?" the Lord Emperor asked. "Do tell me." "I have been escorting the Tang Priest on his journey to the West," Monkey replied, "and our route took us via the Wuzhuang Temple on the Mountain of Infinite Longevity. The youths there were so ill-mannered that I lost my temper and knocked their manfruit tree over. We've been held up for a while as a result, and the Tang Priest cannot get away, which is why I have come to ask you, sir, to give me a formula that will cure it. I do hope that you will be good enough to agree." "You thoughtless ape," the Lord Emperor replied, "you make trouble wherever you go. Master Zhen Yuan of the Wuzhuang Temple has the sacred title Conjoint Lord of the Age, and he is the Patriarch of the Immortals of the Earth. Why ever did you clash with him? That

244

manfruit tree of his is Grass-returning Cinnabar. It was criminal enough of you to steal some of the fruit, and knocking the tree over makes it impossible for him ever to make it up with you."

"True," said Monkey. "When we escaped he caught up with us and swept us into his sleeve as if we were so many sweat-rags, which made me furious. However, he had to let me go and look for a formula that would cure it, which is why I've come to ask your help." "I have a nine-phased returning pill of the Great Monad, but it can only bring animate objects back to life, not trees. Trees are lives compounded of the Wood and Earth elements and nurtured by Heaven and Earth. If it were an ordinary mortal tree I could bring it back to life, but the Mountain of Infinite Longevity is the blessed land of a former heaven, the Wuzhuang Temple is the Cave Paradise of the Western Continent of Cattle-gift, and the manfruit tree is the life-root from the time when Heaven and Earth were separated. How could it possibly be revived? I have no formula, none at all."

[9] "In that case I must take my leave," replied Monkey, and when the Lord Emperor tried to detain him with a cup of jade nectar he said, "This is too urgent to allow me to stay." He rode his cloud back to the island of Yingzhou, another wonderful place, as this poem shows:

> Trees of pearls glowed with a purple haze;
> The Yingzhou palaces led straight to the heavens.
> Blue hills, green rivers, and the beauty of exquisite
> flowers;
> Jade mountains as hard as iron.
> Pheasants called at the sunrise over the sea,
> Long-lived phoenixes breathe in the red clouds.
> People, do not look so hard at the scenery in your jar:
> Beyond the world of phenomena is an eternal spring.

On reaching Yingzhou he saw a number of white-haired Immortals with the faces of children playing chess and drinking under a pearl tree at the foot of a cinnabar cliff. They were laughing and singing. As the poem says, there were

> Light-filled auspicious clouds,
> Perfume floating in a blessed haze.
> Brilliant phoenixes singing at the mouth of a cave,
> Black cranes dancing on a mountain top.
> Pale green lotus-root and peaches helped their wine down,
> Pears and fiery red dates gave them a thousand years of
> life.
> Neither of them had ever heard an imperial edict,
> But each was entered on the list of Immortals.
> They drifted and floated with the waves,
> Free and easy in unsullied elegance.
> The passage of the days could not affect them;
> Their freedom was guaranteed by Heaven and Earth.
> Black apes come in pairs,
> Looking most charming as they present fruit;
> White deer, bowing two by two,
> Thoughtfully offer flowers.

These old men were certainly living a free and happy life. "How about letting me play with you?" Monkey shouted at the top of his voice, and when the Immortals saw him they hurried over to welcome him. There is a poem to prove it that goes:

> When the magic root of the manfruit tree was broken;
> The Great Sage visited the Immortals in search of a cure.
> Winding their way through the vermilion mist, the Nine
> Ancients
> Came out of the precious forest to greet him.

Monkey, who knew the Nine Ancients, said with a smile, "You nine brothers seem to be doing very nicely." "If you had stayed on straight and narrow in the old days, Great Sage," they replied, "and not wrecked the Heavenly Palace you would be doing even better than we are. Now we hear that you have

246

reformed and are going West to visit the Buddha. How did you manage the time off to come here?" Monkey told them how he was searching for a formula to cure the tree. "What a terrible thing to do," they exclaimed in horror, "what a terrible thing. We honestly have no cure at all." "In that case I must take my leave of you."

[10]   The Nine Ancients tried to detain him with jasper wine and jade lotus-root, but Monkey refused to sit down, and stayed on his feet while he drank only one cup of wine and ate only one piece of lotus-root. Then he hurried away from Yingzhou and back to the Great Eastern Ocean. When he saw that Potaraka was not far away, he brought his cloud down to land on the Potara Crag, where he saw the Bodhisattva Guanyin expounding the scriptures and preaching the Buddha's Law to all the great gods of heaven, Moksa, and the dragon maiden in the Purple Bamboo Grove. A poem about it goes:

> Thick the mists round the lofty city of the sea's mistress,
> And no end to the greater marvels to be seen.
> The Shaolin Temple really has the true flavour,
> With the scent of flowers and fruit and the trees all red.

The Bodhisattva saw Monkey arrive and ordered the Great Guardian God of the Mountain to go and welcome him. The god emerged from the bamboo grove and shouted, "Where are you going, Monkey?" "You bear monster," Monkey shouted back, "how dare you address me as 'Monkey'? If I hadn't spared your life that time you'd have been just a demon's corpse on the Black Wind Mountain. Now you've joined the Bodhisattva, accepted enlightenment, and come to live on this blessed island where you hear the Law being taught all the time. Shouldn't you address me as 'sir'?" It was indeed thanks to Monkey that the black bear had been enlightened and was now guarding the Bodhisattva's Potaraka as one of the great gods of heaven, so all he could do was to force a smile and say, "The ancients said, Great Sage, that a gentleman does not bear grudges. Why should you care about what you're called? Anyhow, the Bodhisattva has sent me to welcome you." Monkey then became grave and serious as he went into the Purple Bamboo Grove with the Great God and did obeisance to the Bodhisattva.

"How far has the Tang Priest got, Monkey?" she asked. "He has reached the Mountain of Infinite Longevity in the Western Continent of Cattle-gift," Monkey replied. "Have you met the Great Immortal Zhen Yuan who lives in the Wuzhuang Temple on that mountain?" she asked. "As your disciple didn't meet the Great Immortal Zhen Yuan when I was in the Wuzhuang Temple," replied Monkey, bowing down to the ground, "I destroyed his manfruit tree and offended him. As a result my master is in a very difficult position and can make no progress." "You wretched ape," said the Bodhisattva angrily now that she knew about it, "you have no conscience at all. That manfruit tree of his is the life-root from the time when Heaven and Earth were separated, and Master Zhen Yuan is the Patriarch of the Earth's Immortals, which means even I have to show him a certain respect. Why ever did you harm his tree?" Monkey bowed once more and said, "I really didn't know. He was away that day and there were only two immortal youths to look after us. When Pig heard that they had this fruit he wanted to try one, so I stole three for him and we had one each. They swore at us no end when they found out, so I lost my temper and knocked the tree over. When he came back the next day he chased us and caught us all up in his sleeve. We were tied up and flogged for a whole day. We got away that night but he caught up with us and put us in his sleeve again. All our escape attempts failed, so I promised him I'd put the tree right. I've been searching for a formula all over the seas and been to all three islands of Immortals, but the gods and Immortals are all useless, which is why I decided to come and worship you, Bodhisattva, and tell you all about it. I beg you in your mercy to grant me a formula so that I can save the Tang Priest and have him on his way west again as soon as possible." "Why didn't you come and see me earlier instead of searching the islands for it?" the Bodhisattva asked.

"I'm in luck," thought Monkey with delight when he heard this, "I'm in luck. The Bodhisattva must have a formula." He went up to her and pleaded for it again. "The 'sweet dew' in this pure vase of mine," she said, "is an excellent cure for magic trees and plants." "Has it ever been tried out?" Monkey asked. "Yes," she said. "How?" he asked. "Some years ago Lord Lao Zi beat me at gambling," she replied, "and took my willow sprig away with him. He put it in his elixir-refining furnace and burnt it to a cinder before sending it back to me. I put it back in the vase, and a day and a night later it was as green and leafy as ever." "I'm really in luck," said Monkey, "really in luck. If it can bring a cinder back to life, something that has only been pushed over should be easy." The Bodhisattva instructed her subjects to look after the grove as she was going away for a while. Then she took up her vase, and her white parrot went in front singing while Monkey followed behind. As the poem goes,

> The jade-haired golden one is hard to describe to mortals;
> She truly is a compassionate deliverer.
> Although in aeons past she had known the spotless Buddha,
> Now she had acquired a human form.
> After several lives in the sea of suffering she had purified
> the waves,
> And in her heart there was no speck of dust.
> The sweet dew that had long undergone the miraculous
> Law
> Was bound to give the magic tree eternal life.

【11】 The Great Immortal and the Three Stars were still in lofty conversation when they saw Monkey bring his cloud down and heard him shout, "The Bodhisattva's here. Come and welcome her at once." The Three Stars and Master Zheng Yuan hurried out with Sanzang and his disciples to greet her. On bringing her cloud to a stop, she first talked with Master Zhen Yuan and then greeted the Three Stars, after which she climbed to her seat. Monkey then led the Tang Priest, Pig, and Friar Sand out to do obeisance before the steps, and all the Immortals in the temple came to bow to her as well. "There's no need to dither about, Great Immortal," said Monkey. "Get an incense table ready at once and ask the Bodhisattva to cure that whatever-it-is tree of yours." The Great Immortal Zhen Yuan bowed to the Bodhisattva and thanked her: "How could I be so bold as to trouble the Bodhisattva with my affairs?" "The Tang Priest is my disciple, and Monkey has offended you, so it is only right that I should make up for the loss of your priceless tree." "In that case there is no need for you to refuse," said the Three Stars. "May we invite you, Bodhisattva, to come into our orchard and take a look?"

【12】 The Great Sage had an incense table set up and the orchard swept, then he asked the Bodhisattva to lead the way. The Three Stars followed behind. Sanzang, his disciples, and all the Immortals of the temple went into the orchard to look, and they saw the tree lying on the ground with the earth torn open, its roots laid bare, its leaves fallen and its branches withered. "Put your hand out, Monkey," said the Bodhisattva, and Brother Monkey stretched out his left hand. The Bodhisattva dipped her willow spray into the sweet dew in her vase, then used it to write a spell to revive the dead on the palm of Monkey's hand. She told him to place it on the roots of the tree until he saw water coming out. Monkey clenched his fist and tucked it under the roots; before long a spring of clear water began to form a pool. "That water must not be sullied by vessels made of any of the Five Elements, so you will have to scoop it out with a jade ladle. If you prop the tree up and pour the water on it from the very top, its bark and trunk will knit together, its leaves will sprout again, the branches will be green once more, and the fruit will reappear." "Fetch a jade ladle this moment, young Taoists," said Monkey. "We poor monks have no jade ladle in our destitute temple. We only have jade tea-bowls and wine-cups. Would they do?" "As long as they are jade and can scoop out water they will do," the Bodhisattva replied. "Bring them out and try." The Great Immortal then told some boys to fetch the twenty or thirty tea-bowls and the forty or fifty wine-cups and ladle the clear water out from under the roots. Monkey, Pig and Friar Sand put their shoulders under the tree, raised it upright, and banked it up with earth. Then they presented the sweet spring water cup by cup to the Bodhisattva, who sprinkled it lightly on the tree with her spray of willow and recited an incantation. When a little later the water had all been sprinkled on the tree the leaves really did become as dense and green as ever, and there were twenty-three manfruits growing there. Pure Wind and Bright Moon, the two immortal boys, said, "When the fruit disappeared the other day there were only twenty-two of them; so why is there an extra one now that it has come back to life?" " 'Time shows the truth about a man'," Monkey replied. "I only stole three that day. The other one fell on the ground, and the local deity told me that this treasure always entered earth when it touched it. Pig accused me of taking it as a bit of extra for myself and blackened my reputation, but at long last the truth has come out."

【13】 "The reason why I did not use vessels made from the Five Elements was because I knew that this kind of fruit is allergic to them," said the Bodhisattva. The Great Immortal, now extremely happy, had the golden rod fetched at once and knocked down ten of the fruits. He invited the Bodhisattva and the Three Stars to come to the main hall of the temple to take part a Manfruit Feast to thank them for their labours. All the junior Immortals arranged tables, chairs, and cinnabar bowls. The Bodhisattva was asked to take the seat of honour with the Three Stars on her left, the Tang Priest on her right, and Master Zhen Yuan facing her as the host. They ate one fruit each, and there are some lines about it:

> In the ancient earthly paradise on the Mountain of Infinite Longevity
> The manfruit ripens once in nine thousand years.
> When the magic roots were bared and the branches dead,
> The sweet dew brought leaves and fruit back to life.
> The happy meeting of the Three Stars was predestined;

It was fated that the four monks would encounter one another.

Now that they have eaten the manfruit at this feast,
They will all enjoy everlasting youth.

The Bodhisattva and the Three Stars ate one each, as did the Tang Priest, who realized at last that this was an Immortal's treasure, and Monkey, Pig and Friar Sand. Master Zhen Yuan had one to keep them company and the Immortals of the temple divided the last one between them. Monkey thanked the Bodhisattva, who went back to Potaraka, and saw the Three Stars off on their journey home to the island of Penglai. Master Zhen Yuan set out some non-alcoholic wine and made Monkey his sworn brother. This was a case of "if you don't fight you can't make friends," and their two households were now united.

252

10. 唐三藏路阻火焰山
孙行者一调芭蕉扇

【1】　若干种性本来同，海纳无穷。千思万虑终成妄，般般色色和融。有日功行满，圆明法性高隆。休教差别走西东，紧锁牢笼。收来安放丹炉同，炼得金乌一样红。朗朗辉辉娇艳，任教出入乘龙。

【2】　话表三藏遵菩萨教旨，收了行者，与八戒、沙僧剪断二心，锁笼猿马，同心戮力，赶奔西天。说不尽光阴似箭，日月如梭。历过了夏月炎天，却又值三秋霜景。但见那：

> 薄云断绝西风紧，鹤鸣远岫霜林锦。光景正苍凉，山长水更长。征鸿来北塞，玄鸟归南陌。客路怯孤单，衲衣容易寒。

师徒四众，进前行处，渐觉热气蒸人。三藏勒马道："如今正是秋天，却怎返有热气？"八戒道："原来不知。西方路上有个斯哈哩国，乃日落之处，俗呼为'天尽头'。若到申酉时，国王差人上城，擂鼓吹角，混发海沸之声。日乃太阳真火，落于西海之间，如火淬水，接声滚沸；若无鼓角之声混耳，即振杀城中小儿。此地热气蒸人，想必到日落之处也。"大圣听说，忍不住笑道："呆子莫乱谈！若论斯哈哩国，正好早哩。似师父朝三暮二的，这等担搁，就从小至老，老了又小，老小三生，也还不到。"八戒道："哥啊，据你说，不是日落之处，为何这等酷热？"沙僧道："正是天时不正，秋行夏令故也。"他三个正都争讲，只见那路旁有座庄院，乃是红瓦盖的房舍，红砖砌的垣墙，红漆板榻，一片都是红的。三藏下马道："悟空，你去那人家问个消息，看那炎热之故何也。"

【3】　大圣收了金箍棒，整肃衣裳，扭捏做个斯文气象，绰下大路，径至门前观看。那门里忽然走出一个老者，但见他：

> 穿一领黄不黄、红不红的葛布深衣；戴一顶青不青、皂不皂

253

的篾丝凉帽。手中拄一根弯不弯、直不直、暴节竹杖；足下
踏一双新不新、旧不旧、撯㩮靸鞋。面似红铜，须如白练。
两道寿眉遮碧眼，一张哈口露金牙。

那老者猛抬头，看见行者，吃了一惊，拄着竹杖，喝道："你是那里
来的怪人？在我这门首何干？"行者答礼道："老施主，休怕我。
我不是甚么怪人。贫僧是东土大唐钦差上西方求经者。师徒四
人，适至宝方，见天气蒸热，一则不解其故，二来不知地名，特持
问指教一二。"那老者却才放心，笑云："长老勿罪。我老汉一时
眼花，不识尊颜。"行者道："不敢。"老者又问："令师在那条路
上？"行者道："那南首大路上立的不是！"老者教："请来，请来。"
行者欢喜，把手一抬，三藏即同八戒、沙僧，牵白马、挑行李近前，
都对老者作礼。

老者见三藏丰姿标致，八戒、沙僧相貌奇稀，又惊又喜；只得
请人里坐，教小的们看茶，一壁厢办饭。三藏闻言，起身称谢道：
"敢问公公：贵处遇秋，何返炎热？"老者道："敝地唤做火焰山。
无春无秋，四季皆热。"三藏道："火焰山却在那边？可阻西去之
路？"老者道："西方却去不得。那山离此有六十里远，正是西方
必由之路，却有八百里火焰，四周围寸草不生。若过得山，就是
铜脑盖，铁身躯，也要化成汁哩。"三藏闻言，大惊失色，不敢再
问。

【4】 只见门外一个少年男子，推一辆红车儿，住在门旁，叫声
"卖糕！"大圣拔根毫毛，变个铜钱，问那人买糕。那人接了钱，不
论好歹，揭开车儿上衣裹，热气腾腾，拿出一块糕递与行者。行
者托在手中，好似火盆里的热炭，煤炉内的红钉。你看他左手倒
在右手，右手换在左手，只道："热，热，热！难吃，难吃！"那男子
笑道："怕热，莫来这里。这里是这等热。"行者道："你这汉子，好
不明理。常言道：'不冷不热，五谷不结。'他这等热得很，你这糕
粉，自何而来？"那人道："若知糕粉米，敬求铁扇仙。"行者道：
"铁扇仙怎的？"那人道："铁扇仙有柄'芭蕉扇'。求得来，一扇息
火，二扇生风，三扇下雨，我们就布种，及时收割，故得五谷养生；
不然，诚寸草不能生也。"

【5】 行者闻言，急抽身走入里面，将糕递与三藏道："师父放心，

且莫隔年焦着，吃了糕，我与你说。"长老接糕在手，向本宅老者道："公公请糕。"老者道："我家的茶饭未奉，敢吃你糕？"行者笑道："人家，茶饭倒不必赐。我问你：铁扇仙在那里住？"老者道："你问他怎的？"行者道："适才那卖糕人说，此仙有柄'芭蕉扇'。求将来，一扇息火，二扇生风，三扇下雨，你这方布种收割，才得五谷养生。我欲寻他讨来扇息火焰山过去，且把这时收种，得安生也。"老者道："固有此说；你们却无礼物，恐那圣贤不肯来也。"三藏道："他要甚礼物？"老者道："我这里人家，十年拜求一度。四猪四羊，花红表里，异香时果，鸡鹅美酒，沐浴虔诚，拜到那仙山，请他出洞，至此施为。"行者道："那山坐落何处？唤甚地名？有几多里数？等我问他要扇子去。"老者道："那山在西南方，名唤翠云山。山中有一仙洞，名唤芭蕉洞。我这里众信人等去拜仙山，往回要走一月，计有一千四百五六十里。"行者笑道："不打紧，就去就来。"那老者道："且住，吃些茶饭，办些干粮，须得两人做伴。那路上没有人家，又多狼虎，非一日可到。莫当耍子？"行者笑道："不用，不用！我去也！"说一声，忽然不见。那老者慌张道："爷爷呀，原来是腾云驾雾的神人也！"

【6】　且不说这家子供奉唐僧加倍。却说那行者霎时径到翠云山，按住祥光，正自找寻洞口，忽然闻得丁丁之声，乃是山林内一个樵夫伐木。行者即趋步至前，又闻得他道：

　　"云际依依认旧林，断崖荒草路难寻。
　　西山望见朝来雨，南涧归时渡处深。"

行者近前作礼道："樵哥，问讯了。"那樵子撇了柯斧，答礼道："长老何往？"行者道："敢问樵哥，这可是翠云山？"樵子道："正是。"行者道："有个铁扇仙的芭蕉洞，在何处？"樵子笑道："这芭蕉洞虽有，却无个铁扇仙，只有铁扇公主，又名罗刹女。"行者道："人言他有一柄芭蕉扇，能熄得火焰山，敢是他么？"樵子道："正是，正是。这圣贤有这件宝贝，善能熄火，保护那方人家，故此称为铁扇仙。我这里人家用不着他，只知他叫做罗刹女，乃大力牛魔王妻也。"

【7】　行者闻言，大惊失色。心中暗想道："又是冤家了！当年伏了红孩儿，说是这厮养的。前在那解阳山破儿洞遇他叔子，尚且

不肯与水，要作报仇之意；今又遇他父母，怎生借得这扇子耶？"樵子见行者沉思默虑，嗟叹不已，便笑道："长老，你出家人，有何忧疑？这条小路儿向东去，不上五六里，就是芭蕉洞。休得心焦。"行者道："不瞒樵说，我是东土唐朝差往西天求经的唐僧大徒弟。前年在火云洞，曾与罗刹之子红孩儿有些言语，但恐罗刹怀仇不与，故生忧虑。"樵子道："大丈夫鉴貌辨色，只以求扇为名，莫认往时之渡话，管情借得。"行者闻言，深深唱个大喏道："谢樵哥教海。我去也。"

遂别了樵夫，径至芭蕉洞口。但见那两扇门紧闭牢关，洞外风光秀丽。好去处！正是那：

> 山以石为骨，石做土之精。烟霞含宿润，苔藓助新青。嵯峨势耸欺蓬岛，幽静花香若海棠。千树乔松栖野鹤，数株衰柳语山莺。诚然是千年古迹，万载仙踪。碧梧鸣彩凤，活水隐苍龙。曲径苹萝垂挂，石梯藤葛攀笼。猿啸翠岩忻月上，鸟啼高树喜晴空。两林竹荫凉如雨，一径花浓没绣绒。时见白云来远岫，略无定体漫随风。

行者上前叫道："牛大哥，开门！开门！"呀的一声，洞门开了，里边走出一个毛儿女，手中提着花篮，肩上担着锄子，真个是一身蓝缕无妆饰，满面精神有道心。行者上前迎着，合掌道："女童，累你转报公主一声。我本是取经的和尚，在西方路上，难过火焰山，特来拜借芭蕉扇一用。"那毛女道："你是那寺里和尚？叫甚名字？我好与你通报。"行者道："我是东土来的，叫做孙悟空和尚。"

【8】那毛女即便回身，转于洞内，对罗刹跪下道："奶奶，洞门外有个东土来的孙悟空和尚，要见奶奶，拜求芭蕉扇，过火焰山一用。"那罗刹听见"孙悟空"三字，便似盐入火，火上浇油；骨都都红生脸上，恶狠狠怒发心头。口中骂道："这泼猴！今日来了！"叫："丫环，取披挂，拿兵器来！"随即取了披挂，拿两口青锋宝剑，整束出来。行者在洞外闪过，偷看怎生打扮。只见他：

> 头裹团花手帕，身穿纳锦云袍。腰间双束虎筋绦，微露绣裙偏绡。　凤嘴弓鞋三寸，龙须膝裤金销。手提宝剑怒声高，凶比月婆容貌。

那罗刹出门，高叫道："孙悟空何在？"行者上前，躬身施礼道："嫂嫂，老孙在此奉揖。"罗刹咄的一声道："谁是你的嫂嫂！那个要你奉揖！"行者道："尊府牛魔王，当初曾与老孙结义，乃七兄弟之亲。今闻公主是牛大哥令正，安得不以嫂嫂称之！"罗刹道："你这泼猴！既有兄弟之亲，如何坑陷我子？"行者佯问道："令郎是谁？"罗刹道："我儿是号山枯松涧火云洞圣婴大王红孩儿，被你倾了。我们正没处寻你报仇，你今上门纳命，我肯饶你！"行者满脸陪笑道："嫂嫂原来不察理，错怪了老孙。你令郎因为是捉了师父，要蒸要煮，幸亏了观音菩萨收他去，救出我师。他如今现在菩萨处做善财童子，实受了菩萨正果，不生不灭，不垢不净，与天地同寿，日月同庚。你倒不谢老孙保命之恩，返怪老孙，是何道理！"罗刹道："你这个巧嘴的泼猴！我那儿虽不伤命，再怎生得到我的跟前，几时能见一面？"行者笑道："嫂嫂要见令郎，有何难处？你且把扇子借我，扇息了火，送我师父过去，我借宝贝，走上南海家菩萨处请他来见你，就送扇子还你，有何不可！那时节，你看他可曾损伤一毫。如有些须之伤，你也怪得有理；如比旧时标致，还当谢我。"罗刹道："泼猴！少要饶舌！伸过头来，等我砍上几剑！若受得疼痛，就借扇子与你；若忍耐不得，教你早见阎君！"行者又手向前，笑道："嫂嫂切莫多言。老孙伸着光头，任尊意砍上多少，但没气力便罢。是必借扇子用用。"那罗刹不容分说，双手抡剑，照行者头上乒乒乓乓，砍有十数下，这行者全不认真。罗刹害怕，回头要走。行者道："嫂嫂，那里去？快借我使使！"那罗刹道："我的宝贝原不轻借。"行者道："既不肯借，吃你老叔一棒！"

【9】　好猴王，一只手扯住，一只手去耳内掣出棒来，幌一幌，有碗来粗细。那罗刹挣脱手，举起来相迎。行者随又抢棒便打。两个在翠云山前，不论亲情，却只讲仇隙。这一场好杀：

> 裙钗本是修成怪，为子怀仇恨泼猴。行者虽然生狠怒，因师路阻让娥流。先言拜借芭蕉扇，不展骁雄耐性柔。罗刹无知抡剑砍，猴王有意说亲由。女流怎与男儿斗，到底男刚压女流。这个金箍铁棒多凶émph恶，那个霜刃青锋甚利兜。劈面打，照头丢，恨苦相持不罢休。左挡右遮施武艺，前迎后架骋奇谋。却才斗到沉酣处，不觉西方坠日头。罗刹忙

将真扇子，一扇挥动鬼神愁！

那罗刹女与行者相持到晚，见行者棒重，却又解具周密，料斗他不过，即便取出芭蕉扇，幌一幌，一扇阴风，把行者扇得无影无形，莫想收留得住。这罗刹得胜回归。

【10】　那大圣飘飘荡荡，左沉不能落地，右坠不得存身。就如旋风翻败叶，流水淌残花。滚了一夜，直至天明，方才落在一座山上，双手抱住一块峰石。定性良久，仔细观看，却才认得是小须弥山。大圣长叹一声道："好利害妇人！怎么就把老孙送到这里来了？我当年曾记得在此处告求灵吉菩萨降黄风怪救我师父。那黄山岭自此直南上有三千余里，今在西路转来，乃东南方隅，不知有几万里。等我下去问灵吉菩萨一个消息，好回旧路。"

正踌躇间，又听得钟声响亮，急下山坡，径至禅院。那门前道人认得行者的形容，即人里面报道："前年来请菩萨去降黄风怪的那个毛脸大圣又来了。"菩萨知是悟空，连忙下宝座相迎，人内施礼道："恭喜！取经来耶？"悟空答道："正好未到！早哩，早哩！"灵吉道："既未曾得到雷音，何以回顾荒山？"行者道："自上年蒙盛情降了黄风怪，一路上，不知历过多少苦楚。今到火焰山，不能前进，询问土人，说有个铁扇仙芭蕉扇，扇得火灭，老孙特去寻访。原来那仙是牛魔王的妻，红孩儿的母。他说我把他儿子做了观音菩萨的童子，不得常见，跟我为仇，不肯借扇，与我争斗。他见我的棒重难撑，将一扇子，一扇，扇得我悠悠荡荡，直至于此，才得落住。故此轻造禅院，问个归路。此处到火焰山，不知多少里数？"灵吉笑道："那妇人唤名罗刹女，又叫做铁扇公主。他的那芭蕉扇本是昆仑山后，自混沌开辟以来，天地产成的一个灵宝，乃太阴之精叶，故能灭火气。假若扇着人，要飘八万四千里，方息阴风。我这山到火焰山，只有五万余里。此还是大圣有留云之能，故止住了。若是凡人，正好不得住也。"行者道："利害！利害！我师父却怎生得度那方？"灵吉道："大圣放心。此一来，也是唐僧的缘法，合教大圣成功。"行者道："怎见成功？"灵吉道："我当年受如来教旨，赐我一粒'定风丹'，一柄'飞龙杖'。飞龙杖已降了风魔。这定风丹尚未曾见用，如今送了大圣，管教那厮扇你不动，你却要了扇子，扇息火，却不就立此功也！"行者低头作礼，感谢不尽。那菩萨即于衣袖中取出一个锦袋儿，将那一粒定风丹与行者安在衣领里边，将针线紧紧缝了。送行者出门道："不及留款。往西北上去，就是罗刹的山场也。"

【11】　行者辞了灵吉，驾筋斗云，径返翠云山，顷刻而至。使铁棒打着洞门叫道："开门！开门！老孙来借扇子使使哩！"慌得那门里女童即忙来报："奶奶，借扇子的又来了！"罗刹闻言，心中悚惧道："这泼猴真有本事！我的宝贝，扇着人的，要去八万四千里，方能停止；他怎么一扇去就回来也？这番等我一连扇他两三扇，教他扇不着归路！"急纵身，结束整齐，双手提剑，走出门来道："孙行者！你不怕我，又来寻死！"行者笑道："嫂嫂勿得悭吝，是必借我使使。保得唐僧过山，就送还你。我是个志诚有余的君子，不是那借物不还的小人。"

罗刹又骂道："泼猢狲！好没道理，没分晓！夺子之仇，尚未报得，借扇之意，岂得如心！你不要走！吃我老娘一剑！"大圣全然不惧，使铁棒劈手相迎。他两个往往来来，战经五七回合，罗刹女手软难抢，孙行者身强善敌。他见事势不谐，即取扇子，望行者扇了一扇，行者巍然不动。行者收了铁棒，笑吟吟的道："这番不比那番！任你怎么扇扇，老孙若动一动，就不算汉子！"那罗刹又扇两扇，果然不动。罗刹慌了，急收宝贝，转回走入洞里，将门紧紧关上。

【12】　行者见他闭了门，却就弄个手段，拆开衣领，把定风丹噙在口头，摇身一变，变做一个蟭蟟虫儿，从他门隙处钻进。只见罗刹女叫道："渴了！渴了！快拿茶来！"近侍女童，即将香茶一壶，沙沙的满斟一碗，起个茶沫漕漕。行者见了欢喜，嘤的一翅，飞在茶沫之下。那罗刹女渴极，接过茶，两三气都喝了。行者已到他肚腹之内，现原身厉声高叫道："嫂嫂，借扇子我使使！"罗刹大惊失色，叫："小的们，关了前门否？"俱说："关了。"他又说："即关了门，孙行者如何在家里叫唤？"女童道："在你身上哩。"罗刹道："孙行者，你在那里弄术哩？"行者道："老孙一生不会弄术，都是些真手段，实本事，已在尊嫂尊腹之内耍子，已见其肺肝矣。我知你也饥渴了，我先送你个坐碗儿解渴！"却就把脚往下一蹬。那罗刹小腹之中，疼痛难禁，坐于地下叫苦。行者道："嫂嫂休得

推辞，我再送你个点心充饥！"又把头往上一顶。那罗刹心痛难禁，只在地上打滚，疼得他面黄唇白，只叫"孙叔叔饶命！"

行者却才收了手脚道："你才认得叔叔么？我看牛大哥情上，且饶你性命。快将扇子拿来我使使。"罗刹道："叔叔，有扇！有扇！你出来拿了去！"行者道："拿扇子我看了出来。"罗刹即叫女童拿一柄芭蕉扇，执在旁边。行者探到喉咙之上见了道："嫂嫂，我既饶你性命，先飞出来一柄芭蕉扇，执在旁边。行者探到喉咙之上见了道："嫂嫂，我既饶你性命，先飞出来，我既饶你性命，先飞出来不撑个窟窿出来，还自口出。你把口张三张儿。"那罗刹果张开口。行者还做个蟭蟟虫儿，先飞出来，丁在芭蕉扇上。那罗刹不知，连张三次，叫："叔叔出来罢？"行者化原身，拿了扇子，叫道："我在此间不是？谢借了！谢借了！"拽开步，往前便走。小的们连忙开了门，放他出洞。

【13】这大圣拨转云头，径回东路。霎时按落云头，立在红砖壁下。八戒见了欢喜道："师父，师兄来了！来了！"三藏即与本庄老者同沙僧出门迎接，同至舍内。把芭蕉扇靠在旁边道："老官儿，可是这个扇子？"老者道："正是！正是！"唐僧喜道："贤徒有莫大之功。求此宝贝，甚劳苦了。"行者道："劳苦倒也不说。那厮铁扇仙，你道是谁，那厮原来是牛魔王的妻，红孩儿的母，名唤罗刹女，又唤铁扇公主。我寻到洞外借扇，他就与我讲起仇隙，把我砍了几剑。是我使棒吓他，他就把扇子扇了我一下，飘飘荡荡，直刮到小须弥山。幸见灵吉菩萨，送了我一粒定风丹，指与归路，复至翠云山。又见罗刹女，罗刹女又使扇子，扇我不动，他就回洞。是我孙变做一个蟭蟟虫，飞入洞去。那厮正讨茶吃，是我又钻在茶沫之下，到他肚里，做起手脚。他疼痛难禁，不住口的叫我做叔叔饶命，情愿将扇借与我，我却饶了他，拿将扇来。待过了火焰山，仍送还他。"三藏闻言，感谢不尽。师徒们俱拜辞老者。

【14】一路西来，约行有四十里远近，渐渐酷热蒸人。沙僧只叫："脚底烙得慌！"八戒又道："爪子烫得痛！"马比寻常又快。只因地热难停，十分难进。行者道："师父且请下马。兄弟们莫走，等我扇息了火，待风雨之后，地土冷些，再过山去。"行者果举扇，径至火边，尽力一扇，那山上火光焰烘腾起；再一扇，更著百倍；又一扇，那火足有千丈之高，渐渐烧着身体。行者急回，已

将两股毫毛烧净，径跑至唐僧面前叫："快回去，快回去！火来了，火来了！"

那师父爬上马，与八戒、沙僧，复东来有二十余里，方才歇下，道："悟空，如何了呀！"行者丢下扇子道："不停当！不停当！被那厮哄了！"三藏听说，愁促眉尖，闷添心上，止不住两泪交流，只叫："怎么是好！"八戒道："哥哥，你急急忙忙叫回去是怎么说？"行者道："我将扇子扇了一下，火光烘烘；第二扇，火气愈盛；第三扇，火头飞有千丈之高。若是跑得不快，把毫毛都烧尽矣！"八戒笑道："你常说雷打不伤，火烧不损，如今何又怕火？"行者道："你这呆子，全不知事！那时节用心防备，故此不伤；今日只为扇息火光，不曾捻避火诀，又未使护身法，所以把两股毫毛烧了。"沙僧道："似这般火盛，无路通西，怎生是好？"八戒道："只拣无火处走便罢。"三藏道："那方无火？"八戒道："东方、南方、北方，俱无火。"又问："那方有经？"八戒道："西方有经。"三藏道："我只欲往有经处去哩！"沙僧道："有经处有火，无火处无经，诚是进退两难！"

【15】　师徒们正自胡谈乱讲，只听得有人叫道："大圣不须烦恼，且来吃些斋饭再议。"四众回看时，见一老人，身披飘风氅，头顶偃月冠，手持龙头杖，足踏铁鞣靴，后带着一个雕嘴鱼腮鬼，鬼头上顶着一个铜盆，盆内有些蒸饼糕糜，黄粮米饭，在于西路下躬身道："我本是火焰山土地。知大圣保护圣僧，不能前进，特献下斋。"行者道："吃斋小可，这火光几时灭得，让我师父过去？"土地道："要灭火光，须求罗刹才借芭蕉扇。"行者去路旁拾起扇子道："这不是？那火光越扇越着，何也？"土地笑道："此扇不是真的，被他哄了。"行者道："如何方得真的？"那土地又控背躬身，微微笑道："若还要借真蕉扇，须是寻求大力王。"毕竟不知大力王有甚缘故，且听下回分解。

Chapter 10
Sanzang's Way Is Blocked at
the Fiery Mountains;
Monkey First Tries to Borrow
the Plantain Fan

【1】 *The many species are at root the same;*
All flows into the boundless sea.
Every thought and worry is in vain;
All types and forms together blend.
When the achievement is complete
Great will be the full and shining dharma.
Do not allow your differences to divide:
Keep everything together.
Gather all into the elixir furnace,
Refine it till it is red as darkest gold.
Then in its brilliance and beauty
On dragons it may ride at will.

【2】 The story tells how Sanzang took back Brother Monkey as the Bodhisattva had instructed him and headed towards the Western Heaven, united in heart with Pig and Friar Sand. They were no longer in two minds, and the ape and the horse were firmly under control. Time shot by like an arrow; days and nights alternated with the speed of a shuttle. After the scorching heat of summer they were now in the frosts of late autumn. What they saw was:

The sparse clouds blown away by the wild west wind,
Cranes calling in the distant hills amid the frosty woods.
This is a chilly time
When mountain rivers seem longer than eve.
The swan returns through the northern frontier passes;
Migrating birds go back to their southern fields.

The traveller feels lonely on the road;
Monastic robes do not keep out the cold.

As master and disciples pressed ahead they began to feel
hotter and hotter in the warm air. "It is autumn now, so why is
it getting hotter again?" Sanzang asked, reining in his horse.
"Don't know," said Pig. "There's a country in the west, Sihali,
where the sun sets. People call it 'the end of the sky'. At about
six o'clock every evening the king sends people on the city walls to
bang drums and blow bugles to cover the sound of the sea boiling.
That's because when the fire of the sun falls into the Western
Ocean there's a great seething noise like something burning being
plunged into water. If they didn't cover the noise with their
drums and bugles the shock would kill all the little children in the
city. That's where I think we are—the place where the sun
sets." When the Great Sage heard this he could not help
laughing. "Don't talk such nonsense, you idiot. We're a long way
from Sihali yet. The way our master keeps dithering and changing
his mind we won't get there in three lifetimes, even if we go on
from childhood to old age, then to childhood again, and then to
another old age and a third childhood." "Tell me then, brother,"
said Pig, "if this isn't where the sun sets why's it so scorching
hot?" "The seasons must be out of joint," said Friar Sand. "I
expect they're following summer rituals here although it's
autumn." Just as the three disciples were arguing they saw a farm
by the side of the road. It had a red tiled roof, red brick walls,
and red painted doors, windows and furniture. It was red
everywhere. "Wukong," said Sanzang, dismounting, "go to that
house and find out why it's so burning hot."
【3】 The Great Sage put his gold-banded cudgel away, neatened
his clothes, and swaggered along the road like a fine gentleman.
When he reached the gate to have a look an old man suddenly
appeared from inside. This is what he looked like:

He wore a robe of hemp-cloth,
Not quite brown or red,

A sunhat of woven bamboo,
In between black and green.
The knobby stick in his hand
Was neither crooked nor straight.
His long boots of leather
Were not new, but not yet old.
His face was the colour of copper,
His beard bleached white like yarn.
Long eyebrows shaded his jade-blue eyes
And his smile showed golden teeth.

The old man had a shock when he looked up to see Monkey. "Where are you from, you freak?" he asked, steadying himself on his stick. "What are you doing at my gate?" "Venerable patron," replied Monkey with a bow, "don't be afraid. I'm no freak. My master and we three disciples have been sent by the Great Tang emperor in the east to fetch the scriptures from the west. As we've now reached your residence I have come to ask you why it's so boiling hot here and what this place is called." Only then did the old man stop feeling worried and reply with a smile, "Please don't take offence, reverend sir. My old eyes are rather dim and I failed to recognize your distinguished self." "There's no need to be so polite," said Monkey. "Which road is your master on?" the old man asked. "That's him, standing on the main road due south," Monkey replied. "Ask him over, ask him over," the old man replied, to Monkey's pleasure. Monkey waved to them, and Sanzang came over with Pig and Friar Sand leading the white horse and carrying the luggage. They all bowed to the old man.

The old man was at the same time delighted by Sanzang's fine appearance and alarmed by Pig's and Friar Sand's remarkable ugliness. Inviting them in, he told the younger members of the family to bring tea and cook a meal. Hearing all this Sanzang rose to his feet to thank the old man and ask, "Could you tell me, sir, why it has turned so hot again although it is autumn now?" "These are the Fiery Mountains," the old man replied. "We

265

don't have springs or autumns here. It's hot all the year round."
"Where are the mountains?" Sanzang asked. "Do they block the
way to the west?" "It's impossible to get to the west," the old
man replied. "The mountains are about twenty miles from here.
You have to cross them to get to the west, but they're over 250
miles of flame. Not a blade of grass can grow anywhere around.
Even if you had a skull of bronze and a body of iron you would
melt trying to cross them." This answer made Sanzang turn pale
with horror; he dared not to ask any more questions.

【4】   Just then a young man pushing a red barrow stopped by the
gate, shouting, "Cakes! Cakes!" The Great Sage pulled out one
of his hairs and turned it into a copper coin with which he bought
a cake off the young man. The man accepted the money and
without a worry he lifted the cover off his barrow to release a
cloud of hot steam, took out a cake and passed it to Monkey.
When Monkey took it in his hand it was as hot as a burning coal
or a red-hot nail in a furnace. Just look at him as he keeps tossing
the cake from one hand to another shouting, "It's hot, it's hot, I
can't eat it." "If you can't stand heat don't come here," the
young man replied. "It's always this hot here." "You don't
understand at all, my lad," said Monkey. "As the saying goes,

> *If it's never too cold and it's never too hot*
> *The five kinds of grain will be harvested not.*

If it's so hot here how do you get the flour to make your cakes?"
To this the young man said,

> *"You ask me where we can obtain the flour for the pan:*
> *Politely we request it from Immortal Iron Fan."*

"What can you tell me about this immortal?" Monkey asked.
"The immortal has a plantain fan," the young man replied. "If
you ask it to, the fan puts out the fire at the first wave, makes a
wind blow at the second wave, and brings rain at the third wave.
That is how we can sow and reap the crops to support ourselves.

Without it nothing would be able to grow."

[5] On hearing this Monkey rushed back inside, gave the cakes to Sanzang, and said, "Don't worry, Master: Don't get upset about what's going to happen the year after next. Eat these cakes up and I'll tell you all about it." Sanzang took the cakes and said to the old man, "Please have a cake, sir." "I could not possibly eat one of your cakes before we've offered you any of our tea and food," the old man replied. "Sir," Monkey replied, "there's no need to give us food or tea. But could you tell me where the Iron Fan Immortal lives?" "What do you want to know about the immortal for?" the old man asked. "The cake-seller told me just now that the immortal has a plantain fan," said Monkey. "If you borrow it the first wave puts the fire out, the second raises a wind and the third brings rain. That's why you're able to sow and reap the crops to support yourselves I want to go to ask the immortal to come so we can put out the flames on the Fiery Mountains and cross them. And you'll be able to sow, reap and live in peace." "It's a nice idea," said the old man, "but as you have no presents the immortal wouldn't come." "What sort of presents would be wanted?" Sanzang asked.

"Every ten years," the old man replied, "we go to visit the immortal. We take four pigs and four sheep, all decorated with flowers and red ribbons, delicious fruit in season, chickens, geese and the best wine. We bathe ourselves and go very reverently to pay a respectful visit to the mountain and ask the immortal to leave the cave and come here to perform magic." "Where is this mountain?" Monkey asked. "What's it called? How far is it from here? I'm going there to ask for the fan." "It lies southwest of here," the old man said, "and it's called Mount Turquoise Cloud. When we believers go to worship at the magic mountain the journey takes us a month as it's about 485 miles altogether." "No problem," said Monkey. "I can be there and back in no time." "Wait a minute," said the old man. "Have something to eat and drink first, and we'll get some provisions ready for the journey. You'll need two people to go with you. Nobody lives along the way and there are many wolves and tigers. It'll take you many a day to get there. You must be serious about it." "No need," said Monkey with a laugh, "no need. I'm off." As soon as he had said that he disappeared. "My lord!" the old man said in astonishment. "He's a god who can ride clouds."

【6】 We shall say no more of how the family redoubled their offerings to the Tang Priest, but tell of Monkey, who arrived at Mount Turquoise Cloud in an instant, brought his auspicious light to a stop and started looking for the entrance to the cave. He heard the sound of an axe and saw a woodcutter felling a tree in the forest on the mountainside. Hurrying forward, Monkey heard him saying,

> *'I recognize the ancient woods amid the clouds;*
> *The path is overgrown; the hillside steep*
> *From western hills I see the morning rain:*
> *Returning to the south the ford's too deep."*

Going closer to the woodman Monkey said, "Greetings, woodman." Putting down his axe the woodcutter returned his courtesy and asked him where he was going. "May I ask if this is Mount Turquoise Cloud?" said Monkey. "Yes," the woodcutter replied. "Where is the Iron Fan Immortal's Plantain Cave?" Monkey asked. "There's a Plantain Cave here," the woodcutter replied, "but no Iron Fan Immortal, only a Princess Iron Fan. She's also called Raksasi." "They say the immortal has a plantain fan that can put out the flames of the Fiery Mountains. Is that her?" "Yes, yes," the woodman said. "She's a sage and she has this treasure that puts out fire. Because she protects the people who live over yonder they call her the Iron Fan Immortal. We have no need of her here, so we just call her Raksasi. She's the wife of the Bull Demon King."

【7】 Monkey went pale with shock at the news. "Another person who's got it in for me," he thought. "When I subdued the Red Boy the other year he said this bitch was his mother. When I met the Red Boy's uncle at Childfree Cave on Mount Offspring Dissolved he refused me the water and wanted revenge. Now I'm up against his parents. How am I ever going to borrow the fan?" Seeing Monkey deep in thought and sighing endlessly, the woodcutter said with a smile, "Venerable sir, you're a man of religion. You shouldn't have any worries. Just follow this path east and you'll be at the Plantain Cave within a couple of miles." "I'll be frank with you, woodcutter," said Monkey. "I'm the senior disciple of the Tang Priest who has been sent by the Tang emperor in the east to go to fetch the scriptures from the Western Heaven. The other year I had words with Raksasi's son Red Boy at the Fire-cloud Cave, and I'm afraid that Raksasi may refuse to let me have the fan because she's still nursing a grudge. That's why I'm worried." "A real man knows how to play it by ear," the woodcutter replied. "Just ask for the fan. Forget about your old quarrel. I'm sure you'll be able to borrow it." Monkey made a respectful chant and said, "Thank you very much for your advice. I'm off."

Brother monkey then took his leave of the woodcutter and went straight to the mouth of the Plantain Cave. Both doors were tightly shut, and the scenery outside was magnificent. It was a splendid place. Indeed,

The rocks were the bones of the mountain,
And also the spirit of the earth.
Clouds at sunset held night rain,
And mosses lent the freshness of their green.
The towering peaks outdid those of Penglai;
The fragrant calm was like a magic island's.
Wild cranes were perching in the lofty pines
While warblers sang in the weeping willows.
This was indeed an ancient site,
The home of immortals for ten thousand years.
The resplendent phoenix sang in the parasol trees
While azure dragons hid in the running waters.
Vines hung over the winding paths,
And creepers covered the steps of stone.
Apes on the cliffs screeched to welcome the rising moon;

> In tall trees birds sang for joy at the clear blue sky.
> The groves of bamboo were as cool as if it had rained;
> The flowers along the path were embroidered velvet.
> At times a cloud of white would blow from a distant peak;
> It had no single form as it drifted in the wind.

"Open up, Brother Bull," Monkey shouted as he went up to the doors. They opened with a creak, and out came a young girl carrying a flower basket in her hand and hoe over her shoulder. Indeed,

> Though clad in rags and dressed in no fine array,
> Her face was full of spirit, her heart set on the Way.

Monkey went up to her with his hands together in front of his chest and said, "Would you kindly tell the princess that I'm a monk going to the west to fetch the scriptures. I'm here to beg the loan of her plantain fan as we can't get across the Fiery Mountain." "What monastery are you from," the girl asked, "and what is you name? Please tell me so that I can announce you." "I'm from the east," Monkey replied, "and my name is Sun Wukong."

[8] The girl went back into the cave, knelt to the princess, and said, "Your Highness, there's a monk from the east called Sun Wukong outside who would like to see you to ask for the loan of the plantain fan to cross the Fiery Mountain." The name Sun Wukong was like a pinch of salt thrown into a flame, or oil poured on a fire. Her face went bright red and evil anger flared up in her heart. "So that damned monkey's here at last," she said with hatred. "Girl," she shouted, "fetch me my armour and my weapons." She then put on her armour, tied her pair of blue-tipped swords at her waist, fastened it all firmly, and went out. Monkey slipped over to the entrances to see what she looked like and this is what he saw:

> A flowered kerchief tied around her head,

A cloud-patterned robe of quilted brocade.
A belt of two tiger sinews round her waist,
Revealing a skirt of embroidered silk.
Her shoes like phoenix beaks were but three inches long;
Her trousers in dragon-beard style were adorned with gold.
Brandishing her swords she gave out angry shouts;
She looked as lethal as the goddess of the moon.

"Where's Sun Wukong?" Raksasi shouted as she came out of her cave. Monkey stepped forward, bowed, and replied, "Monkey offers his respectful greetings, sister-in-law." "I'm no sister-in-law of yours," she shouted angrily, "and I'll have no greetings from you." "Your worthy husband the Bull Demon King was once my sworn brother," Monkey replied. "There were seven of us altogether. As I learn that you are my brother Bull's good lady, of course I must call you sister-in-law."

"Damned ape," said Raksasi, "if you're my husband's sworn brother why did you do that terrible thing to our boy?" "Who is you son?" Monkey asked, as if he did not know. "He's the Red Boy, the Boy Sage King of the Fire-cloud Cave by Withered Pine Ravine on Mount Hao," Raksasi replied. "You ruined him, and now you've come to our door to pay with your life. We've been longing to get our revenge on you but didn't know where to find you. You'll get no mercy from me." Putting on the broadest of smiles, Monkey replied, "You haven't gone into it thoroughly enough, sister-in-law. You've no reason to be so angry with me. Your good son had captured my master and would have steamed or boiled him if the Bodhisattva hadn't taken the boy as his disciple and rescued my master. He's now the page Sudhana on the Bodhisattva's island and he's accepted the pursuit of the true reward from her. He is now beyond life and death and above filth and purity. He will live as long as heaven, earth, the sun and the moon. But so far from thanking me for saving his life you're getting at me. That's wrong of you."

"You smooth-tongued ape," Raksasi snapped back. "My boy may be alive, but when is he ever going to come here? When am I going to see him again?" "It'll be easy for you to see your son again," Monkey replied, still smiling. "Just lend me the fan to put the fire out. When I've taken my master across the mountains I'll go to the Bodhisattva's place in the Southern Ocean and ask him to come here to see you and give your fan back. No problem. Then you'll be able to see that he's completely unharmed. If he'd been wounded at all you'd have had every right to be angry with me. But he's as handsome as ever. You ought to be thanking me." To this Raksasi's reply was: "Shut up, ape fiend! Stick your head out for me to hack with my sword. If you can stand the pain I'll lend you the plantain fan. If you can't you'll be going straight down to Hell to see King Yama." Monkey then clasped his hands together in front of him and replied with a smile, "Enough said, sister-in-law. I'll stretch my bald head out and you can take as many hacks as you like until you're exhausted. But you must lend me the fan." With no more argument Raksasi swung both of her swords around and brought them down with loud thunks a dozen or more times on Monkey's head. He was not bothered at all. Raksasi was so frightened by this that she turned to run away. "Where are you going, sister-in-law?" Monkey said. "Hurry up and lend me that fan." "My treasure isn't something to be lent out casually," Raksasi replied. "Well," said Monkey, "if you refuse now you'll just have to try a taste of your brother-in-law's cudgel."

[9] The splendid Monkey King held on to her with one hand while pulling his cudgel out from his ear with the other. With one wave it became as thick as a ricebowl. Raksasi broke free from his grip and raised her swords to strike back at him. Monkey started swinging his cudgel to hit her with and the fight began in front of Mount Turquoise Cloud. All talk of kinship was forgotten and their minds full of hatred alone. It was a fine battle:

> *The woman had worked hard to make herself a monster;*
> *She lothed the ape and would avenge her son.*
> *Although Monkey was seething with fury,*
> *He would have made concessions for his master's sake.*

First he had asked to borrow the plantain fan,
Being patient and gentle, not fierce.
In ignorance Raksasi hacked with her sword,
While Monkey decided to speak of kinship.
Women should never fight with men,
For men are harder and can crush them.
Terrible was the gold-banded cudgel,
Fine were the movements of the blue frost-bladed sword,
With blows to face and head,
As both of them grimly refused to yield.
Blocking to left and right they used their martial skill;
Great was the cunning with which they stood or fell back.
Just when they both were beginning to enjoy themselves
The sun set in the western sky before they noticed.
Raksasi made ghosts and deities feel small
With many a wave of her true magic fan.

Raksasi and Monkey fought it out till evening. As Monkey's cudgel struck so hard and his technique was so flawless she realized that she would never be able to beat him. She brought out her plantain fan and with a single wave blew Monkey right out of sight. There was no way he could stand his ground. With that she went back to her cave in triumph.

[10]   The Great Sage was thrown around in the air, unable to come down to earth or find any refuge. He was like a dead leaf in a whirlwind or a fallen blossom carried along by a torrent. Only after a whole night's buffeting did he manage to land on a mountain the next morning and hold on hard to a rock by putting both arms round it. He needed a long time to calm himself and take a good look around before he realized that he was on Little Mount Sumeru. "What a terrible woman," he said to himself with a deep sigh. "How ever did she get me here? I remember coming here once to ask the Bodhisattva Lingji to subdue the Yellow Wind Monster and rescue my master. The Yellow Wind Ridge is over a thousand miles south of here, so as I've been blown back from the west I must have come thousands

273

and thousands of miles. I'll go down and find out some more from the Bodhisattva Lingji before I go back."

Just as he was making his mind up he heard a resounding gone, so he hurried down the mountain and straight to the dhyana monastery. The lay brother on the gate recognized Monkey and went in to announce, "The hairy-faced Great Sage who asked the Bodhisattva to subdue the Yellow Wind Monster some years back is here again." Realizing that this must be Sun Wukong, the Bodhisattva hurried down from his throne to greet him and lead him inside with the words, "Allow me to congratulate you. I suppose you have fetched the scriptures now." "It'll be a long time yet," said Monkey, "a long time." "But why are you visiting my mountain if you have yet to reach the Thunder Monastery?" the Bodhisattva asked. "Since in your great kindness you subdued the Yellow Wind Monster for me some years ago," Monkey replied, "goodness only knows how much we've suffered on our journey. Now we are at the Fiery Mountains, but we can't cross them. When I asked the local people they told me about an Iron Fan Immortal who had an iron fan that could put the fires out. I went to visit the immortal, only to discover that she's the wife of the Bull Demon King and the Red Boy's mother. I told her that her son is now Guanyin Bodhisattva page, but she has it in for me because she can't see him. She refused to lend me her fan and fought me. When she realized that my cudgel was too much for her she waved her fan and sent me hurling through the air till I landed here. That's why I've come blundering into your monastery to ask the way back. How far is it from here to the Fiery Mountains?"

"The woman is called Raksasi, or Princess Iron Fan," replied Lingji with a smile. "That plantain fan of hers is a miraculous treasure formed by heaven and earth behind Mount Kunlun ever since primal chaos was first separated. This leaf is the very essence of the negative Yin principle, which is why it can put out fire. If she fans somebody with it he'll be blown 27,000 miles before that negative wind drops. But this mountain of mine is only some 17,000 miles from the Fiery Mountains. You must have stopped here because you have the power to delay clouds, Great Sage. No ordinary mortal would have been able to stop." "She's terrible," said Monkey. "How ever is my master going to get across those mountains?" "Don't worry, Great Sage," Lingji replied. "The Tang Priest is fated to succeed on this journey with you." "How can you tell?" Monkey asked. "Many years ago when the Tathagata gave me his instructions," Lingji replied, "he presented me with a Wind-fixing Pill and a Flying Dragon Staff. The Flying Dragon Staff was used to subdue the Yellow Wind Monster, but I haven't yet tried out the Wind-fixing Pill and I'll give it to you today. It'll stop the fan from being able to move you. You'll just have to ask to get it and put the fire out with it. You'll have an instant success." Monkey bowed deeply and expressed profound thanks. The Bodhisattva then produced a brocade bag from his sleeve and took out of it the Wind-fixing Pill. This he gave to Monkey to sew up securely inside the lapel of his tunic. "I won't detain you here any longer," Lingji said as he saw Monkey out through doors. "Head northwest and that will get you to Raksasi's mountain."

[11]   Taking his leave of Lingji Monkey rode his somersault cloud straight back to Mount Turquoise Cloud and was there in a moment. "Open up, open up!" he shouted, hammering on the doors with his iron cudgel. "Monkey's here to borrow the fan." This so alarmed the servant girl inside the doors that she ran back and reported, "Your Highness, he's here to borrow the fan again." The news frightened Raksasi, who thought, "That damned monkey really has got some powers. If I fan anyone else with my treasure they go 27,000 miles before stopping. How can he be back so soon after being blown away? This time I'll fan him two or three times and he'll never be able to find his way back here." She sprang to her feet, tied all her armour firmly on, and went out of the cave with her swords in her hands shouting, "Sun the Novice, aren't you afraid of me? Why have you come back here to get yourself killed?" "Don't be so stingy, sister-in-law," said Monkey with a smile. "You've got to lend me it. I'll bring it back as soon as I've escorted the Tang Priest across the Fiery

275

Mountains. I give you my word as a gentleman. I'm not the sort of low creature who borrows things but doesn't give them back."

"Damned macaque," Raksasi shouted back. "You're outrageous, and you understand nothing. I've got to avenge the loss of my son, so how could I possibly be prepared to lend you my fan? Clear off if you don't want a taste of my sword." The Great Sage, not at all afraid, struck back at her hands with his iron cudgel, and the two of them fought six or seven rounds. By then Raksasi's arms were becoming too tired to wield the swords, while Brother Monkey was feeling strong and fighting well. Seeing that the balance of the fight was tilting against her, Raksasi took out the fan and fanned it once in Monkey's direction. He stood unmoved, put his iron cudgel away, and said with a chuckle, "This time it's different. Fan as much as you like. If I move an inch I'm no man." She fanned twice more and still he did not move. By now she was so alarmed that she put her pride and joy away at once, went straight back into the cave, and shut the doors firmly.

【12】 When Monkey saw this he used magic. He tore the lapel of his tunic open, put the Wind-fixing Pill in his mouth, shook himself, turned into the tiniest of insects, and squeezed in through the crack between the doors, where he saw Raksasi shouting, "I'm thirsty, I'm thirsty. Quick, bring me some tea." The servant girl who attended her fetched a pot of the best tea and poured a large cup of it so noisily that the surface was frothy. Monkey was delighted. With a quiet buzz of his wings he flew under the froth. Raksasi was so parched that she drained the tea in two gulps.

Once inside her stomach Monkey reverted to his own form and shouted at the top of his voice, "Sister-in-law, lend me the fan." Raksasi went pale with shock. "Little ones," she called to her underlings, "are the front doors shut?" "Yes," they all said. "If the doors are shut then how can Sun the Novice be inside the cave and shouting?" she asked. "He's shouting from inside you," the servant girl replied. "Where are you playing your conjuring tricks, Sun the Novice?" Raksasi asked. "I've never been able to do conjuring tricks in all my life," Monkey replied. "My magic and my powers are all real. I'm fooling around in your own insides, good sister-in-law. I've just seen your lungs and your liver. I know you're very hungry and thirsty, so I'll give you a bowlful to quench your thirst." With that he stamped his foot, giving Raksasi an unbearable cramp in her stomach that left her sitting groaning on the floor. "Don't try to say no, sister-in-law," Monkey then said. "I'm giving you a pastry in case you're hungry." He butted upwards, causing such a violent heart pain that she could only roll around on the ground; her face sallow and her lips white from agony. "Spare me, brother-in-law, spare me," was all she could say.

Only then did Monkey stop hitting and kicking. "So you call me brother-in-law now, do you?" he said. "I'll spare your life for my brother Bull's sake. Get me the fan, and quick." "You shall have it, brother-in-law, you shall have it," she said. "Come out and get it." "Fetch it and show it to me," Monkey said. She told the servant girl to fetch a plantain fan and stand holding it beside her. Monkey poked his head up her throat to see it and said, "As I'm sparing your life, sister-in-law, I won't smash my way out under your ribs. I'll come out through your mouth. Open wide three times." With that Raksasi opened her mouth and Monkey turned back into the tiny insect to fly out and alight on the fan. Not realizing what had happened Raksasi went on to open her mouth twice more. "Come out, brother-in-law," she said. Monkey turned back into himself, took the fan and said, "Here I am. Thanks for the loan." With that he strode forward while the underlings opened the doors to let him out of the cave.

[13] The Great Sage then turned his cloud around and headed back east. A moment later he had landed the cloud and was standing by the red brick wall. Pig was very pleased indeed to see him. "Master," he said, "Monkey's here! He's back!" Sanzang went out with the old man of the farm and Friar Sand to greet him, and they all went back inside. Propping the fan against the wall, Monkey asked, "Tell me sir, is this the fan?" "Yes, yes," the old man said. "This is a great achievement, disciple," said

Sanzang. "Fetching this treasure cost you a great deal of trouble." "No trouble at all," said Monkey. "Do you know who that Iron Fan Immortal is? She's Raksasi, the wife of the Bull Demon King and the Red Boy's mother. Her other name is Princess Iron Fan. I found her outside her cave and asked to borrow the fan, but all she could talk of were her old grudges. She took a few cuts at me with her swords, but when I gave her a bit of a scare with the cudgel she fanned me with the fan and blew me all the way to Little Mount Sumeru. I was lucky enough to be able to see the Bodhisattva Lingji who gave me a tablet that stops winds and showed me the way back to Mount Turquoise Cloud. Then I saw Raksasi again, but this time her fan did not move me an inch, so she went back into her cave and I turned into a tiny insect to fly back in after her. When the damned woman asked for some tea I slipped in under the froth at the top, got inside her, and started giving her a few punches and kicks. She couldn't take the pain. She kept saying, 'Spare me, brother-in-law, spare me.' As she agreed to lend me the fan I spared her life and took the fan. I'll give it back to her after we've crossed the Fiery Mountains." When Sanzang heard this he was extremely grateful.

[14]   Master and disciples then took their leave of the old man and travelled about fifteen miles west. The heat was becoming unbearable. "The soles of my feet are being roasted," Friar Sand complained. "My trotters are getting burnt and it hurts," said Pig. The horse was going much faster than usual too. The ground was so hot that they could not stop, but every step was painful. "Please dismount, Master," said Monkey, "and brothers, stay here while I use the fan to put the fire out. When the wind and the rain come the ground will be a lot cooler and we'll be able to get across the mountains." He then raised the fan and fanned it hard once in the direction of the fire: tongues of flame rose above the mountains. He fanned again, and they were a hundred times as high. He fanned a third time, and now they were a couple of miles high and beginning to burn him. Monkey fled, but not before two patches of fur had been burnt away. He ran straight

back to the Tang Priest and said, "Hurry back, hurry back, the flames are coming."

The master remounted and headed back east with Pig and Friar Sand some seven miles before stopping and asking, "What happened, Wukong?" "It's the wrong one," Monkey said, flinging the fan down, "it's the wrong one. The damned woman fooled me." When Sanzang heard this he frowned and felt thoroughly depressed. "What are we to do?" he sobbed, the tears flowing freely down his cheeks. "Brother," said Pig, "why did you come back in such a mad rush and send us back here?" "The first time I fanned there were flames," Monkey replied, "the second time the fire got fiercer, and the third time the flames were a couple of miles high. If I hadn't run fast all my fur would have been burnt off."

"But you're always telling us that you can't be hurt by thunder and lightning and that fire can't burn you," said Pig with a laugh. "How come you're afraid of fire now?" "Idiot," said Monkey, "you don't understand anything. The other times I was ready: that's why I wasn't hurt. Today I didn't make any flame-avoiding spells or use magic to defend myself. That's why two patches of my fur were singed." "If the fire's so fierce and there's no other way to the west what are we going to do?" Friar Sand asked. "We'll just have to find somewhere where there isn't any fire," Pig replied. "Which way will that be?" Sanzang asked. "East, north or south: there's no fire those ways," said Pig. "But which way are the scriptures?" "Only in the west," Pig replied. "I only want to go where the scriptures are," Sanzang said. "We're well and truly struck," said Friar Sand. "Where there are scriptures there's fire, and where there's no fire there are no scriptures."

【15】 While master and disciples were talking this nonsense they heard someone call, "Don't get upset, Great Sage. Come and have some vegetarian food before you take your discussions any further." The four of them looked round to see an old man wearing a cloak that floated in the wind and a hat the shape of a half moon. In his hand he held a dragon-headed stick, and on his

279

legs were boots of iron. With him was a demon with the beak of an eagle and the cheeks of a fish carrying on his head a copper bowl full of steamed buns, millet cakes, cooked millet and rice. The old man bowed to them on the road to the west and said, "I am the local god of the Fiery Mountains. As I know that you are escorting this holy monk, Great Sage, and can't go any further I have brought this meal as an offering." "Eating doesn't matter," Monkey replied. "When are these fires going to be put out so that my master can cross the mountains?" "If you want to put the fires out you must first ask Raksasi to lend you the plantain fan," the local god said. Monkey went to the side of the path, picked the fan up, and said, "This is it, isn't it? The more I fan the flames the more fiercely they burn. Why?" "Because it's not the real one," said the local deity with a laugh when he looked at it. "She fooled you." "Then how am I to get the real one?" Monkey said. The local god bowed again and had a slight smile on his face as he replied, "If you want to borrow the real plantain fan you will have to ask the Strongarm King." If you don't know all about the Strongarm King listen to the explanation in the next instalment.

11. 牛魔王罢战赴华筵
孙行者二调芭蕉扇

【1】 土地说："大力王即牛魔王也。"行者道："这山本是牛魔王放的火，假名火焰山？"土地道："不是，不是。大圣若肯赦小神之罪，方敢直言。"行者道："你有何罪？直说无妨。"土地道："这火原是大圣放的。"行者怒道："我在那里，你这等乱谈！我可是放火之辈？"土地道："是你也认不得我了。此间原无这座山，因大圣五百年前，大闹天宫时，被显圣擒了，压赴老君，将大圣安于八卦炉内，煅炼之后开鼎，被你蹬倒丹炉，落了几个砖来，内有余火，到此处化为火焰山。我本是兜率宫守炉的道人。当被老君怪我失守，降下此间，就做了火焰山土地也。"猪八戒闻言，恨道："怪道你这等打扮！原来是道士变的土地！"

【2】 行者半信不信道："你且说，早寻大力王何故？"土地道："大力王乃罗刹女丈夫。他这向撇了罗刹，现在积雷山摩云洞，有个万岁狐王。那狐王死了，遗下一个女儿，唤做玉面公主。那公主有百万家私，无人掌管；二年前，访着牛魔王神通广大，情愿倒陪家私，招赘为夫。那牛王弃了罗刹，久不回顾。若大圣寻着牛王，拜求来此，方借得真扇。一则扇息火焰，可保师父前进；二来永除火患，可保此地生灵；三者赦我归天，回缴老君法旨。"行者道："积雷山坐落何处？到彼有多少程途？"土地道："在正南方。此间到彼，有三千余里。"行者闻言，即吩咐沙僧、八戒保护师父。又教土地，陪伴为理。随即忽的一声，渺然不见。

【3】 那里消半个时辰，早见一座高山凌汉。按落云头，停立巅峰之上观看，真是好山：

高不高，顶摩碧汉；大不大，根扎黄泉。山前日暖，岭后风寒。山前日暖，有三冬草木无知；岭后风寒，见九夏冰霜不化。龙潭接涧水长流，虎穴依崖花放早。水流千派似飞琼，花放一心如布锦。湾环岭上湾环树，扢扠石外扢扠松。真个是，高的山，峻的岭，陡的崖，深的涧，香的花，美的果，红的藤，紫的竹，青的松，翠的柳：八节四时颜不改，千年万古色如龙。

大圣看彀多时，步下尖峰，入深山，找寻路径。正自没个消息，忽见松阴下，有一女子，手折了一枝香兰，袅袅娜娜而来。大圣闪在怪石之旁，旁睛观看，那女子怎生模样：

娇娇倾国色，缓缓步移莲。貌若王嫱，颜如楚女。如花解语，似玉生香。高髻堆青亸碧鸦，双睛蘸绿横秋水。湘裙半露弓鞋小，翠袖微舒粉腕长。说甚么暮雨朝云，真个是朱唇皓齿。锦江滑腻蛾眉秀，赛过文君与薛涛。

那女子渐渐走近石边，大圣躬身施礼，缓缓而言曰："女菩萨何往？"那女子未曾观看，听得叫问，却自抬头；忽见大圣的相貌丑恶陋，老大心惊，欲退难退，欲行难行，只得战兢兢，勉强答道："你是何方来者？敢在此间问谁？"大圣沉思道："我若说出取经求扇之事，恐这厮与牛王有亲，——且只以假亲托意，来请魔王之言而答方可。……"那女子见他不语，变了颜色，怒声喝道："你是何人，敢来问我！"大圣躬身陪笑道："我是翠云山来的，初到贵处，不知路径。敢问菩萨，此间可是积雷山？"那女子道："正是。"大圣道："有个摩云洞，坐落何处？"那女子道："你寻那洞做甚？"大圣道："我是翠云山芭蕉洞铁扇公主央来请牛魔王的。"

那女子一听铁扇公主请牛魔王之言，心中大怒，彻耳根子通红，泼口骂道："这贱婢，着实无知！牛王自到我家，未及二载，也不知送了他多少珠翠金银，绫罗缎匹；年供柴，月供米，自自在在受用，还不识羞，又来请他怎的！"大圣闻言，情知是玉面公主，故意子掣出铁棒大喝一声道："你这泼贱，将家私买住牛王，诚然是陪钱嫁汉！你倒不羞，却敢骂谁！"那女子见了，唬得魄散魂飞，没好步乱蹁金莲；战兢兢回头便走。这大圣吆吆喝喝，随后相跟。原来穿过松阴，就是摩云洞口。女子跑进去，扑的把门关了。大圣却收了铁棒，咳咳停步看时，好所在：

树林森密，崖削崚嶒。薜萝阴冉冉，兰蕙味馨馨。流泉漱玉穿修竹，巧石知机带落英。烟霞笼远岫，日月照云屏。

龙吟虎啸，鹤唳莺鸣。一片清幽真可爱，琪花瑶草景常明。
不亚天台仙洞，胜如海上蓬瀛。

【4】　且不言行者这里观看景致。却说那女子跑得粉汗淋淋，唬
得兰心吸吸，径入书房里面。原来牛魔王正在那里静玩丹书。
这女子没好气倒在怀里，抓耳挠腮，放声大哭。牛王满面陪笑
道："美人，休得烦恼。有甚话说？"那女子跳天索地，口中骂道：
"泼魔害杀我也！"牛王笑道："你为甚事骂我？"女子道："我因父
母无依，招你护身养命。江湖中说你是条好汉，你原来是个惧内
的庸夫！"牛王闻说，将女子抱住道："美人，我有那些不是处，你
且慢慢说来，我与你陪礼。"女子道："适才我在洞外闲步花阴，折
兰采蕙，忽有一个毛脸雷公嘴的和尚，猛地前来施礼，把我吓了
个呆挣。及定性问是何人，他说是铁扇公主央他来请牛魔王。
被我说了两句，他倒骂了我一场，将一根棍子，赶着我打。若不
是走得快些，几乎被他打死！这不是招你为祸？害杀我也！"牛王
闻言，即与他整容陪礼。温存良久，女子方才息气。魔王却发狠
道："美人在上，不敢相瞒。那芭蕉洞虽是僻静，却清幽自在。我
山妻自幼修持，也是个得道的女仙，却是家门严谨，内无一尺之
童，焉得有雷公嘴的男子央求，这想是那里的怪妖，或者假绰
名声，至此访我。等我出去看看。"

【5】　好魔王，拽开步，出了书房，上大厅取了披挂，结束了。拿
了一条混铁棍，出门高叫道："是谁人在我这里无状？"行者在旁，
见他那模样，与五百年前又大不同。只见：

　　头上戴一顶水磨银亮熟铁盔；身上贯一副绒穿锦绣黄金
　　甲，足下踏一双卷尖粉底麂皮靴；腰间束一条攒丝三股狮
　　蛮带。一双眼光如明镜，两道剑眉艳似红霓。口若血盆，齿
　　排铜板。吼声响震山神怕，行动威风恶鬼慌。四海有名称
　　混世，西方大力号魔王。

这大圣整衣上前，深深的唱个大喏道："长兄，还认得小弟么？"牛
王答礼道："你是齐天大圣孙悟空么？"大圣道："正是，正是，一向
久别未拜。适才到此问一女子，方得见兄。丰采果胜常，真可贺
也！"牛王喝道："且休巧舌！我闻你闹了天宫，被佛祖降压在五
行山下，近解脱天灾，保护唐僧西天见佛求经，怎么在号山枯松

洞火云洞把我小儿牛圣婴害了？正在这里恼你，你却怎么又来寻我？”大圣作礼道：“长兄勿得误怪小弟。当时令郎捉住吾师，要食其肉，小弟近他不得，幸观音菩萨欲救我师，劝他归正。现今做了善财童子，比兄长还高，享极乐之门堂，受逍遥之永寿，有何不可，返怪我耶？”牛王骂道：“这个乖嘴的猢狲！害子之情，被你说过；你才欺我爱妾，打上我门何也？”大圣笑道：“我因拜谒长兄不见，向那女子拜问，不知就是二嫂嫂；因他骂了我几句，是小弟一时粗卤，惊了嫂嫂。望长兄宽恕宽恕！”牛王道：“既如此说，我看故旧之情，饶你去罢。”

【6】 大圣道：“既蒙宽恩，感谢不尽；但尚有一事奉渎，万望周济周济。”牛王骂道：“这猢狲不识起倒！饶了你，倒还不走，反来缠我！甚么周济周济！”大圣道：“实不瞒长兄。小弟因保唐僧西进，路阻火焰山，不能前进。询问土人，知尊嫂罗刹女有一柄芭蕉扇，欲求一用。昨到旧府，奉拜嫂嫂，嫂嫂坚执不借，是以特求长兄。望兄长开天地之心，同小弟到大嫂处一行，千万借扇扇灭火焰，保得唐僧过山，即时完璧。”牛王闻言，心如火发。咬响钢牙骂道：“你说你不无礼，你原来是借扇之故！一定先欺我山妻，山妻想是不肯，故来寻我！且又赶我爱妾！常言道：‘朋友妻，不可欺；朋友妾，不可灭。’你既欺山妻，又灭我妾，多大无礼？上来吃我一棍！”大圣道：“哥要说打，弟也不惧。但求宝贝，是我真心。万乞借我使使！”牛王道：“你若三合敌得我，我着山妻借你；如敌不过，打死你，与我雪恨！”大圣道：“哥说得是。小弟这一向疏懒，不曾与兄相会，不知这几年武艺比昔日如何，我兄弟们请演演棍看。”这牛王那容分说，掣混铁棍，劈头就打。这大圣持金箍棒，随手相迎。两个这场好斗：

金箍棒，混铁棍，变脸不以朋友论。那个说：正怪你这猢狲害子精！”这个说：“你令郎已得道休嗔恨！”那个说：“你无知怎敢上我门？”这个说：“我有因特地来相问。”一个要求扇子保唐僧，一个不借芭蕉忒鄙吝。语去言来失旧情，举家无义皆生忿。牛王棍起赛蛟龙，大圣棒迎神鬼遁。初时争斗在山前，后来齐驾祥云进。半空之内显神通，五彩光中施妙运。两条棍响振天关，不见输赢皆傍寸。

这大圣与那牛王斗经百十回合，不分胜负。正在难解难分之际，只听得山峰有人叫道："牛爷爷，我大王多多拜上，幸赐早临，好安座也。"牛王闻说，使混铁棍支住金箍棒，叫道："猢狲，你且住了，等我去一个朋友家赴会来者！"言毕，按下云头，径至洞里。对玉面公主道："美人，才那雷公嘴的男子乃孙悟空猢狲，被我一顿棍打走了，再不敢来。你放心耍子。我到一个朋友处吃酒去也。"他才卸了盔甲，穿一领鸦青剪绒袄，走出门，跨上"辟水金睛兽"，着小的们看守门庭，半云半雾，一直向西北方而去。

【7】 大圣在高峰上看着，心中暗想道："这老牛不知又结识了甚么朋友，往那里去赴会。等老孙跟他走走。"好行者，将身幌一幌，变做一阵清风赶上，随着同走。不多时，到了一座山中，那牛王寂然不见。大圣聚了原身，入山寻看，那山中有一面清水深潭，潭边有一座石碣，碣上有六个大字，乃"乱石山碧波潭"。大圣暗想道："老牛断然下水去了。水底之精，若不是蛟精，必是龙精、鱼精、或是龟鳖鼋之精。等老孙也下去看看。"

好大圣，捻着诀，念个咒语，摇身一变，变做一个螃蟹，不大不小的，有三十六斤重。扑的跳在水中，径沉潭底。忽见一座玲珑剔透的牌楼，楼下拴着那个辟水金睛兽。进牌楼里面，却就没水。大圣爬进去，仔细看时，只见那壁厢一派音乐之声，但见：

> 朱宫贝阙，与世不殊。黄金为屋瓦，白玉做门枢。屏开玳瑁甲，槛砌珊瑚珠。祥云瑞蔼辉莲座，上接三光下八衢。非是天宫并海藏，果然此处赛蓬壶。高堂设宴罗宾主，大小官员冠冕珠。忙呼玉女捧牙槃，催唤仙娥调律吕。长鲸鸣，巨蟹舞，鳖吹笙，鼍击鼓，骊颔之珠照樽俎。鸟篆之文列翠屏，虾须之帘挂廊庑。八音迭奏寻仙韶，宫商响彻遏云霄。青头鲈妓抚瑶瑟，红眼马郎品玉箫。鳜婆顶献香獐脯，龙女头簪金凤翅。吃的是，天厨八宝珍羞味；饮的是；紫府琼浆熟酝醪。

那上面坐的是牛魔王，左右有三四个蛟精，前面坐着一个老龙精，两边乃龙子、龙孙、龙婆、龙女。正在那里觥筹交错之际，孙大圣一直走将上去，被老龙看见，即命："拿下那个野蟹！"龙子、龙孙一拥上前，把大圣拿住。大圣忽作人言，只叫："饶命！饶命!"老龙道:"你是那里来的野蟹?怎么敢上厅堂,在尊客之前,横行乱走?快早供来,免汝死罪!"大圣,假捏虚言,对众供道:"生自湖中为活,傍崖做窟权居。盖因日久得身舒,官受横行介士。　踏草拖泥落索,从来未习行仪。不知法度冒王威,伏望尊慈恕罪!"

座上众精闻言,都拱હ老龙作礼道:"蟹介士初入瑶宫,不知王礼,望尊公饶他去罢。"老王听谢了。众精即教:"放了那厮,且记打,外面伺候。"大圣应了一声,往外逃命,径至牌楼之下。心中暗想道:"这牛王在此贪杯,那里等得他散?……就是散了,也不肯借扇与我。不如偷了他的金睛兽,变作牛魔王,去哄那罗刹女,骗他扇子,送我师父过山为妙……"

【8】好大圣,即现本像,将金睛兽解了缰绳,扑一把跨上雕鞍,径直骑出水底。离了深潭外,至潭外,将身变做牛王模样。打着兽,纵着云,不多时,已至翠云山芭蕉洞口。叫声"开门!"那洞门里有两个女童,闻得声音开了门,看见是牛魔王嘴脸,即入报:"奶奶,爷爷来家了。"那罗刹听言,忙整云鬓,急移莲步,出门迎接。这大圣下雕鞍,牵进金睛兽;弄大胆,诓骗女佳人。罗刹女肉眼,认他不出,即携手而入。着丫环彀坐看茶,一家子见是主公,无不敬谨。

须臾间,叙及寒温。"牛王"道:"夫人久阔。"罗刹道:"大王万福"又云:"大王宠幸新婚,抛撇奴家,今日是那阵风儿吹你来的?"大圣笑道:"非敢抛撇,只因玉面公主招后,家事繁沉,朋友多顾,是以稽留在外,却也又治得一个家当了。"又道:"近闻悟空那厮,保唐僧,将近火焰山界,恐他来问你借扇子。我恨那厮害子之仇未报,但来时,可差人报我,等我拿他,分尸万段,以雪我夫妻之恨。"罗刹闻言,滴泪告道:"大王,常言说:'男儿无妇财无主,女子无夫身无主。'我的性命,险些儿不着这猴狲害了!"大圣得故子,发怒骂道:"那泼猴几时过去了?"罗刹道:"还未去。昨日到我这里借扇子,我因他害孩儿之故,披挂了,抢宝剑出门,就砍那猴狲。他忍着疼,叫我做嫂嫂,说大王曾与他结义。"大圣道:"是,五百年前曾拜为七兄弟。"罗刹道:"被我骂也不敢回言,砍也不敢动手,后被我一扇子扇去;不知在那里寻得个定风法儿,今早又在门外叫唤。是我又使扇扇,莫想得动。急抡剑砍时,他就不让我了。我怕他棒重,就走入洞里,紧关上门。不知他又从何处,钻在我肚腹之内,险被他害了性命!是我叫他几声叔叔,将扇与他去也。"大圣又假意捶胸道:"可惜!可惜!夫人错了,怎么就把这宝贝与那猢狲?恼杀我也!"

【9】 罗刹笑道:"大王息怒。与他的是假扇,但哄他去了。"大圣问:"真扇在于何处?"罗刹道:"放心!放心!我收着哩。"叫丫环整酒接风贺喜。遂擎杯奉上道:"大王,燕尔新婚,千万莫忘结发,且吃一杯乡中之水。"大圣不敢不接,只得笑吟吟,举觞在手道:"夫人先饮。我因图治外产,久别夫人,早晚蒙护守家门,权为酬谢。"罗刹复接杯斟起,递与大王道:"自古道:'妻者,齐也。'夫乃养身之父,讲甚么谢。"两个谦谦讲讲,方才坐下巡酒。大圣不敢破荤,只吃几个果子,与他言言语语。

酒至数巡,罗刹觉有半酣,色情微动,就和孙大圣挨挨擦擦,搭搭拈拈;携着手,俏语温存;并着肩,低声俯就。将一杯酒,你喝一口,我喝一口,却又哺果。大圣假意虚情,相陪相笑;没奈何,也与他相倚相偎。果然是:

> 钓诗钩,扫愁帚,破除万事无过酒。男儿立节方襟怀,女子忘情开笑口。面赤似夭桃,身摇如嫩柳。絮絮叨叨话语多,捻捻掐掐风情有。时见掠云鬓,又见轮尖手。几番常把脚儿跷,数次每将衣袖抖。粉项自然低,蛮腰渐觉扭。合欢言语不曾丢,酥胸半露松金钮。醉来真个玉山颓,饧眼摩娑几弄丑。

【10】 大圣见他这等酣然,暗自留心,挑斗道:"夫人,真扇子你收在那里?早晚仔细。但恐孙行者变化多端,却又来骗去。"罗刹笑嘻嘻的,口中吐出,只有一个杏叶儿大小,递与大圣道:"这个不是宝贝?"大圣接在手中,却又不信,暗想着:"这些些儿,怎生扇得火灭?……怕又是假的。"罗刹见他看看宝贝沉思,忍不住上前,将粉面揾在行者脸上,叫道:"亲亲,你收了宝贝吃酒罢。只管出神想甚么哩?"大圣就趁脚儿跷,问他一句道:"这般小小之物,如何扇得八百里火焰?"罗刹酒陶真性,无忌惮,就说出方法道:"大王,与你别了二载,你想是昼夜贪欢,被那玉面公主弄

伤了神思，怎么自家的宝贝事情，也都忘了？——只将左手大指头捻着那柄儿上第七缕红丝，念一声'啯嘘呵吸嘻吹呼'，即长一丈二尺长短。这宝贝变化无穷！那怕他八万里火焰，可一扇而消也。"

大圣闻言，切切记在心上。却把扇儿也噙在口里，把脸抹一抹，现了本像。厉声高叫道："罗刹女！你看看我可是你亲老公！就把我缠了这许多丑勾当！不羞！不羞！"那女子一见是孙行者，慌得推倒桌席，跌落尘埃，羞愧无比，只叫"气杀我也！气杀我也！"

【11】 这大圣，不管他死活，捽脱手，拽大步，径出了芭蕉洞。正是无心贪美色，得意笑颜回。将身一纵，踏祥云，跳上高山，将扇子吐出来，演演方法，将左手大指头捻着那柄上第七缕红丝，念了一声"啯嘘呵吸嘻吹呼"，果然长了有一丈二尺长短。拿在手中，仔细看了又看，比前番假的果是不同，只见祥光幌幌，瑞气纷纷，上有三十六缕红丝，穿经度络，表里相联。原来行者只讨了个长的方法，不曾讨他个小的口诀，左右只是那等长短。没奈何，只得扛在肩上，找旧路而回，不题。

【12】 却说那牛魔王在碧波潭底与众精散了筵席，出门了来，不见了辟水金睛兽。老龙王聚众精问道："是谁偷放牛爷的金睛兽也？"众精跪下道："没人敢偷。我等俱在筵前供酒捧盘，供唱奉乐，更无一人在前。"老龙道："家乐儿断乎不敢，可曾有甚生人进来？"龙子、龙孙道："适才安座之时，有个蟹精到此。那个便是生人。"牛王闻说，顿然省悟道："不消讲了！早间贤友着人邀我去时，有个孙悟空保唐僧取经，路遇火焰山难过，曾向我求借芭蕉扇。我不曾与他，他和我赌斗一场，未分胜负，我却丢了他，径赴盛会。那猴子千般伶俐，万样机关，断乎是那厮变做蟹精，来此打探消息，偷了我兽，去山妻处骗了那一把芭蕉扇儿也！"众精听说，一个个胆战心惊，问道："可是那大闹天宫的孙悟空么？"牛王道："正是。列公若在西天路上，有不是处，切要躲避他些儿。"老龙道："似这般说，大王的骏骑，却如之何？"牛王笑道："不妨，不妨，列公各散，等我赶她去来。"

【13】 遂而分开水路，跳出潭底，驾黄云，径至翠云山芭蕉洞。

只听得罗刹女跌脚捶胸，大呼小叫。推开门，又见辟水金睛兽拴在下边，牛王高叫："夫人，孙悟空那厢去了？"众女童看见牛魔，一齐跪下道："爷爷来了？"罗刹女扯住牛王，磕头撞脑，口里骂道："泼老天杀的！怎样这般不谨慎，着那猢狲偷了金睛兽，变做你的模样，到此骗我！"牛王切齿道："猢狲那厢去了？"罗刹捶着胸膛骂道："那泼猴赚了我的宝贝，现出原身走了！气杀我也！"牛王道："夫人保重，勿得心焦。等我赶上猢狲，夺了宝贝，剥了他皮，锉碎他骨，摆出他的心肝，与你出气！"叫："拿兵器来！"女童道："爷爷的兵器，不在这里。"牛王道："拿你奶奶的兵器来罢！"侍婢将两把青锋宝剑捧出。牛王脱了那赴宴的鸦青绒袄，束一束贴身的小衣，双手绰剑，走出芭蕉洞，径奔火焰山上赶来。正是那：忘恩汉，骗了痴心妇；烈性魔，来近木叉人。毕竟不知此去吉凶如何，且听下回分解。

Chapter 11
The Bull Demon King Gives up the Fight to Go to a Feast; Monkey Tries the Second Time to Borrow the Plantain Fan

[1] "The Strongarm King is the Bull Demon King," the local god explained. "Did he set these mountains ablaze and pretend they were the Fiery Mountains?" Monkey asked. "No, no," the local god replied. "If you'll promise to forgive me for doing so, Great Sage, I'll speak frankly." "What's there to forgive?" Monkey said. "Speak frankly." "You started this fire, Great Sage," the local god replied. "That's nonsense," said Monkey angrily. "I wasn't here. Do you take me for an arsonist?" "You don't realize who I am," the local god said. "These mountains haven't always been here. When you made havoc in Heaven five hundred years ago and were captured by the Illustrious Sage Erlang you were escorted to Lord Lao Zi, put in the eight Trigrams Furnace and refined. When the furnace was opened you kicked it over, and some of its bricks that still had fire in them fell here as the Fiery Mountains. I used to be one of the Taoist boys who looked after the furnace in the Tushita Palace, but Lord Lao Zi was so angry with me for failing in my duty that he sent me down to be the local god here." "I was wondering why you were dressed like that," said Pig forcefully, "you're a Taoist turned local god."

[2] "Tell me why I need to find the Strongarm King," said Monkey, only half-convinced. "He's Raksasi's husband," the local god said. "He's abandoned her now and gone to live in the Cloud-touching Cave in Mount Thunder Piled. A fox king there who'd lived for ten thousand years died leaving an only daughter, Princess Jade, with property worth a million but nobody to manage it. Two year ago she visited the Bull Demon King and

found out about his tremendous magical powers. She decided to give him her property if he'd come to live in her cave as her husband. So the Bull Demon King abandoned Raksasi and hasn't been back to see her for ages. If you can find him, Great Sage, and persuade him to come here you'll be able to borrow the real fan. First, you'll be able to blow the flames out to take your master across the mountains. Second, you'll put an end to this disastrous fire so that the land here can come back to life. And third, I'll be pardoned and allowed to go back to Heaven and return to live under Lord Lao Zi's command." "Where is Mount Thunder Piled, and how far is it from here?" "Due south," the local deity said, "and over a thousand miles." Once he knew this Monkey told Friar Sand and Pig to look after the master and ordered the local god to stay with them. There was then a roaring like the wind as he disappeared.

【3】 In less than an hour he saw a high mountain that touched the sky. Bringing his cloud down he stood on the peak to look around, and this is what he saw:

> Was it tall?
> Its peak touched the azure sky.
> Was it big?
> Its roots went down to the Yellow Springs.
> While the sun warmed the front of the mountain
> The winds behind the ridge blew cold.
> On the sun-warmed front of the mountain
> The flowers and trees never knew what winter was;
> In the cold winds behind the ridge
> The ice and frost did not even melt in summer.
> From a dragon pool a river flowed in gullies;
> Flowers bloomed early by the tigers' cave in the crag.
> The river split into a thousand jade streams;
> The flowers bloomed together like brocade.
> On the twisting ridge grew twisted trees;
> Beside the knotted rocks were knotted pines.
> Indeed there were

> *A high mountain,*
> *Steep ridges,*
> *Sheer precipices,*
> *Fragrant flowers,*
> *Fine fruit,*
> *Red creepers,*
> *Purple bamboo,*
> *Green pines,*
> *Turquoise willows.*
> *It looked the same throughout the seasons;*
> *Changeless forever, like a dragon.*

After looking for a long time the Great Sage walked down from the towering peak to find his way through the mountain. Just when he was feeling bewildered a slender young woman came towards him holding a spray of fragrant orchid. The Great Sage slipped behind a grotesque rock and took a good look at her. This is what she was like:

> *A ravishing beauty to enchant a nation*
> *Walking so slowly on her little lotus feet.*
> *Her face was like Wang Qiang or the woman of Chu.*
> *She was a talking flower,*
> *Scented jade.*
> *The hair was swept down from her coiffure like jade-blue crows;*
> *The green of her eyes made one think of autumn floods.*
> *Her silken skirt showed a glimpse of tiny feet;*
> *From her turquoise sleeves came long and elegant wrists.*
> *She would put anyone into the mood for love;*
> *Red were her lips, and white her pearly teeth.*
> *Her skin was as smooth and her brows as fine as the Jinjiang beauty;*
> *She was more than a match for Wenjun or Xue Tao.*

As the young woman slowly approached the rock the Great Sage bowed to her and said, "Where are you going, Bodhisattva?" Before he spoke she had not noticed him; but when she looked up and saw how hideous the Great Sage was she was petrified, unable to move forward or back. All she could do was shiver and force herself to reply, "Where are you from? How dare you question me?" "If I tell her about fetching the scriptures and borrowing the fan," the Great Sage thought, "this damn woman might be some relation of the Bull Demon King's. I'd better pretend to be some kinsman of the Bull Demon King come to invite him to a banquet." When he would not answer her questions the woman turned angry and shouted, "Who are you and how dare you question me?" "I'm from Mount Turquoise Cloud," Monkey replied with a bow and a forced smile. "I don't know the way as it's my first time here. Could I ask you, Bodhisattva, if this is Mount Thunder Piled?" "It is," she replied. "Where might I find the Cloud-touching Cave?" the Great Sage asked. "What do you want to find it for?" the woman asked. "I've been sent by Princess Iron Fan in the Plantain Cave on Mount Turquoise Cloud with an invitation for the Bull Demon King," Monkey replied.

The moment the woman heard him speak of Princess Iron Fan sending an invitation to the Bull Demon King she flared into a rage and went crimson from ear to ear. "She ought to know better, the low bitch. It's less than two years since the Bull Demon King came here, and goodness only knows how much jewellery, gold, silver, fine silk and brocade I've given her since then. I send her firewood every year and rice every month. She's doing nicely thank you. So what's the shameless hussy doing, sending him an invitation?" When the Great Sage heard this and realized that she was Princess Jade he deliberately pulled out his iron cudgel and shouted at her, "You're a damned bitch, using your wealth to buy the Bull Demon King. You could only get him to marry you for your money. You ought to be thoroughly ashamed of yourself instead of being so insulting." At this all of her souls sent flying, and she fled trembling with terror, stumbling and tripping over her shoes, while the Great Sage ran after her, shouting and roaring. Once they were out from under the shade of the pines they were at the entrance to the Cloud-touching Cave. She ran inside and the doors slammed shut behind her. Only then did Monkey put his cudgel away and take a good look:

> A thick forest,
> Sheer precipices,
> Luxuriance of creepers,
> Fragrance of orchids.
> The spring washed over jade and through bamboo,
> Grotesque and cunning rocks held precious stones.
> The distant peaks were wreathed in mists;
> Sun and moon lit up the cloudy crags.
> Dragons howled, tigers roared,
> Cranes called and warblers sang.
> Fresh and lovely was its elegant peace,
> And the scenery was radiant with precious flowers.
> It was a match for Tiantai's magic caves,
> And finer than the Peng and Ying islands in the sea.

[4] We will say nothing of how Brother Monkey admired the view but tell how the young woman, dripping with sweat after running and her heart beating wildly from terror, went straight to the study where the Bull Demon King was quietly perusing a book on cinnabar alchemy. She threw herself into his arms feeling thoroughly put out, scratched and tugged at his face and ears, and howled aloud. "Don't upset yourself so, my lovely," said the Bull Demon King, all smiles. "What do you want to tell me?" She then began to prance and jump about in her fury as she said abusively, "You're killing me, damned monster." "What makes you say that?" he asked, all smiles. "I brought you here to look after me and protect me because I'd lost my parents and people who'd been around all said that you were a tough guy," she said. "But you're just another henpecked hack." The Bull Demon King took her in his arms and said, "How've I done you wrong, my

lovely? Take your time and tell me about it. I'll make it up to you." "I was taking a stroll among the flowers outside the cave just now picking orchids," she said, "when a monk with a face like a thunder god rushed up to me and started bowing. I was to scared I couldn't move. When I calmed down enough to ask him who he was he said he'd been sent by that Princess Iron Fan with an invitation for you. I was so angry I had something to say about that, and he started abusing me and chased me with his cudgel. He'd have just about killed me with it if I hadn't run so fast. So you see, bringing you here was a disaster. It's killing me." At this the Bull Demon King apologized to her very earnestly. It took a long time and many tender attentions from him before she finally calmed down. "I tell you the truth, my lovely," the demon king said forcefully. "The Plantain Cave may be rather out of the way, but it's a place of purity and elegance. That wife of mine has had the highest moral principles since childhood, and she's also an immortal who has attained the Way. She runs her household very strictly. There's not even a page there. She couldn't possibly have sent a monk with a face like a thunder god. I wonder what evil fiend he is. He must have used her name to come and see me. I'm going out to have a look."

[5]   The splendid demon king strode out of the study and into the hall to put on his armour and take his iron cudgel. "Who are you, and why are you behaving so outrageously?" he shouted as he went out through the doors. Monkey, who was watching from one side, saw that he now looked quite different from the way he had five hundred years earlier.

His wrought iron helmet shone like water or silver;
His golden armour was trimmed with silks and brocades.
The toes of his deerskin boots turned up; their soles were white.
The silken belt at his waist included three lion's tails.
His eyes were as bright as mirrors,
His brows as elegant as red rainbows,
His mouth like a bowl of blood,

295

> *His teeth a row of copper plates.*
> *At his resounding roar the mountain gods took fright;*
> *Evil ghosts were overawed by his majestic power.*
> *His fame was known throughout the seas for raising chaos;*
> *He was the Strongarm Demon King here in the west.*

The Great Sage then tidied his clothes, stepped forward, chanted a deep "re-e-er" of respect, and asked, "Can you still recognize me, eldest brother?" "Are you Sun Wukong, the Great Sage Equalling Heaven?" the Bull Demon King replied, returning his bow. "Yes, yes," said Monkey. "It's such a long time since last we met. I only got here to see you because I asked a woman some questions just now. I must congratulate you on how well everything is growing." "Cut that out," the Bull Demon King shouted back. "I heard about you making havoc in Heaven and being crushed under the Five Elements Mountain by the Lord Buddha. Then you were released from your heavenly punishment to protect the Tang Priest on his way to worship the Buddha and fetch the scriptures in the Western Heaven. Why did you have to destroy my son, the Sage Boy Bullcalf? I'm very angry with you. Why are you here looking for me?" "Please don't misjudge me, brother," said the Great Sage with another bow. "Your good son captured my master and was going to eat him. I was no match for him. Luckily the Bodhisattva Guanyin rescued my master and converted your boy. He's now the page Sudhana. He's even taller than you. He lives in a temple of great bliss and enjoys eternal ease. There's nothing wrong with any of that, so why be angry with me?" "Smooth-tongued macaque," retorted the Bull Demon King. "Even if you can talk your way out of having ruined my son, what do you mean by upsetting my beloved concubine and chasing her up to my doors?" "I made a polite inquiry of the lady because I could not find you," Monkey replied. I never realized she was your second wife, so when she was rude to me I acted rough. Please forgive me." "Very well then," the Bull Demon King said. "I'll let you off this time for the sake of our old friendship."

[6] "I'm very grateful indeed for your immense kindness," the Great Sage replied. "But there is one thing I'd like to trouble you with. I hope you'll be able to help me out." "You macaque," the Bull Demon King shouted at him, "you think you can get away with anything! I spare your life, but instead of making yourself scarce you have to keep pestering me. What do you mean by helping out?" "Let me be honest with you," the Great Sage replied. "I'm stuck at the Fiery Mountains on my journey escorting the Tang Priest, and we're not getting anywhere. The local people told me that your good lady Raksasi has a plantain fan. I tried to borrow it. I went to visit my sister-in-law, but she refused to lend it me, which is why I've come to see you. I beg you, brother, in the greatness of your heart to come with me to sister-in-law's place and borrow the fan for me so that I can blow out the fires and get my master across the mountains. Then I'll return it right away."

At this the Bull Demon King's heart blazed with wrath. "You told me you knew how to behave," he said, noisily gnashing his teeth of steel. "I suppose all this was not just to borrow the fan. I'm certain my wife has refused to lend it you because you've mistreated her. So that's why you came to see me. On top of that you send my beloved concubine fleeing in terror. As the saying goes,

> Don't push around
> Your best friend's wife,
> Don't try to destroy
> The joy of his life.

You've been pushing my wife around and trying to destroy the concubine who's the joy of my life. It's an outrage. Take this!" "If you want to hit me, brother, I'm not afraid," said Monkey. "All I want is the treasure. I beg you to lend it me." "If you can last out three rounds with," the Bull Demon King said, "I'll make my wife lend it to you. And if you can't I'll kill you and have my revenge." "Good idea, brother," Monkey replied. "I've

297

been so lazy. I haven't been to see you for ages, and I don't know how your fighting powers now compare with the old days. Let's have a match with our cudgels." The Bull Demon King was in no mood for further argument, and he hit at Monkey's head with his mace. Monkey hit back with his gold-banded cudgel. It was a splendid fight:

> The gold-banded cudgel,
> The rough iron mace,
> Are no longer friends.
> One said, "You destroyed my son, you macaque."
> The other, "Don't be angry: he has found the Way."
> "How could you be so stupid as to come to my door?"
> "I am here to visit you with a special purpose."
> One wanted the fan to protect the Tang Priest;
> The other was too mean to lend the plantain leaf.
> Friendship was lost in the exchange of words;
> In anger neither had any sense of brotherhood.
> The Bull Demon King's mace moved like a dragon:
> The Great Sage's cudgel sent gods and demons fleeing.
> First they fought in front of the mountain,
> Then they both rose on auspicious clouds.
> They showed their great powers up in mid-air,
> Doing wonderful movements in multi-coloured light.
> The clash of their cudgels rocked the gates of Heaven;
> They were too evenly matched for either to win.

The Great Sage and the Bull Demon King fought over a hundred rounds without either emerging as the victor. Just as they were becoming locked in their struggle a voice called from the peak, "King Bull, my king sends his respects and invites you to honour him with your presence at a banquet." At this the Bull Demon King blocked the gold-banded cudgel with his iron mace and called out, "You stay here, macaque. I'm going to a friend's house for a meal. I'll be back." With that he landed his cloud and went straight back into the cave. "My lovely," he said to Princess

Jade, "the man you saw with a face like a thunder god is the macaque Sun Wukong. A bout with my mace has sent him packing: he won't be back. Stop worrying and enjoy yourself. I'm going to a friend's place for some drinks." He then took off his helmet and armour, donned a duck-green jacket of cut velvet, went outside and mounted his water-averting golden-eyed beast. Telling his underlings to look after the palace he headed northwest in clouds and mist.

[7] While the Great Sage watched all this from the peak he thought, "I wonder who the friend is and where he's gone for his banquet. I'll follow him." Splendid Monkey then shook himself and turned into a clear breeze to follow him. He soon reached a mountain, but the Bull Demon King was nowhere to be seen. The Great Sage turned back into himself and started to search the mountain. He found a deep pool of pure water beside which was inscribed in large letters in a tablet of stone

RAGGED ROCK MOUNTAIN
GREEN WAVE POOL

"Old Bull must have gone into the water," Monkey thought, "and underwater spirits are lesser dragons, dragon or fish spirits, or else turtle, tortoise of terrapin spirits. I'd better go down and have a look."

Making a hand-spell and saying the magic words the splendid Great Sage shook himself, turned into a medium-sized crab weighing thirty-six pounds, jumped into the water with a splash, and went straight down to the bottom of the pool. He saw an ornamental arch of delicate tracery to which was tethered a water-averting golden-eyed beast. On the other side of the arch there was no more water. Monkey crawled through and took a careful look. From one side he heard music, and this is what he saw:

Cowry gateways to a palace red,
Like nothing else in the world.
The roof tiles were of yellow gold,

299

The door pivots of whitest jade.
The screens were of tortoise-shell,
The balustrades of coral and of pearl.
Auspicious clouds glowed all around the throne,
From the sky above right down to the ground.
This was not the palace of Heaven or the sea,
Although it more than rivalled an island paradise.
A banquet for host and guests was set in the lofty hall,
Where all the officials wore their hats with pearls.
Jade girls were told to bring ivory bowls,
Exquisite beauties to play fine music.
The great whale sang,
Giant crabs danced,
Turtles played pipes and drums,
While pearls shone over the goblets and boards.
Birdlike script adorned the turquoise screens,
While shrimp-whisker curtains hung along the corridors.
From the eight notes mingled came wonderful music
Whose tones rose up to the clouds above.
Green-headed singsong girls stroked zithers of jasper
While red-eyed dragonflies played jade flutes.
Mandarin fish carried dried venison in on their heads,
While dragon girls had the wings of golden pheasants in
their hair.
What they ate were
The rarest delicacies of the heavenly kitchen;
What they drank were
The finest vintages of the purple palace.

The Bull Demon King was sitting in the seat of honour with three or four lesser dragon spirits on either side. Facing him was an ancient dragon, surrounded by dragon sons, dragon grandsons, dragon wives and dragon daughters. Just as they were feasting and drinking the Great Sage Sun marched straight in, to be spotted by the ancient dragon, who ordered, "Arrest that vagrant crab." The dragon sons and grandsons fell upon him and seized him. "Spare me, spare me," said Monkey, suddenly reverting to human speech. "Where are you from, crab vagrant?" the ancient dragon asked. "How dare you come into my hall and behave in this disgraceful way in front of my distinguished guests? Tell me this moment if you want to be spared the death penalty." The splendid Great Sage then made up a pack of lies to tell him:

"Ever since coming to live in the lake
I've had to make my home in cliffs and caves.
Over the years I've learned to stretch myself out
So now I am known as the Sideways Man-at-arms.
Dragging my way through weeds and through mud,
I have never been taught correct social behaviour.
If in my ignorance I have caused offence
I beg Your Majesty to show me mercy."

When the spirits at the banquet heard this they all bowed to the ancient dragon and said, "This is the first time that the Sideways Man-at-arms has come to your palace of jasper, and he does not understand royal etiquette. We beg Your Excellency to spare him." The ancient dragon thanked the spirits and ordered, "Release the wretch. Put a beating on record against his name, and have him wait outside." The Great Sage acknowledged his kindness then fled for his life till he reached the archway outside. "That Bull Demon King is drinking for all he's worth in there," he thought. "I'm not going to wait till the feast breaks up. And even if I did he still wouldn't lend me the fan. I'd do better to steal his golden-eyed beast and turn myself into a Bull Demon King. Then I can trick Raksasi into lending me the fan and I'll be able to escort my master across the mountains. That'll be best."

[8] The splendid Great Sage then reverted to his original form, untied the golden-eyed beast, leapt into the carved saddle, and rode straight up from the bottom of the water. Once out of the pool he made himself look like the Bull Demon King. Whipping on the beast he set his cloud moving and was soon at the mouth of the Plantain Cave in Mount Turquoise Cloud. "Open up!" he

shouted, and at the sound of his voice the two servant girls inside the gates opened them for him. Taking him for the Bull Demon King they went in to report, "Madam, His Majesty's come home." At the news Raksasi quickly neatened her hair and hurried out on her little lotus feet to meet him. Climbing out of the saddle the Great Sage led the golden-eyed beast inside. He was bold enough to try to deceive the beauty, whose mortal eyes failed to see who he really was as she led him inside, hand in hand. The maids were told to prepare places and bring tea, and as the master was back the whole household tried its hardest.

The Great Sage and Raksasi were soon talking. "My good lady," said the false Bull Demon King, "it's been a long time." "I hope that everything has gone well for Your Majesty," Raksasi replied, going on to ask, "what wind brings you back to your abandoned wife now that you have married your new darling?" "There's no question of having abandoned you," the Great Sage replied with a smile. "It's just that I've been away a long time since Princess Jade invited me to her place. I'm kept very busy with domestic matters to deal with and friends to attend to. I hear that so-and-so Sun Wukong is very near the Fiery Mountains with the Tang Priest, and I'm worried that he might come and ask you to lend him the fan. I can't forgive him for destroying our son. I want my revenge. If he turns up, just send someone to tell me. When I get him we can cut his body up into ten thousand pieces as revenge for what we have suffered." "Your Majesty," replied Raksasi, in tears at what he had just said, "as the saying goes, 'A man with no woman is risking his wealth; a woman with no husband is risking her health.' That macaque practically killed me."

At this the Great Sage pretended to fly into a terrible rage. "When did that bloody monkey go?" he swore. "He hasn't gone yet," Raksasi replied. "He was here yesterday to borrow the fan, and as he'd destroyed our boy I put my armour on and went out to cut him to bits with my swords. But he endured the pain, called me his sister-in-law, and said that you and he were once sworn brothers." "He was my seventh sworn brother five hundred years

ago," the Great Sage replied. "He said not a word when I swore
at him," Raksasi continued, "and didn't strike back when I cut
him. Finally I blew him away with the fan. Goodness only knows
where he got some wind-fixing magic from, but this morning he
was back shouting outside the door again, and the fan wouldn't
move him no matter how hard I waved it. When I swung my
swords around and went for him with them he wasn't being polite
any more. I was so scared of the force of his cudgel I came back
in here and had the doors tightly shut. Somehow or other he
managed to get right into my belly and it practically killed me. I
had to call him brother-in-law and lend him the fan before he'd
go." The Great Sage put on a great show of beating his chest and
saying, "How terrible, how terrible. You did wrong, wife. You
should never have given that treasure to the macaque."

[9] "Don't be angry, Your Majesty," Raksasi replied. "I lent
him a false fan and tricked him into going away." "Where's the
real one?" the Great Sage asked. "Don't worry," she replied,
"don't worry. It's safely put away." She then told the serving
girls to lay on wine and a feast to welcome him back. "Your
Majesty," she then said, offering him a goblet of wine, "please
don't forget the wife of your youth in the joy of your new
marriage. Won't you drink this cup of wine from home?" The
Great Sage had no choice but to accept the goblet and smile as he
raised it. "You drink first, wife," he said. "I've left you looking
after the home by yourself, good lady, for too long, while I've
been busy with my other property. Let this be a gesture of my
gratitude." Raksasi took the goblet back, lifted it again, and
handed it to the king with the words, "As the old saying goes:
The wife is the equal, but the husband is the father who supports
her. You don't need to thank me." It was only after more such
politeness that the two of them sat down and began drinking. Not
wanting to break his vow to avoid meat, the Great Sage only ate
some fruit while he talked to her.

After they had each had several cups Raksasi was feeling a
little drunk and rather sexy. She started to press herself against
the Great Sage, stroking and pinching him. Taking him by the

303

hand, she whispered tender words to him; leaning her shoulder against him, she spoke quietly and submissively. They shared the same cup of wine, drinking a mouthful each at a time, and she fed him fruit. The Great Sage pretended to go along with this and smile. He had no choice but to lean against her. Indeed,

> The book to catch poetry,
> The broom to sweep away sorrow,
> The remover of all difficulties is wine.
> The man, though virtuous, unbuttoned his lapel;
> The woman forgot herself and began to laugh.
> Her face had the complexion of a peach,
> Her body swayed like a willow sapling.
> Many a word came babbling from her mouth
> As she pinched and nipped in her desire.
> Sometimes she tugged at her hair,
> Or waved her delicate fingers.
> She often raised a foot
> And twitched the sleeves of her clothes.
> Her powdered neck sunk lower
> And her fine waist started to wiggle.
> She never stopped talking for a moment
> As she opened gold buttons to half show her breasts.
> In her cups she was like a landslide of jade,
> And as she rubbed her bleary eyes she did not look at her

best.

【10】 Watching her get drunk the Great Sage had kept his wits about him, and he tried to lead her on by saying, "Where have you put the real fan, wife? You must watch it very carefully all the time. I'm worried that Sun the Novice will trick it out of you with some of his many transformations." At this Raksasi tittered, spat it out of her mouth, and handed it to the Great Sage. It was only the size of an apricot leaf. "Here's the treasure," she said.

The Great Sage took it but could not believe that it really was. "How could a tiny little thing like this blow a fire out?" he wondered. "It must be another fake." Seeing him looking at the treasure so deep in thought, Raksasi could not restrain herself from rubbing her powdered face against Monkey's and saying, "Put the treasure away and have another drink, darling. What are you looking so worried about?" The Great Sage took the chance to slip in the question, "How could a little thing like this blow out 250 miles of fire?" She was now drunk enough to have no inhibitions about speaking the truth, so she told him how it was done: "Your Majesty, I expect you've been overdoing your pleasures day and night these last two years since you left me. That Princess Jade must have addled your brains if you can't even remember about your own treasure. You just have to pinch the seventh red silk thread with the thumb of your left hand and say, 'Huixuhexixichuihu.' Then it'll grow twelve feet long. It can do as many changes as you like. It could blow 250,000 miles of flame out with a single wave."

The Great Sage committed all this very carefully to memory, put the fan in his mouth, rubbed his face and turned back into himself. "Raksasi!" he yelled at the top of his voice. "Have a careful look: I'm your brother-in-law. What a disgusting way you've been carrying on in with me, and for what a long time too. You're shameless, quite shameless." In her horror at realizing it was Sun Wukong she pushed the dining table over and fell into the dust, overcome with shame and screaming, "I'm so upset I could die, I could die."

[11] Not caring whether she was dead or alive, the Great Sage broke free and rushed straight out of the Plantain Cave. He was indeed not lusting after that female beauty, and glad to turn away with a smiling face. He sprang on his auspicious cloud that took him up to the top of the mountain, spat the fan out of his mouth, and tried the magic out. Pinching the seventh red tassel with the thumb of his left hand, he said "Huixuhexixichuihu," and indeed it grew to be twelve feet long. On close examination he found it quite different from the false one he had borrowed before. It glittered with auspicious light and was surrounded by lucky vapours. Thirty-six threads of red silk formed a trellis pattern

305

inside and out. But Brother Monkey had only asked how to make it grow and had not found out the spell for shrinking it. So he had to shoulder it as he went back by the way he had come.

[12] When the Bull Demon King's feast with all the spirits at the bottom of the Green Wave Pool ended he went outside to find that the water-averting golden-eyed beast was missing. The ancient dragon king called the spirits together to ask them, "Which of you untied and stole the Bull Demon King's golden-eyed beast?" The spirits all knelt down and replied, "We wouldn't dare steal it. We were all waiting, singing or playing at the banquet. None of us was out here." "I am sure that none of your palace musicians would have dared to take it," the ancient dragon said. "Have any strangers been here?" "A crab spirit was here not long ago during the banquet, and he was a stranger."

At this the Bull Demon King suddenly realized what had happened. "Say no more," he exclaimed. "When you sent your messenger with the invitation this morning there was a Sun Wukong there who'd come to ask to borrow my plantain fan as he couldn't get the Tang Priest he's escorting to fetch the scriptures across the Fiery Mountains. I refused. I was in the middle of a fight with him that neither of us was winning when I shook him off and came straight here to the banquet. That monkey's extremely quick and adaptable. I'm sure that the crab spirit was him here in disguise to do a bit of spying. He's stolen my beast to go and trick the plantain fan out of my wife." This news made all the spirits shake with fright. "Do you mean the Sun Wukong who made havoc in Heaven?" they asked. "Yes," the Bull Demon King replied. "If any of you gentlemen have any trouble on the road west keep your distance from him whatever you do." "But if all that's true, what about Your Majesty's steed?" the ancient dragon asked. "No problem," the Bull Demon King replied with a smile. "You gentlemen may all go home now while I go after him."

[13] With that he parted his way through the waters, sprang up from the bottom of the pool and rode a yellow cloud straight to the Plantain Cave on Mount Turquoise Cloud, where he heard

Raksasi stamping her feet, beating her breast, howling and moaning. He pushed the doors open to see the water-averting golden-eyed beast tethered by them. "Where did Sun Wukong go, wife?" the Bull Demon King said. Seeing that the Bull Demon King was back, the serving girls all knelt down and said, "Are you home, Your Majesty?" Raksasi grabbed hold of him, banged her head against his, and said abusively, "Damn and blast you, you careless fool. Why ever did you let that macaque steal the golden-eyed beast and turn himself into your double to come here and trick me?" "Which way did the macaque go?" the Bull Demon King asked, grinding his teeth in fury. Beating her breast Raksasi continued to pour out abuse: "The damn monkey tricked me out of my treasure, turned back into himself, and went. I'm so angry I could die." "Do look after yourself, wife," the Bull Demon King said, "and don't be so upset. When I've caught the macaque and taken the treasure off him I'll skin him, grind his bones to powder, and bring you his heart and liver. That'll make you feel better." He then called for weapons. "Your Majesty's weapons aren't here," the serving girls replied. "Then bring your mistress' weapons," the Bull Demon King replied. The servants brought her pair of blue-tipped swords, and the Bull Demon King took off the duck-green velvet jacket he had worn to the banquet and tied the little waistcoat he wore next to his skin more tightly. He than strode out of the Plantain Cave, a sword in each hand, and headed straight for the Fiery Mountains in pursuit of Monkey. It was a case of

> The man who forgot a kindness
> Tricking a doting wife;
> The fiery-tempered old demon
> Meeting a mendicant monk.

If you don't know whether this journey was ill-fated or not, listen to the explanation in the next instalment.

12. 猪八戒助力败魔王
孙行者三调芭蕉扇

【1】 话表牛魔王赶上孙大圣，只见他肩膊上掮着那柄芭蕉扇，怡颜悦色而行。魔王大惊道："猢狲原来把运用的方法儿也叨饬得来了。我若当面问他索取，他定然不与。倘若扇我一扇，要去十万八千里远，却不遂了他意？我闻得唐僧在那大路上等候。他二徒弟猪精，三徒弟沙流精，我当年做妖怪时，也曾会他。且变做猪猪精的模样，返骗他一场。料猢狲以得意为喜，必不详细提防。"好魔王，他也有七十二变，武艺也与大圣一般，只是身子狼犹些，欠钻疾，不活达些；把那宝剑藏了，念个咒语，摇身一变，即变做八戒一般嘴脸，抄下路，当面迎着大圣，叫道："师兄，我来也！"

【2】 这大圣果然欢喜。古人云："得胜的猫儿欢似虎"也，只倚着强能，更不察来人的意思。见是个八戒的模样，便就叫道："兄弟，你往那里去？"牛魔王绰着经儿道："师父见你许久不回，恐牛魔王手段大，你斗他不过，难得他的宝贝，教我来迎你的。"行者笑道："不必费心，我已得了手了。"牛王又问道："你怎么得的？"行者道："那老牛与我战经百十合，不分胜负。他就撇了我，去那乱石山碧波潭底，与一伙蛟精、龙精饮酒。是我暗跟他去，变做个螃蟹，偷了他所骑的辟水金睛兽，变了老牛的模样，径至芭蕉洞哄那罗刹女。那女子与老孙结了一场干夫妻，是老孙设法骗将来的。"牛王道："却是生受了。哥哥劳碌太甚，可把扇子我拿。"孙大圣那知真假，也虑不及此，遂将扇子递与他。

【3】 原来那牛王，他知那扇子收放的根本；接过手，不知捻个甚么诀儿，依然小似一片杏叶，现出本像。开言骂道："泼猢狲！认得我么？"行者见了，心中自懊悔："是我的不是了！"恨了一声，跌足高呼道："咦！逐年家打雁，今却被小雁儿鹐了眼睛。"狠得他爆躁如雷，犀铁棒，劈头便打，那魔王就使扇子扇他一下；不知那

308

大圣先前变蟭蟟虫儿入罗刹女腹中之时，将定风丹噙在口里，不觉的咽下肚里，所以五脏皆牢，皮骨皆固，凭他怎么扇，再也扇他不动。牛王慌了，把宝贝丢入口中，双手抢剑就砍。那两个在半空中试一场好杀：

齐天孙大圣，混世泼牛王，只为芭蕉扇，相逢各骋强。粗let
大圣将人骗，大胆牛王把索诓。这一个，金箍棒起无情义；那一个，双刃青锋有智量。大圣施威喷彩雾，牛王放泼吐毫光。齐斗勇，两不良，咬牙锉齿气昂昂。播土扬尘天地暗，飞砂走石鬼神藏。这个说："你敢无知返骗我！"那个说："我妻许你共相将！"言村语浊，性烈情刚。那个说："你哄人妻女真该死！告到官司有罪殃！"伶俐的齐天圣，凶顽的大力士，一心只要杀，更不待商量。棒打剑迎各努力，有些松慢见阎王。

【4】　且不说他两个相斗相嚷。却表唐僧坐在途中，一则火气蒸人，二来心焦口渴，对火焰山土地道："敢问尊神，那牛魔王法力如何？"土地道："那牛王神通不小，法力无边，正是孙大圣的敌手。"三藏道："悟空是个会走路的，往常家二千里路，一霎时便回，怎么如今去了一日？断是与那牛王赌斗。"叫："悟能，悟净！你两个，那一个去迎你师兄一迎？倘或遇敌，就当用力相助，求得扇子来，解我烦躁，早早过山，赶路去也。"八戒道："今日天晚，我想着要去接他，但只是不认得积雷山路。"土地道："小神认得。且教卷帘将军与你师父做伴，我与你去来。"三藏大喜道："有劳尊神，功成再谢。"

【5】　那八戒抖擞精神，束一束皂锦直裰，挈着钯，即与土地纵起云雾，径回东方而去。正行时，忽听得喊杀声高，狂风滚滚。八戒按住云头看时，原来孙行者与牛王厮哩。土地道："天蓬还不上前怎的？"呆子掣钉钯，厉声高叫道："师兄，我来也！"行者恨道："你这弼货，误了我多少大事！"八戒道："师父教我来迎你，因认不得积雷山，商议良久，教土地引我，故此来迟，如何误了大事？"行者道："不是怪你来迟。这泼牛十分无礼！我向罗刹女弄得扇子来，却被这厮变做你的模样，迎着我，我一时欢悦，转把扇子递在他手，他却现了本像，与老孙在此比并，所以误了大事也。"八戒闻言大怒，举钉钯当面骂道："我把你这血皮胀的遭

瘟！你怎敢变做你祖宗的模样，骗我师兄，使我弟兄不睦！"你看他没头没脸的使钉钯乱筑。那牛王，一则是与行者斗了一日，力倦神疲；二则是见八戒的钉钯凶猛，遮架不住，败阵而走。只见那火焰山土地，帅领阴兵，当面挡住道："大力王，且住手。唐三藏西天取经，有神保护，有天护佑，三界通知，十方拥护。快将芭蕉扇扇息火焰，教他无灾无障，早过山去；不然，上天责你罪愆，定遭诛也。"牛王道："你这土地，全不察理！那泼猴夺我子，欺我妾，骗我妻，番番无理，我恨不得囫囵吞他下肚，化做大便喂狗，怎么肯将宝贝借他！"

【6】 说不了，八戒赶上骂道："我把你个结心瘟！快拿出扇来，饶你性命！"那牛王只得回头，使宝剑又战八戒。孙大圣举棒相帮。这一场在那里好杀：

> 成精豕，作怪牛，兼上偷天得道猴。禅性自来能战练，必当用土合元由。钉钯九齿尖还利，宝剑双锋快更柔。铁棒卷舒为主仗，土神助力结丹头。三家刑克相争竞，各展雄才要运筹。捉牛耕地金钱长，唤豕归炉木气收。心不在焉何作道，神常守舍要拴猴。胡乱嚷，苦相求，三般兵刃响嗖嗖。钯筑剑伤无好意，金箍棒起有因由。只杀得星不光兮月不皎，一天寒雾黑悠悠！

那魔王奋勇争强，且行且斗，斗了一夜，不分上下，早又天明。前面是他的积雷山摩云洞口，他三个与土地、阴兵，又喧哗振耳，惊动那玉面公主，唤丫环看是那里人嚷。只见守门小妖来报："是我家爷爷与昨日那雷公嘴汉子并一个长嘴大耳的和尚同火焰山土地等众厮杀哩！"玉面公主听言，即命外护的大小头目，各执枪刀助力。前后点起七长八短，有百十余口。一个个卖弄精神，拈枪弄棒，齐告："大王爷爷，我等奉奶奶内旨，特来助力也！"牛王大喜道："来得好！来得好！"众妖一齐上前乱砍。八戒措手不及，倒拽着钯，败阵而走。大圣纵筋斗云，跳出重围。众阴兵亦四散奔走。老牛得胜，聚众妖归洞，紧闭了洞门不题。

【7】 行者道："这厮骁勇！自午日申时前后，与老孙战起，直到今夜，未定输赢，却又幸这两个来接力。如此苦斗半日一夜，他更不见劳困。才这一伙小妖，却又莽壮。他将洞门紧闭不出，如之奈

何?"八戒道:"哥哥,你昨日巳时离了师父,怎么到申时才与他斗起?你那两三个时辰,在那里的?"行者道:"别你后,顷刻就到这座山上,见一个女子,问讯,原来就是他爱妾玉面公主。被我使铁棒唬他一唬,他就跑进洞,叫出那牛王来。与老孙劖言劖语,嚷了一会,又与他交手,斗了有一个时辰。正打处,有人请他赴宴去了。是我跟他到那乱石山碧波潭底,变做一个螃蟹,探了消息,偷了他辟水金睛兽,假变牛王模样,复至翠云山芭蕉洞,骗了罗刹女,哄得他扇子。出门试演试演方法,把扇子弄长了,只是不会收小。正揣了走处,被他假变做你的嘴脸,返骗了去。故此耽搁两三个时辰也。"

八戒道:"这正是俗语云:'大海里翻了豆腐船,汤里来,水里去。'如今难得他扇子,如何保得师父过山,且回去,转路走他娘罢!"土地道:"大圣休焦恼,天蓬莫懈怠。但说转路,就是入了傍门,不成个修行之类,古语云:'行不由径',岂可转走?你那师父,在正路上坐着,眼巴巴只望你们成功哩!"行者发狠道:"正是,正是!呆子莫要胡谈!土地说得有理。我们正要与他:

　　赌输赢,弄手段,等我施为地煞变。自到西方无对头,牛王本是心猿变。今番正好会源流,断要相借宝扇。趁清凉,息火焰,打破顽空参佛面。行满超升极乐天,大家同赴龙华宴!"那八戒听言,便生努力。殷勤道:

　　"是,是,是!去,去,去!管取牛王会不会,木生在亥配为猪,牵转牛儿归土类。申下生金本是猴,无刑无克多和气。用芭蕉,为水意,焰火消除成既济。昼夜休离苦尽功,功完赶赴'盂兰会'。"

【8】他两个领着土地、阴兵一齐上前,使钉钯,抢铁棒,乒乒乓乓,把一座摩云洞的前门,打得粉碎。唬得那外护头目,战战兢兢,闯入里边报道:"大王!孙悟空率众打破前门也!"那牛王正与玉面公主争言其事,懊恨孙行者哩。听说打破前门,十分发怒,急披挂,拿了铁棍,从里边骂出来道:"泼猢狲!你是多大个人儿,敢这等上门撒泼,打破我门扇?"八戒近前乱骂道:"泼老剥皮!你是个甚样人物,敢量那个大小!不要走!看钯!"牛王喝道:"你这个囔糟食的夯货,不见怎的!快叫那猴儿上来!"行者

道："不知好歹的泼草！我昨日还与你论兄弟，今日就是仇人了！仔细吃吾一棒！"那牛王奋勇而迎。这场比前番更胜。三个英雄，厮混在一处。好杀：

　　钯钉铁棒逞神威，同帅阴兵战老牺。牺牲独展凶强性，遍满同天法力恢。使钯筑，着棍擂，铁棒英雄又出奇。三般兵器叮当响，隔架遮拦谁让谁？他道他为首，我道我夺魁。土兵为证难分解，木土相煎上下随。这两个说："你如何不借芭蕉扇！"那一个道："你焉敢欺心骗我妻！赶妻害儿仇未报，敲门打户又惊疑！"这个说："你仔细提防如意棒，擦着些儿就破皮，翻云覆雨随来往，吐雾喷风任发挥。恨苦这场都拚命，各怀恶念喜相持。丢架手，让高低，前迎后挡总无亏。兄弟二人齐努力，单身一棍施为。卯时战到辰时后，战罢牛魔束手回。

　　他三个含死忘生，斗有百十余合。八戒发起呆性，仗着行者神通！举钯乱筑。牛王遮架不住，败阵回头，就奔洞门，却被土地、阴兵拦住洞门，喝道："大力王，那里走！吾等在此！"那老牛不得进洞，急抽身，又见八戒、行者赶来，慌得卸了盔甲，丢了铁棍，摇身一变，变做一只天鹅，望空飞走。

　　行者看见，笑道："八戒！老牛去了。"那呆子漠然不知，土地亦不能晓，一个个东张西觑，只在积雷山前后乱找。行者指道："那空中飞的不是？"八戒道："那是一只天鹅。"行者道："正是老牛变的。"土地道："既如此，却怎生才好？"行者道："你两个打进此门，把群妖尽情剿除，拆了他的窝巢，绝了他的归路，等老孙与他赌变化去。"那八戒与土地，依言攻破洞门不题。

【9】　这大圣收了金箍棒，捻诀念咒，摇身一变，变做一个海东青，飕的一翅，钻在云眼里，倒飞下来，落在天鹅身上，抱住颈项嗛眼。那牛王也知是孙行者变化，急忙抖抖翅翎，变做一只黄鹰，返来嗛海东青。行者又变做一个乌凤，专一赶黄鹰。牛王识得，又变做一只白鹤，长唳一声，向南飞去。行者立定，抖抖翎毛，又变做一只丹凤，高鸣一声。那白鹤见凤是鸟王，诸禽不敢妄动，刷的一翅，淬下山崖，将身一变，变做一只香獐，乜乜些些，在崖前吃草。行者认得，也就落下翅来，变做一只饿虎，剪尾跑蹄，要

来赶獐做食。魔王慌了手脚，又变做一只金钱花斑的大豹，要伤饿虎。行者见了，迎着风，把头一幌，又变做一只金眼狻猊，声如霹雳，铁额铜头，复转身要食大豹。牛王着了急，又变做一个人熊，放开脚，就来擒那狻猊。行者打个滚，就变做一只赖象，鼻似长蛇，撒开鼻子，要去卷那人熊。

牛王嘻嘻的笑了一笑，现出原身，——只一只大白牛。头如峻岭，眼若闪光。两只角，似两座铁塔。牙排利刃。连头至尾，有千余丈长短；自蹄至背，有八百丈高下。——对行者高叫道："泼猢狲！你如今将奈我何？"行者也现出了原身，抽出金箍棒来，把腰一躬，喝声叫："长！"长得身高万丈，头如泰山，眼如日月，口似血池，牙似门扇，手执一条铁棒，着头就打。那牛王硬着头，使角来触。这一场，真个是撼岭摇山，惊天动地！有诗为证。诗曰：

　　道高一尺魔千丈，奇巧心猿用力降。

　　若得火山无烈焰，必须宝扇有清凉。

　　黄婆矢志扶元老，木母留情扶荡妖。

　　和睦五行归正果，炼魔涤垢上西天。

他两个大展神通，在半山中厮斗，惊得那过往虚空，一切神众与金头揭谛、六甲六丁、一十八位护教伽蓝都来围困魔王。那魔王公然不惧，你看他东一头，西一头，直挺挺，光耀耀的两只铁角，往来抵触；南一撞，北一撞，毛森森，筋暴暴的一条硬尾，左右敲摇。这行者当面迎，众多神明四面打，牛王急了，就地一滚，复本像，便投芭蕉洞去。行者也收了法象，同众多神随后追袭。那魔王闯入洞里，闭门不出。概众把一座翠云山围得水泄不通。

【10】 正都上门攻打，忽听得八戒与土地、阴兵嚷嚷而至。行者见了，问曰："那摩云洞事体如何？"八戒笑道："那老牛的娘子，被我一钯筑死，剥开衣看，原来是个玉面狸精。那伙群狱，俱是些驴、骡、犊、特、獾、狐、狢、獐、羊、虎、麋、鹿等类。已此尽皆剿戮，又将他府府房廊放火烧了。土地说他还有一处家小，住居此山，故又来扫荡也。"行者道："贤弟有功。可喜！可喜！老孙空与那老牛赌变化，未曾得胜。他变做无大牛的大白牛，我变了法天象地的身量。正和他抵触之间，幸蒙诸神下降。围困多时，他却复原身，走进洞去矣。"八戒道："那可是芭蕉洞么？"行者道：

"正是！正是！罗刹女正在此间。"八戒发狠道："既是这般，怎么不打进去，剿除那厮，问他要扇子，倒让他停留长智，两口儿叙情！"

好呆子，抖擞威风，举钯照门一筑，忽辣的一声，将那石崖连山筑倒了一边。慌得那女童忙报："爷爷！不知甚人把前门都打坏了！"牛王方跑进去，喘嘘嘘的，正告诉罗刹女与孙行者夺扇子赌斗之事，闻报，心中大怒。就口中吐出扇子，递与罗刹女。罗刹女接扇在手，满眼垂泪道："大王！把这扇子送与那猢狲，教他退兵去罢。"牛王道："夫人啊，物虽小而恨则深。你且坐着，等我再和他比并去来。"那魔重整披挂，又选两口宝剑，走出门来。正遇着八戒使钯筑门，老牛更不打话，挥剑劈脸便砍。八戒举钯迎着，向后倒退了几步，出门来，早有大圣抢棒当头。那牛魔即驾狂风，跳离洞府，又都在翠云山上相持。众多神四面围绕，土地兵左右攻击。这一场，又好杀哩：

> 云迷世界，雾罩乾坤。飒飒阴风砂石滚，巍巍怒气海波浑。重磨剑二口，复披甲全身。结冤深似海，怀恨越生嗔。你看齐天大圣因功绩，不讲当年古故人。八戒施威求扇子，众神护法捉牛君。牛王双手无停息，左遮右挡弄精神。只杀得那过鸟难飞皆敛翅，游鱼不跃尽潜鳞；鬼泣神嚎天地暗，龙愁虎怕日光昏！

那牛王拚命捐躯，斗经五十余合，抵敌不住，败了阵，往北就走。早有五台山秘魔岩神通广大泼法金刚阻住，喝道："牛魔，你往那里去！我等力释迦牟尼佛祖差来，布列天罗地网，至此擒拿汝也！"正说间，随后有大圣、八戒、众神赶来。那魔王慌转身向南走，又撞着峨眉山清凉洞法力无量胜至金刚挡住，喝道："吾奉佛旨在此，正要拿住你也！"牛王心慌脚软，急抽身往东便走；却遇着须弥山摩耳崖毗卢沙门大力金刚迎住道："你老牛何往！我蒙如来密令，教来捕获你也！"牛王又悚然而退，向西就走；又遇着昆仑山金霞岭不坏尊王永住金刚敌住，道："这厮又弄这精神！我领西天大雷音寺佛老亲言，在此把截，谁放你也！"那老牛心惊胆战，悔之不及。见那四面八方都是佛兵天将，真个似罗网高张，不能脱命。正在仓惶之际，又闻得行者帅众赶来，他就驾云头，望上便走。

【11】　却好有托塔李天王并哪吒太子，领鱼肚药叉、巨灵神将，幔住空中，叫道："慢来！慢来！吾奉玉帝旨意，特来此剿除你也！"牛王急了，依前摇身一变，还变做一只大白牛，使两只铁角去触天王。天王使刀来砍。随后孙行者又到。哪吒太子厉声高叫："大圣，衣甲在身，不能为礼。愚父子昨日见佛如来，发檄奏闻玉帝，言唐僧恭阻火焰山，孙大圣难伏牛魔王，玉帝传旨，特差我父王领众助力。"行者道："这厮神通不小！又变做这等身躯，却怎奈何？"太子笑道："大圣勿疑，你看我擒他。"

　　这太子即喝一声变："变！"变得三头六臂，飞身跳在牛王背上，使斩妖剑望颈项上一挥，不觉得把个牛头斩下。天王收刀，却才与行者上见。那牛王腔子里又钻出一个头来，口吐黑气，目放金光。被哪吒又砍一剑，头落处，又钻出一个头来。一连砍了十数剑，随即长出十数个头。哪吒取出火轮儿挂在那老牛的角上，便吹真火，焰焰烘烘，把牛王烧得张狂哮吼，摇头摆尾。才要变化脱身，又被托塔天王照妖镜照住本像，腾那不动，无计逃生，只叫"莫伤我命！情愿归顺佛家也！"哪吒道："既惜身命，快拿扇子出来！"牛王道："扇子在我山妻处收着哩。"

　　哪吒见说，将缚妖索子解下，跨在他那颈项上，一把拿住鼻头，将索穿在鼻孔里，用手牵着。孙行者却会聚了四大金刚、六丁六甲、护教伽蓝、托塔天王，巨灵神将并八戒、土地、阴兵，簇拥着白牛，回至芭蕉洞口。老牛叫道："夫人，将扇子出来，救我性命！"罗刹听叫，急卸了钗环，脱了色服，挽青丝如道姑，穿缟素似比丘，双手捧着那柄丈二长短的芭蕉扇子，走出门；又见有金刚众圣与天王父子，慌忙跪在地下，磕头礼拜道："望菩萨饶我夫妻之命，愿将此扇奉承孙叔叔成功去也！"行者近前接了扇，同大众共驾祥云，径回东路。

【12】　却说那三藏与沙僧、立一会，坐一会，盼望行者，许久不回，何等忧虑！忽见祥云满空，瑞光满地，飘飘飖飖，盖众神行将近，这长老害怕道："悟净！那壁厢是谁神兵来也？"沙僧认得道："师父啊，那是四大金刚、金头揭谛、六甲六丁、护教伽蓝与过往众神。牵牛的是哪吒三太子。拿镜的是托塔李天王。大师兄执

着芭蕉扇，二师兄并土地随后，其余的都是护卫神兵。”三藏听说，换了毗卢帽，穿了袈裟，与悟净拜迎众圣，称谢道：“我弟子有何德能，敢劳列位尊圣临凡也！”四大金刚道：“圣僧喜了，十分功行将完！吾等奉佛旨差来助汝，汝当竭力修持，勿得须臾怠惰。”三藏叩齿叩头，受身受命。

【13】 孙大圣执着扇子，行近山边，尽气力挥了一扇，那火焰山平平息焰，寂寂除光；行者喜喜欢欢，又扇一扇，只闻得习习潇潇，清风微动；第三扇，满天云漠漠，细雨落霏霏。有诗为证。诗曰：

火焰山遥八百程，火光大地有声名。
火煎五漏丹难熟，火燎三关道不清。
时借芭蕉施雨露，幸蒙天将助神功。
牵牛归佛休颠劣，水火相联性自平。

此时三藏解燥除烦，清心了意。四众皈依，谢了金刚，各转宝山。六丁六甲，升空保护。过往神祇四散。天王、太子，牵牛径归佛地回缴。止有本山土地，押着罗刹女，在旁伺候。

行者道：“那罗刹，你不走路，还立在此等甚？”罗刹跪道：“万望大圣垂慈，将扇子还了我罢。”八戒喝道：“泼贱人，不知高低！饶了你的性命，就彀了，还要讨甚么扇子，我们拿过山去，不会卖钱买点心吃，费了这许多精神力气，又肯与你！雨蒙蒙的，还不回去哩！”罗刹再拜道：“大圣原说扇息了火还我。今此一场，诚悔之晚矣。只因不倜傥，致令劳师动众。我等也修成人道，只是未归正果。见今真身现像归西，我再不敢妄作。愿赐本扇，从立自新，修身养命去也。”土地道：“大圣，趁此女深知息火之法，断绝火根，还他扇子，小神居此苟安，拯救这方生民，求些血食，诚为恩便。”行者道：“我当时问着乡人说：‘这山扇息火，只收得一年五谷，便又火发。’如何治得除根？”罗刹道：“要是断绝火根，只消连扇四十九扇，永远再不发了。”

行者闻言，执扇子，使尽筋力，望山头连扇四十九扇，那山上大雨淙淙。果然是宝贝：有火处下雨，无火处天晴。他师徒们立在这无火处，不遭雨湿。坐了一夜，次早才收拾马匹、行李，把扇子还了罗刹。又道：“老孙若不与你，恐人说我言而无信。你将扇子回山,再休生事。看你得了人身,饶你去罢!"那罗刹接了扇子,念个咒语,捏做个杏叶儿,噙在口里。拜谢了众圣,隐姓修行。后来也得了正果,经藏中万古流名。罗刹、土地,俱感激谢恩,随后相送。行者、八戒、沙僧,保着三藏遂此前进,真个是身体清凉,足下滋润。

Chapter 12
Zhu Bajie Helps to Defeat a Demon King;
Monkey's Third Attempt to Borrow the Fan

[1]   The story tells how the Bull Demon King caught up with the Great Sage Sun and saw him looking very cheerful as he went along with the plantain fan over his shoulder. "So the macaque has also tricked the art of using the fan out of her," the demon king thought. "If I ask him for it back to his face he's bound to refuse, and if he fans me with it and sends me sixty thousand miles away that would be just what he wants. Now I know that the Tang Priest is sitting waiting by the main road. When I was an evil spirit in the old days I used to know his second disciple the Pig Spirit. I think I'll turn myself into a double of the Pig Spirit and play a trick back on him. That macaque will no doubt be so pleased with himself that he won't really be on his guard." The splendid demon king could also do seventy-two transformations and his martial skills were on a par with those of the Great Sage: it was just that he was rather more clumsily built, was less quick and penetrating, and not so adaptable. First he hid the swords then he said the words of the spell, turned himself into the exact likeness of Pig, went down, and met Monkey face to face. "I'm here, brother," he called.

[2]   The Great Sage was indeed delighted. As the ancient saying goes, a cat that's won a fight is more pleased with himself than a tiger. Monkey was so confident of his powers that he did not bother to investigate why the new arrival was here, but seeing that he looked like Pig, called out, "Where are you going, brother?" The Bull Demon King made up an answer on the spot: "You'd been away for so long that the master wondered if the Bull Demon King's magic powers were too much for you and you couldn't get the treasure. So he sent me to meet you." "There was no need to worry," said Monkey. "I've already got it." "How did you manage that?" the Bull Demon King asked. "Old

318

Bull and I fought over a hundred rounds without either of us getting the upper hand till he broke off the fight and went to the bottom of the Green Wave Pool in Ragged Rock Mountain for a banquet with a whole lot of lesser dragons and dragons. I tailed him there, turned into a crab, stole the water-averting golden-eyed beast, made myself look like him, and went to the Plantain Cave to trick Raksasi. She as good as married me on the spot and I conned it out of her." "You had to go to a lot of trouble, brother," the Bull Demon King replied. "Can I hold the fan?" Not realizing that this Pig was an impostor, or even considering the possibility, the Great Sage Sun handed him the fan.

【3】 Now the Bull Demon King knew the secret of making the fan shrink or grow, and as soon as he had the fan in his hands he made a spell with them that nobody could see, shrunk it back to the size of an apricot leaf, and reverted to his true form. "Bloody macaque," he swore, "do you know who I am now?" As soon as he saw this Monkey regretted making so terrible a mistake. With a cry of anguish he stamped his feet and yelled, "Aagh! After all these years I've been hunting wild geese a gosling has pecked out my eye!" He was now leaping around in a thunderous fury, and he took a crack at the Bull Demon King's head with his iron cudgel. The demon king then fanned him with the fan, not realizing that the Great Sage had inadvertently swallowed the wind-fixing pill he had in his mouth when he turned himself into a tiny insect to go into Raksasi's stomach. This had made all his entrails, his skin and his bones so solid and firm that no matter how hard the Bull Demon King fanned he could not move him. This alarmed the Bull Demon King, who put the treasure in his mouth and fought back, swinging a sword in each hand. The two of them fought a splendid battle up in mid-air:

> *The Great Sage Equalling Heaven,*
> *The Bull Demon King of evil,*
> *All for the sake of a plantain-leaf fan.*
> *When they met each showed his powers;*
> *The careless Great Sage got the fan by a trick,*

319

But allowed the Bull King to take it back.
One mercilessly raised the golden cudgel,
The other wielded with skill his blue-tipped swords.
The mighty Great Sage belched out coloured mists
While the evil Bull King breathed brilliant lights.
Well matched in courage,
Both of them wicked,
They gnashed and ground their teeth in terrible wrath.
Heaven and earth were darkened by the dust they kicked up;
Gods and ghosts alike hid from the flying stones.
"How dare you try to turn a trick against me!"
"I'll get you for what my wife promised you!"
Coarse was their language and fierce were their tempers.
"For tricking my wife you deserve to die."
"When I sue you the sentence will surely be death."
The cunning Great Sage Equalling Heaven,
The murderous Strongarm Demon King:
Both of them only wanting to fight,
Neither of them willing to pause and discuss.
Equal the effort of swords and of cudgel;
Had either relaxed he'd have gone straight to Hell.

【4】 The story now tells not of those two locked in their struggle but of the Tang Priest sitting by the road and finding the heat unbearable. He was also very anxious and thirsty. "May I ask you," he said to the local deity, "what that Bull Demon King's powers are like?" "He has very great magic," the local god replied, "and his dharma powers are unlimited. He and the Great Sage Sun are well matched." "Wukong is a very good traveller," Sanzang replied. "He can normally go six or seven hundred miles and back in an instant. Why has he been away all day? I'm sure he must be fighting the Bull Demon King." With that he called for Pig and Friar Sand and asked, "Which of you will go to meet your elder brother? If he is up against an enemy you will have to help him in the fight, get the fan, and come back. I am very

impatient to cross these mountains and continue along our way."
"It's getting late," Pig replied, "and I'd like to go to meet him.
The only thing is that I don't know the way to Mount Thunder
Piled." "But I do," the local god said. "Tell the Curtain-lifting
General to keep your master company while you and I go there."
Sanzang was delighted. "I am most grateful to you for going to
such trouble," he said, "and I shall thank you again when you
have succeeded."

[5] Pig then summoned up his spirits, tightened the belt round
his black brocade tunic, and took his rake in his hands as he rose
up on his cloud with the local god and headed due east. As they
were going along they heard great shouts and were buffeted by
strong winds. Stopping his cloud for a good look he saw that it
was all caused by Monkey and the Bull Demon King fighting.
"Why don't you join in, Marshal Tian Peng?" the local deity
asked. "What are you waiting for?" At that the idiot brandished
his rake and said with a great shout, "Brother, I'm coming."
"Idiot," said Monkey bitterly, "you've ruined things for me."
"But the master told me to come to meet you," Pig protested.
"He asked the local god to guide me as I don't know the way.
That's why I'm a bit late. How can you say I've ruined things for
you?" "I'm not angry with you for being late," Monkey replied.
"It's this damned bull who's a thorough disgrace. I'd got the fan
off Raksasi, but he turned himself into your double and came to
meet me. I was so pleased to see you that I passed him the fan.
He turned back into himself and we've been fighting it out ever
since. That's why I said you'd ruined things for me."

This news put Pig into a flaming temper. Raising his rake he
shouted abuse to the Bull Demon King's face: "I'll get you, you
pox-ridden bag of blood! I'll get you for pretending to be me,
your own ancestor, to trick my brother and stir up trouble
between us." Watch as he starts lashing out wildly with the rake.
The Bull Demon King, who had been fighting Monkey all day,
was tiring, and he also realized that he would never be able to
withstand the onslaught of Pig's rake, so he fled in defeat. But
his way was blocked by a force of spirit soldiers led by the local

god of the Fiery Mountains. "Wait, Strongarm King," the local deity said. "All the gods and heavens are protecting Tang Sanzang on his journey west to fetch the scriptures. The Three Worlds all know about him, and the Ten Directions are supporting him. Please lend him your plantain fan to blow out the flames so that he can cross the mountains without danger or disaster. Otherwise Heaven will hold you criminally responsible and you're bound to be executed." "You haven't looked into the rights and wrongs of this at all," King Demon Bull replied. "That damned ape has done one evil thing after another: he's stolen my son, bullied my concubine, and defrauded my wife. I wish I could swallow him whole and turn him into shit to feed to the dogs. I'll never lend him my treasure."

[6]   Before the words were all out of his mouth Pig had caught up with him and was saying abusively, "I'll get you, you poxy bull. The fan or your life!" The Bull Demon King had to turn round to fight Pig off with his swords while the Great Sage Monkey wielded his cudgel to help him. It was a fine fight they had there:

> A boar turned spirit,
> A bull become monster,
> A monkey who had robbed Heaven and found the Way.
> Dharma-nature can always overcome what has been created;
> Earth must be used to combine with the prime cause.
> Pointed and sharp were the nine teeth of the rake;
> Flexible and keen were the two sword blades.
> The movements of the iron cudgel dominated the fray;
> The local god formed the cinnabar head.
> The three of them struggled to overcome,
> Each of them scheming to give play to his powers.
> Metal money is best at making the bull draw the plough;
> If the boar goes in the oven, wood is finished.
> Unless the heart is in it the Way cannot be completed;
> To keep the spirit controlled the monkey must be tied up.

Amid wild shouts and desperate pleas
The three types of weapon whistled through the air.
There was no kindness in the blows of rake and sword;
The gold-banded cudgel rose for good reason.
Their fight put out the stars and dimmed the moon;
The sky was filled with a cold, dark dreary fog.

The demon king fought hard and courageously for mastery, falling back all the while. When the dawn came after a whole night of battle there was still no victor, and in front of them now was the entrance to the Cloud-touching Cave on Mount Thunder Piled. The ear-splitting noise that the three of them, the local god and the spirit soldiers were making alarmed Princess Jade, who sent her serving girls to see who was causing the din. The little demons on the doors came in to report, "It's our master. He's fighting the man with a face like a thunder god, another monk with a long snout and big ears, and the local god of the Fiery Mountains and his men." The moment Princess Jade heard this she ordered the senior and junior officers of the guard to take their swords and spears and help their lord. "Good to see you," said the Bull Demon King with delight, "good to see you." All the demons rushed wildly into the attack. It was more than Pig could cope with and he fled in defeat, trailing his rake behind him. The Great Sage sprang aloft out of the multiple encirclement on a somersault cloud; the spirit soldiers broke and ran. Old Bull led his host of demons back to the cave in victory and the doors were shut tightly behind them.

[7] "He's tough, damn him," said Monkey. "He started fighting me at about four yesterday afternoon and we were nowhere near a result when you two came along to help last night. He fought for half a day and a whole night without showing any sign of tiring. And that bunch of little devils who came out just now were a rough lot too. Now he's shut the doors of his cave and won't come out. What are we to do?" "It was about ten yesterday morning when you left the master, brother," Pig said, "so why was it four in the afternoon when you started

323

fighting him? What were you doing for the six hours in between?" "I reached this mountain soon after I left you," Monkey replied, "and saw a woman. When I questioned her she turned out to be his favourite concubine Princess Jade. I gave her a bit of a fright with my cudgel, so she fled into the cave and sent her Bull Demon King out. He and I swapped a few insults then started fighting. We'd been at it for a couple of hours when someone came to invite him to a banquet. I tailed him to the bottom of the Green Wave Pool on Ragged Rock Mountain and turned into a crab to do a little spying. Then I stole his water-averting golden-eyed beast and changed myself into the Bull Demon King's double to go back to the Plantain Cave on Mount Turquoise Cloud, where I conned Raksasi into giving me the fan. I went outside to try the magic spell out on the fan and made it grow, but I didn't know how to make it shrink again. As I was walking along with it on my shoulder he turned himself into your spitting image and tricked it back off me again. That's how I wasted six hours."

"As the saying goes," Pig replied, "it's just like a boatful of beancurd sinking: it came out of the wet and it disappeared into the wet. Easy come, easy go. But how are we going to take our master across the mountains if we're having so hard a time getting the fan? We'll just have to go back and make a bloody detour." "Don't get impatient, Great Sage," the local god said, "and don't try to be lazy, Marshal Tian Peng. If you make a detour that will mean leaving the straight and narrow: you'll never cultivate your conduct that way. As the old saying goes, 'In walking never take a short cut.' You mustn't talk about detours. Your master is waiting by the main road, desperate for your success." "Yes, yes," said Monkey, his resolve stiffened, "don't talk nonsense, idiot. The local deity is right. As for that Bull Demon King, we'll have to

> Struggle for mastery,
> Use our powers,
> Until we can make the whole earth change.

Since coming to the west he has never met a rival:
The Bull King was originally the mind-ape transformed.
Only today do the sources flow:
We must hold out till we borrow the fan.
Put out the flames in the cool of the dawn,
Smash through obstinate emptiness to visit the Buddha.
When all is fulfilled we will rise to heavenly bliss,
And all go to the assembly under the Dragon-flower Tree."

These words braced Pig's spirits too, and eagerly he said,

"Yes, yes, yes!
Go, go, go!
Never mind what the Bull King's powers are,
Wood grows in the nor'nor'west and is matched with a pig;
The bull-calf will be led back to the earth.
Metal was born in west sou'west and was an ape,
Without any conflict or conquest and full of peace.
We must use the plantain leaf as if it were water
To put out the flames and bring harmony.
Hard work by night and day with never a rest
Will lead us to success and the Ullambana feast."

[8]   The two of them led the local deity and his spirit soldiers forward, then battered the doors of the Cloud-touching Cave to pieces with the rake and the cudgel. This so terrified the guard commanders that they rushed inside to report, "Your Majesty, Sun Wukong's brought his troops here and has smashed down our front doors." The Bull Demon King was just then telling Princess Jade what had happened and feeling thoroughly fed up with Monkey. The news of the front doors being smashed made him beside himself with fury, so he put his armour on immediately and went outside with his iron mace in his hands shouting abusively, "Damned macaque! You must think you're a very big shot indeed, coming here to play the hooligan and smash down my front door." "Old skinflint," retorted Pig, going forward, "who

do you think you are, trying to put other people in their place? Don't move! Take this!" "Idiot!" the Bull Demon King replied. "Chaff-guzzler! You're not worth bothering with. Tell that monkey to come here." "You don't know what's good for you, cud-chewer," called Monkey. "Yesterday you were still my sworn brother, but today we're enemies. Watch this carefully!" The Bull Demon King met their onslaught with spirit, and the ensuing fight was even finer than the one before. The three heroes were locked in a melee. What a battle!

> Rake and iron cudgel showing their might,
> Leading the spirit soldiers to attack the ancient beast.
> The beast displayed his terrible strength when fighting alone,
> Reviving his powers that rivalled those of Heaven.
> The rake hit hard,
> The mace struck,
> The iron cudgel showed its heroic powers.
> The three weapons rang against each other,
> Blocking and parrying, never giving way.
> One said he was the champion,
> Another claimed, "I am the best."
> The earth soldiers who were watching could hardly tell them apart.
> As wood and earth were locked in combat.
> "Why won't you lend us the plantain fan?"
> "You had the effrontery to mistreat my wife,
> To ruin my son and terrify my concubine.
> I haven't punished you for all of that yet,
> And now you harass us and beat down my doors."
> "Be on your guard against the as-you-will cudgel:
> A touch of it will tear your skin open."
> "Mind you avoid the teeth of my rake:
> One blow, and nine wounds all gush blood."
> The Bull Monster fearlessly gave play to his might,
> Wielding his mace with skill and with cunning.

Their movements turned the rain clouds upside-down,
As each of them snorted out his mists and winds.
This was indeed a battle to the death,
As they fought it out together with hatred in their hearts.
Taking new stances,
Offering openings high and low,
They attacked and they parried with never a mistake.
The two brother disciples were united in their efforts;
The solitary mace showed its might alone.
They battled from dawn till eight in the morning
Till the Bull Demon had to abandon the fight.

With death in their hearts and no thought of survival the three of them fought another hundred or so rounds till Pig took advantage of Monkey's miraculous powers to put all his brute strength into a rain of blows from his rake that were more than the Bull Demon King could withstand. He turned and fled defeated back to his cave, only to find the entrance blocked by the local god and his spirit troops. "Where do you think you're going, Strongarm King?" the local god shouted. "We're here." As he could not get into his cave the Bull Demon King fled, only to be pursued by Pig and Monkey. In his panic the Bull Demon King tore off his helmet and armour, threw away his mace, shook himself, turned into a swan and flew away.

Monkey looked around and said with a grin, "Pig, Old Bull's gone." The idiot had not the faintest idea of what had happened and neither had the local god as they looked all around and aimlessly searched Mount Thunder Piled. "Isn't that him flying up there?" said Monkey, pointing. "It's a swan," Pig replied. "Yes," said Monkey, "it's what Old Bull turned himself into." "So what are we going to do about it?" the local god asked. "You two charge in there, wipe all the demons out without quarter and tear down his den," Monkey replied. "That will cut off his retreat while I go and match transformations with him." We shall say no more of Pig and the local god smashing their way into the cave as they had been instructed.

327

[9] Putting away his gold-banded cudgel and saying the words of a spell while making the necessary hand movements, Monkey shook himself and turned into a vulture who soared up into the clouds with his wings beating noisily, then swooped down on the swan, seizing its neck and gouging at its eyes. Realizing that this was Sun Wukong transformed the Bull Demon King braced himself and turned into a golden eagle who gouged back at the vulture. Then Monkey turned into a black phoenix to chase the eagle, only to be recognized by the Bull King, who turned into a white crane and flew off south with a loud call. Monkey stopped, braced his feathers, and turned into a red phoenix, who called loudly too. At the sight of the phoenix, the king of all the birds whom no bird dared treat with disrespect, the white crane swooped down beside the precipice with a beat of his wings, shook himself, and turned into a river-deer grazing in a timid, stupid way at the foot of the cliff. Monkey spotted him, came swooping down too, and turned into a hungry tiger that came running after the river-deer, swishing his tail hungrily. The demon king had to move fast as he transformed himself into a huge leopard with spots like golden coins who turned to savage the hungry tiger. Seeing this, Monkey faced the wind, shook himself, and turned into a golden-eyed lion with a voice like thunder, a brazen head and an iron brow. He spun round to devour the leopard, at which the Bull Demon King immediately became a giant bear that ran after the lion. Monkey then rolled himself up and became an elephant with tusks shaped like bamboo shoots, and a trunk like a python that he stretched out to wrap round the bear.

The Bull Demon King chuckled and switched back into his own original shape as a great white bull with a craggy head and flashing eyes. Each of his horns was like an iron pagoda, and his teeth were rows of sharp swords. He was about ten thousand feet long from head to tail and stood eight thousand feet high at the shoulder. "What are you going to do to me now, damned macaque?" he shouted to Brother Monkey at the top of his voice; at which Monkey too reverted to his own form, pulled out his gold-banded cudgel, bowed forward and shouted "Grow!" He then grew to be a hundred thousand feet tall with a head like Mount Taishan, eyes like the sun and moon, a mouth like a pool of blood and teeth like doors. He raised his iron cudgel and struck at the Bull Demon King's head; and the Bull Demon King hardened his head and charged Monkey with his horns. This was a ridge-rocking, mountain-shaking, heaven-scaring, earth-frightening battle, and there is a poem to prove it that goes:

> The Way grows by one foot, the demon by ten thousand;
> The cunning mind-ape puts him down by force.
> If the Fiery Mountains' flames are to be put out,
> The precious fan must blow them cool.
> The yellow-wife is determined to protect the primal ancient;
> The mother of wood is set on wiping out the demons.
> When the Five Elements are harmonized they return to the true achievement;
> Evil and dirt are refined away as they travel to the west.

The two of them gave such a great display of their magic powers as they fought on the mountain that they alarmed all the deities, the Gold-headed Protector, the Six Jias, the Six Dings and the Eighteen Guardians of the Faith, who were passing through the air, came to surround the demon king. He was not in the least afraid as he butted to east and west with his straight, shining, iron horns, and lashed to north and south with his strong and hairy tail. Sun Wukong stood up to him head on while all the other gods surrounded him till in his despair the Bull Demon King rolled on the ground, turned back into his usual form, and headed for the Plantain Cave. Monkey too put away his magical form and joined in the chase with all the gods, but once in the cave the demon king shut the doors fast. The gods then threw a watertight encirclement around Mount Turquoise Cloud.

[10]   Just when they were all about to storm the doors they heard the shouts of Pig arriving with the local god and his spirit

329

soldiers. "How are things in the Cloud-touching Cave?" Monkey asked, greeting him. "I finished off Old Bull's woman with one blow from my rake," grinned Pig, "and when I stripped her I found she was a jade-faced fox spirit. Her demons were all donkeys, mules, bulls, badgers, foxes, racoon dogs, river-deer, goats, tigers, elk, deer and things like that. We killed the lot of them and burnt down all the buildings in the cave. The local god tells me he's got another woman who lives here, so we've come here to wipe her out too." "You've done well, brother," said Monkey. "Congratulations. I tried competing with Old Bull in transformations, but I couldn't beat him. He turned into a simply enormous white bull, and I made myself as big as heaven and earth. We were just battling it out when all the gods came down and surrounded him. After a long time he turned back into himself and went into the cave." "Is this Plantain Cave?" Pig asked. "Yes, yes," Monkey replied, "Raksasi's in here." "Then why don't we storm the place and wipe the lot of them out to get the fan?" said Pig, his blood still up. "Are we going to let the two of them live to be any older and wiser and love each other with tender passion?"

The splendid idiot then summoned up his strength to bring his rake down on the doors so hard that doors, rockface and all collapsed with a mighty rumble. The serving girls rushed inside to report, "Your Majesty, someone's smashed the doors in and we don't know who he is." The Bull Demon King himself had just run panting in and was still telling Raksasi about his fight with Monkey for the fan when he heard this report, which made him very angry indeed. At once he spat out the fan and gave it to Raksasi, who took it in her hands and said tearfully, "Your Majesty, give the macaque the fan if he'll call his troops off." "Wife," the Bull Demon King replied, "it may only be a little thing in itself, but I hate and loathe him. Wait here while I have it out with him again." Once more the demon put on his armour, chose another pair of swords, and went out to find Pig smashing the doors down with his rake. Without a word Old Bull raised his swords and cut at Pig's head. Pig parried with his rake and fell back a few paces till he was outside the doors, where Monkey swung his cudgel at the Bull Demon King's head. The Bull Monster then mounted a storm wind and sprang away from the cave to fight Monkey once more on Mount Turquoise Cloud. All the gods surrounded him, while the local god's soldiers joined in the fray from either side. It was a splendid fight:

> Mists obscured the world,
> Fog shrouded heaven and earth.
> A whistling evil wind sent sand and pebbles rolling;
> Towering wrath had the ocean's waves breaking.
> With a newly-sharpened pair of swords,
> And a body encased in armour once more,
> His hatred was deeper than the sea,
> And loathing made his fury greater than ever.
> In his pursuit of glory the Great Sage Equalling Heaven
> No longer regarded the other as an old friend.
> Pig was using his might to obtain the fan
> While the gods and protectors tried to capture the Bull.
> Neither of the Bull King's hands could rest
> As he blocked to left and right with heavenly skill.
> Birds folded their wings, unable to fly past;
> Fish stopped leaping and sank to the bottom.
> Ghosts wept, gods howled; the earth and sky were dark;
> Dragons and tigers were terrified and the sun was dimmed.

The Bull Demon King fought over fifty rounds for all he was worth till he abandoned the field and fled north, unable to hold out any longer. He was soon blocked by the Vajrapani Bofa from the Hidden Demon Cave on Mount Wutai whose magical powers were very extensive. "Bull Monster," he shouted, "Where are you going? I have been commanded by the Lord Sakyamuni Buddha to spread out heaven-and-earth nets and arrest you here." As he spoke the Great Sage, Pig and all the gods caught up. In his desperation the demon king turned and fled south only to find

331

his way blocked by the Vajrapani Shenzhi of the Cave of Cool Purity on Mount Emei, who shouted, "I am here on the Buddha's orders to take you." The Bull Demon King was now so terrified and exhausted that he turned and fled east, only to be blocked by the Vairocana monk, the Vajrapani Dali of Mo'er Cave on Mount Sumeru, who shouted, "Where are you going, Old Bull? I am on a secret mission from the Tathagata to catch you." The Bull Demon King withdrew in terror once more, this time to the west, where he came up against the imperishable king, the Vajrapani Yongzhu from the Golden Brightness Ridge on Mount Kunlun, shouting, "Where are you going, damn you? I have been personally instructed by the venerable Buddha of the Thunder Monastery in the Western Heaven to cut off your escape this way. Nobody will let you pass." The Old Bull was now trembling with fear, but it was too late for regrets. On all sides he was surrounded by the Buddha's troops and heavenly generals. It really was as if he were caught in a high net from which there was no escape. In his despair he heard Monkey coming after him at the head of his forces, so he sprang on his cloud and went up.

[11]　At just that moment Heavenly King Li the Pagoda-carrier was encamped in the sky with Prince Nezha, the Fish-bellied Yaksa and the Mighty Miracle God. "Not so fast," he shouted, "not so fast. I am here on the mandate of the Jade Emperor to exterminate you." In his extremity the Bull Demon King shook himself, turned back into the giant white bull, and tried to gore the Heavenly King with his iron horns, while the Heavenly King hacked at him with his sword. Soon Brother Monkey arrived. "Great Sage," Prince Nezha shouted at the top of his voice, "I can't greet you properly as I'm in armour. Yesterday my father and I went to see the Tathagata Buddha, who sent a note to the Jade Emperor. It said that the Tang Priest was held up by the Fiery Mountains and that you couldn't subdue the Bull Demon King, Great Sage. The Jade Emperor then ordered my father to bring his forces here to help." "But this damned creature's magical powers are tremendous," Monkey replied, "and he's turned himself into this. What are we going to do about him?"

332

"Have no doubts," replied Nezha with a smile. "Watch me catch him."

The prince then shouted, "Change!" gave himself three heads and six arms, and took a flying leap upon the Bull Demon King's back. With one swing of his demon-beheading sword he had the bull's head off before he even realized he had done it. The Heavenly King threw down his sword and went to meet Monkey. But another head grew out from the Bull Demon King's throat, its mouth breathing black vapours and its eyes flashing golden light. Nezha cut again, but as the head fell a new one appeared. Nezha's sword cut a dozen heads off and a dozen new heads immediately grew again. Nezha then hung his fire-wheel on the bull's horns, blew on the magic fire, and made it blaze so fiercely that the Bull Demon King bellowed in desperate pain, shaking his head and tail and trying for all he was worth to escape. Just when he was about to do another transformation and get away his true image was fixed in Heavenly King Li's demon-revealing mirror. Now he could make no more changes and he had no way of escape. He could only call out, "Spare my life! I wish to be converted to the Buddhist faith." "If you value your life, hand the fan over at once," said Nezha. "My wife is looking after it," the Bull Demon King replied.

Hearing this reply, Nezha undid his demon-binding rope and slipped it round his neck, then took him by the nose, ran the rope through it, and led him along by hand. Monkey meanwhile gathered together the four vajrapanis, the Six Dings, the Six Jias, the Guardians of the Faith, Heavenly King Li, the Mighty Miracle God, Pig, the local god and the spirit soldiers to crowd around the white bull and lead him back to the entrance to the Plantain Cave. "Wife," Old Bull called, "bring the fan out and save my life." As soon as she heard this Raksasi took off her jewellery and bright-coloured clothing, dressed her hair like a Taoist nun and put on a white silk habit like a Buddhist one. She came out through the doors carrying the twelve-foot fan with both hands, and at the sight of the vajrapanis, the gods, the Heavenly King and Nezha she fell to her knees in terror, kowtowing in

333

worship and saying, "I beg you Bodhisattvas to spare my husband and me. I present the fan to my brother-in-law Monkey for him to win his glory with." Monkey went forward, took the fan, and rode back east by auspicious cloud with the others.

【12】 Sanzang and Friar Sand had been waiting a very long time, sometimes sitting and sometimes standing, for Monkey to come back. They were extremely anxious by the time the sky was suddenly filled with auspicious clouds and the earth was lit up by blessed light as all the gods came whistling through the air towards them. "Wujing," said the venerable elder in terror, "whose divine soldiers are coming from over there?" "Master," said Friar Sand, who could recognize them, "it's the four vajrapanis, the Golden-headed Protector, the Six Jias, the Six Dings, the Guardians of the Faith and all the other passing gods. The one leading the bull is Prince Nezha, and there's Heavenly King Li the Pagoda-carrier holding a mirror. My eldest brother is carrying the plantain fan, and that's second brother and the local god behind him. The others are all escort troops." Hearing this, Sanzang put on his Vairocana mitre and his cassock then went with Friar Sand to welcome the gods and thank them with these words: "What merits do I, your disciple, have that I put all you holy ones to the trouble of coming down to earth?" To this the four vajrapanis replied, "Congratulations, holy monk. The great task has now been achieved. We were sent to help you on the Buddha's orders. You must now continue your self-cultivation and not slacken for a moment." Sanzang replied amid kowtows that he accepted their commands.

【13】 The Great Sage Sun took the fan close to the Fiery Mountains, waved it as hard as he could, and put the flames out. Their glare disappeared. He waved the fan again and the rustle of a cool breeze could be heard; and at the third wave the sky was overcast with cloud and a fine rain began to fall. There is a poem that bears witness to this:

For hundreds of miles the mountains of fire
Lit heaven and earth with notorious flames.

When fire roasts the five passions the elixir cannot be made.

When flame burns the three passes the Way is not pure.
To borrow the plantain fan and bring down rain,
Heavenly gods had to help with their spiritual power.
When the bull is led to the Buddha it must stop being evil;
When water and fire are allied the nature is calm.

Having been relieved of his cares Sanzang stopped worrying. All the hosts then reverently thanked the vajrapanis, who all returned to their mountains, and the Six Dings and Six Jias went back into the sky to give their protection. The deities who had been passing by all went on their way; and the Heavenly King and Nezha led the bull back to hand him over to the Buddha. This left only the local mountain god waiting there with Raksasi under his guard.

"Why aren't you on your way, Raksasi?" Monkey asked. "What are you standing there waiting for?" "I beg you in your mercy, Great Sage," she replied, "to give me back the fan." "You've got a cheek, damned bitch," roared Pig. "We've spared your life and that should be enough for you. What do you want the fan for? When we've crossed the mountains we'll be able to sell it for food. Do you think we're going to give it to you after all the trouble and effort we've been to? It's raining, so be off home with you." She bowed again and said, "But the Great Sage promised to give it back when he'd put the fire out. I'm very sorry about all that has happened. It was only because I was feeling so upset that I put you to all that trouble. We too have learned to live like human beings. The only thing is that we had not been converted to the pursuit of the true achievement. Now our true bodies have turned to the west, and we will not dare do anything wicked again. I beg you to return the fan so that I can reform and cultivate myself." "Great Sage," said the local deity, "let us make full use of this woman's knowledge of the art of extinguishing fire to put these fires out for good, and give her back her fan. Then I will be able to live here in peace, help the people who live here, and be given offerings of blood and food.

This would truly be a great kindness to me." "I heard the local people saying that when the fan puts the flames out in these mountains they can only gather one harvest before they start burning again," said Monkey. "How are we going to be able to put them out forever?" "All you have to do to put the flames out forever," said Raksasi, "is wave the fan forty-nine times. Then they'll never burn again."

Now that Brother Monkey knew this he took the fan and fanned the mountains with it forty-nine times as hard as he possibly could, whereupon heavy rain began to pour down. The fan really was a treasure: where there were flames it rained, and where there were not the sky was clear. By standing where there no flames master and disciples avoided getting wet. After spending the night sitting there they got the horse and luggage ready the next morning and returned the fan to Raksasi. "If I don't give you it back," Monkey said, "people might say I don't keep my word. Take the fan with you, go back to your mountain and don't make any more trouble. As you've achieved human form I'll spare your life." Taking the fan from him Raksasi said the words of the spell, pinched the thread so that it shrank back to the size of an apricot leaf and put it in her mouth. She then thanked them all and prepared to cultivate her conduct as a hermit. Later she too achieved the true reward and her name was made eternally famous through the scriptures. Raksasi and the local god expressed their deep gratitude to the four sages and escorted them along their way. As Monkey, Pig and Friar Sand escorted Sanzang along his way their bodies felt cool and the ground under their feet was pleasantly damp.

13. 朱紫国唐僧论前世
孙行者施为三折肱

【1】　善正万缘收，名誉传扬四部洲。智慧光明登彼岸，飕飕，霭霭云生天际头。　诸佛共相酬，永住瑶台万万秋。打破人间蝴蝶梦，休休，涤净尘氛不惹愁。

【2】　话表三藏师徒走上逍遥之道路，光阴迅速，又值炎天。正是：

> 海榴舒锦弹，荷叶绽青盘。
> 两路绿杨藏乳燕，行人避暑扇摇纨。

进前行处，忽见有一城池相近。三藏勒马叫："徒弟们，你看那是甚么去处？"行者道："师父原来不识字，亏你怎么领唐王旨意离朝也！"三藏道："我自幼为僧，千经万典皆通，怎么说我不识字？"行者道："既识字，怎么那城头上杏黄旗，明书三个大字，就不认得，却问是甚去处何也？"三藏喝道："这泼猢狲胡说！那旗被风吹得乱摆，纵有字也看不明白！"唐僧道："老孙偏怎看见？"八戒、沙僧道："师父，莫你弄巧捣鬼。这般遥望，城池尚不明白，如何说见是甚字号？"行者道："却不是朱紫国'三字？"三藏道："朱紫国必是西邦王位，却要倒换关文。"行者道："不消讲了。"

【3】　不多时，至城门下马，过桥，入进三层门里，真个好个皇州！但见：

> 门楼高耸，垛迭齐排。周围活水通流，南北高山相对。六街三市货资多，万户千家生意盛。果然是个帝王都会处，天府大京城。绝域梯航至，遐方玉帛盈。形胜连山远，宫垣接汉清。三关严锁钥，万古乐升平。

师徒们在那大街里上行时，但见人物轩昂，衣冠齐整，言语清朗，真不亚大唐世界。那两边做买做卖的，忽见猪八戒相貌丑陋，沙和尚面黑身长，孙行者脸毛额廓，丢了买卖，都来争看。三藏只叫:"不要撞祸!低着头走!"八戒遵依,把个扁子嘴揣在怀里;沙僧不敢仰视;惟行者东张西望,紧随唐僧左右。那些人有知事的,看着儿就回去了。有那游手好闲的并那顽童们,烘烘笑笑,都上前抛瓦丢砖,与八戒做戏。唐僧捏着一把汗,只教:"莫要生事!"那呆子不敢抬头。

不多时,转过隅头,忽见一座门墙,上有"会同馆"三字。唐僧道:"徒弟,我们进这衙门去也。"行者道:"进去怎的?"唐僧道:"会同馆乃天下通会通同之所,我们也好投宿。待我见驾,倒换了关文,再赶出城走路罢。"八戒闻言,掣出嘴来,把那些随看的人,唬倒了数十个。他上前道:"师父说的是。我们且到里边藏下,免得这伙鸟人吵嚷。"遂进馆去。那些人方渐渐而退。

【4】 却说那馆中有两个大使,乃是一正一副,都在厅上查点人夫,要往那里接官。忽见唐僧来到,个个心惊,齐道:"是甚么人?是甚么人?往那里去?"三藏合掌道:"贫僧乃东土大唐驾下,差往西天取经者。今到宝方,不敢私过,有关文欲倒验放行,权借高衙暂歇。"那两个馆使听言,屏退左右,一个个整冠束带,下厅迎上相见。即命打扫客房安歇,教办清素支应。三藏谢了。二官带领人夫,出厅而去。手下人假请老爷客房安歇,三藏便走。行者恨道:"这厮愈懑!怎么不让老孙在正厅?"三藏道:"他这里不服我大唐管属,又不与我国相连,况不时又有上司过客往来,所以不好留此相待。"行者道:"这等说,我偏要他相待了!"

正说处,有管事的送支应来,乃是一盘白米、一盘白面、两把青菜、四块豆腐、两个面筋、一盘干笋、一盘木耳。三藏教徒弟收了,谢了管事的。管事的说:"西房里有干净锅灶,柴火方便,请自去做饭。"三藏道:"我问你一声,国王可在殿上么?"管事的道:"我万岁爷爷久不上朝,今日乃黄道良辰,正与文武多官议出黄榜。你若要倒换关文,趁此急去,还赶上;到明日,就不能彀了,不知还有多少时间候哩。"三藏道:"悟空,你们在此安排斋饭,等我急急去验了关文回来,我们了走路。"八戒急取出袈裟关文。三藏整束了进朝,只是吩咐徒弟们,切不可出外去生事。

【5】 不一时,已到五凤楼前。说不尽那殿阁峥嵘,楼台壮丽。

直至端门外，烦奏事官转达天廷，欲倒验关文。那黄门官果至玉
阶前，启奏道："朝门外有东土大唐钦差一员僧，前往西天雷音寺
拜佛求经，欲倒换通关文牒，听宣。"国王闻言，喜道：寡人久病，
不曾愈甚；今上殿出榜招医，就有高僧来国！"即传旨宣至阶下。
三藏即礼拜俯伏。国王又宣上金殿赐坐，命光禄寺办斋。三藏
谢了恩，将关文献上。

国王看毕，十分欢喜道："法师，你那大唐，几朝君正？几辈
臣贤？至于唐王，因甚作疾回生，道你远涉山川求经？"这长老因
问，即欠身合掌道："贫僧那里：

三皇治世，五帝分伦。尧舜正位，禹汤安民，成周子众，各
立乾坤。倚强欺弱，分国称君。邦君十八，分野边尘。后
成十二，宇宙安淳。因无车马，却又相吞。七雄争胜，六国
归秦。天生鲁沛，各怀不仁。江山属汉，约法钦遵。汉归
司马，晋又纷纭。南北十二，宋齐梁陈。列祖相继，大隋绍
真。赏花无道，涂炭多民。我王李氏，国号唐君。高祖晏
驾，当今世民。河清海晏，大德宽仁。兹因长安城北，有个
怪水龙神，刻减甘雨，应该损身。夜间托梦，告王救迍。王
言准赦，早召贤臣。款留殿内，慢把棋轮。时当日午，那贤
臣梦斩龙身。"

国王闻言，忽作呻吟之声，问道："法师，那贤臣是那邦来者？"三
藏道："就是我王驾前丞相，姓魏名徵。他识天文，知地理，辨阴
阳，乃安邦立国之大宰辅也。因他梦斩了泾河龙王，那龙王告到
阴司，说我王许救又杀之，故我王遂得促病，渐觉身危。魏徵又
写书一封，与我王带至冥司，寄与丰都城判官崔珏。少时，唐王
身死，至三日复得回生。亏了魏徵，感崔判官改了文书，加王二
十年寿。今要做水陆大会，故遣贫僧远路迢遰，询求诸国，拜佛
祖，取《大乘经》三藏，超度孽苦升天也。"那国王又呻吟叹道："诚
乃是天朝大国，君正臣贤！似我寡人久病多时，并无一臣拯救。"
长老听说，偷睛观看，见那皇帝面黄肌瘦，形脱神衰。长老正欲
启问，有光禄寺官，奏请唐僧奉斋。王传旨，教"在披香殿，连宴
之膳摆下，与法师同享。"三藏谢了恩，与王同进膳进斋不题。

【6】　却说行者在会同馆中，着沙僧安排茶饭，并整治素菜。沙

僧道："茶饭易煮，蔬菜不好安排。"行者问道："如何？"沙僧道："油盐、酱、醋俱无也。"行者道："我这里有几文衬钱，教八戒上街买去。"那呆子躲懒道："我不敢去。嘴脸欠俊，恐惹下祸来，师父怪我。"行者道："公平交易，又不讹他，又不抢他，何祸之有！"八戒道："你才不曾看见獐智？在这门前扯出嘴来，把人唬倒了十来个；若到闹市丛中，也不知唬杀多少人是！"行者道："你只知闹市丛中，你可曾看见那市上卖的是甚么东西？"八戒道："师父只教我低着头，莫撞祸，实是不曾看见。"行者道："酒店、米铺、磨坊，并绫罗杂货不消说；着然又好茶房、面店，大烧饼、大馍馍，饭店又有好汤饭、好椒料、好蔬菜，与那异品的糖糕、蒸酥、点心、馔子、油食、蜜食，……无数好东西，我去买些儿请你如何？"那呆子闻说，口内流涎，喉咙里咽咽的咽唾，跳起来道："哥哥！这遭我扰你，待下次趱钱，我也请你回席。"行者暗笑道："沙僧，好生煮饭，等我们去买调和来。"沙僧也知是耍呆子，只得顺口应承道："你们去，须是多买些，吃饱了来。"那呆子捞个碗盏拿了，就跟行者出门。有两个在官人问道："长老那里去？"行者道："买调和。"那人道："这条街往西去，转过拐角鼓楼，那郑家杂货店，凭你买多少，油、盐、酱、醋、姜、椒、茶叶俱全。"

【7】　他二人携手相搀，径上街西而去。行者过了几处茶房，几家饭店，当买的不买，当吃的不吃。八戒叫道："师兄，这里将就买些用罢。"那行者原是耍他，那里肯买，道："贤弟，你好不经纪！再走走，拣大的买吃。"两个人说说话儿，又领了许多人跟随争看。不时，到了鼓楼边，只见那楼下无数人喧嚷，挤挤挨挨，填街塞路。八戒见了道："哥哥，我不去了。那里人嚷得紧，只怕是拿和尚的。又况是面生可疑之人，拿了去，怎的了？"行者道："胡谈！和尚又不犯法，拿我怎的？我们走过去，到郑家店买些调和来。"八戒道："罢！罢！罢！我不撞祸。这一挤到人丛里，把耳朵捽了两捽，唬得他跌跌爬爬，跌死几个，我倒偿命！"行者道："既然如此，你在这壁根下站定，等我过去买了回来，与你买素面烧饼吃罢。"那呆子将碗盏递与行者，把嘴拄着墙根，背着脸，死也不动。

这行者走至楼边，果然挤塞。直挨入人丛里听时，原来是那皇榜张挂楼下，故多人争看。行者挤到近处，闪开火眼金睛，仔细看时，那榜上却云：

> 朕西牛贺洲朱紫国王，自立业以来，四方平服，百姓清安。近因国事不祥，沉疴伏枕，淹延日久难痊。本国太医院，屡选良方，未能调治。今出此榜文，普招天下贤士。不拘北往东来，中华外国，若有精医药者，请登宝殿，疗理朕躬。稍得病愈，愿将社稷平分，决不虚示。为此出给张挂。须至榜者。"

览毕，满心欢喜道："古人云：'行动有三分财气。'早是不在馆中呆坐。即此不必买甚调和，且把取经事宁耐一日，等老孙做个医生耍耍。"好大圣，弯倒腰，丢了碗盏，拈一撮土，往上洒去，念声咒语，使个隐身法，轻轻的上前揭了榜。又朝着巽地上吸口仙气吹来，那阵旋风起处，他却回身，径到八戒站处，只见那呆子嘴拄着墙根，却是睡着了一般。行者更不惊他，将榜文折了，轻轻揣在他怀里，拽转步，先往会同馆去了不题。

【8】　却说那楼下众人，见风起时，各自蒙头闭眼。不觉风过时，没了皇榜，众皆悚惧。那榜原有十二个太监，十二个校尉，早朝领出。才挂上不三个时辰，被风吹去战兢兢左右追寻。忽见猪八戒怀中露出一个纸边儿来，众人近前道："你揭了榜来耶？"那呆子猛抬头，把嘴一捞，唬得那队几个校尉，踉踉跄跄，跌倒在地。他却转身要走，又被面前几个胆大的扯住道："你揭了招医的皇榜，还不进朝医治我万岁去，却待何往？"那呆子慌慌张张道："你儿子便揭了皇榜！你孙子便会医治！"校尉道："你怀中揣的是甚？"呆子却才低头看时，真个有一张字纸。展开一看，咬着牙骂道："那猢狲害杀我也！"恨一声，便要扯破，早被众人架住道："你是死了！此乃当今国王出的榜文，谁敢扯坏？你既揭在怀中，必有医国之手，快同我去！"八戒喝道："汝等不知。这榜不是我揭的，是我师兄孙悟空揭的。他暗暗揣在我怀中，就钟下我去了。若得此事明白，我与你寻他去。"众人道："说甚么乱话！'现钟不打打铸钟'？你现揭了榜文，教我们寻谁！不管你！扯了去见主子！"那伙人不分清白，将呆子推推扯扯。这呆子立定脚，就如生了根一般，十来个人也弄他不动。八戒道："汝等不知高低！再

扯一会，扯得我呆性子发了，你却休怪！"

不多时，闹动了街人，将他围绕。内有两个年老的太监道："你这相貌稀奇，声音不对，是那里来的，这般村强？"八戒道："我们是东土差往西天取经的。我师父乃唐王御弟法师，却才入朝，倒换关文去了。我与师兄来此买办调和，我见楼下人多，未曾敢去，是我师兄教我在此等候。他原来见有榜文，弄阵旋风揭了，暗揣我怀内，先去了。"那太监道："我头前见个白面胖和尚，径奔朝门而去，想就是你师父？"八戒道："正是，正是。"太监道："你师兄往那里去了？"八戒道："我们一行四众。师父去倒换关文，我三众并行囊、马匹俱歇在会同馆。师兄弄了我，他先回馆中去了。"太监道："校尉，不要扯他。我等同到馆中，便知端的。"八戒道："你这两个奶奶知事。"众校尉道："这和尚委不识货！怎么赶着公公叫起奶奶来耶？"八戒笑道："不差！你这反了阴阳的！他二位老妈妈儿，不叫他做婆婆、奶奶，倒叫他做公公！"众人道："莫弄嘴！快寻你师兄去。"

【9】那街上人吵吵闹闹，何止三五百，共扛到馆门首。八戒道："列位住了。我师兄却不比我任你们作戏。他却是个猛烈认真之士。汝等见了，须要行个大礼，叫他声'孙老爷'，他就架起了。不然啊，他就变了嘴脸，这事却弄不成也。"众太监、校尉俱道："你师兄果有手段，医好国王，他也该有一半江山，我等合该下拜。"

那些闲杂人都在门外喧哗。八戒领着一行太监、校尉，径入馆中。只听得行者与沙僧在客房里正说那揭榜之事变笑哩。八戒上前扯住，乱嚷道："你可成个人！哄我去买素面、烧饼、馍馍我吃，原来都是空头！又弄旋风，揭了甚么皇榜，暗暗的揣在我怀里，拿我装胖！这可成个弟兄！"行者笑道："你这呆子，想是错了路，走向别处去。我过鼓楼，买了调和，急回来寻你不见，我先来了。在那里揭甚皇榜？"八戒道："现有看榜的官员在此。"行者道："只见那几个太监、校尉朝上礼拜道：'孙老爷，今日我王有缘，天遣老爷下降，是必大展经纶手，微施三折肱。治得我王病愈，江山有份，社稷平分也。'"行者闻言，正了声色，接了八戒的榜文，对众道："你们想是看榜的官么？"太监叩头道："奴婢乃司礼监内臣。这几个是锦衣校尉。"行者道:"这招医榜,委是我揭的,故遣我师弟引见。即你主有病,常言道:'药不跟卖,病不讨医。'你去教那国王亲来请我。我有手到病除之功。"太监闻言,无不惊骇。校尉道:"口出大言,必有度量。我等着一半在此哑请,着一半入朝启奏。"

【10】　当分了四个太监,六个校尉,更不待宣召,径入朝,当阶奏道:"主公万千之喜!"那国王正与三藏膳毕清谈,忽闻此奏,问道:"喜自何来?"太监奏道:"奴婢等早领出招医榜皇榜,数楼下张挂,有东土大唐远来取经的一个圣僧孙长老揭去了,现在会同馆内,要王亲自去请他,他有手到病除之功。故此特来启奏。"国王闻言,满心欢喜,就问唐僧道:"法师有几位高徒?"三藏合掌答曰:"贫僧有三个顽徒。"国王问"那一位高徒善医?"三藏道:"实不瞒陛下道。我那顽徒,俱是山野庸才,只会挑包背马,转涧寻波,带领贫僧登山跋岭,过背岭,可以伏魔擒怪,捉虎降龙而已;更无一个能知药性者。"国王道:"法师何必太谦?朕当今日登殿,幸遇法师来朝,诚天缘也。高徒既不知医,他怎肯揭我榜文,教寡人亲迎?断然有医国之能也。"叫:"文武众卿,寡人身虚力怯,不敢乘辇;汝等可替寡人,俱到朝外,敢请孙长老,看朕之病。汝等见他,切不可轻慢,称他做'神僧孙长老',皆以君臣之礼相见。"

那众臣领旨,与看榜的太监,校尉径至会同馆,排班参拜。唬得那猪八戒躲在厢房,沙僧闪于壁下。那大圣,看他坐在当中,端然不动。八戒暗地里怨恶道:"这猢狲活活的折杀也!怎么这许多官员礼拜,更不还礼,也不站将起来!"不多时,礼拜毕,分班启奏道:"上告神僧孙长老。我等俱朱紫国王之臣,今奉王旨,敬以洁礼参请神僧,入朝看病。"行者方才立起身来,对众道:"你王如何不来?"众臣道:"我王身虚力怯,不敢乘辇,特令臣等代行君之礼,拜请神僧也。"行者道:"既然如此说,列位请前行,我当随至。"众臣各依品从,作队而走。行者整衣而起。八戒道:"哥哥,切莫攀出我们来。"行者道:"我不攀你,只要你两个与我收药。"沙僧道:"收甚么药?"行者道:"凡有人送药来与我,照数收下,待我回来取用。"二人领诺不题。

【11】 这行者即同多官，顷间便到。众臣先走，奏知那国王，高卷珠帘，闪龙睛凤目，开金口御言，便问："那一位是神僧孙长老？"行者进前一步，厉声道："老孙便是。"那国王听得声音凶狠，又见相貌刁钻，唬得战兢兢，跌在龙床之上。慌得那女官内宫，急扶入宫中。道："唬杀寡人也！"众官都嗔怨行者道："这和尚怎么这等粗鲁村疏！怎敢就擅揭榜！"

行者闻言，笑道："列位错怪了我也。若像这等慢人，你国王之病，就是一千年也不得好。"众臣道："人生能有几多阳寿？就一千年也还不好？"行者道："他如今是个病君，死了是个病鬼，再转世也还是个病人，却不是一千年也还不好？"众臣怒道："你这和尚，甚不知礼！怎么敢这等满口胡柴！"行者笑道："不是胡柴。你都听我道来：

医门理法至微玄，大要心中有转旋。

望闻问切四般事，缺一之时不备全：

第一望他神气色，润枯肥瘦起和眠；

第二闻声清与浊，听他真语及狂言；

三问病原经几日，如何饮食怎生便；

四才切脉明经络，浮沉表里是何般。

我不望闻并问切，今生莫想得安然。"

那两班文武丛中，有太医院官，一闻此言，对众称扬道："这和尚也说得有理。就是神仙看病，也须望、闻、问、切，谨合着神圣功巧也。"众官依此言，着近侍传奏道："长老要用望、闻、问、切之理，方可认病用药。"那国王睡在龙床上，声声唤道："叫他去罢！寡人见不得生人面了！"近侍的出宫来道："那和尚，我王旨意，教你去罢，见不得生人面哩。"行者道："若见不得生人面啊，我会'悬丝诊脉'。"众官暗喜道："悬丝诊脉，我等耳闻，不曾眼见。再奏去来。"那近侍的又入宫奏道："主公，孙长老不见主公之面，他悬丝诊脉。"国王心中暗想道："寡人病了三年，未曾试此，宣他进来。"近侍的即忙传出道："主公已许他悬丝诊脉，快宣孙长老进宫诊视。"

【12】 行者却就上了宝殿。唐僧迎着骂道："你这泼猴，害了我也！"行者笑道："好师父，我倒与你壮观，你返说我害你？"三藏喝

道："你跟我这几年，那曾见你医好谁来！你连药性也不知，医书也未读，怎么大胆撞这个大祸！"行者笑道："师父，你原来不晓得。我有几个草头方儿，能治大病，管情医徒他好便是。就是医杀了，也只问得个庸医杀人罪名，也不该死，你怕怎的！不打紧，不打紧，你且坐下看我的脉理如何。"长老又道："你那曾见《素问》、《难经》、《本草》、《脉诀》，是甚般章句，怎生注解，就这等胡说散道，会甚么悬丝诊脉！"行者笑道："我有金线在身，你不曾见哩。"即伸手下去，尾上拔了三根毫毛，捻一把，叫声"变！"即变做三条丝线，每条各长二丈四尺，按二十四气，托于手内，对唐僧道："这不是我的金线？"近侍宦官在旁道："长老且休讲口，请入宫中诊视去来。"行者别了唐僧，随着近侍入宫看病。正是那：心有秘方能治国，内藏妙诀注长生。毕竟这去不知看出甚么病来，用甚么药品。欲知端的，且听下回分解。

Chapter 13
In the Land of Purpuria the Tang Priest
Discusses History;
Sun the Pilgrim in His Charity Offers to
Be a Doctor

[1] *When good is right all causes disappear;*
Its fame is spread through all four continents.
In the light of wisdom they climb the other shore;
Soughing dark clouds are blown from the edge of the sky.
All the Buddhas give them help,
Sitting for ever on their thrones of jade.
Smash the illusions of the human world,
Cease!
Cleanse the dirt; provoke no misery.

[2]   The story tells how Sanzang and his disciples pressed far
ahead along the road. Time passes quickly and the weather was
scorching again. Indeed,

> *The begonias spread their globes of brocade;*
> *Lotus leaves split their own green dishes.*
> *Fledgling swallows hide in the roadside willows;*
> *Travellers wave their silken fans for relief from the heat.*

As they carried on their way a walled and moated city
appeared before them. Reining in his horse, Sanzang said,
"Disciples, can you see where this is?" "You can't read,
Master," Monkey exclaimed. "How ever did you get the Tang
Emperor to send you on this mission?" "I have been a monk since
I was a boy and read classics and scriptures by the thousand,"
Sanzang replied. "How could you say I can't read?" "Well,"
Monkey replied, "if you can, why ask where we are instead of
reading the big clear writing on the apricot-yellow flag over the

city wall?" "Wretched ape," Sanzang shouted, "you're talking nonsense. The flag is flapping much too hard in the wind for anyone to read what, if anything, is on it." "Then how could I read it?" Monkey asked. "Don't rise to his bait, Master," Pig and Friar Sand said. "From this distance we can't even see the walls and moat clearly, never mind words in a banner." "But doesn't it say Purpuria?" Monkey asked. "Purpuria must be a western kingdom," Sanzang said. "We shall have to present our passport." "Goes without saying," Monkey observed.

[3] They were soon outside the city gates, where the master dismounted, crossed the bridge, and went in through the triple gates. It was indeed a splendid metropolis. This is what could be seen.

> Lofty gate-towers,
> Regular battlements,
> Living waters flowing around,
> Mountains facing to north and south.
> Many are the goods in the streets and markets,
> And all the citizens do thriving business.
> This is a city fit for a monarch,
> A capital endowed by heaven.
> To this distant realm come travellers by land and water;
> Jade and silk abound in this remoteness.
> It is more beautiful than the distant ranges;
> The palace rises to the purity of space.
> Closely barred are the passes leading here,
> When peace and prosperity have lasted for ever.

As master and disciples walked along the highways and through the markets they saw that the people were tall, neatly dressed and well spoken. Indeed, they were not inferior to those of the Great Tang. When the traders who stood on either side of the road saw how ugly Pig was, how tall and dark-featured Friar Sand was, and how hairy and wide-browed Monkey was they all dropped their business and came over to see them. "Don't provoke trouble," Sanzang called to them. "Hold your heads down." Pig obediently tucked his snout into his chest and Friar Sand did not dare look up. Monkey, however, stared all around him as he kept close to the Tang Priest. The more sensible people went away again after taking a look, but the idlers, the curious and the naughty children among the spectators jeered, threw bricks and tiles at the strangers, and mocked Pig. "Whatever you do, don't get into a row," Sanzang said again in great anxiety. The idiot kept his head down.

Before long they turned a corner and saw a gate in a wall over which was written HOSTEL OF MEETING in large letters. "We are going into this government offence," Sanzang said. "Why?" Monkey asked. "The Hostel of Meeting is a place where people from all over the world are received, so we can go and disturb them," said Sanzang. "Let's rest there. When I have seen the king and presented our passport we can leave the city and be on our way again." When Pig heard this he brought his snout out, so terrifying the people following behind that dozens of them collapsed. "The master's right," said Pig, stepping forward. "Let's shelter inside there and get away from these damned mockers." They went inside, after which the people began to disperse.

[4] There were two commissioners in the hostel, a senior one and his assistant, and they were in the hall checking over their personnel before going to receive an official when, to their great consternation, the Tang Priest suddenly appeared. "Who are you?" they asked together. "Who are you? Where are you going?" "I have been sent by His Majesty the Tang Emperor to fetch the scriptures from the Western Heaven," the Tang Priest replied, putting his hands together in front of his chest. "Having reached your illustrious country I did not dare to try to sneak through. I would like to submit my passport for inspection so that we may be allowed to continue our way. Meanwhile we would like to rest in your splendid hostel."

When the two commissioners heard this they dismissed their subordinates, put on their full official dress and went down from the main hall to greet the visitors. They instructed that the guest rooms be tidied up for them to sleep in and ordered vegetarian provisions for them. Sanzang thanked them, and the two officials led their staff out of the hall. Some of their attendants invited the visitors to sleep in the guest rooms. Sanzang went with them, but Monkey complained bitterly, "Damned cheek. Why won't they let me stay in the main hall?" "The people here don't come under the jurisdiction of our Great Tang and they have no connections with our country either. Besides, their superiors often come to stay. It is difficult for them to entertain us." "In that case," Monkey replied, "I insist on them entertaining us properly."

As they were talking the manager brought their provisions: a dish each of white rice and wheat flour, two cabbages, four pieces of beancurd, two pieces of wheat gluten, a dish of dried bamboo shoots and a dish of "tree-ear" fungus. Sanzang told his disciples to receive the provisions and thanked the manager. "There's a clean cooking-stove in the western room," the manager said, "and it's easy to light the firewood in it. Would you please cook your own food?"

"May I ask you if the king is in the palace?" Sanzang asked. "His Majesty has not attended court for a long time," the manager replied. "But today is an auspicious one, and he is discussing the issue of a notice with his civil and military officials. You'd better hurry if you want to get there in time to submit your passport to him. Tomorrow will be too late to do it, and goodness knows how long you'll have to wait." "Wukong," said Sanzang, "you three prepare the meal while I hurry there to have our passport inspected. After we have eaten we can be on our way." Pig quickly unpacked the cassock and passport for Sanzang, who dressed himself and set out for the palace, instructing his disciples not to leave the hostel or make trouble.

【5】 Before long the Tang Priest was outside the Tower of Five Phoenixes at the outer palace gate. The towering majesty of the halls and the splendour of the tall buildings and terraces beggared description. When he reached the main southern gate he requested the reporting officer to announce to the court his wish to have his passport inspected. The eunuch officer at the gate went to the steps of the throne, where he submitted the following memorial: "There is a monk at the palace gate sent by the Great Tang in the east to worship the Buddha and fetch the scriptures at the Thunder Monastery in the Western Heaven. He wishes to submit his passport for approval. I await Your Majesty's command." When the king heard this he replied happily, "For a long time we have been too ill to sit on our throne. Today we are in the throne room to issue a notice sending for doctors, and now a distinguished monk has arrived in our country." He ordered that the monk be summoned to the steps of the throne. Sanzang abased himself in reverence. The king then summoned him into the throne room, invited him to sit down, and ordered the department of foreign relations to arrange a vegetarian meal. Sanzang thanked the king for his kindness and presented his passport.

When he had read it through the king said with great delight, "Master of the Law, how many dynasties have ruled in your land of Great Tang? How many generations of wise ministers have there been? After what illness did the Tang emperor come back to life, so that he sent you on this long and difficult journey to fetch the scriptures?" On being asked all these questions the venerable elder bowed, put his hands together and said, "In my country,

> *The Three Emperors ruled,*
> *The Five Rulers established morality.*
> *Yao and Shun took the throne,*
> *Yu and Tang gave the people peace.*
> *Many were the offspring of Chengzhou*
> *Who each established their own states,*
> *Bullying the weak with their own strength,*
> *Dividing the realm and proclaiming themselves rulers.*
> *Eighteen such lords of local states*
> *Divided the territory up to the borders.*
> *Later they became a dozen,*

Bringing peace to the cosmic order.
But those who had no chariots of war
Were swallowed up by others.
When the seven great states contended
Six of them had to surrender to Qin.
Heaven gave birth to Liu Bang and Xiang Yu,
Each of whom cherished wicked ideas.
The empire then belonged to Han
According to the stipulations agreed between the two.
Power passed from Han to the Sima clan,
Till Jin in its turn fell into chaos.
Twelve states ruled in north and south,
Among them Song, Qi, Liang and Chen.
Emperors ruled in succession to each other
Till the Great Sui restored the true unity.
Then it indulged in evil and wickedness.
Inflicting misery on the common people.
Our present rulers, the House of Li,
Have given the name of Tang to the state.
Since the High Ancestor passed on the throne
The reigning monarch has been Li Shimin.
The rivers have run clear and the seas been calm
Thanks to his great virtue and his benevolence.
North of the city of Chang'an
Lived a wicked river dragon
Who gave the timely rain in short measure,
For which he deserved to pay with his death.
One night he came in a dream to the emperor,
Asking the monarch to spare his life.
The emperor promised to grant a pardon
And sent for his wise minister early next day.
He kept him there inside the palace,
Filling his time with a long game of chess.
But at high noon the minister
Slept, and in a dream cut off the dragon's head."

351

On hearing this the king groaned and asked, "Master of the Law, which country did that wise minister come from?" "He was our emperor's prime minister Wei Zheng, astrologer, geographer, master of the *Yin* and *Yang*, and one of the great founders and stabilizers of our state," Sanzang explained. "Because he beheaded the Dragon King of the Jing River in his dream, the dragon brought a case in the Underworld against our emperor for having him decapitated after granting a pardon. The emperor became very ill and his condition was critical. Wei Zheng wrote him a letter to take to the Underworld and give to Cui Jue, the judge of Fengdu. Soon after that the emperor died, only to come back to life on the third day. It was thanks to Wei Zheng that Judge Cui was persuaded to alter a document and give His Majesty an extra twenty years of life. He held a great Land and Water Mass and despatched me on this long journey to visit many lands, worship the Buddha and fetch the Three Stores of Mahayana scriptures that will raise all the sufferers from evil up to Heaven."

At this the king groaned and sighed again. "Yours is indeed a heavenly dynasty and a great nation," he said, "with a just ruler and wise ministers. We have long been ill, but not one minister do we have who will save us." On hearing this the venerable elder stole a glance at the king and saw that his face was sallow and emaciated; his appearance was going to pieces and his spirits were very low. The venerable elder was going to ask him some questions when an official of the department of foreign relations came to invite the Tang Priest to eat. The king ordered that his food should be set out with Sanzang's in the Hall of Fragrance so that he could eat with the Master of the Law. Thanking the king for his kindness Sanzang took his meal with him.

【6】 Meanwhile, back in the Hostel of Meeting, Brother Monkey told Friar Sand to prepare the tea, the grain and the vegetarian dishes. "There's no problem about the tea and the rice," Friar Sand said, "but the vegetable dishes will be difficult." "Why?" Monkey asked. "There's no oil, salt, soya sauce or vinegar," Friar Sand replied. "I've got a few coins here," Monkey said, "so we can send Pig out to buy them." "I wouldn't dare," said the idiot, who was feeling too lazy to go. "My ugly mug could cause trouble, and then the master would blame me." "If you buy the stuff at a fair price and don't try to get it by asking for alms or theft there couldn't possibly be any trouble," said Brother Monkey. "Didn't you see the commotion just now?" asked Pig. "I only showed my snout outside the gate and about a dozen of them collapsed with fright. Goodness only knows how many I'd scare to death in a busy shopping street." "Well," said Monkey, "as you know so much about the busy shopping streets did you notice what was being sold in them?" "No," said Pig. "The master told me to keep my head down and cause no trouble. Honest, I didn't see anything."

"I won't need to tell you about the bars, grain merchants, mills, silk shops and grocers," said Monkey. "But there are marvellous teahouses and noodle shops selling big sesame buns and steamed bread. You can buy terrific soup, rice, spices and vegetables in the restaurants. Then there are all the exotic cakes, yoghurts, snacks, rolls, fries, and honey sweets. Any number of goodies. Shall I go out and buy you some?"

This description had the idiot drooling; the saliva gurgled in his throat. "Brother," he said, jumping to his feet, "I'll let you pay this time. Next time I'm in the money I'll treat you." "Friar Sand," said Monkey, hiding his amusement, "cook the rice while I go out to buy some other ingredients." Realizing that Monkey was only fooling the idiot, Friar Sand agreed. "Off you go," he said. "Buy plenty and have a good feed." Grabbing a bowl and a dish the idiot went out with Monkey.

"Where are you reverend gentlemen going?" two officials asked him. "To buy some groceries," Monkey replied. "Go west along this street, turn at the drum tower, and you'll be at Zheng's grocery," they said. "You can buy as much oil, salt, soya sauce, vinegar, ginger, pepper and tea as you like there: they've got them all."

【7】 The two of them headed west along the road hand in hand. Monkey went past several tea-houses and restaurants but did not buy any of the things on sale or eat any of the food. "Brother," called Pig, "why don't we make do with what we can buy here?" this was the last thing that Monkey, who had only been fooling him, intended to do. "My dear brother," he said, "you don't know how to get a good bargain. If we go a little further you can choose bigger one." As the two of them were talking a lot of people followed jostling behind them. Before long they reached the drum tower, where a huge and noisy crowd was pushing and shoving and filling the whole road. "I'm not going any further, brother," said Pig when he saw this. "From the way they're shouting they sound as though they're out to catch monks. And we're suspicious-looking strangers. What'll we do if they arrest us?" "Stop talking such nonsense," said Monkey. "We monks haven't broken the law, so monk-catchers would have no reason to arrest us. Let's carry on and buy the ingredients we need at Zheng's." "No," said Pig, "never. I'm not going to ask for trouble. If I try to squeeze through that crowd and my ears get pulled out to their full length they'll collapse with fright. Several of them might get trampled to death, and it would cost me my life." "Very well then," said Monkey. "You stand at the foot of this wall while I go and buy the things. I'll bring you back some wheaten cakes." The idiot handed the bowl and dish to Monkey then stood with his back to the crowd and his snout against the foot of the wall. He would not have moved for anything in the world.

When Monkey reached the drum tower he found that the crowds really were very dense. As he squeezed his way through them he heard people saying that a royal proclamation had been posted at the tower: this was what all the people were struggling to see. Monkey pushed forward till he was close to it, then opened wide his fiery eyes with golden pupils to read it carefully. This is what was written:

> We, the King of Purpuria in the Western Continent of Cattle-gift, from the beginning of our reign gave peace to the four quarters and tranquillity to the people. Recently the

state's misfortunes have confined us to our bed with a chronic
illness that has continued for a very long time. Recovery has
proved impossible, and the many excellent prescriptions of
our country's Royal College of Medicine have not yet effected
a cure. We hereby issue an invitation to all experts in
medicine and pharmacy among the wise men of the world,
whether from the north or the east, from China or from
foreign countries, to ascend to the throne hall and heal our
sickness. In the event of a recovery we will give half our
kingdom. This is no empty promise. All those who can offer
cures should come to this notice.

When Monkey had read this he exclaimed with delight, "As
they used to say in the old days, ' Make a move and your
fortune's one third made.' I was wrong to stay put in the hostel.
There's no need to buy groceries, and fetching the scriptures can
wait for a day while I go and have a bit of fun as a doctor." The
splendid Great Sage bent low, got rid of the bowl and dish, took
a pinch of dust, threw it into the air, said the words of a spell and
made himself invisible. He then went up to the notice, quietly
took it down, and blew towards the southeast with a magic
breath.

Immediately a whirlwind arose that scattered all the people
there. Monkey then went straight back to where Pig was
standing, his nose propped against the foot of the wall as if he
were fast asleep. Brother Monkey folded the notice up, slipped it
inside the lapel of Pig's tunic without disturbing him, turned and
went back to the hostel.

[8] As soon as the whirlwind started blowing all the people in
the crowd at the foot of the drum tower covered their heads and
shut their eyes, never imagining that when the wind fell the royal
proclamation would have disappeared. They were horror-struck.
That morning twelve palace eunuchs and twelve guards officers
had come out to post it, and now it had been blown away after
less than six hours. In fear and trembling the people searched all
around for it until a piece of paper was spotted sticking out of

Pig's lapel. "So you took the proclamation down, did you?" they asked, going up to him.

Looking up with a start the idiot thrust his nose up at them, making the guards officers stagger about and collapse with terror. He turned to flee, only to be grabbed by several bold spirits who blocked his way. "You've taken down the royal proclamation inviting doctors, so you're coming to the palace to cure His Majesty," they said. "Where else d'you think you're going?" "I'm your son if I tore the poster down," said Pig in panic. "I'd be your grandson if I could cure disease." "What's that sticking out of your tunic?" one of the officers asked.

Only then did the idiot look down and see that there really was a piece of paper there. Opening it he ground his teeth and swore, "That macaque is trying to get me killed!" He gave an angry roar and was just about to tear it up when they all stopped him. "You're a dead man," they said. "That's a proclamation His Majesty issued today. How dare you tear it up? As you've put it in your tunic you're no doubt a brilliant doctor. Come with us at once!" "You don't understand," shouted Pig. "It wasn't me that took it down. It was my fellow disciple Sun Wukong. He sneaked it into my tunic then abandoned me. We'll all have to go and find him to get to the bottom of this." "Nonsense," they said. "We've got a bell here—we're not going off to play one that's still being cast. You can say what you like. Drag him off to see His Majesty." Not bothering to get to the truth of the matter they pushed and pulled the idiot, who stood his ground as firmly as if he had taken root there. Over ten of them tried to move him without any success. "You've got no respect," said Pig. "If you go on pulling at me and make me lose my temper I'll go berserk, and don't blame me then."

It had not taken long for this commotion to stir up the whole neighbourhood, and Pig was now surrounded. Two elderly palace eunuchs in the crowd said, "You look very odd and you sound wrong too. Where are you from, you ruffian?" "We're pilgrims sent from the east to fetch the scriptures from the Western Heaven," Pig replied. "My master is the younger brother of the

Tang emperor and a Master of the Law. He's just gone to the palace to hand his passport over for inspection. I came here with my brother disciple to buy some groceries, but there were so many people by the tower that I was scared to go any further. He told me to wait here. When he saw the proclamation he made a whirlwind, took it down, sneaked it into my tunic and went away." "We did see a monk with a plump white face going in through the palace gates," one of the eunuchs said. "Perhaps that was your master." "Yes, yes," said Pig. "Where did your fellow disciple go?" the eunuch asked. "There are four of us altogether," said Pig. "When the master went to present his passport the other three of us stayed with our luggage and our horse in the Hostel of Meeting. My brother's played a trick on me and gone back there ahead of me." "Let go of him, officers," the eunuch said. "We'll all go to the hostel together and find out what's really happening."

"You two ladies are very sensible," said Pig. "Monk, you don't know about anything," said the officers. "How can you address gentlemen as ladies?" "You're shameless," laughed Pig. "You've made them change sex. Fancy calling these two old females gentlemen instead of women or ladies!" "That's enough of your insolence," they all said. "Find your fellow disciple at once."

[9]   The noisy crowd in the street, which was not to be numbered in mere hundreds, carried him to the hostel gates. "Don't come any further, gentlemen," Pig said. "My brother won't let you make a fool of him the way I do. He's a ferocious and serious character. When you meet him you'll have to bow deeply to him and call him 'Lord Sun', then he'll look after you. If you don't he'll turn nasty and this business will fail." To this the eunuchs and officers replied, "If your brother really has the power to cure our king he'll be given half the country and we will all bow to him."

The idlers were still making a commotion outside the hostel gates as Pig led the eunuchs and officers straight inside, where Monkey could be heard laughing with pleasure as he told Friar

357

Sand about how he had taken the proclamation down. Pig went up to him, grabbed him and yelled, "Why won't you act like a man? You said you'd buy me noodles, buns, and steamed bread to lure me out, but it was only an empty promise. Then you made a whirlwind, took down the royal proclamation, and sneakily put it in my tunic. You made a real idiot of me. What kind of brother are you?" "Idiot," laughed Monkey, "you must have got lost and gone the wrong way. I couldn't find you when I rushed back from buying the groceries the other side of the drum tower, so I came back ahead. Where did I tear any royal proclamations down?" "The officials who were guarding it are here," said Pig.

Before he had finished speaking the eunuchs and officers came up, bowed low and said, "Lord Sun, His Majesty is very fortunate today as Heaven has sent you down to us. We are sure that you will display your great skill and give him the benefit of your outstanding mèdical knowledge. If you cure our king you will receive half the country and half the state." On hearing this Monkey composed his face, took the proclamation from Pig and said, "I suppose you are the officials who were guarding the notice." "We slaves are eunuchs in the Bureau of Ritual," said the eunuchs, kowtowing, "and these gentlemen are officers in the royal guard." "I did take the royal proclamation down," Monkey said, "and I used my younger brother to bring you here. So your lord is ill. As the saying goes, 'Don't sell medicine carelessly, and don't send for any old doctor when you're ill.' Tell your king to come here and ask me himself to help him. I can get rid of his illness at a touch." This shocked all the eunuchs. "That is very big talk, so you must be a man of great breadth of spirit," the officers said. "Half of us will remain here to press the invitation in silence while the other half go back to the palace to report."

[10]   Four of the eunuchs and six of the guards officers went straight into the palace without waiting to be summoned and said at the steps of the throne room, "Congratulations, Your Majesty." When the king, who was in the middle of a cultivated conversation with Sanzang after their meal together, heard this he asked, "What on?" "When we, your slaves, took out Your

Majesty's proclamation sending for doctors this morning and posted it at the foot of the drum tower, a holy monk from Great Tang in the east took it down," they replied. "He is now in the Hostel of Meeting and wants Your Majesty to go in person to ask his help. He can get rid of illness at a touch. That is why we have come to submit this report."

This news delighted the king. "How many distinguished disciples do you have, Master of the Law?" he asked. Putting his hands together in front of his chest Sanzang replied, "I have three stupid followers." "Which of them is a medical expert?" the king asked. "To be frank with Your Majesty," Sanzang replied, "they are all country bumpkins fit only for carrying baggage, leading the horse, finding their way along streams, or leading me over mountains and rivers. In dangerous places they can defeat monsters, capture demons, and subdue tigers and dragons. None of them knows anything about medicines." "Aren't you being too hard on them?" the king asked. "It was very fortunate that you came to court when we entered the throne hall this morning: this was surely destined by Heaven. If your disciple knows nothing about medicine why would he have taken down our proclamation and demanded that we go to greet him in person? He must surely be a great physician." He then called, "Civilian and military officers, we are much too weak to ride in our carriage. You must all leave the palace and go on our behalf to invite the Venerable Sun to treat our disease. When you meet him you must on no account show him any disrespect. You must address him as 'Holy monk, Venerable Sun' and treat him with the deference due to your own sovereign."

Having received these orders the officials went straight to the Hostel of Meeting with the eunuchs and guards officers responsible for the proclamation. There they arranged themselves in their companies to kowtow to Monkey. Pig was so frightened that he hid in the wing, while Friar Sand slipped behind the wall. Just look at the Great Sage sitting solemnly and unmoving in the middle of the room. "That macaque is really asking to have his head cut off," Pig thought resentfully. "All those officials

blowing to him, and he's not bowing back or standing up either."
Soon afterwards, when the rituals had been performed, the
officials addressed Monkey as if he were their monarch: "We
report to the holy monk, the Venerable Sun, that we officials of
the Kingdom of Purpuria have come at the command of our king
to do respectful homage to the holy monk and invite him to the
palace to treat our sick king." Only then did Brother Monkey
stand up and reply, "Why hasn't your king come?" "His Majesty
is too weak to ride in his carriage," the officials all replied,
"which is why he ordered us to pay homage to you, holy monk,
as if you were our sovereign, kowtow to you and invite you to
come." "In that case," said Monkey, "will you gentlemen please
lead the way. I'll follow you." The officials then formed
themselves into a column in accordance with their ranks and set
out. Monkey tidied his clothes and got to his feet. "Brother,"
said Pig, "whatever you do, don't drag us in." "I won't,"
Monkey replied, "provided you two accept the medicine for me."
"What medicine?" Friar Sand asked. "You must accept all the
medicine people send me," Monkey replied. "I'll collect it when I
come back." The two of them undertook this commission.

[11]   Monkey was soon at the palace with the officials, who
went in first to inform the king. He raised high the curtains of
pearls, flashed his dragon and phoenix eyes, opened his golden
mouth and spoke majestically, "Which gentleman is the holy
monk, the Venerable Sun?" Taking a step forward, Monkey
shouted at the top of his voice, "I am." The voice was so ugly
and the face so hideous that the king fell back on his dragon
throne. In their alarm the female officials and the palace eunuchs
helped him to the inner quarters. "He's terrified His Majesty to
death," they said. "Monk," all the officials said angrily to
Monkey, "how could you be so rough and crude? How dared you
take the proclamation down?"

When Brother Monkey heard this he replied with a smile,
"You shouldn't be angry with me. If you're going to be so rude to
me your king won't get better in a thousand years." "But how
long does human life last?" the officials asked. "How is it that he

won't get better even in a thousand years?" "He's a sick ruler now," said Monkey. "When he dies he'll be a sick ghost, and whenever he's reincarnated he'll be a sick man again. That's why he won't get better even in a thousand years." "You've got no sense of respect at all," the infuriated officials replied. "How dare you talk such nonsense!" "It's not nonsense," Monkey laughed. "Listen and I'll explain:

> *Mysterious indeed are the principles of medicine;*
> *Flexibility of mind is a quality required.*
> *Use eyes and ears, ask questions, take the pulses:*
> *Omit but one and the examination's incomplete.*
> *First look for outward signs of the patient's vital energy.*
> *Dried? Smooth? Fat? Thin? Active? Does he sleep well?*
> *Secondly, listen to whether the voice is clear or harsh:*
> *Determine if the words he speaks are true or crazed.*
> *Third, you must ask how long the disease has lasted,*
> *And how the patient eats, drinks and relieves himself.*
> *Fourth, feel the pulses and be clear about the veins:*
> *Are they deep, shallow, external or inside?*
> *Should I not look and listen, ask questions, and take the*
> *pulses,*
> *Never in all his days will the king be well again."*

In the ranks of the civil and military officials there were some fellows of the Royal College of Medicine who when they heard these words praised Monkey publicly: "The monk is right. Even a god or an immortal would have to look, listen, ask questions and take the pulses before treating a patient successfully with his divine gifts." All the officials agreed with these remarks, then went up to the king and submitted: "The reverend gentleman wishes to look, listen, ask questions and take the pulses before he can prescribe properly." "Send him away," the king said over and over again as he lay on his dragon bed. "We cannot bear to see any strangers." His attendants then came out from the inner quarters and announced, "Monk, His Majesty commands that

361

you go away. He cannot bear to see a stranger." "If he won't see a stranger," Monkey replied, "I know the art of taking the pulses with hanging threads." "That is something of which we have only heard," exclaimed all the officials, concealing their delight, "but that we have never seen with our own eyes. Please go back in and submit another report." The personal attendants then went back into the inner quarters and reported, "Your Majesty, the Venerable Sun can take your pulses with hanging threads; he does not need to see Your Majesty's face." At this the king reflected, "In the three years we have been ill we have never tried this technique. Send him in." At once the courtiers in attendance announced, "His Majesty has consented to pulse-taking by the hanging threads. Send the Venerable Sun to the inner quarters at once to make his diagnosis."

[12]   Monkey then entered the throne hall, where the Tang Priest met him with abuse: "Wretched ape! You will be the death of me!" "My good master," Monkey replied with a smile, "I'm bringing you credit. How can you say I'll be the death of you?" "In all the years you've been with me," Sanzang shouted, "I have never seen you cure a single person. You know nothing about the nature of drugs, and you have never studied medical books. How can you be so reckless and bring this disaster on us?" "You don't realize, Master," said Monkey with a smile, "that I do know the odd herbal remedy and can treat serious illnesses. I guarantee I can cure him. Even if the treatment kills him I'll only be guilty of manslaughter through medical incompetence. That's not a capital offence. What are you afraid of? There's nothing to worry about, nothing. You sit here and see what my pulse diagnosis is like." "How can you talk all this rubbish," Sanzang asked, "when you have never read the Plain Questions, the Classic of Difficulties, the Pharmacopoeia and the Mysteries of the Pulses, or studied the commentaries to them? How could you possibly diagnose his pulses by hanging threads?" "I've got golden threads on me that you've never seen," Monkey replied, putting out his hand to pull three hairs from his tail, hold them in a bunch, call, "Change!" and turn them into three golden threads each twenty-four feet

long to match the twenty-four periods of the solar year. Holding these in his hand he said to the Tang Priest, "These are golden threads, aren't they?" "Stop talking, reverend gentleman," said the eunuchs in attendance on the king. "Please come inside and make your diagnosis." Taking his leave of the Tang Priest Monkey followed the attendants into the inner quarters to see his patient. Indeed,

> The heart has a secret prescription that will save a country;
> The hidden ad wonderful spell gives eternal life.

If you do not know what illness was diagnosed or what medicines were used and wish to learn the truth listen to the explanation in the next instalment.

14.
心主夜间修药物
君王筵上论妖邪

【1】 话表孙大圣同近侍宦官，到于皇宫内院，直至寝宫门外立定。将三条金线与宦官拿入里面，吩咐："教内宫妃后，或近侍太监，先系在圣躬左手腕上，按寸、关、尺三部上，却将线头从窗棂儿穿出与我。"真个那宦官依此言，请国王坐在龙床，按寸、关、尺，以金线一头系了，一头理出窗外。行者按了线头，以自己右手大指先托着食指，看了寸脉；次将中指按大指，看了关脉；又将大指托定无名指，看了尺脉；调停自家呼吸，分定四气、五郁、七表、八里、九候、浮中沉、沉中浮，辨明了虚实之端；又教解下左手，依前系在右手腕下部位。行者即以左手指，一一从头诊视毕，却将身抖了一抖，把金线收上身来。厉声高呼道："陛下左手寸脉强而紧，关脉涩而缓，尺脉芤且沉；右手寸脉浮而滑，关脉迟而结，尺脉数而牢。夫左寸强而紧者，中虚心痛也；关涩而缓者，汗出肌麻也；尺芤而沉者，小便赤而大便坠血也。右手寸脉浮而滑者，内结经闭也；关迟而结者，宿食留饮也；尺数而牢者，烦满虚寒相持也。——诊此贵恙：是一个惊恐忧思，号为'双鸟失群'之症。"那国王在内闻言，满心欢喜。打起精神，高声应道："指下明白！指下明白！果是此疾！请出外面用药来也。"

【2】 大圣却才缓步出宫。早有在旁听见的太监，已先对众报知。须臾，行者出来，唐僧即问如何。行者道："诊了脉，如今对症制药哩。"众官上前道："神僧长老，适才说'双鸟失群'之症，何也？"行者笑道："有雌雄二鸟，原在一处同飞；忽被暴风骤雨冲散，雌不能见雄，雄不能见雌，雌儿想雄，雄亦想雌：这不是'双鸟失群'也？"众官闻说，齐声喝采道："真是神僧！真是神医！"称赞不已。当有太医官问道："病势已看出矣，但不知用何药治之？"行者道："不必执方，见药就要。"医官道："经云：'药有八百八味，

364

人有四百四病。'病不在一人之身，药岂有全用之理！如何见药就要？"行者道："古人云：'药不执方，合宜而用。'故此全征药品，而随便加减也。"那医官不复再言。即出朝门之外，差本衙当值之人，遍晓满城生熟药铺，即将药品，每味各办三斤，送与行者。行者道："此间不是制药处，可将诸药之数并制药一应器皿，都送入会同馆，交与我师弟二人收下。"医官听命，即将八百八味每味三斤及药碾、药磨、药罗、药乳并乳钵、乳槌之类都送至馆中，一一交付收讫。

　　行者往殿上请师父同至馆中制药。那长老正自起身，忽见内宫传旨，教阁下留住法师，同宿文华殿。待明朝服药之后，病瘥酬谢，倒换关文送行。三藏大惊道："徒弟啊，此意是留我做当头哩。若医得好，欢喜起送，若医不好，我命休矣。你须仔细上心，精度制度也！"行者笑道："师父放心，在此受用。老孙自有医国之手。"

【3】　好大圣，别了三藏，辞了众臣，径至馆中。八戒迎着笑道："师兄，我知道你了。"行者道："你知甚么？"八戒道："知你取经之事不果，欲做生涯无本，今日见此处富庶，设法要开药铺哩。"行者喝道："莫胡说！医好国王，得意处辞朝走路，开甚么药铺！"八戒道："终不然，这八百八味药，每味三斤，共计二千四百二十四斤，只医一人，能用多少？不知多少年代方吃得了哩！"行者道："那里用得许多？他那太医院官都是些愚盲之辈，所以取这许多药品，教他没处捉摸，不知我用的是那几味，难识我神妙之方也。"

　　正说处，只见两个馆使，当面跪下道："请神僧老爷进晚斋。"行者道："早间那殷殷待我，如今却跪而请之，何也？"馆使叩头道："老爷来时，下官有眼无珠，不识尊颜。今闻老爷大展三折之肱，治我一国之主，若主上病愈，老爷江山有分，我辈皆臣子也，礼当拜请。"行者见说，欣然登堂上坐。八戒、沙僧分坐左右。摆上斋来。沙僧低声问道："师兄，师父在那里哩？"行者笑道："师父被国王留在做当头哩。只待医好，方才酬谢送行。"沙僧又问："可有些受用么？"行者道："国王岂无受用！我来时，他已有三个阁老陪侍左右，请入文华殿去也。"八戒道："这等说，还是师父大

365

哩。他倒有阁老陪侍，我们只得两个馆使奉承。——且莫管他，让老猪吃酸饱饭也。"兄弟们遂自在受用一番。

【4】 天色已晚。行者叫馆使："收了家火，多办些油蜡，我等到夜静时，方好制药。"馆使果送若干油蜡，各命散讫。至半夜，天街人静，万籁无声。八戒道："哥哥，制何药？赶早干事。我瞌睡了。"行者道："你将大黄取一两来，碾为细末。"沙僧乃道："大黄味苦，性寒，无毒；其性沉实而不浮，其用走而不守；夺诸郁而无壅滞，定祸乱而致太平；名之曰'将军'。此行者耳。但恐久病虚弱，不可用此。"行者笑道："贤弟不知。此药利痰顺气，荡肚中凝滞之寒热。你莫管我。——你去取一两巴豆，去壳去膜，捶去油毒，碾为细末来。"八戒道："巴豆味辛，性热，有毒；削坚积，荡肺腑之沉寒；通闭塞，利水谷之道路；乃斩关夺门之将，不可轻用。"行者道："贤弟，你也不知。此药破结宣肠，能理心膨水胀。快制来。我还有佐使之味辅之也。"他二人即时将二药研细。行者道："师兄，还用那几十味？"行者道："不用了。"八戒道："八百八味，每味三斤，只用此二两，诚为起夺人了。"行者将一个花磁盏子，道："贤弟莫讲，你拿这个盏儿，将锅脐灰刮半盏过来。"八戒道："要怎的？"行者道："药内要用。"沙僧道："小弟不曾见药内用锅灰。"行者道："锅灰名为'百草霜'，能调百病，你不知道。"那呆子真个刮了半盏，又碾细了。行者又将盏子，递与他道："你再去把我们的马尿等半盏来。"八戒道："要他怎的？"行者道："要丸药。"沙僧又笑道："哥哥，这事不是耍子。马尿腥臊，如何入得药品？我只见醋糊为丸，陈米糊为丸，炼蜜为丸，或只是清水为丸，那曾见马尿为丸。那东西腥腥臊臊，脾虚的人，一闻就吐；再服巴豆、大黄，弄得上吐下泻，可是耍子？"行者道："你不知就里。我那马，不是凡马。他本是西海龙身。若得他肯去便溺，凭你何疾，服之即愈。但急不可得耳。"八戒闻言，真个去到马边。那马斜伏下睡哩。呆子一顿脚踢起，衬在肚下，等了半会，全不见撒尿。他跑将来，对行者说："哥啊，且莫去医皇帝，且快去医医马来。那亡人干结了，莫想尿得出一点儿！"行者笑道："我和你去。"沙僧道："我也去看看。"

【5】 三人都来到马边，那马跳将起来，口吐人言，厉声高叫道："师

兄,你岂不知?我本是西海飞龙,因为犯了天条,观音菩萨救了我,将我锯了角,退了鳞,变做马,驮师父往西天取经,将功折罪。我若过水撒尿,水中游鱼,食了成龙;过山撒尿,山中草头得味,变做灵芝,仙僮采去长寿;我怎肯在此尘俗之处轻抛却也?"行者道:"兄弟谨言。此间乃西方国王,非尘俗也,亦非轻抛弃也。常言道:'众毛攒裘。'要与本国之王治病哩。医得好时,大家光辉。不然,恐俱不得善离此地也。"那马才叫声"等着。"你看他往前扑了一扑,往后蹲了一蹲,咬得那满口牙龊支支的响亮,仅努出几点儿,将身止起。八戒道:"这个亡人! 就是金汁子,再撒些儿也罢!"那行者见有少半盏,道:"彀了! 彀了! 拿去罢。"沙僧方才欢喜。

三人回至厅上,把前项药饵搅和一处,搓了三个大丸子。行者道:"兄弟,忒大了。"八戒道:"只有核桃大。若论我吃,还不彀一口哩!"遂此收在一个小盒儿里。兄弟们连衣睡下,一夜无词。

【6】 早是天晓。却说那国王耽病设朝,请唐僧见了,即命众官快往会同馆参拜神僧孙长老取药去。

多官随至馆中,对行者拜伏于地道:"我王特命臣等拜领妙剂。"行者叫八戒取盒儿,揭开盖子,递与多官。多官启问:"此药何名? 好见王回话?"行者道:"此名'乌金丹。'"八戒二人,暗中作笑道:"锅灰拌的,怎么不是乌金!"多官又问道:"用何引子?"行者道:"引孔两般都下得。有一般易取者,乃六物煎汤送下。"多官问:"是何六物?"行者道:

> "半空飞的老鸦屁,紧水负的鲤鱼尿,王母娘娘搽脸粉,老君炉里炼丹灰,玉皇戴破的头巾要三块,还要五根困龙须:六物煎汤送此药,你王忧病等时除。"

多官闻言道:"此物乃世间所无者。请问那一般引子是何?"行者道:"用无根水送下。"众官笑道:"这个易取。"行者道:"怎见得易取?"多官道:"我这里人家俗论:若用无根水,将一个碗盏,到井边,或河下,舀了满,急转步,到家,不落地,亦不回头,到家与病人吃药,便是。"行者道:"井中河内之水,俱是有根的。我这无根水,非此之论,乃是天上落下者,不沾地就吃,才叫做'无根水'。"多官又道:"这也容易。等到天阴下雨时,再吃药便罢了。"遂拜谢了行者，将持回献上。

国王大喜，即命近侍接上来。看了道："此是甚么丸子？"多官道："神僧说是'乌金丹'，用无根水送下。"国王便教宫人取无根水。众官道："神僧说，无根水不是井河中者，乃是天上落下不沾地的才是。"国王即唤当驾官传旨，教请法官求雨。众官遵依出榜不题。

【7】 却说行者在会同馆厅上，叫猪八戒道："适间允他天落之水，才可用药，此时急忙，怎么得个雨水？我看这王，倒也是个大贤大德之君，我与你助他些儿下药，如何？"八戒道："怎么样助？"行者道："你在我左边立下，做个辅星。"又叫沙僧，"你在我右边立下，做了弼宿。等老孙助他些无根水儿。"好大圣，步了罡诀，念声咒语，早见那正东上，一朵乌云，渐近于头顶。叫道："大圣，东海龙王敖广来见。"行者道："无事不敢烦渎，请你来助些无根水与国王下药。"龙王道："大圣呼唤时，不曾说用水，小龙只身来了，不曾带得雨器，亦未有风云雷电，怎生降雨？"行者道："如今用不着风云雷电，亦不须多雨，只要些须引药之水便了。"龙王道："既如此，待我打两个喷涕，吐些涎津溢，与他吃药罢。"行者大喜道："最好！最好！不必迟疑，趁早行事。"

那老龙在空中，渐渐低下乌云，直至皇宫之上，隐身潜像，噀一口津唾，遂化做甘霖。那满朝官齐声喝采道："我主万千之喜！天公降下甘雨来也！"国王即传旨，教："取器皿盛着。不拘宫内外及官大小，都要等贮仙水，拯救寡人。"你看那文武多官并三宫六院妃嫔与三千彩女，八百娇娥，一个个擎杯托盏，举碗持盘，争接甘雨。那老龙在半空，运化津涎，不离于王宫前后。将有一个时辰，龙王辞了大圣回海。众臣将杯盂碗盏收来，也有等着一点两点者，也有等着三点五点者，也有一点不曾等着者，共合一处，约有三盏之多，总献至御案。真个是异香满袭金銮殿，佳味熏飘天子庭！

【8】 那国王辞了法师，将着"乌金丹"并甘雨至宫中，先吞了一丸，吃了一盏甘雨；再吞了一丸，又饮了一盏甘雨；三次，三丸俱吞了，三盏甘雨俱送。不多时，腹中作响，如辘轳之声不绝，即取净桶，连行了三五次，服了些米饮，软倒在龙床之上。有两个

妃子，将净桶捡看，说不尽那秽污痰涎，内有糯米饭块一团。妃子近龙床前来报："病根都行下来也！"国王闻此言，甚喜，又进一次米饭。少顷，渐觉心胸宽泰，气血调和，就精神抖擞，脚力强健。下了龙床，穿上朝服，即登宝殿，见了唐僧，辄倒身下拜。那长老忙忙还礼。拜毕，以御手搀着，便教阁下："快具简帖，帖上写朕'再拜顿首'字样，差官奉请法师高徒三位。一壁厢大开东阁，光禄寺排宴酬谢。"多官领旨，具简的具简，排宴的排宴，正是国家有倒山之力，霎时俱完。

【9】 却说八戒见官投简，喜不自胜道："哥啊，果是好妙药！今来酬谢，乃兄长之功。"沙僧道："二哥说那里话！常言道：'一人有福，带挈一屋。'我们在此合药，俱是有功之人。只管受用去，再休多话。"咦！你看他弟兄们俱欢欢喜喜，径入朝来。

众官接引，上了东阁，早见唐僧、国王、阁老，已都在那里安排筵宴哩。这行者与八戒、沙僧，对师父唱了个喏，随后众官都至。只见那上面有四张素桌面，都是吃一看十的筵席；前面有一张劳桌面，也是吃一看十的珍馐。左右有四五百张单桌面，真个排得齐整：

> 古云："珍馐百味，美禄千锺。琼膏酥酪，锦缕肥红。"宝妆花彩艳，果品味香浓。斗糖龙缠列狮仙，饼锭拖炉摆凤侣。荤有猪羊鸡鹅鱼鸭般般肉，素有蔬肴笋芽木耳并蘑菇。几样香汤饼，数次透酥糖。滑软黄粱饭，清新菰米糊。色色粉汤香又辣，般般添换美还甜。君臣举盏方安席，名分品级慢传壶。

那国王御手擎杯，先与唐僧安坐。三藏道："贫僧不会饮酒。"国王道："素酒。法师饮此一杯，何如？"三藏道："酒乃僧家第一戒。"国王甚不过意道："法师戒饮，却以何物为敬？"三藏道："顽徒三众代饮罢。"国王却才欢喜，转金卮，递与行者。行者接了酒，对众礼毕，吃了一杯。国王见他吃得爽利，又奉一杯。行者不辞，又吃了。国王笑道："吃个三宝锺儿。"行者不辞，又吃了。国王又叫斟上，"吃个四季杯儿。"

八戒在旁，见酒不到他，忍得他咽咽咽唾；又见那国王苦劝行者，他就叫将起来道："陛下，吃的药也亏了我，那药里有马

——"这行者听说，恐怕呆子走了消息，却将手中酒递与八戒。八戒接着就吃，却不言语。国王问道："神僧说药里有马，是甚么马？"行者接过口来道："我这兄弟，是这般口敞。但有个经验的好方儿，他就要说与人。陛下早间吃药，内有马兜铃。"国王问众官道："马兜铃是何品味？能医何症？"时有太医院官在旁道："主公：

> 兜铃味苦寒无毒，定喘消痰大有功。
>
> 通气最能除血盅，补虚宁嗽又宽中。"

国王笑道："用得当！用得当！猪长老再饮一杯。"呆子亦不言语，却也吃了个三宝锺。国王又递了沙僧酒，也吃了三杯，却俱叙坐。

【10】饮宴多时，国王又擎大爵，奉与行者。行者道："陛下请坐。老孙依巡痛饮，决不敢推辞。"国王道："神僧恩重如山，寡人酬谢不尽。好歹进此一巨觞，朕有话说。"行者道："有甚话说了，老孙好饮。"国王道："寡人有数载忧疑病，被神僧一贴灵丹打通，所以就好了。"行者笑道："昨日老孙看了陛下，已知是忧疑之疾，但不知何事忧惊？"国王道："古人云：'家丑不可外谈。'奈神僧是朕恩主——惟不笑，方可告之。"行者道："怎敢笑话，请说无妨。"国王道："神僧东来，不知经过几个邦国？"行者道："经有五六处。"又问："他国之后，不知是何称呼？"行者道："国王之后，都称为正宫、东宫、西宫。"国王道："寡人不是这等称呼，将正宫称为金圣宫，东宫称为玉圣宫，西宫称为银圣宫。现今只有银、玉二后在宫。"行者道："金圣宫因何不在宫中？"国王滴泪道："不在已三年矣。"行者道："向那厢去了？"国王道："三年前，正值端阳之节，朕与嫔后都在御花园海榴亭下解粽插艾，饮菖蒲雄黄酒，看斗龙舟。忽然一阵风至，半空中现出一个妖精，自称赛太岁，说他在麒麟山獬豸洞居住，洞中少个夫人，访得我金圣宫生得貌美姿妖，要做个夫人，教朕快早送出。如若三声不献出来，就要先吃寡人，后吃众臣，将满城黎民，尽皆伤绝。那时节，朕却忧国忧民，无奈，将金圣宫推出海榴亭外，被那妖响一声摄将去了。寡人为此着了惊恐，把那粽子凝滞在内；况又昼夜忧思不息，所以成此苦疾三年。今得神僧灵丹服后，行了数次，尽是那三年前积

滞之物，所以这会体健身轻，精神如旧。今日之命，皆是神僧所赐，岂但如泰山重之而已乎！"

【11】　行者闻得此言，满心喜悦，将那巨觥之酒，两口吞之，笑问国王曰："陛下原来是这等惊忧！今遇老孙，幸而获愈。但不知可要金圣宫回国？"那国王滴泪道："朕切切思思，无昼无夜，但只是没一个能获得妖精的。岂有不要他回国之理！"行者道："我老孙与你去伏妖邪，那时何如？"国王跪下道："若救得朕后，朕愿领三宫九嫔，出城为民，将一国江山，尽付神僧，让你为帝。"八戒在旁，见出此言，行此礼，忍不住呵呵大笑道："这皇帝失了体统！怎么为老婆就不要江山，跪着和尚？"行者急上前，将国王搀起道："陛下，那妖精自得金圣宫去后，这一向可曾再来？"国王道："他前年五月节摄了金圣宫，至十月间来，要取两个宫娥，是说伏侍娘娘，朕即献出两个。至旧年三月间，又来要两个宫娥；七月间，又要两个；今年二月里，又要去两个；不知到几时又要来也。"行者道："似他这等频来，你们可怕他么？"国王道："寡人见他来得多遭，一则惧怕，二来又恐有伤害之意，旧年四月内，是朕命工起了一座避妖楼，但闻风响，知是他来，即与二后、九嫔，入楼躲避。"行者道："陛下不弃，可携老孙去看那避妖楼一番，何如？"那国王即将左手携着行者出席。众官亦皆起身。猪八戒道："哥哥，你不达理！这般御酒不吃，摇席破坐的，且去看甚么哩！"国王闻说，情知八戒是为嘴，即命当驾官抬两张素菜桌席，看酒在避妖楼外伺候。呆子却才不嚷，同师父、沙僧笑道："翻席去也。"

【12】　一行文武官引导，那国王并行者相搀，穿过皇宫到了御花园后，更不见楼台殿阁。行者道："避妖楼何在？"说不了，只见两个太监，拿两根红漆扛子，往那空地上掘起一块四方石板。国王道："此间便是。这底下有三丈多深，窈成的九间朝殿。内有四个大缸，缸内满注清油，点着灯火，昼夜不息。寡人听得风响，就入里边躲避，外面着人盖上石板。"行者笑道："那妖精还是不害你；若要害你，这里如何躲得？"正问间，只见那正南上，呼呼的，吹得风响，播土扬尘。唬得那多官齐声报怨道："这和尚盐酱口，讲起甚么妖精，妖精就来了！"慌得那国王丢了行者，即钻入地

穴。唐僧也就跟入。众官亦躲个干净。

八戒，沙僧也都要躲，被行者左右手扯住他两个道："兄弟们，不要怕得。我和你认他一认，看是个甚么妖精？"八戒道："可是扯淡！认他怎的？众官躲了，师父藏了，国王避了，我们不去了罢，炫的是那家世！"那呆子左挣右挣，挣不得脱手，被行者拿定多时，只见那半空里闪出一个妖精。你看他怎生模样：

> 九尺长身多恶狞，一双环眼闪金灯。
> 两轮查耳如撑扇，四个钢牙似插钉。
> 鬓绕红毛眉竖焰，鼻垂槽准孔开明。
> 髭髯几缕朱砂线，颧骨崚嶒满面青。
> 两臂红筋蓝靛腿十，十条尖爪把枪擎。
> 豹皮裙子腰间系，赤脚蓬头若鬼形。

行者见了道："沙僧，你可认得他么？"沙僧道："我又不曾与他相识，那里认得！"又问："八戒，你可认得他？"八戒道："我又不曾与他会茶会酒，又不是宾朋邻里，我怎么认得他！"行者道："他却像东岳天齐手下把门的那个醮面金睛鬼。"八戒道："不是！不是！"行者道："你怎知他不是？"八戒道："我岂不知，鬼乃阴灵也，一日至晚，交申酉戌亥时才出。今日还在巳时，那里有鬼敢出来？就是鬼，也不会驾云。纵会弄风，也只是一阵旋风耳，有这等狂风？或者他就是赛太岁也。"行者笑道："好呆子！倒也有些论头！既如此说，你两个护持在此，等老孙去问他个名号，好与国王救取金圣宫来朝。"八戒道："你去自去，切莫供出我们来。"行者昂然不答，急纵祥光，跳将上去。咦！正是：安邦先却君王病，守道须除爱恶心。毕竟不知此去，到于空中，胜败如何，怎么擒得妖怪，救得金圣宫，且听下回分解。

Chapter 14
The Heart's Master Prepares Medicine in the Night;
The Monarch Discusses a Demon at the Banquet

[1]   The story tells how the Great Sage Sun went with the eunuchs in attendance on the king to the inner quarters of the palace and stood outside the doors of the royal bed-chamber. Handing the three golden threads to the eunuchs to take inside he gave them these instructions: "Tell the queens and consorts of the inner palace or the eunuchs in personal attendance to fasten these threads to His Majesty's left wrist at the inch, the bar and the cubit then pass them out of the window to me." The eunuchs did as he said, asking the king to sit on his dragon bed while they fastened one end of the golden threads to the inch, the bar and the cubit and passed the other ends outside.

Monkey took these ends and first held the end of one between the thumb and the forefinger of his right hand and felt the pulse at the inch point. He held the next against his middle finger and felt the pulse at the bar, and then oppressed his thumb against his third finger and felt the cubit pulse. Next he regulated his own breathing to examine the four functions, the five depressions, the seven exterior and eight interior symptoms, the nine tempers, the deep pulses within the floating ones and the floating ones within the deep ones. He thus determined the insufficiencies and excesses of the functioning of organs, then told the eunuchs to take the threads off the king's left wrist and fasten them to the same points on the right wrist. He felt the threads one by one with the fingers of his left hand.

With a shake he put the golden threads back on his body and shouted at the top of his voice, "Your Majesty, the inch pulse on your left wrist is strong and tense, the bar pulse is sluggish and

373

tardy, and the cubit is hollow and deep. On your right wrist the inch is floating and slippery, the bar is slow and knotted, and the cubit is frequent and firm. The left inch being strong and tense means that you have an internal emptiness and pains in the heart. The left bar being sluggish and tardy shows that you sweat and that your muscles feel numb. The hollowness and depth of the cubit suggest red urine and bloody stools. The floating, slippery inch pulse on the right wrist shows internal accumulations and blocked channels. The bar being slow and knotted is from indigestion and retained drinking. The frequency and wiriness of the cubit shows a chronic opposition of irritable fullness and empty coldness. My diagnosis of Your Majesty's ailment is that you are suffering from alarm and worry. The condition is the one known as the 'pair of birds parted'." When the king heard this inside his chamber he was so delighted that his spirits revived and he shouted in reply, "You have understood my illness through your fingers. That is indeed my trouble. Please go out and fetch some medicine."

[2]   Monkey walked slowly out of the inner palace, by when the eunuchs watching him had already given the news to everyone. When Monkey emerged a moment later the Tang Priest asked him how it had gone. "I made a diagnosis from his pulses," Monkey said. "I now have to prepare the medicine for his condition." All the officials then came forward to ask, "Holy monk, reverend sir, what is the 'pair of birds parted' condition of which you spoke just now?" "It's when a cock bird and a hen who were flying together are suddenly separated by a violent storm," replied Monkey with a smile. "The hen misses the cock and the cock misses the hen. Isn't that 'a pair of birds parted'?" At this the officials all cried out over and over again in admiration, "He really is a holy monk! He really is a divine doctor!"

"You have diagnosed the condition," said one of the fellows of the Royal College of Medicine, "but what drugs will you use to treat it?" "There's no need to stick to prescriptions," said Monkey. "I'll choose the drugs when I see them." "According to the medical classic, 'There are 808 varieties of medicine and 404 varieties of sickness,'" said the fellows of the Royal College of Medicine. "How can it be right to use all the medicines when one person does not have all the ailments? You can't just choose your drugs on sight." To this Monkey replied, "The ancients said, 'In preparing medicines do not stick rigidly to the formulae; use them as appropriate.' That's why I've asked for the full range of pharmaceutical materials so that I can make adjustments as I need to." The fellows of the Royal College could say no more to this, but went out through the palace gates and sent those of the college's staff who were on duty to tell all the pharmacies in the city, whether selling raw materials or prepared drugs, to send three pounds of each to Monkey. "This is no place for preparing medicine," said Monkey. "All the medicines and a set of pharmacist's utensils must be sent to the Hostel of Meeting and handed over to my two fellow disciples." The fellows did as they were told. Three pounds of each of the 808 ingredients of medicine together with pharmacist's rollers, hand-mills, sieves, mortars, bowls, pestles and the like were all sent to the hostel, handed over and received.

【3】 Monkey went back into the throne hall and asked his master to return to the hostel with him while he prepared the medicine. Sanzang was just getting up to go when the king sent a command from the inner quarters that the Master of the Law was to stay behind and spend the night in the Hall of Literary Splendour; the next morning, after taking the medicine and recovering from his illness, the king would reward them, inspect the passport and send them on their way. Sanzang was horrified. "Disciple," he said, "he means to keep me here as a hostage. If he is cured he will be happy to send us on our way, but if the treatment fails my life is over. You must be very careful and pay full attention when preparing the medicine." "Don't worry, Master," Monkey said with a smile, "Enjoy yourself here. I'm a superb doctor."

Taking his leave of Sanzang and of all the officials the splendid Great Sage went straight back to the hostel where Pig welcomed him with a grin. "Brother," he said, "I know what you're up to." "What?" Monkey asked. "If fetching the scriptures doesn't come off you'll be left without any capital to start up a business." Pig replied. "Now you've seen how prosperous this place is you're planning to open a chemist's shop here." "Don't talk nonsense," shouted Monkey. "When I've cured the king I'll use my success to leave the court and be on our way. I'm not going to be running a chemist's." "Well," said Pig, "if you're not opening a shop, why get three pounds of each of 808 different ingredients to treat one man? How much of it will you need? How many years will it take for him to finish the lot?" "He'll never finish that much," Monkey replied. "The fellows of their Royal College of Medicine are a load of idiots. The only reason why I sent for so many ingredients was to baffle them and stop them knowing which ones I'm going to use. Then they won't be able to find out what my miraculous prescription is."

As they were talking two of the hostel staff came in and fell to their knees before them to say, "We beg the holy monks and reverend gentlemen to partake of their evening repast." "This morning you treated us rather differently," said Monkey, "so why go on your knees to invite us now?" "When you first came my lords," the hostel orderlies replied, "we were too blind to recognize your illustrious faces. Now we have heard how you are using your outstanding medical powers to treat our king. If His Majesty recovers his health he will share the kingdom with you, so we'll all be your subjects. So it's only proper for us to kowtow to you and to invite you politely to eat." On hearing this Monkey cheerfully took the place of honour while Pig and Friar Sand sat to his left and right. As the vegetarian meal was served Friar Sand asked, "Where's our master, brother?" "The king's kept him as a hostage," Monkey replied. "When the king's cured he'll reward us and send us on our way." "Is he being well looked after?" Friar Sand continued. "His host's a king," Monkey replied, "so of course he's in luxury. When I went there he had three senior ministers looking after him and he was invited into the Hall of Literary Splendour." "In that case," said Pig, "the master's still doing much better than us. He's got ministers looking after him, and we've only got a couple of hostel orderlies to serve us. So I'm going to forget about him and eat a good meal." Thus the three of them enjoyed their meal at ease.

[4] It was now late. "Tidy the dishes away," Monkey said to the hostel orderlies, "and fetch me plenty of oil and candles. The best time for us to make up the medicine will be in the quiet of the night." The orderlies brought oil and candles as instructed and were then dismissed. In the still silence of the middle of the night Pig asked, "Brother, what medicines are we going to make? Let's get on with it. I need my shut-eye." "Get an ounce of rhubarb and grind it to a fine powder with a roller," said Brother Monkey. "Rhubarb has a bitter taste and a cold nature and isn't noxious," said Friar Sand. "Its nature is deep, not superficial; it's an active medicine, not a defensive one. It removes stagnations and clears obstructions, settles disorder and brings about peace, and they call it 'the general'. It's a cathartic drug. But perhaps it's wrong for someone in an empty, weakened state after a long illness." "There's something you don't know, brother," Monkey said. "This drug helps phlegm, makes the vital forces travel smoothly, and calms the heat and cold that become congested in the stomach. Just leave me alone and fetch me an ounce of croton seeds. Shell them, peel them, hammer the poisonous oil out of them, then grind them to a fine powder with a roller." "Croton seed is acrid, hot by nature and poisonous," said Pig. "It cuts away hard accumulations, deals with submerged cold in the lungs and bowels, and clears obstructions. It smooths the way for water and grain. It's a warrior for storming passes and gates. You must be very careful how you use it." "Brother," Monkey replied, "what you don't understand is that this is a drug that destroys knots, opens the intestine and can cure swelling of the heart and dropsy. Hurry up and get it ready. And I'll want an adjuvant to back it up."

The two of them started work on grinding the two drugs to a fine powder. "You'll need dozens more, brother," they said, "so which'll they be?" "That's all," Monkey replied. "But you've got three pounds of each of 808 different medicinal ingredients," Pig said. "If all you're going to use is two ounces you've been making

377

a fool of these people." Monkey then produced a patterned porcelain dish and said, "Stop talking, brothers. Take this dish and fill it half full with soot scraped from a cooking pot." "Whatever for?" Pig asked. "I need it for the medicine," Monkey replied. "I never heard of soot from a cooking pot being used in medicine," said Friar Sand. "It's called 'frost on the flowers'," said Monkey, "and it helps treat all kinds of illness. Didn't you know that?" The idiot then scraped off half a dishful and ground it up to a fine powder.

Monkey then handed him another dish and said, "Now fetch me half a dishful of our horse's piss." "What for?" Pig asked. "To make the medicine up into pills with," Monkey replied. "Brother," said Friar Sand with a smile, "this is no joking matter. Horse piss stinks. You can't use it in medicine. I've only seen vinegar paste, old rice paste, refined honey and clean water used for making pills. Who ever heard of horse piss used to make pills? It's got a terrible stink. Anyone with a weak spleen would throw up at the first sniff. If he goes on and takes the rhubarb and croton seeds he'll be vomiting at one end and having the runs at the other. That'll be no joke." "You don't know the inside story," said Monkey. "That horse of ours is no ordinary horse. He used to be a dragon in the Western Ocean. If he'll give us some of his piss it'll cure any illness you could have. My only worry is that he might refuse." When Pig heard this he went and stood beside the horse, who was lying down asleep. The idiot kicked the horse till he got to his feet then pressed himself against the horse's stomach for a very long time but without seeing any sign of piss. He ran back to Monkey to say, "Brother, never mind about treating the king. Hurry up and cure the horse. He's done for: he's dried right up. There's no way we're going to get a drop of piss out of him." "I'll go with you," smiled Monkey. "I'll come and have a look too," said Friar Sand.

【5】 When the three of them reached the horse he started to jump about and shout in human language at the top of his voice, "How can you be so ignorant, brother? I used to be a flying dragon in the Western Ocean. The Bodhisattva Guanyin saved me after I'd offended against the Heavenly Code. She sawed off my horns, removed my scales and turned me into a horse to carry the master to the Western Heaven to fetch the scriptures. This way I'll be able to redeem my crimes. If I pissed into any river I was crossing the fish in the water would drink it and turn into dragons. The grass on any mountain we were going over that got a taste of it would become magic fungus for immortal boys to gather and give themselves eternal life. So of course I can't casually drop it in a vulgar, worldly place like this." "Watch your words, brother," said Monkey. "This is the city of a western king, not some vulgar, worldly place. You wouldn't be casually dropping it here. As the saying goes, many hands make light work. We've got to cure the king. When we do we'll all be covered in glory. If we fail I'm afraid we won't be able to leave this country with any credit."

"Wait a moment," the horse finally said. Look at him as he springs forward then squats back on his haunches, grinds his teeth noisily and only with the greatest strain manages to squeeze out a few drops before standing up again. "What a deadbeat," said Pig. "You could give us a few more even if they were drops of gold." Seeing that the dish was now about a third full Monkey said, "That'll do, that'll do. Take it away." Only then did Friar Sand feel cheerful.

The three of them then returned to the main hall, mixed the piss with the ingredients that had already been prepared, and rolled the mixture into three large round balls. "They're too big, brothers," said Monkey. "They're only walnut-sized," Pig replied. "That wouldn't be enough for a single mouthful if I were taking them." The three disciples then put the pills into a large box and went to bed fully dressed.

[6]   It was soon dawn, and despite his sickness the king held court, asking the Tang Priest to come to see him and sending all his officials straight to the Hostel of Meeting to pay their respects to the holy monk, the Venerable Sun, and fetch the medicine.

When the officials reached the hostel they prostrated themselves before Brother Monkey with the words, "His Majesty

379

has sent us to pay our respects and fetch the miraculous medicine." Monkey told Pig to fetch the box, which he opened and handed to the officials. "What is this medicine called?" they asked. "We would like to be able to inform His Majesty when we see him." "It's called Black Gold Elixir," Monkey replied, at which Pig and Friar Sand had to hide their grins as they thought, "of course they're black gold—they were made with soot scraped off cooking pots."

"What should be taken with the pills to guide them on their way?" the officials asked. "There are two kinds of guide that can be taken with them," Monkey replied. "One's easily got hold of. That is a decoction of six ingredients to be taken as a hot potion." "What six ingredients?" the officials asked. "A fart from a flying crow," Monkey replied, "piss from a carp in a fast-flowing stream, some of the face-powder used by the Queen Mother of the West, soot from elixir refined in Lord Lao's furnace, three pieces of a worn-out head cloth of the Jade Emperor's, and five whiskers from a trapped dragon's beard. A decoction of those six ingredients taken with the pills would clear up your king's illness straight away."

When the officials heard this they replied, "Those are things that are not to be found in this world, so please tell us what the other guide is." "The pills should be taken with rootless water," said Monkey. "That's very easily got hold of," smiled the officials. "How can you be so sure?" Monkey asked. "We have a saying here," the officials replied, "that if you need rootless water you take a bowl or a dish to a well or a stream, fill it with water, and hurry back with it. Don't spill a drop, don't look behind you, and give it to the patient to take with the medicine." "But well water and stream water both have roots," Monkey said. "The rootless water I'm talking about has to fall from the sky and be drunk before it touches the ground. Only then can it be called rootless." "That easily got too," the officials said. "The medicine shouldn't be taken till the next cloudy, wet day."

The officials then kowtowed to thank Monkey and took the medicine back with them to present to the king, who delightedly ordered his attendants to bring it to him. "What are these pills?" he asked when he saw them. "The holy monk says they are Black Gold Elixir and have to be taken with rootless water," the officials replied. The king then sent some of his palace women to fetch rootless water. "The holy monk says that rootless water can't be got from wells or streams," the officials said. "It has to be water that has come down from the sky and nor yet touched the ground." The king then ordered his aides to issue a decree inviting magicians to summon rain. The officials then issued a proclamation as the king had ordered.

【7】 Back in the hall of the Hostel of Meeting Brother Monkey said to Pig, "He must be given some rain now so he can take his medicine. This is very urgent. How are we going to get some? I reckon he's a very virtuous and worthy king, so why don't we help him get a little rainwater to take his medicine with?" "But how are we going to help him get some rootless water?" Pig asked. "Stand on my left and be my Sustainer Star," Monkey said to him, then told Friar Sand, "stand on my right as my Straightener Star while I help him to get some rootless water."

The splendid Great Sage then paced out a magic pattern and said the words of a spell. Soon a dark cloud appeared to their east that came closer till it was over their heads. "Great Sage," called a voice from it, "Ao Guang, the Dragon King of the Eastern Sea, is here to call on you." "I wouldn't have troubled you if it hadn't been important," Monkey said. "Could I ask you to help by giving the king here some rootless water to take his medicine with?" "When you summoned me, Great Sage," the dragon king replied, "you said nothing about water. I have only come by myself. I haven't brought any rain-making equipment, to say nothing of wind, clouds, thunder and lightning. So how can I make it rain?" "There'll be no call for wind, clouds, thunder or lightning this time," Monkey said, "and we don't need much rain either. We just need enough water for someone to take his medicine with." "In that case I'll do a couple of sneezes and spit out some saliva," the dragon king said. "That ought to be enough for him to take his medicine." "Terrific," said Monkey, delighted. "Don't waste a moment. Do it as soon as you can."

The ancient old dragon gradually brought his dark cloud down till it was just over the palace, though he kept himself entirely concealed. He spat out a mouthful of saliva that turned into timely rain, whereupon all the official at court exclaimed, "Ten million congratulations, Your Majesty. Heaven is sending down timely rain." The king then ordered, "Take vessels out to hold the rain. All officials, whether inside or outside the palace and irrespective of their rank, must gather this sacred water to save our life." Just watch as all the civil and military officials as well as the consorts, concubines, three thousand beauties, and eight hundred charming ladies-in-waiting of the three harems and the six compounds of the inner palace all stood there holding cups, dishes, bowls and plates to catch the timely rain. Up in the sky the ancient dragon so controlled his saliva that all of it fell within the palace. After about two hours the dragon king took his leave of the Great Sage and went back to the sea. When the officials gathered all the cups, dishes, bowls and plates together they found that some had caught one or two drops of water, some three to five, and some none at all. When it was all put together there were a little over three dishes full of it, and this was all presented to the king. Indeed,

> *The throne hall was filled with exquisite fragrance;*
> *Fine scents were wafting round the Son of Heaven's court.*

[8]　　The king then dismissed the Master of the Law and had the Black Gold Elixir and the timely rain carried into the inner quarters, where he took the first pill with the first dish of timely rain, then the second pill with the second dish. In three efforts he finished all three pills and all three dishfuls. Soon afterwards there was a noise from his stomach like the endless turning of a windlass. He sent for his chamber pot and evacuated four or five times before taking some rice porridge and collapsing on his dragon bed. When two of his consorts inspected the chamber pot they saw it contained huge amounts of faeces and mucus, and

amid it all a ball of glutinous rice. "The root of the disorder has come out," the consorts reported, going over to the royal bed. The king was very pleased to hear this and ate some rice. A little later his chest felt eased and his natural forces and blood were in harmonious balance once more. He was full of vigour and the strength came back to his legs, so he rose from his bed, dressed in his court clothes and went into the throne hall, where he greeted the Tang Priest by prostrating himself. The venerable elder returned this courtesy as quickly as he could. When this had been done the king helped Sanzang to his feet with his own hands and told his courtiers, "Write a note at once sending our personal and respectful greetings and have an official go to invite the three illustrious disciples of the Master of the Law to come here. Meanwhile the eastern hall of the palace is to arrange a banquet of thanksgiving." Having been given these commands the officials carried them out. The scribes wrote out the note and the caterers prepared the meal. A state is indeed strong enough to overturn a mountain, and everything was done in an instant.

[9] When Pig saw the officials come to deliver the note he was beside himself with delight. "Brother," he said, "it really must be miracle medicine. From the way they're coming to thank you you must have pulled it off." "You've got it all wrong, brother," said Friar Sand. "As the saying goes, 'One man's good fortune affects his whole household,' We two made up the pills, so we take a share of the credit. So just enjoy yourself and stop talking." Hey! Just look at the three brothers as they all happily go straight to the palace, where all the officials received them and led them to the eastern hall.

Here they saw the Tang Priest with the king and his ministers and the banquet all set out ready. Brother Monkey, Pig and Friar Sand all chanted a "na-a-aw" of respect to their master, after which the officials all came in. In the best place there were set out four tables of vegetarian food. It was the sort of banquet at which there are ten times as many dishes as you can eat. In front of these tables was one of meat dishes, and on this too you could see ten dishes of rare delicacies while you ate one. To either side four or five hundred more single tables were most neatly set out.

As the ancients had it:
"A hundred rare delicacies,
A thousand goblets of fine wine,
Rich cream and yoghurt,
Fat, red meat like brocade."
Precious and many-coloured decorations,
Heavy fragrances of fruit.
Huge sugar dragons coil round sweet lions and immortals:
Ingots of cake draw furnaces escorted by phoenixes.
For meat there was pork and mutton, goose, chicken, duck
and fish;
For vegetables, bamboo shoots, beansprouts, fungus and
button mushrooms.
Delicious noodles in soup,
Translucent creamy sweets,
Succulent millet,
Fresh wild rice congee,
Pungent, tasty soup with rice noodles,
Dishes in which sweetness vied with beauty.
Monarch and subjects raised their cups as the diners took
their seats;
Officials seated by rank slowly passed the jugs.

Holding a cup in his hand the king first seated the Tang
Priest, who said, "As a monk I may not drink liquor." "This is
alcohol-free wine," the king said. "Could you not drink one cup
of this, Master of the Law?" "But wine is the first prohibition for
us monks," said Sanzang. The king felt awkward. "If you may
not drink, Master of the Law, how can I congratulate you?"
"My three badly-behaved disciples will drink on my behalf,"
Sanzang replied. The king then happily passed the golden goblet
to Monkey, who took it, made a courteous gesture to the
assembly, and downed a cupful. Seeing how cheerfully he
downed it the king offered him another cup. Monkey did not

decline it but drank again. "Have a third goblet," said the king with a smile, and Monkey accepted and drank for a third time. The king then ordered that the cup be refilled and said, "Have another to make it four for the four seasons."

Pig, who was standing beside Monkey, had to put up with the saliva gurgling inside him as the wine would not come his way; and now that the king was pressing Monkey so hard to drink he started to shout, "Your Majesty, that medicine you took owes something to me. Those pills include 'orse—" When Monkey heard this he was terrified that the idiot was going to give the game away, so he handed Pig the cup. Pig took the cup, drank and stopped talking. "Holy monk," said the king, "just now you said there was horse in the pills. What sort of horse?" "This brother of mine has a very loose tongue," said Monkey, cutting in. "We've got a really good formula that has been tried and tested, and he wants to give it away. The pills Your Majesty took this morning included not 'orse but Aristolochia." "What class of medicine is Aristolochia?" the king asked. "What conditions can it cure?" One of the fellows of the Royal College of Medicine who was standing beside the king said, "Your Majesty,

> Aristolochia is bitter, cold and free of poison,
> Ends shortness of breath and cures phlegm well,
> Circulates the energy, removes blood infections,
> Fills emptiness, soothes coughs and eases the heart.

"It was the right thing to use, the right thing to use," the king said. "The Venerable Pig must have another cup." The idiot said nothing more, but downed three goblets. The king then gave three cupfuls to Friar Sand, who drank them. Everyone then sat down.

[10] When they all had been feasting and drinking for a long time the king raised a large goblet once more and handed it to Monkey. "Please sit down, Your Majesty," Monkey said. "I've been drinking hard in every round. I'd never refuse." "Holy monk," the king said, "we are under a profound debt of gratitude

385

to you that we will never be able to repay. Please drain this great goblet: we have something to say to you." "Say what you will first," Monkey replied, "I'll drink after." "We suffered from that melancholia for years on end," the king said, "and one dose of your miraculous pills cured it." "When I saw Your Majesty yesterday I realized you were suffering from melancholia," Monkey said, "but I don't know what's getting you down."

"There's an old saying that a family doesn't talk about its dirt to strangers," the king replied. "As you are our benefactor, holy monk, we shall tell you, but please don't laugh." "I'd never dare," Monkey said. "Please speak freely." "How many countries did you holy monks come through on your way here from the east?" the king asked. "Five or six," Monkey replied. "What titles do the queens of the other kings have?" the king went on to ask. "They're called the queens of the Main Palace, East Palace and West Palace," Monkey replied. "We don't use titles like that," the king said. "We call the principal queen the Queen of the Sacred Golden Palace, the eastern queen the Queen of the Sacred Jade Palace and the western queen the Queen of the Sacred Silver Palace. But now only the Jade and Silver Queen are here." "Why isn't the Golden Queen in the palace?" Monkey asked. "She has been gone for three whole years," the king replied in tears. "Where did she go?" Monkey asked. "At the Dragon-boat Festival three years ago," the king said, "we were in the Pomegranate Pavilion of the palace gardens with our queens and consorts, unwrapping rice dumplings, putting artemisia out, drinking calamus and realgar wine and watching the dragon boats race when all of a sudden there was a gust of wind. An evil spirit appeared in mid-air. He said he was the Evil Star Matcher who lives in the Horndog Cave on Mount Unicorn and was short of a wife. Seeing how beautiful and charming our Golden Queen is he wanted her for his wife and insisted we should hand her over at once. If we did not do so by the time he had asked three times he was going to eat us up first, then our officials and all the commoners living in the city. We were so concerned over the fate of our country and our people that there was no alternative: the

Golden Queen had to be pushed outside the pavilion to be carried noisily off by the evil spirit. All this gave us such a fright that the rice dumpling we were eating turned solid inside us. On top of that we have been unable to sleep for worrying, which is why we were ill for three years. Since taking you holy monks' miraculous pills we have evacuated our bowels three times, and the accumulations from three years ago have all been passed. That is why our body now feels light and strong and our spirit is restored to what it was. Our life has today been given to us by you holy monks; this is a gift more weighty than Mount Tai."

[11] When Brother Monkey heard this he was very happy indeed and he downed the huge goblet of wine in two gulps. "Your Majesty," he said with a smile to the king, "so that's what caused your shock and your depression. Today you've been lucky: you met me and you were cured. But I don't know whether you want the Golden Queen back in the palace." To this the king answered with tears, "We have been longing for her night and day, but nobody has ever been able to catch the evil spirit. Of course we want her back in our country." "What if I go to deal with that evil creature for you?" said Monkey. The king fell to his knees and replied, "If you can rescue our queen we will gladly take our three queens and nine consorts away from the capital and go to live as commoners, leaving the whole kingdom to be yours to reign over, holy monk." When Pig, who was sitting beside them, heard all this being said and such great honours being done he could not help bursting into noisy laughter. "This king's got no sense of what's proper," he chortled. "Fancy giving up his kingdom and going on his knees to a monk for the sake of his old woman."

Monkey hurried forward to help the king back on his feet and ask, "Your Majesty, has the evil spirit been back since he got the Golden Queen?" "In the fifth month of the year before last," the king said, "he carried off the Golden Queen. In the tenth month he came back to demand a couple of ladies in waiting to serve her, and we presented him with a couple. In the third month of last year he came to demand another couple, and two

387

more in the seventh month. Then in the second month of this year it was a fourth pair. We do not know when he will be back again." "If he comes that often you must be terrified of him," Monkey replied. "Because he has come so frequently we are afraid of him and of his murderous intentions," said the king. "In the fourth month last year we ordered the building of a demon shelter, so that whenever we hear the wind and know that he's coming we can shelter there with our two queens and nine consorts." "Would Your Majesty mind taking me to see the shelter?" Monkey asked, and the king led Monkey by his left hand from the table. All the officials rose to their feet. "Brother," protested Pig, "you're very unreasonable. Why leave this royal wine and break up the banquet to go looking at something?" Hearing this and realizing that Pig was worried for his stomach the king told his attendants to have two tables of vegetarian food brought along so that Pig could go on being wined outside the demon shelter. Only then did the idiot stop making a fuss and join in with his master and Friar Sand saying, "Let's break up the banquet."

[12]　As a column of civil and military officials led the way the king and Monkey went arm-in-arm through the living quarters of the palace to the back of the royal gardens, but there were no great buildings to be seen. "Where's the demon shelter?" Monkey asked, and before the words were out of his mouth two eunuchs levered open a square flagstone with red lacquered crowbars. "Here it is," said the king. "Twenty feet or more below us a large underground palace hall has been excavated. In it there are four great vats of purified oil in which lights burn night and day. When we hear the wind we take shelter here and the flagstone is put on again from outside." "So the evil spirit doesn't want to kill you," said Monkey with a smile. "If he did this would give you no protection." Just as he was speaking there came the roaring of a wind from due south that made the dust fly. In their alarm all the officials complained, "That monk has the mouth of an oracle. The moment he mentions the evil spirit it turns up." The panic-stricken monarch abandoned Monkey and

scuttled into his underground shelter. The Tang Priest went with him, and all the officials fled for cover.

Pig and Friar Sand wanted to hide too, but Monkey grabbed one of them with each hand and said, "Don't be afraid, brothers. You and I are going to identify him and see what sort of evil spirit he is." "Nonsense," said Pig. "What do we want to identify him for? The officials have all hidden and the king's shut himself away. Why don't we clear off? What kind of hero are you trying to be?" But struggle though he might the idiot could not break free. When Monkey had been holding on to him for some time an evil spirit suddenly appeared in mid-air. Just see what it looked like:

A loathsome great body nine feet tall,
Round eyes flashing like lamps of gold.
Two huge ears sticking out as if they were round fans,
Four steel fangs like very long nails.
Red hair curled at his temples; his brows were as flames;
His nose was a hanging trough; his nostrils flared.
His whiskers were strands of cinnabar thread,
And jutting cheekbones shaped his greeny face.
On red-muscled arms were hands of indigo blue,
And ten sharp claws grasped a spear.
A leopardskin kilt was tied round his waist.
Bare feet and tangled hair completed his fiendish looks.

"Friar Sand," asked Monkey when he saw the evil spirit, "can you recognize him?" "I don't know who he is," Friar Sand replied. "I've never seen him before." "Pig," Monkey next asked, "do you know?" "I've never had a cuppa or a drink with him," Pig replied. "He's no friend or neighbour of mine. How could I know?" "He reminds me of the sallow-faced golden-eyed gate-keeper ghost under the Equal of Heaven of the Eastern Peak." "No he isn't, no he isn't," said Pig. "How do you know he isn't?" Monkey asked. "Because ghosts are spirits of the dark and the underworld," Pig replied. "They only come out at night,

389

between five and midnight. It's only ten in the morning, and no ghost would ever dare come out now. And even if it was a devil it'd never ride a cloud. Ghosts that stir up winds make whirlwinds, not gales. Perhaps he's the Evil Star Matcher." "You're not such an idiot after all," said Monkey. "That sounds sensible, so you two look after the master while I go to ask him his name. That'll help me rescue the Golden Queen and bring her back to the palace for the king." "Go if you must," Pig replied, "but don't tell him anything about us." Monkey did not deign to answer, but leapt straight up on his magic light. Goodness!

> To settle the nation he started by curing the king;
> To preserve the Way love and hatred had to go.

If you don't know who won the battle that followed when Monkey rose up into the sky or how the evil monster was captured and the Golden Queen rescued listen to the explanation in the next chapter.

15. 妖魔宝放烟沙火
悟空计盗紫金铃

【1】　却说那孙行者抖擞神威，持着铁棒，踏祥光，起在空中，迎面喝道："你是那里来的邪魔，待往何方猖獗！"那怪物厉声高叫道："吾党不是别人，乃麒麟山獬豸洞赛太岁大王爷爷部下先锋。今奉大王令，到此取宫女二名，伏侍金圣娘娘。你是何人，敢来问我！"行者道："吾乃齐天大圣孙悟空。因保东土唐僧西天拜佛，路过此国，知你这水脏魔欺压，特展雄才，治国祛邪。正没处寻你，却来此送命！"那怪闻言，不知好歹，提长枪就刺行者。行者举铁棒劈面相迎。在半空里这一场好杀：

> 棍是龙宫镇海珍，枪乃人间转炼铁。凡兵怎敢比仙兵，擦着些儿神气泄。大圣原来太乙仙，妖精本是邪魔孽。鬼祟焉能近正人，一正之时邪就灭。那个弄风播土唬皇王，这个踏雾腾云遮日月。丢开架手赌输赢，无能谁敢夸豪杰！还是齐天大圣能，乒乓一棍枪先折。

那妖精被行者一铁棒把根枪打做两截，慌得顾性命，拨转风头，径往西方败走。

【2】　行者且不赶他，按下云头，来到避妖楼地穴之外，叫道："师父，请同陛下出来。怪物已赶去矣。"那唐僧才扶着君王，同出穴外。见满天清朗，更无妖邪之气。那皇帝即至酒席前，自己拿壶把盏，满斟金杯，奉与行者道："神僧，权谢！权谢！"这行者接杯在手，还未回言，只听得朝门外有官来报："西门上火起了！"行者闻说，将金杯连酒望空一撒，当的一声响喨，那金杯落地。君王着了忙，躬身施礼道："神僧，恕罪！恕罪！是寡人不是了！礼当请上殿拜谢，只因有这方便酒在此，故就奉斗。神僧却把杯子撇了，却不是有见怪之意？"行者笑道："不是这话，不是这话。"少倾间，又有官来报："好雨呀！才西门上起火，被一场大雨，把火

391

灭了。满街上流水，尽都是酒气。"行者又笑道："陛下，你见我撒杯，疑有见怪之意，非也。那妖败走西方，我不曾赶他，他就放起火来。这一杯酒，却是我灭了妖火，救了西城里外人家，岂有他意！"

【3】 国王更十分欢喜加敬。即请三藏四众，同上宝殿，就有推位让国之意。行者笑道："陛下，才那妖精，他称是赛太岁部下先锋，来此取宫女的。他如今战败而回，定然报与那厮。那厮定要来与我相争。我恐他一时兴师帅众，未免又惊伤百姓，恐唬陛下。欲去迎他一迎，就在那半空中擒了他，取回圣后。但不知向那方去，这里到他那山洞有多少远近？"国王道："寡人曾差'夜不收'军马到那里探听声息，往来要行五十余日。坐落南方，约有三千余里。"行者闻言，叫："八戒、沙僧，护持在此，老孙去来。"国王扯住道："神僧且从容一日，待安排些干粮烘炒，与你些盘缠银两，凑一匹快马，方才可去。"行者笑道："陛下说得是巴山转岭步行之话。我老孙不瞒你说，似这三千里路，斟酒在锺不冷，就打个往回。"国王道："神僧，你不要怪我说。你这尊貌，却像个猿猴一般，怎生有这等法力会走路也？"行者道：

> "我身虽是猿猴数，自幼打开生死路。
> 遍访明师把道传，山前修炼无朝暮。
> 倚天为顶地为炉，两般药物团乌兔。
> 采取阴阳水火交，时间顿把玄关悟。
> 全仗天罡搬运功，也凭斗柄迁移步。
> 退炉进火最依时，抽铅添汞相交顾。
> 攒簇五行造化生，合和四象分时度。
> 二气归于黄道间，三家会在金丹路。
> 悟通法律归四肢，本来筋斗如神助。
> 一纵纵过太行山，一打打过凌云渡。
> 何愁峻岭几千重，不怕长江百十数。
> 只因变化没遮拦，一打十万八千路！"

那国王见说，又惊又喜，笑吟吟捧着一杯御酒递与行者道："神僧远劳，进此一杯引意。"这大圣一心要去降妖，那里有心吃酒，只叫："且放下，等我去了回来再饮。"好行者，说声去，唿哨一声，寂然不见。那一国君臣，皆惊讶不题。

【4】　却说行者将身一纵，早见一座高山，阻住雾角。即按云头，立在那巅峰之上。仔细观看，好山：

> 冲天占地，碍日生云。冲天处，尖峰叠叠；占地处，远脉迢迢。碍日的，乃岭头郁郁，生云的，乃崖下石磷磷。松郁郁，四时八节常青；石磷磷，万载千年不改。林中每听猿啼，洞内常闻䖡蟒过。山禽声咽咽，山兽吼呼呼。山獐山鹿，成双作对纷纷走；山鸦山鹊，打阵攒群密密飞。山草山花看不尽，山桃山果映时新。虽然倚险不堪行，却是妖仙隐逸处。

这大圣看看不厌，正欲找寻洞口，只见那山凹里烘烘火光飞出，霎时间，扑天红焰，红焰之中冒出一股恶烟，比火更毒。好烟！但见他：

> 火光进万点金灯，火焰飞千条红虹。那烟不是灶筒烟，不是草木烟，烟却有五色：青红白黑黄。熏着南天门外柱，燎着灵霄殿上梁。烧得那窝中走兽连皮烂，林内飞禽羽尽光。但看这烟如此恶，怎入深山伏怪王！

大圣正自惊惧，又见那山中迸出一道沙来。好沙，真个是遮天蔽日！你看：

> 纷纷絯絯遍天涯，邓邓浑浑大地遮。
> 细尘到处迷人目，粗灰满谷滚芝麻。
> 采药仙僮迷失伴，打柴樵子没寻家。
> 手中就有明珠现，时间刮得眼生花。

这行者只顾看玩，不觉沙灰飞入鼻内，痒斯斯的，打了两个喷嚏，即回头伸手，在岩下摸了两个鹅卵石，塞住鼻子；摇身一变，变做一个撞火的鹞子，飞入烟火中间，蓦了几蓦，却就没了沙灰，烟火也息了。急现本像下来。又看时，只听得丁丁东东的，一个铜锣声响。却道："我走错了路也！这里不是妖精住处。锣声似铺兵之锣。想是通国的大路，有铺兵送下文书。且等老孙去问他一问。"

正走处，忽见是个小妖儿，担着黄旗，背着文书，敲着锣儿，急走如飞而来。行者笑道："原来是这厮打锣。他不知送的是甚么书信，等我听他一听。"好大圣，摇身一变，变做个猛虫儿，轻轻的飞在他书包之上。只听得那妖精敲着锣，绪绪聒聒的自念自诵道："我家大王，忒也心毒。三年前到朱紫国强夺了金圣皇后，一向无缘，未得沾身，只苦了要来的宫女顶缸。两个来弄杀了，四个来也弄杀了。前年要了，去年又要，今年又要；今年还要，却撞个对头来了。那个要宫女的先锋被个甚么孙行者打败了，不发宫女。我大王因此发怒，要与他国争持，教我下甚么战书。这一去，那国王不战则可，战必不利。我大王使烟火飞沙，那国王君臣百姓等，莫想一个得活。那时我等占了他的城池，大王称帝，我等称臣，——虽然也有个大小官爵，只是天理难容也!"

【5】　行者听了，暗喜道："妖精也有存心好的。似恁后边这两句话说，'天理难容'，却不是个好的？——但只说金圣皇后一向无缘，未得沾身，此话却不解其意。等我问他一问。"嘤的一声，一翅飞离了妖精，转向前路，有十数里地，摇身一变，又变做一个道童：

头戴双抓髻，身穿百衲衣。

手敲鱼鼓简，口唱道情词。

转山坡，迎着小妖，打个起手道："长官，那里去？送的是甚么公文？"那妖物就像认得他的一般。住了锣槌，笑嘻嘻的还礼道："我大王差我到朱紫国下战书的。"行者接口问道："朱紫国那话儿，可曾与大王配合哩？"小妖道："自前年摄将来，当时就有了一个神仙，送一件五彩仙衣与金圣皇牧新。他自穿了那衣，就浑身上下都生了针刺，我大王摸也不敢摸他一摸。但挽着些儿，手心就痛，不知是甚缘故。自始至今，尚未沾身。早间差先锋去要宫女伏侍，被一个甚么孙行者战败了。大王奋怒，所以教我下战书，明日与他交战也。"行者道："怎的大王却着恼呵？"小妖道："正在那里着恼哩。你去与他唱个道情词儿解解闷也好。"

那行者拱手抽身就走。那妖依旧敲锣前行。行者就作起凶来，掣出棒，复转身，望小妖脑后一下，可怜就打得头烂血流浆进出，皮开颈折命倾之！收了棍子，却又自悔道："急了些儿！不曾问他叫做甚么名字，——罢了！"却去取下他的战书，藏于袖内；将他黄旗、铜锣，藏在路旁草里；因扯着脚要往涧下掷时，只听当的一声，腰间露出一个镶金的牙牌。牌上有字，写道：

　　"心腹小校一名，有来有去。五短身材，挖挞脸，无须。长川悬挂，无牌即假。"

行者笑道："这厮名字叫做有来有去，这一棍子，打得'有去无来'也！"将牙牌解下，带在腰间，欲要捽下尸骸；却又思量起烟火之毒，且不敢寻他洞府，即将棍子举起，着小妖脑前捣了一下，挑在空中，径回本国，且当报一个头功。你看他自思自念，嗯哨一声，到了国界。

【6】　那八戒在金銮殿前，正护持着王、师，忽回头看见行者半空中将个妖精挑来，他却怨道："嗳！不打紧的买卖！早知老猪去拿来，却不算我一功？"说未毕，行者按落云头，将妖精捽在阶下。八戒跑上去，就筑了一钯道："此是老猪之功！"行者道："是你甚功？"八戒道："莫赖我！我有证见！你不看一钯筑了九个眼子哩！"行者道："你看看可有头没头。"八戒道："原来有没头的！我道如何筑他也不动动儿。"行者道："师父在那里？"八戒道："在殿里与王叙话哩。"行者道："你且请他出来。"八戒急上殿，点点头。三藏即便起身下殿，迎着行者。行者将一封战书，揣在三藏袖里道："师父收下，且莫与国王看见。"

　　说不了，那国王也下殿，迎着行者道："神僧孙长老来了！拿妖之事如何？"行者用手指道："那阶下不是妖精，被老孙打杀了也？"国王道："是便是个妖尸，却不是赛太岁。赛太岁寡人亲见他两次：身长丈八，膊阔五停；面似金光，声如霹雳；那里是这般郎矮。"行者笑道："陛下认得。果然不是。这是一个报事的小妖，撞见老孙，却先打死，挑回来报功。"国王大喜道："好！好！好！该算头功！寡人这里常差人去打探，更不曾得个的实。似神僧一出，就捉了一个回来，真神通也！"叫："看暖酒来！与长老贺功。"

　　行者道："吃酒还是小事。我问陛下，金圣宫别时，可曾留下个甚么表记？你与我些儿。"那国王听说"表记"二字，却似刀剑剜心，忍不住失声泪下，说道：

　　"当年佳节庆朱明，太岁凶妖发喊声。
　　强夺御妻为压寨，寡人献出为苍生。

更无会话并离话，那有长亭共短亭！
表记香囊全没影，至今撇我苦伶仃！"

行者道："陛下在迩，何以为恼？那娘娘既无表记，他在宫内，可有甚么心爱之物，与我一件也罢。"国王道："你要怎的？"行者道："那妖王实有神通。我见他放烟、放火、放沙，果是难收。纵收了，又恐娘娘见我面生，不肯跟我回国。须是得他平日心爱之物一件，他方信我，我好带他回来。为此故要带去。"田王道："昭阳宫里，梳妆阁上，有一双黄金宝串，原是金圣宫手上带的。只因那日端午，要缚五色彩线，故此褪下，不曾带上。此乃是他心爱之物。如今现收在减妆盒里。寡人见他遭此离别，更不忍见，一见即如见他玉容，病又重几分也。"行者道："且休题这话。且将金串取来。如舍得，都与我拿去；如不舍，只拿一只去也。"国王遂命玉圣宫取出。取出即递与国王。国王见了，叫了几声"知疼着热的娘娘"，遂递与行者。行者接了，套在胳膊上。

【7】 好大圣，不吃得功酒，且驾筋斗云，唿哨一声，又至麒麟山上。无心玩景，径寻洞府而去。正行时，只听得人语喧嚷，即伫立凝睛观看。原来那獬豸洞口把门的大小头目，约摸有五百名，在那里：

森森罗列，密密挨排。森森罗列执干戈，映日光明；密密挨排展旌旗，迎风飘闪。虎将熊师能变化，豹头彪帅弄精神。苍狼多猛烈，獭象更骁雄。狡兔乖獐轮剑戟，长蛇大蟒挎刀弓。猩猩能解人言语，引阵安营识汛风。

行者见了，不敢前进，抽身径转旧路。你道他抽身怎么？不是怕他。他却ží那打死小妖之处，又想黄旗、铜锣，即风捏讲，想拿腾那，即摇身一变，变做那有来有去的模样，乒乓敲着锣，大踏步向前，一直前来，径撞至獬豸洞。正欲看看洞景，只闻得猩猩出语道："有来有去，你回来了？"行者只得答应道："来了。"猩猩道："快走！大王爷爷正在剥皮亭上等你回话哩。"行者闻言，拽开步，敲着锣，径入前门里看处，原来是悬崖削壁石屋虚堂，左右有琪花瑶草，前后多古柏乔松。不觉又至二门之内，忽抬头见一座八窗明亮的亭子，亭子中间有一张钹金的交椅，椅子上端坐着一个魔王，真个生得恶像。但见他：

幌幌霞光生顶上，威威杀气迸胸前。

口外獠牙排利刃，鬓边焦发放红烟。

嘴上髭须如插箭，遍体昂毛似迭毡。

眼突铜铃欺太岁，手持铁杵若摩天。

行者见了，公然傲慢那妖精，更不循一些儿礼法。调转脸，朝着外，只管敲锣。妖王问道："你来了？"行者不答。又问："有来有去，你来了？"也不答应。妖王上前扯住道："你怎么到了家还筛锣？问之又不答，何也？"行者把锣往地下一掼道："甚么'何也，何也'！我说我不去，你却教我去。行到那厢，只见无数的人马列成阵势，见了我，就都叫：'拿妖精！拿妖精！'把我揪揪扯扯，拽拽扛扛，拿进城去，见了那国王，国王便教'斩了'，幸亏那两班谋士道：'两家相争，不斩来使。'把我饶了。收了战书，又押出城外，对车前打了三十顺腿，放我来回话。他那里不久就要来此与你交战哩。"妖王道："这等说，是你吃亏了。怪不道问你要不言语。"行者道："却不是怎的？只为护疼，所以不曾答应。"妖王道："那里有多少人马？"行者道："我也唬昏了，又吃他打怕了，那里曾查他人马数目！只见那里森森兵器摆列着：

弓箭刀枪甲与衣，干戈剑戟并缨旗。剽枪月铲兜鍪铠，大斧团牌铁蒺藜。长闷棍，短窝槌，钢叉铣铇及头盔。打扮得鞋鞋护顶并胖袄，简鞭袖弹与锤锤。

那王听了笑道："不打紧！不打紧！似这般兵器，一火皆空。你且去报与金圣娘娘得知，教他莫恼。今早他听见我发狠，要去战斗，他就眼泪汪汪的不干。你如今去说那里人马骁勇，必然胜我，且宽他一时之心。"

【8】　行者闻言，十分欢喜道："正中老孙之意！"你看他偏是路熟，转过角门，穿过厅堂。那里边尽是高堂大厦，更不似前边的模样。直到后面宫里，远见彩门壮丽，乃是金圣娘娘住处。直入里面看时，有两班妖狐、妖鹿，一个个都妆成美女之形，侍立左右。正中间坐着那个娘娘，手托着香腮，双眸滴泪，果然是：

玉容娇嫩，美貌妖娆。懒梳妆，散鬓堆鸦；怕打扮，钗环不戴。面无粉，冷淡了胭脂；发无油，蓬松了云鬓。努樱唇，紧咬银牙；皱蛾眉，泪淹星眼。一片心，只忆着朱紫君王；

一时间，恨不离天罗地网。诚然是：自古红颜多薄命，恹恹无语对东风！

行者上前打了个问讯道："接喑？"那娘娘道："这泼村怪，十分无状！想我在那朱紫国中，与王同享荣华之时，那太师宰相见了，就俯伏尘埃，不敢仰视。这野怪怎么叫声'接喑'？是那里来的这般村泼？"众侍婢上前道："太太息怒。他是大王爷爷心腹的小校，唤名有来有去。今早差下战书的是他。"娘娘听说，忍怒问曰："你下战书，可曾到朱紫国界？"行者道："我持书直至城里，到于金銮殿，面见君王，已讨回音来也。"娘娘道："你面君，君有何言？"行者道："那君王敌战之言，与排兵布阵之事，才与大王言了。只是那君王有思想娘娘之意，有一句合心的话儿，特来上禀。奈何左右人众，不是说处。"

娘娘闻言，喝退两班狐鹿。行者掩上宫门，把脸一抹，现了本像。对娘娘道："你休怕我。我是东土大唐差往大西天天竺国雷音寺见佛求经的和尚。我师父是唐王御弟唐三藏。我是他大徒弟孙悟空。因过你国倒换关文，见你君臣出榜招医，是我大施三折之肱，把他相思之病治好了。排宴谢我，饮酒之间，说出他被妖摄来，我会降龙伏虎，特请我来捉怪，救你回国。那战败先锋是我，打死小妖也是我。我见他们外凶狂，是我变做有来有去模样，舍身到此，与你通信？"那娘娘听说，沉吟不语。行者取出宝串，双手奉上道："你若不信，看此物何来。"娘娘一见垂泪。下座拜谢道："长老，你果是救得我回朝，没齿不忘大恩！"

行者道："我且问你，他那放火，放烟，放沙的，是件甚么宝贝？"娘娘道："那里是甚宝贝！乃是三个金铃。他将头一个幌一幌，有三百丈火光烧人；第二个幌一幌，有三百丈烟光熏人；第三个幌一幌，有三百丈黄沙迷人。烟火还不打紧，只是黄沙最毒。若钻入人鼻孔，就伤了性命。"行者道："利害！利害！我曾经着，打了两个喷嚏，却不知他的铃儿放在何处？"娘娘道："他那肯放下，只是带在腰间，行住坐卧，再不离身。"行者道："你若有意于朱紫国，还要相会国王，把那烦恼忧愁，都且权解，使出个风流喜悦之容，与他叙个夫妻之情，教他把铃儿与你收贮。待我取便偷了，降了这妖怪，那时节，好带你回去，重谐鸾凤，共享安宁也。"

那娘娘依言。

【9】　这行者还变做心腹小校，开了宫门，唤进左右侍婢。娘娘叫："有来有去，快往前亭，请你大王来，与他说话。"好行者，应了一声，即至剥皮亭，对妖精道："大王，圣宫娘娘有请。"妖王欢喜道："娘娘常时只骂，怎么今日有请？"行者道："那娘娘向朱紫国王之事，是我说：'他不要你了，他国中另扶了皇后。'娘娘听说，故此没了想头，方才命我来奉请。"妖王大喜道："你却中用。待我剿除了他国，封你为个随朝的太宰。"

　　行者顺口谢恩，疾与妖王来至后宫门首。那娘娘欢embracedb迎接，就去用手相搀。那妖王嗒嗒而退道："不敢！不敢！多承娘娘下爱，我怕手痛，不敢相傍。"娘娘道："大王请坐，我与你说。"妖王道："有话但说不妨。"娘娘道："我蒙大王厚爱，今已三年，未得共枕同衾。也是前世之缘，做了这场夫妻；谁知大王原来是个真男子，不以夫妻相待。我想着当时在朱紫国为后，外邦凡有进贡之宝，君拿毕，一定与后收之。你这里更无甚么宝贝，左右穿的是貂裘，吃的是血食，那曾见绫锦金珠！只一味铺皮盖毯。或者就有些宝贝，你因外我，也不教我看见，也不与我收着。且如闻得你有三个铃铛，想就是件宝贝，你怎么走也带着，坐也带着？你就拿了去放，待你用时取出，未为不可。此也是做夫妻一场，也有个心腹相托之意。——如此不相托付，非外我而何？"妖王大笑赔礼道："娘娘怪得是！怪得是！宝贝在此，我就当付你收之。"便即揭衣取宝。行者在旁，眼不转睛，看着那怪揭起两三层衣服，贴身带着三个铃儿。他解下来，将些绵花塞了口儿，把一块豹皮做一个包袱儿包了，递与娘娘道："物虽微贱，却要用心收藏，切不可摇幌着他。"娘娘接过手道："我晓得。安在这妆台之上，无人摇动。"叫："小的们，安排酒来，我与大王交欢会喜，饮几杯儿。"众侍婢闻言，即铺排果菜，摆上些獐犯鹿兔之肉，将椰子酒斟来奉上。那娘娘做出妖娆之态，哄着精灵。

【10】　孙行者在旁取事，但挨挨摸摸，行近妆台，把三个金铃轻轻拿过，慢慢移步，溜出宫门，径离洞府。到了剥皮亭前，无人处，展开豹皮幅子看时，中间一个，有茶锺大；两头两个，有拳头大。他不知利害，就把绵花扯了。只闻得当的一声响晬，骨都都

的进出烟火黄沙,急收不住,满亭中烘烘火起。唬得那把门精怪,一拥撞入后宫,惊动了妖王,慌忙教:"去救火!救火!"出来看时,原来是有来有去拿了金铃儿哩。妖王上前喝道:"好贱奴!怎么偷了我的金铃宝贝,在此胡弄!"叫:"拿来!拿来!"那厮前虎将、熊师、豹头、彪帅、獭婆、苍狼、乖獐、狡兔、长蛇、大蟒、猩猩,帅众妖一齐攒簇。

那行者慌了手脚,丢了金铃,现出本像。掣出金箍如意棒,撒开解数,往前乱打。那妖王收了宝贝,传号令,教:"关了前门!"众妖听了,关门的关门,打仗的打仗。那行者难得脱身,收了棒,摇身一变,变做个痴苍蝇儿,钉在那火处石壁上。众妖寻不见。报道:"大王,走了贼也!走了贼也!"妖王问:"可曾自门里走出去?"众妖都说:"前门紧锁牢拴在此,不曾走出。"妖王只说:"仔细搜寻!"有的取水泼火,有的仔细搜寻,更无踪迹。妖王怒道:"是个甚么贼子,好大胆,变做有来有去的模样,进来见我回话,又跟在身边,乘机盗我宝贝!早是不曾拿将出去!若拿出山头,见了天风,怎生是好?"虎将上前道:"大王的洪福齐天,我等的气数不尽,故此知觉了。"熊师上前道:"大王,这贼不是别人,定是那战败先锋的那个孙悟空。想必路上遇着有来有去,伤了性命,夺了黄旗、铜锣、牙牌,变做他的模样,到此欺骗了大王也。"妖王道:"正是!正是!见得有理!"叫:"小的们,仔细搜求防避,切莫开门放出走了!"这才是个有分教:弄巧翻成拙,作耍却为真。毕竟不知孙行者怎么脱得妖门,且听下回分解。

Chapter 15
The Evil Monster's Treasures Emit Smoke,
Sand and Fire;
Wukong Steals the Golden
Bells by Trickery

[1]   The story tells how Brother Monkey summoned up his
divine prestige and rose up into the air on his magic light,
wielding his iron cudgel. "Where are you from, evil monster?" he
asked, shouting in the evil spirit's face. "And where are you
going to wreak havoc?" "I'm the vanguard warrior under the
Great King Evil Star Matcher from Horndog Cave on Mount
Unicorn," shouted the demon at the top of his voice, "that's who
I am. His Majesty has ordered me to fetch two ladies-in-waiting
to serve Her Majesty the Golden Queen. Who are you and how
dare you question me?" "I'm Sun Wukong, the Great Sage
Equalling Heaven," Monkey replied. "I was passing through this
country while escorting the Tang Priest to worship the Buddha in
the Western Heaven. Now I know that your gang of monsters
was oppressing the king I'm going to use my heroic powers to
bring the country back to order and wipe out this evil. And now
you've come along to throw your life away just when I didn't
know where to find you." When the monster heard this he
foolishly thrust his spear at Monkey, who struck back at his face
with the iron cudgel. they fought a splendid battle up in mid-air:

The cudgel was the sea-settler from the dragon's palace;
The spear was of iron tempered by mankind.
An ordinary weapon was no match for that of an
immortal;
In a few clashes its magic powers all drained away.
The Great Sage was an immortal of the Supreme
Ultimate;

The spirit was only an evil monster.
How could a demon approach a True One?
In the face of truth the evil would be destroyed.
One stirred up wind and dust to terrify a king;
The other trod on mist and cloud to blot out sun and moon.
When they dropped their guard to try for victory
Neither of them dared to show off.
The Heaven-equalling Great Sage was the abler fighter:
With a loud clash of his cudgel the spear was broken.

When his spear was quickly broken in two by Monkey's iron cudgel the evil spirit was in fear for his life, so he turned the wind right round and fled westwards.

[2] Instead of chasing him Monkey brought his cloud down to the entrance of the underground demon shelter. "Master," he called, "you and His Majesty can come out now. The monster's run away." Only then did the Tang Priest come out of the underground shelter, supporting the king. The sky was clear, and all traces of the evil spirit had disappeared. The king went over to the table, filled a golden goblet from the wine bottle with his own hands, and presented it to Monkey with the words, "Holy monk, allow us to offer our provisional thanks." Monkey took the cup, but before he could reply an official came in from outside the western gate of the palace to report, "The western gate is on fire."

As soon as he heard this Monkey threw the wine, cup and all, up into the air. The cup fell with a clang. This so alarmed the king that he bowed to Monkey with the words, "Forgive us, holy monk, forgive us. We have treated you shabbily. The proper thing would have been to ask you to the throne hall to bow to you in thanks. We only offered you the wine here because it was to hand. Did you not throw the goblet aside because you were offended, holy monk?" "Nothing of the sort," laughed Monkey, "nothing of the sort." A moment later another official came in to report, "There's been a miraculous fall of rain. No sooner had the western gate caught fire than a heavy rainstorm put it out. The streets are running with water and it all smells of wine." "Your Majesty," said Monkey with another smile, "you thought I'd taken offence when I tossed the cup aside, but you were wrong. When the evil spirit fled westwards I didn't go after him, so he started that fire. I just used the goblet to put out the demon's fire and save the people outside the western gate. It didn't mean anything else."

[3]   The king, even more delighted than before, treated Monkey with still greater respect. He invited Sanzang and his three disciples to enter the throne hall with him, clearly intending to abdicate in their favour. "Your Majesty," said Brother Monkey with a smile, "the demon who was here just now said he was a vanguard warrior under the Evil Star Matcher who'd come here to fetch palace girls. Now he's gone back beaten he's bound to report that damned monster, who's certain to come here fight me. I'm worried that if he comes here at the head of his hordes he'll alarm the common people and terrify Your Majesty. I'd like to go out to meet him, capture him in mid-air and bring back your queen. But I don't know the way. How far is it to his cave from here?" "We once sent some of the horsemen and infantry of our night scouts to find out what was happening," the king replied. "The return journey took them over fifty days. It's over a thousand miles away to the south." "Pig, Friar Sand," said Monkey on learning this, "stay on guard here. I'm off." "Wait another day, holy monk," said the king, grabbing hold of him. "Don't go till we have had some dried provisions prepared for you. We'll give you silver for the journey and a fast horse too." "You're talking as if I'd have to go slogging up mountains and over ridges, Your Majesty," Monkey replied. "I tell you truthfully that I can do the return journey of a thousand miles each way before a cup of wine you've poured out has had time to get cold." "Holy monk," the king replied, "I hope you won't take offence at our saying this, but your distinguished features are very much like those of an ape. How can you have such magical powers of travel?" To this Monkey replied:

403

"Although my body is the body of an ape,
When young I mastered the paths of life and death.
I visited all the great teachers who taught me their Way
And trained myself by night and day beside the mountain.
I took heaven as my roof and the earth as my furnace
And used both kinds of drug to complete the sun and moon,
Taking from positive and negative, joining fire and water,
Until suddenly I was aware of the Mystic Pass.
I relied entirely on the Dipper for success in my movements,
Shifting my steps by relying on the handle of that constellation.
When the time is right I lower or increase the heat,
Taking out lead and adding mercury, watching them both.
By grouping the Five Elements transformations are made;
Through combining the Four Forms the seasons can be distinguished.
The two vital forces returned to the zodiac;
The three teachings met on the golden elixir road.
When understanding of the laws came to the four limbs
The original somersault was given divine assistance.
With a single bound I could cross the Taihang mountains;
At one go I could fly across the Cloud-touching Ford.
A thousand steep ridges are no bother to me,
Nor hundreds of rivers as great as the Yangtse.
Because my transformations are impossible to stop
I can cover sixty thousand miles in a single leap."

The king was both alarmed and delighted to hear this. He presented a cup of royal wine to Monkey with a chuckle and the words, "Holy monk, you have a long and tiring journey ahead of you. Won't you drink this wine to help you on your way?" All the Great Sage had on his mind was going off to defeat the demon, he was not at all interested in drinking. "Put it down," he said. "I'll drink it when I come back." No sooner had the

splendid Monkey said this than he disappeared with a whoosh.
We will not describe the amazement of the king and his subjects.
[4] Instead we tell how with a single leap Monkey was soon in
sight of a tall mountain locked in mists. He brought his cloud
down till he was standing on the summit. When he looked around
he saw that it was a fine mountain:

> *Soaring to the heavens, occupying the earth,*
> *Blocking out the sun and making clouds.*
> *Where it soared to the heavens*
> *The towering peak rose high;*
> *In the earth it occupied*
> *Its ranges spread afar.*
> *What blocked the sun*
> *Was the ridge dark with pines;*
> *Where clouds were made*
> *Was among the boulders glistening underneath the scar.*
> *The dark pines*
> *Were green throughout all seasons;*
> *The glistening boulders*
> *Would never change in many a thousand years.*
> *Apes could often be heard howling in the night,*
> *And evil pythons would often cross the deep ravines.*
> *On the mountains birds sang sweetly*
> *While the wild beasts roared.*
> *Mountain roebuck and deer*
> *Moved around in many a pair.*
> *Mountain magpies and crows*
> *Flew in dense flocks.*
> *There was no end of mountain flowers in sight,*
> *While mountain peaches and other fruit gleamed in season.*
> *Steep it was, and the going impossible,*
> *But this was still a place where evil immortals could live in*
> retirement.

The Great Sage gazed with unbounded delight and was just

about to look for the entrance to the cave when flames leapt out from a mountain hollow. In an instant the red fire blazed to the heavens, and from the flames there poured out evil smoke that was even more terrible than the fire. What splendid smoke! This is what could be seen:

> *The fire glared with a myriad golden lamps;*
> *The flames leapt in a thousand crimson rainbows.*
> *The smoke was not a stove chimney's smoke,*
> *Nor the smoke of grass or wood,*
> *But smoke of many colours,*
> *Blue, red, white, black and yellow.*
> *It blackened the columns outside the Southern Gate of Heaven,*
> *Scorched the roofbeams in the Hall of Miraculous Mist.*
> *It burned so hard that*
> *Wild beasts in their dens were cooked through, skins and all,*
> *And the forest birds lost all their plumage.*
> *At the mere sight of this appalling smoke he wondered*
> *How the demon king could be captured in the mountain.*

Just as the Great Sage was transfixed with terror a sandstorm burst out of the mountain. What magnificent sand! It blotted out the sun and the sky. Look:

> *Swirling masses of it filled the sky,*
> *Dark and turbid as it covered the earth.*
> *The fine grains blinded the people everywhere,*
> *While bigger cinders filled the valleys like rolling sesame seeds.*
> *Immortal boys collecting herbs lost their companions;*
> *Woodmen gathering firewood could not find their way home.*
> *Even if you were holding a bright-shining pearl*
> *It still would have blown too hard for you to see.*

Monkey had been so absorbed in enjoying the view that he did not notice the sand and cinders flying into his nose till it started tickling. Giving two great sneezes he stretched his hand out behind him, felt for two pebbles at the foot of a cliff and blocked his nostrils with them, then shook himself and turned into a fire-grabbing sparrowhawk that flew straight in among the flames and smoke, made a few swoops, and at once stopped the sand and cinders and put out the fires. He quickly turned back into himself, landed, and looked around again. This time he hear a banging and a clanging like a copper gong. "I've come the wrong way," he said to himself. "This is no den of demons. The gong sounds like an official messenger's gong. This must be the main road to some country, and that must be an official messenger on his way to deliver some document. I'll go and question him."

As Monkey went along what looked like a young demon appeared. He was holding a yellow flag, carrying a document on his back and beating a gong as he hurried along so fast he was almost flying. "So this is the so-and-so who was beating that gong," Monkey said. "I wonder what document he's delivering. I'll ask him." The splendid Great Sage shook himself and turned into a grasshopper that lightly flew over and alighted on his document bag. Here Monkey could hear the evil spirit talking garrulously to himself as he beat the gong. "Our king is thoroughly vicious. Three years ago he took the Golden Queen from the Kingdom of Purporia, but fate's been against him and he hasn't been able to get his hands on her. The poor palace ladies he took had to suffer on her behalf. He killed two of them who came, then the next four. He demanded them the year before last, last year and earlier this year. When he sent for two more this time he found his match. The vanguard warrior who went to demand the palace ladies was beaten by someone called Sun the Novice or whatever. He didn't get his palace girls. It made our king so angry he wants to wage a war on Purpuria. He's sent me with this declaration of war. Their king will be all right if he doesn't fight, but if he does fight it'll be a disaster for him. When our king uses his fire, smoke and sandstorms their king, ministers

407

and common people will all die. Then we'll take over their city. Our king will be its monarch and we'll be his subjects. But even though we'll get official posts it goes against Heaven."

【5】 Monkey was very pleased to hear this. "So there are even some decent evil spirits," he thought. "That last remark — 'it goes against Heaven' — was very good. I wonder what he meant when he said that fate has been against their king and he hasn't been able to get his hands on the Golden Queen. Let me ask him some questions." With a whining buzz he flew away from the evil spirit to a point some miles ahead of him on the road, shook himself and turned into a Taoist boy:

> He wore his hair in two bunches
> And a robe of a hundred patches.
> He beat on a fisherman's drum
> As he sang some Taoist snatches.

As Monkey came round the slope towards the little devil he raised his hands in greeting and said, "Where are you going, sir? What official document is that you're delivering?" The devil seemed to recognize him as he stopped beating his gong, returned his greeting and said with a titter, "Our king's sent me to Purpuria with a declaration of war." "Has that woman from Purpuria slept with the king yet?" Monkey asked, pressing on with his questioning. "When he brought her here the other year," the little devil replied, "an immortal gave the Golden Queen a magic robe as her wedding dress. As soon as she put it on she was covered from head to foot with spikes. Our king didn't dare so much as caress her. Even the slightest touch makes his hand hurt. I don't know why it happened. So from that year till this he hasn't had her. When his vanguard fighter was sent this morning to demand two more palace ladies to serve her he was beaten. Our king was so angry he sent me with this declaration of war. He's going to fight him tomorrow." "So is the king in a bad mood?" Monkey asked. "Yes, he's in a bad mood back there," said the little devil. "You ought to go and sing him some Taoist songs to cheer him up."

The splendid Monkey put his arms in his sleeves, ready to go, while the evil spirit went on his way beating his gone as before. Monkey then turned murderous. He brought out his cudgel, turned round and hit the little devil on the back of his head. The unfortunate demon's head was smashed to a pulp. The blood gushed out as his skin split open and his neck was broken. He was dead. Monkey then put his cudgel away and said to himself with regret, "I was in too much of a hurry. I never asked him his name. Too bad." He took the declaration of war from the body and put it in his sleeve. Then he hid the yellow flag and the gong in the undergrowth by the path and was dragging the body by its ankles to throw it down the ravine when he heard something clinking. An ivory tablet inlaid with gold could be seen at the demon's waist. The writing on it read:

> This is our trusted subordinate Gocome. He is of short stature and has a spotty and unbearded face. This tablet is to be kept permanently at his waist. Anyone without this tablet is an impostor.

"So the wretch was called Gocome. But after being hit by this cudgel of mine he's gone and won't be coming back." He then undid the ivory tablet, fastened it at his own waist, and was just about to throw the body down when he remembered the terrible fire and smoke and decided he could not bring himself to look for the cave palace. He raised the cudgel, rammed it into the demon's chest, lifted him up into the air and went straight back to Purpuria to announce his first success. Watch him as he goes whistling back to that country.

[6] Pig was in front of the throne room guarding the king and his master when suddenly he turned round to see Monkey carrying the demon through the air. "Hey," he complained, "that was an easy piece of work. If I'd known you were going to get him I'd have done it and got the credit." Before he had finished speaking Monkey brought the cloud down and threw the demon at the foot

409

of the steps. Pig ran over and struck the body with his rake. "I'll take the credit for that," he said. "You? The credit?" Monkey replied. "Don't try to rob me of it," Pig said. "I've got proof. Can't you see the nine holes I made in him with my rake?" "See if he's got a head," said Monkey. "So he doesn't have a head," Pig replied. "Now I know why he never moved when I hit him." "Where's the master?" Monkey asked. "Talking to the king in the throne hall," said Pig. "Go and ask him to come out," said Monkey, and Pig hurried up into the hall. At pig's nod Sanzang rose to his feet and came out at once to see Monkey, who thrust the declaration of war into his sleeve with the words, "Look after this, Master, and don't let the king see it."

Before the words were all out of his mouth the king too came out of the hall to greet Monkey and say, "You're back, holy monk, venerable sir. How did the capture of the demon go?" "Isn't that a demon at the foot of the steps?" Monkey asked, pointing. "I killed him." "True," said the king, "it is the body of an evil spirit, but it isn't the Evil Star Matcher. We have twice seen the Evil Star Matcher with our own eyes. He is eighteen feet tall and nine feet across the shoulders. His face shines like gold and his voice is like thunder. He's not a miserable little wretch like that." "You Majesty is right," Monkey replied, "this isn't him. It's just a little messenger devil happened to meet. I killed him and brought him back as a trophy." "Splendid," said the king, who was very pleased indeed, "splendid. This is the first success. We have often sent people out to find out what is happening but they never discover anything. Then you just have to go out, holy monk, to bring one straight back. You really do have divine powers." "Fetch some warm wine," he ordered, "and give it to the reverend gentlemen."

"Never mind about the wine," said Monkey. "I want to ask Your Majesty whether the Golden Queen left any keepsakes when she went. If so, give me some." The word "keepsakes" cut the king to the heart. He could not help sobbing aloud with tears pouring down as he replied:

"When we were enjoying the festival that year
The Evil Star Matcher gave a mighty shout,
He took our wife to be his bandit queen;
To save the land we had to send her out.
We had no time for talk or parting words,
Nor could I see her off along her way.
She left no keepsake and no perfume bag;
We would be lonely here until today. "

"Your Majesty is here," Monkey said, "so why upset yourself? If the queen didn't leave any keepsake there must be some things in the palace that she's specially fond of. Give me one of them."
"What do you want it for?" the king asked. "That demon king's magic powers are quite something," said Monkey, "and from what I've seen of his fire, smoke and sand he'll be really hard to capture. Even if I do capture him the queen might refuse to come back here with a stranger like me. I must have some favourite thing of hers so that she'll trust me and let me bring her back. That's why I want it." "There is a pair of gold bracelets in her dressing room in the Sunlight Palace that she used to wear," the king replied. "She only took them off that day as it was the Dragonboat Festival and she was going to wear multicoloured threads instead. She was very fond of those bracelets. They have been put away in her dressing table. We have not been able to bear the sight of them since she left us: seeing them is like seeing her lovely face, and it makes us feel even more ill than ever."
"Say no more," Monkey replied, "and have the bracelets brought here. If you can bring yourself to part with them, give me both. If you can't I'll take just one." The king ordered the Jade Queen to fetch them, which she did, handing them to the king. At the sight of them he called out, "My beloved and tender-hearted queen," several times, then handed them to Monkey, who took them and put them on his arm.

【7】 The splendid Great Sage could not stay to drink the celebratory wine, but whistled back to Mount Unicorn on his somersault cloud. Now he had no interest in the view as he

411

headed straight for the cave palace. While he was walking along he heard noisy shouts so he stopped to take a careful look around. About five hundred of the soldiers of all ranks guarding the entrance to Horndog Cave were

> Drawn up in massed array.
> In close order.
> Drawn up in massed array they held their weapons
> Gleaming in the sun.
> In close order they unfurled their banners
> That fluttered in the breeze.
> Tiger and bear generals did transformations;
> Leopard and tiger-cat marshals were full of spirit.
> Fiercely savage were the wolves;
> The elephants were mighty and imposing.
> Crafty hares and water-deer swung sword and halberd;
> Great snakes and pythons carried cutlass and bow.
> Orang-utans that understood human speech
> Controlled the formations and gathered intelligence.

When Monkey saw this he ventured no closer but went straight back the way he had come. Do you know why? Not because he was afraid of them. He went back to where he had killed the little devil, recovered the yellow flag and the gong, made a hand spell, thought of what he wanted to become, faced the wind, shook himself and turned into the likeness of Gocome. Then he started hitting the gong as he strode straight back towards Horndog Cave. He was going to look at the layout of the cave when he heard an orang-utan say; "You're back, Gocome." "Yes," Monkey had a reply. "Hurry up," the orang-utan said. "Our king is waiting in the Flaying Pavilion to hear what you have to report." As soon as he heard this Monkey hurried straight in through the main gate beating his gong and looking around. He saw that rooms and halls had been carved out of the beetling crag. On either side bloomed rare and precious flowers, while all around stood ancient cypressed and tall pines. Before he realized it he was through the inner gate, and suddenly looking up he saw a pavilion made light by the eight windows in it. In the pavilion was a splendid chair inlaid with gold on which a demon king was sitting upright. He was a truly terrifying sight. This is what he looked like:

A shimmering red glow rose from the top of his head;
A mighty and murderous air burst from his chest.
Sharp were the fangs that protruded from his mouth;
Red smoke rose from the scorched hair at his temples.
The bristles of his moustache were like embedded arrows;
His body was covered with hair like brushed-up felt.
Eyes bulged like bells to rival the Evil Star:
Hands held an iron mace like Mahadeva.

When Monkey saw the evil spirit he acted towards him in an offhand way, showing no trace of respect, but looking away and keeping on hitting his gong. "So you're back, are you?" said the demon king. Monkey did not reply. "Gocome," the demon king asked again, "you're back, are you?" Still Monkey did not reply. The demon king then went over to him, grabbed him and said, "Why are you still beating your gong now you're back home? And why don't you answer when I ask you a question?"

"What do you mean by your 'Why? Why? Why?'" Monkey replied. "I told you I didn't want to go but you insisted. When I got there I saw huge numbers of foot soldiers and cavalry drawn up in order of battle. As soon as I was spotted they shouted, 'Seize the demon! Seize the demon!' They pushed and shoved and dragged and carried me into the city, where I saw their king. He told them to cut my head off, but luckily his two groups of advisers said that in international conflicts envoys should not be executed, so I was spared. They took the declaration of war, marched me out of the city, gave me thirty strokes in front of their army, and let me come back here to report. Before long they'll be here to fight you." "In other words," the monster said, "you had a bad time. I don't blame you for refusing to

413

answer when I asked you those questions." "It wasn't that," said Monkey. "The reason I didn't answer was because of the pain." "How strong are their forces?" the demon king asked. "I was reeling from shock and too badly frightened by the beating to be able to count them," Monkey replied. "All I could see were masses of weapons drawn up there:

> *Bows and arrows, spears and sabres, suits of armour,*
> *Dagger-axes, halberds, swords and tasselled banners.*
> *Pikes, partisans, helmets,*
> *Axes, round shields, and iron caltrops.*
> *Long staves,*
> *Short cudgels,*
> *Steel forks, cannons and casques.*
> *They were wearing tall boots, hats and quilted jackets,*
> *And carrying cudgels, small pellet-bows and maces of*
bronze."

"That's neither here nor there," laughed the demon king when he heard this. "Weapons like that can be finished off in a single blaze. Go and tell the Golden Queen all about it and ask her not to upset herself. Ever since she heard me lose my temper this morning and decide to go to war she's been crying her eyes out. Tell her that their army is so fierce and brave that they're bound to beat us. That'll calm her down for a while."

【8】　　This delighted Monkey, who thought, "Just what I want." Watch him as he goes the way he knows, through the side door and across the hall. Inside there were tall buildings: it was not like outside. He went straight to the women's quarters at the back, where he saw from a distance a handsome and decorated doorway. That was where the Golden Queen lived. When he went to see her there were two groups of fox and deer spirits dressed like beautiful women to wait on her. The queen sat in the middle with her fragrant cheeks in her hands and tears pouring from both her eyes. Indeed, she had

414

> *A beautiful face so soft and charming,*
> *A bewitching countenance so fair.*
> *But her raven-black hair was uncombed*
> *And piled untidily on her head;*
> *She did not want to dress up*
> *And wore no hair ornaments or rings.*
> *Her face was unpowdered,*
> *And she wore no rouge.*
> *Her hair was not oiled*
> *But all in a tangle.*
> *She pouted her cherry lips,*
> *Ground her silver teeth,*
> *Frowned with her brows like moth antennae,*
> *And let her eyes sparkle with tears.*
> *All her heart*
> *Was filled with memories of Purpuria's king;*
> *All the time*
> *She longed to escape from the net that held her.*
> *Truly,*
> *Ill-fated have been many lovely ladies*
> *Left in their wordless grief to face the eastern wind.*

Monkey went up to her and greeted her with a "Hello." "You impudent boorish freak," said the queen. "I remember how when I was living in splendour with my king in Purpuria even the king's tutor and the prime minister had to prostrate themselves in the dust when they met me: they would never have dared look me in the face. How dare you say 'Hello' to me, you lout? Where are you from, you coarse beast?" "Please don't be angry, ma'am," the serving women said. "He's one of His Majesty's most trusted lieutenants. His name is Gocome. He was the one who was sent with the declaration of war this morning." At this the queen controlled her temper and asked, "Did you go inside Purpuria when you delivered the declaration?" "I took it straight to the capital and right into the throne hall," said Monkey. "I saw the king himself and got an answer from him." "What did the king

415

say when you saw him?" the queen asked. "I have already told His Majesty here what he said about war and about the dispositions of their forces," Monkey replied. "But there was also a private message from the king, who misses you, ma'am. There's something private I have come to report to you, but with all these attendants around this is no place to talk."

When the queen heard this she dismissed her foxes and deer. Brother Monkey shut the door of the palace, rubbed his face, and turned back into himself. "Don't be afraid of me," he said to her. "I'm a monk sent by the Great Tang in the east to see the Buddha and fetch the scriptures at the Thunder Monastery in India. My master is Tang Sanzang, the younger brother of the Tang Emperor. I'm Sun Wukong, his senior disciple. When we were in your capital to present our passport for approval I saw a notice calling for doctors that your king and his ministers had posted. Then I used many medical skills to cure the illness he had contracted from missing you. When we were drinking at the banquet he gave to thank me he told me that you had been carried off by the evil spirit. As I can subdue dragons and tigers I was specially invited to capture the demon, rescue you and take you back to your country. I was the one who defeated the vanguard and killed the little devil. When I saw from outside the gates how ferocious the demon king was I turned myself into Gocome's double and came here to bring you a message."

The queen said nothing when she heard this. Then Monkey produced the bracelets and presented them to her with both hands. "If you don't believe me, just look; where did these come from?" he asked. As soon as she saw them the queen burst into tears, came down from where she was sitting, bowed to him in thanks and said, "Reverend sir, if you really can save me and get me back to court I will remember my deep debt of gratitude to you even when I'm old and toothless."

"Let me ask you something," said Monkey. "What treasure does he use to produce that fire, smoke and sand?" "It's no treasure," the queen said, "just three golden bells. As soon as he shakes the first one three thousand feet of burning flames shoot out. When he shakes the second one a three-thousand-foot column of smoke gushes out to kipper people. And when he shakes it the third time a blinding three-thousand-foot sandstorm blows up. The fire and smoke are nothing much, but the sand is lethal. If it gets up your nostrils it can kill you." "It's terrible," Monkey said, "terrible. I've experienced it and I had to sneeze a couple of times. I wonder where he keeps the bells." "He never puts them down," the queen replied. "He keeps them at his waist whether he's going somewhere, staying at home, sitting down or sleeping. They are always with him." "If you still care for Purpuria and want to see your king again you must forget about your distress and grief for the moment," said Monkey. "Make yourself look attractive and happy. Talk to him like a loving wife and get him to give you the bells to look after. When I've stolen them and defeated the monster I'll take you back to be reunited with your royal husband so that you can live in peace together."

[9] The queen did as Monkey said while he turned himself back into the demon king's trusted lieutenant, opened the doors again and called the serving women back in. "Go to the pavilion at the front, Gocome," the queen said, "and ask His Majesty to come here as I've something to say to him." The splendid Monkey assented and went to the Flaying Pavilion, where he said to the evil spirit, "Your Majesty, Her Majesty would like to see you." "All she usually does is curse me, so why is she sending for me now?" the demon king happily asked. "When she asked me about the king of Purpuria I told her, 'He doesn't want you any more: he's got a new queen now.' When she heard that Her Majesty stopped missing him. That's why she sent me out with this invitation." "You're very able," the demon king said, "and when we've destroyed Purpuria I'll make you my high chancellor in personal attendance."

Monkey thanked the demon king for his kindness and hurried to the door of the living quarters at the back, where the queen greeted him with happy smiles and her hands on his arms. The king stepped back with an awkward noise. "Don't," he said, "don't. I'm very grateful for this sign of your affection, ma'am,

417

but I don't dare stand next to you in case it hurts my hand." "Sit down, Your Majesty," the queen said. "I have something to say to you." "There's no objection to you speaking," the demon king replied. "I'm very much obliged to Your Majesty for condescending to love me," she said. "For three years now you have not shared my pillow although we were fated from our earlier lives to be married. I never expected that Your Majesty would treat me as a stranger instead of your wife. I remember that when I was queen of Purpuria the king gave all the valuable tribute from foreign countries to the queen to look after when he had seen it. But you have no treasures here. The servants wear marten hides and feed on blood. I have seen no fine silks, brocades, gold or pearls here. All the covers and blankets are of skins and felt. Or perhaps you do have some treasures that you won't let me see or look after because you regard me as a stranger. They say you have three bells. I think they must be treasures. Why do you always keep them with you, even when you're travelling or sitting down? There's no reason why you shouldn't give them to me to look after. I can give them to you when you need them. That would be one way of being a wife to you and it would show that we trust each other in our hearts. The only reason why you don't do this must because you regard me as an outsider."

At this the demon king burst into loud laughter, then bowed to her and said, "Ma'am, you're justified in your complaint. Here are the treasures, and today I'm giving them to you to look after." He undid his clothing to bring them out. Monkey watch with unwavering eyes as the monster pulled two or three layers of clothing aside to bring out the three bells that he carried next to his skin. Putting cotton-wool in to muffle them he wrapped them up in a piece of leopard skin and handed them to the queen with the words, "They're nothing, but please look after them very carefully. Whatever you do don't shake them." "I understand," the queen replied as she accepted them. "I shall keep them on my dressing table and nobody will move them at all." Then she gave these orders: "My little ones, lay on a banquet. His Majesty and I are going to have a few drinks to celebrate our happy union." At once the serving women brought in fruit, vegetables and the flesh of water deer, raccoon-dogs, deer and hare and poured out coconut toddy that they offered them. The queen made herself so bewitchingly attractive that she swept the evil spirit off his feet.

[10] Monkey meanwhile went to fetch the bells. Feeling and groping, he found his way to the dressing-table, gently took the three bells, crept out through the doors of the inner quarters and left the cave palace. When he reached the Flaying Pavilion there was nobody about, so he opened the leopard-skin wrapper to have a look. One of the bells was as big as a teacup and the other two the size of fists. With reckless folly he tore the cotton-wool apart. There was a loud clang and smoke, fire and sand came gushing out. Desperately Monkey tried to stop them but could do nothing. The pavilion was by now ablaze, sending the evil spirits on the gates all crowding in alarm inside the inner quarters. "Put the fire out," said the demon king, who was badly rattled. As he rushed out to look he saw that Gocome had taken the golden bells, went up to him and shouted, "Dirty slave! Why did you steal my precious golden bells? What sort of nonsense are you up to? Arrest him!" The tiger and bear generals, the leopard and tiger-cat marshals, the elephants, grey wolves, cunning water deer, crafty hares, long snakes, great pythons, orang-utans and all the other troops on the gates rushed him in a crowd.

Monkey was thrown into panic. Dropping the golden bells he turned back into himself, pulled out his gold-banded as-you-will cudgel, went and charged at them, going through his cudgel routines and lashing out wildly. The demon king took his treasures back and ordered, "Shut the main gates." At this some of the demons shut the gates and others went into battle. Unable to get away, Monkey put his cudgel away, shook himself and turned into a silly fly that attached itself to a spot on the stone wall which was not burning. None of the demons could find him. "Your Majesty," they reported, "the thief's got away, the thief's got away." "Did he get out through the gates?" the demon king asked. "The front gates are firmly locked and bolted," the demons replied. "He can't have got out through them." "Make a

419

careful search," said the demon king, and while some of them fetched water to douse the fire the others made a close search but found no trace of him.

"What sort of thief is he?" the demon king asked with fury. "He's got a hell of a nerve, turning himself into Gocome's double, coming in here to report back to me, then staying with me till he found a chance to steal my treasures. It's lucky he didn't take them out, if he'd taken them over the mountain top and there had been a heavenly wind it would have been a disaster." "Your Majesty's good fortune is divine," said the tiger general, stepping forward. "It was because our luck has not yet run out that he was discovered." Then the bear marshal came forward to say, "Your Majesty, the thief was none other than the Sun Wukong who beat our vanguard warrior. I think he must have run into Gocome when he was on his way, killed him, taken his yellow flag, gong and ivory tablet, and turned into his double to come here and deceive Your Majesty." "Yes, yes," the demon king replied, "you're clearly right. Little ones," he ordered, "make another careful search and be on your guard. Whatever you do, don't open the gates and let him out." It is rightly said that

> By being too clever one becomes a fool;
> What was once a joke can turn out to be real.

If you don't know how Brother Monkey got out through the demons' gates, listen to the explanation in the next instalment.

420

16. 行者假名降怪犼
观音现像伏妖王

【1】　色即空兮自古，空言是色如然。人能悟彻色空禅，何用丹砂炮炼。　德行全修休懈，工夫苦用熬煎。有时行满始朝天，永驻仙颜不变。

　　话说那赛太岁，紧关了前后门户，搜寻行者。直嚷到黄昏时分，不见踪迹。坐在那剥皮亭上，点聚群妖，发号施令，都教各门上提铃喝号，击鼓敲梆；一个个弓上弦，刀出鞘，支更坐夜。原来孙大圣变做个痴苍蝇，钉在门旁。见前面防备甚紧，他即抖开翅，飞入后宫门首看处，见金圣娘娘伏在御案上，清清滴泪，隐隐声悲。行者飞进门去，轻轻的落在他那乌云散髻之上，听他哭的甚么。少顷间，那娘娘忽失声道：“主公啊！我和你：

　　前生烧了断头香，今世遭逢泼怪王。
　　拆凤三年何日会？分鸾两处致悲伤。
　　差来长老才通信，惊散佳姻一命亡。
　　只为金铃难解识，相思又比旧时狂。”

行者闻言，即移身到他耳根后，悄悄的叫道：“圣宫娘娘，你休恐惧。我还是你家差来的神僧孙长老，未曾伤命。只因自家性急，近妆台偷了金铃，你与妖王吃酒之时，我却脱身私出了前亭，忍不住打开看看。不期扯动那塞口的绵花，那铃响一声，迸出烟火黄沙。我就慌了手脚，把金铃丢了，现出原身，使铁棒，苦战不出。恐遭毒害，故变做一个苍蝇儿，钉在门枢上，躲到如今。那妖王愈加严紧，不肯开门。你可去再以夫妻之礼，哄他进来安寝，我好脱身行事，别做区处救你也。”

【2】　娘娘一闻此言，战兢兢，发似神揪；虚怯怯，心如杵筑。泪汪汪的道：“你如今是人是鬼？”行者道：“我也不是人，我也不是鬼，如今变做个苍蝇儿在此。你休怕，快去请那妖王也。”娘娘不

421

信,泪滴滴,悄语低声道:“你莫魇寐我。”行者道:“我岂敢魇寐你?你若不信,展开手,等我跳下来你看。”那娘娘真个把左手张开,行者轻轻飞下,落在他玉掌之间,好便似:

菡萏蕊头钉黑豆,牡丹花上歇游蜂;
绣球心里葡萄落,百合枝边黑点浓。

金圣宫高擎玉掌,叫声“神僧。”行者嘤嘤的应道:“我是神僧变的。”那娘娘方才信了。悄悄的道:“我去请那妖王来时,你却怎生行事?”行者道:“古人云:‘断送一生惟有酒。’又云:‘破除万事无过酒。’酒之为用多端。你只以饮酒为上。你将那贴身的侍婢,唤一个进来,指与我看,我就变做他的模样,在旁边伏侍,却好下手。”

那娘娘真个依言,即叫:“春娇何在?”那屏风后转出一个玉面狐狸来,跪下道:“娘娘唤春娇有何使令?”娘娘道:“你去叫他们来点纱灯,焚脑麝,扶我上前庭,请大王安寝也。”那春娇即转前面,叫了七八个怪鹿妖狐,打着两对灯笼,一对提炉,摆列左右。娘娘欠身叉手,那大圣早已飞去。好行者,展开翅,径飞到那玉面狐狸头上,拔下一根毫毛,吹口仙气,叫“变!”变做一个瞌睡虫,轻轻的放在他脸上。原来瞌睡虫到了人脸上,往鼻孔里爬;爬进孔中,即瞌睡了。那春娇果然渐觉困倦,立不住脚,摇桩打盹,即忙寻着原睡处,丢倒头,只情呼呼的睡起。行者跳下来,摇身一变,变做那春娇一般模样,转屏风,与众排立不题。

【3】 却说那金圣宫娘娘往前正走,有小妖看见,即报赛太岁道:“大王,娘娘来了。”那妖王急出剥皮亭外迎迓。娘娘道:“大王啊,烟火既息,贼已无踪,深夜之际,特请大王安置。”那妖满心欢喜道:“娘娘珍重。却才那贼乃是孙悟空。他败了我先锋,打杀我小校,变化进来,哄了我们。我们这般搜检,他却渺无踪迹,故此心上不安。”娘娘道:“那厮想是走脱了。大王放心勿虑,且自安寝去也。”妖精见娘娘侍立敬请,不敢坚辞,只得吩咐群妖,各要小心火烛,谨防盗贼,遂与娘娘径往后宫。行者假变春娇,从两班侍婢引入。娘娘叫:“安排酒来与大王解劳。”妖王笑道:“正是,正是。快将酒来,我与娘娘压惊。”“假春娇”即同众怪铺排了果品,整顿些腥肉,调开桌椅。那娘娘擎杯,这妖王也以一杯奉

上，二人穿换了酒杯。"假春娇"在旁，执着酒壶道："大王与娘娘今夜才递交杯盏，请各饮干，穿个双喜杯儿。"真个又各斟上，又饮干了。"假春娇"又道："大王娘娘喜会，众侍婢会唱的供唱，善舞的起舞来耶。"说未毕，只听得一派歌声，齐调音律，唱的唱，舞的舞。你两个又饮了许多，娘娘叫住了歌舞。众侍婢分班，出屏风外摆列；惟有"假春娇"执壶，上下奉酒。娘娘与那妖王专说得是夫妻之话。你看那娘娘一片云情雨意，哄得那妖王骨软筋麻。只是没福，不得沾身。可怜！真是"猫咬尿胞空欢喜"！

【4】　叙了一会，笑了一会，娘娘问道："大王，宝贝可不曾伤损么？"妖王道："这宝贝乃先天传铸之物，如何得损！只是被那贼扯开塞口之绵，烧了豹皮包袱也。"娘娘说："怎生收拾？"妖王道："不用收拾，我带在腰间哩。""假春娇"闻得此言，即拔下毫毛一把，嚼得粉碎，轻轻挨近妖王，一捻那毫毛放在他身上，吹了三口仙气，暗暗的叫"变！"那些毫毛即变做三样恶物，乃虱子、蛇蚤、臭虫，攻人妖王身内，挨着皮肤乱咬。那妖王燥痒难禁，伸手人怀揣摸揉痒，用指头捏出几个虱子来，拿近灯前观看。娘娘见了，含忖道："大王，想是衬衣襷了，久不曾浆洗，故生此物耳。"妖王惭愧道："我从来不生此物，可可的今宵出丑。"娘娘笑道："大王何为出丑？常言道：'皇帝身上也有三个御虱'哩。且脱下衣服来，等我替你捉捉。"妖王真个与解带脱衣。

【5】　"假春娇"在旁，着意看着妖王身上，衣服层层皆有虱蚤跳，件件皆排大臭虫；子母虱，密密浓浓，就如蝼蚁出窝中。不觉的揭到第三层见肉之处，那金铃上纷纷骇骇的，不胜其数。"假春娇"道："大王，拿铃子来，等我也与你捉捉虱子。"那妖王一则羞，二则慌，却也不认得真假，将三个铃儿递与"假春娇"。"假春娇"接在手中，卖弄多时，见那妖王低着头抖这衣服，他即将金铃藏过了，拔下一根毫毛，变做三个铃儿，一般无二，拿向灯前翻检；却又把身子扭扭捏捏的，抖了一抖，将那虱、臭虫、蛇蚤，收了归在身上，把假金铃儿递与那怪。那怪接在手中，一发опен疑无措，那里认得甚么真假，双手托着那铃儿，递与娘娘道："今番你却收好了。却要仔细仔细，不要像前一番。"那娘娘接过来，轻轻的揭开衣箱，把那假铃收了，用黄金锁儿锁了。却又与妖王叙饮了

几杯酒，教侍婢："净拂牙床，展开锦被，我与大王同寝。"那妖王诺诺连声道："没福！没福！不敢奉陪。我还带个宫女往西宫里睡去。娘娘请自安置。"遂此各归寝处不题。

【6】　却说"假春娇"得了手，将他宝贝带在腰间，现了本像，把身子抖一抖，收去那个瞌睡虫儿，径往前走，只听得梆铃齐响，紧打三更。好行者，捏着诀，念动真言，使个隐身法，直至门边。又见那门上拴锁甚密，却就取出金箍棒，望门一指，使出那解锁之法，那门就轻轻开了。急抽步出门站下，厉声高叫道："赛太岁！还我金圣娘娘来！"连叫两三遍，惊动大小群妖，急急看处，前门开了，即忙掌灯寻锁，把门儿依然锁上，着几个跑入里边去报道："大王！有人在大门外呼唤大王尊号，要金圣娘娘哩！"那里边侍婢，即出宫门，悄悄的传言道："莫吆喝，大王才睡着了。"行者又在门前高叫，那小妖又不敢去惊动。如此者三四遍，俱不敢去通报。那大圣在外嚷嚷闹闹的，直弄到天晓。忍不住，手抡着铁棒，上前打门。慌得那大小群妖，顶门的顶门，报信的报信。那妖王一觉方醒，只闻得乱撺撺的喧哗，起身穿了衣服，即出罗帐之外，问道："嚷甚么？"众侍婢才跪下道："爷爷，不知是甚人在洞外叫骂了半夜，如今却又打门。"

　　妖王走出宫门，只见那几个传报的小妖，慌张张的磕头道："外面有人叫骂，要金圣宫娘娘哩！若说半个'不'字，他就说出无的数诳话，甚不中听。见天晓大王不出，却跑得打门也。"那妖道："且休开门。你去问他是那里来的，姓甚名谁。快来回报。"小妖急出去，隔门问道："打门的是谁？"行者道："我是朱紫国拜请来的外公，来取圣金娘娘回国哩！"那小妖听得，即以此言回报。那妖随往后宫，查问来历，原来那娘娘才起来，还未梳洗。早见侍婢来报："爷爷来了。"那娘娘整整衣，散挽黑云，出宫迎迓。才坐下，还未及问，又听得小妖来报："那来的外公已将门打破矣。"那妖笑道："娘娘，你朝中有多少将帅？"娘娘道："在朝有四十八卫人马，七十千员；各边上元帅总兵，不计其数。"妖王道："可有个姓外的么？"娘娘道："我在宫，只知内里辅理君王，早晚教诲妃嫔，外事无边，我怎记得名姓！"妖王道："这来者称为'外公'，我想着《百家姓》上，更无个姓外的。娘娘赋性聪明，出身高贵，居皇宫之中，必多览书籍。记得那本书上有此姓也？"娘娘道："止《千字文》上有句'外受傅训'，想必就是此矣。"

【7】　妖王喜道："定是！定是！"即起身辞了娘娘，到剥皮亭上，结束整齐，点出妖兵，开了门，直至外面，手持一柄宣花钺斧，厉声高叫道："那个是朱紫国来的'外公'？"行者把金箍棒揽在右手，将左手指定道："贤甥，叫我怎的？"那妖王见了，心中大怒道："你这厮——

相貌若猴子，嘴脸似猢狲。
七分真是鬼，大胆敢欺人！"

行者笑道："你这个诳上欺君的泼怪，原来没眼！想我五百年前大闹天宫时，九天神将见了我，无一个'老'字，不敢称呼；你叫我声'外公'，那里亏了你！"妖王喝道："快早说出姓甚名谁，有些甚么武艺，敢到我这里猖獗！"行者道："你若不问姓名犹可，若要我说出姓名，只怕你立身无地！你上来，站稳着，听我道：

生身父母是天地，日月精华结圣胎。
仙石怀抱无岁数，灵根孕育甚奇哉。
当年产我三阳泰，今日归真万会谐。
曾聚众妖称帅首，能降众怪拜丹崖。
玉皇大帝传宣旨，太白金星捧诏来。
请我上天承职裔，官封'弼马'不开怀。
初心造反谋山洞，托塔天王并太子，交锋一阵尽猥衰。
金星复奏玄穹帝，再降招安敕旨来。
封做齐天真大圣，那时方称栋梁材。
又因搅乱蟠桃会，仗酒偷丹惹下灾。
太上老君亲奏驾，西池王母拜瑶台。
情知是我欺王法，即点天兵发火牌。
十万凶星并恶曜，干戈剑戟密排排。
天field地网漫山布，齐举刀兵大会垓。
恶斗一场无胜败，观音推荐二郎来。
两家对敌分高下，他有梅山兄弟侪。
各逞英雄施变化，天门三圣拨云开。

老君丢了金钢套，众神擒我到金阶。
不须详允书供状，罪犯凌迟碎斩灾。
斧剁锤敲难损命，刀轮剑砍怎伤怀。
火烧雷打只如此，无计摧残长寿胎。
押赴太清兜率院，炉中煅炼尽安排。
日期满足才开鼎，我向当中跳出来。
手挺这条如意棒，翻身打上玉龙台。
各星各象皆潜躲，大闹天宫任我歪。
巡视灵官忙请佛，释伽与我逞英才。
手心之内翻筋斗，游遍周天去复来。
佛使先知赚哄法，被他压住在天崖。
到今五百余年矣，解脱微躯又弄乖。
特保唐僧西域去，悟空行者甚明白。
西方路上降妖怪，那个妖邪不惧哉！"

那妖王听他说出悟空行者，遂道："你原来是大闹天宫的那厮。你既脱身保唐僧西去，你走你的路去便罢了，怎么罗织管事，替那朱紫国为奴，却到我这里寻死！"行者喝道："贼泼怪！说话无知！我受朱紫国拜请之礼，又蒙他称呼管待之恩，我老孙比那王位还高千倍，他敬之如父母，事之如神明，你怎么说出'为奴'二字！我把你这诳上欺君之怪！不要走！吃外公一棒！"那妖慌了手脚，即闪身躲过，使宣花斧劈面相迎。这一场好杀！你看：

> 金箍如意棒，风刃宣花斧。一个咬牙发狠凶，一个切齿施威武。这个是齐天大圣降临凡，那个是作怪妖王来下土。两个喷云嗳雾照天宫，真是走石扬沙遮斗府。往往来来解数多，翻翻复复金光吐。齐来本事施，各把神通赌。这个要取娘娘转帝都，那个喜同皇后居山坞。这场都是没来由，舍死忘生因国主。

他两个战经五十回合，不分胜负。那妖王见行者手段高强，料不能取胜，将斧架住他的铁棒道："孙行者，你且住。我今日还未早膳，待我进了膳，再来与你定雌雄。"行者情知是要取铃铛，收了铁棒道："'好汉子不赶乏兔儿'，你去！你去！吃饱些，好来领死！"

【8】　那妖急转身闯入里边，对娘娘道："快将宝贝拿来！"娘娘道："要宝贝何干？"妖王道："今早叫战者，乃是取经的和尚之徒，叫做孙悟空行者，假称'外公'。我与他战到此时，不分胜负。等我拿宝贝出去，放些烟火，烧这猴头。"娘娘见说，心中悒突：欲不取出铃儿，恐他见疑；欲取出铃儿，又恐伤了孙行者性命。正自踌躇未定，那妖王又催逼道："快拿出来！"这娘娘无奈，只得将锁钥开了，把三个铃儿递与妖王。妖王拿了，就走出洞。娘娘坐在宫中，泪如雨下，思量行者不知可能逃得性命。两人却俱不知是假铃也。

　　那妖出了门，就占起上风，叫道："孙行者，休走！看我摇摇铃儿！"行者笑道："你有铃，我就没铃？你会摇，我就不会摇？"妖王道："你有甚么铃儿，拿出来我看。"行者将铁棒捏做个绣花针儿，藏在耳内，却去腰间解下三个真宝贝来，对妖王说："这不是我的紫金铃儿？"妖王见了，心惊道："跷蹊！跷蹊！他的铃儿怎与我的铃儿就一般无二！纵然是个模子铸的，好道打磨不到，也有多个瘢儿，少个蒂儿，却怎么这等一毫不差？"又问："你那铃儿是那里来的？"行者道："贤甥，你那铃儿却是那里来的？"妖王老实，便说出道："我这铃儿是：

太清仙君道源深，八卦炉中久炼金。

结就铃儿称至宝，老君留下到如今。"

行者笑道："老孙的铃儿，也是那时来的。"妖王道："怎生出处？"行者道："我这铃儿是：

道祖烧丹兜率宫，金铃传炼在炉中。

二三如六循环宝，我的雌来你的雄。"

妖王道："铃儿乃金丹之宝，又不是飞禽走兽，如何辨得雌雄？但只是摇出宝来，就是好的！"行者道："口说无凭，做出便见。且让你先摇。"那妖王真个将头一个铃儿幌了三幌，不见火出；第二个幌了三幌，不见烟出；第三个幌了三幌，也不见沙出。妖王慌了手脚道："怪哉！怪哉！世情变了！这铃儿想是惧内，雄见了雌，所以不出来了。"行者道："贤甥，住了手，等我也摇摇你看。"好猴子，一把撺了三个铃儿，一齐摇起。你看那红火、青烟、黄沙，一齐滚出，骨都都燎树烧山！大圣口里又念个咒语，望巽地上叫："风来！"真个是风催火势，火挟风威，红焰焰，黑沉沉，满天烟火，遍地黄沙！把那赛太岁唬得魄散魂飞，走投无路，在那火当中，怎逃性命！

【9】　只闻得半空中厉声高叫："孙悟空！我来了也！"行者急回头上望，原来是观音菩萨，左手托着净瓶，右手拿着杨柳，洒下甘露救火哩。慌得行者把铃儿藏在腰间，即合掌倒身下拜。那菩萨将柳枝连拂几点甘露，霎时间，烟火俱无，黄沙绝迹。行者叩头道："不知大慈悲兴，有失迎避。敢问菩萨何往？"菩萨道："我特来收寻这个妖怪哩。"

行者道："这怪是何来历，敢劳金身下降收之？"菩萨道："他是我跨的个金毛犼。因牧童盹睡，失于防守，这孽畜咬断铁索走来，却与朱紫国王消灾也。"行者闻言，急欠身道："菩萨反说了。他在这里欺君骗后，败俗伤风，与那国王生灾，却说是消灾，何也？"菩萨道："你不知之。当时朱紫国先王在位之时，这个王还做东宫太子，未曾登基。他年幼间，极好射猎。他率领人马，纵放鹰犬，正来到落凤坡前，有西方佛母孔雀大明王菩萨所生二子，乃雌雄两个雀雏，停翅在山坡之下，被此王弓开处，射伤了雄孔雀，那雌孔雀也带箭归西。佛母忏悔以后，吩咐教他拆凤三年，身耽啾疾。那时节，我跨着这犼，同听此言，不期这孽畜留心，故来骗了皇后，与王消灾。至今三年，冤愆满足，幸你来救治王患。我特来收妖邪也。"行者道："菩萨，虽是这般故事，奈何他玷污了皇后，败俗伤风，坏伦乱法，却是该他死罪。今蒙菩萨亲临，饶他死罪，却绝不得他活罪。让我打他二十棒，以与他带去罢。"菩萨道："悟空，你既知我临见，就当看我分上，一发都饶了罢；也算你一番降妖之功。若是动了棍子，他也就是死了。"行者不敢违言，只得拜道："菩萨既收他回海，再不可令他私降人间，贻害不浅！"

那菩萨才喝了一声"孽畜！还不还原，待何时也！"只见那怪打个滚，现了原身，将毛衣抖抖，菩萨骑上。菩萨又望项下一看，不见那三个金铃。菩萨道："悟空，还我铃来。"行者道："老孙不知。"菩萨喝道："你这贼猴！若不是你偷了这铃，莫说一个悟空，就是十个，也不敢近身！快拿出来！"行者笑道："实不曾见。"菩萨道："既不曾见，等我念念《紧箍儿咒》。"那行者慌了，只教："莫念！莫念！铃儿在这里哩！"这正是：犼项金铃何人解？解铃人还得系铃人。菩萨将铃儿套在犼项下，飞身高坐。你看他四足莲花生焰焰，满身金缕迸森森。大慈悲回南海不题。

【10】　却说孙大圣整束了衣裙，抡铁棒打进獬豸洞去，把群妖众怪，尽情打死，剿除干净。直至宫中，请圣宫娘娘回国。那娘娘顶礼不尽。行者将菩萨降妖并拆洞原由备说了一遍，寻些软草，扎了一条草龙，教："娘娘跨上，合着眼，莫怕，我带你回朝见主也。"那娘娘谨遵吩咐，行者使起神通，只听得耳内风响。

半个时辰，带进城，按落云头，叫："娘娘开眼。"那皇后睁开眼看，认得是凤阁龙楼，心中欢喜，撇了草龙，与行者同登宝殿。那国王见了，急下龙床，就来拉娘娘玉手，欲诉离情，猛然跌倒在地，只叫："手疼！手疼！"八戒哈哈大笑道："嘴脸！没福消受！一见面就蜇杀了也！"行者道："呆子，你敢扯他扯儿么？"八戒道："就扯他扯儿便怎的？"行者道："娘娘身上生了毒刺，手上有蜇阳之毒。自到麒麟山，与那赛太岁三年，那妖更不曾沾身。但沾身就害身疼，但沾手就害手疼。"众官听说，道："似此怎生奈何？"此时外面众官忧虑，内里妃嫔悚惧，旁有玉圣、银圣二宫，将君王扶起。

【11】　俱正在仓皇之际，忽听得那半空中，有人叫道："大圣，我来也。"行者抬头观看，只见那：

　　肃肃冲天鹤唳，飘飘径至朝前。缭绕祥光道道，氤氲瑞气翩翩。棕衣苫体放云烟，足踏芒鞋罕见。手执龙须蝇帚，丝绦腰下围缠。乾坤处处结人缘，大地逍遥游遍。此乃是大罗天上紫云仙，今日临凡解魇。

行者上前迎住道："张紫阳何往？"紫阳真人直至殿前，躬身施礼道："大圣，小仙张伯端起手。"行者答礼道："你从何来？"真人道："小仙三年前曾赴佛会。因打这里过，见朱紫国王有拆凤之忧，我恐那妖将皇后玷辱，有坏人伦，后日难与国王复合。是我将一件旧棕衣变做一领新霞裳，光生五彩，进与妖王，教皇后穿了妆新。那皇后穿上身，即生一身毒刺。毒刺者，乃棕毛也。今知大圣成功,特来解魇。"行者道:"既如此,累你远来,且快解脱。"真人走向前,对娘娘用手一指,即脱下那件棕衣。那娘娘遍体如旧。真人将衣抖一抖,披在身上,对行者道:"大圣勿罪,小仙告辞。"行者道:"且住,待君王谢谢。"真人笑道:"不劳,不劳。"遂长揖一声,腾空而去。慌得那皇帝、皇后及大小众臣,一个个望空礼拜。

【12】 拜毕,即命大开东阁,酬谢四僧。那君王领众跪拜,夫妻才得重谐。正当欢宴时,行者叫:"师父,拿那战书来。"长老袖中取出,递与行者。行者递与国王道:"此书乃那怪差小校送来者。那小校已先被我打死,送来报功。后复至山中,变做小校,进洞回复,因得见娘娘,盗出金铃,几乎被他拿住;又变化,复偷出与他对敌。幸遇观音菩萨将他收去,又与我说拆凤之故。……"从头至尾,细说了一遍。那举国君臣内外,无一人不感谢称赞。唐僧道:"一则是贤王之福,二来是小徒之功。今蒙盛宴,至矣!至矣!就此拜别,不要误贫僧向西去也。"那国王恳留不得,遂换过关文,大排銮驾,请唐僧稳坐龙车,那君王、妃后,俱捧毂推轮,相送而别。正是:有缘洗尽忧疑病,绝念无思心自宁。毕竟这去,后面再有甚么吉凶之事,且听下回分解。

Chapter 16
Under a False Name Monkey Beats
the Demon Hound;
Guanyin Appears to Subdue
the Demon King

[1] *Matter has always been empty;*
Emptiness said to be matter is only natural.
When one penetrates the dhyana of matter's emptiness
There is no need for cinnabar to be refined into elixir.
Rest not when pursuing perfection of virtue and conduct;
Endure suffering to achieve hard-won skills.
Sometimes one only turns to heaven when one's actions are complete,
To win an unchanging and immortal face.

The story tells how the Evil Star Matcher had the front and back gates tightly closed while Monkey was hunted for. The din went on till dusk, but no sign of him did they find. The demon king sat in the Flaying Pavilion, where he called his demons together and issued orders to the guards on all the gates to carry bells, shout passwords, beat drums and strike clappers. Everyone was to have an arrow on his bowstring or a sword unsheathed as he took his turn to keep watch during the night. Sun Wukong, who had turned into a fly, was sitting by the gates. Seeing how strict the security was at the front gates he spread his wings and flew to the gateway of the living quarters to take a look. He saw the Golden Queen slumped across a low table, the tears flowing down as she wept quietly in her sorrow, so he flew inside and landed lightly on the loose black clouds of her hair to listen to what she was crying about. A moment later she said tearfully, "My lord, you and I,

Burnt in an earlier life the incense of separation,
And now I have encountered an evil demon king.

431

> *For three years I have been gone: when will we two be reunited?*
>
> *Great is the grief of mandarin ducks that are parted.*
>
> *Just when the priest had brought me your message*
> *Our union has been severed once more and the monkey is dead.*
>
> *Because he was too curious about the golden bells*
> *I long for you now more desperately than ever."*

When he heard this Monkey went behind her ear, where he whispered, "Don't be afraid, Your Majesty. I'm the holy monk, the venerable Sun Wukong, who was sent from your country. I'm still alive. It was all because I was too impatient. I went to your dressing table and stole the golden bells. While you were drinking with the demon king I sneaked out to the pavilion in the front, but I couldn't restrain myself from opening them up to take a look at them. I didn't mean to, but I tore the cotton wool muffling the bells, and the moment they rang flame, smoke and sand came gushing out. I panicked, threw the bells down, turned back into myself, and tried hard to fight my way out with my iron cudgel. When I failed and was scared they'd kill me I turned into a fly, and hid on the door pivot till just now. The demon king has made the security precautions even stricter and he won't open the doors. Will you act like a wife to him and lure him in here to sleep so that I can escape and find some other way of rescuing you?"

[2] When the queen heard this she shivered and shook, and her hair stood on end as if a spirit were pulling it; she was terrified, as if her heart was being pounded by a pestle. "Are you a man or a ghost?" she asked, the tears streaming down. "Neither man nor ghost," he replied. "At the moment I've turned into a fly and I'm here. Don't be afraid. Hurry up and ask the demon king here." The queen still refused to believe him. "Stop appearing in this nightmare," she said in a low voice through her tears. "I'm not in a nightmare," said Monkey. "If you don't believe me put your hand out and open it. I'll jump down to it for you to see." The queen then put out her open hand. Monkey flew down and

432

landed lightly on her jade palm. He was just like

> *A black bean on a lotus flower,*
> *A bee resting on a peony blossom,*
> *A raisin fallen into a hydrangea,*
> *A black spot on a wild lily stalk.*

The queen raised her hand and said, "Holy monk." "I'm the holy monk transformed," Monkey replied. Only then did the queen believe him. "When I invite the demon king here what are you going to do?" she asked. "There's an old saying that there's nothing like liquor for ending a life," Monkey replied, "and another that there's nothing like liquor for solving any problem. Liquor's very useful stuff. The best thing is to give him plenty to drink. Call one of our personal slave-girls in and let me have a look at her so I can make myself look like her and wait on you. Then I'll be able to make my move."

The queen did as he told her. "Spring Beauty, where are you?" she called, and a fox with a beautiful face came in round the screen, knelt down and said, "What orders did Your Majesty call me in to receive?" "Tell them to come in and light the silk lanterns, burn some musk, and help me into the front room," the queen said. "Then I shall ask His Majesty to bed." Spring Beauty went to the front and called seven or eight deer and fox spirits who lined up on either side of her. They carried two pairs of lanterns and one pair of portable incense-burners. By the time the queen bowed to them with her hands together the Great Sage had already flown off. Spreading his wings, the splendid Monkey flew straight to the top of Spring Beauty's head, where he pulled out one of his hairs, blew a magic breath on it, and called, "Change!" It turned into a sleep insect that landed lightly on Spring Beauty's face. Now when sleep insects reach a human face they crawl into the nostrils, and once they are inside the person goes to sleep. Spring Beauty did indeed start feeling sleepy. She could not keep on her feet, but swayed about and felt down as she hurried to where she had been resting before, collapsed head first and fell into a deep sleep. Brother Monkey then jumped down, shook himself, turned into Spring Beauty's exact likeness and went back round the screen to line up with the others.

[3]   As the Golden Queen walked into the front part of the palace a little devil saw her and reported to the Evil Star Matcher, "The queen's here, Your Majesty." The demon king hurried out of the Flaying Pavilion to greet her. "Your Majesty," the queen said, "the smoke and fire have been put out and there's no sign of the thief. As it's late now I've come to urge you to come to bed." "How considerate you are, my queen," the monster replied, utterly delighted to see her. "The thief was Sun Wukong who defeated my vanguard warrior then killed my lieutenant and came here disguised as him to fool us. We've searched but can't find a trace of him. It makes me feel uneasy." "The wretch must have got away," the queen replied. "Relax, Your Majesty, stop worrying, and come to bed."

Seeing the queen standing there and inviting him so earnestly the demon king could not refuse too insistently, so he told the other demons to be careful with the fires and lamps and be on their guard against robbers before he went to the living quarters at the back with the queen. Monkey, disguised as Spring Beauty, led their way with the other slave girls. "Bring wine for His Majesty," the queen said. "He's exhausted." "Indeed I am," said the demon king with a smile, "indeed I am. Fetch some at once. It'll calm our nerves." The imitation Spring Beauty and the other servants then laid out fruit and high meat and set a table and chairs. The queen raised a cup and the demon king did likewise; each gave the other a drink from their own. The imitation Spring Beauty, who was standing beside them, said as she held the jug, "As tonight is the first time Your Majesties have given each other a drink from your own cups I hope that you will each drain them dry for double happiness." They did indeed both refill their cups and drain them again. "As this is so happy an occasion for Your Majesties why don't we slave girls sing and dance for you?" the imitation Spring Beauty suggested.

Before the words were all out of her mouth melodious voices

could be heard as the singing and dancing began. The two of them drank a lot more before the queen called for the singing and dancing to end. The slave girls divided themselves into their groups and went to line up outside the screen, leaving only the imitation Spring Beauty to hold the jug and serve them wine. The queen and the demon king spoke to each other like husband and wife, and the queen was so full of sensuality that the demon king's bones turned soft and his sinews went numb. The only trouble was that the poor demon was not lucky enough to enjoy her favours. In deed, it was a case of "happiness over nothing, like a cat biting a piss bubble."

[4] After talking and laughing for a while the queen asked, "Were the treasures damaged, Your Majesty?" "Those are treasures that were cast long, long age," the demon king said, "so they couldn't possibly be damaged. All that happened was that the thief tore the cotton wool that was muffling the bells and the leopard skin wrapper was burnt." "Where have they been put away?" the queen asked. "No need for that," the demon king replied. "I carry them at my waist." Hearing this, the imitation Spring Beauty pulled out a handful of his hairs, chewed them up into little bits, crept closer to the demon king, put the pieces of hair on the demon's body, blew three magic breaths, said "Change!" very quietly, and turned the pieces of hair into three revolting pests: lice, fleas and bedbugs. They all made for the demon king's body and started biting his skin wildly. Itching unbearably, the demon king put his hands inside his clothing to rub the irritation. He caught a few of the lice between his fingers and took them to a lamp for a closer look.

When the queen saw them she said mockingly, "Your Majesty, your shirt must be filthy. It can't have been washed for ages. I expect that's why they're there." "I've never had insects like these before," he said in embarrassment. "I would have to make a fool of myself tonight." "What do you mean, making a fool of yourself, Your Majesty?" the queen said with a smile. "As the saying goes, even the emperor has three imperial lice. Undress and I'll catch them for you." The demon king really did

435

undo his belt and take his clothes off.

[5]   The imitation Spring Beauty was standing beside the demon king looking closely at the fleas leaping around between each layer of clothing, on which were rows of enormous bedbugs. Lice and nits were crowded as closely together as ants coming out of their nest. When the demon king took off the third layer of clothing and revealed his flesh the golden bells were also swarming with countless insects. "Your Majesty," said the imitation Spring Beauty, "hand me the bells so that I can catch the lice on them for you." The demon king was so overcome with shame and alarm that he handed the three bells to Spring Beauty, not noticing that she was an impostor.

The imitation Spring Beauty took the bells and made a long show of catching lice. When she saw the demon king looking down to shake his clothes she hid the golden bells, pulled out a hair and turned it into three more bells just like the originals that she carried to the lamp to examine. She then wriggled, braced herself, put the lice, bedbugs and fleas back on her body and returned the imitation bells to the monster. He took them but was still too befuddled to see that they were copies. Passing them with both his hands to the queen he said, "Put them away now, but be very careful with them, not like before." The queen took the bells, quietly opened the chest, put them inside, and locked them in with a golden lock. Then she drank several more cups of wine with the demon king. "Dust and clean the ivory bed," she ordered the serving women, "and spread the brocade quilt. His Majesty and I are going to bed." The demon king expressed his thanks but said, "I have no such luck. I don't dare go with you. I'll take one of the palace women with me and go to bed in the western part of the palace. I wish you a good night by yourself, ma'am." With that each of them went to bed, and we will say no more of that.

[6]   Meanwhile the successful imitation Spring Beauty tucked the treasures into her belt and turned back into Monkey. He shook himself, took back the sleep insect, and headed for the front of the palace, where nightsticks and bells sounded together

to mark the third watch. Splendid Monkey made himself invisible by making a spell with his hands and saying the words of it. Going straight to the gates he saw that they were very firmly locked and bolted, so he brought out his gold-banded cudgel, pointed it at the door and made unlocking magic. The gates swung easily open. Hurrying outside he stood by the gates and shouted two or three times at the top of his voice, "Evil Star Matcher, give us back our Golden Queen."

This startled all the devils, who hurried to look and saw that the gates were open. Quickly they fetched lamps to find the locks and fasten the gates once more. Several of them were sent running back inside to report, "Your Majesty, there's someone outside the main gates shouting your title and demanding the Golden Queen." The slave girls hurried out to say very quietly, "Stop yelling. His Majesty's only just gone to sleep." Monkey gave another loud shout at the front gates, but the little devils dared not disturb their master. This happened three or four times over, but they never went in to report. The Great Sage kept up his din till daybreak, by when his patience was exhausted and he swung his iron cudgel to hit the gates. This so alarmed the demons big and small that while some of them barricaded the gates the others went in to report. As soon as the demon king woke up and heard the cacophonous din he got up, dressed and emerged from his bed-curtains to ask, "What's all the shouting about?" "Sir," said the kneeling slave girls, "someone's been shouting and cursing outside the cave half the night. We don't know who it is. Now he's attacking the gates."

As the demon king went out through the gates of the palace several panic-stricken little devils appeared to kowtow to him and say, "There's someone shouting and cursing outside. He's demanding the Golden Queen, and if we say so much as half a 'no' he goes on and on at us, swearing in a thoroughly horrible way. When Your Majesty still hadn't come out at daybreak he got so desperate he started attacking the gates." "Don't open them," the demon king said. "Go and ask him where he's from and what he's called. Report back as quickly as you can."

The little devils hurried off to ask through the gates, "Who are you, knocking at our gates?" "I'm your grandpa sent by Purpuria to take the Golden Queen back to her own country," Monkey replied. When the little devils heard this they reported it to the demon king, who went back to the living quarters at the back to question the queen about why the attacker had come. The queen had only just arisen and had not yet done her hair or washed when slave girls came in to report, "His Majesty's here." The queen hastily tidied up her clothes and let her black tresses hang loose as she went outside to greet him. He had just sat down and had not yet asked her any questions when little demons were heard again asking, "The Grand Par from over there has smashed the gates down." "How many officers are there in your country, ma'am?" the demon king asked with a smile. "Inside the palace there are forty-eight brigades of horse and foot, and a thousand good officers; and there are ever so many marshals and commanders on the frontiers." the queen replied. "Are any called Grand Par?" the demon king asked. "When I was in the palace all I knew about was helping His Majesty in the inner quarters and instructing the consorts and concubines every morning and evening," the queen said. "There were no end of things happening outside. How could I possibly remember the names?" "This one calls himself Grand Par," the demon king replied. "There's no such name I can think of in the book *The Hundred Surnames*. You're a very intelligent and well-born lady, ma'am, and you've lived in a royal palace. You must have read a lot of books. Can you remember coming across that name in any of them?" "There's a passage in the *Thousand Word Classic* that goes, 'received grand instruction'," the queen replied. "I think that must refer to him."

【7】 "I'm sure you're right," the demon king said with pleasure, "I'm sure you're right." He then got up, took his leave of the queen, went to the Flaying Pavilion, fastened his armour on neatly, mustered his devil soldiers, had the gates opened, and went straight outside with his flower-scattering battle-axe in his hand. "Who's the Grand Par from Purpuria?" he yelled stridently at the top of his voice. Grasping his gold-banded cudgel in his right hand and pointing with his left Monkey replied, "What are you shouting at me for, nephew?" The sight of him drove the demon king into a fury. "Damn you," he shouted:

> *You've a face just like a monkey's;*
> *You resemble a macaque.*
> *A ghost is what you look like;*
> *Don't try to knock me back.*

"Impudent devil," laughed Monkey, "trying to bully your superiors and push your master around. You're blind. I remember how when I made havoc in Heaven five hundred years ago all the nine heavenly generals only dared speak to me with the greatest respect. If I make you call me Grandpa I'm letting you off lightly." "Tell me your name immediately," the demon king shouted. "What fighting skills have you got that give you the nerve to come rampaging here?" "You'd have done better not to ask me what I'm called," Monkey replied. "But as you insist on me telling you I'm afraid you'll be in a hopeless mess. Come here and stand still while I tell you:

> *Heaven and earth were the parents that bore me;*
> *My foetus was formed from the sun and moon's essence.*
> *The magic rock was pregnant for years beyond number;*
> *Strange indeed was the miraculous root's gestation.*
> *When I was born the Three Positives were at their height;*
> *Now I have been converted all is in harmony.*
> *Once I was declared the chief of all the demons,*
> *Who bowed to me by the red cliff as subduer of monsters.*
> *The Jade Emperor issued a decree of summons,*
> *And the Great White Planet came with the edict,*
> *Inviting me to Heaven to take up my office,*
> *But as Protector of the Horses I had no joy.*
> *When I first planned rebellion in my mountain cave*
> *Boldly I led my armies against the Jade Emperor.*

The Pagoda-carrying Heavenly King and Prince Nezha
Were utterly helpless when they fought against me.
Then the White Planet made a new suggestion,
And brought another edict urging me to make peace.
I was made Great Sage Equalling Heaven,
And proclaimed as one of the pillars of the state.
Because I disrupted the banquet of peaches
And stole elixir when drunk I met with disaster.
Lord Lao Zi submitted a memorial in person,
And the Queen Mother of the West did homage to the throne.
Knowing that I was running riot with the law,
They mustered heavenly forces and issued movement orders.
A hundred thousand vicious stars and evil planets
Were packed in close array with their swords and their halberds.
Heaven-and-earth nets were spread across the mountain
As all of the soldiers raised their weapons together.
A bout of bitter fighting left neither side the victor,
So Guanyin recommended the warrior Erlang.
The two of us fought together for mastery;
He was helped by the Seven Brothers who come from Plum Hill.
Each of us played the hero and did our transformations:
The three sages at the gates of Heaven opened the clouds.
Then Lord Lao Zi dropped his diamond noose,
And the gods led me as a prisoner to the steps of the throne-hall.
They did not bother with a detailed indictment:
The sentence was death by a thousand cuts.
Axe and hammer could not kill me,
And I was unharmed by sword or sabre.
Fire and thunderbolts were neither here nor there;
They had no way to destroy my immortal body.
I was taken under escort to the Tushita Heaven,

And all was arranged to refine me in the furnace.
Only when full time was up did they open up the vessel,
And I came bounding out from the middle of the crucible.
In my hands I was wielding this as-you-will cudgel
As I somersaulted up to the Jade Emperor's throne.
All the stars and constellations went into hiding,
And I could play the vandal in the palaces of Heaven.
The Miraculous Investigator rushed to invite the Buddha,
Then Sakyamuni and I both displayed our powers.
Turning my somersaults in the palm of his hand
I roamed all over the heavens before my return.
The Buddha then, using both foresight and deception,
Crushed and held me at the ends of the heavens.
After a period of over five hundred years
My body was delivered and I could once more play up.
Guarding the Tang Priest on his journey to the West,
Brother Sun Wukong is very intelligent,
I subdue the demons on the westward road;
Every evil spirit is struck with terror."

When the demon king heard him tell that he was Sun Wukong he said, "So you're the so-and-so who made havoc in Heaven. If you were released to guard the Tang Priest on his journey west then you should be on your way there. Why are you being such a busybody and making trouble for me? You're acting as if you were the slave of Purpuria. By coming here you've thrown your life away." "Thieving damned monster," Monkey shouted back. "You don't know what you're talking about. I was politely invited to help by the king of Purpuria. He addressed me very respectfully and treated me well. I'm a thousand times higher than that king. He treated me as if I were his father and mother or a god. How can you say I'm acting like a slave? I'll get you, you monster, for bullying your superiors and trying to push your master around. Stay there and take this from your grandpa." The monster then moved his hands and feet as fast as he could, dodged the blow from the cudgel and struck back at

441

Brother Monkey's face with his flower-scattering axe. It was a fine battle. Just watch!

> The gold-banded as-you-will cudgel,
> The flower-scattering axe and its wind-keen blade.
> One ground his teeth with terrible ferocity:
> The other gnashed his molars and displayed his might.
> One was the Great Sage Equalling Heaven descended to earth,
> The other an evil demon king come down to the lower world.
> Both snorted out clouds and shining mists that lit up the heavenly palace,
> Sent stones and sand flying that blotted out the Dipper.
> They came and went through many a movement,
> Twisting and turning and giving off golden light.
> Each used all of his talents to the full;
> Both staked the whole of their magical powers.
> One wanted to take the queen back to the capital;
> The other would happily have stayed with her in the cave.
> There was no deep reason for the struggle:
> He was ready to give his life for the sake of the king.

When the two of them had fought fifty rounds without result the demon king realized that Monkey was too strong a fighter for him to be able to beat. Blocking the iron cudgel with his axe the demon said, "Stop, Sun the Novice. I haven't had my breakfast yet today. Let me eat, then I'll have it out with you." Monkey was well aware that he wanted to fetch the bells, so he put his cudgel away and said, "A hero doesn't chase an exhausted hare. Off you go. have a good meal, and get ready to come back and die."

[8]   The demon quickly turned and rushed inside, where he said to the queen, "Get me my treasures at once." "What for?" she asked. "The man challenging me to battle this morning was a disciple of the monk who's going to fetch the scriptures," he said.

"He's called Sun Wukong, or Sun the Novice, and Grand Par was just a nickname. I've been battling it out with him all this time, but still there's no outcome. Just wait while I take my treasures out and set off smoke and flames to burn that ape." These words made the queen feel very uneasy. If she didn't fetch the bells, she was worried that he might be suspicious, but if she did she feared that Sun the Novice would be killed. As she was hesitating the demon king pressed her again: "Hurry up and fetch them." She had no choice but to undo the lock, bring out the three bells and hand them to the demon king, who took them and went out outside the cave again. The queen sat in the inner quarters, her tears pouring down like rain, as she thought that Monkey would not possibly be able to escape with his life. Neither of them realized that the bells were only copies.

Once outside the cave the demon stood upwind and shouted, "Stay where you are, Sun the Novice. Watch while I ring these bells." "You have your bells, so why shouldn't I have mine?" Monkey replied. "You can ring yours, so why shouldn't I ring mine?" "What bells have you got?" the demon king asked. "Show me." Monkey pinched his iron cudgel to make it into an embroidery needle that he tucked into his ear then brought out the three real treasures from at his waist. "Here are my purple gold bells," he said to the demon king. The sight of them came as a shock to the demon. "That's funny," he thought, "very funny. Why are his bells exactly the same as mine? Even if they'd been cast from the same mould they'd not have been properly smoothed: you'd expect some extra marks or missing knobs. How can they be identical with this?" "Where did you get your bells from?" he went on to ask again. "Where are yours from, dear nephew?" Monkey replied. Being honest, the demon king replied, "These bells of mine,

Come from deep in the Way of the Immortal of Great Purity,

Are made of gold long refined in the Eight Trigrams Furnace

443

> *Formed into bells renowned as ultimate treasures*
> *Left by Lord Lao Zi left till the present day."*

"That's where my bells come from too," Monkey replied with a smile. "How were they made?" the demon king asked. "These bells of mine," said Monkey,

> *"Were made of gold refined in the furnace*
> *When Lord Lao Zi made elixir in the Tushita Palace,*
> *They are cyclical treasures. The two threes make six:*
> *Mine are the female and yours are the male."*

"The bells are golden elixir treasures," the demon king said, "not birds or beasts. They can't be male or female. As long as they yield what's precious when they're rung they're good ones." "Words prove nothing," said Monkey. "Show it by actions. Shake yours first." The demon king then rang his first bell three times. No fire came out. He rang his second three times. No smoke came out. He rang his third three times, and no sand came out either. "Very odd," he said, making wild gestures, "very odd. The world's changed. These bells must be hen-pecked. When the males see the females they don't dare to do their stuff." "Stop, nephew," said Monkey. "Now I'm going to shake mine to show you what happens." The splendid ape then grasped all three bells in one hand and rang them together. Watch as clouds of red flames, black smoke and yellow sand all come gushing out, setting the trees and the mountain ablaze. Monkey then said the words of another spell and shouted "Wind!" towards the southeast; and a wind did indeed spring up that fanned the flames. With the power of the wind behind them the flames and smoke filled the heavens, blazing red and deepest black, and the earth was covered by the yellow sandstorm. The Evil Star Matcher's souls fled from his body in his terror, but he had nowhere to turn: amid that fire there was no way of escaping with his life.

[9]   Then a penetrating shout was heard from mid-air: "Sun

Wukong, I am here." Monkey quickly looked up and saw that it was the Bodhisattva Guanyin holding her vase of pure water in her left hand and a sprig of willow in her right with which to sprinkle sweet dew and put out the flames. In his alarm Monkey hid the bells at his waist, put the palms of his hands together and prostrated himself in a kowtow. The Bodhisattva flicked a few drops of sweet dew from her willow sprig and in an instant both flames and smoke disappeared, while no sign of the yellow sand remained to be seen. "I did not realize, Most Merciful One, that you were coming down to the mortal world," said Brother Monkey as he kowtowed, "and it was wrong of me to fail to keep out of your way. May I venture to ask where you are going, Bodhisattva?" "I am here especially to find and take this evil monster," the Bodhisattva replied.

"What is the monster's background, and how can he put you to the trouble of capturing him in your illustrious person?" Monkey asked. "He is a golden-haired giant hound on which I used to ride," the Bodhisattva replied. "The boy in charge of it fell asleep and failed to keep proper guard over it, so that the wicked beast bit through its iron chains and escaped to save the king of Purpuria from disaster." When Monkey heard this he hastily bowed and said, "You have it the wrong way round, Bodhisattva. He's been mistreating the king and his queen, and thus damaging public morality. So how can you say that he has saved the king from disaster when in fact he has brought him disaster?" "You would not know," the Bodhisattva replied, "that when the previous king of Purpuria was reigning and the present king was the crown prince and had not yet taken the throne he was a superb archer and huntsman. Once he led his men and horses hunting with flacon and hound. They came to the Fallen Phoenix Slope, where a young peacock and peahen, two children of the Buddha's mother in the West, the Bodhisattva Maurya Vidya Rani were resting. When the king shot with his bow he wounded the cock, while the hen died with an arrow still in her. After the Buddha's mother realized to her regret what had happened she ordered that the prince should be separated from his wife for three years and suffer himself the way birds do when they are parted from their mates. At the time I was riding that hound and we both heard her say that. I never imagined that the beast would remember it and come back to mistreat the queen and thus save the king from disaster. That was three years ago, and now that the misdeed has been paid for it was fortunate that you came along to cure the king. I am here to recover the wicked and evil creature." "Bodhisattva," said Monkey, "this may well be so, but he did sully the queen, damage public morality, offend ethics and break the law. You can't let him off a non-capital punishment. Let me give him twenty blows before handing him over for you to take back." "Wukong," said the Bodhisattva, "as you know I am here to really ought to show me the respect I deserve and spare him completely. This still counts as one of your success in subduing a demon. If you hit him with your cudgel it'll kill him." Monkey dared not disobey, but bowed and said, "If you're taking him back to the ocean with you, Bodhisattva, you mustn't let him escape and come down to the human world again. That would be quite a catastrophe."

Only then did the Bodhisattva shout, "Wicked beast! Turn back into your own form! What are you waiting for?" The monster could be seen doing a roll and turning back into himself. Then he shook his fur for the Bodhisattva to mount on his back. The Bodhisattva looked down at his neck to see that the three golden bells were missing. "Wukong," she said, "give me my bells back." "I don't know where they are," Monkey said. "Thieving ape," the Bodhisattva shouted. "If you hadn't stolen those bells then ten Sun Wukongs, never mind one, would have dared go nowhere near him. Hand them over at once." "I really haven't seen them," Monkey replied with a smile. "In that case I'll have to recite the Band-tightening Spell," said the Bodhisattva. This scared Monkey, who could only plead, "Don't say it, don't say it. The bells are here." This was indeed a case of

Who could untie the bells from neck of the giant hound?
To find that out ask the one who first fastened them on.

The Bodhisattva then placed the bells round the giant hound's neck, and flew up to her high throne. Watch as the

Four-stalked lotus flowers blazed with fire;
Her whole body was thickly clad in cloth of gold.

We will say no more of how the Great Merciful One returned to the Southern Ocean.

[10]　The Great Sage Sun Wukong then tidied up his clothing and charged into the Horndog Cave swinging his iron cudgel and killing to his heart's content. He wiped all the demons out till he reached the inner quarters of the palace and asked the Golden Queen to go back to her country. She prostrated herself to him for a long time. Monkey told her all about how the Bodhisattva had subdued the demon and why she had been separated from her husband. Then he gathered some soft grasses that he twisted together into a long straw dragon. "Sit on this, ma'am," he said, "and shut your eyes. Don't be afraid. I'm taking you back to court to see your master." The queen followed his instructions carefully while he used his magic power. There was a sound of the wind whistling in her ears.

An hour later he brought her into the city. Bringing his cloud down he said, "Open your eyes, ma'am." When the queen opened her eyes and looked she recognized the phoenix buildings and dragon towers. She was very happy, and getting off the straw dragon she climbed the steps of the throne hall. When the king saw her he came straight down from his dragon throne to take the queen by her jade hand. He was just going to tell her how much he had missed her when he suddenly collapsed, shouting: "My hand hurts, my hand hurts." "Look at that mug," Pig said, roaring with laughter, "he's out of luck. No joy for him. The moment he meets her again he gets stung." "Idiot," said Monkey, "would you dare grab her?" "What if I did?" Pig asked. "The queen's covered with poisonous spikes," Monkey replied, "and she has poison on her hands. In the three years she was with the Evil Star Matcher in Mount Unicorn the monster never had her. If he had, his whole body would have been in agony. Even touching her with his hand made his hand ache." "Then what is to be done about it?" the officials asked. While all the officials were wondering what to do in the outer palace and the consorts and concubines in the inner palace were full of terror, the Jade and the Silver Queen helped their king to his feet.

【11】   Amid the general alarm a voice was heard in the sky shouting, "Great Sage, I'm here." Brother Monkey looked up, and this is what was to be seen:

> The cry of a crane soaring through the heavens,
> Then flying straight down to the palace of the king.
> Beams of auspicious light shone about;
> Cloud of holy vapours drifted all around.
> Mists came from the cloak of coir that covered his body:
> Rare were the straw sandals on which he trod.
> The fly-whisk in his hand was made of dragon whiskers,
> And silken tassels hung around his waist.
> He joined human destinies together throughout heaven and earth
> As he roamed free and easy all over the world.
> He was the Purple Clouds Immortal of the Daluo Heaven,
> Come down to earth today to lift an enchantment.

Monkey went over to him to greet him with, "Where are you going, Zhang Boduan of the Ziyang sect?" The True Man of Ziyang came to the front of the hall, bowed and replied, "Great Sage, the humble immortal Zhang Boduan greets you." "Where have you come from?" Monkey replied. "Three years ago I passed this way when going to a Buddha assembly," the True Man said. "When I saw that the King of Purpuria was suffering the agony of being parted from his wife I was worried that the demon would defile the queen. That would have been an affront to morality and made it hard for the queen to be reunited with the king later on. So I turned an old coir cloak into a new dress of many colours and gave it to the demon king. He made the queen wear it as here wedding dress. As soon as she put it on poisonous barbs grew all over her body. They were the coir cloak. Now that you have been successful, Great Sage, I've come to lift the spell." "In that case," said Monkey, "thank you for coming so far. Please remove the barbs at once." The True Man stepped forward, pointed at the queen, and removed the coir cloak. The queen's body was once more as it had originally been. The True Man shook the cloak, put it over his shoulders, and said to Monkey, "Please forgive me if I leave now, Great Sage." "Don't go yet," said Monkey. "Wait till the king has thanked you." "I won't trouble him," said the True Man with a smile, then raised his hands together in salute, rose up into the sky and went. The king, queen and the officials high and low were so astonished that they all bowed to the sky.

[12]　　When the bowing was over the king ordered that the eastern hall of the palace be thrown open so that they could give thanks to the four monks. The king led all his officials to go down on their knees and kowtow to them, and husband and wife were reunited. In the middle of the celebratory banquet Monkey said, "Master, bring out that declaration of war." The venerable elder produced it from his sleeve and handed it to Monkey, who passed it in turn to the king. "This was a letter that the demons sent his lieutenant to deliver," Monkey said. "He was the officer I killed and brought here as a trophy. Then I turned myself into the officer and went back to the cave to report. That was how I saw Her Majesty and stole the golden bells. He almost caught me, but I did another change, stole them again, got them out and fought him. It was lucky for him that the Bodhisattva Guanyin came to collect him and tell me why you and Her Majesty were parted." He told the whole story from beginning to end in great detail. Everyone in the country—whether ruler or ministers, whether within the palace or outside—expressed admiration and gratitude. "In the first place," said the Tang Priest, "it was because of Your Majesty's own good fortune, and in the second place it was thanks to my disciple's efforts. We are deeply obliged to you for

449

this sumptuous banquet today, and now we must take our leave of you. Please do not delay us poor monks on our pilgrimage to the West." When the king realized that his efforts to keep them there would be of no avail he inspected and returned the passport and arranged a great procession of royal coaches. The Tang Priest was invited to sit in his own dragon carriage, while the king, his queens and his consorts themselves all pushed it along as they saw them on their way then bade them farewell. Indeed,

> He was fated to have his melancholy washed clean away:
> The mind finds peace of itself when thought and worrying cease.

If you do not know what of good or ill lay in store for them on the way ahead listen to the explanation in the next instalment.

17. 盘丝洞七情迷本 濯垢泉八戒忘形

【1】 话表三藏别了朱紫国王，整顿鞍马西出。行彀多少山原，历尽无穷水道，不觉的秋去冬残，又值春光明媚。师徒们正在路踏青玩景，忽见一座庵林。三藏滚鞍下马，站立大道之旁。行者问道："师父，这条路平坦无邪，因何不走？"八戒道："师兄好不通情！师父在马上坐得困了，也让他下来关关风是。"三藏道："不是关风；我看那里是个人家，意欲自去化些斋吃。"行者笑道："你看师父说的是那里话。你要吃斋，我自去化。俗语云：'一日为师，终身为父。'岂有为弟子者高坐，教师父去化斋之理？"三藏道："不是这等说。平日间一望无边无际，你们没远没近的去化斋，今日人家逼近，可以叫应，也让我去化一个来。"八戒道："师父没主张。常言道：'三人出外，小的儿苦。'你况是个父辈，我等俱是弟子。古书云：'有事弟子服其劳。'等我老猪去。"三藏道："徒弟啊，今日天气晴明，与那风雨之时不同。那时节，汝等必定远去；此个人家，等我去。有斋无斋，可以就回走路。"沙僧在旁笑道："师兄，不必多讲。师父的心性如此，不必违拗。若恼了他，就化将斋来，他也不吃。"

【2】 八戒依言，即取出钵盂，与他换了衣帽。拽开步，直至那庄前观看，却也好座住场。但见：

> 石桥高耸，古树森齐。石桥高耸，潺潺流水接长溪；古树森齐，聒聒幽禽鸣远岱。桥那边有数椽茅屋，清清雅雅若仙庵；又有那一座蓬窗，白白明明欺道院。窗前忽见四佳人，都在那里刺凤描鸾做针线。

长老见那人家没个男儿，只有四个女子，不敢进去。将身立定，闪在乔林之下。只见那女子，一个个：

> 闺心坚似石，兰性喜如春。

娇脸红霞衬，朱唇绛脂匀。
峨眉横月小，蝉鬓逶迤新。
若对花间立，游蜂错认真。

少停有半个时辰，一发静悄悄，鸡犬无声。自家思虑道："我若没本事化顿斋饭，也惹着徒弟笑我：敢道为师的化不出斋来，为徒的怎能去拜佛。"

长老没计奈何，也带了几分不是，趋步上桥。又走了几步，只见那茅屋里面有一座木香亭子，亭子下又有三个女子在那里踢气球哩。你看那三个女子，比那四个又生得不同。但见那：

飘扬翠袖，摇拽缃裙。飘扬翠袖，低笼着玉笋纤纤；摇拽缃裙，半露出金莲窄窄。形容体势十分全，动静脚跟千样踢。拿头过论有高低，张泛送来真又楷。转身踢个出墙花，退步翻成大过海。轻接一团泥，单枪急对拐。明珠上佛头，实提来尖捽。窄砖偏会拿，卧鱼将脚挖。平腰折膝蹲，扭顶翘跟踢。扳爱能喧泛，披肩甚脱洒。绞裆任往来，锁项随摇摆。踢的是黄河水倒流，金鱼滩上买。那个错认是儿，这个转身就打拐。端然捧上臁，周正尖来捽。提跟濺草鞋，倒插回头采。退步泛肩妆，钩儿只一歹。版婆下来长，便把夺门掐。踢到美心时，佳人齐喝采。一个个汗流粉腻透罗裳，兴懒情疏方叫海。

言不尽，又有诗为证。诗曰：

蹴踘当场三月天，仙风吹下素婵娟。
汗沾粉面花含露，尘染峨眉柳带烟。
翠袖低垂笼玉笋，缃裙斜拽露金莲。
几回踢罢娇无力，云鬓蓬松且鬓偏。

三藏看得时辰久了，只得走上桥头来，应声高叫道："女菩萨，贫僧这里随缘布施些儿斋吃。"那些女子听见，一个个喜喜欢欢抛了针钱，撇了气球，都笑笑吟吟的接出门来道："长老，失迎了。今到荒庄，决不敢拦路斋僧，请里面坐。"三藏闻言，心中暗道："善哉，善哉！西方正是佛地！女流尚且注意斋僧，男子岂不虔心向佛？"

【3】长老向前问讯了，相随众女入茅屋。过木香亭看处，呀！

原来那里边没甚房廊，只见那：

> 峦头高耸，地脉遥长。峦头高耸接云烟，地脉遥长通海岳。门近石桥，九曲九弯流水顾；园栽桃李，千株千颗斗秋华。藤薜挂悬三五树，芝兰香散万千花。远观洞府欺蓬岛，近睹山林压太华。正是妖仙寻隐处，更无邻舍独成家。

有一女子上前，把石头门推开两扇，请唐僧里面进去。忽抬头看时，铺设的都是石桌、石凳，冷气阴阴。长老心惊，暗自思忖道："这去处少吉多凶，断然不善。"众女子喜笑吟吟，都道："长老请坐。"长老没奈何，只得坐了。少时间，打个冷禁。众女问道："长老是何宝山？化甚么缘？还是修桥补路，建寺礼塔，还是造佛印经？请缘簿出来看看。"长老道："我不是化缘的和尚。"女子道："既不化缘，到此何干？"长老道："我是东土大唐差去西天大雷音求经者。适过宝方，腹间饥馁，特造檀府，募化一斋，贫僧就行也。"众女子道："好！好！好！常言道：'远来的和尚好看经。'妹妹们！不可怠慢，快办斋来。"

此时有三个女子陪着，言来语去，论说些因缘。那四个到厨中撩衣敛袖，炊火刷锅。你道他安排的是些甚么东西？原来是人油炒炼，人肉煎熬；熬得黑糊充做面筋样子，剜的人脑煎做豆腐块片。两盘儿捧到石桌上放下，对长老道："请了。仓卒间，不曾备得好斋，且将就吃些充饥。后面还有添换来也。"那长老闻了一闻，见那腥膻，不敢开口，欠身合掌道："女菩萨，贫僧是胎里素。"众女子笑道："长老，此是素的。"长老道："阿弥陀佛！若像这等素的啊，我和尚吃了，莫想见得世尊，取得经卷。"众女子道："长老，你出家人，切莫拣人布施。"长老道："怎敢，怎敢！我和尚奉大唐旨意，一路西来，微生不损，见苦就救；遇谷粒手拈入口，逢丝缕联缀遮身，怎敢拣主布施！"众女子笑道："长老虽不拣人布施，却只有些上门怪人。莫嫌粗淡，吃些儿罢。"长老道："实是不敢吃，诚破了戒。望菩萨养生不杀为念，放我和尚出去罢。"

【4】 那长老挣着要走，那女子拦住门，怎么肯放，俱道："上门的买卖，倒不好做！'放了屁儿，却使手掩。'你往那里去？"他一个个都会些武艺，手脚又活，把长老扯住，顺手牵羊，扑的损倒在地。众人按住，将绳子捆了，悬梁高吊。这吊有个名色，叫做"仙

人指路"。原来是一只手向前，牵丝吊起，一只手拦腰捆住，将绳吊起；两只脚向后一条绳吊起；三条绳把长老吊在梁上，却是脊背朝上，肚皮朝下。那长老忍着疼，噙着泪，心中暗暗道："我和尚这等命苦！只说是好人家化顿斋吃，岂知道落了火坑！徒弟啊！速来救我，还得见面；但迟两个时辰，我命休矣！"

那长老虽然苦恼，却还留心看着那些女子。那些女子把他吊得停当，便去脱剥衣服。长老心惊，暗自忖道："这一脱了衣服，是要打我的情了。或者夹生儿吃我的情也有哩。"原来那女子们只解了上身罗衫，露出肚腹，各显神通：一个个脐眼中冒出丝绳，有鸭蛋粗细，骨都都的，进玉飞银，时下把庄门罩了不题。

【5】 却说那行者、八戒、沙僧，都在大道之旁。他二人都放马看担，惟行者是个顽皮，他且跳树攀枝，摘叶寻果。忽回头，只见一片光亮，慌得跳下树来，吆喝道："不好，不好！师父造化低了！"行者用手指道："你看那庄院如何？"八戒、沙僧共目视之，那一片，如雪又亮如雪，似银又光似银。八戒道："罢了，罢了！师父遇着妖精了！我们快去救他也！"行者道："贤弟莫嚷。你都不见怎的，等老孙去来。"沙僧道："哥哥仔细。"行者道："我自有处。"

好大圣，束一束虎皮裙，掣出金箍棒，拽开脚，两三步跑到前边，看见那丝绳缠得有千百层厚，穿穿道道，却似经纬之势；用手按一按，有些粘软沾人。行者更不知是甚么东西，他即举棒道："这一棒，莫说是几千层，就是几万层，也打断了！"正欲打，又停住手道："若是硬的便可打断，这个软的，只好打圆罢了。——假如惊了他，缠住老孙，反为不美。等我且问他一问再打。"

你道他问谁？即捻一个诀，念一个咒，拘得个土地老儿在庙里似推磨的一般乱转。土地婆儿道："老儿，你转怎的？好道是羊儿风发了！"土地道："你不知！你不知！有一个齐天大圣来了，我不曾接他，他那拘我哩。"婆儿道："你去见他便了，却如何在这里打转？"土地道："若去见他，他那棍子好不重，他管你好歹就打哩！"婆儿道："他见你这等老了，那里就打你？"土地道："他一生好吃没钱酒，偏打老年人。"两口儿讲一会，没奈何只得走出去，战兢兢的，跪在路旁，叫道："大圣，当境土地叩头。"行者道："你且起来，不要假忙。我且不打你，寄下在那里。我问你，此间是甚地方?"土地道:"大圣从那厢来?"行者道:"我自东土往西来的。"土地道:"大圣东来,可曾在那山岭上?"行者道:"正在那山岭上。我们行者、马匹还都歇在那岭上不是!"土地道:"那岭叫做盘丝岭。岭下有洞,叫做盘丝洞。洞里有七个妖精。"行者道:"是男怪女怪?"土地道:"是女怪。"行者道:"他有多大神通?"土地道:"小神力薄威短,不知他有多大手段;只知那正南上,离此有三里之遥,有一座濯垢泉,乃天生的热水,原是上方七仙姑的浴池。自妖精到此居住,占了他的濯垢泉,仙姑更不曾与他争竞,平白地就让与他了。我见天仙不惹妖魔怪,必定精灵有大能。"行者道:"占了此泉何干?"土地道:"这怪占了浴池,一日三遭,出来洗澡。如今巳时已过,午时将来哩。"行者听言道:"土地,你且回去,等我自家拿他罢。"那土地老儿磕了一个头,战兢兢的,回本庙去了。

【6】这大圣独显神通,摇身一变,变做个麻苍蝇儿,钉在路旁草梢上等待。须臾间,只听得呼呼吸吸之声,犹如蚕食叶,却似海生潮。只好有半盏茶时,丝绳皆尽,依然现出丝村,还像当初模样。又听得呀的一声,柴扉响处,里边笑语喧哗,走出七个女子。行者在暗中细看,见他一个个携手相搀,挨肩执袂,有说有笑的,走过桥来,果是标致。但见:

> 比玉香尤胜,如花语更真。柳眉横翠岫,檀口破樱唇。钗头翘翡翠,金莲闪绛裙。却似嫦娥临下界,仙子落凡尘。

行者笑道:"怪不得我师父要来化斋,原来是这一般好处。这七个美人儿,假若留住我师父,要吃也不勾一顿吃,要用也不勾两日用;要动手轮流一摆布就是死了。且等我去听他一听,看他怎的算计。"

好大圣,嘤的一声,飞在那前面走的女子云髻上钉住。才过桥来,后边的走向前来呼道:"姐姐,我们洗了澡,来蒸那胖和尚吃去。"行者暗笑道:"这怪物好没算计!煮还省些柴,怎么转要蒸了吃!"那些女子采花斗草向南来。不多时,到了浴池。但见一座石墙,十分壮丽。遍地野花香艳艳,满旁兰蕙密森森。后面一个女子,走上前,唿哨的一声,把两扇门儿推开,那中间果有一塘热水。这水:

自开辟以来，太阳星原贞有十，后被羿善开弓，射落九乌坠
地，止存金乌一星，乃太阳之真火也。天地有九处汤泉，俱
是众乌所化。那九阳泉，乃香冷泉、伴山泉、温泉、东合泉、
潢山泉、孝安泉、广汾泉、汤泉，此泉乃濯垢泉。

有诗为证。诗曰：

> 一气无冬夏，三秋永注春。
> 炎波如鼎沸，热浪似汤新。
> 分溜滋禾稼，停流荡俗尘。
> 涓涓珠泪泛，滚滚玉团津。
> 润滑原非酿，清平还自温。
> 瑞祥本地秀，造化乃天真。
> 佳人洗处冰肌滑，涤荡尘烦玉体新。

那浴池约有五丈余阔，十丈多长，内有四尺深浅，但见水清彻底。
底下水一似滚珠泛玉，骨都都冒将上来。四面有六七个孔窍通
流。流去二三里之遥，淌到田里，还是温水。亭子中近后壁放着一张八只脚的板凳。两山头放着两个
金彩漆的衣架。行者暗中喜嘤嘤的，一翅飞在那衣架头上钉住。

【7】　那些女子见水又清又热，便要洗浴，即一齐脱了衣服，搭在
衣架上。一齐下去，被行者看见：

> 褪放纽扣儿，解开罗带结。
> 酥胸白似银，玉体浑如雪。
> 肘膊赛冰铺，香肩欺粉贴。
> 肚皮软又绵，脊背光还洁。
> 膝腕半圆团，金莲三寸窄。
> 中间一段情，露出风流穴。

那女子都跳下水去，一个个跃浪翻波，负水顽耍。行者道："我若
打他啊，只消把这棍子往池中一搅，就叫做'滚汤泼老鼠，一窝儿
都是死。'可怜！可怜！便打打死他，只是低了老孙的名头。常
言道：'男不与女斗。'我这般一个汉子，打杀这几个丫头，着实不
济。不要打他，只送他一个绝科计，教他动不得身，出不得水，多
少是好。"好大圣，捏着诀，念个咒，摇身一变，变做一个饿老鹰，
但见：

毛犹霜雪，眼若明星。妖狐见处魂皆丧，狡兔逢时胆尽倾。
钢爪锋芒快，雄姿猛气横。会使老拳供口腹，不辞亲手逐
飞腾。万里寒空随上下，穿云检物任他行。

呼的一翅，飞向前，轮开利爪，把他那衣架上搭的七套衣服，尽情
雕去，径转岭头，现出本相来见八戒、沙僧道："你看！"那呆子迎
着对沙僧笑道："师父原来是典当铺里拿了去的。"沙僧道："怎见
得？"八戒道："你不见此把他些衣服都抢将来也？"行者放下
道："此是妖精穿的衣服。"八戒道："怎么就有这许多？"行者道：
"七套。"八戒道："如何这般剥得容易，又剥得干净？"行者道："那
曾用剥。原来此处唤做盘丝岭。那庄村唤做盘丝洞。洞中有七
个女怪，把你师父拿住，吊在洞里，都向濯垢泉去洗浴。那泉却
是天地产成的一塘子热水。他都算计着洗了澡要把师父蒸吃。
是我跟到那里，见他脱了衣服下水，我要打他，恐怕污了棍子，又
怕坏了名头，是以不曾动棍，只变做一个饿老鹰，雕了他的衣服。
他都忍辱含羞，蹲在水中哩。我等快去解下师父走路
罢。"八戒笑道："师兄，你凡干事，只要留根。既见妖精，如何不
打杀他，却就去解师父！他如今纵然藏羞不出，到晚间必定出
来。他家里还有旧衣服，穿上一套，来赶我们。纵然不赶，他久住
在此，我们取了经，还从那条路回来。常言道：'宁少路边钱，
莫少路边拳。'那时节，他拦住了吵闹，却不是个仇人也？"行者
道："凭你如何主张？"八戒道："依我，先打杀了妖精，再去解放师
父；此乃'斩草除根'之计。"行者道："我是不打他。你要打，你去
打他。"

【8】　八戒抖擞精神，欢天喜地，举着钉钯，拽开步，径直跑到那
里。忽的推开门看时，只见那七个女子，蹲在水里，口中乱骂那
鹰哩，道："这个匾毛畜生！猫嚼头的亡人！把我们衣服都雕去
了，教我们怎的动手！"八戒忍不住笑道："女菩萨，在这里洗澡
哩。也携带我和尚洗洗，何如？"那怪见了，作怒道："你这和尚，
十分无礼！我们是在家的女流，你是个出家的男子。古书云：
'七年男女不同席。'你好和我们同塘洗澡？"八戒道："天气炎热，
没奈何，将就容我洗洗儿罢。那里调甚么书担儿，同席不同席！"
呆子不容说，丢了钉钯，脱了皂锦直裰，扑的跳下水来。那怪心中

烦恼，一齐上前要打。不知八戒水势极熟，到水里摇身一变，变做一个鲇鱼精。那怪就都摸鱼，赶上拿他不住：东边摸，忽的又溜了西去；西边摸，忽的又溜了东去；滑扢虀的，只在那腿裆里乱钻。原来那水有搀胸之深，水上盘了一会，又盘在水底，都盘倒了，喘嘘嘘的，精神倦怠。

八戒却才跳将上来，现了本相，穿了直裰，执着钉钯，喝道："我是那个？你把我当鲇鱼精哩！"那怪见了，心惊胆战，对八戒道："你先来是个和尚，到水里变做鲇鱼，及拿你不住，却又这般打扮；你端的是从何到此？是必留名。"八戒道："这伙泼怪当真的不识我！我是东土大唐取经的唐长老之徒弟，乃天蓬元帅悟能八戒是也。他把我师父吊在洞里，算计要蒸他受用！我的师父，又好蒸吃？快早伸过头来，各筑一钯，教你断根！"那些妖闻此言，魂飞魄散，就在水中跪拜道："望老爷方便方便！我等有眼无珠，误投了你家父，虽然居在那里，不曾造甚受苦。望慈悲饶了我的性命，情愿贴些盘费，送你师父往西天去也。"八戒摇手道："莫说这话！俗语说得好：'曾着卖糖君子哄，到今不信口甜人。'是便筑一钯，各人走路！"

【9】 呆子一味粗夯，显手段，那有怜香惜玉之心，举着钯，不分好歹，赶上前乱筑。那怪慌了手脚，那里顾甚么羞耻，只是性命要紧，随用手侮着羞处，跳出水来，都跑在亭子里站立，作出法来：脐孔中骨都都冒出丝绳，瞒天搭了个大丝篷，把八戒罩在当中。那呆子忽抬头，不见天日，即抽身往外便走。那里早得跨步？原来放了绊脚索，满地都是丝绳，动动脚，跌个踉跄：左边去，一个面磕地；右边去，一个倒栽葱；急转身，又跌了个嘴揾地；忙爬起，又跌了个竖蜻蜓。也不知跌了多少跟头，把个呆子跌得身麻脚软，头晕眼花，爬也爬不动，只睡在地下呻吟。那怪物却将他困住，也不打他，也不伤他，一个个跳出门来，将丝篷遮住天光，各回本洞。

到了石桥上站下，念动真言，霎时间，把丝篷收了，赤条条的，跑入洞里，侮着那话，从唐僧面前笑嘻嘻的跑过去。走入石房，取几件旧衣穿了，径至后门口立定，叫："孩儿们何在？"原来那妖精一个有一个儿子，却不是他养的，都是他结拜的干儿子。

有名唤做蜜、蚂、蠦、班、蜢、蜡、蜻：蜜是蜜蜂，蚂是蚂蜂，蠦是蠦蜂，班是班毛，蜢是牛蜢，蜡是抹蜡，蜻是蜻蜓。原来那妖精幔天结网，掳住这七般虫蛭，却要吃他。古云："禽有禽言，兽有兽语。"当时这些虫哀告饶命，愿拜为母，遂此春采百花供怪物，夏寻诸卉孝妖精。忽闻一声呼唤，都到面前，问："母亲有何使令？"众怪道："儿啊，早间我们错惹了唐朝来的和尚，才然被他徒弟拦在池里，出了多少丑，几乎丧了性命！汝等努力，快出门前去退他一退。如得胜后，可到你舅舅家来会我。"那些怪既得逃生，往他师兄处，孳嘴生灾不题。你看这些虫蛭，一个个摩拳擦掌，出来迎敌。

【10】 却说八戒跌得昏头昏脑，猛抬头，见丝篷丝索俱无，他才一步一探，爬将起来，忍着疼，找回原路。见了行者，用手扯住道："哥哥，我的头可肿，脸可青么？"行者道："你怎的来？"八戒道："我被那厮将丝绳罩住，放了绊脚索，不知跌了多少跟头，跌得我腰拖背折，寸步难移。却才丝篷索子俱空，方得了性命回来也。"沙僧见了道："罢了，罢了！你闯下祸来也！那怪一定往洞里去伤害师父，我等快去救他！"

行者闻言，急拽步便走。八戒牵着马，急急来到庄前。但见那石桥上有七个小妖儿挡住道："慢来，慢来！吾等在此！"行者看了道："好笑！干净都是些小人儿！长的也只有二尺五六寸，不满三尺；重的也只有八九斤。不满十斤。"喝道："你是谁？"那怪道："我乃七仙姑的儿子。你把我母亲欺辱了，还敢无知，打上我门！不要走！仔细！"好怪物，一个个手之舞之，足之蹈之，乱打将来。八戒见了生嗔，本是跌恼了的性子，又见那伙虫蛭小巧，就发狠举钯来筑。

那些怪见呆子凶猛，一个个现了本像，飞将起去，叫声"变！"须臾间，一个变十个，十个变百个，百个变千个，千个变万个，个个都变成无穷之数。只见：

满天飞抹蜡，遍地舞蜻蜓。
蜜蚂追头额，蠦蜂扎眼睛。
班毛前后咬，牛蜢上下叮。
扑面漫漫黑，翛翛神鬼惊。

八戒慌了道："哥啊，只说经好取，西方路上，虫儿也欺负人哩！"行者道："兄弟，不要怕，快上前打！"八戒道："扑头扑脸，浑身上下，都叮有十数层厚，却怎么打？"行者道："没事！没事！我自有手段！"沙僧道："哥啊，有甚手段，快使出来罢。一会子光头上都叮肿了！"

【11】　好大圣，拔了一把毫毛，嚼得粉碎，喷将出去，即变做些黄、麻、䍶、白、雕、鱼、鹞。八戒道："师兄，又打甚么市语——黄啊、麻啊哩？"行者道："你不知。黄是黄鹰，麻是麻鹰，䍶是䍶鹰，白是白鹰，雕是雕鹰，鱼是鱼鹰，鹞是鹞鹰。那妖精的儿子是七样虫，我的毫毛是七样鹰。"鹰最能嗛虫，一嘴一个，爪打翅敲，须臾，打得磬尽，满空无迹，地积尺余。

三兄弟方才闯过桥去，径入洞里。只见老师父吊在那里哼哼的哭哩。八戒近前道："师父，你是要来这里吊了耍子，不知作成我跌了多少跟头哩！"沙僧道："且解下师父再说。"行者即将绳索挑断，放下唐僧，都问道："妖精那里去了？"唐僧道："那七个怪都赤条条的往后边叫儿子去了。"行者道："兄弟们，跟我来寻去。"

三人各持兵器，往后园里寻处，不见踪迹。都到那桃李树上寻遍不见。八戒道："去了！去了！"沙僧道："不必寻他，等我扶师父去也。"弟兄们复来前面，请唐僧上马去了，再不自专了。八戒道："你们扶师父走着，等老猪一顿钯筑倒他这房子，教他来时没处安身。"行者笑道："筑还费力，不若寻些柴来，与他个断根罢。"好呆子，寻了些朽松、破竹、干柳、枯藤，点上一把火，烘烘的都烧得干净。师徒却才放心前来。咦！毕竟这去，不知那怪的吉凶如何，且听下回分解。

Chapter 17
The Seven Emotions Confuse the Basic in Gossamer Cave; At Filth-cleansing Spring Pig Forgets Himself

【1】 The story tells how Sanzang took his leave of the king of Purpuria, got everything ready, saddled the horse and headed westwards. They crossed many a mountain and river. Before they realized it autumn and winter were over and spring's brightness and charm were back. Master and disciples were enjoying the scenery as their way led them across the greenery when they suddenly noticed a building amid trees. Sanzang dismounted and stood beside the main track. "Master," Brother Monkey asked, "the road is easy and there is no evil about, so why have you stopped?" "You aren't at all understanding, brother," Pig said. "The master is feeling sleepy after being in the saddle for so long. You ought to let him come down and have a rest." "It's not that," Sanzang said. "I can see a house over there. I was thinking of going there myself to beg for some food."

"What a thing for the master to say," said Monkey with a smile. "If you want some food I'll go and beg some for you. As the saying goes, 'Your teacher for a day is your father for the rest of your life.' It would be outrageous for me, your disciple, so sit here idly and let my master go begging." "There's no need to say that," Sanzang replied. "Usually you three have to cross enormous distances as far as the eye can see to beg for our food. Today there's a house so close it's in shouting distance, so let me beg this time." "But, Master, you wouldn't know what to do," said Pig. "As the saying goes, when three people go travelling it's the youngest who does the rough jobs. You're the senior one and we're all only disciples. As the old book says, 'When there is a job to be down the disciple does it.' Let me go." "Disciples," said

Sanzang, "the weather is good today. It's not at all like the times when you all have to go far away in wind and rain. Let me go to this house. Whether I get any food or not I shall soon be back and we shall be on our way." Friar Sand, who was standing beside them, smiled and said, "Stop arguing so much, brother. As the master has made his mind up you shouldn't disobey him. If you upset him he won't eat any of the food you are able to beg."

[2]   Pig accepted this suggestion and brought out the begging bowl and a change of hat and cassock for the master, who went straight to the farm building to look at it. It really was a fine place. He could see:

> A high-rising stone bridge,
> Ancient trees growing close together.
> Where the stone bridge rose high
> A babbling brook joined a long stream;
> Amid close-growing ancient trees
> Hidden birds sang sweetly on the distant hill.
> Across the bridge were several thatched houses
> As pure and elegant as an immortal's hermitage.
> There was also a thatched hut
> So pure and white it would put a Taoist temple to shame.
> Before the hut could be seen four beauties
> All busily embroidering phoenix designs.

As there were no males but only these four girls to be seen the reverend gentleman did not dare go inside, but slipped back under the tall trees and stood stock still. He could see that each of the girls

> Were rock-hard in their ladylike propriety,
> And happy as the spring in their orchid natures.
> Red glows set off their tender cheeks;
> Crimson make-up was spread on their lips.
> Their moth brows were as fine as a crescent moon,
> While their clouds of hair were piled up like cicada wings.

463

> *Had any of them stood among the flowers*
> *Wandering bees would have taken them for blossoms.*

He stood there for an hour. The silence was complete, unbroken by dog or cock. "If I'm not even capable of begging us a meal my disciples will laugh at me," he thought. "If the master can't beg a meal, what hope do his disciples have of ever getting to see the Buddha?"

He did not know what to do, but it seemed wrong to stay there any longer, so he went back towards the bridge, only to notice a pavilion inside the compound of thatched cottages. In the pavilion three more girls were juggling a ball with their feet. Look at them. They were different from the other four:

> *Their turquoise sleeves are waving*
> *And their embroidered skirts are swaying.*
> *The waving turquoise sleeves*
> *Cover their delicate jade bamboo-shoots of fingers,*
> *The swaying embroidered skirts*
> *Half show their tiny golden lotus feet.*
> *Perfect are their faces and bodies,*
> *Endless the movements of their slippered heels.*
> *As they grab for the head they vary in height;*
> *They pass the ball around most smoothly.*
> *One turns around and kicks an "over-the-wall flower,"*
> *Then does a backward somersault called "crossing the sea."*
> *After lightly taking a pass like a lump of clay*
> *A single spear is hard pressed by a pair of sticks.*
> *A shining pearl is put on the Buddha's head*
> *And held between the tips of their fingers.*
> *Skilfully they hold the ball as a narrow brick,*
> *Twisting their feet in the sleeping fish position.*
> *Their backs held level, they squat with bended knee;*
> *Turning their necks they kick their heels in the air.*
> *They can make benches fly around;*
> *Very stylish are the capes upon their shoulders.*

Their trouser-legs are bound with tapes to let them move,
While their necklaces swing as they sway.
They kick the ball like the Yellow River flowing
backwards,
Or goldfish purchased on the beach.
When you mistake one of them for the leader
Another one turns to carry the ball away.
They all hold their calves so trimly in the air,
Pointing their toes to catch the ball.
They raise their heels to spin straw sandals,
Planting them upside-down and picking them up in a
turn.
As they step back their shoulder-capes spread out
Fastened only with a hook.
The pedlar's basket comes down long and low,
Then they grab for the goal.
At the really magnificent footwork
All the beauties shout with admiration.
The silken clothes of all are soaked in sweat;
Feeling tired and relaxed they ended their game.

The description could go on and on. There is another poem that tells more:

Kicking the ball in the April weather,
Beauties blown along by the magical wind.
Sweat stained their powdered faces like dew on a flower;
The dust on their moth eyebrows was mist hiding willows.
Their turquoise sleeves hanging low covered jade fingers;
Trailing embroidered skirts showed golden lotus feet.
After kicking the ball many times they were charmingly
tired;
Their hair was dishevelled and their topknots askew.

After watching for a long time Sanzang could only go to the bridge and call loudly, "Bodhisattvas, fate brings me here as a poor monk to beg for the gift of some food." As soon as the women heard him they cheerfully put aside their needlework and balls to come out smiling and giggling through the gates to greet him. "Reverend sir," they said, "we're sorry we didn't welcome you sooner. As you have come to our poor farm we couldn't possibly feed you on the path. Please come inside and sit down." When Sanzang heard this he thought, "Splendid, this is splendid. The West really is Buddha's land. If even these womenfolk are so diligent about feeding monks the men are bound to be pious followers of the Buddha."

[3] Sanzang stepped forward to greet the women and followed them into the thatched cottages. As he passed the pavilion and looked he saw that on the other side of it there were no buildings. All that could be seen were

> *Towering mountain-tops,*
> *Distant ranges of the earth.*
> *The towering mountain-tops touch the clouds;*
> *The distant ranges of the earth lead to peaks in the ocean.*
> *From the stone bridge by the gates*
> *One looks on a stream that bends nine times;*
> *The peach and plum trees in the orchard*
> *Vie in abundance of blossom.*
> *Creepers and vines hang from three or four trees;*
> *The fragrance of orchids is spread by thousands of flowers*
> *From afar this retreat rivals Penglai's fairyland;*
> *Seen from close to the mountain beats Tai and Hua.*
> *This is truly a retreat for demon immortals,*
> *An isolated house with no neighbours around.*

One woman came forward to push the stone gates open and invite the Tang Priest to come in and sit down. All he could do was go inside. When he looked up he saw that the tables and seats were all of stone, and the atmosphere was oppressively cold. This alarmed the venerable elder, who thought, "This is a thoroughly sinister place. I'm sure it's evil." "Please sit down, venerable elder," the women all said with simpering smiles. He had no choice but to sit down. A little later he found himself shuddering.

"What monastery are you from, reverend sir?" the women asked. "For what purpose are you collecting alms? Are you repairing roads and bridges, founding monasteries, worshipping at pagodas, or having Buddha statues made and sutras printed? Won't you show us your donation book?" "I am not a monk collecting donations," the venerable elder replied. "If you're not here to ask for charity then why are you here?" the women asked. "We have been sent by Great Tang in the east to the Thunder Monastery in the Western Heaven to fetch the scriptures," Sanzang replied. "As our stomachs were empty when we happened to be passing this distinguished place I have come to beg a vegetarian meal from you in your kindness. After that we poor monks will be on our way again." "Splendid, splendid," the women all said. "As the saying goes, monks from afar most love to read the scriptures. Sisters! We must treat them well. Let's give them some vegetarian food as quickly as we can."

While three of the women kept him company, talking about such matters as primary and secondary causation, the other four went into the kitchen, where they tucked up their clothes, rolled up their sleeves, fanned the fire and scrubbed the cooking pots. Do you know what it was they prepared? They were frying in human fat, and what they cooked was human flesh, stewed into black paste as if it were wheat gluten, and human brain but out to fry like pieces of beancurd. Then they placed the two dishes on a stone table and said to Sanzang, "Do eat. We were too rushed to prepare anything good, so please make do with this. It'll stave off the pangs of hunger. There will be some more dishes to follow."

As soon as Sanzang used his nose and smelled the stench of flesh he would not eat, but bowed with his hands together before his chest and said, "Bodhisattvas, I have been a vegetarian since birth." "But this is vegetarian food, reverend sir," the women all replied with smiles. "Amitabha Buddha!" exclaimed Sanzang. "If as a monk I ate vegetarian food like that I would never have any hope of seeing the Buddha or fetching the sutras." "Reverend sir," the women said, "as a monk you shouldn't be so choosy about what you're given." "I never could be," Sanzang said, "I never could be. I am under the orders of the Great Tang emperor to harm not even the tiniest life, to save all I see suffering, to put all the food-grain I am given into my mouth with my fingers, and to cover my body with the threads of silk that come my way. I would never dare pick and choose among my benefactors' gifts." "Even if you're not picking and choosing," the women replied with smiles, "you do seem to have come here to complain. Please eat some of the food and don't mind if it's a little coarse and flavourless." "It's not that I don't want to eat it," Sanzang said, "it's that I'm afraid I'd be breaking my vows. I hope that you Bodhisattvas will remember that setting living beings free is better than keeping them with you and let me go on my way."

[4] As Sanzang struggled to get out the women blocked the gateway and refused to let him go. "Business bringing itself to our door!" they all said. "You've no more chance of getting away from here than of covering up a fart with your hands. Where do you think you're going?" They were all quite skilled in the martial arts and quick movers too, and after they had grabbed Sanzang they dragged him like a sheep and threw him to the ground. Then they all held him down, tied him up, and suspended him from the rafters. There is a special name for the way they hung him up there: The Immortal Shows the Way. One hand was strung up by a rope so that it pointed forward. The other hand was fastened to his waist by another rope that was also holding him aloft, and his legs were both held up by a third rope behind him. The three ropes had him suspended from a beam with his back on top and his belly pointing down. As Sanzang endured the agony and held back his tears he thought with bitter regret, "How evil my destiny is. I thought I was coming to beg for a vegetarian meal from good people. I never imagined I'd be falling into the fiery pit. Disciples! Rescue me as soon as you can if I am ever to see you again. If you don't get here within four hours I shall be dead."

Despite his misery Sanzang kept a careful eye on the women.

When they had him tied up securely and hanging there they started to remove their clothes. This alarmed the venerable elder, who thought, "They must be taking their clothes off because they are going to beat me. Perhaps they are going to eat me too." The women only unbuttoned their gauze blouses, exposing their stomachs. Then each of them produced a silken rope about as thick as a duck egg from her navel. These they made move like bursting jade or flying silver as they fastened the gates of the farm.

[5] We leave them and go back to Monkey, Pig and Friar Sand, who were all still waiting by the main road. While the other two were pasturing the horse and looking after the baggage Monkey was amusing himself by leaping from tree to tree and climbing around the branches as he picked leaves and looked for fruit. Suddenly he turned round and saw a sheet of light. This so alarmed him that he jumped out of the tree with a shout of "This is terrible! Terrible! The master's luck is out." He pointed as he continued, "Look at the farm. What do you think?" When Pig and Friar Sand both looked they saw a sheet of something like snow but brighter and like silver but shinier. "That's done it," said Pig, "that's done it. The master's run into evil spirits. We'd better go and rescue him straight away." "Stop yelling, brother," said Monkey. "Neither of you can see just what's there. Wait while I go and take a look." "Do be careful, brother," said Friar Sand. "I can cope," Monkey replied.

The splendid Great Sage tightened his tigerskin kilt, pulled out his gold-banded cudgel and took a few strides forward to see that the silken ropes had formed something like a web with thousands of strands. When he felt it with his hands it was somewhat soft and sticky. Not knowing what it was, Monkey raised his cudgel and said, "Never mind thousands of strands. This cudgel could break through tens of thousands of them." He was just about to strike when he stopped to think, "If they were hard I could certainly smash them, but then soft ones would only be knocked flat, and if I alarm the demons and get caught myself that would be a disaster. I'd better make some enquiries before I do any hitting."

Who do you think he asked? He made a spell with his hands, said the words of it and sent for an old local god, who ran round and round in his shrine just as if turning a mill. "Old man," his wife asked, "what are you rushing round and round for? You must be having a fit." "You don't understand," the local god replied. "There's a Great Sage Equalling Heaven here. I didn't go to meet him. But he's sending for me." "Go and see him then," his wife replied, "and that'll be that. Why charge round and round in here?" "But if I go and see him that cudgel of his hits very hard," the local deity said. "He doesn't care what you're like—he just hits you." "He won't possibly hit you when he sees how old you are," his wife replied. "He's been cadging free drinks all his life," the local god said, "and he really loves hitting old people."

After talking for a while with his wife the local god had no choice but to go outside and kneel shivering and shaking by the roadside, calling out, "Great Sage, the local deity kowtows to you." "Get up," Brother Monkey replied, "and stop pretending to be so keen. I'm not going to hit you. I'm just passing through. Tell me where this is." "Which way have you come, Great Sage?" the local deity asked. "I've come from the east and I'm heading west," said Monkey. "Which mountain have you reached on your journey from the east?" the local deity asked. "That ridge there," Monkey replied. "Our baggage and the horse are there, aren't they?" "That is Gossamer Ridge," the local deity replied. "Under the ridge there's a cave called Gossamer Cave where seven evil spirits live." "Male or female ones?" Monkey asked. "She-devils," the local deity replied. "How powerful is their magic?" Monkey asked. "I'm much too weak and insignificant to know that," the local god replied. "All I can tell you is that a mile due south of here there is a natural hot spring called the Filth-cleansing Spring," the local god said, "where the Seven Fairies from on high used to bathe. When the seven evil spirits settled here and took over the Filth-cleansing Spring the good spirits didn't try to fight them for it. They let the spirits have it for nothing. I reckon that if even good spirits from Heaven don't dare offend them the evil spirits must have tremendous powers." "What have they taken the spring over for?" Monkey asked. "Ever since taking the bathing pool over the monsters have been coming to bathe there three times a day," the local god replied. "It's already after eleven. They'll be along at noon." "Go back now, local god," Monkey said when he heard all this, "and wait while I capture them." The old local god kowtowed to him and went back to his shrine all of a tremble.

[6]   The Great Sage then gave a solo display of his magical powers, shaking himself, turning into a fly, and landing on the tip of a blade of grass to wait beside the path. A little later he heard a rustling, hissing sound like that of silkworms eating leaves or an ocean tide coming in. In the time it takes to drink half a cup of tea the silken ropes had all gone, and the farm looked just the same as it had before. Then there was a creaking noise as the wicker gate opened and the seven women came out laughing and talking noisily. Monkey watched carefully from where he was hiding and saw them talking and laughing as they held each other by the hand and walked shoulder to shoulder across the bridge. They were real beauties:

> *Compare them with jade and they were more fragrant;*
> *They were like flowers but able to talk.*
> *Their willowy brows were like distant hills;*
> *Sandalwood-scented mouths were bursting cherries.*
> *Hair ornaments were of jade;*
> *Golden lotus feet darted out under crimson skirts.*
> *They were like the moon goddess come down to earth,*
> *Immortal girls descending to the world.*

"No wonder the master wanted to come begging for food," thought Monkey with a laugh, "with all these lovelies here. If these seven beauties have captured him he won't be enough for a single meal for them. They couldn't make him last a couple of days. And if they take it in turns to have their way with him

471

they'll kill him straight off. I'd better go and listen to what they're plotting."

The splendid Great Sage flew over with a high-pitched buzz and landed on the topknot of the woman who was walking in front. When she was over the bridge the women behind her caught up with her and called out, "Sister, let's have a bath before we steam the fat monk and eat him up." "These monsters aren't at all economical," Monkey smiled to himself. "They'd save a lot of firewood if they boiled him. Why steam him instead?" The women walked south, picking flowers and throwing grass at each other, and were soon at the bathing pool, where a very magnificent wall and gateway appeared, with fragrant flowers, among them a bed of orchids, growing all around. One of the women behind him stepped forward and with a whistling sound pushed the double gates open, revealing the pond of naturally hot water inside. As for this water,

> *When heaven and earth were first separated*
> *There were ten suns in the sky*
> *Till Yi, the fine archer,*
> *Shot nine of the sun-crows down to the earth,*
> *Leaving only one golden crow star,*
> *The true fire of the sun.*
> *The nine hot springs in heaven and earth*
> *Are the other nine crows transformed.*
> *These nine hot springs are*
> *Cool Fragrance Spring,*
> *Mountain-companions Spring,*
> *Warm Spring,*
> *Donghe Spring,*
> *Mount Huang Spring,*
> *Xiao'an Spring,*
> *Guangfen Spring,*
> *Hot Water Spring,*
> *And this filth-cleansing Spring.*

There is a poem about it that goes:

> The same vital force runs in all four seasons;
> Spring continues throughout the autumn.
> The scalding water bubbles like a cauldron;
> The snow-white waves are boiling hot.
> If the waters are spread they help the crops to grow;
> Left where they are they wash worldly dust away.
> Little bubbles spread out like pearls,
> Rolling ones rise like pieces of jade.
> It is rich and smooth although not wine,
> Clear, calm and naturally warm.
> The whole place thrives on its air of good omen:
> It brings good fortune and the natural truth.
> When the beauties wash their flesh is smooth as ice;
> As dirt is soaked away their jade-like bodies are made new.

The bathing pool was about fifty feet across, a hundred feet long and four feet deep. The water was pure and translucent, and from the bottom of it came up bubbles like rolling pearls or floating jade. In the four sides of the pool there were six or seven pipes through which the water flowed out, keeping warm even when it reached fields up to a mile away. Beside the pool was a three-roomed pavilion, next to the back wall of which stood an eight-legged bench. At each end of the pavilion was a clothes stand painted in coloured lacquers. All this secretly delighted Monkey, who flew straight to one of the stands and landed on it.

[7] When the women saw how clear and warm the water was they wanted to bathe in it, so they all took their clothes off and hung them on the stands before going into the pool together. This is what Monkey saw:

> They undid the buttons on their clothes,
> Loosened the knots in their gauzy sashes. .
> Silvery white were their creamy breasts,
> Snowy their bodies that looked like jade.

Their arms and elbows were cool as ice,
And scented shoulders more lovely than if powdered.
Soft and supple the skin on their stomachs,
Glistening and clean their backs.
Their knees and wrists were rounded and soft;
Only three inches long were their golden lotus feet.
And as for what lay in between,
They showed a glimpse of the cave of pleasure.

The women all jumped into the water and enjoyed themselves as they frolicked in the waves. "If I wanted to hit them," Monkey thought, "I'd only need to stir the water with my cudgel. It would be like pouring boiling water on a nest of mice: I could kill the lot of them. What a pity. If I hit them I'd kill them, but it wouldn't do my reputation any good. As they say, a real man doesn't fight women. It'd be hopeless if a man like me killed these girls. If I'm not going to hit them I'll have to make things difficult for them so that they can't move." The splendid Great Sage made a spell with his hands, said the words of it, shook himself and turned into a hungry eagle.

His feathers were like frost or snow,
His eyes like bright stars.
When evil foxes saw him their souls were scared out of them;
And crafty hares were struck with terror.
His steely claws were sharp as spear-points;
His air was both majestic and ferocious.
He used his talons to seize his food,
And was ready to catch his flying prey himself.
He could fly high and low across the chilly sky,
Swooping through clouds and on his quarry at will.

With a whoosh of his wings he flew towards them, stretched his sharp talons to seize all seven sets of clothes that were hung on the stands and flew straight back to the ridge with them. Here he reverted to his own form to see Pig and Friar Sand.

Just look at the idiot as he comes up to Brother Monkey and says with a grin, "The master must have been taken to a pawn-broker's." "How can you tell?" asked Friar Sand. "Can't you see all those clothes our brother's grabbed?" Pig replied. "These are the evil spirits' clothes," said Monkey, putting them down. "How on earth did you get so many?" Pig asked. "There are seven outfits," said Monkey. "How did you strip them so easily, and strip them naked at that?" Pig asked. "I didn't have to strip them," said Monkey. "This place is called Gossamer Ridge, and the farm is called Gossamer Cave. The seven she-devils who live there captured the master, hung him up in their cave and all went off to bathe in the Filth-cleansing Spring. It's a natural hot spring. Their plan was to have a bath then steam the master and eat him. I went there with them and watched them undress and get into the water. I wanted to hit them, but I was worried it would contaminate my cudgel and ruin my reputation so I didn't. I just turned myself into a hungry eagle and grabbed their clothes in my talons. Now they're all squatting in the water, too embarrassed to come out. Let's rescue the master and be on our way as quickly as we can."

"Brother," grinned Pig, "you always leave something undone. You could see that they were evil spirits, so why didn't you kill them first then rescue the master? Even if they're too embarrassed to come out now they'll certainly come out after nightfall. They're bound to have enough old clothes at home to be able to put on an outfit each and come after us. Even if they don't come after us they live here permanently and we'll have to come this way back after we've fetched the scriptures. As the saying goes, it's better to get into debt on a journey than to get into a fight. When they stop us and make a row they'll really have it in for us." "So what do you suggest?" Monkey asked. "If you ask me we should kill the demons then rescue the master," said Pig. "That's what's called cutting down weeds and digging them out by the roots." "I'm not going to hit them," Monkey replied. "If you want them hit go and do it yourself."

【8】 Pig then summoned up his spirits and in high delight rushed straight there, his rake held aloft. As he suddenly pushed the gates open and looked inside he saw 7the seven women squatting in the water and wildly cursing the eagle. "Feathery beast," they were saying, "cat-headed monster. What the hell can we do now you've carried our clothes off?" Pig could not help laughing as he said to them, "Bodhisattvas, carry on with your bath. Do you mind if I join you?" "You monk, you're a disgrace," the devils retorted angrily as they saw him. "We're lay women and you're a man of religion. As the ancient book has it, 'From the age of seven boys and girls do not share the same mat.' You mustn't possibly bathe in the same pool as us." "But the weather's so scorching hot I've got no choice," said Pig. "You'll have to make the best of it and let me take a wash. What do you have to show off all that book-learning about sharing mats for?"

With no further argument the idiot dropped his rake, stripped off his cotton tunic and jumped in with a splash, to the fury of the demons who all rushed at him to hit him. Little did they realize how expert Pig was in the water. Once in the pool he shook himself and turned into a catfish spirit. The demons then tried to grab him but even when they caught him they could not get a firm grip. If they grabbed to the east he suddenly shot westwards, and if they tried to grab him to the west he went east. The funny thing was that he kept wriggling around their crotches. The water was about chest-high, and after swimming around at the surface and then at the bottom of the pool for a while he had covered all of it and was panting and exhausted.

Only then did Pig jump out, turn back into himself, put his tunic back on, pick up his rake and shout, "Who am I then? You thought I was a catfish spirit!" At the sight of him the demons all trembled with fright and said to Pig, "When you came here first you were a monk, then you turned into a catfish in the water and we couldn't catch you. Now you've dressed like that . Where have you come from? You must tell us your name." "Bloody demons, you really don't know who I am," said Pig. "I'm a disciple of the Venerable Tang Priest, who has been sent from

Tang in the east to fetch the scriptures. My title is Marshal Tian Peng and I'm called Zhu Wuneng, or Pig. You've hung my master up in your cave and you're planning to steam him and eat him. Is my master just a meal for you to cook? Stretch your heads out at once. I'm going to smash you all with my rake and wipe the lot of you out."

At this the demons were scared out of their wits. They fell to their knees in the water, kowtowed to him and said, "Please be kind, reverend sir. We were blind and we captured your master by mistake. Although we did hang him up we haven't tortured him. We beg you in your compassion to spare our lives. We'll gladly give you some money for the journey and send your master on his way to the Western Heaven." "Cut that talk out," said Pig, waving his hands. "It's quite right what they say: 'Once you've been tricked by a confectioner you won't believe sweet-talkers again.' I'm going to hit you with my rake, then we can all go our separate ways."

[9] The idiot was thoroughly rough and crude and wanted to show off his powers. He was unmoved by their fragrant feminine beauty. Raising his rake he charged them, lashing out wildly without caring what he was doing. The demons acted desperately. Forgetting about their modesty they cared only about saving their living as covering their private parts with their hands they jumped out of the water and ran into the pavilion. Standing there they used magic to make thick silken ropes come out of their navels, filling the sky with a huge silken canopy under which Pig was caught. When the idiot looked up he could not see the sun in the heavens. He tried to run outside, but he could not lift his feet, which were tangled in silken ropes that covered the ground. When he tried to move his feet he tripped and staggered. He tried going left, but his head crashed to the ground, then tried going right and came a cropper. So he turned round as quickly as he could and kissed the dirt, got himself back on his feet, and collapsed head first once more. Goodness only knows how many times he stumbled and fell till his whole body was numb, his feet sore, his head aching and his eyes blurred. He could no longer

even crawl, but lay groaning on the floor. Then the demons tied him up. They neither beat him up nor wounded him, but sprang outside to rush back to their cave, leaving the silken canopy to blot out the daylight.

When they reached the stone bridge they stopped and said the words of a spell. In an instant the silk canopy had been put away, and they all rushed stark naked into the cave, covering their private parts with their hands as they ran giggling past the Tang Priest. Once inside their bedrooms carved out of the rock they put on old clothes and went straight to the back door of the cave, where they stood and called, "Where are you, children?"

Now each she-devil had a child, not one that she had borne, but an adopted child who had taken her as a mother. They were called Bee, Hornet, Cockroach, Spanish-fly, Grasshopper, Wax-insect and Dragonfly, for such they were. The evil spirits had spread their nets across the sky, caught these seven insects and been on the point of eating them. But as the old saying goes, "Birds have bird language and beasts have beast language." The insects had pleaded for their lives and volunteered to take the spirits as their own mothers. Ever since then they had gathered blossoms in the spring and summer flowers for the evil spirits, and as soon as they heard the shouts they appeared and asked, "What orders do you have for us, mothers?" "Sons," the demons replied, "this morning we made a mistake and provoked the monk from Tang. His disciples trapped us in the pool and disgraced us. We were almost killed. You must do your utmost. Go outside and drive them away. When you've beaten them come to your uncle's to meet us." The she-devils then fled for their lives and went to the home of their teacher's senior disciple, where their wicked tongues were to give rise to more disasters, but of that we shall not now speak. Watch while the insects rub their fists in their hands and go out to confront their enemies.

[10] Pig, meanwhile, whose head was spinning after falling over so often, looked up and suddenly saw that the silken canopy and ropes had all disappeared. Groping around he picked himself up and despite his pain he made his way back the way he had

come. As soon as he saw Monkey he grabbed him and said, "Brother, is my head bulging? Is my face all blue?" "What happened to you?" Monkey asked. "Those damned creatures caught me under a silken net and tripped me up goodness knows how many times with silk ropes," Pig replied. "My waist was twisted, my back felt broken and I couldn't move an inch. Then the silk canopy and the ropes all disappeared, so I could escape and come back." "Forget about it," said Friar Sand when he saw him, "forget about it. You asked for trouble. I'm sure the demons have all gone back to the cave to harm the master. We must go and rescue him straight away."

When Monkey heard this he set out at once as fast as he could and rushed back to the farm while Pig led the horse. Here the seven little devils could be seen standing on the bridge, blocking their way and saying, "Not so fast, not so fast. We're here." "What a joke!" said Pig when he saw them. "They're just a bunch of kids. They're only two foot five or six, well under three foot, and they can only weigh eight or nine pounds, not even ten." "Who are you?" he shouted. "We're the sons of the seven immortal ladies," the little devils replied. "You've insulted our mothers, and now you've got the effrontery to attack us, you ignorant fools. Stay where you are, and watch out." The splendid monsters then launched a wild onslaught on Pig, who was in a flaming temper after falling over so often. Seeing how tiny the insects were he lifted his rake to strike furious blows at them.

When the little devils saw how ferocious the idiot was they all reverted to their original forms, flew into the air and shouted, "Change!" In an instant each of them became ten, each ten became a hundred, each hundred became a thousand, and each thousand became ten thousand. Every one became a countless number. This is what could be seen:

> The sky was full of wax-flies,
> Dragonflies danced all over the land.
> Bees and hornets went for the head,

479

> *Cockroaches jabbed at the eyes.*
> *Spanish-flies bit before and behind,*
> *While grasshoppers stung above and below.*
> *His face was black and crawling with insects;*
> *Even devils or deities would have been scared by their*
> *speed.*

"Brother," said Pig in alarm, "you can say what you like about it being easy to fetch the scriptures, but on this road to the west even the insects give you a bad time." "Don't be afraid, brother," said Monkey. "Go for them." "But they're flying into my head and my face and all over my body," replied Pig. "They're at least ten layers deep and all stinging me. How can I go for them?" "No problem," said Monkey, "no problem. I know a trick." "Whatever it is, brother," said Friar Sand, "use it right now. His shaven head has swollen up with those bites in no time at all."

[11] The splendid Great Sage pulled out a handful of hairs, chewed them into little bits and blew them out, telling them to turn to golden eagles, falcons, hawks, white eagles, vultures, ospreys and sparrowhawks." "Brother," said Pig, "what's that jargon about goldens and all that?" "Something you don't know about," Monkey replied. "Golden eagles, falcons, hawks, white eagles, vultures, ospreys and sparrowhawks are the seven birds of prey that my hairs turned into. That's because the she-devils' children are insects." Because the birds were so good at catching insects they got one every time they opened their beaks, grabbed at them with their claws or struck them with their wings. They wiped all the insects out in an instant, leaving no trace of them in the sky. The ground was piled over a foot deep with their bodies.

Only then could the three brothers charge across the bridge and into the cave, where they found their master hanging groaning and sobbing in mid-air. "Master," said Pig, going up to him, "are you hanging around here for fun? I don't know how many times I've had to fall over on your account." "Untie the master before we take this conversation any further," said Friar

Sand. Brother Monkey then snapped the ropes and set the master free, asking, "Where did the evil spirits go?" "All seven of them ran stark naked through to the back," the Tang Priest replied. "They were calling for their sons." "After them, brother!" said Monkey. "Follow me!"

The three of them, each holding his weapon, went searching in the back garden, but no sign of them could be found. They looked for them without success under all the peach and plum trees. "They've gone," said Pig, "they've gone. We can stop looking for them," said Friar Sand. "I'm going to help the master away from here." The three brothers then went back to the front, where they asked the Tang Priest to mount up. "You two help the master along the way," said Pig. "I'm going to smash these buildings to the ground with my rake. Then they'll have nowhere to live when they come back." "Smashing the place would be too much effort," said Monkey. "The best way to cut off their roots would be to find some firewood." The splendid idiot then gathered some dead pine, broken-off bamboo, dried-out willow and withered creepers that he set alight. The roaring blaze destroyed everything. Only then did master and disciples feel easy enough to be on their way. If you don't know what of good or evil the demons were to do to them, listen to the explanation in the next instalment.

18. 情因旧恨生灾毒
心主遭魔幸破光

【1】 话说孙大圣扶持着唐僧，与八戒、沙僧奔上大路，一直西来。不半晌，忽见一处楼阁重重，宫殿巍巍。唐僧勒马道："徒弟，你看那是个甚么去处？"行者举头观看，忽然见：

> 山环楼阁，溪绕亭台。门前杂树密森森，宅外野花香艳艳。柳间栖白鹭，浑如烟里玉无瑕；桃内啭黄莺，却似火中金有色。双双野鹿，忘情闲踏绿莎茵；对对山禽，飞语高鸣红树杪。真如刘阮天台洞，不亚神仙阆苑家。

行者报道："师父，那所在也不是王侯第宅，也不是豪富人家，却像一个庵观寺院。到那里方知端的。"三藏闻言，加鞭纵马。师徒们来至门前观看，门上嵌着一块石板，上有"黄花观"三字。三藏下马。八戒道："黄花观乃道士之家。我进去会他一会也好，他与我们衣冠虽别，修行一般。"沙僧道："说得是。一则进去看看景致，二来也当散货头口。看方便处，安排些斋饭，与师父吃。"

【2】 长老依言，四众共入。但见二门上有一对春联："黄芽白雪神仙府，瑶草琪花羽士家。"行者笑道："这个是烧茅炼药，弄炉火，提罐子的道士。"三藏捻他一把道："谨言！谨言！我们不与他相识，又不认亲，左右暂时一会，管他怎的？"说不了，进了二门，只见那正殿谨闭，东廊下坐着一个道士，在那里丸药。你看他怎生打扮：

> 戴一顶红艳艳戗金冠；穿一领黑淄淄乌皂服，踏一双绿阵阵云头履；系一条黄拂拂吕公绦。面如瓜铁，目若朗星。准头高大类回回，唇口翻张如达达。道心一片隐轰雷，伏虎降龙真羽士。

三藏见了，厉声高叫道："老神仙，贫僧问讯了。"那道士猛抬头，一见心惊，丢了手中之药，按簪儿，整衣服，降阶迎接道："老师父，失迎了。请里面坐。"长老欢喜上殿。推开门，见有三清圣像，供桌有炉有香，即拈香注炉，礼拜三匝，方与道士行礼。遂至客位中，同徒弟们坐下。急唤仙童看茶。当有两个小童，即入里边，寻茶盘，洗茶盏，擦茶匙，办茶果。忙忙的乱走，早惊动那几个冤家。

【3】　原来那盘丝洞七个女怪与这道士同堂学艺。自从穿了旧衣，唤出儿子，径来此处。正在后面裁剪衣服，忽见那童子看茶，便问道："童儿，有甚客来了，这般忙冗？"仙童道："适问有四个和尚进来，师父教来看茶。"女怪道："可有个白胖和尚？"——道："有。"又问："可有个长嘴大耳朵的？"——道："有。"女怪道："你快去递了茶，对你师父丢个眼色，着他进来，我有要紧的话说。"

　　果然那仙童将五杯茶拿出去。道士敛衣，双手拿一杯递与三藏，然后与八戒、沙僧、行者。茶罢，收锺。小童丢个眼色。那道士就欠身道："列位请坐。"教："童儿，放了茶盘陪侍。等我去去就来。"此时长老与徒弟们，并一个小童出殿上观玩不题。

【4】　却说道士走进方丈中，只见七个女子齐齐跪倒，叫："师兄！师兄！听小妹子一言！"道士用手搀起道："你们早来时，要与我说甚么话，可可的今日丸药，这枝药忌见阴人，所以不曾答你。如今又有客在外面，有话且慢慢说罢。"众怪道："告禀师兄。这桩事，专为客来，方敢告诉；若客去了，纵说也没用了。"道士笑道："你看贤妹说话，怎么专为客来才说？却不疯了？且莫说我是个清静修仙之辈，就是个俗人家，有妻子老小家务事，也等客去了再处。怎么这等不贤，替我装幌子哩！且让我出去。"众怪又一齐扯住道："师兄息恕。我问你，前边过客，是那方来的？"道士唾着脸，不答应。众怪道："方才小童进来取茶，我闻得他说，是四个和尚。"道士作怒道："和尚便怎么？"众怪道："四个和尚，内有一个白面胖的，有一个长嘴大耳的，师兄可曾问他是那里的？"道士道："内中是有这两个，你怎么知道？想是在那里见他来？"

　　女子道："师兄原不知这个委曲。那和尚乃唐朝差往西天取经去的。今早到我洞里化斋，委是妹子们闻得唐僧之名，将他拿了。"道士道："你拿他怎的?"女子道："我等久闻人说,唐僧乃十世修行的真体,有人吃他一块肉,延寿长生,故此拿了他。后被那个长嘴大耳朵的和尚把我们拦在濯垢泉里,先抢了衣服,后弄本事,强要同我等洗浴,也止他不住。他就跳下水,变做一个鲇鱼,在我们腿裆里钻来钻去,欲行奸骗之事。果有十分急燥!他又跳出水去,现了本相。见我们不肯相从,他就使一柄九齿钉钯,要伤我们性命。若不是我们有些见识,几乎遭他毒害。故此战兢兢逃生,又着你愚外甥与他敌斗,不知存亡如何。我们特来投兄长,望兄长念昔日同窗之雅,与我今日做个报冤之人!"

【5】 那道士闻此言,却就恼恨,遂变了声色道："这和尚原来这等无礼!这等急燥!你们都放心,等我摆布他!"众女子谢道："师兄如若动手,等我们都来相帮打他。"道士道："不用打!不用打!常言道:'一打三分低。'你们都跟我来!"

众女子相随左右。他入房内,取了梯子转过床后,爬上屋梁,拿下一个小皮箱儿。那箱儿有八寸高下,一尺长短,四寸宽窄,上有一把小铜锁儿锁住。即于袖中拿出一方鹅黄绫汗巾儿来。汗巾须上系着一把小钥匙儿。开了锁,取出一包儿药来,此药乃是:

> 山中百鸟粪,扫积上千斤。
> 是用铜锅煮,煎熬火候匀。
> 千斤熬一杓,一杓炼三分。
> 三分还要炒,再煅再重熏。
> 制成此毒药,贵似宝和珍。
> 如若尝他味,入口见阎君!

道士对七个女子道："妹妹,我这宝贝,若与凡人吃,只消一厘,入腹就死;若与神仙吃,也只消三厘就绝;这些和尚,只怕也有些道行,须得三厘。快取等子来。"内一女子,急拿了一把等子道："称出一分二厘,分作四分。"却拿了十二个红枣儿,将枣掐破些儿,捏上一厘;分在四个茶钟内,又将两个黑枣儿做一个茶锺,着一个托盘安了,对众女说道:"等我去问他。不是唐朝的便罢;若是唐朝来的,就教换茶,你却将此茶令童儿拿出。但吃了,个个身亡,就与你报了此仇,解了烦恼也。"七女感激不尽。

【6】　那道士换了一件衣服，虚礼谦恭，走将出来，请唐僧等又至客位坐下，道："老师父莫怪。适间去后面吩咐小徒，教他们挑些青菜、萝卜、实排一顿素斋供养，所以supplies久陪。"三藏道："贫僧素手进拜，怎么敢劳赐斋？"道士笑云："你我都是出家人，见山门就有三升俸粮，何言素手？敢问老师父，是何宝山？到此何干？"三藏道："贫僧乃东土大唐驾下差往西天大雷音寺取经者。却才路过仙宫，竭诚进拜。"道士闻言，满面生春道："老师乃忠诚大德之佛，小道不知，失于远候。想罪！想罪！"叫："童儿，快去换茶来。一面作速办斋。"那小童走将进去，众女子招呼他来道："这里有现成好茶，拿出去。"那童子果然将五锺茶拿出。道士连忙双手拿一个红枣儿茶锺奉与唐僧。他见八戒身躯大，就认做大徒弟；沙僧认做二徒弟；见行者身量小，认做三徒弟：所以第四锺才奉与行者。

　　行者眼乖，接了茶锺，早已见盘子里那茶锺是两个黑枣儿。他道："先生，我与你穷换一杯。"道士笑道："不瞒长老说。山野中贫僧士，茶果一时不备。才然在后面亲自寻果子，止有这十二个红枣，做四锺茶奉敬。小道又不可空陪，所以将两个下色枣儿做一杯奉陪。此乃贫道恭敬之意也。"行者笑道："说那里话？古人云：'在家不是贫，路上贫杀人。'你是在家儿的，何以言贫！像我们这行脚僧，才是真贫哩。我和你换些。我和你换些。"三藏闻言道："悟空，这仙长实乃爱客之意，你吃了罢，换些怎么？"行者无奈，将左手接了，右手盖住，看着他们。

　　却说那八戒，一则饥，二则渴，原来是食肠大大的，见那锺子里有三个红枣儿，拿起来咽的都咽在肚里。师父也吃了。沙僧也吃了。一霎时，只见八戒脸上变色，沙僧满眼流泪，唐僧口中吐沫。他们都坐不住，晕倒在地。

【7】　这大圣情知是毒，将茶锺，手举起来，望道士劈脸一掼。道士将袍袖隔起，当的一声，把个锺子跌得粉碎。道士怒道："你这和尚，十分村卤！怎么把我锺子碎了？"行者骂道："你这畜生！你看我那三个人是怎么说！我与你有甚相干，你却将毒药茶药倒我的人？"道士道："你这个村畜生，闯下祸来，你岂不知？"行者道："我们才进你门，方叙了坐次，道及乡贯，又不曾有个高言，那

里闯下甚祸?"道士道:"你可曾在盘丝洞化斋么?你可曾在濯垢泉洗澡么?"行者道:"濯垢泉乃七个女怪。你既说出这话,必定与他苟合,必定也是妖精!不要走!吃我一棒!"好大圣,去耳朵里摸出金箍棒,幌一幌,碗来粗细,望道士劈脸打来。那道士急转身躲过,取一口宝剑来迎。

他一个厮骂厮打,早惊动那里边的女怪。他七个一拥出来,叫道:"师兄且莫劳心,待小妹子拿他。"行者见了,越生嗔怒,双手轮铁棒,丢开解数,滚将进去乱打。只见那七个敞开怀,腆着雪白肚子,脐孔中作出法来:骨都都丝绳乱冒,搭起一个天篷,把行者盖在底下。

行者见事不谐,即翻身念声咒语,打个筋斗,扑的撞破天篷走了;忍着性气,淤淤的立在空中看处,见那怪丝绳幌亮,穿穿道道,却是穿梭的经纬,顷刻间,把黄花观的楼台殿阁都遮得无影无形。行者道:"利害!利害!却才这般,怪道猪八戒跌了若干!似这般怎生是好!我师父与师弟却又中了毒药。这伙怪合意同心,却不知是个甚来历,待我还去问那土地神也。"

【8】好大圣,按落云头,捻着诀,念声"唵"字真言,把个土地老儿又拘来了,战兢兢跪下路旁,叩头道:"大圣,你去救你师父的,为何又转来了?"行者道:"早间救了师父,前去不远,遇一座黄花观。我与师父等进去看看,那观主迎接。才叙话间,被他把毒药茶药倒我师父。我幸不曾吃茶,使棒就打,他却说出盘丝洞化斋、濯垢泉洗澡之事,我就知明厮是怪。才举手相打,只见那七个女子跑出,吐放丝绳,老孙亏有见识走来。我想你在此间为神,定知他的来历。是个甚么妖精,老实说来,免打!"土地叩头道:"那妖精到此,住不上十年。小神自三年前检点之后,方见他的本相,乃是七个蜘蛛精。他吐那些丝绳,乃是蛛丝。"行者闻言,十分欢喜道:"据你说,却是小可。既这般,你回去,等我作法降他也。"那土地叩头而去。

行者却到黄花观外,将尾巴上毛捋下七十根,吹口仙气,叫"变!"即变做七十个小行者;又将金箍棒吹口仙气,叫"变!"即变做七十个双角叉儿棒。每一个小行者,与他一根。他自家使一根,站在外边,将叉儿搅那丝绳,一齐着力,打个号子,把那丝绳都搅断，各搅了有十余斤。里面拖出七个蜘蛛，足有巴斗大的身躯。一个个攒着手脚，索着头，只叫："饶命！饶命！"此时七十个小行者，按住七个蜘蛛，那里肯放。行者道："且不要打他，只教还我师父、师弟来。"那怪厉声高叫道："师兄，还他唐僧，救我命也！"那道士从里边跑出道："妹妹，我要吃唐僧哩，救不得你了。"行者闻言，大怒道："你既不还我师父，且看你妹妹的样子！"好大圣，把又儿棒幌一幌，复了一根铁棒，把七个蜘蛛精，尽情打烂，却似七个剜肉布袋儿，脓血淋淋。却又将尾巴摇了两摇，收了毫毛，单身抢棒，赶入里边来打道士。

【9】　那道士见他打死了师妹，心甚不忍，即发狠举剑来迎。这一场各怀忿怒，一个个大展神通。这一场好杀：

> 妖精抢宝剑，大圣举金箍。都为唐朝三藏，先教七女呜呼。如今大圣经纶手，施威弄法逞金吾。大圣神光壮，妖仙胆气粗。浑身解数如花锦，双手腾那似辘轳。乒乓剑棒响，惨淡野云浮。剜言语，使机谋，一来一往如画图。杀得风响沙飞狼虎怕，天昏地暗斗星无。

那道士与大圣战经五六十合，渐觉手软；一时间松了筋节，便解开衣带，忽辣的响一声，脱了皂袍。行者笑道："我儿子！打不过人，就脱剥了也是不能毅的！"原来这道士剥了衣裳，把手一齐抬起，只见那两胁下有一千只眼，眼中放出金光，十分利害：

> 森森黄雾，艳艳金光。森森黄雾，两边胁下似喷云；艳艳金光，千只眼中放捷火。左右却如金桶，东西犹似铜钟。此乃妖仙施法力，道士显神通：幌眼迷天遮日月，罩人爆燥气朦胧；把个齐天孙大圣，困在金光黄雾中。

行者慌了手脚，只在那金光影里乱转，向前不能举步，退后不能动脚，却便似在个桶里转的一般。无奈又爆燥不过，他急了，往上着实一跳，却撞破金光，扑的跌了一个倒栽葱；觉道撞的头疼，急伸手摸头，把顶梁皮都撞软了。自家心焦道："晦气！晦气！这颗头今日也不济了！常时刀砍斧剁，莫能伤损，却怎么被这金光撞软了皮肉？久以后定要脓溃。纵然好了，也是个破伤风。"一会家爆燥难禁。却又自家计较道："前去不得，后退不得，左行不得，右行不得，往上又撞不得，却怎么好？——往下走他

487

娘罢!"

好大圣,念个咒语,摇身一变,变做个穿山甲,又名鲮鲤鳞。真个是:

四只铁爪,钻山碎石如挝粉;满身鳞甲,破岭穿岩似切葱。

两眼光明,好便似双星幌亮;一嘴尖利,胜强如钢钻金锥。

药有性穿山甲,俗语呼为鲮鲤鳞。

你看他硬着头,往地下一钻,就钻了有二十余里,方才出头。原来那金光只罩得十余里。出来现了本相,力软筋麻,浑身疼痛,止不住眼中流泪。忽失声叫道:"师父啊!

当年秉教出山中,共往西来苦用工。

大海洪波无恐惧,阳沟之内却遭风!"

【10】 美猴王正当悲切,忽听得山背后有人啼哭,即欠身揩了眼泪,回头观看。但见一个妇人,身穿重孝,左手托一盏凉浆水饭,右手执几张烧纸黄钱,从那пів 一步一声,哭着走来。行者点头嗟叹道:"正是'流泪眼逢流泪眼,断肠人遇断肠人!'这一个妇人,不知何事,待我问他一问。"那妇人不一时走上路来,迎着行者。行者躬身问道:"女菩萨,你哭的是甚人?"妇人噙泪道:"我丈夫因与黄花观观主买竹竿争讲,被他将毒药茶药死,我将这陌纸钱烧化,以报夫妇之情。"行者听言,眼中泪下。那妇女见了作怒道:"你甚无知!我丈夫烦恼生悲,你怎么泪眼愁眉,欺心戏我?"

行者躬身道:"女菩萨息怒。我本是东土大唐钦差御弟唐三藏大徒弟孙悟空行者。因往西天,行过黄花观歇马。那观中道士,不知是个甚么妖精,他与七个蜘蛛精,结为兄妹。蜘蛛精在盘丝洞害骂我师父,是我与师弟八戒、沙僧,救解得脱。那蜘蛛精走到他这里,背了是非,说我等有欺骗之意。道士将毒药茶药倒我师父、师弟共三人,连马四口,陷在他观里。惟我不曾吃他茶,将茶锺摜碎,他就与我相打。正嚷时,那七个蜘蛛精跑出来吐放丝绳,将我捆住,是我使法力走脱。问及土地,说他本相,我却又使分身法摆绝丝绳,拖出妖精,一顿棒打死。这道士却与他报仇,举宝剑与我相斗。斗经六十回合,他败了阵,随脱了衣裳,两胁下放出千只眼,有万道金光,把我罩定。所以进退两难,才变做一个鲅鲤鳞，从地下钻出来。正自悲切，忽听得你哭，故此相问。因见你为丈夫，有此纸钱报答，我师父丧身，更无一物相酬，所以自怨生悲。岂敢相戏！"

【11】那妇女放下水饭、纸钱，对行者陪礼道："莫怪，莫怪，我不知你是被难者。才据你说将起来，你不认得那道士。他本是个百眼魔君，又唤做多目怪。你既然有此变化，脱得金光，战得许久，必定有大神通，却只是还不得那厮。我教你去请一位圣贤，他能破得金光，降得道士。"行者闻言，连忙唱喏道："女菩萨知此来历，烦为指教指教。果是那位圣贤，我去请求，救我师父之难，就报你丈夫之仇。"妇人道："我就说出来，你去请他，降了道士，只可报仇而已，恐不能救你师父。"行者道："怎不能救？"妇人道："那厮毒药最狠：药倒人，三日之间，骨髓俱烂。你此往回恐迟了，故不能救。"行者道："我会走路，凭他多远，千里只消半日。"女子道："你既会走路，听我说：此处到那里有千里之遥。那厢有一座山，名唤紫云山。山中有个千花洞。洞里有位圣贤，唤做毗蓝婆。他能降得此怪。"行者道："那山坐落何方？却从何方去？"女子用手指定道："那直南上便是。"行者回头看时，那女子早不见了。

行者慌忙礼拜道："是那位菩萨？我弟子钻昏了，不能相识，千乞留名，好谢！"只见那半空中叫道："大圣，是我。"行者急抬头看处，原是黎山老姆。赶至空中谢道："老姆从何来指教我也？"老姆道："我才自龙华会上回来，见你师父有难，假做孝妇，借夫丧之名，……免他一死。你快去请他。但不可说出是我指教，那圣贤有些怪人。"

【12】行者谢了。辞别，把筋斗云一纵，随到紫云山上。按定云头，就见那千花洞。那洞外：

青松遮胜境，翠柏绕仙居。绿柳盈山道，奇花满涧渠。香兰围石屋，芳草映岩嵎。流水连溪碧，云封古树虚。野禽声聒聒，幽鹿步徐徐。修竹枝枝秀，红梅叶叶舒。寒鸦栖古树，春鸟噪高樗。夏麦盈田广，秋禾遍地余。四时无叶落，八节有花如。每生瑞霭连霄汉，常放祥云接太虚。

这大圣喜喜欢欢走将进去，一程一节，看不尽无边的景致。直入里面，更没个人儿，见静静悄悄的，鸡犬之声也无。心中暗道："这圣贤想是不在家了。"又进数里看时，见一个女道姑坐在榻上。你看他怎生模样：

> 头戴五花纳锦帽，身穿一领织金袍。
> 脚踏云尖凤头履，腰系攒丝双穗绦。
> 面似秋容霜后老，声如春燕社前娇。
> 腹中久谙三乘法，心上常修四谛饶。
> 悟出空空真古果，炼成了了自逍遥。
> 正是千花洞里佛，毗蓝菩萨姓名高。

行者止不住脚，近前叫道："毗蓝婆菩萨，问讯了。"那菩萨即下榻，合掌回礼道："大圣，失迎了。你从那里来的？"行者道："你怎么就认得我是大圣？"毗蓝婆道："你当年大闹天宫时，普地里传了你的形象，谁人不知，那个不识？"行者道："正是'好事不出门，恶事传千里。'像我如今皈正佛门，你就不晓的了！"毗蓝道："几时皈正？恭喜！恭喜！"行者道："近些脱命，保师父唐僧上西天取经，师父遇黄花观道士，将毒药茶药倒。我与那厮赌斗，他就放金光罩住我，是我使神通走脱了。闻菩萨能灭他的金光，特来拜请。"菩萨道："是谁与你说的？我自赴了盂兰会，到今三百余年，不曾出门。我隐姓埋名，更无一人知得，你却怎么得知？"行者道："我是个地里鬼，不管那里，自家都会访着。"毗蓝道："也罢，也罢。我本当不去，奈蒙大圣下临，不可灭了的求经之善，我和你去来。"

行者称谢了。道："我忒无知，擅自催促，但不知曾带甚么兵器？"菩萨道："我有个绣花针儿，能破那厮。"行者忍不住道："老姆误了我，早知是绣花针，不须劳você，就问老孙要一担也是有的。"毗蓝道："你那绣花针，无非是钢铁金针，用不得。我这宝贝，非钢、非铁、非金，乃是我小儿日眼里炼成的。"行者道："令郎是谁？"毗蓝道："小儿乃昴日星官。"行者惊骇不已。早望见金光艳艳，即回向毗蓝道："金光处便是黄花观也。"毗蓝随于衣领里取出一个绣花针，似眉毛粗细，有五六分长短，拈在手，望空抛去。少时间，响一声，破了金光。行者喜道："菩萨，妙哉，妙哉！寻针，寻针！"毗蓝托在手掌内道："这不是？"行者却同按下云头，走人观里，只见那道士合了眼，不能举步。行者骂道："你这泼怪装瞎子哩！"耳朵里取出棒来就打。毗蓝扯住道："大圣莫打。且看你师父去。"

【13】　行者径至后面客位里看时，他三人都睡在地上吐痰吐沫哩。行者垂泪道："却怎么好！却怎么好！"毗蓝道："大圣休悲。也是我今日出门一场，索性积个阴德，我这里有解毒丹，送你三丸。"行者转身拜谢。那菩萨袖中取出一个破纸包儿，内将三粒红丸子递与行者，教放人口里。行者把药扳开他们牙关，每人塞了一丸。须臾，药味入腹，便就一齐呕哕，遂吐出毒味，得了性命。那八戒先爬起道："闷杀我也！"三藏、沙僧俱醒了道："好晕也！"行者道："你们那茶里中了毒了。亏这毗蓝菩萨搭救，快都来拜谢。"三藏欠身整衣谢了。

八戒道："师兄，那道士在那里？等我问他一问，为何这般害我。"行者把蜘蛛精上项事，说了一遍。八戒发狠道："这厮既与蜘蛛为姊妹，定是妖精！"行者指道："他在那殿外立定装瞎子哩。"八戒拿钯就筑，又被毗蓝止住道："天蓬息怒。大圣知我洞里无人，待我收他去看守门户也。"行者道："感蒙大德，岂不奉承！但只是教他现本像，我们看看。"毗蓝道："容易。"即上前用手一指，那道士扑的倒在尘埃，现了原身，乃是一条七尺长短的大蜈蚣精。毗蓝使小指头挑起，驾祥云，径转千花洞去。八戒打仰道："这妈妈儿却也利害，怎么就降这般恶物？"行者笑道："我问他有甚兵器破他金光，他道有个绣花针儿，是他儿子在日眼里炼的。乃问他令郎是谁，他道是昴日星官。我想昴日星是只公鸡，这老妈妈子必定是个母鸡。鸡最能降蜈蚣，所以能收伏也。"

三藏闻言，顶礼不尽。教："徒弟们，收拾去罢。"那沙僧即在里面寻了些米粮，安排了些斋，俱饱餐一顿。牵马挑担，请师父出门。行者从中厨中放了一把火，把一座观宇时烧得煨烬，却拽步长行。正是：唐僧得命感毗蓝，了性消除多目怪。毕竟向前去还有甚么事体，且听下回分解。

Chapter 18
The Emotions Bear a Grudge and
Inflict Disaster;
The Heart's Master Smashes the Light
when He Meets the Demons

【1】 The story tells how the Great Sage Sun supported the Tang Priest as they hurried along the main road to the west together with Pig and Friar Sand. Within a few hours they were in sight of a compound with many tall towers and imposing buildings. "Disciple," said Sanzang, reining in his horse, "what's that place?" Monkey looked up to gaze at it and this is what he saw:

> Tall towers girdled by hills,
> Streams winding round pavilions.
> Dense grew the wood in front of the gates,
> And outside the buildings the scent of flowers hung heavy.
> White egrets perched among the willows,
> Like flawless jades half hidden in a mist;
> Golden orioles sang in the peach-trees,
> Flashes of gold in the fiery blossom.
> Wild deer in couples
> Trod lost to the world across cushions of greenery;
> Pairs of mountain birds
> Sang as they flew among the red tree-tops,
> It was like the Tiantai Cave of Liu and Ruan,
> And rivalled the home of the immortals in fairyland.

"Master," Brother Monkey reported, "that's no princely palace or rich man's mansion. It looks like a Taoist temple or Buddhist monastery. We'll know for sure when we get there." On hearing this Sanzang whipped on his horse, and when master and disciples reached the gates to look there was a stone tablet set over the gateway on which was written YELLOW FLOWER TEMPLE.

492

Sanzang dismounted. "Yellow Flower Temple means it's a Taoist place," said Pig, "so it's all right for us to go in and see them. Although we wear different clothes we cultivate our conduct the same way." "You're right," said Friar Sand. "We can go in and have a look round, and at the same time the horse can have a feed. If it looks suitable we can arrange a meal for the master."

[2]   The master accepted their suggestions and the four of them went inside. A couplet was pasted up on either side of the inner gates:

> *Palace of immortals: yellow shoots and white snow.*
> *Home of men who can fly: rare and wonderful flowers.*

"So the Taoist here refines drugs, plays with a furnace and totes a crucible," said Monkey with a grin. "Watch your words," said Sanzang, giving him a pinch, "watch your words. We don't know them and they are no relations of ours. This is only a passing encounter. Never mind what they are like." Before he had finished saying these words he went in through the inner gate, where he found the doors of the main hall shut tight and a Taoist master sitting under a covered walkway making elixir pills. Just look at how he was dressed:

> *On his head a bright red hat all set with gold,*
> *On his body a jet-black Taoist robe,*
> *On his feet a pair of deep green cloud-treading shoes,*
> *Round his waist a brilliant yellow Lu Dongbin sash.*
> *His face was round like a golden melon,*
> *His eyes like bright stars.*
> *His nose was as big and as high as a Muslim's,*
> *And his lips turned back like a Tartar's.*
> *His heart, set on the Way, was hidden thunder;*
> *He was a true immortal, subduer of tigers and dragons.*

As soon as he saw him Sanzang shouted at the top of his voice, "My respectful greetings, venerable Taoist master." The

Taoist looked up with a start and was so alarmed by what he saw that he dropped the elixir on which he was working. Then he neatened his hair-pins and clothes, came down the steps and greeted Sanzang: "Venerable sir, excuse me for failing to meet you. Please come inside and sit down." The venerable elder happily went up into the main hall. On pushing the doors open he saw the statues of the Three Pure Ones and an altar on which stood incense burner and incense, so he planted some joss-sticks in the burner and performed a triple set of obeisances to the Pure Ones before bowing to the Taoist master. He then went to the guest seats, where he sat down with his disciples. Immortal boys were told to bring tea at once, whereupon two boys went inside to fetch the tea-tray, wash the teacups, wipe the teaspoons and prepare some refreshments to eat with it. Their rushing about soon disturbed the pilgrims' enemies.

【3】 Now the seven devils from Gossamer Cave had been fellow-students of the Taoist master here, and it was here that they had hurried after putting on their old clothes and calling for their sons. They were making themselves new clothes at the back of the temple when they noticed the boys preparing the tea and asked, "What visitors have arrived, boys? What are you in such a rush for?" "Four Buddhist monks have just turned up," the boys replied, "and the master has told us to prepare tea for them." "Is one of the monks pale and fat?" the she-devils asked. "Yes." "Does one of them have a long snout and big ears?" they asked again. "Yes." "Then take the tea in as quickly as you can," the she-devils said, "and tip your master a wink to come in here. We've got something urgent to say to him."

The boys took five cups of tea out to the Taoist master, who tucked back his sleeves and passed a cup with both hands first to Sanzang and then to Pig, Friar Sand and Brother Monkey. After the tea had been drunk the cups were collected and the boys gave their master a look, at which he bowed and said, "Please sit down, gentlemen. Boys, put the tray down and keep them company. I have to go out. I'll be back." Sanzang and his disciples went out of the hall to look around, guided by one boy.

[4]   When the Taoist master went back to the abbot's lodgings the seven women all fell to their knees and said, "Brother, brother, please listen to what we have to say." The Taoist master helped them to their feet and said, "When you came here this morning you wanted to tell me something, but because of the elixir pills I was making I couldn't see any women. That's why I had to refuse. I have visitors out there now, so you can tell me later." "We have to report, elder brother," the she-devils said, "that it's because the strangers are here that we're talking to you. If the strangers go away there'll be no point in telling you." "What are you talking about, sisters?" the Taoist master said. "Why do you have to talk to me just now, when the strangers are here? Have you gone off your heads? I'm a man who lives in peace and quiet cultivating immortality, but even if I were a layman with wife and children and family responsibilities I'd wait till my visitors had left before attending to them. How can you be so ill-behaved and disgrace me? Now let me go." All the she-devils grabbed him and said, "Please don't lose your temper, elder brother. Tell us where the visitors come from." The Taoist master pulled a long face and ignored them. "When the boys came in for the tea just now they told us the visitors are four Buddhist monks," the she-devils said. "They're monks," said the Taoist master angrily, "what of it?" "Does one of the four monks have a pale, fat face," the she-devils asked, "and one of them a long snout and big ears? Did you ask them where they're from?" "Yes," the Taoist said, "there are two like that among them. How did you know? I suppose you've seen them somewhere."

"You don't know the terrible things that have happened, brother," the devils said. "That monk was sent by the Tang court to fetch the scriptures from the Western Heaven. He came to our cave this morning begging for food. We captured him because we'd heard of this Tang Priest." "Why did you capture him?" the Taoist asked. "We've long known that the Tang Priest has a pure body because he has cultivated his conduct for ten successive incarnations," the devils replied. "Anyone who eats a piece of his flesh will live for ever. That's why we captured him.

495

Later the monk with a long snout and big ears kept us in the Filth-cleansing Spring. First he stole our clothes and then he used his magical powers to insist on bathing with us. He jumped into the water and turned himself into a catfish. From the way he kept swimming around between our thighs he obviously had very improper ideas. He was thoroughly disgraceful. Then he jumped out of the water and turned back into himself. As we weren't going to let him have his way he tried to kill us all with his nine-pronged rake. If we hadn't known a thing or two he'd have murdered the lot of us. We fled in fear and trembling and sent your nephews into battle. We don't know whether they are alive or dead. We have come here to fling ourselves on your mercy and beg you to avenge your fellow-students from long ago."

[5]   On hearing this the Taoist was furious, as could be seen from his changed expression. "What outrageous monks!" he exclaimed. "What hooligans! Don't you worry: I'm going to sort them out." "If you're going to fight them," said the she-devils in gratitude, "you must let us help you." "There'll be no need to fight," said the Taoist, "no need. As the saying goes, you have to lower yourself to fight someone. Come with me."

The women went with him to his room, where he carried a ladder behind the bed, climbed up to the rafters and brought down a little leather box. It was eight inches high, a foot long, four inches wide and locked with a tiny brass lock. From his sleeve he produced a square handkerchief of goose-yellow silk, to the fringes of which a tiny key was tied. Unlocking the box he brought out a packet containing a drug. This drug was:

> *A thousand pounds of droppings*
> *From all kinds of mountain birds,*
> *Boiled in a copper cauldron,*
> *Reduced on an even fire,*
> *Till the thousand pounds were only a spoonful*
> *That was then reduced to a third.*
> *This was fried even longer,*
> *Refined and smoked once again,*

To make the poisonous drug,
More precious than treasures or jewels.
Were you to try out its flavour,
One taste would send you to Hell.

"Sisters," said the Taoist master, "any mortal who eats one grain of this treasure of mine will be dead when it reaches his stomach. Only three grains would be enough to kill a god or an immortal. As these monks may have mastered something of the Way they'll need three grains. Fetch my balance." One of the women brought a balance at once. "Weigh out twelve grains," he said, "and divide that into four portions." Then he took twelve red jujubes, pinched holes in them, stuffed a grain of the drug in each, and put them into four teacups. These were then placed with a fifth cup containing two black jujubes on a tray. "Let me question them," he said. "If they aren't from Tang that'll be the end of it; but if they are I'll ask for fresh tea and you can give this tea to the boys to bring in. Once they drink it they'll all die and you'll be avenged. That'll cheer you up." The seven women were beside themselves with gratitude.

【6】 The Taoist changed into another robe and walked out again with a great show of feigned courtesy. He urged the Tang Priest and the others to sit down in the guest seats again. "Please excuse me, venerable sir," the Taoist said. "The reason why I neglected you just now was because I was at the back telling my disciples to choose some greens and radishes to cook as a vegetarian meal for you." "We Buddhist monks came empty-handed," said Sanzang. "We could not possibly trouble you for a meal." "We are all men of religion," replied the Taoist master with a smile. "Whenever we go to a monastery or temple we are entitled to three pints of rice, so why talk of being empty-handed? May I ask you, reverend sir, what monastery you are from, and why you are here?" "I have been sent by His Majesty the Great Tang emperor to fetch the scriptures from the Great Thunder Monastery in the Western Heaven," Sanzang replied. "As we were passing your Taoist temple we came in to pay our respects." At this news the

497

Taoist's face was full of animation, as he said, "It was only because I did not realize you were so faithful to the most virtuous Buddha that I failed to come out a long way to meet you. Please forgive me. Please forgive me." Then he told the boys to bring fresh tea at once and get a meal ready as soon as possible, at which the boys went straight inside to fetch the tea. "Here's some good tea that's all ready," the women called to them. "Take this in." The boys did indeed take the five cups in, and the Taoist master hurriedly passed a cup of red jujube tea to the Tang Priest. As Pig was so big the Taoist took him for the senior disciple, and he thought Friar Sand was the next senior. Thinking that Monkey was the junior one the Taoist only handed him his cup fourth.

By the time the sharp-eyed Brother Monkey took his cup he had already noticed that there were two black jujubes in the cup left on the tray. "Let's change cups, sir," he said. "To be honest with you," the Taoist replied with a smile, "as a poor Taoist living out here in the wilds I am rather short of tea and food at the moment. I was looking for fruit out at the back just now and I could only find these twelve red jujubes to put into four cups of tea to offer you. As I had to take something with you I made another cup with these inferior jujubes to keep you company. This is just a gesture of respect." "What nonsense," said Monkey with a smile. "As the ancients said, 'You are never poor if you are at home; but poverty on a journey is killing.' You're at home here, so why all this talk about being poor? It's wandering monks like us who are really poor. I'll swop with you. I insist." "Wukong," said Sanzang when he heard this, "this immortal gentleman is being very hospitable. You have yours. There is no need for a swop." Monkey had no choice. Taking the cup with his left hand he covered it with his right and watched them.

Pig, however, who apart from feeling hungry and thirsty had an enormous appetite at the best of times, picked the three red jujubes out of the cup as soon as he saw them and swallowed them noisily. The master ate his too, as did Friar Sand. In that very instant Pig's face changed colour, tears started pouring from

Friar Sand's eyes and the Tang Priest began of foam at the mouth. Unable to sit upright, all three of them fainted and fell to the floor.

[7]   Realizing that they had been poisoned, the Great Sage raised his teacup in his hands and threw it at the Taoist master's face. The Taoist stopped it with his sleeve and it shattered noisily as it fell to the floor. "You lout, monk," said the Taoist in fury, "how dare you smash my cup?" "Animal," said Monkey abusively, "just look what you've done to those three! What have I ever done to you for you to give my people poisoned tea?" "Beast," said the Taoist master, "you asked for it. Don't you realize that?" "We've only just come here and talked about things like where we should sit and where we're from," said Monkey. "We didn't talk big. How can you say we asked for this trouble?" "Did you beg for food in Gossamer Cave?" the Taoist master asked. "Did you bathe in the Filth-cleansing Spring?" "There were seven she-devils in the Filth-cleansing Spring," Monkey replied. "From what you're saying you must be in cahoots with them. I'm sure you're an evil spirit yourself. Stay where you are and take this!" The splendid Great Sage felt in his ear for his gold-banded cudgel, waved it to make it as thick as a rice-bowl, and struck at the Taoist master's face. The Taoist rapidly turned and dodged the blow, then produced a fine sword with which he fought back.

Their cursing and fighting had by now disturbed the seven she-devils inside, who all rushed out shouting, "Spare yourself the trouble, elder brother. Let us catch him." At the sight of them Monkey became angrier than ever. Whirling his iron cudgel around with both hands he dropped his guard and tumbled in among them, lashing out wildly. The seven women then undid their clothes, revealing their white stomachs, and from their navels they produced by magic thick silken ropes that came reeling out in such abundance that they formed a canopy under which Brother Monkey was confined.

Seeing that things were going badly Monkey got up, said the words of a spell, did a somersault, smashed through the canopy and escaped. Then he stood gloomily in mid-air, controlling his temper and watching as the flashing silken ropes criss-crossed like the warp and weft of cloth on the loom. Within a moment the Yellow Flower Temple's towers and halls were all completely concealed. "Terrible," said Monkey, "they're terrible. I've never been up against anything like that before. No wonder Pig fell over so often. What am I to do now? The master and my brothers have been poisoned. This gang of devils are all hand in glove, and I know nothing about their background. I'll go back and question that local god."

[8] The splendid Great Sage brought his cloud down to land, made a spell with his fingers, said the sacred syllable Om, and forced the old local god to come to him again. The old deity knelt beside the path, trembling with fear and kowtowing as he said, "Great Sage, you went to rescue your master. Why are you back again?" "I rescued him this morning," Monkey replied, "and a little way ahead from there we reached a Yellow Flower Temple. When I went in with the master to look around, the head Taoist of the temple greeted us, and in the middle of our conversation he knocked out my master and the other two with poisoned tea. Luckily I didn't drink any, but when I was going to hit him with my cudgel he started talking about begging for food at Gossamer Cave and bathing at the Filth-cleansing Spring, so I knew he was a monster. No sooner had he raised his hand to fight back than the seven women came out and set off their silken ropes. It was a good thing I had the know-how to get away. I reckon that as you're a god who lives round here you're bound to know their background. What sort of evil spirit are they? Tell me the truth if you don't want to be hit." "It's less than ten years since those evil spirits came here," said the local deity, kowtowing. "When I was making an inspection three years ago I saw what they really are: seven spider spirits. The silken ropes that come out of them are spiders' webs." The news thoroughly delighted Monkey, who said, "From what you tell me they're no problem. Very well then. You can go back while I use magic to subdue him." The local god kowtowed and went.

Monkey then went to the outside of the Yellow Flower Temple, pulled seventy hairs out of his tail, blew on them with magic breath and shouted, "Change!" The hairs turned into seventy little Monkeys. He then blew a magic breath on his gold-banded cudgel, called "Change!" and turned it into seventy two-pronged forks, one of which he gave to each of the little Monkeys. Monkey himself used one of the forks to twist the silken ropes as he stood outside, then they all attacked together to the rhythm of a tune, tearing the ropes to pieces, each of them tearing off over ten pounds of rope. They dragged seven spiders out from inside. Each was about the size of a wicker basket. All of them held their hands and feet together and had ropes round their necks. "Spare us, spare us," they said. The seventy little Monkeys then pressed the seven spiders to the ground, refusing to let them go. "Don't hit them," said Monkey. "All we want is to make them give my master and my brothers back." "Elder Brother," shrieked the demons at the tops of their voices, "give the Tang Priest back and save our lives." The Taoist master rushed outside saying, "Sisters, I'm going to eat the Tang Priest. I can't save you."

This infuriated Brother Monkey. "If you won't give my master back just watch what happens to your sisters." The splendid Great Sage waved his fork, turned it back into an iron cudgel that he lifted with both hands and smashed the seven spider spirits to pulp. Then he shook his tail a couple of times, put the hairs back on it and charged inside alone, swinging his cudgel to fight the Taoist master.

[9] When the Taoist master saw Monkey kill his seven fellow-students it was more than he could bear. Goaded to fury, he raised his sword to fight back. In this battle each of them was seething with anger and giving full play to his divine powers. It was a fine battle.

> *The evil spirit swung a fine sword;*
> *The Great Sage raised his gold-banded cudgel.*
> *Both were fighting for Sanzang of the Tang,*

> *On whose account the seven women had been killed.*
> *Now they were fighting with all-round skill,*
> *Showing their mighty powers with their weapons.*
> *Powerful was the Great Sage's aura,*
> *And rough the courage of the evil immortal.*
> *Their vigorous moves were as rich as brocade,*
> *And both hands moved as fast as a windlass.*
> *Noisily clanged the sword and cudgel,*
> *And ominously pale were the floating clouds.*
> *Few were the words they spoke*
> *As they used their cunning,*
> *Moving to and fro like brush-strokes in a painting.*
> *The wind and dust they raised scared wolves and tigers;*
> *The stars disappeared as heaven and earth went dark.*

When the Taoist master had fought fifty or sixty rounds with the Great Sage he felt his hand weakening and his sinews getting slack, so he undid his belt and with a loud flapping noise took off his black robe. "Well, my lad," said the Great Sage with a laugh, "if you can't beat me you still won't be able to when you strip off." Once the Taoist master had striped off his clothes he raised both hands to reveal under his ribs a thousand eyes flashing golden light. It was terrible:

> *Dense yellow smoke,*
> *Brilliant golden light.*
> *The dense yellow smoke*
> *Gushed out as clouds from under his ribs;*
> *The brilliant golden light*
> *Came from a thousand eyes like fire.*
> *To left and right they seemed like golden pails;*
> *To east and west they resembled bells of bronze.*
> *Thus an evil immortal used his magic power,*
> *A Taoist master showed divine ability,*
> *Dazzling the eyes, blotting out sun, moon and sky,*
> *Blanketing people with acrid vapours.*

The Great Sage Equalling Heaven
Was caught in the golden light and yellow smoke.

Monkey started lashing out desperately with his hands and feet, but could only spin around inside the golden light, unable to take a step either forwards or backwards. It was as if he were turning round and round in a bucket. It was hopeless. He was unbearably hot. In his anxiety he leapt into the air, smashing against the golden light, and crashing head first to the ground. His head ached where he had hit it, and felt anxiously to find that the top of his scalp was tender. "What lousy luck," he thought, "what lousy luck. This head's useless today. Usually swords and axes can't hurt it, so why has golden light bruised it now? After a while it's bound to go septic, and even if it does get better I might have tetanus." He was still feeling unbearably hot. "I can't move forward or back," he thought, working out a plan, "or to left or right, and I can't smash my way through by going up. Whatever shall I do? I'll bloodly well have to get out by going down."

The splendid Great Sage said the words of a spell, shook himself, and turned into one of those scaly diggers called pangolins. Indeed,

> *Four sets of iron claws*
> *Dug through the mountain, smashing rocks like powder.*
> *The scales covering his body*
> *Carved through ridges and crags like slicing scallions.*
> *His eyes were as bright*
> *As two gleaming stars;*
> *His mouth was sharper*
> *Than a steel drill or brazen auger.*
> *He was the scaly mountain-borer used in medicine,*
> *The creature known as the pangolin.*

Watch him as he burrows into the ground with his head, not coming out again till he has covered over six miles. The golden light could only enclose about three miles. When he emerged and

503

turned back into himself he was exhausted. His muscles ached, his whole body was in pain, and he could not help weeping. Suddenly he burst out with, "Master,

> *Since leaving the mountain and joining the faith*
> *I've worked very hard on our way to the West.*
> *The waves of the ocean are nothing to fear,*
> *But in this dry gulch I've come out second best.*"

[10] Just as the Handsome Monkey King was feeling miserable the sound of sobs could suddenly be heard from the other side of the mountain. Leaning forward and drying his tears he turned to look. A woman appeared, dressed in deep mourning and sobbing at every step as she came from the other side of the mountain. She was holding a dish of cold rice gruel in her left hand and several pieces of yellow paper money for burning to the dead in her right. Monkey sighed and nodded as he said to himself, "This is a case of

> *Weeping eyes meeting weeping eyes,*
> *One broken heart coming across another.*

I wonder what this woman is crying about. I'll ask her." Before long the woman was coming along the path towards him. "Lady Bodhisattva," asked Brother Monkey with a bow, "who are you weeping for?" Through her tears the woman replied, "My husband was murdered by the master of the Yellow Flower Temple with poisoned tea because he got into a quarrel with him over the purchase of some bamboo poles. I'm going to burn this paper money as a mark of my love for him." This made Monkey's tears flow. The sight made the woman say angrily, "You ignorant fool. I'm grieving over my husband, but what business do you have to be weeping and looking so miserable? Are you mocking me?"

"Please don't be angry, Bodhisattva," said Monkey with a bow. "I'm Sun Wukong the Novice, the senior disciple of Tang

Sanzang, the younger brother of the Great Tang Emperor in the east. When we passed the Yellow Flower Temple on our way to the Western Heaven we stopped to rest, but the Taoist master there is some kind of evil spirit who's the sworn brother of seven spider spirits. When the spider spirits wanted to kill my master in Gossamer Cave I and my brother disciples Pig and Friar Sand managed to save him. The spider spirits fled to the Taoist's place and told him a pack of lies about us bullying them, so the Taoist knocked out my master and brothers. The three of them and the horse are now prisoners in his temple. I was the only one who didn't drink the tea. I smashed the cup and he attacked me. Because of the noise the seven spider spirits rushed outside to give out their silken ropes and catch me in the web they wove. I only got away by magic. After I'd found out who they really were I used my power of giving myself extra bodies to tear the silken ropes to pieces, drag the demons out and beat them to death. The Taoist master wanted revenge, so he went for me with his sword. When we'd gone sixty rounds he fled beaten, took off his clothes, and used the thousand eyes he has under his ribs to give off countless beams of golden light. I was caught under them, unable to move forwards or backwards, so I turned into a pangolin and burrowed my way out underground. It was when I was feeling thoroughly depressed that I heard you weeping, which was why I asked you those questions. When I saw that you had paper money to give your husband I felt wretched and miserable because I've got nothing for my master when he dies. Making fun of you was the last thing on my mind!"

[11] Putting down the gruel and the paper money the woman returned Brother Monkey's bow and said, "Please forgive me. I didn't realize that you were a sufferer too. From what you've just said you don't know who that Taoist is. He's really the Demon King Hundred-eye, who's also known as the Many-eyed Monster. You must have tremendous magical powers to have escaped from the golden light and fought so long, but you couldn't get near him. I'll tell you about a sage you can send for who would be able to smash the golden light and defeat the Taoist."

Monkey's immediate response was to chant a "na-a-aw" of respect and say, "If you know the sage's background, lady Bodhisattva, may I trouble you to tell me about it? If there is such a sage I'll fetch him to rescue my master and avenge your husband." "I'll tell you," the woman said, "and you can fetch the sage, who will subdue the Taoist, but that will only bring revenge. I'm afraid the sage won't be able to rescue your master." "Why not?" Monkey asked. "His poison is truly lethal," the woman replied. "When people are laid low by it the very marrow of their bones rots within three days. I'm afraid that by the time you've been to see the sage and come back again you'll be too late to save him." "I know how to travel," Monkey replied. "However far it is I'll only take half a day." "If you can travel then listen to this," the woman said. "About three hundred miles from here there's a mountain called Mount Purple Clouds, and in the mountain there's a Thousand Flower Cave where there lives a sage called Vairambha who will be able to defeat that demon." "Where's the mountain?" Monkey asked. "Which direction should I take?" "It's due south of here," the woman replied, pointing; and by the time Brother Monkey looked back at her she had disappeared.

Monkey quickly did a kowtow and said, "Which Bodhisattva was that? After all that burrowing your disciple was feeling too stupid to recognize you. I beg you to tell me your name so that I can thank you." At this there came a shout from mid-air, "Great Sage, it's me." Monkey quickly looked up to see that it was the Old Lady of Mount Li. Catching up with her in the sky he thanked her with the words, "Where have you come from to give me these instructions?" "On my way back from Dragon Flower Assembly I noticed that your master was in trouble," the Old Lady replied. "It was to save his life that I pretended to be a woman in mourning for her husband. Hurry up and fetch the sage. But don't tell her I sent you: she is rather difficult."

[12] Thanking her, Monkey took his leave and set off straight away on his somersault cloud. Once at Mount Purple Clouds he brought his cloud down and saw the Thousand Flower Cave.

Outside the cave:

> Blue pines masked the splendid view,
> Turquoise cypresses surrounded the immortal's home.
> Green willows were packed close along the mountain paths,
> Rare flowers filled the watercourses.
> Orchids grew all around stone buildings,
> And scented blooms gave colour to the crags.
> Flowing water linked ravines with green,
> While clouds enclosed the emptiness of trees.
> Noisily sang wild birds,
> Slowly strolled the deer,
> Elegant grew the bamboo,
> And all the red plums were open.
> Rooks perched in ancient woods,
> While spring birds chirped in the tree of heaven.
> Summer wheat filled spreading acres,
> And autumn millet grew all over the land.
> No leaf fell in all four seasons,
> And flowers bloomed throughout the year.
> Auspicious rosy glows joined with the Milky Way,
> And clouds of good omen were linked with the Great
Emptiness.

The Great Sage was delighted as he went inside, seeing boundless beauty at every stage. He went straight on, but found it deserted and completely silent. Not even a chicken or a dog could be heard. "I think that this sage must be out," Monkey thought. When he had gone a mile or two further on he saw a Taoist nun sitting on a couch. This is what she looked like:

> She wore a five-flowered hat of brocade,
> And a robe of golden silk.
> Her cloud-treading shoes were patterned with phoenixes
> And round her waist was a sash with double tassels.
> Her face looked as old as autumn after a frost,

But her voice was as charming as swallows in the spring.
Long had she mastered the Dharma of Three Vehicles,
And she was ever mindful of the Four Truths.
She knew true achievement, that emptiness is empty,
And through her training had acquired great freedom.
She was the Buddha of the Thousand Flower Cave,
The illustrious Vairambha of great fame.

Monkey went straight up to her without stopping and said, "Greetings, Bodhisattva Vairambha." The Bodhisattva then came down from her couch, put her hands together to return his greeting and said, "Great Sage, it was remiss of me not to come out to greet you. Where have you come from?" "How do you know that I'm the Great Sage?" Monkey asked. "When you made havoc in Heaven the other year," Vairambha replied, "your picture was circulated everywhere. That's why everyone can recognize you." "How true it is," Monkey said, "that

While good deeds stay at home
Bad deeds are known far and wide.

Take my conversion to Buddhism, for example. You didn't know about that." "Congratulations," said Vairambha. "When did that happen?" "Not long ago my life was spared to escort my master the Tang Priest on his journey to the Western Heaven to fetch the scriptures," Monkey replied. "My master has been laid low with poisoned tea by the Taoist of the Yellow Flower Temple. When I was fighting with him he caught me in his golden light, and I had to use magic to escape. I have come here to pay you my respects, Bodhisattva, and ask your help because I've heard that you are able to destroy his golden light." "Who told you that?" the Bodhisattva asked. "I have not left here since the Ullambana assembly over three hundred years ago. I've lived in complete secrecy and nobody has heard of me, so how is it that you know of me?" "I'm an underground devil," Monkey replied, "and I can make my own enquiries anywhere at all." "Never

508

mind," Vairambha said, "never mind. I shouldn't really go, but as you have honoured me with a visit, Great Sage, and as the great cause of fetching the scriptures must not be allowed to fail I'll go with you."

Monkey thanked her and said, "It's very ignorant of me to hurry you along in this way. I wonder what weapon you use." "I have an embroidery needle that will put an end to that damned creature," said the Bodhisattva.

This was too much for Monkey. "Old Lady, you've been wasting my time," he said. "Had I known it was an embroidery needle I wouldn't have had to trouble you. I could have provided a hundredweight of them." "Your embroidery needles are all made of iron, steel or gold," the Bodhisattva replied. "They're no use. My treasure isn't iron and isn't steel and isn't gold. It was tempered by my son in the Sun." "Who is he?" asked Monkey. "He is the Star Lord of the Mane," Vairambha replied. This came as a shock to Monkey, who gazed at the golden light then turned to Vairambha and said, "The Yellow Flower Temple is where that golden light is coming from." Vairambha then took from the lapel of her gown an embroidery needle about the thickness of an eyebrow hair and half an inch long. Holding it between her fingers she threw it into the air. A few moments later there was a loud noise and the golden light was shattered. "That's wonderful, Bodhisattva, wonderful!" exclaimed a delighted Monkey. "Let's find your needle now." "Isn't this it here?" asked Vairambha, who was holding it in her hand. Brother Monkey brought his cloud down to land with hers and went into the temple, where he found the Taoist with his eyes shut, unable to move. "Stop playing blind, damned demon," he said abusively, taking his cudgel from his ear ready to hit the Taoist with. "Don't hit him, Great Sage," said Vairambha. "Go and see your master."

[13]　On going straight to the reception room at the back Monkey found the three of them bringing up mucus and spittle where they lay on the floor. "What am I to do?" wept Monkey. "What am I to do?" "Don't grieve, Great Sage," said

Vairambha. "As I've come out today I think I might as well accumulate some merit by giving you three of these pills that are an antidote to the poison." Monkey turned round to bow down and beg her for them, whereupon she produced a torn paper packet from her sleeve containing three red pills that she handed to Monkey, telling him to put one in each of their mouths. This he did, forcing their teeth apart. A few moments later they all started vomiting as the drug reached their stomachs, bringing up the poison and coming back to life. Pig was the first to scramble to his feet. "I feel suffocated," he said. Sanzang and Friar Sand both came round too, saying that they felt very dizzy. "Your tea was poisoned," Brother Monkey explained. "It was the Bodhisattva Vairambha who saved you. Hurry up and bow to her in thanks." Sanzang bowed to her to show his gratitude as he straightened up his clothes.

"Brother," said Pig, "where's that Taoist? I've got some questions to ask him about why he tried to murder me." Monkey then told him all about the spider spirits. "If spider spirits are his sisters that damned creature must be an evil spirit too," said Pig with fury. "He's standing outside the main hall pretending to be blind," said Monkey, pointing. Pig grabbed his rake and was about to hit the Taoist with it when Vairambha stopped him and said, "Control your temper, Marshal Tian Peng. As the Great Sage knows, I have no servants in my cave. I am going to take him as my doorkeeper." "We are deeply indebted to your great power," Monkey replied, "and we will of course obey. But we would like you to turn him back into his real self so that we can have a look at him." "Easily done," said Vairambha, stepping forward and pointing at the Taoist, who collapsed into the dust and reverted to his real form of a giant centipede spirit seven feet long. Picking him up with her little finger Vairambha rode her auspicious cloud straight back to the Thousand Flower Cave. "That old lady's a real terror," said Pig, looking up. "How did she manage to subdue that evil creature?" "When I asked her what weapon she had to smash the golden light with," Monkey replied, "she told me about a golden embroidery needle of hers that her son had tempered in the sun. When I asked her who her son was she told me he was the Star Lord of the Mane. As I remember, the Mane Star is a cock, so his mother must be a hen. Hens are very good at dealing with centipedes, which is why she could subdue him."

On hearing this Sanzang performed no end of kowtows. "Disciples," he ordered, "go and get things ready." Friar Sand then went inside to find some rice and prepare a vegetarian meal, so that they could all eat their fill. Then they led the horse up, shouldered the carrying-pole, and asked the master to set out. Monkey started a blaze in the kitchen that in an instant burnt the whole temple to ashes. He then set out on his way. Indeed,

The Tang Priest thanked Vairambha for saving his life;
The emotions were eliminated and the Many-eyed Monster removed.

As for what happened on the way ahead, listen to the explanations in the next instalment.

19. 长庚传报魔头狠
行者施为变化能

【1】　情欲原因总一般，有情有欲自如然。
　　　　沙门修炼纷纷士，断欲忘情即是禅。
　　　　须着意，要心坚，一尘不染月当天。
　　　　行功进步休教错，行满功完大觉仙。

【2】　话表三藏师徒们打开欲网，跳出情牢，放马西行。走多时，又是夏尽秋初，新凉透体。但见那：

　　　急雨收残暑，梧桐一叶惊。
　　　萤飞莎径晚，蛩语月华明。
　　　黄葵开映露，红蓼遍沙汀。
　　　蒲柳先零落，寒蝉应律鸣。

三藏正然行处，忽见一座高山，峰插碧空，真个是摩星碍日。长老心中害怕，叫悟空道："你看前面这山，十分高耸，但不知有路通行否？"行者笑道："师父说那里话。自古道：'山高自有客行路，水深自有渡船人。'岂无通达之理？可放心前去。"长老闻言，喜笑花生，扬鞭策马而进，径上高岩。

　　　行不数里，见一老者，鬓蓬松，白发飘搔；须稀朗，银丝摆动；项挂一串数珠子，手持拐杖龙头；远远的立在那山坡上高呼："西进的长老，且暂住骅骝，紧兜玉勒。这山上有一伙妖魔，吃尽了阎浮世上人，不可前进！"三藏闻言，大惊失色。一是马的足下不平，二是坐个雕鞍不稳，扑的跌下马来，挣挫不动，睡在草里哼哩。行者近前搀起道："莫怕，莫怕！有我哩！"长老道："你听那高岩上老者，报道这山上有伙妖魔，吃尽阎浮世上人，谁敢去问他一个真实端的？"行者道："你且坐地，等我去问他。"三藏道："你的相貌丑陋，言语粗鄙，怕冲撞了他，问不出个实信。"行者笑道："我变个俊些儿的去问他。"三藏道："你是变了我看。"好大

512

圣，捻着诀，摇身一变，变做个干干净净的小和尚儿，真个是目秀眉清，头圆脸正；行动有斯文之气象，开口无俗类之言辞；抖一抖锦衣直裰，拽步上前。向唐僧道："师父，我可变得好么？"三藏见了大喜道："变得好！"八戒道："怎么不好！只是把我们都比下去了。老猪就滚上二三年，也变不得这等俊俏！"

【3】　好大圣，躲离了他们，径直近前，对那老者躬身道："老公公，贫僧问讯了。"那老儿见他生得俊雅，年少身轻，待答不答的，还了他个礼，用手摸着他头儿，笑嘻嘻问道："小和尚，你是那里来的？"行者道："我们是东土大唐来的，特上西天拜佛求经。适到此间，闻得公公报道有妖怪，我师父胆小怕惧，着我来问一声：端的是甚妖精，他敢这般短路！烦公公细说与我知之，我好把他贬解起身。"那老儿笑道："你这小和尚年纪，说话不知好歹，言不帮衬。那妖魔神通广大得紧，怎敢就说贬解他起身！"行者笑道："据你之言，似有护他之意，必定与他有亲，或是紧邻契友；不然，怎么长他的威智，兴他的节概，不肯倾心吐胆说他个来历。"公公点头笑道："这和尚倒会弄嘴！想是跟你师父游方，到处儿学些法术，或者会驱缚魍魉，与人家镇宅降邪，你不曾撞见十分狠怪哩！"行者道："怎的狠？"公公道："那妖精一封书到灵山，五百阿罗都来迎接；一纸简上天宫，十一大曜个个相钦。四海龙曾与他为友，八洞仙常与他会合。十地阎君以兄相称，社令、城隍为宾朋相爱。"

【4】　大圣闻言，忍不住呵呵大笑，用手扯着老者道："不要说！不要说！那妖精与我后生小厮为兄弟、朋友，也不见十分高作。若知是我小和尚啊，他连夜就搬起身去了！"公公道："你这小和尚胡说！不当人子！那个神圣是你的后生小厮？"行者笑道："实不瞒你说。我小和尚祖居傲来国花果山水帘洞，姓孙，名悟空。当年也曾做过妖精，干过大事。曾因一会众魔，多饮了几杯酒睡着，梦中见二人将批勾我去到阴司。一时怒发，将金箍棒打伤鬼判，唬倒阎王，几乎掀翻了森罗殿。吓得那掌案的判官拿纸，十阎王金名画字，教我饶他打，情愿与我做后生小厮。"那公公闻说道："阿弥陀佛！这和尚说了过过头话，莫想再长得大了。"行者道："官儿，似我这般大也够了。"公公道："你年几岁了？"行者

道："你猜猜看。"老者道："有七八岁罢了。"行者笑道："有一万个七八岁！我把旧嘴脸拿出来你看看，你即莫怪。"公公道："怎么又有个嘴脸？"行者道："我小和尚有七十二副嘴脸哩。"

那公公不识窍，只管问他，他就把脸抹一抹，即现出本像，咨牙徕嘴，两股通红，腰间系一条虎皮裙，手里执一根金箍棒，立在石崖之下，就像个活雷公。那老者见了，吓得面容失色，腿脚酸麻，站不稳，扑的一跌；爬起来，又一个蹦踵。大圣上前道："老官儿，不要虚惊。我等山恶人善。莫怕！莫怕！适间蒙你好意，报有妖魔。委的有多少怪，一发累你说说，我好谢你。"那老儿战战兢兢，口不能言，又推耳聋，一句不应。

【5】 行者见他不言，即抽身回坡。长老道："悟空，你来了？所问如何？"行者笑道："不打紧！不打紧！西天有便有个把妖精儿，只是这里人胆小，把他放在心上。没事，没事！有我哩！"长老道："你可曾问他此处是甚么山，甚么洞，有多少妖怪，那条路通得雷音？"八戒道："师父，莫怪我说。若论赌变化，使捉掐，捉弄人，我们三五个也不如师兄；若论老实，像师兄就摆一队伍，也不如我。"唐僧道："正是！正是！你还老实。"八戒道："他不知怎么钻过头不顾尾的，问了两声，不尴不尬的就跑回来了。等老猪去问他个实信来。"唐僧道："悟能，你仔细着。"

好呆子，把钉钯撒在腰里，整一整皂直裰，扭扭捏捏，奔上山坡，对老者叫道："公公，唱喏了。"那老儿见行者回去，方拄着杖挣得起来，战战兢兢的要走，忽见八戒，愈觉惊怕道："爷爷呀！今夜做的甚么恶梦，遇着这伙恶人！为先的那和尚丑便丑，还有三分人相；这个和尚，怎么这等个碓梃嘴，蒲扇耳朵，铁片脸，鬃毛颈项，一分人气儿也没有了！"八戒笑道："你这老公公不高兴，有些儿好褒贬人。你是怎的看我哩？丑便丑，奈看，再停一时就俊了。"那老者见他说出人话来，只得开言问他："你是那里来的？"八戒道："我是唐僧第二个徒弟，法名叫做悟能八戒。才自先问的，叫做悟空行者，是我师兄。师父怪他冲撞了公公，不曾问得实信，所以特着我来拜问。此处果是甚山、甚洞，洞里果是甚妖精，那里是西去大路，烦尊一指示指示。"老者道："可老实么？"八戒道："我生平不敢有一毫虚的。"老者道："你莫像才来的那个和尚走花弄水的胡缠。"八戒道:"我不像他。"

公公拄着杖,对八戒说:"此山叫做八百里狮驼岭。中间有座狮驼洞。洞里有三个魔头。"八戒唖了一声:"你这老儿却也多心!三个妖魔,也费心劳力的来报遭信!"公公道:"你不怕么?"八戒道:"不瞒你说,这三个妖魔,我师兄一棍就打死一个;我一钯就筑死一个;我还有个师弟,他一降妖杖又打死一个:三个都打死,我师父就过去了,有何难哉!"那老者笑道:"这和尚不知深浅!那三个魔头,神通广大得紧哩!他手下小妖,南岭上有五千,北岭上有五千;东路口一万,西路口一万;巡哨的有四五千,把门的也有一万;烧火的无数,打柴的也无数:共计算有四万七八千。这都是有名字带牌儿的,专在此吃人。"

【6】　那呆子闻得此言,战兢兢跑将转来,相近唐僧,不回话,放下钯,在那里出恭。行者见了,喝道:"你不回话,却跑去那里怎的?"八戒道:"唬出屎来了!如今也不消说,赶早儿各自顾命去罢!"行者道:"这个呆根!我问信偏不惊恐,你去问就这等慌张失智!"长老道:"端的何如?"八戒道:"这老儿说:此山叫做八百里狮驼山。中间有座狮驼洞。洞里有三个老妖,有四万八千小妖,专在那里吃人。我们若蹭着他些山边儿,就是他口里食了。莫想去得!"三藏闻言,战兢兢,毛骨悚然,道:"悟空,如何是好?"行者笑道:"师父放心,没大事。想是这里有便有几个妖精,只是这里人胆小,把他就说说出许多人,许多大,所以自惊自怪。有我哩!"八戒道:"哥哥说的是那里话!我比你不同:我问的是实,决无虚谬之言。满山满谷都是妖魔,怎生前进?"行者笑道:"呆子嘴脸!不要虚惊!若论满山满谷之魔,只消老孙一路棒,半夜打个罄尽!"八戒道:"不羞,不羞!莫说大话!那些妖精点卯也得七八日,怎么就打得罄尽?"行者道:"你说怎样打?"八戒道:"凭你抓倒,捆倒,使定身法定倒,也没有这等快的。"行者笑道:"不用甚么抓拿捆缚。这把这棍子两头一扯,叫'长!'就有四十丈长短;幌一幌,叫'粗!'就有八丈围圆粗细。往山南一滚,滚杀五千;山北一滚,滚杀五千;从东往西一滚,只怕四五万砑做肉泥烂酱!"八戒道:"哥哥,若是这等赶面打,或者二更时也都了了。"沙僧在旁笑道:"师父,有大师兄恁样神通,怕他怎的!请上

马走啊。"唐僧见他们讲论手段，没奈何，只得宽心上马而走。

【7】　正行间，不见了那报信的老者。沙僧道："他就是妖怪，故意狐假虎威的来传报，恐唬我们哩。"行者道："不要忙，等我去看看。"好大圣，跳上高峰，四顾无迹，急转面，见半空中有彩霞幌亮，即纵云赶上看时，乃是太白金星。走到身边，用手扯住，口口声声只叫他的小名道："李长庚！李长庚！你好惫懒！有甚话，当面来说便好；怎么装做个山林之老，魔样混我！"金星慌忙施礼道："大圣，报信来迟，乞勿罪！乞勿罪！这魔头果是神通广大，势要峥嵘，只看你挪移变化，乖巧机谋，可便过去；如若急慢些儿，其实难去。"行者谢道："感激！感激！果然此处难行，望老星上界与玉帝说声，借些天兵帮助老孙帮助。"金星道："有！有！有！你只口信带去，就是十万天兵，也是有的。"

大圣别了金星，按落云头，见了三藏道："适才那个老儿，原是太白星来与我们报信的。"长老合掌道："徒弟，快赶上他，问他那里另有一个路，我们转了去罢。"行者道："转不得。此山径过有八百里，四周围不知更有多少路哩。怎么转得？"三藏闻言，止不住眼中流泪道："徒弟，似此艰难，怎生拜佛！"行者道："莫哭！莫哭！一哭便脓包行了！他这报信，必有几分虚话，只是要我们着意留心，诚所谓'以告者，过也。'你且下马来坐着。"八戒道："又有甚商议？"行者道："没甚商议。你且在这里用心保守师父。沙僧好生看守行李、马匹。等老孙上岭打听打听，看有几多妖怪，拿住一个，问他个详细，教他写个执结，开个花名，把他老老小小，一一查明，盼吩他关了洞门，不许阻路，却请师父静静悄悄的过去，方显得老孙手段！"沙僧听教："仔细！仔细！"行者笑道："不消嘱咐。我这一去，就是东洋大海也荡开路，就是铁裹银山也撞透门！"

【8】　好大圣，嗖哨一声，纵筋斗云，跳上高峰。扳藤负葛，平山观看，那山里静悄无人。忽失声道："错了！错了！不该放这金星老儿去了。他原来想唬我。他就说出来跳风顽爱，必定拈枪弄棒，操演武艺；如何没有一个？……"正自家揣度，只听得山背后，叮叮当当，辟辟剥剥，梆铃之声。急回头看处，原来是个小妖儿，掮着一杆"令"字旗，腰间悬着铃子，手里

敲着梆子，从北向南而走。仔细看他，有一丈二尺的身子。行者暗笑道："他必是个铺兵。想是送公文下报帖的。且等我去听他一听，看他说些甚话。"

好大圣，捻着诀，念个咒，摇身一变，变做个苍蝇儿，轻轻飞在他帽子上，侧耳听之。只见那小妖走上大路，敲着梆，摇着铃，口里作念道："我等寻山的，各人要谨慎堤防孙行者：他会变苍蝇！"行者闻言，暗自惊疑道："这厮看见我了；若未看见，怎么就知我的名字，又知我会变苍蝇！……"原来那小妖也不曾见他，只是那魔头不知怎么就吩咐他这话，却是个谣言，着他这等胡念。行者不知，反疑他看见，就要取出棒来打他，却又停住，暗想道："曾记得八戒问金星时，他说老妖三个，小妖有四万七八千名。似这小妖，再多几万，也不打紧，却不知这三个老魔有多大手段。……等我问他一问，动手不迟。"

【9】　好大圣！你道他怎么合弄：跳下他的帽子来，钉在树头上，让那小妖先行几步，急转身腾那，也变做个小妖儿，照依他敲着梆，摇着铃，捎着旗，一般衣服，只是比他略长了三五寸，口里也那般念着，赶上前叫道："走路的，等我一等。"那小妖回头道："你是那里来的？"行者笑道："好人呀！一家人也不认得！"小妖道："我家没你呀。"行者道："怎的没有？你认认看。"小妖道："面生，认不得！认不得！"行者道："可知道面生。我是烧火的，你会得我少。"小妖摇头道："没有！没有！我洞里就是烧火的那些兄弟，也没有这个嘴尖的。"行者暗想道："这个嘴的变尖了些了。"即低头，把手侮着嘴揉一揉道："我的嘴不尖哩。"真个就不尖了。那小妖道："你刚才是个尖嘴，怎么揉一揉就不尖了？疑惑人子！大不好认！不是我一家的！少会，少会！可疑，可疑！我那大王法甚严，烧火的只管烧火，巡山的只管巡山，终不然教你烧火，又教你来巡山？"行者口乖，就趁过来道："你不知道。大王见我烧得火好，就升我来巡山。"

小妖道："也罢；我们这巡山的，一班有四十名，十班共四百名，各自年貌，各有名色。大王怕我们乱了班次，不好点卯，一家与我们一个牌儿为号。你可有牌儿？"行者只见他那般打扮，那般报事，遂照他的模样变了；因不曾看见他的牌儿，所以身上没有。好大圣，更不说没有，就满口应承道："我怎么没牌？但只是刚才领的新牌。拿你的出来我看。"那小妖那里知这个机括，即揭起衣服，贴身带着个金漆牌儿，穿条绒线绳儿，扯与行者看看。行者见那牌背是个"威镇诸魔"的金牌，正面有三个真字，是"小钻风"，他却心中暗想道："不消说了！但是巡山的，必有个'风'字坠脚。"便道："你且放下衣走过，等我拿牌儿你看。"即转身，插下手，将尾巴梢儿的小毫毛拔下一根，捻他把，叫"变！"即变做个金漆牌儿，也穿上个绿绒绳儿，上书三个真字，乃"总钻风"，拿出来，递与他看了。小妖大惊道："我们都叫做个小钻风，偏你又叫做个甚么'总钻风'！"行者干事找绝，说话合宜，就道："你实不知。大王见我烧得火好，把我升个巡风；又与我个新牌，叫做'总巡风'，教我管你这一班四十名兄弟里。"那妖闻言，即忙唱喏道："长官，长官，新点出来的，实是面生。言语冲撞，莫怪！"行者还礼笑道："怪便不怪你，只是一件：见面钱却要哩，每人拿出五两来罢。"小妖道："长官不要忙，待我向南岭头会了我这一班的人，一总打发罢。"行者道："既如此，我和你同去。"那小妖真个走，大圣随后相跟。

【10】　不数里，忽见一座笔峰。何以谓之笔峰？那山头上长出一条峰来，约有四五丈高，如笔插在架上一般，故以为名。行者到边前，把尾巴掬一掬，跳上去，坐在峰尖儿上。叫道："钻风！都过来！"那些小钻风在下面躬身道："长官，伺候。"行者道："你可知大王点我出来之故？"小妖道："不知。"行者道："大王要吃唐僧，只怕孙行者神通广大，说他会变化，只恐他变做小钻风，来这里蹲着路径，打探消息，把我升做总钻风，来查勘你们这一班可有假的。"小钻风连声应道："长官，我们俱是真的。"行者道："你既是真的，大王有甚本事，你可晓得？"小钻风道："我晓得。"行者道："你晓得，快说来我听。如若说得合着我，便是真的；若说差了一些儿，便是假的。我定拿去见大王处治。"那小钻风见他坐在高处，弄獐弄智，呼呼喝喝的，没奈何，只得实说道："我大王神通广大，本事高强，一口曾吞了十万天兵。"行者闻说，吐出一声道："你是假的！"小钻风慌了道："长官老爷，我是真的，怎么说是假的？"行者道："你既是真的，如何胡说！大王身子能有多大，一

口都吞了十万天兵？"小钻风道："长官原来不知。我大王会变化：要大能撑天堂，要小能如菜子。因那年王母娘娘设蟠桃大会，邀请诸仙，他不曾具柬来请，我大王意欲争天，被玉皇差十万天兵来降我大王；是我大王变化法身，张开大口，似城门一般，用力吞将去，唬得众天兵不敢交锋，关了南天门：故此是一口曾吞十万兵。"行者闻言暗笑道："若是讲手头之话，老孙也曾干过。"又应声道："二大王有何本事？"小钻风道："二大王身高三丈，卧蚕眉，丹凤眼，美人声，匾担牙，鼻似蛟龙。若与人争斗，只消一鼻子卷去，就是铁背铜身，也就魂亡魄丧！"行者道："鼻子卷人的妖精也好拿。"又应声道："三大王也有几多手段？"小钻风道："我三大王不是凡间之怪物，名号云程万里鹏，行动时，抟风运海，振北图南。随身有一件儿宝贝，唤做'阴阳二气瓶'。假若是把人装在瓶中，一时三刻，化为浆水。"

行者听说，心中暗惊道："妖魔倒也不怕，只是仔细防他瓶儿。"又应声道："三个大王的本事，你倒也说得不差，与我知道的一样；但只是那个大王要吃唐僧哩？"小钻风道："长官，你不知道？"行者喝道："我比你不知些儿！因恐汝等不知底细，吩咐我来着实盘问你哩！"小钻风道："我大王与二大王久住在狮驼岭狮驼洞。三大王不在这里住。他原住处离此西下有四百里远近。那厢有座城，唤做狮驼国。他五百年前吃了这城国王及文武官员，满城大小男女也尽被他吃了干净，因此上夺了他的江山。如今尽是些妖怪。不知那一年打听得东土唐朝差一个僧人去西天取经，说那唐僧乃十世修行的好人，有人吃他一块肉，就延寿长生不老；只因怕他一个徒弟孙行者十分利害，自家一个难为，径来此处与我这两个大王结为兄弟，合意同心，打伙儿捉那个唐僧也。"

行者闻言，心中大怒道："这泼魔十分无礼！我保唐僧成正果，他怎么算计要吃我的人！"恨一声，咬响钢牙，掣出铁棒，跳下高峰，把棍子望小妖头上砑了一砑，可怜砑得像一个肉陀！自家见了，又不忍道："咦！他倒是个好意，把些家常话儿都与我说了，我怎么却这一下子就结果了他？——也罢，也罢！左右是左右！"好大圣，只为师父阻路，没奈何干出这件事来。就把他牌儿解下，带在自家腰里，将"令"字旗掮在背上，腰间挂了铃，手里敲着梆子，迎风捻个诀，口里念个咒语，摇身一变，变的就像小钻风模样；拽动步，径转旧路，找寻洞府，去打探那三个老妖魔的虚实。这正是：千般变化美猴王，万样腾那真本事！

【11】　闯入深山，依着旧路，正走处，忽听得人喊马嘶之声，即举目观之，原来是狮驼洞口有万数小妖排列着枪刀剑戟，旗帜旌旄。这大圣心中暗喜道："李长庚之言，真是不寒！真是不妄！"原来这摆列的有些路数：二百五十名做一大队伍。他只见有四十名杂彩长旗，迎风乱舞，就知有万名人马；却又自揣自度道："老孙变做小钻风，这一进去，那老魔若问我巡山的话，我必随机答应。倘或一时言语差讹，认得我啊，怎生脱体？就要往外跑时，那伙把门的挡住，如何出得门去？——要拿洞里妖王，必先除了门前众怪！"你道他怎么除得众怪？好大圣，……想着："那老魔不曾与我会面，就知我老孙的名头，我且倚着我这个名头，仗着威风，说些大话，吓他一吓看。果然中土众僧有缘有分，取得经回，这一去，只消我几句英雄之言，就吓退那门前若干之怪；假若众僧无缘无分，取不得真经啊，就是纵然说得莲花现，也除不得西方洞外精。"心问口，口问心，思量此计，敲着梆，摇着铃，径直闯到狮驼洞口，早被前营上小妖挡住道："小钻风来了？"行者不应，低着头就走。

走至二层营里，又被小妖扯住道："小钻风来了？"行者道："来了。"众妖道："你今早巡风去，可曾撞见甚么孙行者么？"行者道："撞见的。正在那里磨扛子哩。"众妖害怕道："他怎么个模样？磨甚么扛子？"行者道："他蹲在那涧边，还似个开路神；若站起来，好道有十数丈长！手里拿着一条铁棒，就似碗来粗细的一根大扛子，在那石崖上抄一把水，磨一磨，口里又念着：'扛子啊！这一向不曾拿你出来显显神通，这一去就有十万妖精，也都替我打死！等我杀了那三个魔头祭你！'他要磨得明了，先打死你们前一万精哩！"那些小妖闻得此言，一个个心惊胆战，魂散魄飞。行者又道："列位！那863僧的肉也不多几斤，也分不到我处，把我也替他顶这个缸怎的！不如我各自散一散罢。"众妖都道："说得是。我们各自顾命去来。"假若是些军民人等，服了圣化，就死也不敢走。原来此辈都是些狼虫虎豹，走兽飞禽，鸣的一声，都哄然而去了。这个倒不像孙大圣几句铺头话，却就如楚歌声吹散了八千兵！行者暗自喜道："好了！老妖是死了！闻言就走，怎敢觌面相逢？这进去还似此方才好；若说差了，才这伙小妖有一两个倒走进去听见，却不走了风汛？……"你看他存心来古洞，仗胆入深门。毕竟不知见那个老魔头有甚吉凶，且听下回分解。

Chapter 19
Li Changgeng Reports
the Demons' Vicious Nature;
The Novice Displays His Powers
of Transformation

[1] *Emotions and desires are in origin all the same;*
   Both emotions and desires are completely natural.
   Many a gentleman refines himself in the Buddhist faith;
   When desire and emotions are forgotten, dhyana comes.
   Don't be impatient; be firm of heart;
   Be free of dust like the moon in the sky.
   Make no mistake in your labours and your progress;
   When your efforts are completed you will be an enlightened
immortal.

[2]   The story tells how Sanzang and his disciples, having broken through the net of desires and escaped from the prison-house of the emotions, let the horse travel west. Before they had been going for very long the summer was over and the new coolness of early autumn was refreshing their bodies. What they saw was:

   Driving rains sweeping away the last of the heat,
   Alarming the leaf of the parasol tree.
   At evening glow-worms flew by the sedgy path
   While crickets sang beneath the moon.
   The golden mallows opened in the dew;
   Red knotweed covered the sandbanks.
   Rushes and willows were the first to lose their leaves
   As cold cicadas sang in tune.

As Sanzang was travelling along a high mountain appeared in front of him. Its peak thrust up into the azure void, touching the stars and blocking out the sun. In his alarm the venerable elder said to

Monkey, "Look at that mountain in front of us. It's very high. I don't know whether the path will take us across." "What a thing to say, Master," said Monkey with a smile. "As the old saying goes,

> However high the mountain there will be a way across;
> However deep the river there's always a ferryman.

There's no reason why we shouldn't get over it. Stop worrying and carry on." When Sanzang heard this his face broke out in smiles and he whipped his horse forward to climb straight up the high crag.

After a mile or two an old man appeared. His white hair was tangled and flying in the wind while his sparse whiskers were being blown about like silver threads. He wore a string of prayer-beads round his neck and held a dragon-headed walking-stick as he stood far away at the top of the slope shouting, "Venerable gentleman travelling west, stop your worthy steed. Rein in. There is a band of demons on this mountain who have eaten all the people in the continent of Jambu. Go no further!" At this Sanzang turned pale with terror, and because the horse was not standing steadily and he himself was not well seated in the carved saddle he crashed to the ground and lay in the grass, moaning but unable to move.

Monkey went over to help him to his feet with the words, "Don't be afraid, don't be afraid. I'm here." "Did you hear the old man up on the crag telling us that there's a band of demons on this mountain who have eaten everyone in the continent of Jambu?" said Sanzang. "Who'll dare go to ask him what this is early all about?" "Sit there while I go and ask him," Monkey replied. "With your ugly face and coarse language I'm afraid you may shock him," said Sanzang, "so you won't get the truth from him." "I'll make myself a bit better looking before questioning him," laughed Brother Monkey. "Do a change to show me," said Sanzang, and the splendid Great Sage made a spell with his fingers, shook himself, and turned into a very neat little monk, clear-eyed, fine-browed, round-headed and regular of features. He moved in a most refined way and said nothing vulgar when he opened his mouth. Brushing his brocade tunic he stepped forward and said to the Tang Priest, "Master, have I changed for the better?" "Yes," said the delighted Sanzang. "Marvellous," said Pig, "but the rest of us look shabby by comparison. Even if I rolled around for two or three years on end I couldn't make myself look as elegant as that."

【3】 The splendid Great Sage left them behind as he went straight up to the old man, bowed to him and said, "Greetings, venerable sir." Seeing how young and cultivated he looked, the old man returned his greeting and stroked his head in an offhand way. "Little monk," the old man said with a smile, "where have you come from?" "We are from the Great Tang in the east," Monkey replied, "going to worship the Buddha and fetch the scriptures. When we came here and heard you tell us that there are demons here my master was terrified. He sent me to ask you about them. What sort of evil spirits would dare go in for that sort of crime? I would trouble you, venerable sir, to tell me all the details so that I can put them in their palace and send them on their way." "You're much too young, little monk," said the old man with a smile, "to know what's good for you. Your remarks aren't helpful. Those evil spirits have tremendous magical powers. How can you have the nerve to talk of putting them in their place and sending them on their way?" "From what you are saying," Monkey replied with a smile, "you seem to be trying to protect them. You must be a relation of theirs, or else a neighbour or a friend. Why else would you be promoting their prestige and boosting their morale, and refusing to pour out everything you know about their background?" "You certainly know how to talk, monk," said the old man, nodding and smiling. "I suppose you must have learned some magic arts while travelling with your master. Perhaps you know how to drive away and capture goblins, or have exorcised people's houses for them. But you've never come up against a really vicious monster." "What sort of vicious?" Monkey said. "If those evil spirits send a letter to Vulture Mountain the five hundred arhats all come out to meet them," the old man said. "If they send a note to the Heavenly Palace the Ten Bright Shiners all turn out to pay their respects. The dragons of the Four Oceans were their friends and they often meet the immortals of the Eight Caves. The Ten Kings of the Underworld call them brothers; the local gods and city gods are good friends of theirs."

[4] When the Great Sage heard this he could not help bursting into loud guffaws. "Stop talking," he said, grabbing hold of the old man, "stop talking. Even if that demon is friends with all those young whipper-snappers, my juniors, that's nothing really remarkable. If he knew I was coming he'd clear off the same night." "You're talking nonsense, little monk," the old man said. "How can any of those sages be juniors and young whipper-snappers to you?" "To be truthful with you," Monkey replied with a grin, "my people have lived for many generations in the Water Curtain Cave on the Mountain of Flowers and Fruit in the land of Aolai. My name is Sun Wukong. In the old days I used to be an evil spirit too and did some great things. Once I fell asleep after drinking too much at a feast with the other demons and dreamed that two men came to drag me off to the World of Darkness. I got so angry that I wounded the demon judges with my gold-banded cudgel. The kings of the Underworld were terrified and I practically turned the Senluo Palace upside-down. The judges in charge of the case were so scared that they fetched some paper for the Ten Kings to sign. They promised to treat me as their senior if I let them off a beating." "Amitabha Buddha!" exclaimed the old man when he heard this. "If you talk big like that you won't be able to grow any older." "I'm old enough, fellow," said Monkey. "How old are you then?" the old man asked. "Guess," Monkey replied. "Six or seven," the old man said. "I'm ten thousand times as old as that," laughed Monkey, "I'll show you my old face, then you'll believe me." "How can you have another face?" the old man asked. "This little monk has seventy-two faces," Monkey replied.

Not realizing that Monkey really had these powers the old

man went on questioning him till Monkey rubbed his face and turned back into himself, with his protruding teeth, big mouth, red thighs and tigerskin kilt round his waist. As he stood there at the foot of the rocky scar, holding his gold-banded cudgel, he was the living image of a thunder god. The sight of him made the old man turn pale with terror and go so weak at the knees that he could not keep himself upright but collapsed to the ground. When he got to his feet again he lost his balance once more. "Old man," said the Great Sage, going up to him, "don't get yourself so frightened over nothing. I may look evil but I'm good inside. Don't be afraid! You were kind enough just now to tell us that there are demons here. Could I trouble you to let me know how many of them there are? I'll thank you very much if you do." The old man trembled, unable to speak and acting as if deaf. He replied not a word.

[5] Getting no answer from him, Monkey went back down the slope. "So you are back, Wukong," Sanzang said. "What did you find out?" "It's nothing," said Monkey with a smile, "nothing. Even if there are one or two evil spirits on the way to the Western Heaven, the people here only worry so much about them because they're such cowards. No problem! I'm here!" "Did you ask him what mountain this was and what cave," said Sanzang, "how many monsters there are, and which is the way to Thunder Monastery?" "Please excuse me if I speak frankly, Master," put in Pig. "When it comes to transformations, trickery and deception then four or five of us would be no match for Brother Monkey. But a whole parade of Monkeys couldn't touch me for honesty." "That's right," said the Tang Priest, "that's right. You're honest." "Goodness knows why," said Pig, "but he just rushed in without a second thought, asked a couple of questions, and came running back in an awful mess. I'm going to find out the truth." "Do be careful, Wuneng," said the Tang Priest.

The splendid idiot put his rake in his belt, straightened up his tunic, and swaggered straight up the slope to call to the old man, "Respectful greetings, sir." The old man had finally managed to get back on his feet with the help of his stick after seeing that Monkey had gone, and was still shaking and about to depart when Pig suddenly appeared. "Sir," he said, more shocked than ever, "whatever kind of nightmare am I in the middle of? The first monk was ugly enough, but at least he looked a little bit human. But this one's got a snout like a pestle, ears like rush fans, a face like iron plates, and a neck covered in bristles. It doesn't look at all human." "You must be in a very bad mood to run me down like that, old man," laughed Pig. "Is that how you see me? Ugly I may be, but if you can bear to look at me for a while you'll find I get quite handsome."

Only when the old man heard Pig using human speech did he address him by asking, "Where are you from?" "I'm the Tang Priest's second disciple," Pig replied, "and my Buddhist names are Wuneng or Bajie. The one who came and asked you questions just now was Sun Wukong the Novice, the senior disciple. My master has sent me to pay my respects to you because he's angry with Sun Sukong for offending you and not finding out the truth. Could you please tell me, sir, what mountain this is, what caves there are on it, what demons live in them, and which is the main route west?" "Are you honest?" the old man asked. "I've never been false in all my life," Pig replied. "You mustn't talk a whole lot of fancy nonsense like the other monk just now," said the old man. "I'm not like him," Pig replied.

Leaning on his stick, the old man said to Pig, "This is Lion Ridge, and it is 150 miles around. In it there is a Lion Cave where there are three demon chieftains." "You're worrying over nothing, old man," said Pig, spitting. "Why go to all that trouble just to tell us about three demons?" "Aren't you afraid?" the old man said. "To tell you the truth," Pig replied, "my elder brother'll kill one with one swing of his cudgel, I'll kill another with one bash from my rake, and the other disciple will kill the third one with his demon-quelling staff. And with the three of them dead our master will be able to cross the ridge. No problem!" "You don't know the whole story, monk," said the old man with a smile. "Those three demon chiefs have the most

527

tremendous magic powers. As for the little demons under their command, there are five thousand on the southern end of the ridge, five thousand on the northern end, ten thousand on the road east, ten thousand on the road west, four or five thousand patrollers and another ten thousand on the gates. Then there are any number who work in the kitchen and gather firewood. There must be 47,000 or 48,000 altogether. They all have names and carry passes, and all they do is eat people. "

[6]   On learning this the idiot ran back, shivering and shaking. As soon as he was near the Tang Priest he put down his rake and started shitting instead of reporting back. "What are you squatting there for instead of making your report?" shouted Monkey when he saw the idiot. "Because I'm shit scared," Pig replied. "No time to talk now. The sooner we all run for our lives the better." "Stupid fool," said Monkey. "I wasn't frightened when I questioned him, so why should you be in such a witless panic?" "What is the situation?" Sanzang asked. "The old man says that this is Lion Mountain," Pig replied, "and that there's a Lion Cave in it. There are three chief demons there, and they have 48,000 little devils under them. All they do is eat people. So if we step on their mountain we'll just be serving ourselves up as a meal to them. Let's forget about it." On hearing this Sanzang shivered, his hairs standing on end. "What are we to do, Wukong?" he asked. "Don't worry, Master," said Monkey. "It can't be anything much. There are bound to be a few evil spirits here. It's just that the people here are such cowards that they exaggerate about how many demons there are and how powerful they are. They get themselves into a funk. I can cope."

"You're talking nonsense, brother," said Pig. "I'm not like you. What I found out was the truth. I wasn't making any of it up. The hills and valleys are all crawling with demons. How are we going to move ahead?" "You're talking like an idiot," said Monkey with a grin. Don't scare yourself over nothing. Even if the hills and valleys were crawling with demons I'd only need half a night to wipe them all out with my cudgel." "You're shameless," said Pig, "quite shameless. Stop talking so big. It would take seven or eight days just to call the roll. How could you wipe them all out?" "Tell me how you'd do it," laughed Monkey. "However you grabbed them, tied them up, or fixed them where they are with fixing magic you'd never be able to do it so fast," said Pig. "I wouldn't need to grab them or tie them up," said Monkey. "I'll give my cudgel a tug at both ends, say 'Grow!', and make it over four hundred feet long. Then I'll wave it, say 'Thicken!', and make it eighty feet around. I'll roll it down the southern slope and that'll kill five thousand of them. I'll roll it down the northern slope and kill another five thousand. Then I'll roll it along the ridge from east to west, and even if there are forty or fifty thousand of them I'll squash them all to a bloody pulp." "Brother," said Pig, "if you kill them that way, like rolling out dough for noodles, you could do it in four hours." "Master," said Friar Sand with a laugh, "as my elder brother has such divine powers we've got nothing to fear. Please mount up so that we can be on our way." Having heard them discussing Monkey's powers Sanzang could not but mount with an easy heart and be on his way.

[7] As they travelled along the old man disappeared. "He must have been an evil spirit himself," said Friar Sand, "deliberately coming to frighten us with cunning and intimidation." "Take it easy," said Monkey. "I'm going to take a look." The splendid Great Sage leapt up to a high peak but saw no trace of the old man when he looked around. Then he suddenly turned back to see a shimmering coloured glow in the sky, shot up on his cloud to look, and saw that it was the Great White Planet. Walking over and grabbing hold of him, Monkey kept addressing him by his personal name: "Li Changgeng! Li Changgeng! You rascal! If you had something to say you should have said it to my face. Why did you pretend to be an old man of the woods and make a fool of me?" The planet hastened to pay him his respects and said, "Great Sage, I beg you to forgive me for being late in reporting to you. Those demon chiefs really have tremendous magical abilities and their powers are colossal. With your skill in transformations and your cunning you may just be able to get over, but if you

529

slight them it will be very hard." "I'm very grateful," Monkey thanked him, "very grateful. If I really can't get across this ridge I hope that you'll go up to Heaven and put in a word with the Jade Emperor so he'll lend me some heavenly soldiers to help me." "Yes, yes, yes," said the Great White Planet. "Just give the word and you can have a hundred thousand heavenly troops if you want them."

The Great Sage then took his leave of the planet and brought his cloud down to see Sanzang and say, "The old man we saw just now was actually the Great White Planet come to bring us a message." "Disciple," said Sanzang, putting his hands together in front of his chest, "catch up with him quick and ask him where there's another path we could make a detour by." "There's no other way round," Monkey relied. "This mountain is 250 miles across, and goodness knows how much longer it would be to go all the way around it. How ever could we?" at this Sanzang could not restrain himself from weeping. "Disciple," he said, "if it's going to be as hard as this how are we going to worship the Buddha?" "Don't cry," Monkey said, "don't cry. If you cry you're a louse. I'm sure he's exaggerating. All we have to do is be careful. As they say, forewarned is forearmed. Dismount and sit here for now." "What do you want to talk about now?" Pig asked. "Nothing," replied Monkey. "You stay here and look after the master carefully while Friar Sand keeps a close eye on the baggage and the horse. I'm going up the ridge to scout around. I'll find out how many demons there are in the area, capture one, ask him all the details, and get him to write out a list with all of their names. I'll check out every single one of them, old or young, and tell them to shut the gates of the cave and not block our way. Then I can ask the master to cross the mountain peacefully and quietly. That'll show people my powers." "Be careful," said Friar Sand, "do be careful!" "No need to tell me," Brother Monkey replied with a smile. "On this trip I'd force the Eastern Ocean to make way for me, and I'd smash my way in even if it were a mountain of silver cased in iron."

[8]   The splendid Great Sage went whistling straight up to the

peak by his somersault cloud. Holding on to the vines and creepers, he surveyed the mountain only to find it silent and deserted. "I was wrong," he said involuntarily, "I was wrong. I shouldn't have let that old Great White Planet go. He was just trying to scare me. There aren't any evil spirits here. If there were they'd be out leaping around in the wind, thrusting with their spears and staves, or practising their fighting skills. Why isn't there a single one?" As he was wondering about this there was a ringing of a bell and a banging of clappers. He turned round at once to see a little devil boy with a banner on which was written BY ORDER over his shoulder, a bell at his waist and clappers in his hands that he was sounding. He was coming from the north and heading south. A closer look revealed that he was about twelve feet tall. "He must be a runner," thought Monkey, grinning to himself, "delivering messages and reports. I'll take a listen to what he's talking about."

The splendid Great Sage made a spell with his hands, said the magic words, shook himself and turned into a fly who landed lightly on the devil's hat and tilted his head for a good listen. This is what the little devil was saying to himself as he headed along the main road, sounding his clappers and ringing his bell: "All we mountain patrollers must be careful and be on our guard against Sun the Novice. He can even turn into a fly!" Monkey was quietly amazed to hear this. "That so-and-so must have seen me before. How else could he know my name and know that I can turn into a fly?" Now the little devil had not in fact seen him before. The demon chief had for some reason given him these instructions that he was reciting blindly. Monkey, who did not know this, thought that the devil must have seen him and was on the point of bringing the cudgel out to hit him with when he stopped. "I remember Pig being told," he thought, "when he questioned the planet that there were three demon chieftains and 47,000 or 48,000 junior devils like this one. Even if there were tens of thousands more juniors like this it would be no problem. But I wonder how great the three leaders' powers are. I'll question him first. There'll be time to deal with them later."

[9]   Splendid Great Sage! Do you know how he questioned the demon? He jumped off the devil's hat and landed on a tree top, letting the junior devil go several paces ahead. Then Monkey turned round and did a quick transformation into another junior devil, sounding clappers, ringing a bell and carrying a flag over his shoulder just like the real one. He was also dressed identically. The only difference was that he was a few inches taller. He was muttering the same things as the other as he caught him up, shouting, "Hey, you walking ahead, wait for me." Turning round the junior devil asked, "Where have you come from?" "You're a nice bloke," Monkey said with a smile, "not even recognizing one of your own people." "You're not one of ours," said the demon. "What do you mean?" Monkey asked. "Take a look and see if you can recognize me." "I've never seen you before," the demon said. "I don't know you." "It's not surprising you don't know me," said Monkey. "I work in the kitchens. We've rarely met." "You don't," said the demon, shaking his head, "you don't. None of the brothers who do the cooking has got a pointy face like yours." "I must have made my face too pointy when I did the transformation," thought Monkey, so he rubbed it with his hands and said, "It isn't pointy." Indeed it was not. "But it was pointy just now," the little devil said. "How did you stop it being pointy just by rubbing it? You're a very shady character. I don't have the faintest idea who you are. You're not one of us. I've never met you. Very suspicious. Our kings run the household very strictly. The kitchen staff only work in the kitchen and the mountain patrols keep to patrolling the mountain. How could you possibly be a cook and a patroller?" "There's something you don't know," said Monkey, improvising a clever answer. "I was promoted to patrolling because the kings saw how well I'd worked in the kitchens."

"Very well then," said the little devil. "We patrollers are divided into ten companies of forty each, which makes four hundred in all. We're all known by our ages, appearances, names and descriptions. Because Their Majesties want to keep the organization neat and roll-calls convenient they've given us all passes. Have you got one?" Monkey, who had seen what the devil looked like and heard what he had said, had been able to turn himself into the devil's double. But not having seen the devil's pass he was not carrying one himself. Instead of saying that he did not have one the splendid Great Sage claimed that he had. "Of course I've got one," he said. "But it's a new one that's only just been issued to me. Show me yours."

Not realizing what Monkey was up to, the little devil lifted his clothes to reveal a gold-lacquered pass with a silken cord through it fastened next to his skin that he lifted out to show Monkey. Monkey saw that on the back of it were the words "Demon-suppressor," while on the front was handwritten "Junior Wind-piercer." "Goes without saying," Brother Monkey thought, "all the ones in mountain patrols have 'Wind' at the end of their names. Put your clothes down now," he said, "and come over here while I show you my pass." With that he turned away, put a hand down to pull a little hair from the tip of his tail, rubbed it between his fingers, called "Change!" and turned it into another gold-lacquered pass on a green silken cord on which were handwritten the words "Senior Wind-piercer." With his liking for taking things to extremes and his gift of finding the right thing to say, Monkey remarked, "There's something you don't know. When Their Majesties promoted me to patrolling for doing so well in the kitchen they gave me a new pass as a Senior Patroller and put me in charge of you forty lads in this company." At this the demon at once gave a "na-a-aw" of respect and said, "Sir, I didn't recognize you as you've only just been appointed. Please forgive me if anything I said offended you." "I'm not angry with you," said Monkey, returning his courtesy. "There's just one thing. I want some money from you all to mark our first meeting: five ounces of silver each." "Please be patient, sir," the little devil replied. "When I get back to the southern end of the ridge to meet the rest of our company we'll all give it to you together." "In that case I'm coming with you," said Monkey, and he followed behind as the demon led the way.

[10] After a mile or two a writing-brush peak was seen. Why

was it called a writing-brush peak? Because on the top of the mountain there was a pinnacle about forty or fifty feet high that looked just like a writing brush standing upright on a brush stand. Going up to it Monkey lifted his tail, jumped to the top of the pinnacle, sat down and called, "Come here, all of you." The young Wind-piercers all bowed low beneath him and said, "We're at your service, sir." "Do you know why Their Majesties appointed me?" Monkey asked. "No," they replied. "Their Majesties want to eat the Tang Priest," said Monkey, "but they're worried about Sun the Novice's tremendous magic powers. They've heard that he can do transformations and are worried that he might turn himself into a young Wind-piercer and come along the path here to find out what's going on. That's why they've made me senior Wind-piercer to check up on you and find out if there are any impostors among you." "We're all genuine, sir," the junior Wind-piercers all replied at once. "If you're all genuine do you know what powers His Senior Majesty has?" Monkey asked. "Yes," one of the young Wind-piercers said. "In that case," said Monkey, "tell me about them at once. If what you say matches what I know, you're genuine. If it's at all wrong you're impostors, and I'll take you to Their Majesties for punishment."

Seeing him sitting up on high, playing wise and cunning as he shouted at them, the young devils had nothing for it but to tell him the truth. "His Majesty has vast magical abilities and enormous powers," one of the young devils replied. "He once devoured a hundred thousand heavenly warriors in a single mouthful." "You're an impostor," Monkey spat out when he heard this. "Sir, Your Honour," said the young devil in panic, "I'm real. How can you call me an impostor?" "If you're genuine why did you talk such nonsense?" Monkey replied. "No matter how big he is His Majesty couldn't have swallowed a hundred thousand heavenly soldiers in a single mouthful." "This is something you don't know about, sir," the young devil replied. "His Majesty can do transformations. He can make himself tall enough to hold up the sky or as small as a cabbage seed. Some years ago when the Queen Mother invited all the immortals to a peach banquet she didn't send him an invitation, so His Majesty wanted to fight Heaven. The Jade Emperor sent a hundred thousand heavenly soldiers to subdue His Majesty, gave himself a magical body and opened his mouth that was as big as a city gate. He made as if to swallow hard, which frightened the heavenly soldiers so much that they dared not give battle, and the Southern Gate of Heaven was shut. That's how he could have swallowed a hundred thousand heavenly soldiers at a single mouthful. "

Monkey grinned to himself and thought, " Frankly, I've done that too. What powers does His Second Majesty have?" he asked. "His Second Majesty is thirty feet tall with brows like sleeping silkworms, phoenix eyes, a voice like a beautiful woman, tusks like carrying-poles and a nose like a dragon. If he's in a fight he only needs to wrinkle his nose for his enemy to be scared witless even if he's covered in bronze and iron. " "Evil spirits who get people with their noses are easy enough to catch, " said Monkey, who then asked, "and what powers does His Third Majesty have?" "He's no monster from the mortal world," the young devil replied. "His name is Ten Thousand Miles of Cloud Roc. When he moves he rolls up the wind and shifts the waves, shaking the north as he heads for the south. He carries a treasure about with him called the Male and Female Vital Principles Jar. Anyone who's put in that jar is turned liquid in a few moments. "

That news gave Monkey something to worry about. " I'm not scared of the monsters, " he thought, "but I'll have to watch out for his jar. " Then he said aloud, "Your account of Their Majesties' powers isn't bad—it fits exactly with what I know. But which of them wants to eat the Tang Priest?" "Don't you know, sir?" said the young Wind-piercer. "As if I didn't know better than you!" shouted Monkey. "I was told to come and question you because they're worried that you don't know all the details. " "Our Senior King and Second King have long lived in Lion Cave on Lion Mountain, " the young devil replied, "but the Third King doesn't live here. He used to live over a hundred miles to the west of here in the capital of a country called Leonia. Five

535

hundred years ago he ate the king of the country, his civil and military officials, and everybody else in the city, young and old, male and female. So he seized their country, and now all the people there are evil monsters. I don't know which year it was in which he heard that the Tang court has sent a priest to the Western Heaven to fetch the scriptures. They say this priest is a good man who has cultivated his conduct for ten incarnations, and anyone who eats a piece of his flesh will live for ever and never grow old. But the Third King is worried about the priest's disciple Sun the Novice who's a real terror, so he's come to swear brotherhood with our two kings. All three are now working together to catch the Tang Priest."

"Damn this thoroughly ill-behaved monster," thought Brother Monkey with great fury. "I'm protecting the Tang Priest while he works for the true achievement. How dare they plot to eat my man?" With a snort of fury he ground his steel teeth and brandished his iron cudgel as he leapt down from the high pinnacle and smashed the poor young devil's head into a lump of meat. When he saw what he had done Monkey felt sorry. "Oh dear," he thought, "he meant well, telling me all about the house. Why did I finish him off all of a sudden like that? Oh well! Oh well! That's that." The splendid Great Sage had been forced to do this because his master's way ahead had been blocked. He took the little devil's pass off him, tied it round his own waist, put the "By order" flag over his shoulder, hung the bell from his waist and sounded the clappers with his hand. Then he made a hand-spell into the wind, said a spell, shook himself, turned into the exact likeness of the junior Wind-piercer, and went straight back the way he had come, looking for the cave to find out about the three demon chieftains. Indeed,

The Handsome Monkey King had a thousand transformations
And the true power of magic to make ten thousand changes.

[11] Monkey was rushing deep into the mountains along the way he had come when suddenly he heard shouts and whinnies. As he looked up he saw tens of thousands of little devils drawn up outside the entrance to the Lion Cave with their spears, sabres, swords, halberds, flags and banners. Monkey was delighted. "Li Changgeng, the planet, was telling the truth," he thought. "He wasn't lying at all." The devils were drawn up in a systematic way, each 250 forming a company, so that from the forty standards in many colours that were dancing in the wind he could tell that there were ten thousand infantry and cavalry there. "If I go into the cave disguised as a junior Wind-piercer and one of the demon chiefs questions me about my mountain patrol," Monkey thought, "I'll have to make up answers on the spur of the moment. The moment I say anything at all wrong he'll realize who I am and I won't be able to get away. That army on the gates would stop me and I'd never get out. If I'm going to catch the demon kings I'll have to get rid of the devils on the gates first." Do you know how he was going to do that? "The old demons have never seen me," he thought, "they've only heard of my reputation. I'll talk big and scare them with my fame and prestige. If it's true that all living beings in the middle land are destined to have the scriptures brought to them, then all I need do is talk like a hero and scare those monsters on the gate away. But if they're not destined to have the scriptures brought to them I'll never get rid of the spirits from the gates of this cave in the west even if I talk till lotus flowers appear." Thus he thought about his plans, his mind questioning his mouth and his mouth questioning his mind, as he sounded the clappers and rang the bell. Before he could rush in through the entrance to Lion Cave he was stopped by the junior devils of the forward camp, who said, "You're back, young Wind-piercer." Monkey said nothing but kept going with his head down.

When he reached the second encampment more young devils grabbed hold of him and said, "You're back, young Wind-piercer." "Yes," Monkey replied. "On your patrol this morning did you meet a Sun the Novice?" they asked. "I did," Monkey

537

replied. "He was polishing his pole." "What's he like?" the terrified devils asked. "What sort of pole was he polishing?" "He was squatting beside a stream," Monkey replied. "He looked like one of those gods that clear the way. If he'd stood up I'm sure he'd have been hundreds of feet tall, and the iron cudgel he was holding was a huge bar as thick as a rice-bowl. He'd put a handful of water on a rocky scar and was polishing the cudgel on it muttering, 'Pole, it's ages since I got you out to show your magic powers: This time you can kill all the demons for me, even if there are a hundred thousand of them. Then I'll kill the three demon chiefs as a sacrificial offering to you.' He's going to polish it till it shines then start by killing the ten thousand of you on the gates."

On hearing this the little devils were all terror-struck and their souls all scattered in panic. "Gentlemen," Monkey continued, "that Tang Priest has only got a few pounds of flesh on him. We won't get a share. So why should we have to carry the can for them? We'd do much better to scatter." "You're right," the demons said. "Let's all run for our lives." If they had been civilized soldiers they would have stayed and fought to the death, but as they were all really wolves, tigers and leopards, running beasts and flying birds, they all disappeared with a great whoosh. Indeed, it wasn't as if the Great Sage Sun had merely talked big: it was like the time when Xiang Yu's army of eight thousand soldiers disappeared, surrounded by foes who were former comrades. "Splendid," said Monkey to himself with self-congratulation, "the old devils are as good as dead now. If this lot run away at the sound of me they'll never dare look me in the face. I'll use the same story when I go in there. If I said anything different and one or two of the young devils had got inside and heard me that would give the game away." Watch him as he carefully approaches the ancient cave and boldly goes deep inside. If you don't know what of good or ill was to come from the demon chieftains listen to the explanation in the next instalment.

20. 心猿钻透阴阳窍 魔王还归大道真

【1】 却说孙大圣进于洞口，两边观看。只见：

骷髅若岭，骸骨如林。人头发中踹成毡片，人皮肉烂作泥尘。人筋缠在树上，干焦晃如银。真是个尸山血海，果然腥臭难闻。东边小妖，将活人拿了剐肉；西下泼魔，把人肉鲜煮鲜烹。若非美猴王如此英雄胆，第二个凡夫也进不得他门。

不多时，行入二层门里看时，呀！这里却比外面不同：清奇幽雅，秀丽宽平；左右有瑶草仙花，前后有乔松翠竹。又行七八里远近，才到三层门。闪着身，偷着眼看处，那上面高坐三个老妖，十分狞恶。中间的那个生得：

凿牙锯齿，圆头方面。声吼若雷，眼光如电。仰鼻朝天，赤眉飘焰。但行处，百兽心慌；若坐下，群魔胆战。这一个是兽中王，青毛狮子怪。

左手下那个生得：

凤目金睛，黄牙粗腿。长鼻银毛，看头似尾。圆额皱眉，身躯磊磊。细声如窈窕佳人，玉面似牛头恶鬼。这一个是藏齿修身多年的黄牙老象。

右手下那一个生得：

金翅鲲头，星睛豹眼。振北图南，刚强勇敢。变生翱翔，鷃笑龙惨。抟风翮百鸟藏头，舒利爪诸禽丧胆。这个是云程九万的大鹏雕。

那两下列着有百十大小头目，一个个全装披挂，介胄整齐，威风凛凛，杀气腾腾。行者见了，心中欢喜。一些儿不怕，大踏步，径直进门，把梆铃卸下。朝上叫声“大王。”三个老魔，笑呵呵问道：“小钻风，你来了？”行者应声道：“来了。”——“你去巡山，打听孙行者的下落何如?"行者道:"大王在上,我也不敢说起。"老魔道:"怎么不敢说?"行者道:"我奉大王命,敲着梆铃,正然走处,猛抬头,只看见一个人,蹲在那里磨杠子,还像个开路神,若站将起来,足有十数丈长短。他就着那洞崖石上,抄一把水,磨一磨,口里又念一声,说他那杠子到此还不曾显个神通,他要磨明,就来打大王。我因此知他是孙行者,特来报知。"

【2】 那老魔闻此言,浑身是汗,唬得战呵呵的道:"兄弟,我说莫惹唐僧。他徒弟神通广大,预先做了准备,磨棍打我们,却怎生是好?"教:"小的们,把洞外大小俱叫进来,关了门,让他过去罢。"那头目中有知道的报:"大王,门外小妖,已都散了。"老魔道:"怎么都散了? 想是闻得风声不好也。快早关门! 快早关门!"众妖乒乒乓乓把前后门尽皆牢拴紧闭。

【3】 行者自心惊讶:"这一关了门,他再问我家长里短的事,我对不上来,却不弄走了风,被他拿住? 且再唬他一唬,教他开着前门,好跑。"又上前道:"大王,他还说得不好。"老魔道:"他又说甚么?"行者道:"他说拿大大王剥皮,二大王剐骨,三大王抽筋。你们若关了门不出去啊,他会变化,一时变了个苍蝇儿,自门缝里飞进,把我们都拿出去,却怎生是好?"老魔道:"兄弟们仔细。我这洞里,递年家没个苍蝇,但是有苍蝇进来,就是孙行者。"行者暗笑道:"就变个苍蝇唬他一唬,好开门。"大圣闪在旁边,伸手去脑后拔了一根毫毛,吹一口仙气,叫"变!"即变做一个金苍蝇,飞去望老魔劈脸撞了一头。那老怪慌了道:"兄弟! 不停当! 那话儿进门来了!"惊得那大小群妖,一个个丫钯扫帚,都上前乱扑苍蝇。

这大圣忍不住,赥赥的笑出声来。干净他不宜笑,这一笑笑出原嘴脸来了,却被那第三个老妖魔,跳上前,一把扯住道:"哥哥,险些儿被他瞒了!"老魔道:"贤弟,谁瞒谁?"三怪道:"刚才这个回话的小妖,不是小钻风,他就是孙行者。必定撞见小钻风,不知是他怎么打杀了,却变化来哄我们哩。"行者慌了道:"他认得我了!"把手摸摸,对老怪道:"我怎么是孙行者? 我是小钻风。大王错认了!"老魔笑道:"兄弟,他是小钻风。他一日三次在面前点卯,我认得他。"又问:"你有牌儿么?"行者道:"有。"掳着衣服，就拿出牌子。老怪一发认实道："兄弟，莫屈了他。"三怪道："哥哥，你不曾看见他？他才子闪着身，笑了一声，我见他就露出个雷公嘴来。见我扯住时，他又变做个这等模样。"叫："小的们，拿绳来！"众头目即使绳索。三怪把行者扳翻倒，四马攒蹄捆住；揭起衣裳看时，足足是个弼马温。原来行者有七十二般变化，若是变飞禽、走兽、花木、器皿、昆虫之类，却就连身子滚去了；但变人物，却只是头脸变了，身子变不过来。果然一身黄毛，两块红股，一条尾巴。老妖看着道："是孙行者的身子，小钻风的脸皮，是他了！"教："小的们，先安排酒来，与你三大王递个得功之杯。既拿倒了孙行者，唐僧坐定是我们口里食也。"三怪道："且不要吃酒。孙行者溜撒，他会逃遁之法，只怕走了。教小的们抬出瓶来，把孙行者装在瓶里，我们才好吃酒。"

老魔大笑道："正是！正是！"即点三十六个小妖，入里面开了库房门，抬出瓶来。你说那瓶有多大？只得二尺四寸高。怎么用得三十六个人抬？那瓶乃阴阳二气之宝，内有七宝八卦、二十四气，要三十六人，按天罡之数，才抬得动。不一时，将宝瓶抬出，放在三层门外，展得干净，揭开盖，把行者解了绳索，剥了衣服，就着那瓶中仙气，飕的一声，吸入里面，将盖子盖上，贴了封皮。却去吃酒道："猴儿今番入我宝瓶之中，再莫想那西方之路！若还能勠拜佛求经，除是转背摇车，再去投胎夺舍是。"你看那大小群妖，一个个笑呵呵都去贺功不题。

【4】　却说大圣到了瓶中，被那宝贝将身束得小了，索性变化，蹲在当中；半晌，倒还荫凉，忽失声道："这妖精外有虚名，内无实事。怎么告诉人说这瓶装了人，一时三刻，化为脓血？若似这般凉快，就住上七八年也无事！"咦！大圣原来不知那宝贝根由：假若装了人，一年不语，一年荫凉；但闻得人言，就有火来烧了。大圣未曾说完，只见满瓶都是火焰。幸得他有本事，坐在中间，捻着避火诀，全然不惧。耐到半个时辰，四周围钻出四十条蛇来咬。行者轮开手，抓将过来，尽力一捻，撮做八十段，都不动了。少顷间，又有三条火龙出来，把行者上下盘绕，着实难禁，自觉慌张无措道："别事好处，这三条火龙难为。再过一会不出，弄得火气攻心，怎了？"他又想道："我把身子长一长，券破罢。"好大圣，捻着诀，

念声咒，叫"长！"即长了丈数高下，那瓶紧靠着身，也就长起去；他把身子往下一小，那瓶儿也就小下来了。行者心惊道："难！难！难！怎么我长他也长，我小他也小？如之奈何！"说不了，孤拐上有些疼痛，急伸手摸摸，却被火烧软了，自己心焦道："怎么好？孤拐烧软了！弄做个残疾之人了！"忍不住吊下泪来，——这正是：遭魔遇苦怀三藏，着难临危虑圣僧。——道："师父啊！当年饭正，蒙观音菩萨劝善，脱离天灾，我与你苦历诸山，收珍多怪，降八戒得沙僧，千辛万苦，指望同证西方，共成正果。何期今日遭此毒魔，老孙误入于此，倾了性命，撇你在半山之中，不能前进！想是我昔日名高，故有今朝之难！"正比凄怆，忽想起："菩萨当年在蛇盘山曾赐我三根救命毫毛，不知有无，且等我寻一寻看。"即伸手浑身摸了一把，只见脑后有三根毫毛，十分挺硬。忽喜道："身上毛都如彼软熟，只此三根如此硬棱，必然是救我命的。"即便咬着牙，忍着疼，拔下一根，叫"变！"一根即变做金钢钻，一根变做竹片，一根变做绵匹。扳张篾片儿儿，牵着那钻，照瓶底下飕飕的一顿钻，钻成一个眼孔，透进光亮。喜道："造化！造化！却好出去也！"才变化出身，那瓶复荫凉。怎么就凉？原来被他钻了，把阴阳之气泄了，故此遂凉。

【5】 好大圣，收了毫毛，将身一小，就变做个蟭蟟虫儿，十分轻巧，细如须发，长似眉毛，自孔中钻出；且还不走，径飞在老魔头上钉着？那老魔头正饮酒，猛然放下杯儿道："三弟，孙行者这回化了么？"三魔笑道："还到此时哩？"老魔头教传令教抬上瓶来。那下面三十六个小妖即便抬起，瓶就轻了许多，慌得众小妖报道："大王，瓶轻了！"老魔喝道："胡说！宝贝乃阴阳二气之全功，如何轻了！"内中有一个勉强的小妖，把瓶提上来道："你看这不轻了？"老魔揭盖看时，只见里面透亮，忍不住失声叫道："这瓶里空者，控也！"大圣在他头上，也忍不住道一声"我的儿啊！搜者，走也！"众怪听见道："走了！走了！"即传令："关门！关门！"

那行者将身一抖，收了剥去的衣服，现本相，跳出洞来。回头骂道："妖精不要无礼！瓶子钻破，装不得人了，只好拿了出恭！"喜喜欢欢，嚷嚷闹闹，踏着云头，径转唐僧处。那长老正在那里撮土为香，望空祷视。行者且停云头，听他祷祝甚的。那长老合掌朝天道：

"祈请云霞众位仙，六丁六甲与诸天。

愿保贤徒孙行者，神通广大法无边。"

大圣听得这般言语，更加努力，收敛云光，近前叫道："师父，我来了！"长老揽住道："悟空，劳碌！你远探高山，许久不回，我甚忧虑。端的这山中有何吉凶？"行者笑道："师父，才这一去，一则是东土众僧有缘有分，二来是师父功德无量无边，三也亏弟子法力！……"将前项妆钻风、陷瓶里及脱身之事，细陈了一遍。"今得见尊师之面，实为两世之人也！"长老感谢不尽道："你这番不曾与妖精赌斗么？"行者道："不曾。"长老道："这等保不得我过山了？"行者是个好胜的人，叫喊道："我怎么保你出山不得？"长老道："不曾与他斗个胜负，只这般含糊，我怎敢前进！"大圣笑道："师父，你也忒不通变。常言道：'单丝不线，孤掌难鸣。'那魔三个，小妖千万，教老孙一人，怎生与他赌斗？"长老道："寡不敌众，是你一人也难处。八戒、沙僧他也都有本事，教他们都去，与你协力同心，扫净山路，保我过去罢。"行者沉吟道："师言最当。着沙僧保护你，着八戒跟我去罢。"那呆子慌了道："哥哥没眼色！我又粗夯，无甚本事，走路扛风，跟你何益？"行者道："兄弟，你虽无甚本事，好道也是个人。俗云：'放屁添风。'你也可壮我些胆气。"八戒道："也罢，也罢。你带挈带挈。但只急溜处，莫捉弄我。"长老道："八戒在意，我与沙僧在此。"

【6】那呆子抖擞神威，与行者纵着狂风，驾着云雾，跳上高山，即至洞口。早见那洞口紧闭，四顾无人。行者上前，执铁棒，厉声高叫道："妖怪开门！快出来与老孙打耶！"那洞里小妖报入，老魔心惊胆战道："几年前说猴儿狠，话不虚传果是真！"二老怪在旁问道："哥哥怎么说？"老魔道："那行者早间变小钻风混进来，我等不曾认得。幸三贤弟认得，把他装在瓶里。他弄本事，钻破瓶儿，却又摄去衣服走了。如今在外叫战，我与他打个头仗？"更无一人答应。又问，又无人答，都是那装聋推哑。老魔发怒道："我等在西方大路上，忝着个丑名，今日孙行者这般藐视，若不出去与他见阵，也低了名头。等我舍了这老命去与他战上三合！三合战得过，唐僧还是我们口里食；战不过，那时关了门，

让他过去罢。"遂取披挂结束了，开门前走。

行者与八戒在门旁观看，真是好一个怪物：

铁额铜头戴宝盔，盔缨飘舞甚光辉。

辉辉掣电双睛亮，亮亮铺霞两鬓飞。

勾爪如银尖且利，锯牙似凿密还齐。

身披金甲无丝缝，腰束龙绦有见机。

手执钢刀明晃晃，英雄威武世间稀。

一声吆喝如雷震，问道"敲门者是谁？"

大圣转身道："是你孙爷爷齐天大圣也。"老魔笑道："你是孙行者？大胆泼猴！我不惹你，你却为何在此叫战？"行者道："'有风方起浪，无潮水自平'你不惹我，我好寻你？只因你狐群狗党，结为一伙，算计吃我师父，所以来此施为。"老魔道："你这等雄纠纠的，嚷上我门，莫不是要打么？"行者道："正是。"老魔道："你休猖獗！我若调出妖兵，摆开阵势，摇旗擂鼓，与你交战，显得我是坐家虎，欺负你了。我只与你一个对一个，不许帮丁！"行者闻言，叫："猪八戒走过，看他把老孙怎的！"那呆子真个闪在一边。老魔道："你过来，先与我做个桩儿，让我尽力气着光头砍上三刀，就让你唐僧过去；假若禁不得，快送你唐僧来，与我做一顿下饭！"行者闻言笑道："妖怪，你洞里若有纸笔，取出来，与你定个合同。自今日起，就砍到明年，我也不与你当真！"

【7】那老魔抖擞威风，丁字步站定，双手举刀，望大圣劈顶就砍。这大圣把头往上一迎，只闻扢扠一声响，头皮儿红也不红。那老魔大惊道："这猴子好个硬头儿！"大圣笑道："你不知。"老孙是：

"生就铜头铁脑盖，天地乾坤世上无。

斧砍锤敲不得碎，幼年曾入老君炉。

四斗星官监临造，二十八宿用工夫。

水浸几番不得坏，周围扢搭板筋铺。

唐僧还恐不坚固，预先又上紫金箍。"

老魔道："猴儿不要说嘴！看我这二刀来！决不容你性命！"行者道："不见怎的，左右也只这般砍罢了。"老魔道："猴儿，你不知这刀：

金火炉中造，神功百炼熬。锋刃依三略，刚强按六韬。却
似苍蝇尾，犹如白蟒腰。入山多荡荡，下海浪滔滔。琢磨
无遍数，煎熬几百遭。深山古洞放，上阵有功劳。搀着你
这和尚天灵盖，一削就是两个瓢！"

大圣笑道："这妖精没眼色！把老孙认做个瓢头哩！——也罢，
误砍误让，教你再砍一刀看怎么。"

那老魔举刀又砍，大圣把头迎一迎，乒乒的劈做两半个；大
圣就地打个滚，变做两个身子。那妖一见慌了，手按下钢刀。猪
八戒远远望见，笑道："老魔好砍两刀的！却不是四个人了？"老
魔指定行者道："闻你能使分身法，怎么把这法儿拿出在我面前
使！"大圣道："何为分身法？"老魔道："为甚么先砍你一刀不动，
如今砍你一刀，就是两个人了？"大圣笑道："妖怪，你切莫害怕。砍
上一万刀，还你二万个人！"老魔道："你这猴儿，只会分身，不
会收身。你若有本事收做一个，打我一棍去罢。"大圣道："不许
说谎。你要砍三刀，只砍了我两刀；教我打一棍，若打了棍半，就
不姓孙！"老魔道："正是，正是。"

【8】　好大圣，就把身搂上来，打个滚，依然一个身，掣棒劈头就
打。那老魔举刀架住道："泼猴无礼！甚么样个哭丧棒，敢上门
打人？"大圣喝道："你若问我这条棍，天上地下，都有名声。"老魔
道："怎见名声？"他道：

棒是九转镔铁炼，老君亲手炉中煅。
禹王求得号'神珍'，四海八河为定验。
中间星斗暗铺陈，两头箝裹黄金片。
花纹密布鬼神惊，上造龙纹与凤篆。
名号'灵阳棒'一条，深藏海藏人难见。
成形变化要飞腾，飘飘五色霞光现。
老孙得道取归山，无穷变化多经验。
时间要大瓮来粗，小些微如铁线。
粗如南岳细如针，长短随吾心意变。
轻轻举动彩云生，亮亮飞腾如闪电。
攸攸冷气逼人寒，条条杀雾空中现。
降龙伏虎谨随身，天涯海角都游遍。

曾将此棍闹天宫，威风打散蟠桃宴。

天王赌斗未曾赢，哪吒对敌难交战。

棍打诸神没躲藏，天兵十万都逃窜。

雷霆众将护灵霄，飞身打上通明殿。

掌朝天使尽皆惊，护驾仙卿俱搅乱。

举棒掀翻北斗宫，回首揪开南极院。

金阙天皇见棍凶，特请如来与我见。

兵家胜负自如然，困苦灾危无可辨。

整整挨排五百年，亏了南海菩萨劝。

大唐有个出家僧，对天发下洪誓愿。

枉死城中度鬼魂，灵山会上求经卷。

西方一路有妖魔，行动甚是不方便。

已知铁棒世无双，央我途中为侣伴。

邪魔汤着赴幽冥，肉化红尘骨化面。

处处妖精棒下亡，论万成千无打算。

上方击坏斗牛宫，下方压损森罗殿。

天将曾将九曜追，地府打伤催命判。

半空丢下振山川，胜如太岁新华剑。

全凭此棍保唐僧，天下妖魔都打遍。"

那魔闻言，战兢兢舍着性命，举刀就砍。猴王笑吟吟，使铁棒前迎。他两个先时在洞前撑持，然后跳起去，都在半空里厮杀。这一场好杀：

天河定底神珍棒，棒名如意世间高。夸称手段魔头恼，大捍刀擎法力豪。门外争持还可近，空中赌斗怎相饶！一个随心更面目，一个立地长身腰。杀得满天云气重，遍野雾飘飘。那一个几番立意吃三藏，这一个广施法力保唐朝。都因佛祖传经典，邪正分明恨苦交。

那老魔与大圣斗经二十余合，不分输赢。原来八戒在底下见他两个战到好处，忍不住掣钯架风，跳将起去，望妖魔劈脸就筑。那魔慌了，不知八戒是个呼头性子，冒冒失失的唬人，他只道嘴长耳大，手硬钯凶，败了阵，丢了刀，回头就走。大圣喝道："赶上！赶上！"这呆子仗着威风，举着钉钯，即忙赶下怪去。老魔见他赶的相近，在坡前立定，迎着风头，幌一幌现了原身，张开大口，就要来吞八戒。八戒害怕，急抽身往草里一钻，也管不得荆针棘刺，也顾不得刮破头疼，战兢兢的，在草里听着梆声。随后行者到了，那怪物也张口来吞，却中了他的机关，收了铁棒，迎将上去，被老魔一口吞之。唬得个呆子在草里囊囊咄咄的埋怨道："这个弼马温，不识进退！那怪来吃你，你如何不走，反去迎他！这一口吞在肚中，今日还是个和尚，明日就是个大恭也！"那魔得胜而去。这呆子才钻出草来，溜回旧路。

却说三藏在那山坡下，正与沙僧盼望，只见八戒喘呵呵的跑来。三藏大惊道："八戒，你怎么这等狼狈？悟空如何不见？"呆子哭哭啼啼道："师兄被妖精一口吞下肚去了！"三藏听言，唬倒在地。半晌间跌脚拳胸道："徒弟呀！只说你善会降妖，领我西天见佛，怎知今日死于此怪之手！苦哉，苦哉！我弟子同众的功劳，如今都化做尘土矣！"那师父十分苦痛。你看那呆子，他也不来劝解师父，却叫："沙和尚，你拿将行李来，我两个分了罢！"沙僧道："二哥，分怎的？"八戒道："分开了，各人散火：你往流沙河，还去吃人；我往高老庄，看看我浑家。将白马卖了，与师父买个寿器送终。"长老气哼哼的，闻得此言，叫皇天放声大哭。且不题。

【9】　却说那老魔吞了行者，以为得计，径回本洞。众妖迎问出战之功。老魔道："拿了一个来了。"二魔喜道："拿在何处？"老魔道："被我一口吞在腹中哩。"第三个魔头大惊道："大哥啊，我就不曾吩咐你。孙行者不中吃！"那大圣肚里道："忒中吃！又禁饥，再不得饿哩！"慌得那小妖道："大王，不好了！孙行者在你肚里说话哩！"老魔道："怕他说话！有本事吃了他，没本事摆布他不成？你们快去烧些盐白汤，等我灌下肚去，把他哕出来，慢慢的煎了吃酒。"小妖真个冲了半盆盐汤。老怪一饮而干，注着口，着实一呕，那大圣在肚里生了根，动也不动；却又拦着喉咙，往外呈声，吐得头晕眼花，黄胆都破了，行者越发不动。老魔喘息了，叫声："孙行者，你不出来？"行者道："早哩！正好不出来哩！"老魔道："你怎么不出？"行者道："你这妖精，甚不通变。我自做和尚，十分淡薄：如今秋凉，我还穿个单直裰。这肚里倒暖，又不透风，

等我住过冬才好出来。"

众妖听说，都道："大王，孙行者要在你肚里过冬哩！"老魔道："他要过冬，我就打起禅来，使个搬运法，一冬不吃饭，就饿杀那弼马温！"大圣道："我儿子，你不知事！老孙保唐僧取经，从广里过，带了个折迭锅儿，进来煮杂碎吃。将你这里边的肝、肠、肚、肺、细细儿受用，还彀盘缠到清明哩！"那二魔大惊道："哥啊，这猴子他干得出来！"三魔道："哥啊，吃了杂碎也罢，不知在那里支锅。"行者道："三叉骨上好支锅。"三魔道："不好了！假若支起锅，烧动火烟，到鼻孔里，打嚏喷么？"行者笑道："没事！等老孙把金箍棒往顶门里一搠，搠个窟窿：一则当天窗，二来当烟洞。"

老魔听说，虽说不怕，却也心惊。只得硬着胆叫："兄弟们，莫怕，把我那药酒拿来，等我吃几盅下去，把猴儿药杀了罢！"行者暗笑道："老孙五百年前大闹天宫时，吃老君丹，玉皇酒，王母桃，及凤髓龙肝，——一那样东西我不曾吃过？是甚么药酒，敢来药我？"那小妖真个将药酒筛了两壶，满满斟了一盅，递与老魔。老魔接在手中，大圣在肚里就闻得酒香，道："不要与他吃！"好大圣，把头一扭，变做个喇叭口子，张在他喉咙之下。那怪咽的咽下，被行者咽的接吃了。第二盅咽下，被行者咽的又接吃了。一连咽了七八盅，都是他接吃了。老魔放下盅道："不吃了。这酒常时吃两盅，腹中如火；却才吃了七八盅，脸上红也不红！"原来这大圣吃不多酒，接了他七八盅吃了，在肚里撒起酒风来，不住的支架子，跌四平，踢飞脚；抓住肝花打秋千，竖蜻蜓，翻根斗乱舞。那怪物疼痛难禁，倒在地下。毕竟不知死活如何，且听下回分解。

Chapter 20
The Mind-ape Bores a Hole in the Male and Female Jar;
The Demon King Returns and the Way Is Preserved

【1】   The story tells how the Great Sage Sun went in through the entrance of the cave and looked to either side. This is what he saw:

> *Hills of skeletons,*
> *Forests of bones,*
> *Human heads and hair trampled into felt,*
> *Human skin and flesh rotted into mud,*
> *Sinews twisted round trees,*
> *Dried and shining like silver.*
> *Truly there was a mountain of corpses, a sea of blood,*
> *An unbearable stench of corruption.*
> *The little devils to the east*
> *Sliced the living flesh off human victims;*
> *The evil demons to the west*
> *Boiled and fried fresh human meat.*
> *Apart from the heroic Handsome Monkey King*
> *No common mortal would have dared go in.*

He was soon inside the second gates, and when he looked around here he saw that things were different from outside. Here was purity, quiet elegance, beauty and calm. To left and right were rare and wonderful plants; all around were tall pines and jade-green bamboo. After another two or three miles he reached the third gates, slipped inside for a peep, and saw the three old demons sitting on high. They looked thoroughly evil. The one in the middle

Had teeth like chisels and saws,
A round head and a square face.
His voice roared like thunder;
His eyes flashed like lightning.
Upturned nostrils faced the sky;
Red eyebrows blazed with fire.
Wherever he walked
The animals were terrified;
If he sat down
The demons all trembled.
He was the king among the beasts,
The Blue-haired Lion Monster.

The one sitting on his left was like this:

Phoenix eyes with golden pupils,
Yellow tusks and powerful thighs.
Silver hair sprouting from a long nose,
Making his head look like a tail.
His brow was rounded and wrinkled,
His body massively heavy.
His voice as delicate as a beautiful woman's,
But his face was as fiendish as an ox-headed demon's.
He treasured his tusks and cultivated his person for many
years,
The Ancient Yellow-tusked Elephant.

The one on the right had

Golden wings and a leviathan's head,
Leopard eyes with starry pupils.
He shook the north when he headed south,
Fierce, strong and brave.
When he turned to soaring
Quails laughed but dragons were terrified.
When he beat his phoenix wings the birds all hid their

heads,

    And the beasts all lost their nerve when he spread his talons.

    He could fly thirty thousand miles through the clouds,
    The Mighty Roc.

Beneath these two were ranged a hundred and ten commanders high and low, all in full armour and looking most imposing and murderous. The sight delighted Brother Monkey, who strode inside, quite unafraid, put down his clappers and bell, and called, "Your Majesties." The three old demons chuckled and replied, "So you're back, young Wind-piercer." "Yes," monkey replied. "When you were patrolling what did you find out about where Sun the Novice is?" "Your Majesties," Monkey replied, "I don't dare tell you." "Why not?" the senior demon chief asked. "I was walking along sounding my clappers and ringing my bell following Your Majesties' orders," Monkey said, "when all of a sudden I looked up and saw someone squatting and polishing a pole there. He looked like one of the gods that clear the way. If he'd stood up he'd have been well over a hundred feet tall. He'd scooped up some water in his hand and was polishing his iron bar on the rocky scar. He was saying to himself that his cudgel still hadn't the chance to show its magical powers here and that when he'd shined it up he was coming to attack Your Majesties. That's how I realized he was Sun the Novice and came here to report."

【2】 On hearing this the senior demon chief broke into a sweat all over and shivered so that his teeth chattered as he said, "Brothers, I don't think we should start any trouble with the Tang Priest. His disciple has tremendous magical powers and he's polishing his cudgel to attack us. Whatever are we to do?" "Little ones," he shouted, "call everybody, high and low, who's outside the cave to come inside and shut the gates. Let them pass." "Your Majesty," said one of the subordinate officers who knew what had happened, "the little devils outside should have all scattered." "Why?" the senior demon asked. "They must have heard about his terrible reputation. Shut the gates at once! At once!" The

hosts of demons noisily bolted all the front and back gates firmly.
[3] "Now they've shut the gates they might ask me all sorts of
questions about things in here," Monkey thought with alarm. "If
I don't know the right answers I'll give the game away and they'll
catch me. I'd better give them another scare and get them to open
the gates to let me out." "Your Majesty," he said, stepping
forward, "there were some other wicked things he said." "What
else?" the senior demon chief asked. "He said he was going to
skin Your Senior Majesty," replied Brother Monkey, "slice up
the bones of His Second Majesty, and rip out His Third Majesty's
sinews. If you shut the gates and refuse to go out he can do
transformations. He might turn himself into a fly, get in through
a crack between the gates and catch us all. Then we'll be done
for." "Be very careful, brothers," said the senior demon. "We
haven't had a fly here for years, so any fly that gets in will be Sun
the Novice." "So I'll change into a fly and frighten them into
opening the gates," thought Monkey, smiling to himself. The
splendid Great Sage then slipped aside, reached up to pull a hair
from the back of his head, blew on it with a magic breath, called
"Change!" and turned it into a golden fly that flew straight into
the old demon's face. "Brothers," said the old demon in a panic,
"this is terrible! He's inside!" All the demons great and small
were so alarmed that they rushed forward to swat the fly with
their rakes and brooms.

The Great Sage could not help giggling aloud, which was
just what he should not have done as it revealed his true face. The
third demon chief leapt forward, grabbed him and said,
"Brothers, he almost had us fooled." "Who had who fooled?" the
senior demon asked. "The young devil who reported just now was
no junior Wind-piercer," the third chief replied, "but Sun the
Novice himself. He must have run into a junior Wind-piercer and
somehow or other murdered him and done this transformation to
trick us." "He's rumbled me," thought Monkey with alarm,
rubbing his face. "What do you mean, I'm Sun the Novice?"
Monkey said to the senior demon chief. "I'm a junior Wind-
piercer. His Majesty's mistaken." "Brother," side the senior

demon, "he really is a junior Wind-piercer. He's in the roll-call out front three times a day. I know him. Do you have a pass?" he went on to ask Monkey. "Yes," Monkey replied, pulling his clothes apart to produce it. Seeing that it looked genuine the senior demon said, "Brother, don't mistreat him." "Elder brother," the third demon chief replied, "didn't you see him slip aside just now and giggle? I saw him show his face: it's like a thunder god's. When I grabbed hold of him he turned back into what he looks like now. Little one's," he called, "fetch ropes!" The officers then fetched ropes.

The third demon chief knocked Monkey over and tied his hands and feet together. When his clothes were striped off he was most evidently the Protector of the Horses. Now of the seventy-two transformations that Monkey could perform, when he turned himself into a bird, a beast, a plant, a tree, a vessel or an insect he changed his whole body. When he turned into another person, however, he could only change his head and face but not his body, and indeed he was still covered with brown hair and had red thighs and a tail. "That's Sun the Novice's body," the senior demon chief said when he saw this, "and a junior Wind-piercer's face. It's him! Little ones," he ordered, "bring wine and give His Third Majesty a cup of it to congratulate him. Now that we've captured Sun the Novice the Tang Priest is as good as a meal in our mouths." "We mustn't drink now," said the third demon chief. "Sun the Novice is a slippery customer and is good at escaping by magic. I'm worried he might get away. Tell the juniors to bring the jar out and put him inside. Then we can drink."

"Yes, yes," said the senior demon chief with a smile, who then chose thirty-six little demons to go inside, open the store-rooms, and carry the jar out. Do you know how big the jar was? It was only two feet four inches high. So why were thirty-six people needed to carry it? It was because the jar was a treasure of the two vital forces, male and female, and contained the seven precious things, the eight trigrams and the twenty-four periods of the year that thirty-six carriers were required to match the number of the stars of the Dipper. Before long the precious jar had been carried out, set down outside the third pair of gates, cleaned up and opened. Monkey was untied, stripped bare and sucked inside the jar with a hiss by magical vapour that came out of it. The lid was then put back on and sealed on with a label, after which the demons went off to drink, saying, "Now that he's in our jar that monkey can forget all about his journey west. The only way he'll be able to pay his respects to the Buddha and fetch the scriptures now will be by pushing the wheel of destiny backwards and being reborn." Watch how all the demons great and small go laughing off to celebrate. But of that no more.

【4】 Once inside the jar the Great Sage, who was very cramped, decided to transform himself and squat down in the middle, where he found it very cool. "Those evil spirits don't live up to their reputation," he said to himself, laughing aloud. "Why ever do they tell people that anyone put in this jar will be turned to pus and blood in a few moments. It's so cool that spending seven or eight years here would be no problem."

Alas! The Great Sage did not know about this treasure. Anyone put inside it who said nothing for a year would stay cool for a year; but the moment a voice was heard fires began to burn. Before Monkey had finished speaking the whole jar was full of flame. Luckily he could use the knack of making fire-averting magic with his hands as he sat in the middle of the jar completely unafraid. When he had endured the flames for an hour forty snakes emerged from all around to bite him. Swinging his arms about him Monkey grabbed hold of all of them, twisted with all his strength, and broke them into eighty pieces. A little later three fire dragons appeared to circle above and below Monkey, which was really unbearable. It drove Monkey into a helpless desperation of which he was only too conscious. "The other things were no trouble," he said, "but these three fire dragons are a real problem. If I don't get out soon the fire will attack my heart, and what then? I'll make myself grow," he went on to think, "and push my way out." The splendid Great Sage made a spell with his hands, said the words of a spell and called out,

"Grow!" He made himself over a dozen feet tall, but as he grew the jar grew with him, enclosing him tightly. When he made himself smaller, the jar shrank too. "This is terrible," Brother Monkey thought with alarm, "terrible. It grows when I grow and shrinks when I get smaller. Why? What am I to do?" Before he had finished speaking his ankle began to hurt. Putting his hand down at once to feel it he found that it had been burnt so badly it had gone soft. "I don't know what to do," he said with anxiety. "My ankle's been cooked tender. I'm a cripple now." He could not stop the tears from flowing. Indeed,

> When suffering at the demons' hands he thought of his master;
> In facing deadly peril he worried about the Tang Priest.

"Master," he exclaimed, "since I was converted by the Bodhisattva Guanyin and delivered from my heavenly punishment you and I have toiled over many a mountain. I've beaten and wiped out a lot of monsters, subdued Pig and Friar Sand, and gone through no end of suffering. All this was done in the hope of reaching the west and completing the true achievement together. Never did I expect to meet these vicious demons today. Now I've been stupid enough to get myself killed in here I've left you stuck in the middle of the mountains. What a mess to be in for someone who used to be as famous as I was!" Just when he was feeling thoroughly miserable he suddenly remembered, "Years ago the Bodhisattva gave me three life-saving hairs on the Coiled Snake Mountain. I wonder if I've still got them. I'd better look for them." He felt all over his body and found three very rigid hairs on the back of his head. "All the other hair on my body is soft except for these three that are as hard as spears," he said with delight. "They must be my life-savers." Gritting his teeth against the pain, he pulled the three hairs out, blew on them with magic breath and called, "Change!" One of them turned into a steel drill, one into a strip of bamboo, and one into a silken cord. He made the bamboo strip into a bow to which he fixed the drill.

After a noisy spell of drilling at the bottom of the jar he made a hole through which the light came in. "I'm in luck," he said with glee, "I'm in luck. Now I can get out." No sooner had he transformed himself ready to escape then the jar became cool again. Why was that? It cooled because the hole he had bored in it let the male and female vital forces escape.

[5]　　The splendid Great Sage put his hairs back, made himself small by turning into the tiniest of insects, a very delicate creature as thin as a whisker and as long as an eyebrow hair, and slipped out through the hole. Instead of making his escape Monkey flew straight to the senior demon chief's head and landed on it. The senior demon, who was drinking, slammed his goblet down and asked, "Third brother, has Sun the Novice been liquefied yet?" "Is the time up?" the third demon chief asked. The senior demon told his messengers to carry the jar in. When the thirty-six young devils picked the jar up they found that it was far lighter. "Your Majesty," they reported with alarm, "the jar's lighter." "Nonsense!" the senior demon shouted. "It has the full powers of the male and female vital forces. It couldn't possibly get lighter." One of the junior demons who liked showing off picked the jar up and said, "Look. It is lighter, isn't it?" When the senior demon took the lid off to look in he saw that it was bright inside. "It's empty," he could not help shouting aloud, "it's leaked." And Monkey, sitting on his head, could not help shouting, "Search, my lads! He's escaped." "He's escaped," all the monsters shouted, "he's escaped!" The order was then given to shut the gates.

With that Monkey shook himself, took back the clothes that had been taken off him, turned back into himself and leapt out of the cave. "Behave yourselves, evil spirits," he flung back insultingly. "I've bored through the jar and you can't keep anyone in it any more. You'll have to take it outside and shit in it." Shouting and yelling with glee he went straight back on his cloud to where the Tang Priest was. Here he found the venerable gentleman making symbolic incense with a pinch of earth and praying to the sky. Monkey stopped his cloud to listen to what he was saying. Sanzang had his hands together in front of his chest and was saying to Heaven,

> *"All you immortals up there in the clouds,*
> *The Dings and the Jias and each god and goddess,*
> *Protect my disciple, whose powers are enormous,*
> *And magic is boundless, the good Sun the Novice."*

When the Great Sage heard this he decided to redouble his efforts. Putting his cloud away he went up to Sanzang and called, "Master, I'm back." Sanzang held him as he said, "Wukong, you have been to great trouble. I was very concerned because you had gone so far into these high mountains and not come back for so long a time. How dangerous is the mountain in fact?" "Master," Monkey replied with a smile, "that trip just now depended in the first place on the good destiny of all the living beings in the east, secondly on your boundless achievement and great virtue, and thirdly on your disciple's magical powers." Then he told the whole story of how he had pretended to be a Wind-piercer, been drawn into the jar and escaped. "Now I've seen your face again, Master, it's like having a second life."

Sanzang expressed endless thanks then asked, "Did you not fight the evil spirits this time?" "No, I didn't," replied Brother Monkey. "Then you won't be able to escort me safely across this mountain," Sanzang said, at which Monkey, who hated to admit he was beaten, shouted, "What do you mean, I won't be able to escort you?" "If you and they have not yet had it out and you can only give me evasive answers I will never dare press ahead," the venerable elder replied. "Master," laughed the Great Sage, "you really don't understand. As the saying goes, you can't spin a thread from a single strand of silk, and you can't clap one-handed. There are three demon chiefs and thousands of the little devils. How could I fight them all single-handed?" "If you are that outnumbered you would indeed find it hard by yourself," Sanzang replied. "Pig and Friar Sand also have their talents. I shall tell them to go with you to help you clean up the path across the mountain and escort me over it." "What you say is completely right, Master," replied Monkey with a smile. "Tell Friar Sand to protect you while Pig comes with me." "Brother," said Pig in alarm, "you're a poor judge. I'm rough and I can't do anything much. I'd just get in the way as I walked along. What use would I be to you?" "You may not be up to much, brother," Monkey replied, "but you're someone. As the saying goes, even a fart can swell the wind. You'd make me feel a bit braver." "All right," Pig said, "all right. You can take me with you. But don't play any of your tricks on me when the going gets tough." "Don't forget that Friar Sand and I will be waiting here," said Sanzang.

【6】 The idiot braced himself and set off a gale with Monkey that carried them by cloud up to the top of the mountain where the entrance to the cave was. They saw at once that the gates were shut tight. There was nobody in sight anywhere around. Monkey went forward, his iron cudgel in his hands, to shout at the top of his voice, "Open up, evil monsters! Come out right now and fight Monkey!" When the young devils in the cave went inside to report the senior demon shook with terror as he commented,

> *'I've heard tell for years of that monkey's ferocity;*
> *Now I can vouch for the story's veracity."*

"What do you mean, elder brother?" the second demon chief asked. "When that Sun the Novice first turned himself into a fly to sneak in here none of us realized who he was except our Third Brother, who put him in the jar. He used his skills to drill a hole in the jar, pick up his clothes and get out. Now he's outside challenging us to battle. Who's brave enough to be the first to take him on?" Nobody replied. The senior demon asked again; again there was no response. Everyone was pretending to be deaf and dumb. "We've got ourselves a lousy reputation in the West already," the senior demon chief said in fury. "Now that Sun the Novice has treated us with such contempt today our reputation will stand even lower if we don't fight him. I'm going out there to chance my old life on three rounds with him. If I can hold out for those three rounds the Tang Priest will still be a meal in our mouths. If I can't then shut the gates and let them pass." He then kitted himself out in his armour, had the gates opened and went out. As Monkey and Pig watched from beside the gates they saw that he was a fine monster:

> On iron brow and brazen head a precious helmet
> With tassels dancing brightly in the wind.
> His eyes both flashed as if with lightning,
> And ruddy glowed the hair at his temples.
> Pointed and sharp were his silvery claws,
> And his saw-like teeth were set close and neat.
> His armour was golden, without any seam,
> Bound with a dragon sash that could foresee the future.
> In his hand flashed a cutlass of steel.
> Such martial might is rare in the world.
> With a voice that roared like thunder he asked,
> "Who is that knocking at my gates?"

"Your grandfather, Lord Sun, the Great Sage Equalling Heaven," said Monkey, turning to face the gate. "Are you Sun the Novice?" asked the demon with a laugh. "You've got a cheek, ape. I never gave you any trouble, so why are you here challenging me to battle?" " 'No waves come without a wind; without the tide the waters are still,' " Monkey replied. "Would I have come looking for you if you hadn't given me trouble? The reason why I'm here to fight is because your gang of foxes and dogs is plotting to eat my master." "From the way you're acting so fierce and shouting at our gates you must want a fight," the old demon replied. "Yes," Monkey said. "Stop all that ranting and raving then," said the demon. "It would be most unfair if I brought out my devil soldiers and drew them up in battle order with flags flying and drums beating to fight you as I'm on my own territory. I'll fight you single-handed with no helpers for either side." When Monkey heard this he shouted, "Keep out of the way, Pig, and let's see how he copes with me." The idiot did indeed get out of the way. "Come over here," the senior demon shouted, "and be a chopping block for me. Let me hack you three times as hard as I can with sword on your bare head. After that I'll let your Tang Priest pass. If you can't take it then hand your Tang Priest over at once. He'll be a tasty morsel to help our rice down." "Bring out a brush and some paper if you have them in your cave and I'll give you a bond. You can hack at me from today till next year, but it'll be nothing to me."

[7]   The old demon then summoned up all his might, took up a stance with his feet apart, lifted his sword with both hands and hacked at the top of the Great Sage's head. The Great Sage raised his head, and though there was a mighty crash his scalp did not even go red. "That monkey really does have a hard head," exclaimed the old demon with shock. "You wouldn't know about it," said Monkey with a laugh. "I was

> Born with a skull of bronze and iron,
> Like nobody else's in all the world.
> Hammer and axe will never smash me;
> I went in Lord Lao Zi's furnace when I was a boy.
> The Star Lords of the Four Dippers helped mould me,
> The twenty-eight constellations all used their skill.
> I've often been soaked in water but never come to harm,
> And all over my body the sinews are knotty.
> The Tang Priest, fearing I would not stand firm,
> Placed a golden band around my head."

"Cut out that insolence, ape," the senior demon said, "and take these two blows from my sword. I'm most certainly not going to spare your life." "It's nothing," Monkey replied. "Have another cut like that if you like." "You monkey," the old demon said, "you don't know about this sword,

> Created in furnaces of metal and fire,
> A hundred times tempered by divine craftsmanship.

560

Its sharp blade follows the Three Strategies,
And it is as strong as described in the Six Plans.
The point is as fine as a housefly's tail,
And supple as the body of a white dragon.
When it goes to the mountains dense clouds arise;
If it plunges into the sea the great waves roll.
It has been burnished times beyond number,
Heated and tempered many hundred times over.
Deep in the mountains it is kept in the caves;
Great is the glory it has won when in battle.
If I use it to strike at your monkish pate
I'll cut it into a pair of gourd ladles."

"You're blind, evil spirit," laughed the Great Sage, "if you think my head is just gourd ladles. I'll let you hack at me if you're silly enough to want to. Have another go and see what happens."

The senior demon raised his sword for another hack, which the Great Sage moved his head forward to meet. With a loud bang his head was split into two, whereupon the Great Sage rolled on the ground and gave himself a second body. The sight so alarmed the demon that he lowered his sword. Watching all this from a distance Pig said with a laugh, "Give him a couple more hacks, old devil, then there'll be four of him." Pointing at Brother Monkey the senior demon said, "I'd heard that you can use self-dividing magic. Why are you showing it off to me now?" "What self-dividing magic?" Monkey asked. "Why was it that the first time I hacked you it made no impact, but this time I cut you in two?" the senior demon asked. "Don't worry, evil spirit," said the Great Sage with a smile. "If you cut me ten thousand times there'll be twenty thousand of me." "You ape," the demon said, "you may be able to divide yourself but you can't put yourself together again. If you can, hit me with your cudgel." "Don't talk nonsense," said the Great Sage. "You asked to take three cuts at me but only took two. Now you've invited me to hit you once I'm not Monkey if I hit you one and a half times." "Very well," said the senior demon.

【8】 The splendid Great Sage hugged his two bodies together, rolled, became one body again and struck with his cudgel at the demon's head. The old demon raised his sword to parry the blow. "Damned ape," he said, "you've got a cheek! How dare you come here attacking me with a mourner's staff like that?" "If you ask about this cudgel of mine," shouted the Great Sage, "everybody in heaven and earth has heard of it." "What's it famous for?" the senior demon asked. To this Monkey replied:

> *The cudgel is made of nine-cycled wrought iron*
> *Tempered by Lord Lao Zi himself in his furnace.*
> *King Yu called it a divine treasure when he obtained it*
> *To hold the eight rivers and four oceans in place.*
> *In its middle the constellations are secretly set out,*
> *And each end is banded with yellow gold.*
> *Ghosts and gods are amazed at its intricate decorations,*
> *Dragon patterns and phoenix signs.*
> *Known as the Divine Male Cudgel,*
> *It was inaccessibly deep in the bed of the sea.*
> *Its shape can change and it knows how to fly,*
> *Sending clouds of many colours drifting through the air.*
> *Once it was mine I took it back to my mountain,*
> *Where I discovered how its infinite changes.*
> *When I want size it's as thick as a vat,*
> *Or it can be as thin as an iron wire,*
> *Huge as a mountain or small as a needle,*
> *Adapting its length to the wishes of my heart.*
> *Lightly I lift it and coloured clouds spring up,*
> *Or it flies through the sky and flashes like lightning.*
> *The cold air it gives off chills all who feel it,*
> *And ominous mists appear in the sky.*
> *I have carried it with me to beat dragons and tigers,*
> *Travelling to all of the ends of the earth.*
> *Once with this cudgel I made havoc in heaven,*
> *And used its great might to wreck the peach banquet.*
> *The heavenly kings were unable to beat me,*

And Nezha was hard pressed to match me in combat.
With this cudgel against them the gods had no safe refuge;
A hundred thousand heavenly troops all scattered and fled.
The gods of thunder guarded the Hall of Miraculous Mist
When the cudgel attacked the Palace of Universal
Brightness.
All of the angels at court were flustered
And the Jade Emperor's ministers were thrown into panic.
I raised my cudgel to overturn the Palace of the Dipper,
Then turned back to shake up the South Pole compound.
Seeing my dread cudgel at his golden gates
The Jade Emperor invited the Buddha to see me.
The soldier takes defeat and victory in his stride;
There is nothing to choose between suffering and disaster.
I stuck it out for full five hundred years
Until I was converted by the Bodhisattva Guanyin.
Then a holy monk appeared in Tang
Who swore a mighty oath to heaven,
To save the souls in the City of the Unjustly Slain
And fetch the sutras at an assembly on Vulture Mountain.
On the journey to the west are many evil monsters
Whose actions would be a great obstacle to him.
So, knowing that my cudgel is matchless in the world,
He begged me to be his companion on the journey.
When it struck down evil spirits they were sent to the
Underworld,
Their flesh turned to red dust and their bones all to
powder.
Evil spirits everywhere were killed by the cudgel,
In thousands upon thousands too numerous to count.
Up above it wrecked the Dipper and Bull Palace,
And below it ruined the Senluo Court in Hell.
Of the heavenly generals it routed the Nine Bright Shiners,
And it wounded all of the Underworld's judges.
Dropped from mid-air it shakes mountains and rivers;
It is stronger than the sword of an evil star.

563

With this cudgel alone I protect the Tang Priest
And kill all the evil monsters in the world."

When the monster heard this he trembled, lifted his sword and struck with all his strength. Chuckling, Monkey blocked the blow with his iron cudgel. At first the two of them struggled in front of the cave, but then they both sprang up and fought in mid-air. It was a splendid battle.

The divine rod had once secured the bed of Heaven's River;
The as-you-will cudgel is the finest in the world.
Praise of its powers enraged the demon chief,
Whose mighty cutlass was full of great magic.
When they fought outside the gates they were still open to
reason,
But no mercy was shown in their battle in the sky.
One could change his appearance at will;
The other could make himself grow on the spot.
The fight was so intense that the sky filled with clouds,
And all of the plains were enveloped in mist.
One had often determined to devour the monk Sanzang;
The other used his magic to protect the Tang Priest.
All because the Lord Buddha transmitted the scriptures
Evil and good were opposed in harsh conflict.

The senior demon and the Great Sage fought over twenty rounds without either emerging the victor while Pig admired their magnificent battle from down below until, unable to restrain himself, he grabbed his rake and leapt up into the air, riding on the wind to strike at the evil monster's face. The demon panicked, not realizing that Pig had no staying power, but could only rush recklessly in and give people a fright. All the demon could see was that Pig had a long snout, big ears and a vicious way with his rake, so he abandoned the struggle, threw his sword away, turned and fled. "After him," the Great Sage shouted, "after him!" The idiot raised his rake and went down in

564

all his ferocious might straight after the monster. Seeing how close Pig was to him the old demon stood still in front of the mountainside, faced the wind, shook himself, resumed his real appearance and opened his mouth to devour Pig. This so terrified Pig that he fled as fast as he could into the undergrowth, not caring that brambles and thorns were tearing his head. He sat there trembling and listening out for the sound of the cudgel. When Monkey caught up with him the monster opened his jaws to eat Monkey up too. This was just what Monkey intended. Putting his cudgel away he went straight towards the demon, who swallowed him in a single gulp. This gave idiot such a fright as he was hiding in the undergrowth that he grumbled to himself, "You've got no common sense, Protector of the Horses. Why did you go towards the monster when he wanted to eat you up instead of running away? Now he's swallowed you. Today you're still a monk, but tomorrow you'll be a turd." Only when the monster had departed in triumph did Pig emerge from the undergrowth and slip back by the way he had come.

Sanzang and Friar Sand were still waiting for Pig at the foot of the mountain when they saw him come running breathless towards them. "Pig," said Sanzang with horror, "why are you in this terrible state? Why is Wukong not here?" "My brother was swallowed up by the evil spirit in a single gulp," Pig replied amid sobs, at which Sanzang collapsed in terror. A little later he stamped and beat his chest, saying, "Disciple, I thought you were good at subduing demons and were going to take me to see the Buddha in the Western Heaven. Who would have thought that you would die at this demon's hand today? Alas! Alas! All the efforts of my disciples have now turned to dust." The master was thoroughly miserable.

Just look at the idiot. Instead of coming over to comfort his master he calls, "Friar Sand, fetch the luggage. Let's split it between us." "Why, brother?" Friar Sand asked. "Divide it up," Pig replied, "and all of us can go our separate ways. You can go back to the River of Flowing Sand and carry on eating people. I'll go back to Gao Village and see my wife. We can sell

565

the white horse to buy the master a coffin to be buried in." The master was so upset when he heard this that he wept aloud to Heaven.

[9] We shall leave them and return to the senior demon chief. When he had swallowed Monkey he thought he had won, so he went straight back to his cave, where all the other demons came out to ask him how the fight had gone. "I've got one of them," the senior demon said. "Which one is that?" asked the second demon with delight. "Sun the Novice," the senior demon replied. "Where have you got him?" the second demon chief said. "In my stomach," said the senior demon, "I swallowed him." "Elder brother," said the third demon chief with horror, "I forgot to tell you that Sun the Novice wasn't worth eating." "I'm delicious," said the Great Sage from inside the demon's stomach, "and I'll stop you from ever feeling hungry again." This caused the junior devils such a shock that they reported. "This is terrible, Your Senior Majesty. Sun the Novice is talking inside your stomach." "That doesn't frighten me," said the senior demon. "If I'm clever enough to catch him do you think I'm not clever enough to deal with him? Make me some hot salty water at once. I'll pour it into my stomach, vomit him out, and have him fried at my leisure to eat as a snack with some drinks."

The junior devils soon had ready half a bowl of hot salty water that the old demon drained in one, filling his mouth. He then really did vomit, but the Great Sage, who had taken root in his stomach, did not even move. The monster then pressed his throat and vomited again till his head was spinning, his eyes in a daze and his gall-bladder split, but still Monkey would not be shifted. By now the senior demon was gasping for breath. "Sun the Novice," he called, "won't you come out?" "Not yet," Monkey replied. "I don't want to come out now." "Why not?" the old demon asked. "You really don't understand, evil spirit," said Monkey. "Ever since I've been a monk I've had scant food and clothing. Although it's autumn now and getting cool I'm still only wearing a thin tunic. But it's warm in your stomach and there are no draughts down here. I think I'll spend the winter here before coming out."

When the evil spirits heard this they all said, "Your Majesty, Sun the Novice wants to spend the winter in your stomach." "If he wants to spend the winter there I'll take to meditation and use magic to shift him," the senior demon said. "I won't eat anything all winter. The Protector of the Horses will starve to death." "You just don't understand, my boy," the Great Sage said. "I came via Guangzhou when I started escorting the Tang Priest and I've got a folding cooking pan with me that I brought in here to cook myself a mixed grill. I'll take my time enjoying your liver, bowels, stomach and lungs. They'll be enough to keep me going till spring." "Brother," said the second demon chief with shock, "that ape would eat it too." "Brother," said the third demon, "perhaps he can eat up some bits and pieces, but I don't know where is he going to set up his pan." "The collar bone is an ideal stand," replied Monkey. "This is terrible," said the third demon. "If he sets up his pan and lights a fire won't the smoke get into your nose and make you sneeze?" "That'll be no problem," said Monkey with a laugh. "I'll use my gold-banded cudgel to push a hole through his skull. That'll be a skylight for me and serve as a chimney too."

The old demon heard this and was most alarmed despite saying that he was not afraid. All he could do was to summon up his courage and call, "Don't be scared, brothers. Bring me some of that drugged wine. When I down a few goblets of that the drugs will kill the monkey." At this Monkey smiled to himself and thought, "When I made havoc in Heaven five hundred years ago I drank the Jade Emperor's wine and ate Lord Lao Zi's elixir, the Queen Mother's peaches, the marrow of phoenix bones and dragon livers. I've eaten everything. What kind of drugged wine could do me any harm?" By then the junior devils had strained two jugfuls of drugged wine, a goblet of which they handed to the senior demon chief, who took it in his hands. Monkey, who could smell it from inside the demon's belly, called out, "Don't give it to him!" The splendid Great Sage then tipped his head back and turned it into the bell of a trumpet that he placed wide

567

open below the demon's throat. The demon gulped the wine down noisily and Monkey noisily received it. The demon swallowed the second cupful and Monkey noisily drank that too. This went on till Monkey had drunk all of the seven or eight cupfuls that the demon downed. "That's enough," the demon said, putting the goblet down. "Normally my stomach feels as if it's on fire after a couple of cups of this wine," he said, "but this time my face hasn't even gone red after seven or eight." Now the Great Sage was not a heavy drinker, so after taking these seven or eight cupfuls he started to act drunk in the demon's stomach, propping himself up, falling flat on his face, kicking about him, swinging on the demon's liver, doing headstands and somersaults, and dancing wildly. This caused the monster such unbearable pain that he collapsed. If you don't know whether he lived or died listen to the explanation in the next instalment.

21. 心神居舍魔归性
木母同降怪体真

【1】　话表孙大圣在老魔肚里支吾一会，那魔头倒在尘埃，无声无气，若不言语，想是死了，却又把手放放。魔头回过气来，叫一声："大慈大悲齐天大圣菩萨！"行者听见道："儿子，莫废工夫，省几个字儿，只叫孙外公罢。"那妖魔惜命，真个叫："外公！外公！是我的不是了！一差二误吞了你，你如今却反害我。万望大圣慈悲，可怜蝼蚁贪生之意，饶了我命，愿送你师父过山也。"大圣虽是英雄，甚为唐僧进步。他见妖魔哀告，好奉承的人，也就回了善念，叫道："妖怪，我饶你，你怎么送我师父？"老魔道："我这里也没甚么金银、珠翠、玛瑙、珊瑚、琉璃、琥珀、玳瑁珍奇之宝相送；我兄弟三个，抬一乘香藤轿儿，把你师父送过此山。"行者笑道："既是抬轿相送，强如要宝。你张开口，我出来。"那魔头真个就张开口。那三魔走近前，悄悄的对老魔道："大哥，等他出来时，把口往下一咬，将猴儿嚼碎，咽下却不得磨害你了。"

原来行者在里面听得，便不先出去。却把金箍棒伸出，试他一试。那怪果往下一口，迸喳的一声，把个门牙都迸碎了。行者抽出棒道："好妖怪！我倒问饶你性命出来，你反咬我，要害我命！我不出来，活活的只弄杀你！不出来！不出来！"老魔报怨三魔道："兄弟，你是自家人弄自家人了。且是请他出来的时候，你教我咬他。他倒不曾咬着，却迸得我牙龈疼痛。这是怎么起的！"

三魔见老魔怪他，他又作个激将法，厉声高叫道："孙行者，闻你名如轰雷贯耳，说你在南天门外施威，灵霄殿下逞势；如今在西天路上降妖缚怪，原来是个小辈的猴头！"行者道："我何为小辈？"三怪道："'好汉千里客，万里去传名。'你出来，我与你赌斗，才是好汉；怎么在人肚里做勾当！非小辈而何？"行者闻言，心中暗想道："是，是，是！我若如今扯断他肠，搠破他肝，弄杀这怪，有何难哉？但真是坏了我的名头。……也罢！也罢！——你张口，我出来与你比并。但只是你这洞口窄逼，不好使火，须往宽处去。"三魔闻说，即点大小怪，前前后后，有三万多精，都执着精锐器械，出洞摆开一个三才阵势，专等行者出口，一齐上阵。那二怪搀着老魔，径至门外，叫道："孙行者！好汉出来！此间有战场，好斗？"

【2】 大圣在他肚里，闻得外面鸦鸣鹊噪，鹤唳风声，知道是宽阔之处。想着："我不出去，是失信与他；若出去，这妖精人面兽心：先时说送我师父，哄我出来咬我，今又调兵在此。——也罢！也罢！与他个两全其美：出去便出去，还与他肚里生下一个根儿。"即转手，将尾上毫毛拔下一根，吹口仙气，叫"变！"即变一条绳儿，只有头发粗细，倒有四十丈长短。那绳儿理出去，见风就长粗了。把一头拴着妖怪的心肝系上，打做个活扣儿。那扣儿不扯不紧，扯紧就痛。却拿着一头，笑道："这一出去，他送我师父便罢；如若不送，乱动刀兵，我也没工夫与他打，只消扯此绳儿，就如我在肚里一般！"又将身子变得小小的，往外爬；爬到咽喉之下，见妖精大张着方口，上下钢牙，排如利刃，忽思量道："不好！不好！若从口里出去扯这绳儿，他怕疼，往下一嚼，却不咬断了？我打他没牙齿的所在出去。"好大圣，理着绳儿，从他那上腭子往前爬，爬到他鼻孔里。那老魔鼻子作痒，"阿嚏"的一声，打了个喷嚏，却迸出行者。

【3】 行者见了风，把腰躬一躬，就长了有三丈长短，一只手扯着绳儿，一只手拿着铁棒。那妖头不知好歹，见他出来了，就举钢刀，劈脸来砍。这大圣一只手使铁棒相迎。又见那二怪使枪，三怪使戟，没头没脸的乱上。大圣放松了绳，收了铁棒，急纵身驾云走了。原来怕那伙小妖围绕，不好干事。他却跳出营外，去那空阔山头上，落下云，双手把绳尽力一扯，老魔心里才疼。他害疼，往上一挣，大圣复往下一扯。众小妖远远看见，齐声高叫道："大王，莫惹他！让他去罢！这猴儿不按时景：清明还未到，他却那里放风筝也！"大圣闻言，着力气蹬了一蹬，那老魔从空中，忽剌剌，似纺车儿一般，跌落尘埃。就把那山坡下死硬的黄土跌做个二尺浅深之坑。

慌得那二怪、三怪，一齐按下绳儿，上前拿住绳儿，跪在坡下，哀告道："大圣啊，只说你是个宽洪海量之仙，谁知是个鼠腹蜗肠之辈。实实的哄你出来，与你见阵，不期在我家兄心上拴了一根绳子！"行者笑道："你这伙泼魔，十分无礼！前番哄我出去便就咬我，这番哄我出来，却又摆阵敌我。似你这几万妖兵，战我一个，理上也不通。扯了去！扯了去！扯了去见你师父！"那怪一齐叩头道："大圣慈悲，饶我性命，愿送老师父过山！"行者笑道："你要性命，只消拿刀把绳子割断罢了。"老魔道："爷爷呀，割断外边的，这里边的拴在心上，喉咙里又梆梆的恶心，怎生是好？"行者道："既如此，张开口，等我再进去解出绳来。"老魔慌了道："这一进去，又不肯出来，却难也！却难也！"行者道："我有本事外边就可以解得里面绳头也。解了可实实的送我师父么？"老魔道："但解就送，并不敢打诳语。"大圣审得是实，即便将身一抖，收了毫毛，那怪的心就不疼了。这是孙大圣掩样的法儿，使毫毛拴着他的心；收了毫毛，所以就不害疼。三个妖仙身而起，谢道："大圣清回，上复唐僧，收拾下行李，我们就抬轿来送。"众怪偃干戈，尽皆归洞。

【4】　大圣收绳子，径转山东，远远的看见唐僧睡在地下打滚痛哭；猪八戒与沙僧解了包袱，将行李搭分儿，在那里分哩。行者暗暗嗟叹道："不消讲了。这定是八戒对师父说我被妖精吃了，师父today痛哭，那呆子悬分东西散火哩。——咦！不知可是此意，且等我叫他一声看。"落下云头，叫声："师父！"沙僧听见，报怨八戒道："你是个'棺材座子，专一害人'！师父不曾死，你却说他死了，在这里干这个勾当！那里不叫将来了？"八戒道："我分明看见他被妖精一口吞了。想是日辰不好，那猴子来显魂哩。"行者到跟前，一把揪住八戒脸，一个巴掌打了个跟跄，道："夯货！我显甚么魂？"呆子侮着脸道："哥哥，你实是那怪吃了，你——你怎么又活了？"行者道："像你这个不济事的脓包！他吃了我，我就抓他肠，捏他顺，又把这条绳儿穿住他的心，扯他疼痛难禁，一个个叫头哀告，我才饶了他性命。如今抬轿来送我师父过山也。"那三藏闻言，一骨鲁爬起来，对行者躬身道："徒弟啊，累杀你了！若信悟能之言，我已绝矣！"行者轮拳打着八戒骂道：

"这个馕糠的呆子,十分懈怠,甚不成人!师父,你切莫恼。那怪就来送你也。"沙僧也甚生惭愧。连忙遮掩,收拾行李,扣背马匹,都在途中等候不题。

【5】 却说三个魔头,帅群精入洞来。二怪道:"哥哥,我只道是个九头八尾的孙行者,原来是恁的个小小猴儿!你不该吞他:只与他斗时,他那里斗得过你哩!洞里这几万妖精,吐唾沫也可淬杀他。你却将他吞在肚里,他便弄起法来,教你受苦,怎么敢与他比较!才自说送唐僧,都是假意,实为兄长性命要紧,所以哄他出来。决不送他!"老魔道:"贤弟不送之故,何也?"二怪道:"你与我三千小妖,摆开阵势,我有本事拿住这个猴头!"老魔道:"莫说三千,凭你起老营去;只是拿住他,便大家有功!"

那二魔即点三千小妖,径到大路旁闪开,着一个蓝旗手往来传报,教:"孙行者!赶早出来,与我二大王爷爷交战!"八戒听见,笑道:"哥啊,常言道:'说谎不瞒当乡人。'就来弄虚头,捣鬼!怎么说降了妖精,就抬轿来送师父,却又来叫战,何也?"行者道:"老怪已被我降了,不敢出头,闻着个'孙'字儿,也害头疼。这定是二妖魔不伏气送我们,故此叫战。我道兄弟,这妖精有弟兄三个,这般义气;我弟兄也是三个,就没些义气。我已降了大魔,二魔出来,你就与他战战,未为不可。"八戒道:"怕他怎的!等我去与他打他一仗来!"行者道:"要去便去罢。"八戒笑道:"哥啊,去便去,你把那金箍儿借与我使使。"行者道:"你要怎的?你又没本事钻在肚里,你又没本事拴在他心上,要他何用?"八戒道:"我要扣在这腰里,做个救命索。你与沙僧扯住后手,放我出去,与他交战。估着赢了他,你便放松,我把他拿住;若是输与他,你把我扯回来,莫教他拉了去。"真个行者暗笑道:"也是捉弄呆子一番!"就把绳儿扣在他腰里,撺将他出战。

【6】 那呆子举钉钯跑上山崖,叫道:"妖精!出来!与你猪祖宗打来!"那蓝旗手急报道:"大王,有一个长嘴大耳朵的和尚来了。"二怪即出营,见了八戒,更不打话,挺枪劈面刺来。这呆子举钯上前迎住。他两个在山坡前搭上手,斗不上七八回合,呆子手软,架不得妖魔,急回头叫:"师兄,不好了!扯救命索,扯救命索!"这壁厢大圣闻言,转把绳子放松了,抛将去。那呆子败

了阵往后就跑。原来那绳子拖着走，还不觉；转回来，因松了倒有些绊脚，自家绊倒了一跌，爬起来又一跌。始初还跌个踉踪，后面就跌了个嘴抢地。被妖精赶上，捽开鼻子，就如蛟龙一般，把八戒一鼻子卷住，得胜回洞。众怪凯歌齐唱，一拥而出。

这坡下三藏看见，又恼行者道："悟空，怪不得悟能咒你死哩！原来你弟弟全无相亲相爱之意，专怀相嫉相妒之心！他那般说，教你扯扯救命索，你怎么不扯，还将索子丢去？如今教他被害，却如之何？"行者笑道："师父也忒护短，忒偏心！罢了，像老孙拿去时，你略不挂念，左右是舍命之材；这呆子才遭擒，你就怪我。也教他受些苦恼，方见取经之难。"三藏道："徒弟啊，你去，我岂不挂念？想着你会变化，断然不至伤身。那呆子生得狼犺，又不会腾那，这一去，少吉多凶。你还去救他一救，他一不会腾那。"行者道："师父不得报怨，等我去救他一救。"

【7】　急纵身，赶上山，暗中恨道："这呆子咒我死，且莫与他个快活！且跟去看那妖精怎么摆布他，等他受些罪，再去救他。"即捻诀念起真言，摇身一变，即变做个蟭蟟虫，飞将去，钉在八戒耳朵根上，同那妖精到了洞里。二魔帅三千小怪，大吹大打的，至洞口屯下。自将八戒拿入里边道："哥哥，我拿了一个来了。"老怪道："拿来我看。"他把鼻子放松，捽下八戒道："这不是？"老怪道："这厮没用！"八戒闻言道："大王，没用的放出去，寻那有用的捆将来罢！"三怪道："虽是没用，也是唐僧的徒弟猪八戒。且捆了，送在后边池塘里浸着。待浸退了毛，破开肚子，使盐腌了晒干，等天阴下酒。"八戒大惊道："罢了！罢了！撞见那腌腌的妖怪也！"众怪一齐下手，把呆子四马攒蹄捆住，扛扛抬抬，送至池塘边，往中间一推，尽皆退去了。

大圣却飞起来寻着处，那呆子四肢朝上，揭着嘴，半浮半沉，嘴里哼哼的，着处皮笑，倒像八九月经霜落了子儿的一个大黑莲蓬。大圣见他那嘴脸，又恨他，又怜他，说道："怎的好么？他也是龙华会上的一个人。但只恨他动不动分行李散火，又要揭拨师父念《紧箍咒》咒我。我前日曾闻得沙僧说，他攒了些私房，不知可有否。等我且吓他一吓看。"

【8】　好大圣，飞近他耳边，假捏声音，叫声："猪悟能！猪悟能！"

八戒慌了道："晦气呀！我悟能是观世音菩萨起的，自跟了唐僧，又呼做八戒，此间怎么有人知道我叫做悟能？"呆子忍不住问道："是那个叫我的法名？"行者道："是我。"呆子道："你是那个？"行者道："我是勾司人。"那呆子慌了道："长官，你是那里来的？"行者道："我是五阎王差来勾你的。"呆子道："长官，你且回去，上复五阎王，他与我师兄孙悟空交得甚好，教他让我一日儿，明日来勾罢。"行者道："胡说！'阎王注定三更死，谁敢留人到四更'！趁早跟我去，免得套上绳子扯拉。"呆子道："长官，那里不是方便，看我这般嘴脸，还想活哩。死是一定死，只等一日，这妖精连我师父们都拿来，会一会，就都了帐也。"行者暗道："也罢，我这批上有三十个人，都在这前后，等我拘将来就你，便有一日耽阁。你可有盘缠，把些儿我去？"八戒道："可怜啊！出家人那里有甚么盘缠？"行者道："若无盘缠，索了去！跟着我走！"呆子慌了道："长官不要索。我晓得你这绳儿叫做'追命绳'，索上就要断气。有！有！有！——有便有些儿，只是不多。"行者道："在那里？快拿出来！"八戒道："可怜，可怜！我自做了和尚，如今，有些善信的人家斋僧，见我食肠大，衬钱比他们略多些儿，我拿了攒在这里，零零碎碎有五钱银子；因不好收拾，前者到城中，央了个银匠煎在一处，他又没天理，偷了我几分，只得四钱六分一块儿。你拿了去罢。"行者暗笑道："这呆子裤子也没得穿，却藏在何处？……咄！你银子在那里？"八戒道："在我左耳朵里揣着哩。我捆了拿不得，你自家拿了去罢。"

行者闻言，即伸手往耳窍中摸出，真个是块马鞍儿银子，足有四钱五六分重；拿在手里，忍不住哈哈的一声大笑。那呆子认是行者声音，在水里乱骂道："天杀的弼马温！到这们苦处，还来打诈财物哩！"行者又笑道："我把你这馕糟的！老孙保师父，不知受了多少艰难，你倒攒下私房！"八戒道："嘴脸！这是甚么私房！都是牙齿上刮下来的，我不舍得买了嘴吃，留了买匹布与做件衣服，你却吓了我的。还分些儿与我。"行者道："半分也没得与你！"八戒道："买命钱让与你罢，好道也救我出去是了。"行者道："莫发急，等我救你。"将银子藏了，即现原身，掣铁棒，把呆子划拢，用手提着脚，扯上来，解了绳。八戒跳起来，脱下衣裳，整干了水,抖一抖,潮漉漉的披在身上,道:"哥哥,开后门走了罢。"行者道:"后门里走,可是个长进的?还打前门上去。"八戒道:"我的脚捆麻了,跑不动。"行者道:"快跟我来。"

【9】 好大圣,把铁棒一路丢开解数,打将出去。那呆子忍着麻,只得跟定他。只见二门下靠着的是他的钉钯,走上前,推开小妖,捞过来往前乱筑;与行者打出三四层门,不知打杀了多少小妖。那老魔听见,对二魔道:"拿好人!拿得好人!你看孙行者劫了猪八戒,门上打伤小妖也!"那二魔急纵身,绰枪在手,赶出门来,应声骂道:"泼猢狲!这般无礼!怎敢渺视我等!"大圣听得,即应声站下。那怪物不容讲,使枪便刺。行者正是会家不忙,掣铁棒,劈面相迎。他两个在洞门外,这一场好杀:

> 黄牙老獠变人形,义结狮王为弟兄。因为大魔来说合,同心计较吃唐僧。妖魔无能遭毒手,悟空拯救出门行。妖王赶上施英猛,枪棒交加各显能。这一个枪来好似穿林蟒,这一个棒起犹如出海龙。龙出海门云霭霭,蟒穿林树雾腾腾。算来都为唐和尚,恨苦相持太没情。

那八戒见大圣与妖精交战,他在山嘴上竖着钉钯,不来帮打,只管呆呆的看着。那妖精见行者棒重,满身解数,全无破绽,就把枪架住。捽开鼻子,要来卷他。行者知道他的勾当,双手把金箍棒横起来,往上一举,被妖精一鼻子卷住腰胯,不曾卷手。你看他两只手在妖精身头上丢花棒儿耍子。

【10】 八戒见了,捶胸道:"咦!那妖怪晦气呀!卷我这夯的,连手都卷住了,不能得动;卷那厮滑的,倒不卷手。他那两只手拿着棒,只消往鼻里一捣,那孔子里害疼流涕,怎能卷得他住?"行者原无此意,倒是八戒教了他。他就把棒幌一幌,小如鸡子,长有丈余,真个往他鼻孔里一捣。那妖精害怕,沙的一声,把鼻子捽回,一把挝住,用力力往前一拉。那妖精却疼,随着手,举步跟来。八戒方才敢近,拿钉钯望妖精颈子上乱筑。行者道:"不好!不好!那钯齿儿尖,恐筑破皮,淌出血来,师父看见,又说我们伤生,只调柄子来打罢。"

真个呆子举钯柄,走一步,打一下,行者牵着鼻子,就似两个象奴,牵至坡下。只见三藏凝睛盼望,见他两个嚷嚷闹闹而来,即唤:“悟净,你看悟空牵的是甚么?”沙僧见了,笑道:“师父,大师兄把妖精揪着鼻子拉来,真爱杀人也!”三藏道:“善哉!善哉!那般大个妖精!那般长个鼻子!你且问他:他若喜喜欢欢送我等过山呵,饶了他,莫伤他性命。”沙僧急纵前迎着,高声叫道:“师父说:那怪果送师父过山,教不要伤他命哩。”那怪闻说,连忙跪下,口里呜呜的答应。原来被行者揪着鼻子,捏齈了,就如重伤风一般。叫道:“唐老爷,若肯饶命,即便抬轿相送。”行者道:“我师徒俱是善胜之人,依你言,且饶你命。快抬轿来。如再变卦,拿住决不再饶!”那怪得脱手,磕头而去。行者同八戒见唐僧,备言前事。八戒惭愧不胜,在坡前晾晒衣服,等候不题。

【11】 那二魔战战兢兢回洞,未到时,已有小妖报知老魔、三魔,说二魔被行者揪着鼻子拉去。老魔悚惧,与三魔帅众方出,见二魔独回,又皆接入,问及放回之故。二魔把三藏慈悯善胜之言,对众说了一遍。一个个面面相觑,更不敢言。二魔道:“哥哥可送唐僧么?”老魔道:“兄弟,你说那里话!孙行者是个广施仁义的猴头,他先在我肚里,若肯害我性命,一千个也被他弄杀了。却才揪住你鼻子,若是扯了去不放回,只捏破你的鼻子头儿,却也惶恐。快早安排送他去罢。”三魔笑道:“送!送!送!”老魔道:“贤弟这话,却又像尚气的了。你不送,我两个送去罢。”

三魔又笑道:“二位兄长在上:那和尚倘不要我们送,只这等瞒过去,还是他的造化;若要送,不知正中了我的‘调虎离山’之计哩。”老怪道:“何为‘调虎离山’?”三怪道:“如今把满洞群妖,点将起来,万中选千,千中选百,百中选十六个,又选三十个。”老怪道:“怎么既要十六,又要三十?”三怪道:“要三十个会烹煮的,与他些精米、细面、竹笋、茶芽、香蕈、蘑菇、豆腐、面筋,着他二十里,或三十里,搭下窝铺安排茶饭,管待唐僧。”老怪道:“又要十六个何用?”三怪道:“着八个抬,八个喝路。我弟兄相随左右,送他一程。此去向西四百余里,就是我的城池。我那里自有接应的人马。若至城边,……如此如此,着他师徒首尾不能相顾。要捉唐僧,全在此十六个鬼成功。”老怪闻言,欢欣不已。真是如醉方醒,似梦方觉。道:“好!好!好!”即点众妖,先选三十,与他物件；又选十六，抬一顶香藤轿子。同出门来，又吩咐众妖："俱不许上山闲走：孙行者是个多心的猴子，若见汝等往来，他必生疑，识破此计。"

老怪遂帅众至大路旁高叫道："唐老爷，今日不犯红沙，请老爷早早过山。"三藏闻言道："悟空，是甚人叫我？"行者指定道："那厢是老孙降伏的妖精抬轿来送你哩。"三藏合掌朝天道："善哉！善哉！若不是贤徒如此之能，我怎生得去！"径直向前，对众妖作礼道："多承列位之爱，我弟子取经东回，向长安当传扬善果也。"众妖叩首道："请老爷上轿。"那三藏肉眼凡胎，不知是计；孙大圣又是太乙金仙，忠正之性，只以为擒纵之功，降了妖怪，亦岂期他都有异谋，却也不曾详察，尽着师父之意。即命八戒将行囊捎在马上，与沙僧紧随。他使铁棒向前开路，顾盼吉凶。八个抬起轿子，八个一递一声喝道。三个妖扶着轿扛。师父喜喜欢欢的端坐轿上。上了高山，依大路而行。

【12】 此一去，岂知欢喜之间愁又至。经云："泰极否还生。"时运相逢真太岁，又值丧门吊客星。那伙妖魔，同心合意的，侍卫左右，早晚殷勤。行经三十里献斋，五十里又斋，未晚请歇，沿路齐齐整整。一日三餐，遂心满意；良宵一宿，好处安身。

西进有四百里余程，忽见城池相近。大圣举铁棒，离轿仅有一里之遥，见城池，把他吓了一跌，挣挫不起。你道他只这般大胆，如何见此着唬？原来望见那城中有许多恶气。乃是：

攒攒簇簇妖魔怪，四门都是狼精灵。
斑斓老虎为都管，白面雄彪做总兵。
丫叉角鹿传文引，伶俐狐狸当道行。
千尺大蟒围城走，万丈长蛇占路程。
楼下苍狼呼令使，台前花豹作人声。
摇旗擂鼓皆妖怪，巡更坐铺尽山精。
狡兔开门弄买卖，野猪挑担干营生。
先年原是天朝国，如今翻作虎狼城。

那大圣正当悚惧，只听得耳后风响，急回头观看，原来是三魔双手举一柄画杆方天戟，往大圣头上打来。大圣急翻身爬起，使金箍棒劈面相迎。他两个各怀恼怒，气呼呼，更不打话；咬着牙，各要相争。又见那老魔头，传声号令，举钢刀便砍八戒。八戒慌得丢了马，抢着钯，向前乱筑。那二魔缠长枪，望沙僧刺来。沙僧使降妖杖支开架子敌住。三个魔头与三个和尚，一个敌一个，在那山头舍死忘生苦战。那十六个小妖却遵号令，各各效能：抢了白马、行囊，把三藏一拥，抬着轿子，径至城边，高叫道："大王爷爷定计，已拿得唐僧来了！"那城上大小妖精，一个个跑下，将城门大开，吩咐各营卷旗息鼓，不许呐喊筛锣，说："大王原有令在前，不许吓了唐僧；唐僧禁不得恐吓，一吓就肉酸不中吃了。"众精都欢天喜地邀三藏，控背躬身接主僧。把唐僧一轿子抬上金銮殿，请他坐在当中，一壁厢献茶，献饭，左右旋绕。那长老昏昏沉沉，举眼无亲。毕竟不知性命何如，且听下回分解。

Chapter 21
When the Heart Spirit Stays in the Home
the Demons Submit;
The Mother of Wood Helps Bring
Monsters to the Truth

[1]   The story tells how after the Great Sage had struggled in his stomach for a while the senior demon collapsed in the dust. He made no sound and was not breathing either. As he said nothing Monkey thought the demon was dead, so he stopped hitting him. When the demon chief recovered his breath he called out, "Most merciful and most compassionate Bodhisattva, Great Sage Equalling Heaven." "My boy," said Monkey when he heard this, "don't waste your effort. You could save yourself a few words by simply calling me Grandpa Sun." Desperate to save his skin, the evil monster really did call out, "Grandpa! Grandpa! I was wrong. I shouldn't have eaten you, and now you're destroying me. I beg you, Great Sage, in your mercy and compassion to take pity on my antlike greed for life and spare me. If you do I'll escort your master across the mountain."

Although the Great Sage was a tough hero he was most eager to help the Tang Priest in his journey, so on hearing the evil monster's pathetic pleas and flattery he decided once more to be kind. "Evil monster," he shouted, "I'll spare your life. How are you going to escort my master?" "We don't have any gold, silver, pearls, jade, agate, coral, crystal, amber, tortoise-shell or other such treasures here to give him, but my two brothers and I will carry him in a rattan chair across the mountain." "If you could carry him in a chair that would be better than treasure," said Monkey with a smile. "Open you mouth: I'm coming out." The demon then opened his mouth, whereupon the third chief went over to him and whispered in his ear, "Bite him as he comes out, brother. Chew the monkey to bits and swallow him. Then he

579

won't be able to hurt you. "

Now Monkey could hear all this from inside, so instead of coming straight out he thrust his gold-banded cudgel out first as a test. The demon did indeed take a bite at it, noisily smashing one of his front teeth in the process. "You're a nice monster, aren't you!" exclaimed Monkey, pulling his cudgel back. "I spare your life and agree to come out, but you try to murder me by biting me. I'm not coming out now. I'm going to kill you. I won't come out!" "Brother," the senior demon chief complained to the third one, "what you've done is destroy one of your own kind. I'd persuaded him to come out but you would have to tell me to bite him. Now I'm in agony from my broken tooth. What are we to do?"

In the face of the senior demon chief's complaints the third demon chief tried the method of making the enemy lose his temper. "Sun the Novice," he yelled at the top of his voice, "you have a thundering reputation. They tell of how mighty you were outside the Southern Gate of Heaven and at the Hall of Miraculous Mist. I'd heard that you've been capturing demons along your way to the Western Heaven. But now I see that you're only a very small-time ape. " "What makes me small-time?" Monkey asked. " 'A hero who only roams three hundred miles around will go three thousand miles to make his fame resound, " the third chief replied. "Come out and fight me if you're a real tough guy. What do you mean by messing about in someone else's stomach? If you're not small-time what are you?" "Yes, yes, yes," thought Monkey when he heard this. "It wouldn't be at all difficult for me to tear this demon's bowels to bits, rip up his liver, and kill him. But I'd destroy my own reputation in the process. I'll have to forget about it. Open your mouth and I'll come out and fight you. The only problem is that this cave of yours is much too cramped for me to use my weapons. We'll have to go somewhere where there's more room." On hearing this the third demon chief mustered all the demons young and old from all around. There were over thirty thousand of them armed with the finest and sharpest weapons who came out of the cave to form a line of battle symbolizing heaven, earth and mankind. They were all waiting for Monkey to come out of the senior demon's mouth before rushing him. The second demon chief then helped the senior demon out through the entrance of the cave, where he shouted, "Sun the Novice! If you're a tough guy come out. There's a good battlefield here for us to fight on."

[2] The Great Sage could tell that this was an open area from the calls of crows, magpies and cranes that he could hear in the monster's belly. "If I don't come out I'll be breaking faith with them," he thought. "But if I do these demons are beasts at heart behind their human faces. They tried to lure me out and bite me when they promised to carry the master across the ridge. Now they've got their army here. Oh well! I'll let them have it both ways. I'll go out but I'll leave a root in his stomach too." With that he put his hand behind him to pluck a tiny hair from his tail, blew on it with magic breath, called "Change!" and made it into a string as fine as a hair but some four hundred feet long. As the string came outside it grew thicker in the wind. One end Monkey fastened round the evil monster's heart in a slip-knot that he did not tighten—if he had it would have caused great pain. The other end he held in his hand as he said to himself, "If they agree to escort my master across the ridge when I come out this time I'll leave it at that. But if they refuse and go for me with their weapons so hard that I can't cope with them I'll just need to pull this rope. I'll get the same results as if I were still inside." He then made himself tiny and crawled up as far as the throat, from where he could see that the evil spirit had opened his mouth wide. Rows of steel teeth were set above and below like sharp knives. "This is no good," he thought at once, "no good at all. If I take this rope out through his mouth and he can't stand the pain he'll be able to cut through it with a single bite. I'll have to go out where there aren't any teeth." The splendid Great Sage paid out the string as he crawled up the demon's upper palate and into his nostril, which made his nose itch. The demon sneezed with a loud "atishoo," blowing Monkey out.

[3] As he felt the wind blowing him Monkey bowed and grew

over thirty feet long, keeping the string in one hand and holding the iron cudgel in the other. The wicked monster raised his steel sword as soon as he saw Monkey appear and hacked at his face. The Great Sage met the blow one-handed with his cudgel. Then the second demon chief with his spear and the third chief with his halberd went for him furiously. The Great Sage relaxed his pull on the rope, put his iron cudgel away and made off at speed by cloud, afraid that he would be unable to fight properly when surrounded by so many young devils. Once he had leapt out of the demons' camp he brought his cloud down on a spacious and empty mountain top and pulled with both hands on the rope as hard as he could. This gave the senior demon a pain in the heart. The demon struggled upwards in agony, whereupon the Great Sage pulled him down again. As they all watched from afar the junior demons all shouted, "Don't provoke him, Your Majesty! Let him go. That ape has no sense of when things ought to be done. He's flying a kite before the beginning of April." When the Great Sage heard this he gave a mighty stamp, at which the senior demon came whistling down out of the sky like a spinning-wheel to crash into the dust, making a crater some two feet deep in the hard earth at the foot of the mountain.

[4] This gave the second and third demon chiefs such a fright that they landed their clouds together and rushed forward to grab hold of the rope and kneel at the foot of the mountain. "Great Sage," they pleaded, "we thought you were an immortal of vast and boundless generosity. We'd never dreamed that you would be as small-minded as a rat or a snail. It's true that we lured you out to give battle, but we never expected that you would tie a rope round our eldest brother's heart." "You're a thorough disgrace, you damned gang of demons," said Monkey with a laugh. "Last time you tried to trick me into coming out so you could bite me and this time you've lured me out to face an army ready for battle. It's obvious that you've got tens of thousands of soldiers here to tackle me when I'm alone. Most unreasonable. I'll pull him away. I'm going to drag him off to see my master." "If in your mercy and compassion you spare our lives, Great Sage," the

demons said, all kowtowing together, "we vow to escort your master across this mountain."

"If you want to live all you have to do is cut the rope with your sword," said Monkey with a laugh. "My lord," the senior monster said, "I can cut the rope outside, but it's no good having the length inside that's tied round my heart. It sticks in my throat so uncomfortably that it makes me feel sick." "In that case," said Monkey, "open your mouth and I'll go back inside to undo the rope." This alarmed the senior demon, who said, "If you don't come out when you go in this time I'll be in a mess, a real mess." "I know how to undo the end of the rope that's in you from the outside," Monkey replied. "But when I've undone it will you really escort my master across?" "We will as soon as you've undone it," the senior demon chief replied. "I wouldn't dare lie about this." Now that he had satisfied himself the demon was telling the truth Monkey shook himself and put the hair back on his body, where upon the monster's heart pains stopped. It was the Great Sage Sun's transforming magic that had tied the hair round his heart in the first place, which was why the pain ended as soon as the hair was put back on Monkey. The three demon chiefs then rose up into the air to thank him with the words, "Please go back now, Great Sage, and pack your luggage. We will carry a chair down to fetch him." The demon horde then all put their weapons down and went back into the cave.

Having put his rope away the Great Sage went straight back to the eastern side of the ridge, and when he was still a long way away he saw the Tang Priest lying on the ground, rolling around and howling. Pig and Friar Sand had opened the bundles of luggage and were dividing it up. "Don't tell me," thought Monkey with a quiet sigh. "No doubt Pig has told the master that I've been eaten up by evil spirits. The master's sobbing his heart out because he can't bear to be without me and the idiot's dividing the things ready for us all to split up. Oh dear! I can't be sure, so I'd better go down and give the master a shout." Bringing his cloud down, Monkey shouted, "Master!" As soon as Friar Sand heard this he started complaining to Pig. "All you want is to see people dead, just like a coffin stand," he said. "Our elder brother wasn't killed but you said he was and started this business here. Of course he's bound to kick up a row." "But I saw him with my own eyes being eaten up by the evil spirit in one mouthful," Pig replied. "I'm sure we're just seeing that ape's spirit because it's an unlucky day." Monkey then went up to Pig and hit him in the face with a slap that sent him staggering. "Cretin!" he said. "Is this my spirit you can see?" Rubbing his face, the idiot replied, "But the monster really did eat you up, brother. How can you, how can you have come back to life?" "Useless gumboil!" said Monkey. "After he ate me I grabbed his bowels, twisted his lungs, tied a rope round his heart and tore at him till he was in horrible agony. Then they all kowtowed and pleaded with me, so I spared his life. Now they're bringing a carrying-chair here to take the master over the mountain." As soon as Sanzang heard this he scrambled to his feet, bowed to Monkey and said, "Disciple, I've put you to enormous trouble. If I had believed what Wuneng said we would have been finished." "Chaff-guzzling idiot," Monkey said abusively, taking a swing at Pig with his fist, "you're thoroughly lazy and barely human. But don't get upset, Master. The monsters are coming to take you across the mountain." Friar Sand too felt deeply ashamed, and quickly trying to cover it up he packed up the luggage and loaded the horse to wait on the road.

[5] The story returns to the three demon chiefs, who led their devilish hosts back into the cave. "Elder brother," said the second demon, "I'd imagined that Sun the Novice had nine heads and eight tails, but he turns out to be nothing but that pipsqueak of a monkey. You shouldn't have swallowed him. You should have fought him. He'd have been no match for us. With our tens of thousands of goblins we could have drowned him in our spit. But by swallowing him you let him use his magic and cause you agony, so that you didn't dare have it out with him. When I said we'd take the Tang Priest across the mountains just now I didn't mean it. It was only a way of luring him out because your life was in danger. I most certainly won't escort the Tang Priest." "Why

not, good brother?" the senior demon chief asked. "If you and I draw up three thousand junior devils ready for battle I can capture that ape," the second demon replied. "Never mind about three thousand," the senior demon chief said. "You can have our whole force. If we capture him it'll be a credit to us all."

The second demon chief then mustered three thousand junior demons whom he led to a place beside the main road, where they were put into battle formation. He sent a herald with a blue flag to carry a message. "Sun the Novice," the herald said, "come out at once and fight His Second Majesty." When Pig heard this he said with a laugh, "As the saying goes, brother, liars don't fool the people at home. You lied to us when you came back, you trickster. You said you'd beaten the evil spirits and that they'd be bringing a carrying-chair to take the master across. But here they are challenging you to battle. Why?" "The senior demon did surrender to me," Monkey replied, "and he wouldn't dare show his face. The sound of my name alone is enough to give him a headache. The second demon chief must be challenging me to battle because he can't bring himself to escort us across. I tell you, brother, those three evil spirits are brothers and they have a sense of honour. We're three brothers but we don't. I've beaten the senior demon, so the second demon's come out. There's no reason why you shouldn't fight him."

"I'm not scared of him," Pig said. "I'll go and give him a fight." "If you want to, go ahead," Monkey replied. "Brother," said Pig with a laugh, "I'll go, but lend me that rope." "What do you want it for?" Monkey asked. "You don't know how to get into his belly or tie it to his heart, so what use would it be to you?" "I want it tied round my waist as a lifeline," replied Pig. "You and Friar Sand are to hold on to it and let it out for me to fight him. If you think I'm beating him pay more rope out and I'll capture him, but if he's beating me, pull me back. Don't let him drag me off." At this Monkey smiled to himself and thought, "Another chance to make a fool of the idiot." Monkey then tied the rope round Pig's waist and sent him off into battle.

[6]   The idiot lifted his rake and rushed up the steep slope

585

shouting, "Come out, evil spirit! Come and fight your ancestor Pig!" The herald with the blue flag rushed back to report, "Your Majesty, there's a monk with a long snout and big ears here." The second demon chief came out of the encampment, saw Pig, and without a word thrust his spear straight at Pig's face. The idiot raised his rake and went forward to parry the blow. The two of them joined battle in front of the mountainside, and before they had fought seven or eight rounds the idiot began to weaken. He was no longer able to hold the evil spirit off. "Brother," he shouted, turning back in a hurry, "pull in the lifeline, pull in the lifeline!" When the Great Sage heard this from where he stood he loosened his hold on the rope and dropped it. The idiot started to run back now that he was defeated. At first he had not noticed the rope trailing behind him, but after he turned back, relaxing the tension on it, it started to get tangled round his legs. He tripped himself over, climbed to his feet and tripped over again. At first he only staggered, but then he fell face-down into the dust. The evil spirit caught up with him, unwound his trunk that was like a python, wrapped it round Pig and carried him back in triumph to the cave. The devilish host chorused a paean of victory as they swarmed back.

When Sanzang saw all this from the foot of the slope he became angry with Monkey. "Wukong," he said, "no wonder Wuneng wishes you were dead. You brother-disciples don't love each other at all. All you feel is jealousy. He told you to pull in his lifeline, so why didn't you? Why did you drop the rope instead? What are we to do now you have got him killed?" "You're covering up for him again, Master," said Monkey, "and showing favouritism too. I'm fed up. When I was captured it didn't bother you at all. I was dispensable. But when that idiot gets himself caught you blame me for it. Let him suffer. It'll teach him how hard it is to fetch the scriptures." "Disciple," said Sanzang, "was I to worried when you went? I remembered that you could change into other things, so I was sure you would come to no harm. But the idiot was born clumsy and can't transform himself, which makes this a very dangerous business. You must

586

go and rescue him." "Stop complaining, Master," said Brother Monkey. "I'll go and save him."

【7】 Monkey rushed up the mountain thinking resentfully, "I'm not going to make life easy for that idiot if he wishes me dead. I'll go and see what the evil spirits are doing with him. Before I rescue him I'll let him suffer a bit." He then made magic with his hands, said the words of a spell, shook himself, turned into the tiniest of insects and flew into the cave, where he landed at the bottom of one of Pig's ears to be taken inside with the evil spirit. The second demon chief had led his three thousand junior devils trumpeting and drumming louding to the cave, where they stopped. He now took Pig inside and said, "I've got one, elder brother." "Show me," the senior demon replied. Unwinding his trunk the second demon chief flung Pig to the ground and said, "There he is." "That one's useless," said the senior demon. "Your Majesty," put in Pig when he heard this, "if I'm no use let me go and find a more useful one to capture." "He may not be any use," said the third demon chief, "but he is the Tang Priest's disciple Zhu Bajie. Tie him up and put him to soak in the pool at the back. When his bristles have been soaked off we can open his belly up, salt him and dry him in the sun. He'll go down well with some wine on a rainy day." "That's that then," exclaimed Pig in horror. "I've fallen into the clutches of a demon who's a salt-pork pedlar." The demon hordes fell on him, tied his hands and feet together, carried him to the pool at the back, pushed him in and went back.

When the Great Sage flew there to have a look he saw the idiot with his four limbs pointing upwards and his snout downwards as he half floated and was half sinking, grunting through his snout. He really was a ridiculous sight, like a big blackened frost-bitten lotus pod that has shed its seeds in September or October. Seeing his face the Great Sage felt both loathing and pity for him. "What shall I do?" he wondered. "After all, he is another member of the Dragon Flower Assembly. I just wish he wouldn't keep trying to divide up the luggage, split our band, and incite the master to say the Band-tightening spell. The other day I heard Friar Sand say that he'd stashed some money away for himself. I wonder if it's true. I'll give him a scare and find out."

[8] The splendid Great Sage flew down to his ear and called in a disguised voice, "Zhu Wuneng, Zhu Wuneng." "This is terrible," thought Pig in alarm. "Wuneng is the name the Budhisattva Guanyin gave me. I've been called Zhu Bajie all the time I've been with the Tang Priest. How can there be anyone here who knows my name is Wuneng?" So he could not restrain himself from asking, "Who's that calling my Buddhist name?" "Me," said Monkey. "Who are you?" the idiot asked. "I'm a catcher," Monkey replied. "Where from, sir?" asked Pig in terror. "From the Fifth King of the Underworld, and he's sent me to fetch you," said Monkey. "Then please go back and ask the Fifth King as he's such a good friend of my senior fellow-disciple Sun Wukong to give me a day's grace. You can come for me tomorrow." "You're talking nonsense," Monkey replied. "If King Yama of Hell decides you're to die in the third watch nobody will keep you till the fourth. Come with me at once if you don't want me to put a rope round your neck and drag you off."

"Do me a favour," said the idiot. Even with a face like mine still want to go on living. I'll certainly die if I have to, but give me a day till these evil spirits have captured my master and the rest of us, so I can see them again before we're all done for." "Very well then," said Monkey, grinning to himself. "I've got about thirty people to capture around here in this batch. When I've caught them I'll come back for you. That'll give you a day's grace. Give me some money. I'm sure you've got some." "Oh dear," said Pig, "we monks don't have money." "If you haven't then I'm dragging you off," said Brother Monkey. "Come with me." "Don't be so impatient, sir," said the idiot, panicking. "I know that rope of yours is what they call the life-taking rope. Once it's round you you're dead. Yes, I have got some money. I've got a bit, but not much." "Where is it?" Monkey demanded. "Give it me at once." "Oh dear, what a pity!" said Pig. "From when I became a monk right up till now the kind people who feed monks have given me a bit more alms than the others because my belly's so big. I saved all the little bits of silver till I had about half an ounce. They were awkward to keep, so when we were in a city some time ago I asked a silversmith to melt them all together. The wicked man stole a few grains of it, so the ingot he made only weighed forty-six hundredths of an ounce. Take it." "The idiot hasn't even got his trousers on," grinned Monkey to himself, "so where can he have hidden it? Hey, where's your silver?" "It's stuffed inside my left ear," Pig replied. "I can't get it myself because I'm tied up, so take it out yourself."

When Monkey heard this he put his hand out and took the silver from inside Pig's ear. It was indeed an ingot shaped like a saddle that weighed only forty-five or forty-six hundredths of an ounce. As he held it in his hands Monkey could not help roaring with laughter. Recognizing Monkey's voice the idiot started cursing him wildly from the water: "Damn and blast you, Protector of the Horse, for coming to extort money from me when I'm in such misery." "I've got you now, you dreg-guzzler!" said Monkey. "Goodness only knows what I've had to suffer for the sake of protecting the master, while you've been making your fortune." "Nonsense!" Pig retorted. "Call this a fortune? It's just what I've scraped off my teeth. I resisted spending it on my stomach, so I saved it to but myself some cloth to get a tunic made. You've got it out of me by intimidation. You ought to share it with." "You won't get a cent of it," Monkey replied. "I've paid you to spare my life," said Pig, "so now you damn well ought to rescue me." "Don't be so impatient," said Monkey. "I'll rescue you all in good time." Putting the silver away he turned back into himself and used his cudgel to bring Pig close enough to grab him by his feet, drag him ashore and untie him. Pig then sprang up, took off his clothes, wrung them out, shook them, and draped them still dripping wet over his shoulders. "Brother," he said, "open the back gates. Let's go." "There's no glory in sneaking out the back way," replied Monkey. "We'll leave by the front gates." "My feet are still

589

numb after being tied up." said Pig. "I can't run." "Buck up and come with me," said Monkey.

[9] The splendid Great Sage charged out, clearing his way by swinging his cudgel. The idiot had no choice but to endure the pain and keep close to him. When he saw the rake propped up by the second pair of gates he went over to it, pushed the junior devils aside, retrieved it and rushed forward, lashing out wildly. He and Brother Monkey charged through three or four pairs of gates, and goodness only knows how many junior devils they killed. When the senior demon chief heard all this he said to the second chief, "You captured a fine one! A fine one indeed! Look! Sun the Novice has rescued Pig and they've wounded or killed the juniors on the gates." The second demon at once sprang to his feet and rushed out through the gates brandishing his spear. "Damned macaque," he shouted at the top of his voice. "What a bloody cheek! How dare you treat us with such contempt!" As soon as the Great Sage heard this he stopped still. The monster thrust his spear straight at him without allowing any argument. With the unhurried skill of the expert Monkey raised his iron cudgel to hit back at the demon's face. The two of them fought a splendid battle outside the entrance to the cave:

> The yellow-tusked elephant in human form
> Had sworn brotherhood with the Lion King.
> Persuaded by the senior monster
> They plotted together to eat the Tang Priest.
> Huge were the powers of the Great Sage, Heaven's equal,
> Who helped the good against the bad and killed off
demons,
> The incompetent Pig had met with disaster,
> So Monkey saved him and led him outside.
> When the demon king pursued them with great ferocity
> The spear and the cudgel each showed off its powers.
> The spear moved like a snake in the woods;
> The cudgel arose like a dragon from the sea.
> Where the dragon emerged the clouds were thick;

Dense hung the mist where the snake went through the woods.

It was all for the sake of the Tang Priest
That they fought each other with ferocity and hatred.

When he saw the Great Sage start fighting the evil spirit, Pig stood on the spur, his rake upright. Instead of joining in to help, he watched with stupefied amazement. Monkey's cudgel was so powerful and his martial skills so faultless the evil spirit used his spear to parry Monkey's blows while unrolling his trunk to wrap round him. As Monkey knew about this trick he held his gold-banded cudgel out horizontally in both hands and raised them. The evil spirit's trunk caught Monkey round the waist but missed his hands. Just watch how Monkey belabours the evil spirit's trunk with his cudgel.

[10] When Pig saw this he beat his chest and said, "Oh dear! That monster's got lousy luck. When he caught me he got my arms too because I'm so clumsy, but he didn't when he caught that slippery character. He's got his cudgel in both hands, and all he needs to do is shove it up the monster's trunk to give him such a pain in the nostrils that it'll make the snot run. The monster'll never be able to hold him." Monkey had not thought of this before Pig gave him the idea, but now he waved his cudgel to make it as thick as a hen's egg and over ten feet long and actually did shove it hard up the monster's trunk. This gave the evil spirit such a shock that he unravelled his trunk with a swishing noise. Monkey brought his hand round to grab the trunk and drag it forcefully towards him. To spare himself any more agony the monster steeped out and moved with Monkey's hand. Only then did Pig dare approach, raising his rake to hit wildly at the monster's flanks. "No," said Brother Monkey, "that's no good. The prongs of your rake are so sharp they might break his skin. If he starts bleeding heavily and the master sees it he'll say we've been killing again. You'd better turn it round and hit him with the handle."

The idiot then raised the handle of his rake and struck the

monster at every step while Monkey dragged him by the trunk. They looked like a pair of elephant boys as they led him down to the foot of the mountain, where Sanzang could be seen gazing with concentration at the two of them coming noisily towards him. "Wujing," he said to Friar Sand, "what is it Wukong is leading?" "Master," replied Friar Sand when he saw them, "big brother is dragging an evil spirit here by the nose. He really enjoys slaughter." "Splendid, splendid," said Sanzang. "What a big evil spirit, and what a long nose! Go and ask him if he's happy and willing to escort us over the mountain. If he is he must be spare and not be killed." Friar Sand at once rushed straight towards them shouting, "The master says you mustn't kill the monster if he's really willing to escort him across the mountain." As soon as he heard this the demon fell to his knees and promised to do so in a very nasal voice. His voice was like this because Monkey was pinching his nostrils shut, making it sound as though he had a heavy cold. "Lord Tang," he said, "I'll carry you across by chair if you spare my life." "My master and we disciples are good people," Monkey replied. "As you've said this we'll spare your life. Fetch the chair at once. If you break your word again we most certainly won't spare your life when we catch you next time." The freed monster kowtowed and left. Monkey and Pig went to report to the Tang Priest on everything that had happened to them. Pig was overcome with shame as he spread his clothes out to dry in the sun while he waited.

[11]   The second demon chief returned trembling and shaking to the cave. Even before his return some junior devils had reported to the senior and the third demon chiefs that Monkey had dragged him off by the trunk. In his anxiety the senior demon had led his hosts out with the third demon when they saw the second chief coming back alone. As they brought him inside and asked him why he had been released the second chief told them all about Sanzang's words of mercy and goodness. They looked at each other, at a loss for words. "Elder brother," said the second demon chief, "shall we take Sanzang across?" "What a thing to say, brother," replied the senior chief. "Sun the Novice is a

monkey who shows the greatest benevolence and sense of justice. If he had wanted to kill me when he was in my stomach he could most certainly have done so. He only grabbed your trunk. He might have dragged you off and not let you go. All he did was to pinch your trunk and break its skin, and that's given you a scare. Get ready at once to take them across." The third demon chief smiled and said, "Yes, yes, yes!" "From the way you're talking, my good brother," said the senior demon, "it sounds as though you're reluctant to let the Tang Priest go. If you don't, we'll take him across."

The third demon chief smiled again and said, "Elder brothers, it would have been luckier for those monks if they hadn't asked us to escort them but had slipped quietly across instead. By asking us to escort them they've fallen in with our plan to lure the tiger down from the mountain." "What do you mean by 'luring the tiger from the mountain'?" the senior demon asked. "Summon all the demons in our cave," the third demon chief continued. "Choose one thousand from the ten thousand of them, then a hundred from the thousand, then sixteen and thirty from the hundred." "Why do you want sixteen and thirty?" the senior demon asked. "The thirty must be good cooks," the third demon chief replied. "Give them the best rice and flour, bamboo shoots, tea, gill fungus, button mushrooms, beancurd and wheat gluten. Send them to put up a shelter seven to ten miles along the way and lay on a meal for the Tang Priest." "And what do you want the sixteen for?" the senior demon asked. "Eight to carry the chair and eight to shout and clear the way," the third demon replied. "We brothers will accompany them for a stage of their journey. About 150 miles west of here is my city, and I've plenty of troops there to greet them. When they get to the city we'll do such and such and so on.... The Tang Priest and his disciples won't be able to see what's happening to them. Whether we catch the Tang Priest or not depends completely on those sixteen demons."

The senior demon was beside himself with delight on hearing this. It was as if he had recovered from a drunken stupor or woken up from a dream. "Excellent, excellent," he said, whereupon he mustered the demons, chose thirty to whom he gave the food and another sixteen to carry a rattan chair. As they set out the senior demon gave the following instructions to the rest of the demons: "None of you are to go out on the mountain. Sun the Novice is a very cautious ape, and if he sees any of you around he'll be suspicious and see through our plan."

The senior demon then led his underlings to a place beside the main road, where he called aloud, "Lord Tang, today's not an unlucky one, so please come across the mountain straight away." "Who is that calling me, Wukong?" Sanzang asked when he heard this. "It's the demons I beat," Monkey replied. "They're bringing a chair to carry you." Putting his hands together in front of his chest Sanzang looked up to the sky and said, "Splendid, splendid! But for my worthy disciple's great abilities I could not proceed on my journey." He then walked forward to greet the demons with the words, "I am most grateful for the consideration you gentlemen are showing. When my disciples and I return to Chang'an we will praise your admirable achievements." "Please get into the carrying-chair, my lord," the demons said, kowtowing. Having mortal eyes and body Sanzang did not realize that this was a trick. The Great Sage Sun, a golden immortal of the Supreme Monad with a loyal nature, thought that because he had captured and released the demons they were now won over. He never imagined that they had other plots in mind, so he did not investigate closely but went along with his master's ideas. He told Pig to tie the luggage on the horse and keep close to the master with Friar Sand while he cleared the way with his iron cudgel, watching out to see if all was well. While eight devils carried the chair and eight shouted in turn to clear the way the three demon chiefs steadied the poles of the chair. The master was delighted to sit upright in it and go up the high mountain by the main track, little realizing that

> Great grief would return in the midst of rejoicing;
> "Extremes," says the classic, "create their negation."

Fated they were to meet with disaster,
A star of ill-omen to mark desolation.

The band of demons worked with one mind to escort them and serve them diligently at all times. After ten miles there was a vegetarian meal and after fifteen more miles another one. They were invited to rest before it grew late, and everything along their way was neat and tidy. Each day they had three most satisfactory and delightful meals and spent a comfortable night where they were able to sleep well.

【12】 When they had travelled about 150 miles west they found themselves near a walled city. Raising his iron cudgel the Great Sage, who was only a third of a mile ahead of the carrying-chair, was so alarmed by the sight of the city that he fell over and was unable to rise to his feet. Do you know why someone of his great courage was so frightened by what he saw? It was because he saw a very evil atmosphere hanging over the town.

Crowds of evil demons and monsters,
Wolf spirits at all four gates.
Striped tigers are the commanders;
White-faced tiger-cats are senior officers.
Antlered stags carry documents around;
Cunning foxes walk along the streets.
Thousand-foot pythons slither round the walls;
Twenty-mile serpents occupy the roads.
At the base of high towers grey wolves shout commands;
Leopards speak in human voices by pavilions.
Standard-bearers and drummers—all are monsters;
Mountain spirits patrol and stand sentry.
Crafty hares open shops to trade;
Wild boars carry their loads to do business.
What used to be the capital of a heavenly dynasty
Has now become a city of wolves and tigers.

Just as he was being overcome by terror the Great Sage heard a wind from behind him and turned quickly to see the third demon chief raising a heaven-square halberd with a patterned handle to strike at his head. Springing to his feet, the Great Sage struck back at the monster's face with his gold-banded cudgel. Both of them were snorting with rage and fury as they ground their teeth and fought a wordless struggle. Monkey then saw the senior demon chief giving out orders as he lifted his steel sabre to hack at Pig. Pig was in such a rush that he had to let the horse go as he swung his rake around to hit wildly back. Meanwhile the second demon chief was thrusting with his spear at Friar Sand, who parried with his demon-quelling staff.

The three demon chiefs and the three monks were now all fighting in single combat, ready to throw away their lives. The sixteen junior devils obeyed their orders, each giving play to his talents as they grabbed hold of the white horse and the luggage and crowded round Sanzang, lifting up his chair and carrying him straight to the city. "Your Senior Majesty, please decide what to do now we've captured the Tang Priest," they shouted. All the demons of every rank on the city walls came rushing down to throw the city gates wide open. Every battalion was ordered to furl its flag, silence its drums, and on no account shout war-cries or strike gongs. "His Senior Majesty has given orders that the Tang Priest is not to be frightened. He can't endure being scared. If he is, his flesh will turn sour and be inedible." The demons were all delighted to welcome Sanzang, bowing and carrying him into the throne hall of the palace, where he was invited to sit in the place of honour. They offered him tea and food as they bustled around him in attendance. The venerable elder felt dizzy and confused as he looked about and saw no familiar faces. If you don't know whether he was to escape with his life listen to the explanation in the next instalment.

22. 群魔欺本性
一体拜真如

【1】　且不言唐长老困苦。却说那三个魔头，齐心竭力，与大圣兄弟三人，在城东半山内，努力争持。这一场，正是那"铁刷帚刷铜锅，家家挺硬。"好杀：

六般体相六般兵，六样形骸六样情。六恶六根565六欲，六门六道赌输赢。三十六宫春自在，六六形色恨有名。这一个金箍棒，千般解数；那一个方天戟，百样峥嵘。八戒钉钯凶更猛，二怪长枪俊又能。小沙僧宝杖非凡，有心打死；老魔禽钢刀快利，举手无情。这个是护卫真僧无敌将，那三个是乱法欺君泼野精。起初犹可，向后弥凶。六枚都使升空法，云端里面各翻腾。一时间吐雾喷云天地暗，哮哮吼吼只闻声。

他六个斗罢多时，渐渐天晚。却又是风雾漫漫，霎时间，就黑暗了。原来八戒耳大，盖着眼皮，越发昏蒙；手脚慢，又遮架不住，拖着钯，败阵就走，被老魔举刀砍去，几乎伤命；幸躲过头脑，被老口刀削断八根鬃毛，赶上张开口咬着领头，拿入城中，丢与小怪，捆在金銮殿。老妖又驾云，起在半空助力。沙和尚见事不谐，虚幌着宝杖，顾本身回头便走，被二怪捽开鼻子，响一声，连手卷住，拿到城里，也叫小妖捆在殿下。却又腾空去叫拿行者。行者见两个兄弟遭擒，他自家独力难撑，正是"好手不敌双拳，双拳难敌四手。"他喊一声，把棍子隔开三个妖魔的兵器，纵筋斗云走了。三怪见行者驾筋斗时，即抖抖身体，现了本像，扇开两翅，赶上大圣。你道他怎能赶上？当时如行者闹天宫，十万天兵也拿他不住者，以他会驾筋斗云，一去有十万八千里路，这个精怪一翅就有九万里，两扇就过去了，所以被他一把挝住，拿在手中，左右挣挫不得。欲思要走，莫能逃脱。即使变化法通法，又往来难行：变大些儿，他

597

就放松了挡住；变小些儿，他又搽紧了挡住。复拿了径回城内，放了手，捽下尘埃。吩咐群妖，也把八戒、沙僧捆在一处。那老魔、二魔俱下来迎接。三个魔头，同上宝殿。噫！这一番倒不是捆住行者，分明是与他送行。

【2】　此时有二更时候，众怪一齐相见毕，把唐僧推下殿来。那长老于灯光前，忽见三个徒弟都捆在地下，老师父伏于行者身边，哭道："徒弟啊！常时逢难，你却在外运用神通，到那里取救降魔；今番你亦遭擒，我贫僧怎么得命！"八戒、沙僧听见师父这般苦楚，便也一齐放声痛哭。行者微微笑道："师父放心，兄弟莫哭；凭他怎的，决然无伤。等那老魔安静了，我们走路。"八戒道："哥啊，又来捣鬼了！麻绳捆住，松些儿还着水喷，想你这瘦人儿不觉，我这胖的遭瘟哩！不信，你看两膊上。入肉已有二寸，如何脱身！"行者笑道："莫说是麻绳捆的，就是碗粗的棕缆，只也当秋风过耳，何足挂齿！"

师徒们正说处，只闻得那老魔道："三贤弟有力量，有智谋，果成妙计，拿将唐僧来了！"叫："小的们，着五个打水，七个刷锅，十个烧火，二十个抬出铁笼来，把那四个和尚蒸熟，我兄弟们受用，各散一块儿与小的们吃，也教他个个长生。"八戒听见，战兢兢的道："哥哥，你听。那妖精计较要蒸我们吃哩！"行者道："不要怕，等我看他是雏儿妖精，是把势妖精。"沙和尚哭道："哥呀！且不要说宽话，如今已与阎王隔壁哩，且讲甚么'雏儿'、'把势'！"说不了，二怪道："猪八戒不好蒸。"八戒欢喜道："阿弥陀佛，是那个积阴骘的，说我不好蒸？"三怪道："不好蒸，剥了皮蒸。"八戒慌了，厉声喊道："不要剥皮！粗自粗，汤滚就烂了！"老怪道："不好蒸的，安在底下一格。"行者笑道："八戒莫怕，是'雏儿'，不是'把势'。"沙僧道："怎么认得？"行者道："大凡蒸东西，都从上边起。不好蒸的，安在上头一格，多烧把火，圆了气，就好了；若安在底下，一住了气，就烧半年也是不得气上的。他说八戒不好蒸，安在底下，不是雏儿是甚的！"八戒道："哥啊，依你说，就活活的弄杀人了！他打紧，我不好蒸，抬开了，把我翻转过来，再烧起火，弄得我两边俱熟，中间不夹生了？"

正讲时，又见小妖来报："汤滚了。"老怪传令叫抬。众妖一齐上手,将八戒抬在底下一格,沙僧抬在二格。行者估着来抬他,他就脱身道:"此灯光前好做手脚!"拔下一根毫毛,吹口仙气,叫声"变!"即变做一个行者,捆了麻绳;将真身出神,跳在半空里,低头看着。那群妖那知真假,见人就抬。把个"假行者"抬在上三格;才将唐僧揪翻倒捆住,抬上第四格。干柴架起,烈火气焰腾腾。大圣在云端里嗟叹道:"我那八戒、沙僧,还捱得两滚;我那师父,只消一滚就烂。若不用法救他,顷刻我矣!"

【3】 好行者,在空中捻着诀,念一声"唵蓝净法界,乾元亨利贞"的咒语,拘唤得北海龙王早至。只见那云端里一朵乌云,应声高叫道:"北海小龙敖顺叩头。"行者道:"请起! 请起! 无事不敢相烦,今与唐师父到此,被毒魔拿住,上铁笼蒸哩。你去与我护持护持,莫教蒸坏了。"龙王随即将身变做一阵冷风,吹入锅下,盘旋围护,更没火气烧锅,他三人方不损命。

将有三更尽时,只闻得老魔发放道:"手下的,我等用计劳形,拿了唐僧四众;又因相送辛苦,四昼夜未曾得睡。今已捆在笼里,料应难脱,汝等用心看守,着十个小妖轮流烧火,让我们退宫,略略安寝。到五更天色将明,必然烂了,可安排下蒜泥盐醋,请我们起来,空心受用。"众妖各各遵命。三个魔头,却去转寝宫而去。

【4】 行者在云端里,明明听着这等吩咐,却低下云头,不听见笼里人声。他想着:"火气上腾,必然也热,他们怎么不怕,又无言语?——哼嘴! 莫敢是蒸死了? 等我近前再听。"好大圣,踏着云,摇身一变,变做一个黑苍蝇儿,钉在铁笼格外听时,只闻得八戒在里面道:"晦气,晦气! 不知是闷气蒸,又不知是出气蒸哩。"沙僧道:"二哥,怎么叫做'闷气'、'出气'?"八戒道:"'闷气蒸'是盖了笼头,'出气蒸'不盖。"三藏在浮上一层应声道:"徒弟,不曾盖。"八戒道:"造化! 今夜还不得死! 这是出气蒸了!"行者听得他三人都说话,未曾伤命,便就飞了去,把个铁笼盖,轻轻儿盖上。三藏慌了道:"徒弟! 盖上了!"罢了! 这是闷气蒸,今夜也是死了!"沙僧与长老嘤嘤的啼哭。八戒道:"且不要哭,这一会烧火的换了班了。"沙僧道:"你怎么知道?"八戒道:"早先抬上来时,正合我意:我有些儿寒湿气的病,要他腾腾。这

会子反冷气上来了。——咦！烧火的长官，添上些柴便怎的？要了你的哩！"

行者听见，忍不住暗笑道："这个夯货！冷还발捱，若热就要伤命。再说两遭，一定走了风了，快早救他。——且住！要救他须是要现本相。假如现了，这十个烧火的看见，一齐乱喊，惊动老怪，却不又费事？……等我先送他个法儿。……"忽想起："我当初做大圣时，曾在北天门与护国天王猜枚耍子，赢得他瞌睡虫儿，还有几个，送了他罢。"即往腰间顺带里摸摸，还有十二个。"送他十个，还留两个做种。"即将虫儿抛了去，散在十个小妖脸上，钻入鼻孔，渐渐打盹，都睡倒了。只有一个拿火叉的，睡不稳，揉头搓脸，把鼻子左捏右捏，不住的打喷嚏。行者道："这厮晓得勾当了，我再与他个'双椽灯'。"又将一个虫儿抛在他脸上。"两个虫儿，左进右出，右出左进，谅有一个安住。"那小妖两三个大呵欠，把腰伸一伸，丢了火叉，也扑的睡倒，再不翻身。

【5】 行者道："这法儿真是妙而且灵！"即现原身，走近前，叫声"师父。"唐僧听见道："悟空，救我啊！"沙僧道："哥哥，你在外面叫哩？"行者道："我不在外面，好和你们在里边受罪？"八戒道："哥啊，溜撒的溜了，我们都是顶缸的，在此受闷气哩！"行者笑道："呆子莫嚷，我来救你。"八戒道："哥啊，救便要脱根救，莫又要复笼蒸。"行者却揭开笼头，解了师父，将假变的毫毛，抖了一抖，收上身来；又一层层放了沙僧，放了八戒。那呆子才解了，巴不得就要跑。行者道："莫忙！莫忙！"却又念声咒语，发放了龙神，才对八戒道："我们这去到西天，还有高山峻岭。师父没脚力难行，等我还捎马来。"

你看他轻手轻脚，走到金銮殿下，见那些大小群妖俱睡着了。却解了缰绳，更不惊动。那马原是龙马，若是生人，飞踢两脚，便嘶几声。行者曾养过马，授弼马温之官，又是自家一伙，所以不跳不叫。悄悄的牵来，束紧了肚带，扣备停当，请师父上马。长老战战兢兢的骑上，也就要走。行者道："也且莫忙。我们西去还有国王，我们去看看；不然，我们还去寻行李来。"唐僧道："我记得进门时，众怪将行李放在金殿左手下，担儿也在那一边。"行者道："我晓得了。"即抽身跳在宝殿寻时，忽见光彩飘飘。行者知是行李，——怎么就知？以唐僧的锦襕袈裟上有夜明珠，故此放光。——急前前，见担儿原封未动，连忙拿下去，付与沙僧挑着。

八戒牵着马，他引了路，径奔正阳门。只听得梆铃乱响，门上有锁，锁上贴了封皮。行者道："这等防守，如何去得？"八戒道："后门里去罢。"行者引路，径奔后门："后宰门外，也有梆铃之声，门上也有封锁，却怎生是好？我这一番，若不为唐僧是个凡体，我三人不管怎的，也驾云弄风走了。只为唐僧本超三界外，见在五行中，一身都是父母浊骨，所以不得升驾，难逃。"八戒道："哥哥，不消商量，我们到那没梆铃，不防卫处，撮着师父爬过墙去罢。"行者笑道："这个不好：此时无奈，撮他过去；到取经回来，你这呆子口敞，延地里就对人说，我们是爬墙头的和尚了。"八戒道："此时也顾不得行检，且逃命去罢。"行者也没奈何，只得依他。到那净墙边，算计爬出。

【6】 噫！有这般事！也是三藏灾星未脱。那三个魔头，在宫中正睡，忽然惊觉，说走了唐僧，一个个披衣忙起，急登宝殿。问曰："唐僧蒸了几滚了？"那些烧火的小妖已是有睡熟虫，都睡着了，就是打也莫想打得一个醒来。其余没执事的，惊醒几个，冒冒失失的答应道："七——七——七——七滚了！"急跑近锅边，只见笼格子乱丢在地下，烧火的还都睡着，慌得又来报道："大王，走——走——走——走了！"三个魔头都下殿，近锅前仔细看时，果见那笼格子乱丢在地下，汤锅尽冷，火脚俱无。那烧火的俱呼呼鼾睡如泥。慌得众怪一齐呐喊，都叫："快拿唐僧！快拿唐僧！"这一片喊声振起，把些前前后后，大大小小妖精，都惊起来。刀枪簇拥，至正阳门下，见那封锁不动，梆铃不绝，问外边巡夜的道："唐僧从那里走了？"俱道："不曾走出人来。"急赶至后宰门，封锁、梆铃，一如前门；复乱抢抢的，灯笼火把，漠天通红，就如白日，却明明的照见他四众爬墙哩！老魔赶近，喝声"那里走！"那长老唬得脚软筋麻，跌下墙来，被老魔拿住。二魔捉了沙僧，三魔擒倒八戒，众妖抢了行李、白马，只是走了行者。那八戒口里咽咽哝哝的报怨行者道："天杀的！我说要救便脱根救，如今却又复笼蒸了！"

众魔把唐僧擒至殿上,却不蒸了。二怪吩咐把八戒绑在殿前檐柱上,三怪吩咐把沙僧绑在殿后檐柱上;惟老魔把唐僧抱住不放。三怪道:“大哥,你抱住他怎的?终不然就活吃?却也没些趣味。此物比不得那愚夫俗子,拿了可以当饭;此是上邦稀奇之物,必须待天阴闲暇之时,拿他出来,整制精洁,猜枚行令,细吹细打的吃方可。”老魔笑道:“贤弟之言虽当,但孙行者又要来偷哩。”三魔道:“我这皇宫里面有一座锦香亭子,亭子内有一个铁柜。依着我,把唐僧藏在柜里,关了亭子,却传出谣言,说唐僧已被我们夹生吃了。令小妖满城讲说;那行者必然来探听消息,若听见这话,他必死心塌地而去。待三五日不来搅扰,却拿出来,慢慢受用,如何?”老怪、二怪俱大喜道:“是,是,是!兄弟说得有理!”可怜把个唐僧连夜拿将进去,藏在柜中,闭了亭子。传出谣言,满城里都乱讲不题。

【7】　却说行者自夜半顾不得唐僧,驾云走脱。径至狮驼洞里,一路棍,把那万数小妖,尽情剿绝。急回来,东方日出。到城边,不敢叫战,正是“单丝不线,孤掌难鸣”。他落下云头,摇身一变,变做个小妖儿,演入门里,大街小巷,缉访消息。满城里俱道:“唐僧被大王夹生儿连夜吃了。”前前后后,都是这等说。行者着实心焦,行至金銮殿前观看,那里边有许多精灵,都戴着皮金帽子,穿着黄布直身,手拿着红漆棍,腰挂着象牙牌,一往一来,不住的乱走。行者暗想道:“此必是穿宫的妖怪。就变做这个模样,进去打听打听。”好大圣,果然变得一般无二,混入金门。正走处,只见八戒绑在殿前柱上哼哩。行者近前,叫声“悟能。”那呆子认得声音,道:“师兄,你来了?救我一救!”行者道:“我救你。你可知师父在那里?”八戒道:“师父没了。昨夜被妖精夹生儿吃了。”行者闻言,忽失声泪似泉涌。八戒道:“哥哥莫哭;我也是听得小妖乱讲,未曾眼见。你休误了,再去寻问寻问。”这行者却才收泪,又往里面找寻。忽见沙僧绑在后檐柱上,即近前摸着他胸脯子叫道:“悟净。”沙僧也识得声音,道:“师兄,你变化进来了?救我!救我!”行者道:“救你容易。你可知师父在那里?”沙僧滴泪道:“哥啊!师父被妖精等不得蒸,就夹生儿吃了!”

【8】　大圣听得两个言语相同,心如刀搅,泪似水流,急纵身望空

跳起，且不救八戒、沙僧，回至城东山上，按落云头，放声大哭。叫道："师父啊！

恨我欺天困网罗，师来救我脱沉疴。

潜心笃志同参佛，努力修身共炼魔。

岂料一朝遭蜇害，不能保你上婆娑。

西方胜境无缘到，气散魂消怎奈何！"

行者凄凄惨惨的，自思自忖，以心问心道："这都是我佛如来坐在那极乐之境，没得事干，弄了那三藏之经！若果有心劝善，理当送上东土，却不是个万古流传？只是舍不得送去，却教我等来取。怎知道苦历千山，今朝到此丧命！——罢！罢！罢！老孙且驾个筋斗云，去见如来，备言前事。若肯把经与我送上东土，一则传扬善果，二则了我等心愿；若不肯与我，教他把《松箍咒》念念，退下这个箍子，交还与他，老孙还归本洞，称王道寡，耍子儿去罢。"

好大圣，急翻身驾起筋斗云，径投天竺。那里消一个时辰，早望见灵山不远。须臾间，按落云头，直至鹫峰之下。忽抬头，见四大金刚挡住道："那里走？"行者施礼道："有事要见如来。"当头又有昆仑山金霞岭不坏尊王永住金刚喝道："这泼猴甚是粗狂！前者大困牛魔，我等为汝劳力，今日面见，全不为礼！有事且待入奏，奉召方行。这里比南天门不同，教你进去出来，两边乱走！咄！还不靠开！"那大圣正是烦恼处，又遭此抢白，气得哮吼如雷，忍不住大呼小叫，早惊动如来。

【9】　如来佛祖正端坐在九品宝莲台上，与十八尊轮世的阿罗汉讲经，即开口道："孙悟空来了，汝等出去接待接待。"大众阿罗，遵佛旨，两路幢幡宝盖，即出山门应声道："孙大圣，如来有旨相唤哩。"那山门口四大金刚却才闪开开路，让行者前进。众阿罗引至宝莲台下，见如来倒身下拜，两泪悲啼。如来道："悟空，有何事这等悲啼？"行者道："弟子屡蒙教训之恩，托庇在佛爷爷之门下，自归正果，保护唐僧，拜为师范，一路上苦不可言！今至狮驼山狮驼洞狮驼城，有三个毒魔，乃狮王、象王、大鹏，把我师父捉将去，连弟子一概遭ого，都捆在蒸笼里，受汤火之灾。幸弟子脱逃，唤龙王救免。是夜偷出师等，不料灾星难脱，复又擒回。及

至天明，入城打听，回耐那魔十分狠毒，万样骁勇：把师父连夜夹生吃了，如今骨肉无存。又况师弟悟能、悟净，见绑在那厢，不久性命亦皆倾矣。弟子没及奈何，特地到此参拜如来。望大慈悲，将《松箍咒儿》念念，退下我这头上箍儿，交还如来，放我弟子回花果山宽闲耍子去罢！"说未了，泪如泉涌，悲声不绝。如来笑道："悟空少得烦恼。那妖精神通广大，你胜不得他，所以这等心痛。"行者跪在下面，捶着胸膛道："不瞒如来说。弟子当年闹天宫，称大圣，自为人以来，不曾吃亏，今番却遭这毒魔之手！"

【10】　如来闻言道："你且休恨。那妖精我认得他。"行者猛然失声道："如来！我听见人讲说，那妖精与你有亲哩。"如来道："这个刁猢狲！怎么这妖精与我有亲？"行者笑道："不与你有亲，如何认得？"如来道："我慧眼观之，故此认得。那老怪与二怪有主。"叫："阿傩、迦叶，来！你两个分头驾云，去五台山、峨眉山宣文殊、普贤来见。"二尊者即奉旨而去。如来道："这是老魔、二怪之主。但那三怪，说将起来，也是与我有些亲处。"行者道："亲是父党？母党？"如来道："自那混沌分时，天开于子，地辟于丑，人生于寅，天地再交合，万物尽皆生。万物有走兽飞禽。走兽以麒麟为之长，飞禽以凤凰为之长。那凤凰又得交合之气，育生孔雀、大鹏。孔雀出世之时，最恶，能吃人，四十五里路，把人一口吸之。我在雪山顶上，修成丈六金身，早被他也把我吸下肚去。我欲从他便门而出，恐污真身，是我剖开他脊背，跨上灵山。欲伤他命，当被诸佛劝解：伤孔雀就是伤我母。故此留他在灵山会上，封他做佛母孔雀大明王菩萨。大鹏与他是一母所生，故此有些亲处。"行者闻言笑道："如来，若这般比论，你还是妖精的外甥哩。"如来道："那怪须是我去，方可收伏。"行者叩头，启上如来："千万望挪玉一降！"

如来即下莲台，同诸佛众，径出山门。又见阿傩、迦叶，引文殊、普贤来见。二菩萨对佛礼拜。如来道："菩萨之兽，下山多少时了？"文殊道："七日了。"如来道："山中方七日，世上几千年。不知在那厢伤了多少生灵，快随我收他去。"二菩萨相随左右，同众飞空。只见那：

满天缥缈瑞云分，我佛慈悲降法门。

明示开天生物理,细言辟地化身文。
面前五百阿罗汉,脑后三千揭谛神。
迦叶阿傩随左右,普文菩萨殄妖氛。

大圣有此人情,请得佛祖与众前来,不多时,早望见城池。行者报道:"如来,那放黑气的乃是狮驼国也。"如来道:"你先下去,到那城中与妖精交战,许败不许胜。败上来,我自收他。"

【11】 大圣即按云头,径至城上,脚踏着垛儿骂道:"泼孽畜!快出来与老孙交战!"慌得那城楼上小妖急跳下城中报道:"大王,孙行者在城上叫战哩。"老魔道:"这猴儿两三日不来,今朝却又叫战,莫不是请了些救兵来耶?"三怪道:"怕他怎的!我们都去看来。"三个魔头,各执兵器,赶上城来;见了行者,更不打话,举兵器一齐乱刺。行者抡铁棒掣手相迎。斗经七八回合,行者佯输而走。那魔王喝声大振,叫道:"那里走!"大圣筋斗一纵,跳上半空,三个精即驾云来赶。行者将身一闪,藏在佛爷爷金光影里,全然不见。只见那过去、未来、见在的三尊佛像与五百阿罗汉、三千揭谛神,布散左右,把那三个妖王围住,水泄不通。老魔慌了手脚,叫道:"兄弟,不好了!那猴子真是个地里鬼!那里请得个主人公来也!"三魔道:"大哥休得惊怕。我们一齐上前,使枪刀捣倒如来,夺他那雷音宝刹!"这魔头不识起倒,真个举刀上前乱砍。却被文殊、普贤,念动真言,喝道:"这孽畜还不皈正,更待怎生!"唬得老怪、二怪,不敢撑持,丢了兵器,打个滚,现了本相。二菩萨将莲花台抛在那怪的脊背上,飞身跨坐,二怪遂泯耳皈依。

【12】 二菩萨既收了青狮、白象。只有那第三个妖魔不伏。腾开翅,丢了方天戟,抟摇直上,轮利爪要一捉猴王。原来大圣藏在光中,他怎敢近,如来情知此意,即闪金光,把那鹊巢贯顶之头,迎风一幌,变做鲜红的一块血肉。妖精轮利爪刁他一下,被佛爷把手往上一指,那妖翅膊上就了筋,飞不去,只在佛顶上,不能远遁,现了大鹏金翅雕。即开口对佛应声叫道:"如来,你怎么使大法力困住我也?"如来道:"你在此处多生孽障,跟我去,有进益之功。"妖精道:"你那里持斋把素,极贫极苦;我这里吃人肉,受用无穷;你若饿坏了我,你有罪愆。"如来

道:"我管四大部洲,无数众生瞻仰,凡做好事,我教他先祭汝口。"那大鹏欲脱难脱,要走怎走,是以没奈何,只得皈依。

　　行者方才转出,向如来叩头道:"佛爷,你今收了妖精,除了大害,只是没了我师父也。"大鹏咬着牙根道:"泼猴头!寻这等狠人困我!你那老和尚几曾吃他?如今在那锦香亭铁柜里不是?"行者闻言,忙叩头谢了佛祖。佛祖不敢松放了大鹏,也只教他在光焰上做个护法,引众回云,径归宝刹。

【13】　行者却按落云头,直入城里。那城里一个小妖儿也没有了。正是"蛇无头而不行,鸟无翅而不飞。"他见佛祖收了妖王,各自逃生而去。行者才解救了八戒、沙僧,寻着行李、马匹,与他二人说:"师父不曾吃。都跟我来。"引他两个径入内院,找着锦香亭,打开门看,内有一个铁柜,只听得三藏有啼哭之声。沙僧使降妖杖打开铁锁,揭开柜盖,叫声"师父"。三藏见了,放声大哭道:"徒弟啊!怎生降得妖魔?如何得到此寻我也?"行者把上项事,从头至尾,细陈了一遍。三藏感谢不尽。师徒们在那宫殿里寻了些米粮,按排些茶饭,饱吃一餐,收拾出城,找大路投西而去。

Chapter 22
The Demon Host Mistreats the Fundamental Nature;
The One Body Pays His Respects to the Buddha

[1]   We will tell now not of the sufferings of the venerable Tang Elder but of the three demon chiefs in strenuous combat with the Great Sage and his two brother disciples in the low hills to the east outside the city. It was indeed a good hard battle, like an iron brush against a copper pan:

> *Six types of body, six types of weapon,*
> *Six physical forms, six feelings.*
> *The six evils arise from the six sense organs and the six desires;*
> *The six gates to nirvana and the six ways of rebirth are struggling for victory.*
> *In the thirty-six divine palaces spring comes of itself;*
> *The six times six forms do not want to be named.*
> *This one holding a gold-banded cudgel*
> *Performs a thousand movements;*
> *That one wielding a heaven-square halberd*
> *Is exceptional in every way.*
> *Pig is even more ferocious with his rake;*
> *The second demon's spear-play is superb and effective.*
> *There is nothing commonplace about young Friar Sand's staff*
> *As he tried to inflict a blow that is fatal;*
> *Sharp is the senior demon's sabre*
> *Which he raises without mercy.*
> *These three are the true priest's invincible escorts;*
> *The other three are evil and rebellious spirits.*

At first the fight is not so bad,
But later it becomes more murderous.
All six weapons rise up by magic
To twist and turn in the clouds above.
They belch out in an instant clouds that darken the sky,
And the only sounds to be heard are roars and bellows.

After the six of them had been fighting for a long time evening was drawing in, and as the wind was also bringing cloud it became dark very quickly. Pig was finding it harder and harder to see as his big ears were covering his eyelids. His hands and feet were besides too slow for him to be able to hold off his opponent, so he fled from the fight, dragging his rake behind him. The senior demon chief took a swing at him with his sword that almost killed him. Luckily Pig moved his head out of the way, so that the blade only cut off a few of his bristles. The monster then caught up with Pig, opened his jaws, picked Pig up by the collar, carried him into the city and threw him to the junior demons to tie up and take to the throne hall. The senior demon chief then rose back into the air by cloud to help the other two.

Seeing that things were going badly Friar Sand feinted with his staff and turned to flee only to be caught, hands and all, when the second demon unravelled his trunk and noisily wrapped it round him. The demon took him too into the city, ordering the junior demons to tie him up in the palace before rising up into the sky again to tell the others how to catch Monkey. Seeing that both his brother disciples had been captured Monkey realized that it was going to be impossible for him to hold out single-handed. Indeed,

A couple of fists can defeat a good hand,
But cannot a competent foursome withstand.

With a shout Brother Monkey pushed the three demons' weapons aside, set off his somersault cloud and fled. When the third demon chief saw Monkey ride off by somersault he shook himself,

609

resumed his real form, spread his wings and caught up with the Great Sage. You may well ask how the demon could possibly catch up with him. When Monkey made havoc in heaven all that time ago a hundred thousand heavenly soldiers had failed to capture him. Because he could cover 36,000 miles in a single somersault of his cloud, none of the gods had been able to catch up with him. But this evil spirit could cover 30,000 miles with one beat of his wings, so that with two beats he caught up with Monkey and seized him. Monkey could not get out of the demon's talons no matter how hard he struggled or how desperately he longed to escape. Even when he used his transformation magic he still could not move. If he made himself grow the demon opened his grip but still held firmly to him; and if he shrank the demon tightened his clutch. The demon took him back inside the city, released his talons, dropped him into the dust, and told the fiendish hordes to tie him up and put him with Pig and Friar Sand. The senior and the second demon chiefs both came out to greet the third chief, who went back up into the throne hall with them. Alas! This time they were not tying Monkey up but sending him on his way.

【2】 It was now the second watch of the night, and after all the demons had exchanged greetings the Tang Priest was pushed out of the throne hall. When he suddenly caught sight in the lamplight of his three disciples all lying tied up on the ground the venerable master leaned down beside Brother Monkey and said through his tears, "Disciple, when we meet with trouble you normally go off and use your magic powers to subdue the monsters causing it. Now that you too have been captured can I survive, poor monk that I am?" As soon as Pig and Friar Sand heard their master's distress they too began to howl together. "Don't worry, Master," said Monkey with a hint of a smile, "and don't cry, brothers. No matter what they do they won't be able to hurt us. When the demon chiefs have settled and are asleep we can be on our way." "You're just making trouble again, brother," replied Pig. "We're trussed up with hempen ropes. If we do manage to work them a bit loose they spurt water on them to shrink them again. You might be too skinny to notice, but fat old me's having a terrible time. If you don't believe me take a look at my arms. The rope's cut two inches deep into them. I'd never get away."

"Never mind hempen ropes," said Monkey with a laugh, "even if they were coir cables as thick as a rice-bowl they'd be no more than an autumn breeze to me. What's there to make a fuss about?"

As master and disciples were talking the senior demon could be heard saying, "Third brother, you really are strong and wise. Your plan to capture the Tang Priest was brilliant and it worked." "Little ones," he called, "five of you carry water, seven scrub the pans, ten get the fire burning and twenty fetch the iron steamer. When we've steamed the four monks tender for my brothers and me to enjoy we'll give you juniors a piece so that you can all live for ever." "Brother," said Pig, trembling, when he heard this, "listen. That evil spirit's planning to steam and eat us." "Don't be afraid," said Monkey. "I'm going to find out whether he's an evil spirit still wet behind the ears or an old hand."

"Brother," said Friar Sand, sobbing, "don't talk so big. We're next door to the king of Hell. How can you talk about whether he's wet behind the ears or an old hand at a time like this?" The words were not all out of his mouth before the second demon chief was heard to say, "Pig won't steam well." "Amitabha Buddha!" said Pig with delight. "I wonder who's building up good karma by saying I won't steam well." "If he won't steam well," the third chief said, "skin him before steaming him." This panicked Pig, who screamed at the top of his voice, "Don't skin me. I may be coarse but I'll go tender if you boil me." "If he won't steam well," the senior demon chief said, "put him on the bottom tray of the steamer." "Don't worry, Pig," said Monkey with a laugh, "he's wet behind the ears. He's no old hand." "How can you tell?" Friar Sand asked. "Generally speaking you should start from the top when steaming," Monkey replied. "Whatever's hardest to steam should be put on the top tray. Add a bit of extra fuel to the fire, get up

611

a good steam and it'll be done. But put it at the bottom and lower the steam and you won't get the steam up even if you cook it for six months. He must be wet behind the ears if he says that Pig should be on the bottom tray because he's hard to cook."

"Brother," Pig replied, "if he followed your advice I'd be slaughtered alive. When he can't see the steam rising he'll take the lid off, turn me over and make the fire burn hotter. I'll be cooked on both sides and half done in the middle."

As they were talking a junior devil came in to report that the water was boiling. The senior chief ordered that the monks be carried in, and all the demons acted together to carry Pig to the lowest shelf of the steamer and Friar Sand to the second shelf. Guessing that they would be coming for him next Brother Monkey freed himself and said, "This lamplight is just right for some action." He then pulled out a hair, blew on it with magic breath, called, "Change!" and turned it into another Monkey he tied up with the hempen rope while extracting his real self in spirit form to spring up into mid-air, look down and watch. Not realizing that he was an imitation the crowd of demons picked up the false Monkey they saw and carried him to the third tray of the steamer, near the top. Only then did they drag the Tang Priest to the ground, tie him up, and put him into the fourth tray. As the dry firewood was stacked up a fierce fire blazed. "My Pig and Friar Sand can stand a couple of boilings," sighed the Great Sage up in the clouds, "but that master of mine will be cooked tender as soon as the water boils. If I can't save him by magic he'll be dead in next to no time."

【3】 The splendid Great Sage made a hand-spell in mid-air, said the magic words "Om the blue pure dharma world; true is the eternal beneficence of Heaven", and summoned the Dragon King of the Northern Ocean to him. A black cloud appeared among the other clouds, and from it there came at once an answering shout, "Ao Shun, the humble dragon of the Northern Ocean, kowtows in homage." "Arise, arise," said Monkey. "I would not have ventured to trouble you for nothing. I've now got this far with my master the Tang Priest. He's been captured by vicious monsters and put into an iron steamer to be cooked. Go and protect him for me and don't let the steam harm him." The dragon king at once turned himself into a cold wind that blew underneath the cooking pot and coiled around to shield it from all the heat of the fire. Thus were the three of them saved from death.

As the third watch was drawing to an end the senior demon chief announced a decision. "My men," he said, "we have worn out brains and brawn to capture the Tang Priest and his three disciples. Because of the trouble we went to in escorting them we have not slept for four days and nights. I don't think that they'll be able to escape now that they're tied up and being steamed. You are all to guard them carefully. Ten of your junior devils are to take it in turns to keep the fires burning while we withdraw to our living quarters for a little rest. By the fifth watch, when it's about to get light, they're bound to be cooked tender. Have some garlic paste, salt and vinegar ready and wake us up; then we'll be able to eat them with a good appetite." The devils did as they had been ordered while the three demon chiefs returned to their sleeping chambers.

[4] Up in the clouds Brother Monkey clearly heard these instructions being given, so he brought his cloud down. As there was no sound of voices from inside the steamer he thought, "The fire is blazing away and they must be feeling hot. Why aren't they afraid? Why aren't they saying anything? Hmm ... Could they have been steamed to death? Let me go closer and listen." The splendid Great Sage shook himself as he stood on his cloud and turned into a black fly. As he slighted on the outside of the iron steamer's trays to listen he heard Pig saying inside, "What lousy luck! What lousy luck! I wonder whether we're being closed-steamed or open-steamed." "What do you mean by 'closed' and 'open', brother?" Friar Sand asked. "Closed steaming is when they cover the steamer and open steaming is when they don't," Pig replied. "Disciples," said Sanzang from the top tray, "the cover is off." "We're in luck!" said Pig. "We won't be killed tonight. We're being open-steamed." Having heard all three of

them talking Monkey realized that they were still alive, so he flew away, fetched the iron steamer lid and placed it lightly on the steamer. "Disciples," exclaimed Sanzang in alarm, "they've covered us up." "That's done it," said Pig. "That means closed steaming. We're bound to die tonight." Friar Sand and the venerable elder started to sob. "Don't cry," said Pig. "A new shift of cooks has come on duty." "How can you tell?" Friar Sand asked. "I was delighted at first when they carried me here," Pig replied. "I've got a bit of a feverish chill and I wanted warming up. But all we're getting at the moment is cold air. Hey! Mr. Cook, sir! What are you making such a fuss about putting more firewood on for? Am I asking for what's yours?"

When Monkey heard this he could not help laughing to himself. "Stupid clod," he thought. "Being cold is bearable. If it got hot you'd be dead. The secret will get out if he goes on talking. I'd better rescue him.... No! I'd have to turn back into myself to rescue them, and if I did that the ten cooks would see me and start shouting. That would disturb the old monsters and I'd be put to a lot more trouble. I'll have to use some magic on the cooks first." Then a memory came back to him. "When I was the Great Sage in the old days I once played a guessing game with the Heavenly King Lokapala at the Northern Gate of Heaven and won some of his sleep insects off him. I've got a few left I can use on them." He felt around his waist inside his belt and found that he had twelve of them left. "I'll give them ten and keep two to breed from," Monkey thought. Then he threw the insects into the ten junior devils' faces, where the insects went up their nostrils, so that they all started feeling drowsy, lay down and went to sleep. One of them, however, who was holding a fire-fork slept very fitfully, kept rubbing his head and face, pinching his nose and continuously sneezing. "That so-and-so knows a trick or two," thought Monkey. "I'll have to give him a double dose." He threw one of his remaining insects into the demon's face. "With two insects the left one can go in when the right one comes out and vice versa," Monkey thought. "That should keep him quiet." With that the junior demon gave two or three big yawns,

614

stretched himself, dropped the fork and slumped down, fast asleep. He did not get up again.

[5] "What marvellous magic; it really works," said Monkey, turning back into himself. Then he went close to the steamer and called, "Master." "Rescue me, Wukong," said the Tang Priest when he heard him, "Is that you calling to us from outside?" Friar Sand asked. "If I weren't out here would you prefer me to be suffering in there with you?" Monkey replied. "Brother," said Pig, "you sloped off and left us to carry the can. We're being closed-steamed in here." "Stop yelling, idiot," said Monkey with a laugh. "I'm here to rescue you." "Brother," said Pig, "if you're going to rescue us do it properly. Don't get us put back in here for another steaming." Monkey then took the lid off, freed the master, shook the hair of his that he had turned into an imitation Monkey and put it back on his body, then released Friar Sand and Pig, taking one tray at a time. As soon as he was untied, the idiot wanted to run away. "Don't be in such a hurry!" said Monkey, who recited the words of a spell that released the dragon before going on to say to Pig, "We've still got high mountains and steep ridges ahead of us on our way to the Western Heaven. The going's too heavy for the master—he isn't a strong walker. Wait till I've fetched the horse."

Watch him as with light step he goes to the throne hall, where he saw that all the demons young and old were asleep. He undid the rope attached to the horse's reins, being even more careful not to alarm him. Now the horse was a dragon horse, so had Monkey been a stranger he would have given him a couple of flying kicks and whinnied. But Monkey had kept horses and held the office of Protector of the Horses, and this horse was besides their own. That was why the animal neither reared nor whinnied. Monkey led the horse very quietly over, tightened the girth and got everything ready before inviting his master to mount. Trembling and shaking, the Tang Priest did so. He too wanted to go. "Don't you be in such a hurry either," Monkey said. "There'll be plenty more kings along our journey west and we'll need our passport if we're to get there. What other identity papers do we have? I'm going back to find the luggage." "I remember that when we came in the monsters put the luggage to the left of the throne hall," said the Tang Priest. "The loads must still be there."

"Understood," said Monkey, who sprang off at once to search for it by the throne hall. When he suddenly saw shimmering lights of many colours brother Monkey knew that they came from the luggage. How did he know? Because the light came from the night-shining pearl on the Tang Priest's cassock. He rushed towards it and found that their load was unopened, so he took it out and gave it to Friar Sand to carry, while Pig led the horse and he took the lead.

They were hurrying to go straight out through the main southern gate when they heard the noise of watchmen's clappers and bells. They found the gates locked and paper seals over the locks. "How are we going to get out if the place is so closely guarded?" Monkey wondered. "Let's get out the back door," said Pig. With Monkey leading the way they rushed straight to the back gates. "I can hear clappers and bells outside the back gates as well, and they're sealed too," Monkey said. "What are we to do? If it weren't for the Tang Priest's mortal body it wouldn't bother us three: we could get away by cloud and wind. But the Tang Priest hasn't escaped from the Three Worlds and is still confined within the Five Elements. All his bones are the unclean ones he got from his mother and father. He can't lift himself into the air and he'll never get away." "No time for talking now, brother," said Pig. "Let's go somewhere where there aren't any bells, clappers or guards, lift the master up and climb over the wall." "That won't do," said Monkey. "We could lift him over now because we've got to, but you've got such a big mouth you'd tell people everywhere when we're taking the scriptures back that we're the sort of monks who sneak over people's walls." "But we can't bother about behaving properly now," replied Pig. "We've got to save our skins." Monkey had no choice but to do as he suggested, so they went up to wall and worked out how to climb over.

[6] Oh dear! Things would have to work out this way: Sanzang was not yet free of his unlucky star. The three demon chiefs who had been fast asleep in their living quarters suddenly awoke and heard that the Tang Priest had escaped, got up, threw on their clothes and hurried to the throne hall of the palace. "How many times has the Tang Priest been steamed?" they asked. The junior devils who were looking after the fires were all so soundly asleep because the sleep insects were in them that not even blows could wake them up. The chiefs woke up some others who were not on duty, who answered rashly, "Ss ... ss ... seven times." Then they rushed over to the steamer to see the steamer trays lying scattered on the floor and the cooks still asleep. In their alarm they rushed back to report, "Your Majesties, th ... th ... they've escaped."

The three demon chiefs came out of the throne hall to take a close look around the cauldron. They saw that the steamer trays were indeed scattered on the floor, the water was stone-cold and the fire completely out. The cooks supposed to be tending the fire were still so fast asleep that they were snoring noisily. The fiends were all so shocked that they all shouted, "Catch the Tang Priest! At once! Catch the Tang Priest!" Their yells woke up the demons senior and junior all around. They rushed in a crowd to the main front gates carrying their swords and spears. Seeing that the sealed locks had not been touched and that the night watchmen were still sounding their clappers and bells they asked the watchman, "Which way did the Tang Priest go?" "Nobody's come out," the watchmen all replied. They hurried to the back gates of the palace, only to find that the seals, locks, clappers and bells were the same as at the front. With a great commotion they grabbed lanterns and torches, making the sky red and the place as bright as day. The four of them were clearly lit up as they climbed over the wall. "Where do you think you're going?" the senior demon chief shouted, running towards them and so terrifying the reverend gentleman that the muscles in his legs turned soft and numb and he fell off the wall to be captured by the senior demon. The second demon chief seized Friar Sand and the

617

third knocked Pig over and capture him. The other demons took the luggage and the white horse. Only Monkey escaped. "May Heaven kill him," Pig grumbled under his breath about Monkey. "I said that if he was going to rescue us he ought to do a thorough job of it. As it is we're going to be put back in the steamer for another steaming."

The monsters took the Tang Priest into the throne hall but did not steam him again. The second demon chief ordered that Pig was to be tied to one of the columns supporting the eaves in front of the hall and the third chief had Friar Sand tied to one of the columns holding up the eaves at the back. The senior chief clung to the Tang Priest and would not let go of him. "What are you holding him for, elder brother?" the third demon asked. "Surely you're not going to eat him alive. That wouldn't be at all interesting. He's no ordinary idiot to be gobbled up just to fill your stomach. He's rare delicacy from a superior country. We should keep him till we have some free time one rainy day, then bring him out to be carefully cooked and enjoyed with drinking games and fine music." "A very good suggestion, brother," replied the senior demon with a smile, "but Sun the Novice would come and steal him again." "In our palace we have a Brocade Fragrance Pavilion," said the third demon, "and in the pavilion is an iron chest. I think we should put the Tang Priest into the chest, shut up the pavilion, put out a rumour that we have already eaten him half raw, and get all the junior devils in the city talking about it. That Sun the Novice is bound to come back to find out what's happening, and when he hears this he'll be so miserably disappointed that he'll go away. If he doesn't come to make trouble for another four or five days we can bring the Tang Priest out to enjoy at our leisure. What do you think?" The senior and second demon chiefs were both delighted. "Yes, yes, you're right, brother," they said. That very night the poor Tang Priest was taken inside the palace, put into the chest and locked up in the pavilion. We will not tell how the rumour was spread and became the talk of the town.

[7] Instead the story tells how Monkey escaped that night by

cloud, unable to look after the Tang Priest. He went straight to Lion Cave where he wiped out all the tens of thousands of junior demons with his cudgel to his complete satisfaction. By the time he had hurried back to the city the sun was rising in the east. He did not dare challenge the demons to battle because

> No thread can be spun from a single strand;
> Nobody can clap with a single hand.

So he brought his cloud down, shook himself, turned himself into a junior demon and slipped in through the gates to collect news in the streets and back alleys. "The Tang Priest was eaten raw by the senior king during the night," was what all the people in the city were saying wherever he went. This made Brother Monkey really anxious. When he went to look at the throne hall in the palace he saw that there were many spirits constantly coming and going. They were wearing leather and metal helmets and yellow cotton tunics. In their hands they held red lacquered staves, and ivory passes hung at their waists. "These must be evil spirits who are allowed in the inner quarters of the palace," thought Monkey. "I'll turn myself into one, go in and see what I can find out."

The splendid Great Sage then made himself identical to the demons and slipped in through the inner gates of the palace. As he was walking along he saw Pig tied to one of the columns of the throne hall, groaning. "Wuneng," Monkey said, going up to him. "Is that you, brother?" asked the idiot, recognizing his voice. "Save me!" "I'll save you," said Monkey. "Do you know where the master is?" "He's done for," Pig replied. "The evil spirits ate him raw last night." At this Monkey burst into sobs and the tears gushed out like water from a spring. "Don't cry, brother," said Pig. "I've only heard the junior devils gossiping. I didn't see it with my own eyes. Don't waste any more time. Go on and find out more." Only then did Monkey dry his tears and go to search in the inner part of the palace. Noticing Friar Sand tied to a column at the back of the palace he went up to him felt his chest and said, "Wujing." Friar Sand also recognized his voice

619

and said, "Brother, is that you here in disguise? Save me! Save me!" "Saving you will be easy," said Monkey, "but do you know where the master is?" "Brother!" said Friar Sand in tears. "The evil spirits couldn't even wait to steam the master. They've eaten him raw."

[8] Now that both of them had told him the same story the Great Sage was cut to the heart. Instead of rescuing Pig and Friar Sand he sprang straight up into the sky and went to mountain east of the city, where he landed his cloud and let himself weep aloud. "Poor Master," he said:

> *I fought against heaven, was caught in its net,*
> *Till you came along and delivered me, Master.*
> *It became my ambition to worship the Buddha;*
> *I strove to eliminate fiendish disaster.*
> *I never imagined that now you'd be murdered*
> *And I would have failed on your journey to keep you.*
> *The lands of the West were too good for your fate.*
> *Your life's at an end: in what way can I help you?"*

Deep in misery, Monkey said to himself, "It's all the fault of our Buddha, the Tathagata, who had nothing better to do in his paradise than make the three stores of scriptures. If he really wanted to convert people to be good he ought to have sent them to the east himself. Then they would have been passed on for ever. But he couldn't bring himself to part with them. He had to make us go to fetch them. Who'd ever have thought that after all the trouble of crossing a thousand mountains the master would lose his life here today? Oh well! I'll ride my somersault cloud to see the Tathagata Buddha and tell him what's happened. If he's willing to give me the scriptures to deliver to the east then the good achievement will be propagated and we'll be able to fulfil our vow. If he won't give me them I'll get him to recite the Band-loosening Spell. Then I can take the band off, return it to him and go back to my own cave to play the king and enjoy myself again."

The splendid Great Sage jumped to his feet and went straight to India on his somersault cloud. In less than a couple of hours he could see the Vulture Peak in the near distance, and an instant later he had landed his cloud and was heading straight for the foot of the peak. He looked up and saw the four vajrapanis blocking his way and asking him where he was going. "There's something I want to see the Tathagata about," Monkey replied with a bow. Next he was faced by the Vajrapani Yongzhu, the indestructible king of Golden Glow Ridge on Mount Kunlun, who shouted, "Macaque, you're an outrage! When the Bull Demon King was giving you such terrible trouble we all helped you, but now you've come to see us today you're showing no manners at all. If you're here on business you should submit a memorial first and wait till you're summoned before going any further. This isn't like the Southern Gate of Heaven, where you can come and go as you please. Clear off! Out of the way!" Being told off like this when he was feeling so depressed drove Monkey into thunder roars of fury, and his uncontrollable shouts and yells soon disturbed the Tathagata.

[9] The Tathagata Buddha was sitting on his nine-level lotus throne expounding the sutras to his eighteen arhats when he said, "Sun Wukong is here. You must all go out to receive him." In obedience to the Buddha's command the arhats went out in two columns with their banners and canopies. "Great Sage Sun," they said in greeting, "the Tathagata has commanded us to summon you to his presence." Only then did the four vajrapanis at the monastery gates step aside to let Monkey enter. The arhats led him to the foot of the lotus throne, where he went down to kowtow on seeing the Tathagata. He was sobbing and weeping. "Wukong," said the Buddha, "what makes you weep so miserably?"

"Your disciple has often received the grace of your instruction," Brother Monkey replied, "and has committed himself to the school of Lord Buddha. Since being converted to the true achievement I have taken the Tang Priest as my master and been protecting him on our journey. No words could describe what we have suffered. We have now reached the city of Leonia near Lion Cave on Lion Mountain where three vicious monsters, the Lion King, the Elephant King and the Great Roc, seized my master. All of us disciples of his were in a very bad way too, tied up and put in a steamer to suffer the agony of fire and boiling water. Fortunately I was able to get away and summon a dragon king to save the others. But we could not escape our evil star: the master and the others were recaptured when I was trying to sneak them out last night. When I went back into the city this morning to find out what had happened I learned that those utterly evil and ferocious monsters ate my master raw during the night. Nothing is left of his flesh and bones. On top of that my fellow-disciples Wuneng and Wujing are tied up there and will soon be dead too. I'm desperate. That's why your disciple has come to visit the Tathagata. I beg you in your great compassion to recite the Band-loosening Spell so that I can take the band off my head and give it back to you. Let your disciple go back to the Mountain of Flowers and Fruit and enjoy himself." Before he had finished saying this the tears welled up again. There was no end to his howls of misery.

"Don't upset yourself so, Wukong," said the Tathagata with a smile. "You can't beat those evil spirits. Their magical powers are more than you can handle. That is why you are so unhappy." Monkey knelt below the Buddha and beat his breast as he replied, "Truly, Tathagata, I made havoc in Heaven all those years ago and was called Great Sage. Never in all my life had I been beaten before I met these vicious monsters."

[10] "Stop being so sorry for yourself," said the Tathagata. "I know those evil spirits." "Tathagata!" Monkey suddenly blurted out. "They say those evil spirits are relations of yours." "Wicked macaque!" said the Tathagata. "How could an evil spirit be any relation of mine?" "If they're not relations of yours how come you know them?" retorted Monkey with a grin. "I know them because I see them with my all-seeing eyes," the Buddha replied. "The senior demon and the second demon have masters. Ananda, Kasyapa, come here. One of you is to take a cloud to Mount Wutai and the other to Mount Emei. Summon Manjusri and

Samantabhadra to come and see me." The two arhats left at once as they had been commanded. "They are the masters of the senior and the second demon chiefs. But the third demon does have some connection with me." "On his mother's or his father's side?" Monkey asked. "When the primal chaos was first separated the heavens opened up in the hour of the rat and the earth at the hour of the ox," the Buddha replied. "Mankind was born at the tiger hour. Then heaven and earth came together again and all living creatures were born, including beasts that walk and birds that fly. The unicorn is the most senior of the beasts that walk and the phoenix is the most senior of the birds that fly. When the phoenixes combined their essential spirit they gave birth to the peafowl and the Great Roc. When the peafowl came into the world she was the most evil of creatures and a man-eater. She could devour all the people for fifteen miles around in a single mouthful. When I was cultivating my sixteen-foot golden body on the peak of the snowy mountain she swallowed me as well. I went down into her belly. I wanted to escape through her backside, but for fear of soiling my body I cut my way out through her backbone and climbed Vulture Peak. I would have killed her, but all the Buddha host dissuaded me: to kill the peahen would have been like killing my own mother. So I kept her at my assembly on Vulture Peak and appointed her as the Buddha-mother, the Great Illustrious Peahen Queen Bodhisattva. The Great Roc was born of the same mother as she was. That is why we are relations of a kind." When Monkey heard this he said with a smile, "By that line of argument, Tathagata, you're the evil spirit's nephew." "I shall have to go and subdue that demon in person," the Tathagata said. Monkey kowtowed as he respectfully replied, "I beg you to condescend to grant us your illustrious presence."

The Tathagata then came down from his lotus throne and went out through the monastery gates with all the Buddha host just as Ananda and Kasyapa arrived bringing Manjusri and Samantabhadra. These two Bodhisattvas bowed to the Tathagata, who asked them, "How long have your animals been away from your mountains, Bodhisattvas?" "Seven days," said Manjusri.

"A mere seven days on your mountains is several thousand years in the mortal world," the Tathagata replied. "Goodness knows how many living beings they have destroyed there. Come with me to recapture them at once." The two Bodhisattvas travelled at the Buddha's left and right hand as they flew through the air with the host. This is what could be seen:

> The shimmering clouds of blessing parted for Lord Buddha
> As in his great compassion he came down from his shrine.
> He taught the truth about all beings since creation,
> Explaining how everything had been transformed in time.
> Before him went five hundred holy arhats;
> Behind him were three thousand guardians of the faith.
> Ananda and Kasyapa were both in close attendance;
> Samantabhadra and Manjusri came to conquer monsters.

The Great Sage had been granted this favour and succeeded in bringing the Lord Buddha and his host with him. It was not long before the city was in sight. "Tathagata," said Monkey, "that's Leonia, where the black vapours are coming from." "You go down into the city first," said the Tathagata, "and start a fight with the evil spirits. Do not win. You must lose and come back up. Leave it to us to recapture them."

[11] The Great Sage then brought his cloud straight down to land on the city wall, and shouted abusively, "Evil beasts! Come out and fight me at once!" This caused such consternation among the junior demons in the towers on the wall that they jumped straight down into the city to report, "Your Majesties, Sun the Novice is on the wall, challenging us to battle." "That ape hasn't been here for two or three days," the senior demon replied. "Now he's back challenging us to battle. Can he have fetched some reinforcements?" "He's nothing to be scared of," said the third demon chief. "Let's all go and have a look." The three chieftains, all carrying their weapons, hurried up on the wall where they saw Monkey. Without a word they raised their

weapons and thrust at him. Monkey held them off by swinging his iron cudgel. When they had fought seven or eight rounds Monkey feigned defeat and fled. "Where do you think you're going?" the demon king asked with a mighty shout, and with a somersault Monkey sprang up into mid-air. The three spirits went after him on clouds, but Monkey slipped aside and disappeared completely in the Lord Buddha's golden aura.

All that could be seen were the images of the Three Buddhas of Past, Future and Present, the five hundred arhats and the three thousand Protectors of the Faith who spread all around, encircling the three demon kings so closely that not even a drop of water could leak through. "This is terrible, my brother," said the senior demon chief, lashing out wildly, "that ape is a really sharp operator. How did he manage to bring my master here?" "Don't be afraid, elder brother," said the third demon. "If we all charge together we can cut down the Tathagata with our swords and spears and seize his Thunder Monastery." The demons, who had no sense of proper behaviour, really did raise their swords to charge forward, hacking wildly. Manjusri and Samantabhadra recited the words of a spell and shouted, "Won't you repent now, evil beasts? What else do you hope for?" The senior and the second demon chiefs gave up the struggle, threw down their weapons, rolled and reverted to their true images. The two Bodhisattvas threw their lotus thrones on the demons' backs and flew over to sit on them. The two demons then gave up and submitted.

[12] Now that the blue lion and the white elephant had been captured only the third evil monster was still unsubdued. Spreading its wings it dropped its heaven-square halberd and rose straight up to try to catch the Monkey King with a swing of its sharp talons, but as the Great Sage was hiding in the golden aura the demon dared get nowhere near him. When the Tathagata realized what it was trying to do he made his golden aura flash and shook his head that was the supreme meditator in the wind to turn it into a bright red lump of bloody meat. The evil spirit seized it with a flourish of its sharp talons, whereupon the Lord Buddha

pointed upwards with his hand, destroying the muscles in the monster's wings. It could not fly or get away from the top of the Buddha's head, and it reverted to its true appearance as a golden-winged vulture. Opening its beak it said to the Buddha, "Tathagata, why did you use your great dharma powers to catch me like this?" "You have been doing much evil here," the Tathagata replied. "Come with me and you will win credit for a good deed." "You eat vegetarian food in great poverty and suffering at your place," the evil spirit replied, "but here I can eat human flesh and live in no end of luxury. If you kill me by starvation you'll be guilty of a sin." "In the four continents I control countless living beings who worship me," the Buddha replied, "and whenever they are going to perform a service to me I shall tell them to make a sacrifice to you first." The Great Roc would have escaped and got away if it could. As it was he had no choice but to accept conversion.

Only then did Monkey emerge to kowtow to the Tathagata and say, "Lord Buddha, today you have captured the evil spirits and removed a great bane, but my master is dead." At this the Great Roc said bitterly as it ground its teeth, "Damned ape! Why did you have to bring these ferocious men here to persecute me? I never ate that old monk of yours. He's in the Brocade Fragrance Pavilion now, isn't he?" When Monkey heard this he quickly kowtowed to thank the Lord Buddha. Not daring to release the Great Roc, the Buddha made him into a guardian of the dharma in his brilliant halo then led his host back to his monastery on their clouds.

【13】 Monkey landed his cloud and went straight into the city, where there was not a single junior demon left. Indeed,

> A snake cannot move without its head;
> A bird cannot fly without its wings.

They had all fled for their lives when they saw the Buddha capturing their evil kings. Monkey then freed Pig and Friar Sand, found the luggage and the horse, and said to his fellow-disciples,

"The master hasn't been eaten. Come with me." He took the two of them straight into the inner compound where they found the Brocade Fragrance Pavilion. Opening the door and looking inside they saw an iron trunk from which could be heard the sound of Sanzang weeping. Friar Sand used his demon-quelling staff to open the iron cage over the chest and raise its lid. "Master," he called. At the sight of them Sanzang wept aloud and said, "Disciples, how were the demons beaten? How did you manage to find me here?" Monkey told him all the details of what had happened from beginning to end and Sanzang expressed boundless gratitude. Then master and disciples found some rice in the palace and ate their fill of it before packing their things and leaving the city along the main road west.